MICROECONOMIC THEORY

BASIC PRINCIPLES AND EXTENSIONS

Ninth Edition

WALTER NICHOLSON

THOMSON

SOUTH-WESTERN

Australia · Canada · Mexico · Singapore · Spain · United Kingdom · United States

Microeconomic Theory: Basic Principles and Extensions

Ninth Edition

Walter Nicholson

VP/Editorial Director:
Jack W. Calhoun

VP/Editor-in-Chief:
Mike Roche

Publisher of Economics:
Michael B. Mercier

Acquisitions Editor:
Peter Adams

Developmental Editor:
Susanna C. Smart

Marketing Manager:
Jenny Freuchtenicht

Production Editor:
Cliff Kallemeyn

Technology Project Editor:
Peggy Buskey

Media Editor:
Pam Wallace

Manufacturing Coordinator:
Sandee Milewski

Internal and Cover Design:
Justin Klefeker

Cover Images:
©PhotoDisc

Production House:
Shepherd, Inc.

Printer:
RR Donnelley
Willard, OH

For permission to use material from this text or product, submit a request online at http://www.thomsonrights.com.

For more information contact South-Western, 5191 Natorp Boulevard, Mason, Ohio 45040.
Or you can visit our Internet site at:
http://www.swlearning.com

To Beth, Sarah, and David, who behave as if they understood microeconomics.

About the Author

Walter Nicholson is the Ward H. Patton Professor of Economics at Amherst College. He received his B.A. in mathematics from Williams College and his Ph.D. in economics from MIT. Professor Nicholson's principal research interests are in the econometric analyses of labor market problems including unemployment, job training, and the impact of international trade. He is also the author of *Intermediate Microeconomics and Its Application, Ninth Edition* (South-Western/Thomson Learning, 2004).

Professor Nicholson and his wife, Susan, live in Amherst, Massachusetts, and Naples, Florida. What was previously a very busy household, with four children everywhere, is now rather empty, with only one rather aged Labrador Retriever still underfoot. But an ever-increasing number of grandchildren breathe some life into these places whenever they visit, which seems far too seldom.

Brief Contents

Contents

Preface

The ninth edition of *Microeconomic Theory: Basic Principles and Extensions* provides students with a comprehensive and accessible summary of modern microeconomics. This is accomplished by including clear and intuitive explanations of all of the major theoretical results and by stressing the mathematical structure that is common to many microeconomic problems. Links to more advanced literature and to empirical applications are provided through a number of "extensions" that gather together many results that are often assumed in the professional literature. Ideally, the inclusion of this material should make that literature more approachable.

New to the Ninth Edition

The most important changes in this edition occur in its first nine chapters. In these I have tried to improve and expand the basic material on utility maximization and on the theory of the firm. One important change from prior editions is the adoption of a more streamlined and consistent notation for these parts of the book. Although apparently there is no "standard" notation in microeconomics, I believe that the new notation adopted here conforms well to current practice. Other major changes in the core theory sections of the text include:

- A thorough revision of demand theory with special attention to expenditure functions and the envelope relationships that can be derived from them;

- A more comprehensive coverage of cost functions, focusing on how substitutability among inputs is reflected in such functions;

- An expanded coverage of the profit function concept with a detailed examination of how that function generates input demand functions; and

- A number of new mathematical examples that focus on widely used functional forms.

Changes in the final 12 chapters were significant in the eighth edition, but a number of important improvements have been made to this edition as well, such as:

- Introduction of a number of simple two-good models of general equilibrium;

- New material on the economics of information—especially an extended presentation of principal-agent issues and of more general aspects of incentive-compatible mechanism design;

- Many new shorter sections on such subjects as durable goods, risk aversion, and labor market equilibrium;

- Many new problems and mathematical examples to accompany the new theoretical material being introduced.

The thoroughly revised ancillaries for this edition include:

- The comprehensive student *Study Guide and Workbook,* by David C. Stapleton of Cornell University. Included are Key Concepts and numerous Problems for each chapter, with answers at the end of the *Study Guide.*

- The *Solutions Manual and Test Bank,* by the text author. The *Solutions Manual* contains Comments and Solutions to all problems, available to all adopting instructors in print and electronic versions. The *Solutions Manual and Test Bank* is available for download only by qualified instructors at the textbook support Web site (*http://nicholson.swlearning.com*).

- New! PowerPoint Lecture Presentation Slides, by Linda Ghent of Eastern Illinois University. PowerPoint slides for each chapter of the text provide a thorough set of outlines for classroom use, or for students as a study aid. Available to instructors and students via download at the book's Web site.

Online Resources

Thomson Business and Professional Publishing/Thomson Learning provides students and instructors with a set of valuable online resources that make an effective complement to this text. Each new copy of the book comes with two registration cards. One is for Economics Applications, and the other is for InfoTrac College Edition.

Economic Applications

The purchase of this new textbook includes complimentary access to South-Western's Economic Applications (EconApps) Web site (*http://econapps.swlearning.com*).

The EconApps Web site includes a suite of regularly updated Web features for economics students and instructors: EconDebate Online, EconNews Online, EconData Online, and EconLinks Online. These resources can help students to deepen their understanding of economic concepts by analyzing current news stories, policy debates, and economic data. These resources can also help instructors to develop assignments, case studies, and examples based on real-world issues.

EconDebate Online provides current coverage of economics policy debates, including a primer on the issues, links to background information, and commentaries.

EconNews Online summarizes recent economics news stories and offers questions for further discussion.

EconData Online presents current and historical economic data with accompanying commentary, analysis, and exercises.

EconLinks Online offers a navigation partner for exploring economics on the Web, with a list of key topic links.

The South-Western/Thomson Learning Economics Web site (*http://economics. swlearning.com*) also includes free access to *Newsedge,* which culls and organizes the most recent news and economic information.

Students buying a used book can purchase access to the EconApps site at *http://econapps.swlearning.com*

InfoTrac College Edition

The purchase of this new textbook also comes with four months of access to InfoTrac. This powerful, searchable online database provides access to full text articles from more than 1,000 different publications, from popular press to scholarly journals. Each chapter includes suggested InfoTrac Keywords for study with the chapters. In addition, instructors can search topics and select readings for students and students can search articles and readings for homework assignments and projects.

The publications cover a variety of topics, with articles that range from current events to theoretical developments. InfoTrac College Edition offers instructors and students the ability to integrate scholarship and applications of economics into the learning process.

Acknowledgments

In preparation for undertaking this revision, I received very helpful reviews from:

Ronald S. Warren, Jr., University of Georgia

Nick Feltovich, University of Houston

Steven Marc Goldman, University of California, Berkeley

Gerald M. Lage, Oklahoma State University

Ying Chi Chan, Johns Hopkins University

Carrie Meyer, George Mason University

Stephen Morris, Yale University

James J. Murphy, University of Massachusetts, Amherst

Norman K. Thurston, Brigham Young University

It was these reviewers who suggested that I consider modifying some of the notation in the early chapters in the book and spend more space on the expenditure and profit function concepts. I have tried to follow this good advice, but, of course, none of these individuals bears any responsibility for the final outcome.

This is the first edition of this book that has been completely produced by South-Western/Thompson Learning and I have been very pleased with the working relationship we have developed. I am especially indebted to Susan Smart for keeping the book on schedule and for addressing my concerns about how the notational changes might be accommodated. Copyediting of this manuscript was, I know, a real chore. But copyeditor Michelle Livingston, along with Shepherd Inc., did a great job of penetrating my messy manuscript to obtain something that actually makes sense. The design of the text by Justin Klefeker succeeded in achieving two seemingly irreconcilable goals—making the text easy to read and compact. The end result looks great, I think. Cliff Kallemeyn did a fine job in keeping the production of this edition on track. I especially appreciated his handling of some errors of forgetfulness I made in several spots. I also thank David Stapleton, at Cornell, for his continued work on the *Study Guide,* and Brett Katzman, at Kennesaw State, for creating the Online Quizzes.

As always, my Amherst College colleagues and students bear some responsibility for this new edition. Frank Westhoff has been my most faithful user of this text over many years and he still manages to read it closely enough to point out many potential improvements.

This year Steve Rivkin also joined the list of instructor-critics and I really gained quite a bit from having a new pair of eyes look at the text. To the list of former students whose efforts still appear here (Mark Bruni, Eric Budish, Adrian Dillon, David Macoy, Jordan Milev, Tatyana Mamut, Katie Merrill, and Jeff Rodman) I can now add the name of Doug Norton, who helped me to assemble most of the new extensions in this edition.

Special thanks again go to my wife Susan, who, seeing now 18 editions of my microeconomics texts come and go, has given up all hope of neatness (or, it should be added, of finding me in a good mood). My children (Kate, David, Tory, and Paul) all seem to be living happy and productive lives despite a severe lack of microeconomic education. As the next generation (Beth, Sarah, and David) gets older, perhaps they will seek enlightenment—at least to the extent of wondering what the books dedicated to them are all about.

Walter Nicholson
Amherst, Massachusetts
February, 200

Part 1

INTRODUCTION

This part contains only two chapters. Chapter 1 examines the general philosophy of how economists build models of economic behavior. Chapter 2 then reviews some of the mathematical tools used in the construction of such models. These tools will be used throughout the remainder of this book.

Chapter 1

ECONOMIC MODELS

The main goal of this book is to introduce you to the most important models that economists use to explain the behavior of consumers and firms. These models are central to the study of all areas of economics. So it is essential to understand both the need for such models and the basic framework used to develop them. The goal of this chapter is to begin this process by outlining some of the conceptual issues that determine the ways in which economists proceed to study practically every question that interests them.

Theoretical models

A modern economy is a very complicated entity. Thousands of firms engage in producing millions of different goods. Millions of individuals work in all sorts of occupations and make decisions about which of these goods to buy. Take peanuts, for example. They must be harvested at the right time and shipped to processors who turn them into peanut butter, peanut oil, peanut brittle, and numerous other peanut delicacies. These processors, in turn, must make certain that their products arrive at thousands of retail outlets in the proper quantities to meet demand.

Because it would be impossible to describe the features of just these peanut markets in complete detail, economists have chosen to abstract from the complexities of the real world and to develop rather simple models that capture the "essentials." Just as a road map is helpful even though it does not record every house or every store, economic models of, say, the market for peanuts are also very useful even though they do not record every minute feature of the peanut economy. In this book we shall be studying the most widely used economic models. We will see that, even though they often make heroic abstractions from the complexities of the real world, they nonetheless capture many essential features that are common to all economic activities.

The use of models is widespread in both the physical and social sciences. In physics, the notion of a "perfect" vacuum or an "ideal" gas is an abstraction that permits scientists to study real-world phenomena in simplified settings. In chemistry, the idea of an atom or a molecule is in actuality a very simplified model of the structure of matter. Architects use mock-up models to plan buildings. Television repairers refer to wiring diagrams to locate problems. Economists' models perform similar functions. They portray the way individuals make decisions, the way firms behave, and the way in which these two groups interact to establish markets.

Verification of economic models

Of course, not all models prove to be "good." For example, the earth-centered model of planetary motion devised by Ptolemy was eventually discarded because it proved incapable of explaining accurately how the planets move around the sun. An important purpose of scientific investigation is to sort out the "bad" models from the "good." Two general methods have been used for verifying economic models: (1) a direct approach, which seeks to establish the validity of the basic assumptions on which a model is based; and (2) an indirect approach, which attempts to confirm validity by showing that a simplified model correctly predicts real-world events. To illustrate the basic differences in the two approaches, let's briefly examine a model that we will use extensively in later chapters of this book—the model of a firm that seeks to maximize profits.

The profit-maximization model

The model of a firm seeking to maximize profits is obviously a simplification of reality. It ignores the personal motivations of a firm's managers and does not consider conflicts among them. It assumes that profits are the only relevant goal of a firm; other possible goals, such as obtaining power or prestige, are treated as unimportant. The model also assumes that a firm has sufficient information about its costs and the nature of the market to which it sells to discover what its profit-maximizing options actually are. Most real-world firms, of course, do not have this information readily available. Yet, such shortcomings in the model are not necessarily serious. No model can describe reality exactly. The real question is whether this simple model has any claim to being a good one.

Testing assumptions

One test of the model of a profit-maximizing firm investigates its basic assumption: Do firms really seek maximum profits? Some economists have examined this question by sending questionnaires to executives asking them to specify what goals they pursue. The results of such studies have been varied. Businesspeople often mention goals other than profits or claim they only do "the best they can" given their limited information. On the other hand, most respondents also mention a strong "interest" in profits and express the view that profit maximization is an appropriate goal. Testing the profit-maximizing model by testing its assumptions has therefore provided inconclusive results.

Testing predictions

Some economists, most notably Milton Friedman, deny that a model can be tested by inquiring into the "reality" of its assumptions.[1] They argue that all theoretical models are based on "unrealistic" assumptions; the very nature of theorizing demands that we make certain abstractions. These economists conclude that the only way to determine the validity of a model is to see whether it is capable of explaining and predicting real-world events. The ultimate test of an economic model comes when it is confronted with data from the economy itself.

Friedman provides an important illustration of that principle. He asks what kind of a theory one should use to explain the shots expert pool players will make. He argues that the laws of velocity, momentum, and angles from theoretical classical physics would be a suitable model. Pool players shoot shots *as if* they followed these laws. But if we ask players whether they understand the physical principles behind the game of pool, most will undoubtedly answer that they do not. Nonetheless, Friedman argues, the physical laws

[1]See M. Friedman, *Essays in Positive Economics* (Chicago: University of Chicago Press, 1953), chap. 1. For an alternative view stressing the importance of using "realistic" assumptions, see H. A. Simon, "Rational Decision Making in Business Organizations," *American Economic Review 69*, no. 4 (September 1979): 493–513.

provide very accurate predictions and therefore should be accepted as appropriate theoretical models of how pool is played by experts.

A test of the profit-maximization model, then, would be provided by predicting the behavior of real-world firms by assuming that these firms behave *as if* they were maximizing profits. (see Example 1.1 later in this chapter). If these predictions are reasonably in accord with reality, we may accept the profit-maximization hypothesis. However, if real-world data seem inconsistent with the model, we would reject it. Hence, the ultimate test of either theory is its ability to predict *real-world events.*

Importance of empirical analysis

The primary concern of this book is the construction of theoretical models. But the goal of such models is always to learn something about the real world. Although the inclusion of a lengthy set of applied examples would needlessly expand an already bulky book,[2] the Extensions included at the end of many chapters are intended to provide a transition between the theory presented here and the ways in which that theory is actually applied in empirical studies.

General features of economic models

The number of economic models in current use is, of course, very large. Specific assumptions used and the degree of detail provided vary greatly depending on the problem being addressed. The types of models employed to explain the overall level of economic activity in the United States, for example, must be considerably more aggregated and complex than those that seek to interpret the pricing of Arizona strawberries. Despite this variety, however, practically all economic models incorporate three common elements: (1) the *ceteris paribus* (other things the same) assumption; (2) the supposition that economic decision makers seek to optimize something; and (3) a careful distinction between "positive" and "normative" questions. Because we will encounter these elements throughout this book, it may be helpful at the outset to describe briefly the philosophy behind each of them.

The ceteris paribus assumption

As is the case in most sciences, models used in economics attempt to portray relatively simple relationships. A model of the market for wheat, for example, might seek to explain wheat prices with a small number of quantifiable variables, such as wages of farmworkers, rainfall, and consumer incomes. This parsimony in model specification permits the study of wheat pricing in a simplified setting in which it is possible to understand how the specific forces operate. Although any researcher will recognize that many "outside" forces (presence of wheat diseases, changes in the prices of fertilizers or of tractors, or shifts in consumer attitudes about eating bread) affect the price of wheat, these other forces are held constant in the construction of the model. It is important to recognize that economists are *not* assuming that other factors do not affect wheat prices; but rather, such other variables are assumed to be unchanged during the period of study. In this way the effect of only a few forces can be studied in a simplified setting. Such ceteris paribus (other things equal) assumptions are used in all economic modeling.

Use of the ceteris paribus assumption does pose some difficulties for the verification of economic models from real-world data. In other sciences such problems may not be so severe because of the ability to conduct controlled experiments. For example, a physicist who wishes to test a model of the force of gravity would probably not do so by dropping objects from the Empire State Building. Experiments conducted in that way would be subject to too many extraneous forces (wind currents, particles in the air, variations in

[2]For an intermediate-level text containing an extensive set of real world applications, see W. Nicholson, *Microeconomics Theory and Its Application,* 9th ed. (Mason, Ohio: Thompson/Southwestern, 2004).

temperature, and so forth) to permit a precise test of the theory. Rather, the physicist would conduct experiments in a laboratory, using a partial vacuum in which most other forces could be controlled or eliminated. In this way the theory could be verified in a simple setting, without needing to consider all the other forces that affect falling bodies in the real world.

With a few notable exceptions, economists have not been able to conduct controlled experiments to test their models. Instead, economists have been forced to rely on various statistical methods to control for other forces when testing their theories. Although these statistical methods are in principle as valid as the controlled experiment methods used by other scientists, in practice they raise a number of thorny issues. For that reason, the limitations and precise meaning of the ceteris paribus assumption in economics are subject to somewhat greater controversy than in the laboratory sciences.

Optimization assumptions

Many economic models start from the assumption that the economic actors being studied are rationally pursuing some goal. We briefly discussed such an assumption previously when investigating the notion of firms maximizing profits. Example 1.1 shows how that model can be used to make testable predictions. Other examples we will encounter in this book include consumers maximizing their own well-being (utility), firms minimizing costs, and government regulators attempting to maximize public welfare. Although, as we will show, all of these assumptions are somewhat controversial, all have won widespread acceptance as good starting places for developing economic models. There seem to be two reasons for this acceptance. First, the optimization assumptions are very useful for generating precise, solvable models. A primary reason for this is that such models can draw on a variety of mathematical techniques suitable for optimization problems. Many of these techniques, together with the logic behind them, are reviewed in Chapter 2. A second reason for the popularity of optimization models concerns their apparent empirical validity. As some of our Extensions show, such models seem to be fairly good at explaining reality. In all, then, optimization models have come to occupy a prominent position in modern economic theory.

 EXAMPLE 1.1

Profit Maximization

The profit-maximization hypothesis provides a good illustration of how optimization assumptions can be used to generate empirically testable propositions about economic behavior. Suppose that a firm can sell all the output that it wishes at a price of p per unit and that the total costs of production, C, depend on the amount produced, q. Then, profits are given by

rev. - cost

$$\textbf{Profits} = \pi = pq - C(q). \tag{1.1}$$

Maximization of profits consists of finding that value of q which maximizes the profit expression in Equation 1.1. This is a simple problem in calculus. Differentiation of Equation 1.1 and setting that derivative equal to 0 gives the following first-order condition for a maximum:

$$\frac{d\pi}{dq} = p - C'(q) = 0 \quad \text{or} \quad p = C'(q). \qquad \frac{dc}{dq} \tag{1.2}$$

In words, the profit-maximizing output level (say q^*) is found by selecting that output level for which price is equal to marginal cost, that is, the change in C for a change in q, which is $C'(q)$. This result should be familiar to you from your introductory economics course. Notice that in this derivation the price for the firm's output is treated as a constant because the firm is a price taker.

Equation 1.2 is only the first order condition for a maximum. Taking account of the second-order condition can help us to derive a testable implication of this model. The second-order condition for a maximum is that at q^* it must be the case that

$$\frac{d^2\pi}{dq^2} = -C''(q) < 0 \quad \text{or} \quad C''(q^*) > 0. \qquad (1.3)$$

That is, marginal cost must be increasing at q^* for this to be a true point of maximum profits.

Our model can now be used to "predict" how a firm will react to a change in price. To do so, we differentiate Equation 1.2 with respect to price (p), assuming that the firm continues to choose a profit-maximizing level of q:

$$\frac{d[p - C'(q^*) = 0]}{dp} = 1 - C''(q^*) \cdot \frac{dq^*}{dp} = 0. \qquad (1.4)$$

Rearranging terms a bit gives

$$\frac{dq^*}{dp} = \frac{1}{C''(q^*)} > 0. \qquad (1.5)$$

Here the final inequality again reflects the fact that marginal cost must be increasing if q^* is to be a true maximum. This then is one of the testable propositions of the profit-maximization hypothesis—if other things do not change, a price-taking firm should respond to an increase in price by increasing output. On the other hand, if firms respond to increases in price by reducing output, there must be something wrong with our model.

Although this is a very simple model, it reflects the way we will proceed throughout much of this book. Specifically, the fact that the primary implication of the model is derived by calculus and amounts to showing what sign a derivative should have is an outcome we will see many times.

Query: In general terms how would the implications of this model be changed if the price a firm obtains for its output were a function of how much it sold? That is, how would the model work if the price-taking assumption were abandoned.

Positive-normative distinction

A final feature of most economic models is the attempt to differentiate carefully between "positive" and "normative" questions. So far we have been concerned primarily with *positive* economic theories. Such "scientific" theories take the real world as an object to be studied, attempting to explain those economic phenomena that are observed. Positive economics seeks to determine how resources are *in fact* allocated in an economy. A somewhat different use of economic theory is *normative,* taking a definite stance about what *should be* done. Under the heading of normative analysis, economists have a great deal to say about how resources *should be* allocated. For example, an economist engaged in positive analysis might investigate how prices are determined in the U.S. health-care economy. The economist might also want to measure the costs and benefits of devoting even more resources to health care. But when he or she specifically advocates that more resources *should* be allocated to health care, this becomes normative analysis.

Some economists believe that the only proper economic analysis is positive analysis. Drawing an analogy with the physical sciences, they argue that "scientific" economics should concern itself only with the description (and possibly prediction) of real-world economic events. To take moral positions and to plead for special interests are considered to be outside the competence of an economist acting as an economist. Other economists, however, believe strict application of the positive-normative distinction to economic matters is inappropriate. They believe that the study of economics necessarily involves the researchers' own views about ethics, morality, and fairness. According to these economists, searching for scientific "objectivity" in such circumstances is hopeless. Despite some ambiguity, this book adopts a mainly positivist tone, leaving normative concerns to you to decide for yourself.

Development of the economic theory of value

Although economic activity has been a central feature of all societies, it is surprising that these activities were not studied in any detail until fairly recently. For the most part, economic phenomena were treated as a basic aspect of human behavior that was not sufficiently interesting to deserve specific attention. It is, of course, true that individuals have always studied economic activities with a view toward making some kind of personal gain. Roman traders were not above making profits on their transactions. But investigations into the basic nature of these activities did not begin in any depth until the eighteenth century.[3] Because this book is about economic theory as it stands today, not about the history of economic thought, our discussion of the evolution of economic theory will be brief. Only one area of economic study will be examined in its historical setting: the *theory of value.*

Early economic thought

The theory of value, not surprisingly, concerns the determinants of the "value" of a commodity. The study of this subject is at the center of modern microeconomic theory and is closely intertwined with the fundamental economic problem of allocating scarce resources to alternative uses. The logical place to start is with a definition of the word *value.* Unfortunately, the meaning of this term has not been consistent throughout the development of the subject. Today we regard value as being synonymous with the price of a commodity.[4] Earlier philosopher-economists, however, made a distinction between the market price of a commodity and its value. The term "value" was then thought of as being in some sense synonymous with "importance," "essentiality," or (at times) "godliness." Because "price" and "value" were separate concepts, they could differ, and most early economic discussions centered on these divergences. For example, St. Thomas Aquinas believed value to be divinely determined. Since prices were set by humans, it was possible for the price of a commodity to differ from its value. A person accused of charging a price in excess of a good's value was guilty of charging an "unjust" price. For example, St. Thomas believed the "just" rate of interest to be zero. Any lender who demanded a payment for the use of money was charging an unjust price and could be—and sometimes was—prosecuted by church officials.

The founding of modern economics

During the latter part of the eighteenth century, philosophers began to take a more scientific approach to economic questions. The publication of *The Wealth of Nations* by Adam Smith (1723–1790) in the eventful year 1776 is generally considered the beginning of modern economics. In his vast, all-encompassing work, Smith laid the foundation for thinking about market forces in an ordered and systematic way. Still, Smith and his immediate successors, such as David Ricardo (1772–1823), continued to distinguish between value and price. To Smith, for example, the value of a commodity meant its "value in

---

[3]For a detailed treatment of early economic thought, see the classic work by J. A. Schumpeter, *History of Economic Analysis* (New York: Oxford University Press, 1954), pt. II, chaps. 1, 2, and 3.

[4]This is not completely true when "externalities" are involved and a distinction must be made between private and social value (see Chapter 20).

use," whereas the price represented its "value in exchange." The distinction between these two concepts was illustrated by the famous water-diamond paradox. Water, which obviously has great value in use, has little value in exchange (it has a low price); diamonds are of little practical use but have a great value in exchange. The paradox with which early economists struggled derives from the observation that some very useful items have low prices whereas certain nonessential items have high prices.

Labor theory of exchange value

Neither Smith nor Ricardo ever satisfactorily resolved the water-diamond paradox. The concept of value in use was left for philosophers to debate, while economists turned their attention to explaining the determinants of value in exchange (that is, to explaining relative prices). One obvious possible explanation is that exchange values of goods are determined by what it costs to produce them. Costs of production are primarily influenced by labor costs—at least this was so in the time of Smith and Ricardo—and therefore it was a short step to embrace a labor theory of value. For example, to paraphrase an example from Smith, if catching a deer takes twice the number of labor-hours as catching a beaver, then one deer should exchange for two beavers. In other words, the price of a deer should be twice that of a beaver. Similarly, diamonds are relatively costly because their production requires substantial labor input.

To students with even a passing knowledge of what we now call the *law of supply and demand,* Smith's and Ricardo's explanation must seem incomplete. Didn't they recognize the effects of demand on price? The answer to this question is both yes and no. They did observe periods of rapidly rising and rapidly falling prices and attributed such changes to demand shifts. However, they regarded these changes as abnormalities that produced only a temporary divergence of market price from labor value. Because they had not really developed a theory of value in use, they were unwilling to assign demand any more than a transient role in determining relative prices. Rather, long-run exchange values were assumed to be determined solely by labor costs of production.

The marginalist revolution

Between 1850 and 1880, economists became increasingly aware that to construct an adequate alternative to the labor theory of value, they had to come to devise a theory of value in use. During the 1870s several economists discovered that it is not the total usefulness of a commodity that helps to determine its exchange value, but rather the usefulness of the *last unit consumed.* For example, water is certainly very useful—it is necessary for all life. But, because water is relatively plentiful, consuming one more pint (ceteris paribus) has a relatively low value to people. These "marginalists" redefined the concept of value in use from an idea of overall usefulness to one of marginal, or incremental, usefulness—the usefulness of an *additional unit of a commodity*. The concept of the demand for an incremental unit of output was now contrasted to Smith's and Ricardo's analysis of production costs to derive a comprehensive picture of price determination.[5]

Marshallian supply-demand synthesis

The clearest statement of these marginal principles was presented by the English economist Alfred Marshall (1842–1924) in his *Principles of Economics,* published in 1890. Marshall showed that demand and supply *simultaneously* operate to determine price. As Marshall noted, just as you cannot tell which blade of a scissors does the cutting, so too you cannot say that either demand or supply alone determines price. That analysis is illustrated

---

[5]Ricardo had earlier provided an important first step in marginal analysis in his discussion of rent. Ricardo theorized that as the production of corn increased, land of inferior quality would be used and this would cause the price of corn to rise. In his argument Ricardo implicitly recognized that it is the marginal cost—the cost of producing an additional unit—that is relevant to pricing. Notice that Ricardo implicitly held other inputs constant when discussing diminishing land productivity; that is, he employed one version of the ceteris paribus assumption.

FIGURE 1.1   **The Marshallian Supply-Demand Cross**

Marshall theorized that demand and supply interact to determine the equilibrium price (p^*) and the quantity (q^*) that will be traded in the market. He concluded that it is not possible to say that either demand or supply alone determines price or therefore that either costs or usefulness to buyers alone determines exchange value.

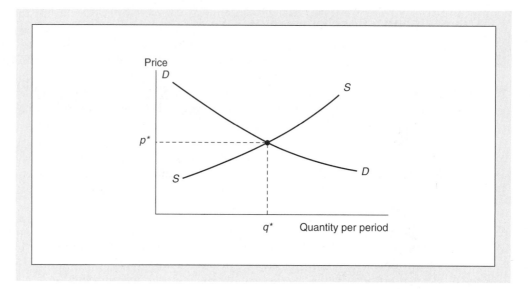

by the famous Marshallian cross shown in Figure 1.1. In the diagram the quantity of a good purchased per period is shown on the horizontal axis, and its price appears on the vertical axis. The curve *DD* represents the quantity of the good demanded per period at each possible price. The curve is negatively sloped to reflect the marginalist principle that as quantity increases, people are willing to pay less and less for the last unit purchased. It is the value of this last unit that sets the price for all units purchased. The curve *SS* shows how (marginal) production costs rise as more output is produced. This reflects the increasing cost of producing one more unit as total output expands. In other words, the upward slope of the *SS* curve reflects increasing marginal costs, just as the downward slope of the *DD* curve reflects decreasing marginal value. The two curves intersect at p^*, q^*. This is an *equilibrium* point—both buyers and sellers are content with the quantity being traded and the price at which it is traded. If one of the curves should shift, the equilibrium point would shift to a new location. Thus price and quantity are simultaneously determined by the joint operation of supply and demand.

Paradox resolved

Marshall's model resolves the water-diamond paradox. Prices reflect both the marginal evaluation that demanders place on goods and the marginal costs of producing the goods. Viewed in this way, there is no paradox. Water is low in price because it has both a low marginal value and a low marginal cost of production. On the other hand, diamonds are high in price because they have both a high marginal value (because people are willing to pay quite a bit for one more) and a high marginal cost of production. This basic model of supply and demand lies behind much of the analysis presented in this book.

General equilibrium models

Although the Marshallian model is an extremely useful and versatile tool, it is a *partial equilibrium model,* looking at only one market at a time. For some questions this narrowing of perspective gives valuable insights and analytical simplicity. For other, broader questions, such a narrow viewpoint may prevent the discovery of important relationships

EXAMPLE 1.2

Supply-Demand Equilibrium

Although graphical presentations are adequate for some purposes, economists often use algebraic representations of their models both to clarify their arguments and to make them more precise. As a very elementary example, suppose we wished to study the market for peanuts and, on the basis of statistical analysis of historical data, concluded that the quantity of peanuts demanded each week (q—measured in bushels) depended on the price of peanuts (p—measured in dollars per bushel) according to the equation

$$\text{quantity demanded} = q_D = 1000 - 100p. \qquad (1.6)$$

Because this equation for q_D contains only the single independent variable p, we are implicitly holding constant all other factors that might affect the demand for peanuts. Equation 1.6 indicates that, if other things do not change, at a price of $5 per bushel people will demand 500 bushels of peanuts, whereas at a price of $4 per bushel they will demand 600 bushels. The negative coefficient for p in Equation 1.6 reflects the marginalist principle that a lower price will cause people to buy more peanuts.

To complete this simple model of pricing, suppose that the quantity supplied of peanuts also depends on price:

$$\text{quantity supplied} = q_S = -125 + 125p. \qquad (1.7)$$

Here the positive coefficient of price also reflects the marginal principle that a higher price will call forth increased supply—primarily because (as we saw in Example 1.1) it permits firms to incur higher marginal costs of production without incurring losses on the additional units produced.

Equilibrium price determination. Equations 1.6 and 1.7 therefore reflect our model of price determination in the market for peanuts. An equilibrium price can be found by setting quantity demanded equal to quantity supplied:

$$q_D = q_S \qquad (1.8)$$

or

$$1000 - 100p = -125 + 125p \qquad (1.9)$$

or

$$225p = 1125 \qquad (1.10)$$

so,

$$p^* = 5. \qquad (1.11)$$

At a price of $5 per bushel, this market is in equilibrium—at this price people want to purchase 500 bushels, and that is exactly what peanut producers are willing to supply. This equilibrium is pictured graphically as the intersection of D and S in Figure 1.2.

A more general model. In order to illustrate how this supply-demand model might be used, let's adopt a more general notation. Suppose now that the demand and supply functions are given by

$$q_D = a + bp \quad and \quad q_S = c + dp \qquad (1.12)$$

(*continued*)

EXAMPLE 1.2 CONTINUED

where a and c are constants that can be used to shift the demand and supply curves respectively and b (<0) and d (>0) represent demanders' and suppliers' reactions to price. Equilibrium in this market requires

$$q_D = q_S$$

or

$$a + bp = c + dp \tag{1.13}$$

So, equilibrium price is given by[6]

$$p^* = \frac{a - c}{d - b}. \tag{1.14}$$

Notice that, in our prior example, $a = 1000$, $b = -100$, $c = -125$, and $d = 125$, so

$$p^* = \frac{1000 + 125}{125 + 100} = \frac{1125}{225} = 5. \tag{1.15}$$

With this more general formulation, however, we can pose questions about how the equilibrium price might change if either the demand or supply curve shifted. For example, differentiation of Equation 1.14 shows that

and

$$\frac{dp^*}{da} = \frac{1}{d - b} > 0$$

$$\frac{dp^*}{dc} = \frac{-1}{d - b} < 0 \tag{1.16}$$

That is, an increase in demand (an increase in a) increases equilibrium price whereas an increase in supply (an increase in c) reduces price. This is exactly what a graphical analysis of supply and demand curves would show. For example, Figure 1.2 shows that when the constant term, a, in the demand equation increases to 1450, equilibrium price increases to $p^* = 7$ [$=(1450 + 125)/225$].

Query: How might you use Equation 1.16 to "predict" how each unit increase in the constant a affects p^*? Does this equation correctly predict the increase in p^* when the constant a increases from 1000 to 1450?

among markets. To answer more general questions we must have a model of the whole economy that suitably mirrors the connections among various markets and various economic agents. The French economist Leon Walras (1831–1910), building on a long Continental tradition in such analysis, created the basis for modern investigations into those broad questions. His method of representing the economy by a large number of simultaneous equations forms the basis for understanding the interrelationships implicit in *general equilibrium* analysis. Walras recognized that one cannot talk about a single market in isolation; what is needed is a model that permits the effects of a change in one market to be followed through other markets.

---

[6]Equation 1.14 is sometimes called the "reduced form" for the supply-demand structural model of Equations 1.12 and 1.13. It shows that the equilibrium value for the endogenous variable p ultimately depends only on the exogenous factors in the model (a and c) and on the behavioral parameters b and d. A similar equation can be calculated for equilibrium quantity.

FIGURE 1.2   **Changing Supply-Demand Equilibria**

The initial supply-demand equilibrium is illustrated by the intersection of D and S ($p^* = 5$, $q^* = 500$). When demand shifts to $q_D = 1450 - 100p$ (denoted as D'), the equilibrium shifts to $p^* = 7$, $q^* = 750$.

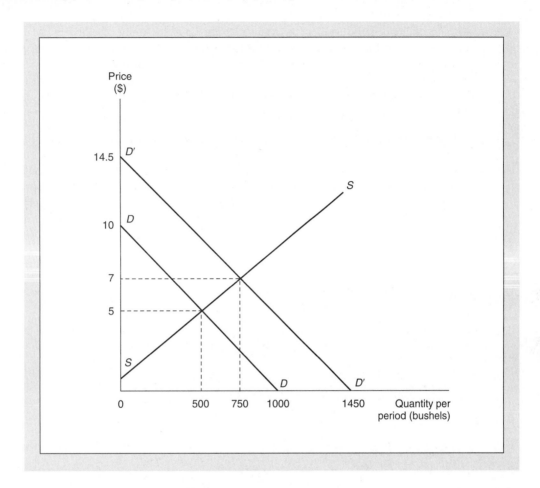

For example, suppose that the demand for peanuts were to increase. This would cause the price of peanuts to increase. Marshallian analysis would seek to understand the size of this increase by looking at conditions of supply and demand in the peanut market. General equilibrium analysis would look not only at that market but also at repercussions in other markets. A rise in the price of peanuts would increase costs for peanut butter makers, which would, in turn, affect the supply curve for peanut butter. Similarly, the rising price of peanuts might mean higher land prices for peanut farmers, which would affect the demand curves for all products that they buy. The demand curves for automobiles, furniture, and trips to Europe would all shift out, and that might create additional incomes for the providers of those products. Consequently, the effects of the initial increase in demand for peanuts eventually would spread throughout the economy. General equilibrium analysis attempts to develop models that permit us to examine such effects in a simplified setting. Several models of this type are described in Part 4.

Production possibility frontier

Here we briefly introduce some general equilibrium ideas by using another graph you should remember from introductory economics—the *production possibility frontier.* This graph shows the various amounts of two goods that an economy can produce using its available resources during some period (say, one week). Because the production possibility frontier shows two goods, rather than the single good in Marshall's model, it is used as a basic building block for general equilibrium models.

Figure 1.3 shows the production possibility frontier for two goods, food and clothing. The graph illustrates the supply of these goods by showing the combinations that can be produced with this economy's resources. For example, 10 pounds of food and 3 units of clothing could be produced, or 4 pounds of food and 12 units of clothing. Many other combinations of food and clothing could also be produced. The production possibility frontier shows all of them. Combinations of food and clothing outside the frontier cannot be produced because not enough resources are available. The production possibility frontier reminds us of the basic economic fact that resources are scarce—there are not enough resources available to produce all we might want of every good.

This scarcity means that we must choose how much of each good to produce. Figure 1.3 makes clear that each choice has its costs. For example, if this economy produces 10 pounds of food and 3 units of clothing at point *A*, producing 1 more unit of clothing would "cost" ½ pound of food—increasing the output of clothing by 1 unit means the production of food would have to decrease by ½ pound. So, the *opportunity cost* of 1 unit of clothing at point *A* is ½ pound of food. On the other hand, if the economy initially produces

---

FIGURE 1.3   **Production Possibility Frontier**

The production possibility frontier shows the different combinations of two goods that can be produced from a certain amount of scarce resources. It also shows the opportunity cost of producing more of one good as the amount of the other good that cannot then be produced. The opportunity cost at two different levels of clothing production can be seen by comparing points *A* and *B*.

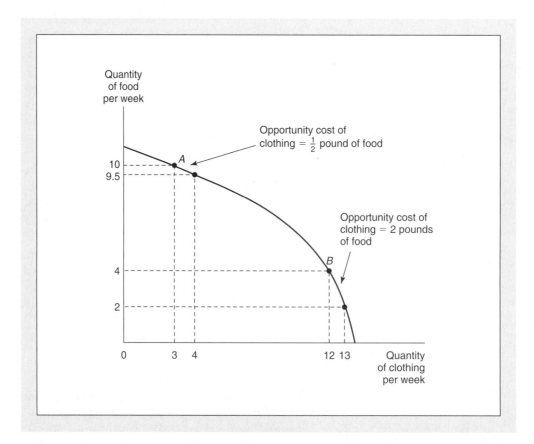

4 pounds of food and 12 units of clothing at point *B*, it would cost 2 pounds of food to produce 1 more unit of clothing. The opportunity cost of 1 more unit of clothing at point *B* has increased to 2 pounds of food. Because more units of clothing are produced at point *B* than at point *A*, both Ricardo's and Marshall's ideas of increasing incremental costs suggest that the opportunity cost of an additional unit of clothing will be higher at point *B* than at point *A*. This effect is just what Figure 1.3 shows.

The production possibility frontier provides two general equilibrium insights that are not clear in Marshall's supply and demand model of a single market. First, the graph shows that producing more of one good means producing less of another good because resources are scarce. Economists often (perhaps too often!) use the expression "there is no such thing as a free lunch" to explain that every economic action has opportunity costs. Second, the production possibility frontier shows that opportunity costs depend on how much of each good is produced. The frontier is like a supply curve for two goods—it shows the opportunity cost of producing more of one good as the decrease in the amount of the second good. The production possibility frontier is therefore a particularly useful tool for studying several markets at the same time.

 EXAMPLE 1.3

A Production Possibility Frontier

Suppose the production possibility frontier for two goods (*x* and *y*) is given by

$$2x^2 + y^2 = 225. \qquad (1.17)$$

A graph of this production possibility frontier would have the shape of a quarter ellipse and would resemble the frontier shown in Figure 1.3. Some points on the frontier include $(x = \sqrt{112.5} = 10.6, y = 0)$, $(x = 10, y = 5)$, $(x = 5, y = \sqrt{175} = 13.2)$, and $(x = 0, y = 15)$. There are infinitely many such points that satisfy Equation 1.17. To find the slope of the frontier at any point, we can solve for *y*,

$$y = \sqrt{225 - 2x^2} \qquad (1.18)$$

and then differentiate to obtain

$$\frac{dy}{dx} = \frac{1}{2}(225 - 2x^2)^{-1/2} \cdot (-4x)$$
$$= \frac{-4x}{2y} = \frac{-2x}{y}. \qquad (1.19)$$

Hence, at *x* = 10, *y* = 5, the slope is –2(10)/5 = –4, and the opportunity cost of producing 1 more unit of *x* is a decrease in *y* production of 4 units. At *x* = 5, $y = \sqrt{175}$, the opportunity cost of *x* is $-2(5)/\sqrt{175} = -0.76$—when less *x* is produced, it has a lower opportunity cost in terms of the number of units of *y* that must be forgone in order to produce 1 more unit of *x*. At many places in this text, we will calculate slopes in this way to illustrate the trade-offs inherent in all economic problems.

Query: Use your calculator together with Equation 1.18 to show that the slope of this function is indeed approximately –4 at the point (*x* = 10, *y* = 5). That is, calculate how much *y* can be produced if *x* = 9.99 or if *x* = 10.01. Why does your calculator permit you to calculate only an approximate value for the exact slope at the point (*x* = 10, *y* = 5)?

Welfare economics

In addition to their use in examining positive questions about how the economy operates, the tools used in general equilibrium analysis have also been applied to the study of normative questions about the welfare properties of various economic arrangements. Although such questions were a major focus of the great eighteenth- and nineteenth-century economists (Smith, Ricardo, Marx, Marshall, and so forth), perhaps the most significant advances in their study were made by the British economist Francis Y. Edgeworth (1848–1926) and the Italian economist Vilfredo Pareto (1848–1923) in the early years of the twentieth century. These economists helped to provide a precise definition for the concept of "economic efficiency" and to demonstrate the conditions under which markets will be able to achieve that goal. By clarifying the relationship between the allocation of resources and the pricing of resources, they provided some support for the idea, first enunciated by Adam Smith, that properly functioning markets provide an "invisible hand" that helps allocate resources efficiently. Later sections of this book focus on some of these welfare issues.

Modern developments

Research activity in economics expanded rapidly in the years following World War II. A major purpose of this book is to summarize much of this research. By illustrating how economists have tried to develop models to explain increasingly complex aspects of economic behavior, this book seeks to put you in a better position to recognize some of the unanswered questions that remain.

The mathematical foundations of economic models

A major postwar development in microeconomic theory was the clarification and formalization of the basic assumptions that are made about individuals and firms. A major landmark in this development was the 1947 publication of Paul Samuelson's *Foundations of Economic Analysis,* in which the author (the first American Nobel Prize winner in economics) laid out a number of models of optimizing behavior.[7] Samuelson demonstrated the importance of basing behavioral models on well-specified mathematical postulates so that various optimization techniques from mathematics could be applied. The power of his approach made it inescapably clear that mathematics had become an integral part of modern economics. In Chapter 2 of this book we review some of the mathematical techniques most often used.

New tools for studying markets

A second feature that has been incorporated into this book is the presentation of a number of new tools for explaining market equilibria. These include techniques for describing pricing in single markets, such as increasingly sophisticated models of monopolistic pricing or game theory models of the strategic relationships among firms that use game theory. They also include general equilibrium tools for exploring relationships among many markets simultaneously. As we shall see, all of these new techniques help to provide a more complete and realistic picture of how markets operate.

The economics of uncertainty and information

A final major theoretical advance during the postwar period was the incorporation of uncertainty and imperfect information into economic models. Some of the basic assumptions used to study behavior in uncertain situations were originally developed in the 1940s in connection with the theory of games. Later developments showed how these ideas could be used to explain why individuals tend to be adverse to risk and how they might gather

---

[7]Paul A. Samuelson, *Foundations of Economic Analysis* (Cambridge, MA: Harvard University Press, 1947).

information in order to reduce the uncertainties they face. In this book, problems of uncertainty and information enter the analysis on many occasions.

Computers and empirical analysis

One final aspect of the postwar development of microeconomics should be mentioned—the increasing use of computers to analyze economic data. As computers have become able to handle larger amounts of information and carry out complex mathematical manipulations, economists' ability to test their theories has dramatically improved. Whereas previous generations had to be content with rudimentary tabular or graphical analyses of real-world data, today's economists have available a wide variety of sophisticated techniques together with extensive microeconomic data with which to develop appropriate tests of their models. To examine these techniques and some of their limitations would be beyond the scope and purpose of this book. But, Extensions at the end of most chapters are intended to help you get started on reading about some of these applications.

SUMMARY

This chapter has provided some background on how economists approach the study of the allocation of resources. Much of the material discussed here should be familiar to you from introductory economics—and that's the way it should be. In many respects, the study of economics represents acquiring increasingly sophisticated tools for addressing the same basic problems. The purpose of this book (and, indeed, of most upper-level books on economics) is to provide you with more of these tools. As a starting place, this chapter reminded you of the following points:

- Economics is the study of how scarce resources are allocated among alternative uses. Economists seek to develop simple models to help understand that process. Many of these models have a mathematical basis because the use of mathematics offers a precise shorthand for stating the models and exploring their consequences.

- The most commonly used economic model is the supply-demand model first thoroughly developed by Alfred Marshall in the latter part of the nineteenth century. This model shows how observed prices can be taken to represent an equilibrium balancing of the production costs incurred by firms and the willingness of demanders to pay for those costs.

- Marshall's model of equilibrium is only "partial"—that is, it looks only at one market at a time. To look at many markets together requires that we develop an expanded set of general equilibrium tools.

- Testing the validity of an economic model is perhaps the most difficult task economists face. Occasionally, a model's validity can be appraised by asking whether it is based on "reasonable" assumptions. More often, however, models are judged by how well they can explain economic events in the real world.

SUGGESTIONS FOR FURTHER READING

On Methodology

Blaug, Mark. *The Methodology of Economics or How Economists Explain*. Cambridge, Cambridge University Press, 1992. A nice summary of several current controversies.

Boland, Lawrence E. "A Critique of Friedman's Critics." *Journal of Economic Literature* (June 1979): 503–22.
Good summary of criticisms of positive approaches to economics and of the role of empirical verification of assumptions.

Friedman, Milton. "The Methodology of Positive Economics." In *Essays in Positive Economics,* pp. 3–43. Chicago: University of Chicago Press, 1953.
Basic statement of Friedman's positivist views.

Harrod, Roy F. "Scope and Method in Economics." *Economic Journal* 48 (1938): 383–412.
Classic statement of appropriate role for economic modeling.

Hausman, David M., and Michael S. McPherson. "Taking Ethics Seriously: Economics and Contemporary Moral Philosophy." *Journal of Economic Literature* (June 1993): 671–731.
Argues strongly that economists should be concerned with ethical questions both because ethics may influence the behavior of economic actors and because moral principles may be needed to determine the relevance of findings from positive economics.

McCloskey, Donald N. *If You're So Smart: The Narrative of Economic Expertise.* Chicago: University of Chicago Press, 1990.
Discussion of McCloskey's view that economic persuasion depends on rhetoric as much as on science. For an interchange on this topic see also the articles in The Journal of Economic Literature, June 1995.

Primary Sources on the History of Economics

Edgeworth, F. Y. *Mathematical Psychics.* London: Kegan Paul, 1881.
Initial investigations of welfare economics, including rudimentary notions of economic efficiency and the contract curve.

Marshall, A. *Principles of Economics,* 8th ed. London: Macmillan & Co., 1920.
Complete summary of neoclassical view. A long-running, popular text. Detailed mathematical appendix.

Marx, K. *Capital.* New York: Modern Library, 1906.
Full development of labor theory of value. Discussion of "transformation problem" provides a (perhaps faulty) start for general equilibrium analysis. Presents fundamental criticisms of institution of private property.

Ricardo, D. *Principles of Political Economy and Taxation.* London: J. M. Dent & Sons, 1911.
Very analytical, tightly written work. Pioneer in developing careful analysis of policy questions, especially trade-related issues. Discusses first basic notions of marginalism.

Smith, A. *The Wealth of Nations.* New York: Modern Library, 1937.
First great economics classic. Very long and detailed, but Smith had the first word on practically every economic matter. This edition has helpful marginal notes.

Walras, L. *Elements of Pure Economics.* Translated by W. Jaffé. Homewood, IL: Richard D. Irwin, 1954.
Beginnings of general equilibrium theory. Rather difficult reading.

Secondary Sources on the History of Economics

Backhouse, Roger E. *The Ordinary Business of Life: The History of Economics from the Ancient World to the 21st Century.* Princeton, NJ: Princeton University Press, 2002.
An iconoclastic history. Quite good on the earliest economic ideas, but some blind spots on recent uses of mathematics and econometrics.

Blaug, Mark. *Economic Theory in Retrospect,* 5th ed. Cambridge: Cambridge University Press, 1997.
Very complete summary stressing analytical issues. Excellent "Readers' Guides" to the classics in each chapter.

Heilbroner, Robert L. *The Worldly Philosophers,* 7th ed. New York: Simon and Schuster, 1999.
Fascinating, easy-to-read biographies of leading economists. Chapters on Utopian Socialists and Thorstein Veblen highly recommended.

Keynes, John M. *Essays in Biography.* New York: W. W. Norton, 1963.
Essays on many famous persons (Lloyd George, Winston Churchill, Leon Trotsky) and on several economists (Malthus, Marshall, Edgeworth, F. P. Ramsey, and Jevons). Shows the true gift of Keynes as a writer.

Schumpeter, J. A. *History of Economic Analysis.* New York: Oxford University Press, 1954.
Encyclopedic treatment. Covers all the famous and many not-so-famous economists. Also briefly summarizes concurrent developments in other branches of the social sciences.

Chapter 2

THE MATHEMATICS OF OPTIMIZATION

Many economic models start with the assumption that an agent is seeking to find the optimal value of some function. For consumers that function measures the utility provided by their purchases; for firms it measures their profits. But in both cases the formal, mathematical aspects of the solution are very similar. In this chapter we examine the mathematics common to all such problems. For those familiar with multivariable calculus, this chapter will be largely in the nature of a review. For those who are familiar only with some concepts from basic calculus, this chapter should provide enough background to start looking at the ways in which calculus is used to construct microeconomic models. More generally, the chapter is intended to provide a reference that may be useful as these various mathematical concepts are encountered later in the text.

Maximization of a function of one variable

Let's start with a simple example. Suppose that a manager of a firm desires to maximize[1] the profits received from selling a particular good. Suppose also that the profits (π) received depend only on the quantity (q) of the good sold. Mathematically,

$$\pi = f(q). \tag{2.1}$$

Figure 2.1 shows a possible relationship between π and q. Clearly, to achieve maximum profits, the manager should produce output $q^\star$, which yields profits $\pi^\star$. If a graph such as that of Figure 2.1 were available, this would seem to be a simple matter to be accomplished with a ruler.

Suppose, however, as is more likely, the manager does not have such an accurate picture of the market. He or she may then try varying q to see where a maximum profit is obtained. For example, by starting at q_1, profits from sales would be π_1. Next, the manager may try output q_2, observing that profits have increased to π_2. The commonsense idea that profits have increased in response to an increase in q can be stated formally as

$$\frac{\pi_2 - \pi_1}{q_2 - q_1} > 0 \quad \text{or} \quad \frac{\Delta\pi}{\Delta q} > 0, \tag{2.2}$$

where the Δ notation is used to mean "the change in" π or q. As long as $\Delta\pi/\Delta q$ is positive, profits are increasing and the manager will continue to increase output. For increases in

---

[1]In this chapter we will generally explore maximization problems. A virtually identical approach would be taken to study minimization problems because maximization of $f(x)$ is equivalent to minimizing $-f(x)$.

| FIGURE 2.1 | Hypothetical Relationship Between Quantity Produced and Profits |

If a manager wishes to produce the level of output that maximizes profits, q^* should be produced. Notice that at q^*, $d\pi/dq = 0$.

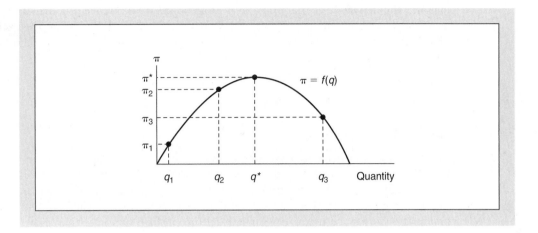

output to the right of q^*, however, $\Delta\pi/\Delta q$ will be negative, and the manager will realize that a mistake has been made if he or she continues to expand q.

Derivatives

As you probably know, the limit of $\Delta\pi/\Delta q$ for very small changes in q is called the *derivative* of the function, $\pi = f(q)$, and is denoted by $d\pi/dq$ or df/dq or $f'(q)$. More formally, the derivative of a function $\pi = f(q)$ at the point q_1 is defined as

$$\frac{d\pi}{dq} = \frac{df}{dq} = \lim_{b \to 0} \frac{f(q_1 + b) - f(q_1)}{b}. \tag{2.3}$$

Notice that the value of this ratio obviously depends on the point q_1 that is chosen.

Value of the derivative at a point

A notational convention should be mentioned: Sometimes one wishes to note explicitly the point at which the derivative is to be evaluated. For example, the evaluation of the derivative at the point $q = q_1$ could be denoted by

$$\frac{d\pi}{dq}\bigg|_{q = q_1} \tag{2.4}$$

At other times one is interested in the value of $d\pi/dq$ for all possible values of q, and no explicit mention of a particular point of evaluation is made.

In the example of Figure 2.1,

$$\frac{d\pi}{dq}\bigg|_{q = q_1} > 0,$$

whereas

$$\frac{d\pi}{dq}\bigg|_{q = q_3} < 0.$$

What is the value of $d\pi/dq$ at q^*? It would seem to be 0, because the value is positive for values of q less than q^* and negative for values greater than q^*. The derivative is the slope of the curve in question; this slope is positive to the left of q^* and negative to the right of q^*. At the point q^*, the slope of $f(q)$ is 0.

First-order condition for a maximum

This result is quite general. For a function of one variable to attain its maximum value at some point, the derivative at that point (if it exists) must be 0. Hence, if a manager could estimate the function $f(q)$ from some sort of real-world data, it would be theoretically possible to find the point where $df/dq = 0$. At this optimal point (say q^*), it would be the case that

$$\frac{df}{dq}\bigg|_{q \,=\, q^*} = 0. \tag{2.5}$$

Second-order conditions

An unsuspecting manager could be tricked, however, by a naive application of this rule alone. For example, suppose that the profit function looks like that shown in either Figure 2.2a or 2.2b. If the profit function is that shown in Figure 2.2a, the manager, by producing where $d\pi/dq = 0$, will choose point q_a^*. This point in fact yields minimum, not maximum, profits for the manager. Similarly, if the profit function is that shown in Figure 2.2b, the manager will choose point q_b^*, which, although it yields a profit greater than that for any output lower than q_b^*, is certainly inferior to any output greater than q_b^*. These situations illustrate the mathematical fact that $d\pi/dq = 0$ is a *necessary* condition for a maximum, but not a *sufficient* condition. To ensure that the chosen point is indeed a maximum point, a second condition must be imposed.

FIGURE 2.2   **Two Profit Functions That Give Misleading Results If the First Derivative Rule Is Applied Uncritically**

In (a) the application of the first derivative rule would result in point q_a^* being chosen. This point is in fact a point of minimum profits. Similarly, in (b) output level q_b^* would be recommended by the first derivative rule, but this point is inferior to all outputs greater than q_b^*. This demonstrates graphically that finding a point at which the derivative is equal to 0 is a necessary, but not a sufficient, condition for a function to attain its maximum value.

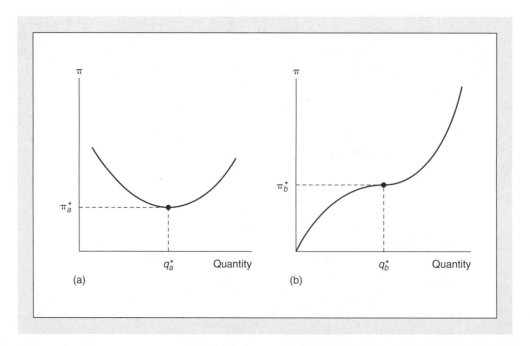

Intuitively, this additional condition is clear: The profit available by producing either a bit more or a bit less than q^* must be smaller than that available from q^*. If this is not true, the manager can do better than q^*. Mathematically, this means that $d\pi/dq$ must be greater than 0 for $q < q^*$ and must be less than 0 for $q > q^*$. Therefore, at q^*, $d\pi/dq$ must be decreasing. Another way of saying this is that the derivative of $d\pi/dq$ must be negative at q^*.

Second derivatives

The derivative of a derivative is called a *second derivative* and is denoted by

$$\frac{d^2\pi}{dq^2} \text{ or } \frac{d^2 f}{dq^2} \text{ or } f''(q).$$

The additional condition for q^* to represent a (local) maximum is therefore

$$\frac{d^2\pi}{dq^2}\bigg|_{q\,=\,q^*} = f''(q)\bigg|_{q\,=\,q^*} < 0, \tag{2.6}$$

where the notation is again a reminder that this second derivative is to be evaluated at q^*.

Hence, although Equation 2.5 ($d\pi/dq = 0$) is a necessary condition for a maximum, that equation must be combined with Equation 2.6 ($d^2\pi/dq^2 < 0$) to ensure that the point is a local maximum for the function. Equations 2.5 and 2.6 together are therefore sufficient conditions for such a maximum. Of course, it is possible that by a series of trials the manager may be able to decide on q^* by relying on market information rather than on mathematical reasoning (remember Friedman's pool-player analogy). In this book we shall be less interested in how the point is discovered than in its properties and how the point changes when conditions change. A mathematical development will be very helpful in answering these questions.

Rules for finding derivatives

Here are a few familiar rules for taking derivatives. We will use these at many places in this book.

1. If b is a constant, then

$$\frac{db}{dx} = 0.$$

2. If b is a constant, then

$$\frac{d[bf(x)]}{dx} = bf'(x).$$

3. If b is a constant, then

$$\frac{dx^b}{dx} = bx^{b-1}.$$

4. $\dfrac{d \ln x}{dx} = \dfrac{1}{x}$

   where ln signifies the logarithm to the base e ($= 2.71828$).

5. $\dfrac{da^x}{dx} = a^x \ln a$ for any constant a.

   A particular case of this rule is $de^x/dx = e^x$.

Now suppose that $f(x)$ and $g(x)$ are two functions of x and that $f'(x)$ and $g'(x)$ exist. Then

6. $\dfrac{d[f(x) + g(x)]}{dx} = f'(x) + g'(x).$

7. $\dfrac{d[f(x) \cdot g(x)]}{dx} = f(x)g'(x) + f'(x)g(x).$

8. $\dfrac{d\left(\dfrac{f(x)}{g(x)}\right)}{dx} = \dfrac{f'(x)g(x) - f(x)g'(x)}{[g(x)]^2},$

provided that $g(x) \neq 0$.

Finally, if $y = f(x)$ and $x = g(z)$ and if both $f'(x)$ and $g'(z)$ exist, then

9. $\dfrac{dy}{dz} = \dfrac{dy}{dx} \cdot \dfrac{dx}{dz} = \dfrac{df}{dx} \cdot \dfrac{dg}{dz}.$

This result is called the *chain rule*. It provides a convenient way to study how one variable (z) affects another variable (y) solely through its influence on some intermediate variable (x). Some examples are

10. $\dfrac{de^{ax}}{dx} = \dfrac{de^{ax}}{d(ax)} \cdot \dfrac{d(ax)}{dx} = e^{ax} \cdot a = ae^{ax}.$

11. $\dfrac{d[\ln(ax)]}{dx} = \dfrac{d[\ln(ax)]}{d(ax)} \cdot \dfrac{d(ax)}{dx} = \ln(ax) \cdot a = a\ln(ax).$

12. $\dfrac{d[\ln(x^2)]}{dx} = \dfrac{d[\ln(x^2)]}{d(x^2)} \cdot \dfrac{d(x^2)}{dx} = \dfrac{1}{x^2} \cdot 2x = \dfrac{2}{x}.$

Functions of several variables

Economic problems seldom involve functions of only a single variable. Most goals of interest to economic agents depend on several variables, and trade-offs must be made among these variables. For example, the *utility* an individual receives from activities as a consumer depends on the amount of each good consumed. For a firm's *production function*, the amount produced depends on the quantity of labor, capital, and land devoted to production. In these circumstances this dependence of one variable (y) on a series of other variables ($x_1, x_2, \ldots, x_n$) is denoted by

$$y = f(x_1, x_2, \ldots, x_n). \tag{2.10}$$

Partial derivatives

We are interested in the point at which y reaches a maximum and in the trade-offs that must be made to reach that point. It is again convenient to picture the agent as changing the variables at his or her disposal (the x's) in order to locate a maximum. Unfortunately, for a function of several variables, the idea of *the* derivative is not well defined. Just as in climbing a mountain the steepness of ascent depends on which direction you go, so does the slope (or derivative) of the function depend on the direction in which it is taken. Usually, the only directional slopes of interest are those that are obtained by increasing one of the x's while holding all the other variables constant (the analogy of mountain climbing might be to measure slopes only in a north-

EXAMPLE 2.1

Profit Maximization

Suppose that the relationship between profits (π) and quantity produced (q) is given by

$$\pi(q) = 1{,}000q - 5q^2. \tag{2.7}$$

A graph of this function would resemble the parabola shown in Figure 2.1. The value of q that maximizes profits can be found by differentiation:

$$\frac{d\pi}{dq} = 1{,}000 - 10q = 0 \tag{2.8}$$

so

$$q^* = 100. \tag{2.9}$$

At $q = 100$, Equation 2.7 shows that profits are 50,000—the largest value possible. If, for example, the firm opted to produce $q = 50$, profits would be 37,500. At $q = 200$, profits are precisely 0.

That $q = 100$ is a "global" maximum can be shown by noting that the second derivative of the profit function is –10 (see Equation 2.8). Hence, the rate of increase in profits is always decreasing—up to $q = 100$ this rate of increase is still positive, but beyond that point it becomes negative. In this example, $q = 100$ is the only local maximum value for the function π. With more complex functions, however, there may be several such maxima.

Query: Suppose that a firm's output (q) is determined by the amount of labor (l) it hires according to the function $q = 2\sqrt{l}$. Suppose also that the firm can hire all of the labor it wants at \$10 per unit and sells its output at \$50 per unit. Profits are therefore a function of l given by $\pi(l) = 100\sqrt{l} - 10l$. How much labor should this firm hire in order to maximize profits, and what will those profits be?

south or east-west direction). These directional slopes are called *partial derivatives.* The partial derivative of y with respect to (that is, in the direction of) x_1 is denoted by

$$\frac{\partial y}{\partial x_1} \text{ or } \frac{\partial f}{\partial x_1} \text{ or } f_{x_1} \text{ or } f_1.$$

It is understood that in calculating this derivative all of the other x's are held constant. Again it should be emphasized that the numerical value of this slope depends on the value of x_1 and on the (preassigned) values of $x_2, \ldots, x_n$.

A somewhat more formal definition of the partial derivative is

$$\left.\frac{\partial f}{\partial x_1}\right|_{\bar{x}_2,\ldots,\bar{x}_n} = \lim_{h \to 0} \frac{f(x_1 + h, \bar{x}_2, \ldots, \bar{x}_n) - f(x_1, \bar{x}_2, \ldots, \bar{x}_n)}{h}, \tag{2.11}$$

where the notation is intended to indicate that $x_2, \ldots, x_n$ are all held constant at the preassigned values $\bar{x}_2, \ldots, \bar{x}_n$ so the effect of changing x_1 only can be studied. Partial derivatives with respect to the other variables ($x_2, \ldots, x_n$) would be calculated in a similar way.

Calculating partial derivatives

It is easy to calculate partial derivatives. The calculation proceeds as for the usual derivative by *treating x_2, . . . , x_n as constants* (which indeed they are in the definition of a partial derivative). Consider the following examples:

1. If $y = f(x_1, x_2) = ax_1^2 + bx_1x_2 + cx_2^2$, then

$$\frac{\partial f}{\partial x_1} = f_1 = 2ax_1 + bx_2$$

and

$$\frac{\partial f}{\partial x_2} = f_2 = bx_1 + 2cx_2.$$

Notice that $\partial f/\partial x_1$ is in general a function of both x_1 and x_2 and therefore its value will depend on the particular values assigned to these variables. It also depends on the parameters a, b, and c, which do not change as x_1 and x_2 change.

2. If $y = f(x_1, x_2) = 5\, e^{ax_1 + bx_2}$, then

$$\frac{\partial f}{\partial x_1} = f_1 = ae^{ax_1 + bx_2}$$

and

$$\frac{\partial f}{\partial x_2} = f_2 = be^{ax_1 + bx_2}.$$

3. If $y = f(x_1, x_2) = a \ln x_1 + b \ln x_2$, then

$$\frac{\partial f}{\partial x_1} = f_1 = \frac{a}{x_1}$$

and

$$\frac{\partial f}{\partial x_2} = f_2 = \frac{b}{x_2}.$$

Notice here that the treatment of x_2 as a constant in the derivation of $\partial f/\partial x_1$ causes the term $b \ln x_2$ to disappear upon differentiation because it does not change when x_1 changes. In this case, unlike our previous examples, the size of the effect of x_1 on y is independent of the value of x_2. In other cases the effect of x_1 on y will depend on the level of x_2.

Partial derivatives and the ceteris paribus assumption

In Chapter 1 we described the way in which economists use the ceteris paribus assumption in their models to hold constant a variety of outside influences so the particular relationship being studied can be explored in a simplified setting. Partial derivatives are a precise mathematical way of representing this approach; that is, they show how changes in one variable affect some outcome when other influences are held constant—exactly what economists need for their models. For example, Marshall's demand curve shows the relationship between price (p) and quantity (q) demanded when other factors are held constant. Using partial derivatives, we could represent the slope of this curve by $\partial q/\partial p$ to indicate the *ceteris paribus,* assumptions that are in effect. The fundamental law of demand—that price and quantity move in opposite directions when other factors do not change—is therefore reflected by the mathematical statement "$\partial q/\partial p < 0$." Again, the use of a partial derivative serves as a reminder of the ceteris paribus assumptions that surround the law of demand.

Partial derivatives and units of measurement

In mathematics relatively little attention is paid to how variables are measured. In fact, most often no explicit mention is made of the issue. But the variables used in economics usually refer to real-world magnitudes and therefore we must be concerned with how they are measured. Perhaps the most important consequence of choosing units of measurement is that the partial derivatives often used to summarize economic behavior will reflect these units. For example, if q represents the quantity of gasoline demanded by all U.S. consumers during a given year (measured in billions of gallons) and p represents the price in dollars per gallon, then $\partial q/\partial p$ will measure the change in demand (in billions of gallons per year) for a dollar per gallon change in price. The numerical size of this derivative depends on how q and p are measured. A decision to measure consumption in millions of gallons per year would multiply the size of the derivative by 1,000 whereas a decision to measure price in cents per gallon would reduce it by a factor of 100.

The dependence of the numerical size of partial derivatives on the units of measurement chosen poses problems for economists. Although many economic theories make predictions about the sign (direction) of partial derivatives, any predictions about the numerical magnitude of such derivatives would be contingent on how authors chose to measure their variables. Making comparisons among studies could prove practically impossible, especially given the wide variety of measuring systems that are in use around the world. For this reason, economists have chosen to adopt a different, unit-free way to measure quantitative impacts.

Elasticity—A general definition

Economists use elasticities to summarize virtually all of the quantitative impacts that are of interest to them. Because such measures focus on the proportional effect of a change in one variable on another, they are unit-free—the units "cancel out" when the elasticity is calculated. Suppose, for example, that y is a function of x and, possibly, other variables. Then the elasticity of y with respect to x (denoted as $e_{y,x}$) is defined as

$$e_{y,x} = \frac{\dfrac{\Delta y}{y}}{\dfrac{\Delta x}{x}} = \frac{\Delta y}{\Delta x} \cdot \frac{x}{y} = \frac{\partial y}{\partial x} \cdot \frac{x}{y}. \tag{2.12}$$

Notice that, no matter how the variables y and x are measured, the units of measurement cancel out because they appear in both a numerator and a denominator. Notice also that, because y and x are positive in most economic situations, the elasticity, $e_{y,x}$ and the partial derivative $\partial y/\partial x$ will have the same sign. Hence, theoretical predictions about the direction of certain derivatives will apply also to their related elasticities.

Specific applications of the elasticity concept will be encountered throughout this book. These include ones with which you should be familiar such as the market price elasticity of demand or supply. But many new concepts that can be expressed most clearly in elasticity terms will also be introduced.

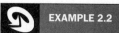 **EXAMPLE 2.2**

Elasticity and Functional Form

The definition in Equation 2.12 makes clear that elasticity should be evaluated at a specific point on a function. In general the value of this parameter would be expected to vary across different ranges of the function. This observation is most clearly shown in the case where y is a linear function of x of the form

$$y = a + bx + \text{other terms.}$$

In this case,

$$e_{y,x} = \frac{\partial y}{\partial x} \cdot \frac{x}{y} = b \cdot \frac{x}{y} = b \cdot \frac{x}{a + bx + \cdots} \qquad (2.13)$$

which makes clear that $e_{y,x}$ is not constant. Hence, for linear functions it is especially important to note the point at which elasticity is to be computed.

If the functional relationship between y and x is of the exponential form

$$y = ax^b$$

then the elasticity is a constant, independent of where it is measured:

$$e_{y,x} = \frac{\partial y}{\partial x} \cdot \frac{x}{y} = abx^{b-1} \cdot \frac{x}{ax^b} = b.$$

A logarithmic transformation of this equation also provides a very convenient alternative definition of elasticity. Because

$$\ln y = \ln a + b \ln x,$$

we have

$$e_{y,x} = b = \frac{\partial \ln y}{\partial \ln x}. \qquad (2.14)$$

Hence, elasticities can be calculated through "logarithmic differentiation." As we shall see, this is frequently the easiest way to proceed in making such calculations.

Query: Are there any functional forms in addition to the exponential that have a constant elasticity, at least over some range?

Second-order partial derivatives

The partial derivative of a partial derivative is directly analogous to the second derivative of a function of one variable and is called a *second-order partial derivative*. This may be written as

$$\frac{\partial(\partial f / \partial x_i)}{\partial x_j}$$

or more simply as

$$\frac{\partial^2 f}{\partial x_j \partial x_i} = f_{ij}. \qquad (2.15)$$

For the examples above:

1. $$\frac{\partial^2 f}{\partial x_1 \partial x_1} = f_{11} = 2a$$
$$f_{12} = b$$
$$f_{21} = b$$
$$f_{22} = 2c.$$

2. $f_{11} = a^2 e^{ax_1 + bx_2}$
$f_{12} = abe^{ax_1 + bx_2}$
$f_{21} = abe^{ax_1 + bx_2}$
$f_{22} = b^2 e^{ax_1 + bx_2}$

3. $f_{11} = \dfrac{-a}{x_1^2}$
$f_{12} = 0$
$f_{21} = 0$
$f_{22} = \dfrac{-b}{x_2^2}.$

Young's theorem

These examples illustrate the mathematical result that, under quite general conditions, the order in which partial differentiation is conducted to evaluate second-order partial derivatives does not matter. That is,

$$f_{ij} = f_{ji} \tag{2.16}$$

for any pair of variables x_i, x_j. This result is sometimes called "Young's theorem." For an intuitive explanation of the theorem, we can return to our mountain-climbing analogy. In this example the theorem states that the gain in elevation a hiker experiences depends on the directions and distances traveled, but not on the order in which these occur. That is, the gain in altitude is independent of the actual path taken as long as the hiker proceeds from one set of map coordinates to another. He or she may, for example, go one mile north, then one mile east or proceed in the opposite order by going one mile east first, then a mile north. In either case, the gain in elevation is the same since in both cases the hiker is moving from one specific place to another. In later chapters we will make quite a bit of use of this result because it provides a very convenient way of showing some of the predictions that economic models make about behavior.[2]

Uses of second-order partials

Second-order partial derivatives will play an important role in many of the economic theories that are developed throughout this book. Probably the most important examples relate to the "own" second-order partial, f_{ii}. This function shows how the marginal influence of x_i on $y\left(\text{that is, }\dfrac{\partial y}{\partial x_i}\right)$ changes as the value of x_i increases. A negative value for f_{ii} is the mathematical way of indicating the economic idea of diminishing marginal effectiveness. Similarly, the cross-partial f_{ij} indicates how the marginal effectiveness of x_i changes as x_j increases. The sign of this effect could be either positive or negative. Young's theorem

---

[2]Young's theorem implies that the matrix of the second-order partial derivatives of a function is symmetric. This symmetry offers a number of economic insights. For a brief introduction to the matrix concepts used in economics, see the Extensions to this chapter.

indicates that, in general, such cross-effects are symmetric. More generally, the second-order partial derivatives of a function provide information about the curvature of the function. Later in this chapter we will see how such information plays an important role in determining whether various second-order conditions for a maximum are satisfied.

Maximization of functions of several variables

Using partial derivatives, we can now discuss how to find the maximum value for a function of several variables. To understand the mathematics used in solving this problem, an analogy to the one-variable case is helpful. In this one-variable case, we can picture an agent varying x by a small amount, dx, and observing the change in y (call this dy). This change is given by

$$dy = f'(x)\ dx. \tag{2.17}$$

The identity in Equation 2.17 records the fact that the change in y is equal to the change in x times the slope of the function. This formula is equivalent to the *point-slope* formula used for linear equations in basic algebra. As before, the necessary condition for a maximum is that $dy = 0$ for small changes in x around the optimal point. Otherwise, y could be increased by suitable changes in x. But because dx does not necessarily equal 0 in Equation 2.7, $dy = 0$ must imply that at the desired point, $f'(x) = 0$. This is another way of obtaining the first-order condition for a maximum that we already derived.

Using this analogy, let's look at the decisions made by an economic agent who must choose the levels of several variables. Suppose that this agent wishes to find a set of x's that will maximize the value of $y = f(x_1, x_2, \ldots, x_n)$. The agent might consider changing only one of the x's, say x_1, while holding all the others constant. The change in y (that is, dy) that would result from this change in x_1 is given by

$$dy = \frac{\partial f}{\partial x_1}\ dx_1 = f_1 dx_1.$$

This says that the change in y is equal to the change in x_1 times the slope measured in the x_1 direction. Using the mountain analogy again, this would say that the gain in altitude a climber heading north would achieve is given by the distance northward traveled times the slope of the mountain measured in a northward direction.

Total differential

If all the x's are varied by a small amount, the total effect on y will be the sum of effects such as that shown above. Therefore the total change in y is defined to be

$$\begin{aligned} dy &= \frac{\partial f}{\partial x_1}\ dx_1 + \frac{\partial f}{\partial x_2}\ dx_2 + \cdots + \frac{\partial f}{\partial x_n}\ dx_n \\ &= f_1 dx_1 + f_2 dx_2 + \cdots + f_n dx_n. \end{aligned} \tag{2.18}$$

This expression is called the *total differential* of f and is directly analogous to the expression for the single-variable case given in Equation 2.17. The equation is intuitively sensible: The total change in y is the sum of changes brought about by varying each of the x's.[3]

---

[3]The total differential in Equation 2.18 can be used to derive the chain rule as it applies to functions of several variables. Suppose that $y = f(x_1, x_2)$ and that $x_1 = g(z)$ and $x_2 = h(z)$. If all these functions are differentiable, it is possible to calculate the effects of a change in z on y. The total differential of y is

$$dy = f_1 dx_1 + f_2 dx_2.$$

Dividing this equation by dz gives

$$\frac{dy}{dz} = f_1 \frac{dx_1}{dz} + f_2 \frac{dx_2}{dz} = f_1 \frac{dg}{dz} + f_2 \frac{dh}{dz}.$$

Hence, calculating the effect of z on y requires calculating how z affects both of the determinants of y (that is, x_1 and x_2). If y depends on more than two variables, an analogous result holds. This result acts as a reminder to be rather careful to include all possible effects when calculating derivatives of functions of several variables.

First-order condition for a maximum

A necessary condition for a maximum (or a minimum) of the function $f(x_1, x_2, \ldots, x_n)$ is that $dy = 0$ for any combination of small changes in the x's. The only way this can happen is if at the point being considered

$$f_1 = f_2 = \cdots = f_n = 0. \qquad (2.19)$$

A point where Equations 2.19 hold is called a *critical point*. Equations 2.19 are the necessary conditions for a local maximum. To see this intuitively, note that if one of the partials (say, f_i) were greater (or less) than 0, then y could be increased by increasing (or decreasing) x_i. An economic agent then could find this maximal point by finding the spot where y does not respond to very small movements in any of the x's. This is an extremely important result for economic analysis. It says that any activity

 EXAMPLE 2.3

Finding a Maximum

Suppose that y is a function of x_1 and x_2 given by

$$y = -(x_1 - 1)^2 - (x_2 - 2)^2 + 10 \qquad (2.20)$$

or

$$y = -x_1^2 + 2x_1 - x_2^2 + 4x_2 + 5.$$

For example, y might represent an individual's health (measured on a scale of 0 to 10), and x_1 and x_2 might be daily dosages of two health-enhancing drugs. We wish to find values for x_1 and x_2 that make y as large as possible. Taking the partial derivatives of y with respect to x_1 and x_2 and applying the necessary conditions given by Equations 2.19 yields

$$\frac{\partial y}{\partial x_1} = -2x_1 + 2 = 0$$

$$\frac{\partial y}{\partial x_2} = -2x_2 + 4 = 0 \qquad (2.21)$$

or

$$x_1^* = 1$$
$$x_2^* = 2.$$

The function is therefore at a critical point when $x_1 = 1$, $x_2 = 2$. At that point, $y = 10$ is the best health status possible. A bit of experimentation provides convincing evidence that this is the greatest value y can have. For example, if $x_1 = x_2 = 0$, then $y = 5$, or if $x_1 = x_2 = 1$, then $y = 9$. Values of x_1 and x_2 larger than 1 and 2, respectively, reduce y because the negative quadratic terms in Equation 2.20 become large. Consequently, the point found by applying the necessary conditions is in fact a local (and global) maximum.[4]

Query: Suppose y took on a fixed value (say, 5). What would the relationship implied between x_1 and x_2 look like? How about for $y = 7$? Or $y = 10$? (These graphs are *contour lines* of the function and will be examined in more detail in several later chapters. See also Problem 2.1.)

---

[4]More formally, the point $x_1 = 1$, $x_2 = 2$ is a global maximum because the function described by Equation 2.20 is concave (see our discussion later in this chapter).

(that is, the x's) should be pushed to the point where its "marginal" contribution to the objective (that is, y) is 0. To stop short of that point would fail to maximize y.

Second-order conditions

Again, however, the conditions of Equations 2.19 are not sufficient to ensure a maximum. This can be illustrated by returning to an already overworked analogy: All hilltops are (more or less) flat, but not every flat place is a hilltop. A second-order condition similar to Equation 2.6 is needed to ensure that the point found by applying Equations 2.19 is a local maximum. Intuitively, for a local maximum, y should be decreasing for any small changes in the x's away from the critical point. As in the single-variable case, this necessarily involves looking at the second-order partial derivatives of the function f. These second-order partials must obey certain restrictions (analogous to the restriction that was derived in the single-variable case) if the critical point found by applying Equations 2.19 is to be a local maximum. Later in this chapter we will look at these restrictions.

Implicit functions

Although mathematical equations are often written with a "dependent" variable (y) as a function of one or more independent variables (x), this is not the only way to write such a relationship. As a trivial example, the equation

$$y = mx + b \tag{2.22}$$

can also be written as

$$y - mx - b = 0 \tag{2.23}$$

or, even more generally, as

$$f(x, y, m, b) = 0 \tag{2.24}$$

where this functional notation indicates a relationship between x and y that also depends on the slope (m) and intercept (b) parameters of the function, which do not change. Functions written in these forms are sometimes called *implicit functions* because the relationships between the variables and parameters are implicitly present in the equation rather than being explicitly calculated as, say, y as a function of x and the parameters m and b.

Often it is a simple matter to translate from implicit functions to explicit ones. For example, the implicit function

$$x + 2y - 4 = 0 \tag{2.25}$$

can easily be "solved" for x as

$$x = -2y + 4 \tag{2.26}$$

or for y as

$$y = \frac{-x}{2} + 2. \tag{2.27}$$

Derivatives from implicit functions

In many circumstances it is helpful to compute derivatives directly from implicit functions without solving for one of the variables directly. For example, the implicit function $f(x, y) = 0$ has a total differential of $0 = f_x dx + f_y dy$ so

$$\frac{dy}{dx} = -\frac{f_x}{f_y}. \tag{2.28}$$

Hence, the implicit derivative dy/dx can be found as the negative of the ratio of the partial derivatives of the implicit function, providing $f_y \neq 0$.

EXAMPLE 2.4

A Production Possibility Frontier—Again

In Example 1.3 we examined a production possibility frontier for two goods of the form

$$2x^2 + y^2 = 225 \qquad (2.29)$$

or, written implicitly,

$$f(x, y) = 2x^2 + y^2 - 225 = 0. \qquad (2.30)$$

Hence,

$$f_x = 4x,$$
$$f_y = 2y$$

and, by Equation 2.28, the opportunity cost trade-off between x and y is

$$\frac{dy}{dx} = \frac{-f_x}{f_y} = \frac{-4x}{2y} = \frac{-2x}{y}, \qquad (2.31)$$

which is precisely the result we obtained earlier, with considerably less work.

Query: Why does the trade-off between x and y here depend only on the ratio of x to y, but not on the "size of the economy" as reflected by the 225 constant?

Implicit function theorem

It may not always be possible to solve implicit functions of the form $g(x, y) = 0$ for unique explicit functions of the form $y = f(x)$. Mathematicians have analyzed the conditions under which a given implicit function can be solved explicitly with one variable being a function of other variables and various parameters. Although we will not investigate these conditions here, they involve requirements on the various partial derivatives of the function that are sufficient to ensure that there is indeed a unique relationship between the dependent and independent variables.[5] In many economic applications, these derivative conditions are precisely those required to ensure that the second-order conditions for a maximum (or a minimum) hold. Hence, in these cases, we will assert that the *implicit function theorem* holds and that it is therefore possible to solve explicitly for trade-offs among the variables involved.

The envelope theorem

One major application of the implicit function theorem, which will be used at many places in this book, is called the *envelope theorem;* it concerns how the optimal value for a particular function changes when a parameter of the function changes. Because many of the economic problems we will be studying concern the effects of changing a parameter (for example, the effects that changing the market price of a commodity will have on an individual's purchases), this is a type of calculation we will frequently make. The envelope theorem often provides a nice shortcut.

---

[5]For a detailed discussion of the implicit function theorem in various contexts, see Carl P. Simon and Lawrence Blume, *Mathematics for Economists* (New York: W. W. Norton, 1994), chap. 15.

A specific example

Perhaps the easiest way to understand the envelope theorem is through an example. Suppose y is a function of a single variable (x) and a parameter (a) given by

$$y = -x^2 + ax. \qquad (2.32)$$

For different values of the parameter a, this function represents a family of inverted parabolas. If a is assigned a specific value, Equation 2.32 is a function of x only, and the value of x that maximizes y can be calculated. For example, if $a = 1$, $x^* = \frac{1}{2}$ and, for these values of x and a, $y = \frac{1}{4}$ (its maximal value). Similarly, if $a = 2$, $x^* = 1$ and $y^* = 1$. Hence, an increase of 1 in the value of the parameter a has increased the maximum value of y by $\frac{3}{4}$. In Table 2.1, integral values of a between 0 and 6 are used to calculate the optimal values for x and the associated values of the objective, y. Notice that as a increases, the maximal value for y also increases. This is also illustrated in Figure 2.3, which shows that the relationship between a and y^* is quadratic. Now we wish to calculate explicitly how y^* changes as the parameter a changes.

A direct, time-consuming approach

The envelope theorem states that there are two equivalent ways we can make this calculation. First, we can calculate the slope of the function in Figure 2.3 directly. To do so, we must solve Equation 2.32 for the optimal value of x for any value of a:

$$\frac{dy}{dx} = -2x + a = 0;$$

hence,

$$x^* = \frac{a}{2}.$$

Substituting this value of x^* in Equation 2.32 gives

$$y^* = -(x^*)^2 + a(x^*)$$

$$= -\left(\frac{a}{2}\right)^2 + a\left(\frac{a}{2}\right)$$

$$= -\frac{a^2}{4} + \frac{a^2}{2} = \frac{a^2}{4},$$

TABLE 2.1   **Optimal Values of *y* and *x* for Alternative Values of *a* in *y* = −*x*² + *ax***

Value of a	Value of x^*	Value of y^*
0	0	0
1	$\frac{1}{2}$	$\frac{1}{4}$
2	1	1
3	$\frac{3}{2}$	$\frac{9}{4}$
4	2	4
5	$\frac{5}{2}$	$\frac{25}{4}$
6	3	9

FIGURE 2.3	**Illustration of the Envelope Theorem**

The envelope theorem states that the slope of the relationship between y^* (the maximum value of y) and the parameter a can be found by calculating the slope of the auxiliary relationship found by substituting the respective optimal values for x into the objective function and calculating $\partial y/\partial a$.

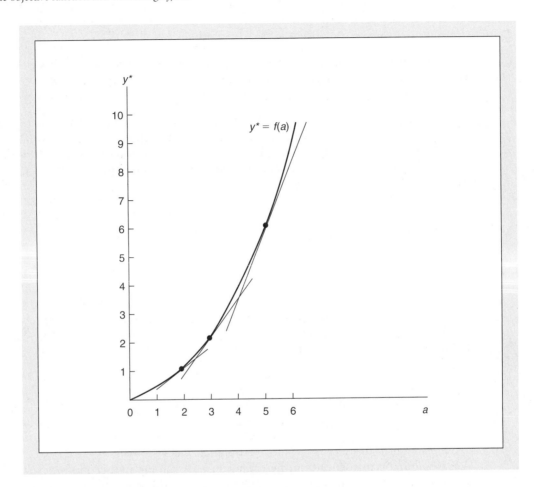

and this is precisely the relationship shown in Figure 2.3. From the previous equation, it is easy to see that

$$\frac{dy^*}{da} = \frac{2a}{4} = \frac{a}{2} \tag{2.33}$$

and, for example, at $a = 2$, $dy^*/da = 1$. That is, near $a = 2$ the marginal impact of increasing a is to increase y^* by the same amount. Near $a = 6$, any small increase in a will increase y^* by three times this change. Table 2.1 illustrates this result.

The envelope shortcut

Arriving at this conclusion was a bit complicated. We had to find the optimal value of x for each value of a and then substitute this value for x^* into the equation for y. In more general cases this may be quite burdensome since it requires repeatedly maximizing the objective function. The envelope theorem, providing an alternative approach, states that for small changes in a, dy^*/da can be computed by holding x constant *at its optimal value* and simply calculating $\partial y/\partial a$ from the objective function directly.

Proceeding in this way gives

$$\frac{\partial y}{\partial a} = x \qquad (2.34)$$

and, at x^* we have

$$\frac{\partial y^*}{\partial a} = x^* = \frac{a}{2}. \qquad (2.35)$$

This is precisely the result obtained earlier. The reason that the two approaches yield identical results is illustrated in Figure 2.3. The tangents shown in the figure report values of y for a *fixed* x^*. The tangents' slopes are $\partial y/\partial a$. Clearly, at y^* this slope gives the value we seek.

This result is quite general, and we will use it at several places in this book to simplify our results. To summarize, the envelope theorem states that the change in the optimal value of a function with respect to a parameter of that function can be found by partially differentiating the objective function while holding x (or several x's) constant at its optimal value. That is,

$$\frac{dy^*}{da} = \frac{\partial y}{\partial a} \{x = x^*(a)\}, \qquad (2.36)$$

where the notation provides a reminder that $\partial y/\partial a$ must be computed at that value of x that is optimal for the specific value of the parameter a being examined.

Many-variable case

An analogous envelope theorem holds for the case where y is a function of several variables. Suppose that y depends on a set of x's ($x_1, \ldots, x_n$) and on a particular parameter of interest, say, a,

$$y = f(x_1, \ldots, x_n, a). \qquad (2.37)$$

Finding an optimal value for y would consist of solving n first-order equations of the form

$$\partial y/\partial x_i = 0 \quad (i = 1, \ldots, n), \qquad (2.38)$$

and a solution to this process would yield optimal values for these x's ($x_1^*, x_2^*, \ldots, x_n^*$) that would implicitly depend on the parameter a. Assuming the second-order conditions are met, the implicit function theorem would apply in this case and ensure that we could solve each x_i^* as a function of the parameter a:

$$x_1^* = x_1^*(a)$$
$$x_2^* = x_2^*(a)$$
$$\vdots \qquad (2.39)$$
$$x_n^* = x_n^*(a).$$

Substituting these functions into our original objective (Equation 2.37) yields an expression in which the optimal value of y (say, y^*) depends on the parameter a both directly and indirectly through the effect of a on the x^*'s.

$$y^* = f[x_1^*(a), x_2^*(a), \ldots, x_n^*(a), a]$$

Totally differentiating this expression with respect to a yields

$$\frac{dy^*}{da} = \frac{\partial f}{\partial x_1} \cdot \frac{dx_1}{da} + \frac{\partial f}{\partial x_2} \cdot \frac{dx_2}{da} \cdots + \frac{\partial f}{\partial x_n} \cdot \frac{dx_n}{da} + \frac{\partial f}{\partial a}. \qquad (2.40)$$

But, because of the first-order conditions all of these terms except the last are equal to 0 if the x's are at their optimal values. Hence, again we have the envelope result:

$$\frac{dy^*}{da} = \frac{\partial f}{\partial a}, \tag{2.41}$$

where this derivative is to be evaluated at the optimal values for the x's.

 EXAMPLE 2.5

The Envelope Theorem: Health Status Revisited

Earlier, in Example 2.3, we examined the maximum values for the health status function

$$y = -(x_1 - 1)^2 - (x_2 - 2)^2 + 10 \tag{2.42}$$

and found that

$$x_1^* = 1$$
$$x_2^* = 2 \tag{2.43}$$

and

$$y^* = 10.$$

Suppose now we use the arbitrary parameter a instead of the constant 10 in Equation 2.42. Here a might represent a measure of the best possible health for a person, but this value would obviously vary from person to person. Hence,

$$y = f(x_1, x_2, a) = -(x_1 - 1)^2 - (x_2 - 2)^2 + a. \tag{2.44}$$

In this case the optimal values for x_1 and x_2 do not depend on a (they are always $x_1^* = 1$, $x_2^* = 2$), so at those optimal values we have

$$y^* = a \tag{2.45}$$

and

$$\frac{dy^*}{da} = 1. \tag{2.46}$$

People with "naturally better health" will have concomitantly higher values for y^*, providing they choose x_1 and x_2 optimally. But this is precisely what the envelope theorem indicates, because

$$\frac{dy^*}{da} = \frac{\partial f}{\partial a} = 1 \tag{2.47}$$

from Equation 2.44. Increasing the parameter a simply increases the optimal value for y^* by an identical amount (again, assuming the dosages of x_1 and x_2 are correctly chosen).

Query: Suppose we focused instead on the optimal dosage for x_1 in Equation 2.42—that is, suppose we used a general parameter, say b, instead of 1. Explain in words and using mathematics why $\partial y^*/\partial b$ would necessarily be 0 in this case.

Constrained maximization

So far we have focused our attention on finding the maximum value of a function without restricting the choices of the x's available. In most economic problems, however, not all values for the x's are feasible. In many situations, for example, it is required that all the x's be positive. This would be true for the problem faced by the manager choosing output to maximize profits; a negative output would have no meaning. In other instances the x's may be constrained by economic considerations. For example, in choosing the items to consume, an individual is not able to choose any quantities desired. Rather, choices are constrained by the amount of purchasing power available; that is, by this person's budget constraint. Such constraints may lower the maximum value for the function being maximized. Because we are not able to choose freely among all the x's, y may not be as large as it can be. The constraints would be said to be "nonbinding" if we could obtain the same level of y with or without imposing the constraint.

Lagrangian multiplier method

One method for solving constrained maximization problems is the *Lagrangian multiplier method,* which involves a clever mathematical trick that also turns out to have a useful economic interpretation. The rationale of this method is quite simple, although no rigorous presentation will be attempted here.[6] In a prior section the necessary conditions for a local maximum were discussed. We showed that at the optimal point all the partial derivatives of f must be 0. There are therefore n equations ($f_i = 0$ for $i = 1, \ldots, n$) in n unknowns (the x's). Generally, these equations can be solved for the optimal x's. When the x's are constrained, however, there is at least one additional equation (the constraint) but no additional variables. The set of equations therefore is overdetermined. The Lagrangian technique introduces an additional variable (the Lagrangian multiplier), which not only helps to solve the problem at hand (because there are now $n + 1$ equations in $n + 1$ unknowns), but also has an interpretation that is useful in a variety of economic circumstances.

The formal problem

More specifically, suppose that we wish to find the values of $x_1, x_2, \ldots, x_n$ that maximize

$$y = f(x_1, x_2, \ldots, x_n), \tag{2.48}$$

subject to a constraint that permits only certain values of the x's to be used. A general way of writing that constraint is

$$g(x_1, x_2, \ldots, x_n) = 0, \tag{2.49}$$

where the function[7] g represents the relationship that must hold among all the x's.

First-order conditions

The Lagrangian multiplier method starts with setting up the expression

$$\mathcal{L} = f(x_1, x_2, \ldots, x_n) + \lambda g(x_1, x_2, \ldots, x_n), \tag{2.50}$$

where λ is an additional variable that is called the Lagrangian multiplier. Later we will interpret this new variable. First, however, notice that when the constraint holds, $\mathcal{L}$ and f have the same value [because $g(x_1, x_2, \ldots, x_n) = 0$]. Consequently, if we restrict our attention only to values of the x's that satisfy the constraint, finding the constrained maximum value of f is equivalent to finding a critical value of $\mathcal{L}$. Let us proceed then to do so,

---

[6]For a detailed presentation, see A. K. Dixit, *Optimization in Economic Theory,* 2nd ed. (Oxford: Oxford University Press, 1990), Chap. 2.

[7]As we pointed out earlier, any function of $x_1, x_2, \ldots, x_n$ can be written in this implicit way. For example, the constraint $x_1 + x_2 = 10$ could be written $10 - x_1 - x_2 = 0$. In later chapters we shall usually follow this procedure in dealing with constraints. Often the constraints we examine will be linear.

treating λ also as a variable (in addition to the x's). From Equation 2.50 the conditions for a critical point are

$$\frac{\partial \mathcal{L}}{\partial x_1} = f_1 + \lambda g_1 = 0$$

$$\frac{\partial \mathcal{L}}{\partial x_2} = f_2 + \lambda g_2 = 0$$

$$\vdots$$

$$\frac{\partial \mathcal{L}}{\partial x_n} = f_n + \lambda g_n = 0$$

$$\frac{\partial \mathcal{L}}{\partial \lambda} = g(x_1, x_2, \ldots, x_n) = 0.$$

(2.51)

Equations 2.51 are then the conditions for a critical point for the function $\mathcal{L}$. Notice that there are $n + 1$ equations (one for each x and a final one for λ) in $n + 1$ unknowns. The equations can generally be solved for $x_1, x_2, \ldots, x_n$, and λ. Such a solution will have two properties: (1) the x's will obey the constraint because the last equation in 2.51 imposes that condition; and (2) among all those values of x's that satisfy the constraint, those that also solve Equations 2.51 will make $\mathcal{L}$ (and hence f) as large as possible (assuming second-order conditions are met). The Lagrangian multiplier method therefore provides a way to find a solution to the constrained maximization problem we posed at the outset.[8]

The solution to Equations 2.51 will usually differ from that in the unconstrained case (see Equations 2.19). Rather than proceeding to the point where the marginal contribution of each x is 0, Equations 2.51 require us to stop short because of the constraint. Only if the constraint were ineffective (in which case, as we show below, λ would be 0) would the constrained and unconstrained equations (and their respective solutions) agree. These revised marginal conditions have economic interpretations in many different situations.

Interpretation of the Lagrangian multiplier

So far we have used the Lagrangian multiplier (λ) only as a mathematical "trick" to arrive at the solution we wanted. In fact, that variable also has an important economic interpretation, which will be central to our analysis at many points in this book. To develop this interpretation, rewrite the first n equations in 2.51 as

$$\frac{f_1}{-g_1} = \frac{f_2}{-g_2} = \cdots = \frac{f_n}{-g_n} = \lambda.$$

(2.52)

In other words, at the maximum point, the ratio of f_i to g_i is the same for every x_i. The numerators in Equations 2.52 are the marginal contributions of each x to the function f. They show the *marginal benefit* that one more unit of x_i will have for the function that is being maximized (that is, for f).

A complete interpretation of the denominators in Equations 2.51 is probably best left until we encounter these ratios in actual economic applications. There we will see that these usually have a "marginal cost" interpretation. That is, they reflect the added burden on the constraint of using slightly more x_i. As a simple illustration, suppose the constraint required that total spending on x_1 and x_2 (say) be given by a fixed dollar amount, F.

---

[8]Strictly speaking, these are the necessary conditions for an interior local maximum. In some economic problems, it is necessary to amend these conditions (in fairly obvious ways) to take account of the possibility that some of the x's may be on the boundary of the region of permissible x's. For example, if all the x's are required to be nonnegative, it may be that the conditions of Equations 2.51 will not hold exactly, because these may require negative x's. We look at this situation later in this chapter.

Hence, the constraint would be $p_1x_1 + p_2x_2 = F$ (where p_i is the per unit cost of x_i). Using our present terminology, this constraint would be written in implicit form as

$$g(x_1, x_2) = F - p_1x_1 - p_2x_2 = 0. \qquad (2.53)$$

In this situation, then

$$-g_i = p_i \qquad (2.54)$$

and the derivative $-g_i$ does indeed reflect the per unit, marginal cost of using x_i. Practically all of the optimization problems we will encounter in later chapters have a similar interpretation for the denominators in Equations 2.52.

Lagrangian multiplier as a benefit-cost ratio

Now we can give Equations 2.52 an intuitive interpretation. They indicate that, at the optimal choices for the x's, the ratio of the marginal benefit of increasing x_i to the marginal cost of increasing x_i should be the same for every x. To see that this is an obvious condition for a maximum, suppose that it were not true: Suppose that the "benefit-cost ratio" were higher for x_1 than for x_2. In this case slightly more x_1 should be used in order to achieve a maximum. Consider using more x_1 but giving up just enough x_2 to keep g (the constraint) constant. Hence, the marginal cost of the additional x_1 used would equal the cost saved by using less x_2. But because the benefit-cost ratio (the amount of benefit per unit of cost) is greater for x_1 than for x_2, the additional benefits from using more x_1 would exceed the loss in benefits from using less x_2. The use of more x_1 and appropriately less x_2 would then increase y because x_1 provides more "bang for your buck." Only if the marginal benefit–marginal cost ratios are equal for all the x's will there be a local maximum, one in which no small changes in the x's can increase the objective. Concrete applications of this basic principle are developed in many places in this book. The result is fundamental for the microeconomic theory of optimizing behavior.

The Lagrangian multiplier (λ) can also be interpreted in the light of this discussion. λ is the common benefit-cost ratio for all the x's. That is,

$$\lambda = \frac{\textbf{marginal benefit of } x_i}{\textbf{marginal cost of } x_i} \qquad (2.55)$$

for every x_i. If the constraint were relaxed slightly, it would not matter exactly which x is changed (indeed, all the x's could be altered), because, at the margin, each promises the same ratio of benefits to costs. The Lagrangian multiplier then provides a measure of how such an overall relaxation of the constraint would affect the value of y. λ in essence assigns a "shadow price" to the constraint. A high λ indicates that y could be increased substantially by relaxing the constraint, because each x has a high benefit-cost ratio. A low value of λ, on the other hand, indicates that there is not much to be gained by relaxing the constraint. If the constraint is not binding at all, λ will have a value of 0, thereby indicating that the constraint is not restricting the value of y. In such a case, finding the maximum value of y subject to the constraint would be identical to finding an unconstrained maximum. The shadow price of the constraint is 0. This interpretation of λ can also be shown using the envelope theorem as described later in this chapter.[9]

Duality

This discussion shows that there is a clear relationship between the problem of maximizing a function subject to constraints and the problem of assigning values to constraints. This reflects what is called the mathematical principle of "duality": Any constrained maximization problem has associated with it a dual problem in constrained *minimization* that focuses attention on the constraints in the original (primal) problem. For example, to

---

[9]The discussion in the text concerns problems involving a single constraint. In general, one can handle m constraints ($m < n$) by simply introducing m new variables (Lagrangian multipliers) and proceeding in an analogous way to that discussed above.

jump a bit ahead of our story, economists assume that individuals maximize their utility, subject to a budget constraint. This is the consumer's primal problem. The dual problem for the consumer is to minimize the expenditure needed to achieve a given level of utility. Or, a firm's primal problem may be to minimize the total cost of inputs used to produce a given level of output, whereas the dual problem is to maximize output for a given cost of inputs purchased. Many similar examples will be developed in later chapters. Each illustrates that there are always two ways to look at any constrained optimization problem. Sometimes taking a frontal attack by analyzing the primal problem can lead to greater insights. In other instances the "back door" approach of examining the dual problem may be more instructive. Whichever route is taken, the results will generally, though not always, be identical, so the choice made will mainly be a matter of convenience.

 EXAMPLE 2.6

Constrained Maximization: Health Status Yet Again

Let's return once more to our (perhaps tedious) health maximization problem. As before, the individual's goal is to maximize

$$y = -x_1^2 + 2x_1 - x_2^2 + 4x_2 + 5,$$

but now assume that choices of x_1 and x_2 are constrained by the fact that he or she can only tolerate one drug dose per day. That is,

$$x_1 + x_2 = 1 \tag{2.56}$$

or

$$1 - x_1 - x_2 = 0.$$

Notice that the original optimal point ($x_1 = 1$, $x_2 = 2$) is no longer attainable because of the constraint on possible dosages: other values must be found. To do so we first set up the Lagrangian expression:

$$\mathscr{L} = -x_1^2 + 2x_1 - x_2^2 + 4x_2 + 5 + \lambda\,(1 - x_1 - x_2). \tag{2.57}$$

Differentiation of $\mathscr{L}$ with respect to x_1, x_2, and λ yields the following necessary condition for a constrained maximum:

$$\frac{\partial \mathscr{L}}{\partial x_1} = -2x_1 + 2 - \lambda = 0$$

$$\frac{\partial \mathscr{L}}{\partial x_2} = -2x_2 + 4 - \lambda = 0$$

$$\frac{\partial \mathscr{L}}{\partial \lambda} = 1 - x_1 - x_2 = 0. \tag{2.58}$$

These equations must now be solved for the optimal values of x_1, x_2, and λ. Using the first and second equations gives

$$-2x_1 + 2 = \lambda = -2x_2 + 4$$

or

$$x_1 = x_2 - 1. \tag{2.59}$$

Substitution of this value for x_1 into the constraint yields the solution:

$$x_2 = 1$$
$$x_1 = 0. \tag{2.60}$$

(continued)

EXAMPLE 2.6 CONTINUED

In words, if this person can tolerate only one dose of drugs, he or she should opt for taking only the second drug. By using either of the first two equations, it is easy to complete our solution by showing that

$$\lambda = 2. \tag{2.61}$$

This, then, is the solution to the constrained-maximum problem. If $x_1 = 0$, $x_2 = 1$, then y takes on the value 8. Constraining the values of x_1 and x_2 to sum to 1 has reduced the maximum value of health status, y, from 10 to 8.

Query: Suppose this individual could tolerate two doses per day. Would you expect y to increase? Would increases in tolerance beyond three doses per day have any effect on y?

 EXAMPLE 2.7

Optimal Fences and Constrained Maximization

Suppose a farmer had a certain length of fence, P, and wished to enclose the largest possible rectangular area. What shape area should the farmer choose? This is clearly a problem in constrained maximization. To solve it, let x be the length of one side of the rectangle and y be the length of the other side. The problem then is to choose x and y so as to maximize the area of the field (given by $A = x \cdot y$), subject to the constraint that the perimeter is fixed at $P = 2x + 2y$.

Setting up the Lagrangian expression gives

$$\mathscr{L} = x \cdot y + \lambda(P - 2x - 2y), \tag{2.62}$$

where λ is an unknown Lagrangian multiplier. The first-order conditions for a maximum are

$$\frac{\partial \mathscr{L}}{\partial x} = y - 2\lambda = 0$$

$$\frac{\partial \mathscr{L}}{\partial y} = x - 2\lambda = 0 \tag{2.63}$$

$$\frac{\partial \mathscr{L}}{\partial \lambda} = P - 2x - 2y = 0.$$

The three equations in 2.63 must be solved simultaneously for x, y, and λ. The first two equations say that $y/2 = x/2 = \lambda$, showing that x must be equal to y (the field should be square). They also imply that x and y should be chosen so that the ratio of marginal benefits to marginal cost is the same for both variables. The benefit (in terms of area) of one more unit of x is given by y (area is increased by $1 \cdot y$), and the marginal cost (in terms of perimeter) is 2 (the available perimeter is reduced by 2 for each unit that the length of side x is increased). The maximum conditions that state that this ratio should be equal for each of the variables.

Since we have shown that $x = y$, we can use the constraint to show that

$$x = y = \frac{P}{4}, \tag{2.64}$$

and, because $y = 2\lambda$,

$$\lambda = \frac{P}{8}. \tag{2.65}$$

INTERPRETATION OF THE LAGRANGIAN MULTIPLIER. If the farmer were interested in knowing how much more field could be fenced by adding an extra yard of fence, the Lagrangian multiplier suggests that he could find out by dividing the present perimeter by 8. Some specific numbers might make this clear. Suppose that the field currently has a perimeter of 400 yards. If the farmer has planned "optimally," the field will be a square with 100 yards ($= P/4$) on a side. The enclosed area will be 10,000 square yards. Suppose now that the perimeter (that is, the available fence) were enlarged by one yard. Equation 2.65 would then "predict" that the total area would be increased by approximately 50 ($= P/8$) square yards. That this is indeed the case can be shown as follows: Because the perimeter is now 401 yards, each side of the square will be 401/4 yards. The total area of the field is therefore $(401/4)^2$, which, according to the author's calculator, works out to be 10,050.06 square yards. Hence, the "prediction" of a 50-square-yard increase that is provided by the Lagrangian multiplier proves to be remarkably close. As in all constrained maximization problems, here the Lagrangian multiplier provides useful information about the implicit value of the constraint.

DUALITY. The dual of this constrained maximization problem is that for a given area of a rectangular field, the farmer wishes to minimize the fence required to surround it. Mathematically, the problem is to minimize

$$P = 2x + 2y, \tag{2.66}$$

subject to the constraint

$$A = x \cdot y. \tag{2.67}$$

Setting up the Lagrangian expression

$$\mathcal{L}^D = 2x + 2y + \lambda^D(A - x \cdot y) \tag{2.68}$$

(where the D denotes the dual concept) yields the following first-order conditions for a minimum:

$$\frac{\partial \mathcal{L}^D}{\partial x} = 2 - \lambda^D \cdot y = 0$$

$$\frac{\partial \mathcal{L}^D}{\partial y} = 2 - \lambda^D \cdot x = 0 \tag{2.69}$$

$$\frac{\partial \mathcal{L}^D}{\partial \lambda^D} = A - x \cdot y = 0.$$

Solving these equations as before yields the result

$$x = y = \sqrt{A}. \tag{2.70}$$

Again, the field should be square if the length of fence is to be minimized. The value of the Lagrangian multiplier in this problem is

$$\lambda^D = \frac{2}{y} = \frac{2}{x} = \frac{2}{\sqrt{A}}. \tag{2.71}$$

As before, this Lagrangian multiplier indicates the relationship between the objective (minimizing fence) and the constraint (needing to surround the field). If the field were 10,000 square yards, as we saw before, a fence 400 yards long would be needed. Increasing the field by one square yard would require about .02 more yards of fence ($= 2/\sqrt{A} = 2/100$).

(*continued*)

EXAMPLE 2.7 CONTINUED

The reader may wish to fire up his or her calculator to show this is indeed the case—a fence 100.005 yards on each side will exactly enclose 10,001 square yards. Here, as in most duality problems, the value of the Lagrangian in the dual is the reciprocal of the value for the Lagrangian in the primal problem. Both provide the same information, although in somewhat different form.

Query: An implicit constraint here is that the farmer's field be rectangular. If this constraint were not imposed, what shape field would enclose maximal area? How would you prove that?

Envelope theorem in constrained maximization problems

The envelope theorem, which we discussed previously in connection with unconstrained maximization problems, also has important applications in constrained maximization problems. Here we will provide only a brief presentation of the theorem. Later we will look at a number of applications.

Suppose we seek the maximum value of

$$y = f(x_1 \ldots x_n; a), \tag{2.72}$$

subject to the constraint

$$g(x_1 \ldots x_n; a) = 0, \tag{2.73}$$

where we have made explicit the dependence of the functions f and g on some parameter, a. As we have shown, one way to solve this problem is to set up the Lagrangian expression

$$\mathcal{L} = f(x_1 \ldots x_n; a) + \lambda g(x_1 \ldots x_n; a) \tag{2.74}$$

and solve the first-order conditions (see Equations 2.51) for the optimal, constrained values $x_1^* \ldots x_n^*$. Alternatively, it can be shown that

$$\frac{dy^*}{da} = \frac{\partial \mathcal{L}}{\partial a} (x_1^* \cdots x_n^*; a). \tag{2.75}$$

That is, the change in the maximal value of y that results when the parameter a changes (and all the x's are recalculated to new optimal values) can be found by partially differentiating the Lagrangian expression (Equation 2.74) and evaluating the resultant partial derivative at the optimal point.[10] Hence, the Lagrangian expression plays the same role in applying the envelope theorem to constrained problems as does the objective function alone in unconstrained problems. As a simple exercise the reader may wish to show that this result holds for the problem of fencing a rectangular field described in Example 2.7.[11]

---

[10]For a more complete discussion of the envelope theorem in constrained maximization problems, see Eugene Silberberg and Wing Suen, *The Structure of Economics: A Mathematical Analysis,* 3rd ed. (Boston: Irwin/McGraw-Hill, 2001), pp. 159–61.

[11]For the primal problem the perimeter P is the parameter of principal interest here. By solving for the optimal values of x and y and substituting into the expression for the area (A) of the field, it is easy to show that $dA/dP = P/8$. Differentiation of the Lagrangian expression (Equation 2.62) yields $\dfrac{\partial \mathcal{L}}{\partial P} = \lambda$ and, at the optimal values of x and y, $\dfrac{dA}{dP} = \dfrac{\partial \mathcal{L}}{\partial P} = \lambda = \dfrac{P}{8}$. The envelope theorem in this case then offers further proof that the Lagrangian multiplier can be used to assign an implicit value to the constraint.

Inequality constraints

In some economic problems the constraints need not hold exactly. For example, an individual's budget constraint requires that he or she spend no more than a certain amount per period, but it is at least possible to spend less than this amount. Inequality constraints also arise in the values permitted for some variables in economic problems. Usually, for example, economic variables must be nonnegative (though they can take on the value of zero). In this section we will show how the Lagrangian technique can be adapted to such circumstances. Although we will encounter problem later in the text that require this mathematics at only a few places, development here will illustrate a few general principles that are quite consistent with economic intuition.

A two-variable example

In order to avoid much cumbersome notation, we will explore inequality constraints only for the simple case involving two choice variables. The results derived are readily generalized. Suppose that we seek to maximize $y = f(x_1, x_2)$ subject to three inequality constraints:

$$1.\ g(x_1, x_2) \geq 0;$$
$$2.\ x_1 \geq 0;\ \text{and} \qquad\qquad (2.76)$$
$$3.\ x_2 \geq 0.$$

Hence, we are allowing for the possibility that the constraint we introduced before need not hold exactly (a person need not spend all of his or her income) and for the fact that both of the x's must be nonnegative (as in most economic problems).

Slack variables

One way to solve this optimization problem is to introduce three new variables (a, b, and c) that convert the inequality constraints in Equation 2.76 into equalities. To ensure that the inequalities continue to hold, we will square these new variables ensuring that their values are positive. Using this procedure, the inequality constraints become

$$1.\ g(x_1, x_2) - a^2 = 0;$$
$$2.\ x_1 - b^2 = 0;\ \text{and} \qquad\qquad (2.77)$$
$$3.\ x_2 - c^2 = 0.$$

Any solution that obeys these three equality constraints will also obey the inequality constraints. It will also turn out that the optimal values for a, b, and c will provide several insights on the nature of the solutions to a problem of this type.

Solution by the method of Lagrange

By converting the original problem involving inequalities into one involving equalities, we are now in a position to use Lagrangian methods to solve it. Because there are three constraints, we must introduce three Lagrangian multipliers: λ_1, λ_2, and λ_3. The full Lagrangian expression is

$$\mathscr{L} = f(x_1, x_2) + \lambda_1 \left[g(x_1, x_2) - a^2\right] + \lambda_2(x_1 - b^2) + \lambda_3(x_2 - c^2). \quad (2.78)$$

We wish to find the values of x_1, x_2, a, b, c, λ_1, λ_2, and λ_3 that constitute a critical point for this expression. This will necessitate eight first-order conditions.

$$\frac{\partial \mathscr{L}}{\partial x_1} = f_1 + \lambda_1 g_1 + \lambda_2 = 0$$

$$\frac{\partial \mathscr{L}}{\partial x_2} = f_2 + \lambda_1 g_2 + \lambda_3 = 0$$

$$\frac{\partial \mathscr{L}}{\partial a} = -2a\lambda_1 = 0$$

$$\frac{\partial \mathscr{L}}{\partial b} = -2b\lambda_2 = 0$$

$$\frac{\partial \mathscr{L}}{\partial c} = -2c\lambda_3 = 0 \qquad (2.79)$$

$$\frac{\partial \mathscr{L}}{\partial \lambda_1} = g(x_1, x_2) - a^2 = 0$$

$$\frac{\partial \mathscr{L}}{\partial \lambda_2} = x_1 - b^2 = 0$$

$$\frac{\partial \mathscr{L}}{\partial \lambda_3} = x_2 - c^2 = 0$$

In many ways these conditions resemble those we derived earlier for the case of a single equality constraint (see Equation 2.51). For example, the final three conditions merely repeat the three revised constraints. This ensures that any solution will obey these conditions. The first two equations also resemble the optimal conditions developed earlier. If λ_2 and λ_3 were 0, the conditions would in fact be identical. But the presence of the additional Lagrangian multipliers in the expressions shows that the customary optimality conditions may not hold exactly here.

Complementary slackness

The three equations involving the constants a, b, and c provide the most important insights into the nature of solutions to problems involving inequality constraints. For example, the third line in Equation 2.79 implies that, in the optimal solution, either λ_1 or a must be 0.[12] In the second case ($a = 0$), the constraint $g(x_1, x_2) = 0$ holds exactly and the calculated value of λ_1 indicates its relative importance to the objective function, f. On the other hand, if $a \neq 0$, then $\lambda_1 = 0$ and this shows that the availability of some slackness in the constraint implies that its value to the objective is 0. In the consumer context this means that if a person does not spend all his or her income, even more income would do nothing to raise his or her well-being.

Similar complementary slackness relationships also hold for the choice variables x_1 and x_2. For example, the fourth line in Equation 2.79 requires that the optimal solution have either b or λ_2 be 0. If $\lambda_2 = 0$ then the optimal solution has $x_1 > 0$, and this choice variable meets the precise benefit-cost test that $f_1 + \lambda_1 g_1 = 0$. Alternatively, solutions where $b = 0$ have $x_1 = 0$, and also require that $\lambda_2 > 0$. So, such solutions do not involve any use of x_1 because that variable does not meet the benefit-cost test as shown by the fact that $f_1 + \lambda_1 g_1 < 0$. An identical result holds for the choice variable x_2.

These results, which are sometimes called *Kuhn-Tucker conditions* after their discoverers, show that the solutions to optimization problems involving inequality constraints will differ from similar problems involving equality constraints in rather simple ways. Hence,

---

[12]We will not examine here the degenerate case where both of these variables are 0.

we cannot go far wrong by working primarily with constraints involving equalities and assuming that we can rely on intuition to state what would happen if the problems actually involved inequalities. That is the general approach we will take in this book.[13]

Second-order conditions

So far our discussion of optimization has focused primarily on necessary (first-order) conditions for finding a maximum. That is indeed the practice we will follow throughout much of this book because, as we shall see, most economic problems involve functions for which the second-order conditions for a maximum are also satisfied. In this section we give a brief analysis of the connection between second-order conditions for a maximum and the related curvature conditions that functions must have to ensure that these hold. The economic explanations for these curvature conditions will be discussed throughout the text.

Functions of one variable

First consider the case in which the objective, y, is a function of only a single variable, x. That is,

$$y = f(x). \tag{2.80}$$

A necessary condition for this function to attain its maximum value at some point is that

$$\frac{dy}{dx} = f'(x) = 0 \tag{2.81}$$

at that point. To ensure that the point is indeed a maximum, we must have y decreasing for movements away from it. We already know (by Equation 2.81) that for small changes in x, the value of y does not change; what we need to check is whether y is increasing before that "plateau" is reached and declining thereafter. We have already derived an expression for the change in y (dy), which is given by the total differential

$$dy = f'(x)\, dx. \tag{2.82}$$

What we now require is that dy be decreasing for small increases in the value of x. The differential of Equation 2.82 is given by

$$d(dy) = d^2y = \frac{d[f'(x)\,dx]}{dx} \cdot dx = f''(x)\,dx \cdot dx = f''(x)\,dx^2. \tag{2.83}$$

But

$$d^2y < 0$$

implies that

$$f''(x)\, dx^2 < 0 \tag{2.84}$$

and since dx^2 must be positive (because anything squared is positive), we have

$$f''(x) < 0 \tag{2.85}$$

as the required second-order condition. In words, this condition requires that the function f have a concave shape at the critical point (contrast Figures 2.1 and 2.2). Similar curvature conditions will be encountered throughout this section.

---

[13]The situation can become much more complex when calculus cannot be relied upon to give a solution, perhaps because some of the functions in a problem are not differentiable. For a discussion, see Avinask K. Dixit, *Optimization in Economic Theory*, 2nd ed. (Oxford: Oxford University Press, 1990).

 **EXAMPLE 2.8**

Profit Maximization Again

In Example 2.1 we considered the problem of finding the maximum of the function

$$\pi = 1{,}000q - 5q^2. \qquad (2.86)$$

The first-order condition for a maximum requires

$$\frac{d\pi}{dq} = 1{,}000 - 10q = 0 \qquad (2.87)$$

or

$$q^* = 100. \qquad (2.88)$$

The second derivative of the function is given by

$$\frac{d^2\pi}{dq^2} = -10 < 0, \qquad (2.89)$$

and hence the point $q^* = 100$ obeys the sufficient conditions for a local maximum.

Query: Here the second derivative is not only negative at the optimal point, but it is always negative. What does that imply about the optimal point? How should the fact that the second derivative is a constant be interpreted?

Functions of two variables

As a second case we consider y as a function of two independent variables:

$$y = f(x_1, x_2). \qquad (2.90)$$

A necessary condition for such a function to attain its maximum value is that its partial derivatives, in both the x_1 and the x_2 directions, be 0. That is,

$$\frac{\partial y}{\partial x_1} = f_1 = 0$$
$$\frac{\partial y}{\partial x_2} = f_2 = 0. \qquad (2.91)$$

A point that satisfies these conditions will be a "flat" spot on the function (a point where $dy = 0$) and therefore will be a candidate for a maximum. To ensure that the point is a local maximum, y must diminish for movements in any direction away from the critical point: In pictorial terms there is only one way to leave a true mountaintop, and that is to go down.

An intuitive argument

Before describing the mathematical properties required of such a point, an intuitive approach may be helpful. If we consider only movements in the x_1 direction, the required condition is clear: The slope in the x_1 direction (that is, the partial derivative f_1) must be diminishing at the critical point. This is simply an application of our discussion of the single-variable case, and it shows that for a maximum, the second partial derivative in the x_1 direction must be negative. An identical argument holds for movements only in the

x_2 direction. Hence, both own second partial derivatives (f_{11} and f_{22}) must be negative for a local maximum. In our mountain analogy, if attention is confined only to north-south or east-west movements, the slope of the mountain must be diminishing as we cross its summit—the slope must change from positive to negative.

The particular complexity that arises in the two-variable case involves movements through the optimal point that are not solely in the x_1 or in the x_2 directions (say, movements from northeast to southwest). In such cases the second-order partial derivatives do not provide complete information about how the slope is changing near the critical point. Conditions must also be placed on the cross-partial derivative ($f_{12} = f_{21}$) to ensure that dy is decreasing for movements through the critical point in any direction. As we shall see, those conditions amount to requiring that the own second-order partial derivatives be sufficiently negative so as to counterbalance any possible "perverse" cross-partial derivatives that may exist. Intuitively, if the mountain falls away steeply enough in the north-south and east-west directions, relatively minor failures to do so in other directions can be compensated for.

A formal analysis

We now proceed to make these points more formally. What we wish to discover are the conditions that must be placed on the second partial derivatives of the function f to ensure that d^2y is negative for movements in any direction through the critical point. Recall first that the total differential of the function is given by

$$dy = f_1\ dx_1 + f_2\ dx_2. \tag{2.92}$$

The differential of that function is given by

$$d^2y = (f_{11}\ dx_1 + f_{12}\ dx_2)\ dx_1 + (f_{21}\ dx_1 + f_{22}\ dx_2)\ dx_2 \tag{2.93}$$

or

$$d^2y = f_{11}\ dx_1^2 + f_{12}\ dx_2\ dx_1 + f_{21}\ dx_1\ dx_2 + f_{22}\ dx_2^2. \tag{2.94}$$

Because, by Young's theorem, $f_{12} = f_{21}$, we can arrange terms to get

$$d^2y = f_{11}\ dx_1^2 + 2\ f_{12}\ dx_1\ dx_2 + f_{22}\ dx_2^2. \tag{2.95}$$

For Equation 2.95 to be unambiguously negative for any change in the x's (that is, for any choices of dx_1 and dx_2), it is obviously necessary that f_{11} and f_{22} be negative. If, for example, $dx_2 = 0$, then

$$d^2y = f_{11}\ dx_1^2 \tag{2.96}$$

and $d^2y < 0$ implies

$$f_{11} < 0. \tag{2.97}$$

An identical argument can be made for f_{22} by setting $dx_1 = 0$. If neither dx_1 nor dx_2 is 0, we then must consider the cross partial, f_{12}, in deciding whether or not d^2y is unambiguously negative. Relatively simple algebra can be used to show that the required condition is[14]

$$f_{11}\ f_{22} - f_{12}^2 > 0. \tag{2.98}$$

---

[14]The proof proceeds by adding and subtracting the term $(f_{12}dx_2)^2/f_{11}$ to Equation 2.95 and factoring. But this approach is only applicable to this special case. A more easily generalized approach that uses matrix algebra recognizes that Equation 2.95 is a "Quadratic Form" in dx_1 and dx_2, and that Equations 2.97 and 2.98 amount to requiring that the Hessian matrix

$$\begin{bmatrix} f_{11} & f_{12} \\ f_{21} & f_{22} \end{bmatrix}$$

be "negative definite." In particular, Equation 2.98 requires that the determinant of this Hessian be positive. For a discussion, see the Extensions to this chapter.

Concave functions

Intuitively, what Equation 2.98 requires is that the own second partial derivatives (f_{11} and f_{22}) be sufficiently negative so that they outweigh any possible perverse effects from the cross-partial derivatives ($f_{12} = f_{21}$). Functions which obey such a condition are called *concave functions*. In three dimensions, such functions resemble inverted teacups (for an illustration, see Example 2.10). This image makes it clear that a flat spot on such a function is indeed a true maximum because the function always slopes downward from such a spot. More generally, concave functions have the property that they always lie below any plane that is tangent to them—the plane defined by the maximum value of the function is simply a special case of this property.

 EXAMPLE 2.9

Second-Order Conditions: Health Status for the Last Time

In Example 2.3 we considered the health status function

$$y = f(x_1, x_2) = -x_1^2 + 2x_1 - x_2^2 + 4x_2 + 5. \qquad (2.99)$$

The first-order conditions for a maximum are

$$f_1 = -2x_1 + 2 = 0$$
$$f_2 = -2x_2 + 4 = 0 \qquad (2.100)$$

or

$$x_1^* = 1$$
$$x_2^* = 2. \qquad (2.101)$$

The second-order partial derivatives for Equation 2.99 are

$$f_{11} = -2$$
$$f_{22} = -2 \qquad (2.102)$$
$$f_{12} = 0.$$

These derivatives clearly obey Equations 2.97 and 2.98, so both necessary and sufficient conditions for a local maximum are satisfied.[15]

Query: Describe the concave shape of the health status function and indicate why it has only a single global maximum value.

Constrained maximization

As a final case, consider the problem of choosing x_1 and x_2 to maximize

$$y = f(x_1, x_2), \qquad (2.103)$$

subject to the linear constraint

$$c - b_1x_1 - b_2x_2 = 0 \qquad (2.104)$$

(where c, b_1, b_2 are constant parameters in the problem). This problem is of a type that will be frequently encountered in this book and is a special case of the constrained maximum

---

[15]Notice that Equations 2.102 obey the sufficient conditions not only at the critical point but also for all possible choices of x_1 and x_2. That is, the function is concave. In more complex examples this need not be the case: The second-order conditions need be satisfied only at the critical point for a local maximum to occur.

problems that we examined earlier. There we showed that the first-order conditions for a maximum may be derived by setting up the Lagrangian expression

$$\mathscr{L} = f(x_1, x_2) + \lambda(c - b_1 x_1 - b_2 x_2). \tag{2.105}$$

Partial differentiation with respect to x_1, x_2, and λ yields the familiar results:

$$f_1 - \lambda b_1 = 0$$
$$f_2 - \lambda b_2 = 0 \tag{2.106}$$
$$c - b_1 x_1 - b_2 x_2 = 0.$$

These equations can in general be solved for the optimal values of x_1, x_2, and λ. To ensure that the point derived in that way is a local maximum, we must again examine movements away from the critical points by using the "second" total differential:

$$d^2 y = f_{11}\, dx_1^2 + 2 f_{12}\, dx_1\, dx_2 + f_{22}\, dx_2^2. \tag{2.107}$$

In this case, however, not all possible small changes in the *x*'s are permissible. Only those values of x_1 and x_2 that continue to satisfy the constraint can be considered valid alternatives to the critical point. To examine such changes, we must calculate the total differential of the constraint:

$$-b_1\, dx_1 - b_2\, dx_2 = 0 \tag{2.108}$$

or

$$dx_2 = -\frac{b_1}{b_2}\, dx_1. \tag{2.109}$$

This equation shows the relative changes in x_1 and x_2 that are allowable in considering movements from the critical point. To proceed further on this problem, we need to use the first-order conditions. The first two of these imply

$$\frac{f_1}{f_2} = \frac{b_1}{b_2}, \tag{2.110}$$

and combining this result with Equation 2.109 yields

$$dx_2 = -\frac{f_1}{f_2}\, dx_1. \tag{2.111}$$

We now substitute this expression for dx_2 in Equation 2.107 to demonstrate the conditions that must hold for $d^2 y$ to be negative:

$$
\begin{aligned}
d^2 y &= f_{11} dx_1^2 + 2 f_{12} dx_1 \left(-\frac{f_1}{f_2}\, dx_1 \right) + f_{22} \left(-\frac{f_1}{f_2}\, dx_1 \right)^2 \\
&= f_{11} dx_1^2 - 2 f_{12} \frac{f_1}{f_2}\, dx_1^2 + f_{22} \frac{f_1^2}{f_2^2}\, dx_1^2.
\end{aligned} \tag{2.112}
$$

Combining terms and putting each over a common denominator gives

$$d^2 y = (f_{11} f_2^2 - 2 f_{12} f_1 f_2 + f_{22} f_1^2) \frac{dx_1^2}{f_2^2}. \tag{2.113}$$

Consequently, for $d^2 y < 0$, it must be the case that

$$f_{11} f_2^2 - 2 f_{12} f_1 f_2 + f_{22} f_1^2 < 0. \tag{2.114}$$

Quasi-concave functions

Although this equation appears to be little more than an inordinately complex mass of mathematical symbols, in fact the condition is quite an important one. It characterizes a set of functions termed *quasi-concave functions*. These have the property that the set of all points for which such a function takes on a value greater than any specific constant is a convex set (that is, any two points in the set can be joined by a line contained completely within the set). Many economic models are characterized by such functions and, as we will see in considerable detail in Chapter 3, in these cases the condition for quasi-concavity has a relatively simple economic interpretation. Problems 2.9 and 2.10 examine two specific quasi-concave functions that we will frequently encounter in this book. Example 2.10 shows the relationship between concave and quasi-concave functions.

 EXAMPLE 2.10

Concave and Quasi-Concave Functions

The differences between concave and quasi-concave functions can be illustrated with the function[16]

$$y = f(x_1, x_2) = (x_1 \cdot x_2)^k \qquad (2.115)$$

where the x's take on only positive values, and the parameter k can take on a variety of positive values.

No matter what value k takes, this function is quasi-concave. One way to show this is to look at the "level curves" of the function by setting y equal to a specific value, say c. In this case

$$y = c = (x_1 x_2)^k \quad \text{or} \quad x_1 x_2 = c^{\frac{1}{k}} = c'. \qquad (2.116)$$

But this is just the equation of a standard rectangular hyperbola. Clearly the set of points for which y takes on values larger than c is convex because it is bounded by this hyperbola.

A more mathematical way to show quasi-concavity would apply Equation 2.114 to this function. Although the algebra of doing this may be a bit messy, it may be worth the struggle. Here are the various components of Equation 2.114:

$$
\begin{aligned}
f_1 &= kx_1^{k-1}x_2^k \\
f_2 &= kx_1^k x_2^{k-1} \\
f_{11} &= k(k-1)x_1^{k-2}x_2^k \\
f_{22} &= k(k-1)x_1^k x_2^{k-2} \\
f_{12} &= k^2 x_1^{k-1} x_2^{k-1}
\end{aligned}
\qquad (2.117)
$$

So,

$$
\begin{aligned}
f_{11}f_2^2 - 2f_{12}f_1f_2 + f_{22}f_1^2 &= k^3(k-1)x_1^{3k-2} x_2^{3k-2} - 2k^4 x_1^{3k-2}x_2^{3k-2} \\
&\quad + k^3(k-1)x_1^{3k-2} x_2^{3k-2} \\
&= 2k^3 x_1^{3k-2} x_2^{3k-2} (-1)
\end{aligned}
\qquad (2.118)
$$

which is clearly negative, as is required for quasi-concavity.

Whether or not the function f is concave depends on the value of k. If $k < 0.5$ the function is indeed concave. An intuitive way to see this is to consider only points where $x_1 = x_2$. For these points,

$$y = (x_1^2)^k = x_1^{2k} \qquad (2.119)$$

which, for $k < 0.5$, is concave. Alternatively, for $k > .5$, this function is convex.

---

[16]This function is a special case of the Cobb-Douglas function. See also Problem 2.9 and the Extensions to this chapter for more details on this function.

A more definitive proof makes use of the partial derivatives from Equation 2.117. In this case the condition for concavity can be expressed as

$$f_{11}f_{22} - f_{12}^2 = k^2(k-1)^2 \, x_1^{2k-2} \, x_2^{2k-2} - k^4 \, x_1^{2k-2} \, x_2^{2k-2}$$
$$= x_1^{2k-2} \, x_2^{2k-2} \, [k^2(k-1)^2 - k^4] \qquad (2.120)$$
$$= x_1^{2k-1} \, x_2^{2k-1} \, [k^2(-2k+1)]$$

and this expression is positive (as is required for concavity) for

$$(-2k+1) > 0 \quad \text{or} \quad k < 0.5.$$

On the other hand, the function is convex for $k > 0.5$.

A Graphic Illustration

Figure 2.4 provides three dimensional illustrations of three specific examples of this function: for $k = .2$, $k = .5$, and $k = 1$. Notice that in all three cases the level curves of the function have hyperbolic, convex shapes. That is, for any fixed value of y the functions are quite similar. This shows the quasi-concavity of the function. The primary differences among the functions are illustrated by the way in which the value of y increases as both x's increase together. In Figure 2.4a (when $k = .2$) the increase in y slows as the x's increase. This gives the function a rounded, teacuplike shape that indicates its concavity. For $k = .5$, y appears to increase linearly with increases in both of the x's. This is the borderline between concavity and convexity. Finally, when $k = 1$ (as in Figure 2.4c) simultaneous increases in the values of both of the x's increase y very rapidly. The spine of the function looks convex to reflect such increasing returns.

A careful look at Figure 2.4a suggests that any function that is concave will also be quasi-concave. You are asked to prove that this is indeed the case in Problem 2.8. This example shows that the converse of this statement is not true—quasi-concave functions need not necessarily be concave. Most functions we will encounter in this book will also illustrate this fact—most will be quasi-concave, but not necessarily concave.

Query: Explain why the functions illustrated both in Figure 2.4a and 2.4c would have maximum values if the x's were subject to a linear constraint, but only the graph in Figure 2.4a would have an unconstrained maximum.

Homogeneous functions

Many of the functions that arise naturally out of economic theory have additional mathematical properties. One particularly important set of properties relates to how the functions behave when all (or most) of their arguments are increased proportionally. Such situations arise when we ask questions such as what would happen if all prices increased by 10 percent or how would a firm's output change if it doubled all of the inputs that it uses. Thinking about these questions leads naturally to the concept of homogeneous functions. Specifically, a function $f(x_1, x_2, \ldots x_n)$ is said to be homogeneous of degree k if

$$f(tx_1, tx_2 \ldots tx_n) = t^k f(x_1, x_2 \ldots x_n). \qquad (2.121)$$

The most important examples of homogeneous functions are those for which $k = 1$ or $k = 0$. In words, when a function is homogeneous of degree one, a doubling of all of its arguments doubles the value of the function itself. For functions that are homogeneous of

FIGURE 2.4   Concave and Quasi-Concave Functions

In all three cases these functions are quasi-concave. For a fixed *y*, their level curves are convex. But only for $k = 0.2$ is the function strictly concave. The case $k = 1.0$ clearly shows nonconcavity because the function is not below its tangent plane.

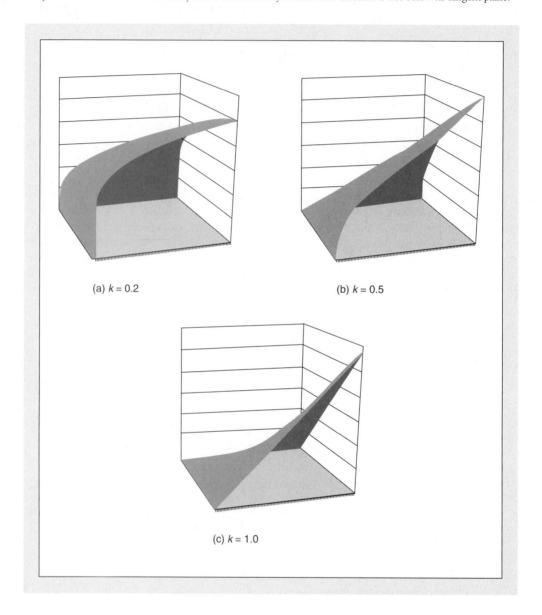

(a) $k = 0.2$

(b) $k = 0.5$

(c) $k = 1.0$

degree 0, a doubling of all of its arguments leaves the value of the function unchanged. Functions may also be homogeneous for changes in only certain subsets of their arguments—that is, a doubling of some of the *x*'s may double the value of the function if the other arguments of the function are held constant. Usually, however, homogeneity applies to changes in all of the arguments in a function.

Homogeneity and derivatives

If a function is homogeneous of degree *k* and can be differentiated, the partial derivatives of the function will be homogeneous of degree *k* − 1. A proof of this follows directly from the definition of homogeneity. For example, differentiating Equation 1.121 with respect to its first argument gives

$$\frac{\partial f(tx_1, \ldots tx_n)}{\partial x_1} \cdot t = t^k \frac{\partial f(x_1 \ldots x_n)}{\partial x_1}$$

or

$$f_1(tx_1 \ldots tx_n) = t^{k-1} f_1(x_1 \ldots x_n) \qquad (2.122)$$

which shows that f_1 meets the definition for homogeneity of degree $k - 1$. Because marginal ideas are so prevalent in microeconomic theory, this property shows that some important properties of marginal effects can be inferred from the properties of the underlying function itself.

Euler's theorem

Another useful feature of homogeneous functions can be shown by differentiating the definition for homogeneity with respect to the proportionality factor, t. In this case, we differentiate the right side of Equation 2.121 first:

$$kt^{k-1} f(x_1 \ldots x_n) = x_1 f_1(tx_1 \ldots tx_n) + \ldots + x_n f_n(tx_1 \ldots tx_n)$$

and, if we let $t = 1$, this equation becomes

$$kf(x_1 \ldots x_n) = x_1 f_1(x_1 \ldots x_n) + \ldots + x_n f_n(x_1 \ldots x_n) \qquad (2.123)$$

This equation is termed Euler's theorem (after the mathematician who also discovered the constant e) for homogeneous functions. It shows that, for a homogeneous function, there is a definite relationship between the values of the function and the values of its partial derivatives. Several important economic relationships among functions are based on this observation.

Homothetic functions

A homothetic function is one that is formed by taking a monotonic transformation of a homogeneous function.[17] Monotonic transformations, by definition, preserve the order of the relationship between the arguments of a function and the value of that function. If certain sets of x's yield larger values for f, they will also yield larger values for a monotonic transformation of f. Because monotonic transformations may take many forms, however, they would not be expected to preserve an exact mathematical relationship such as that embodied in homogeneous functions. Consider, for example, the function $f(x, y) = x \cdot y$. Clearly this function is homogeneous of degree 2—a doubling of its two arguments will multiply the value of the function by 4. But the monotonic transformation, F, that simply adds 1 to f (that is, $F(f) = f + 1 = xy + 1$) is not homogeneous at all. Hence, except in special cases, homothetic functions do not possess the homogeneity properties of their underlying functions. Homothetic functions do, however, preserve one nice feature of homogeneous functions. This property is that the implicit trade-offs among the variables in a function depend only on the ratios of those variables, not on their absolute values. Here we show this for the simple two-variable, implicit function $f(x, y) = 0$. It will be easier to demonstrate more general cases when we get to the economics of the matter later in this book.

---

[17]Because a limiting case of a monotonic transformation is to leave the function unchanged, all homogeneous functions are also homothetic.

Equation 2.28 showed that the implicit trade-off between x and y for a two-variable function is given by

$$\frac{dy}{dx} = -\frac{f_x}{f_y}.$$

If we assume f is homogeneous of degree k, its partial derivatives will be homogeneous of degree $k - 1$ and the implicit trade-off between x and y is

$$\frac{dy}{dx} = -\frac{t^{k-1} f_x(tx, ty)}{t^{k-1} f_y(tx, ty)} = -\frac{f_x(tx, ty)}{f_y(tx, ty)}. \qquad (2.124)$$

But now let $t = \dfrac{1}{y}$ and Equation 1.124 becomes

$$\frac{dy}{dx} = -\frac{f_x\left(\dfrac{x}{y}, 1\right)}{f_y\left(\dfrac{x}{y}, 1\right)} \qquad (2.125)$$

which shows that the trade-off depends only on the ratio of x to y. Now if we apply any monotonic transformation, F (with $F' > 0$), to the original homogeneous function f, we have

$$\frac{dy}{dx} = -\frac{F' f_x\left(\dfrac{x}{y}, 1\right)}{F' f_y\left(\dfrac{x}{y}, 1\right)} = -\frac{f_x\left(\dfrac{x}{y}, 1\right)}{f_y\left(\dfrac{x}{y}, 1\right)} \qquad (2.126)$$

and this shows both that the trade-off is unaffected by the monotonic transformation and that it remains a function only of the ratio of x to y. In Chapter 3 (and elsewhere) this property will make it very convenient to discuss some theoretical results with simple two-dimensional graphs, for which we need not consider the overall levels of key variables, but only their ratios.

 EXAMPLE 2.11

Cardinal and Ordinal Properties

In applied economics it is sometimes important to know the exact numerical relationship among variables. For example, in the study of production, one might wish to know precisely how much extra output would be produced by hiring another worker. This is a question about the "cardinal" (i.e., numerical) properties of the production function. In other cases, one may only care about the order in which various points are ranked. In the theory of utility, for example, we assume that people can rank bundles of goods and will choose the bundle with the highest ranking, but that there are no unique numerical values assigned to these rankings. Mathematically, ordinal properties of functions are preserved by any monotonic transformation because, by definition, a monotonic transformation preserves ordinal rankings. Usually, however, cardinal properties are not preserved by arbitrary monotonic transformations.

These distinctions are illustrated by the functions we examined in Example 2.10. There we studied monotonic transformations of the function

$$f(x_1, x_2) = (x_1 x_2)^k \qquad (2.127)$$

by considering various values of the parameter k. We showed that quasi-concavity (an ordinal property) was preserved for all values of k. Hence, when approaching problems that focus on maximizing or minimizing such a function subject to linear constraints we need not worry about precisely which transformation is used. On the other hand, the function in Equation 1.127 is concave (a cardinal property) only for a narrow range of values of k. Many monotonic transformations destroy the concavity of f.

The function in Equation 1.127 also can be used to illustrate the difference between homogeneous and homothetic functions. A proportional increase in the two arguments of f would yield

$$f(tx_1, tx_2) = t^{2k}x_1x_2 = t^{2k}f(x_1, x_2). \qquad (2.128)$$

Hence, the degree of homogeneity for this function depends on k—that is, the degree of homogeneity is not preserved independently of which monotonic transformation is used. Alternatively, the function in Equation 1.127 is homothetic because

$$\frac{dx_2}{dx_1} = -\frac{f_1}{f_2} = -\frac{kx_1^{k-1}x_2^k}{kx_1^k x_2^{k-1}} = \frac{x_2}{x_1}. \qquad (2.129)$$

That is, the trade-off between x_2 and x_1 depends only on the ratio of these two variables and is unaffected by the value of k. Hence, homotheticity is an ordinal property. As we shall see, this property is quite convenient when developing graphical arguments about economic propositions.

Query: How would the discussion in this example be changed if we considered monotonic transformations of the form $f(x_1, x_2, k) = x_1x_2 + k$ for various values of k?

SUMMARY

Despite the formidable appearance of some parts of this chapter, this is not a book on mathematics. Rather, the intention here was to gather together a variety of tools that will be used to develop economic models throughout the remainder of the text. Material in this chapter will then be useful as a handy reference.

One way to summarize the mathematical tools introduced in this chapter is by stressing again the economic lessons that these tools illustrate:

- Using mathematics provides a convenient, shorthand way for economists to develop their models. Implications of various economic assumptions can be studied in a simplified setting through the use of such mathematical tools.

- The mathematical concept of the derivatives of a function is widely used in economic models because economists are often interested in how marginal changes in one variable affect another variable. Partial derivatives are especially useful for this purpose because they are defined to represent such marginal changes when all other factors are held constant. In this way, partial derivatives incorporate the ceteris paribus assumption found in most economic models.

- The mathematics of optimization is an important tool for the development of models that assume that economic agents rationally pursue some goal. In the unconstrained case, the first-order conditions state that any activity that contributes to the agent's goal should be expanded up to the point at which the marginal contribution of further expansion is zero. In mathematical terms, the first-order condition for an optimum requires that all partial derivatives be zero.

- Most economic optimization problems involve constraints on the choices agents can make. In this case the first-order conditions for a maximum suggest that each activity be operated at a level at which the ratio of the marginal benefit of the activity to its marginal cost is the same for all activities actually used. This common marginal benefit–marginal cost ratio is also equal to the Lagrangian multiplier, which is often introduced to help solve constrained optimization problems. The Lagrangian multiplier can also be interpreted as the implicit value (or shadow price) of the constraint.

- The implicit function theorem is a useful mathematical device for illustrating the dependence of the choices that result from an optimization problem on the parameters of that problem (for example, market prices). The envelope theorem is useful for examining how these optimal choices change when the problem's parameters (prices) change.

- Some optimization problems may involve constraints that are inequalities rather than equalities. Solutions to these problems often illustrate "complementary slackness." That is, either the constraints hold with equality and their related Lagrangian multipliers are nonzero or, the constraints are strict inequalities and their related Lagrangian multipliers are zero. Again this illustrates how the Lagrangian multiplier implies something about the "importance" of constraints.

- The first-order conditions shown in this chapter are only the necessary conditions for a local maximum or minimum. One must also check second-order conditions that require that certain curvature conditions be met.

- Certain types of functions occur in many economic problems. Quasi-concave functions (those functions for which the level curves form convex sets) obey the second-order conditions of constrained maximum or minimum problems when the constraints are linear. Homothetic functions have the useful property that implicit trade-offs among the variables of the function depend only on the ratios of these variables.

PROBLEMS

2.1

Suppose $U(x,y) = 4x^2 + 3y^2$.

a. Calculate $\partial U/\partial x$, $\partial U/\partial y$.

b. Evaluate these partial derivatives at $x = 1$, $y = 2$.

c. Write the total differential for U.

d. Calculate dy/dx for $dU = 0$—that is, what is the implied trade-off between x and y holding U constant?

e. Show $U = 16$ when $x = 1$, $y = 2$.

f. In what ratio must x and y change to hold U constant at 16 for movements away from $x = 1$, $y = 2$?

g. More generally, what is the shape of the $U = 16$ contour line for this function? What is the slope of that line?

2.2

Suppose a firm's total revenues depend on the amount produced (q) according to the function

$$R = 70q - q^2.$$

Total costs also depend on q:

$$C = q^2 + 30q + 100$$

a. What level of output should the firm produce in order to maximize profits ($R - C$)? What will profits be?

b. Show that the second-order conditions for a maximum are satisfied at the output level found in part (a).

c. Does the solution calculated here obey the "marginal revenue equals marginal cost" rule? Explain.

2.3

Suppose that $f(x,y) = xy$. Find the maximum value for f if x and y are constrained to sum to 1. Solve this problem in two ways: by substitution and by using the Langrangian multiplier method.

2.4

The dual problem to the one described in Problem 2.3 is

Minimize $x + y$
Subject to $xy = 0.25$

Solve this problem using the Lagrangian technique. Then compare the value you get for the Lagrangian multiplier to the value you got in Problem 2.3. Explain the relationship between the two solutions.

2.5

The height of a ball that is thrown straight up with a certain force is a function of the time (t) from which it is released given by $f(t) = -0.5gt^2 + 40t$ (where g is a constant determined by gravity).

a. How does the value of t at which the height of the ball is at a maximum, depend on the parameter g?

b. Use your answer to part a to describe how maximum height changes as the parameter g changes.

c. Use the envelope theorem to answer part b directly.

d. On the Earth $g = 32$, but this value varies somewhat around the globe. If two locations had gravitational constants that differed by 0.1, what would be the difference in the maximum height of a ball tossed in the two places?

2.6

A simple way to model the construction of an oil tanker is to start with a large rectangular sheet of steel that is x feet wide and $3x$ feet long. Now cut a smaller square that is *t* feet on a side out of each corner of the larger sheet and fold up and weld the sides of the steel sheet to make a traylike structure with no top.

a. Show that the volume of oil that can be held by this tray is given by

$$V = t(x - 2t)(3x - 2t) = 3tx^2 - 8t^2x + 4t^3.$$

b. How should *t* be chosen so as to maximize *V* for any given value of *x*?

c. Is there a value of *x* that maximizes the volume of oil that can be carried?

d. Suppose that a shipbuilder is constrained to use only 1,000,000 square feet of steel sheet to construct an oil tanker. This constraint can be represented by the equation $3x^2 - 4t^2 = 1,000,000$ (because the builder can return the cut out squares for credit). How does the solution to this constrained maximum problem compare to the solutions described in parts b and c?

2.7

Consider the constrained maximization problem:

$$\text{Maximize } y = x_1 + 5 \ln x_2$$
$$\text{Subject to } k - x_1 - x_2 = 0$$

Where *k* is a constant that can be assigned any specific value.

a. Show that if $k = 10$, this problem can be solved as one involving only equality constraints.

b. Show that solving this problem for $k = 4$ requires that $x_1 = -1$.

c. If the *x*'s in this problem must be nonnegative, what is the optimal solution when $k = 4$?

d. What is the solution for this problem when $k = 20$? What do you conclude by comparing this solution to the solution for part a?

(Note: This problem involves what is called a "quasi-linear function." Such functions provide important examples of some types of behavior in consumer theory—as we shall see.)

2.8

Show that if $f(x_1, x_2)$ is a concave function, it is also a quasi-concave function. Do this by comparing Equation 2.114 (defining quasi-concavity) to Equation 2.98 (defining concavity). Can you give an intuitive reason for this result? Is the converse of the statement true? Are quasi-concave functions necessarily concave?

2.9

One of the most important functions we will encounter in this book is the Cobb-Douglas function:

$$y = (x_1)^\alpha (x_2)^\beta$$

where α and β are positive constants that are each less than one.

a. Show that this function is quasi-concave using a "brute force" method by applying Equation 2.114.

b. Show that the Cobb-Douglas function is quasi-concave by showing that the any contour line of the form $y = c$ (where *c* is any positive constant) is convex and therefore that the set of points for which $y > c$ is a convex set.

c. Show that if $\alpha + \beta > 1$ then the Cobb-Douglas function is not concave (thereby illustrating that not all quasi-concave functions are concave). (Note: The Cobb-Douglas function is discussed further in the Extensions to this chapter.)

2.10

Another function we will encounter often in this book is the "power function":

$$y = x^\delta$$

where $0 \leq \delta \leq 1$ (at times we will also examine this function for cases where δ can be negative too, in which case we will use the form $y = x^\delta/\delta$ to ensure that the derivatives have the proper sign).

a. Show that this function is concave (and therefore also, by the result of problem 2.8, quasi-concave). Notice that the $\delta = 1$ is a special case and that the function is "strictly" concave only for $\delta < 1$.

b. Show that the multivariate form of the power function

$$y = f(x_1, x_2) = (x_1)^\delta + (x_2)^\delta$$

is also concave (and quasi-concave). Explain why, in this case, the fact that $f_{12} = f_{21} = 0$ makes the determination of concavity especially simple.

c. One way to incorporate "scale" effects into the function described in part b is to use the monotonic transformation

$$g(x_1, x_2) = y^\gamma = [(x_1)^\delta + (x_2)^\delta]^\gamma$$

where γ is a positive constant. Does this transformation preserve the concavity of the function? Is g quasi-concave?

SUGGESTIONS FOR FURTHER READING

Dixit, A. K. *Optimization in Economic Theory*, 2nd ed. New York: Oxford University Press, 1990.
A complete and modern treatment of optimization techniques. Uses relatively advanced analytical methods.

Mas-Colell, Andreu, Michael D. Whinston, and Jerry R. Green. *Microeconomic Theory*. New York: Oxford University Press, 1995.
Encyclopedic treatment of mathematical microeconomics. Extensive mathematical appendices cover relatively high-level topics in analysis.

Samuelson, Paul A. *Foundations of Economic Analysis*. Cambridge, MA: Harvard University Press, 1947. Mathematical Appendix A.
A basic reference. Mathematical Appendix A provides an advanced treatment of necessary and sufficient conditions for a maximum.

Silberberg, E., and W. Suen. *The Structure of Economics: A Mathematical Analysis*, 3rd ed. Boston: Irwin/McGraw-Hill, 2001.
A mathematical microeconomics text that stresses the observable predictions of economic theory. The text makes extensive use of the envelope theorem.

Simon, Carl P., and Lawrence Blume. *Mathematics for Economists*. New York: W. W. Norton, 1994.
A very useful text covering most areas of mathematics relevant to economists. Treatment is at a relatively high level. Two topics discussed better here than elsewhere are differential equations and basic point-set topology.

Sydsaeter, K., A. Strom, and P. Berck. *Economists' Mathematical Manual*, 3rd ed. Berlin: Springer-Verlag, 2000.
An indispensable tool for mathematical review. Contains 32 chapters covering most of the mathematical tools that economists use. Discussions are very brief, so this is not the place to encounter new concepts for the first time.

Taylor, Angus E., and W. Robert Mann. *Advanced Calculus*, 3rd ed. New York: John Wiley, 1983, pp. 183–95.
A comprehensive calculus text with a good discussion of the Lagrangian technique.

Thomas, George B., and Ross L. Finney. *Calculus and Analytic Geometry*, 8th ed. Reading, MA: Addison-Wesley, 1992.
Basic calculus text with excellent coverage of differentiation techniques.

Second-Order Conditions and Matrix Algebra

The second-order conditions described in Chapter 2 can be written in very compact ways by using matrix algebra. In this extension we look briefly at that notation. We return to this notation at a few other places in the extensions and problems for later chapters.

Matrix algebra background

The extensions presented here assume some general familiarity with matrix algebra. A succinct reminder of these principles might include:

1. An $n \times k$ *matrix,* **A,** is a rectangular array of terms of the form

$$A = [a_{ij}] = \begin{bmatrix} a_{11} & a_{12} & \cdots & a_{1k} \\ a_{21} & a_{22} & \cdots & a_{2k} \\ \vdots & & & \\ a_{n1} & a_{n2} & & a_{nk} \end{bmatrix}.$$

Here $i = 1, n; j = 1, k$. Matrices can be added, subtracted, or multiplied providing their dimensions are conformable.

2. If $n = k$, **A** is a square matrix. A square matrix is symmetric if $a_{ij} = a_{ji}$. The *identity matrix,* $\mathbf{I}_n$, is an $n + n$ square matrix where $a_{ij} = 1$ if $i = j$ and $a_{ij} = 0$ if $i \neq j$.

3. The **determinant** of a square matrix (denoted by $|\mathbf{A}|$) is a scalar (i.e., single term) found by suitably multiplying together all of the terms in the matrix. If **A** is 2×2,

$$|\mathbf{A}| = a_{11} a_{22} - a_{21} a_{12}.$$

Example: If $A = \begin{bmatrix} 1 & 3 \\ 5 & 2 \end{bmatrix}$

$$|\mathbf{A}| = 2 - 15 = -13.$$

4. The *inverse* of an $n \times n$ square matrix, **A,** is another $n \times n$ matrix, $\mathbf{A}^{-1}$ such that

$$\mathbf{A} \cdot \mathbf{A}^{-1} = \mathbf{I}_n.$$

Not every square matrix has an inverse. A necessary and sufficient condition for the existence of $\mathbf{A}^{-1}$ is that $|\mathbf{A}| \neq 0$.

5. The *leading principal minors of an* $n \times n$ square matrix **A** is the series of determinants of the first p rows and columns of **A,**

where $p = 1, n$. If **A** is 2×2, then the first leading principal minor is a_{11} and the second is $a_{11} a_{22} - a_{21} a_{12}$.

6. An $n \times n$ square matrix, **A,** is *positive definite* if all of its leading principal minors are positive. The matrix is *negative definite* if its principal minors alternate in sign starting with a minus.[1]

7. A particularly useful symmetric matrix is the *Hessian matrix* formed by all of the second-order partial derivatives of a function. If f is a continuous and twice differentiable function of n variables, then its Hessian is given by

$$H(f) = \begin{bmatrix} f_{11} & f_{12} & \cdots & f_{1n} \\ f_{21} & f_{22} & \cdots & f_{2n} \\ \vdots & & & \\ f_{n1} & f_{n2} & \cdots & f_{nn} \end{bmatrix}$$

Using these notational ideas we can now examine again some of the second-order conditions derived in Chapter 2.

E2.1 Concave and convex functions

A concave function is one that is always below (or on) any tangent to it. Alternatively, a *convex function* is always above (or on) any tangent. The concavity or convexity of any function is determined by its second derivative(s). For a function of a single variable, $f(x)$, the requirement is straightforward. Using the Taylor approximation at any point (x_0)

$$f(x_0 + dx) = f(x_0) + f'(x_0)dx + f''(x_0)\frac{dx^2}{2} + \text{higher order terms.}$$

Assuming that the higher order terms are 0, we have

$$f(x_0 + dx) \leq f(x_0) + f'(x_0)dx$$

if $f''(x_0) \leq 0$ and

$$f(x_0 + dx) \geq f(x_0) + f'(x_0)dx$$

---

[1] If some of the determinants in this definition may be 0, the matrix is said to be positive semidefinite or negative semidefinite. To keep our discussion simple we will not use this terminology here.

if $f''(x_0) \geq 0$. Because the expressions on the right of these inequalities are in fact the equation of the tangent to the function at x_0, it is clear that the function is (locally) concave if $f''(x_0) \leq 0$ and (locally) convex if $f''(x_0) \geq 0$.

Extending this intuitive idea to many dimensions is cumbersome in terms of functional notation, but relatively simple when matrix algebra is used. Concavity requires that the Hessian matrix be negative definite whereas convexity requires that this matrix be positive definite. As in the single variable case, these conditions amount to requiring that the function move consistently away from any tangent to it no matter what direction is taken.[2]

If $f(x_1, x_2)$ is a function of two variables, the Hessian is given by

$$H = \begin{bmatrix} f_{11} & f_{12} \\ f_{21} & f_{22} \end{bmatrix}.$$

This is negative definite if

$$f_{11} < 0 \text{ and } f_{11}f_{22} - f_{21}f_{12} > 0,$$

which is precisely the condition described in Chapter 2 in Equation 2.98. Generalizations to functions of three or more variables follow the same matrix pattern.

Example 1

For the health status function in Chapter 2 (Equation 2.20), the Hessian is given by

$$H = \begin{bmatrix} -2 & 0 \\ 0 & -2 \end{bmatrix},$$

and the first and second leading principal minors are

$$H_1 = -2 < 0$$
$$H_2 = (-2)(-2) - 0 = 4 > 0.$$

Hence, the function is concave.

Example 2

The Cobb-Douglas function $x^a y^b$ where $a, b \in (0,1)$ is used to illustrate utility functions and production functions in many places in this text. The first- and second-order derivatives of the function are

$$f_x = ax^{a-1}y^b$$
$$f_y = bx^a y^{b-1}$$
$$f_{xx} = a(a-1)x^{a-2}y^b$$
$$f_{yy} = b(b-1)x^a y^{b-2}.$$

Hence, the Hessian for this function is

$$H = \begin{bmatrix} a(a-1)x^{a-2}y^b & abx^{a-1}y^{b-1} \\ abx^{a-1}y^{b-1} & b(b-1)x^a y^{b-2} \end{bmatrix}.$$

The first leading principal minor of this Hessian is

$$H_1 = a(a-1)x^{a-2}y^b < 0,$$

so the function will be concave providing

$$H_2 = a(a-1)(b)(b-1)x^{2a-2}y^{2b-2} - a^2b^2x^{2a-2}y^{2b-2}$$
$$= ab(1-a-b)x^{2a-2}y^{2b-2} > 0.$$

This condition clearly holds if $a + b < 1$. That is, in production function terminology, the function must exhibit diminishing returns to scale to be concave. Geometrically, the function must turn downward as both inputs are increased together.

E2.2 Maximization

As we saw in Chapter 2, the first-order conditions for an unconstrained maximum of a function of many variables requires finding a point at which the partial derivatives are zero. If the function is concave it will be below its tangent plane at this point and therefore the point will be a true maximum.[3] Because the health status function is concave, for example, the first-order conditions for a maximum are also sufficient.

E2.3 Constrained maxima

When the x's in a maximization or minimization problem are subject to constraints, these constraints have to be taken into account in stating second-order conditions. Again, matrix algebra provides a compact (if not very intuitive) way of denoting these conditions. The notation involves adding rows and columns of the Hessian matrix for the unconstrained problem and then checking the properties of this augmented matrix.

Specifically, we wish to maximize

$$f(x_1 \ldots x_n)$$

subject to the constraint[4]

$$g(x_1 \ldots x_n) = 0.$$

We saw in Chapter 2 that the first-order conditions for a maximum are of the form

---

[2] A proof using the multivariable version of Taylor's approximation provided in Simon and Blume (1994), Chap. 21.

[3] This will be a "local" maximum if the function is concave only in a region, or "global" if the function is concave everywhere.

[4] Here we look only at the case of a single constraint. Generalization to many constraints is conceptually straightforward but notationally complex. For a concise statement see Sydsaeter A. and P. Berck (2000) page 93.

$$f_i + \lambda \, g_i = 0$$

where λ is the Lagrangian multiplier for this problem. Second-order conditions for a maximum are based on the augmented ("bordered") Hessian[5]

$$H_b = \begin{bmatrix} 0 & g_1 & g_2 & \cdots & g_n \\ g_1 & f_{11} & f_{12} & & f_{1n} \\ g_2 & f_{21} & f_{22} & & f_{2n} \\ \vdots & & & & \\ g_n & f_{n1} & f_{n2} & \cdots & f_{nn} \end{bmatrix}$$

For a maximum, $(-1) H_b$ must be negative definite—that is, the leading principal minors of H_b must follow the pattern $- + - + -$ and so forth starting with the second such minor.[6]

The second-order conditions for minimum require that $(-1) H_b$ be positive definite—that is, all of the leading principal minors of H_b (except the first) should be negative.

Example

The Lagrangian for the constrained health status problem (Example 2.6) is

$$\mathcal{L} = -x_1^2 + 2x_1 - x_2^2 + 4x_2 + 5 + \lambda (1 - x_1 - x_2)$$

and the bordered Hessian for this problem is

$$H_b = \begin{bmatrix} 0 & -1 & -1 \\ -1 & -2 & 0 \\ -1 & 0 & -2 \end{bmatrix}.$$

The second leading principal minor here is

$$H_{b2} = \begin{bmatrix} 0 & -1 \\ -1 & -2 \end{bmatrix} = -1$$

and the third is

$$H_{b3} = \begin{vmatrix} 0 & -1 & -1 \\ -1 & -2 & 0 \\ -1 & 0 & -2 \end{vmatrix} = 0 + 0 + 0 - (-2) - 0 - (-2) = 4,$$

so the leading principal minors of the H_b have the required pattern and the point

$$x_2 = 1, \, x_1 = 0$$

is a constrained maximum.

Example

In the optimal fence problem (Example 2.7) the bordered Hessian is

$$H_b = \begin{bmatrix} 0 & -2 & -2 \\ -2 & 0 & 1 \\ -2 & 1 & 0 \end{bmatrix}$$

and

$$H_{b2} = -4$$
$$H_{b3} = 8$$

so, again, the leading principal minors have the sign pattern required for a maximum.

E2.4 Quasiconcavity

If the constraint, g, is linear, the second-order conditions explored in Extension 2.3 can be related solely to the shape of the function to be optimized, f. In this case the constraint can be written

$$g(x_1 \ldots x_n) = c - b_1 x_1 - b_2 x_2 - \ldots - b_n x_n = 0$$

and the first-order conditions for a maximum are

$$f_i = \lambda b_i \qquad i = 1 \ldots n.$$

Using the conditions, it is clear that the bordered Hessian H_b and the matrix

$$H' = \begin{bmatrix} 0 & f_1 & f_2 & \cdots & f_n \\ f_1 & f_{11} & f_{12} & & f_{1n} \\ f_2 & f_{21} & f_{22} & & f_{2n} \\ f_n & f_{n1} & f_{n2} & \cdots & f_{nn} \end{bmatrix},$$

have the same leading principal minors except for a (positive) constant of proportionality.[7] The conditions for a maximum of f subject to a linear constraint will be satisfied providing H' follows the same sign conventions as H_b—that is, $(-1)H'$ must be negative definite. A function, f, for which H' does follow this pattern is called *quasi-concave*. As we shall see, it has the property that the set of points x for which $f(x) \geq c$ (where c is any constant) is convex. For such a function, the necessary conditions for a maximum are also sufficient.

---

[5]Notice that, if $g_{ij} = 0$ for all i and j, H_b can be regarded as the simple Hessian associated with the Lagrangian expression given in Equation 2.50, which is a function of the $n + 1$ variables $\lambda, x_1 \ldots x_n$.

[6]Notice that the first leading principal minor of H_b is 0.

[7]This can be shown by noting that multiplying a row (or a column) of a matrix by a constant multiplies the determinant by that constant.

Example

For the fences problem $f(x, y) = xy$ and $\mathbf{H}'$ is given by

$$\mathbf{H}' = \begin{bmatrix} 0 & y & x \\ y & 0 & 1 \\ x & 1 & 0 \end{bmatrix}.$$

So

$$H'_2 = -y^2 < 0$$
$$H'_3 = 2xy > 0$$

and the function is quasi-concave.[8]

---

[8]Since $f(x,y) = xy$ is a form of a Cobb-Douglas function that is not concave, this shows that not every quasi-concave function is concave. Notice that a monotonic function of f (such as $f^{1/3}$) would be concave, however.

Example

More generally, if f is a function of only two variables, quasi-concavity requires

$$H'_2 = -(f_1)^2 < 0$$
$$H'_3 = -f_{11} f_2^2 - f_{22} f_1^2 + 2f_1 f_2 f_{12} > 0,$$

which is precisely the condition stated in Equation 2.114. Hence, we have a fairly simple way of determining quasi-concavity.

References

Simon, C. P., and L. Blume. *Mathematics for Economists.* New York: W. W. Norton, 1994.

Sydsaeter, R., A. Strom, and P. Berck. *Economists' Mathematical Manual.* 3rd ed. Berlin: Springer-Verlag, 2000.

Part 2

CHOICE AND DEMAND

In Part 2 we will investigate the economic theory of choice. One goal of this examination is to develop the notion of demand in a formal way so that this concept can be used in later sections of the text when we turn to the study of markets. A more general goal of this part is to illustrate the theory economists use to explain how individuals make choices in a wide variety of contexts.

Part 2 begins with a description of the way economists model individual preferences, which are usually referred to by the formal term utility. *Chapter 3 shows how economists are able to conceptualize utility in a mathematical way. This permits the development of "indifference curves," which show the various exchanges that individuals are willing to make voluntarily.*

The utility concept is then used in Chapter 4 to illustrate the theory of choice. The fundamental hypothesis of the chapter is that people who are faced with limited incomes will make economic choices in such a way as to achieve as much utility as possible. Chapter 4 uses both mathematical and intuitive analyses to indicate the insights that this hypothesis provides about economic behavior.

Chapters 5 and 6 use the model of utility maximization to investigate how individuals will respond to changes in their circumstances. Chapter 5 is primarily concerned with responses to changes in the price of a commodity, an analysis that leads directly to the demand curve notion. Chapter 6 continues this type of analysis and applies it to developing an understanding of demand relationships among different goods.

Chapter 3

PREFERENCES AND UTILITY

In this chapter we look at the way in which economists characterize individuals' preferences. We begin with a fairly abstract discussion of the "preference relation," but quickly turn to the economists' primary tool for studying individual choices—the utility function. We look at some general characteristics of that function and at a few simple examples of specific utility functions we will encounter throughout this book.

Axioms of rational choice

One way to begin an analysis of individuals' choices is to state a basic set of postulates, or axioms, that characterize "rational" behavior. Although a number of sets of such axioms have been proposed, all have similarities in that they begin with the concept of "preference": When an individual reports that "A is preferred to B," it is taken to mean that all things considered, he or she feels better off under situation A than under situation B. This preference relation is assumed to have three basic properties:

I. *Completeness:* If A and B are *any* two situations, the individual can always specify exactly one of the following three possibilities:

1. "A is preferred to B,"
2. "B is preferred to A," or
3. "A and B are equally attractive."

People are consequently assumed not to be paralyzed by indecision: They completely understand and can always make up their minds about the desirability of any two alternatives. The assumption also rules out the possibility that an individual can report both that A is preferred to B and that B is preferred to A.

II. *Transitivity:* If an individual reports that "A is preferred to B" and that "B is preferred to C," then he or she must also report that "A is preferred to C."

This assumption states that the individual's choices are internally consistent. Such an assumption can be subjected to empirical study. Generally, such studies conclude that a person's choices are indeed transitive, but that conclusions must be modified in cases where the individual may not fully understand the consequences of the choices he or she is making. Because, for the most part, we will assume choices are fully informed (but see the discussion of uncertainty in Part 7 and elsewhere), the transitivity property seems an appropriate assumption to make about preferences.

III. *Continuity:* If an individual reports "A is preferred to B," then situations suitably "close to" A must also be preferred to B.

This rather technical assumption is required if we wish to analyze individuals' responses to relatively small changes in income and prices. The purpose of the assumption is to rule out certain kinds of discontinuous, knife-edge preferences that pose problems for a mathematical development of the theory of choice. Assuming continuity does not seem to run the risk of missing types of economic behavior that are important in the real world.

Utility

Given the assumptions of completeness, transitivity, and continuity, it is possible to show formally that people are able to rank in order all possible situations from the least desirable to the most.[1] Following the terminology introduced by the nineteenth-century political theorist Jeremy Bentham, economists call this ranking *utility*.[2] We also will follow Bentham by saying that more desirable situations offer more utility than do less desirable ones. That is, if a person prefers situation A to situation B, we would say that the utility assigned to option A, denoted by $U(A)$, exceeds the utility assigned to B, $U(B)$.

Nonuniqueness of utility measures

We might even attach numbers to these utility rankings. But these numbers will not be unique. Any set of numbers we arbitrarily assign that accurately reflects the original preference ordering will imply the same set of choices. It makes no difference whether we say that $U(A) = 5$ and $U(B) = 4$ or that $U(A) = 1,000,000$ and $U(B) = 0.5$. In either case the numbers imply that A is preferred to B. In technical terms, our notion of utility is defined only up to an order-preserving ("monotonic") transformation.[3] Any set of numbers that accurately reflects a person's preference ordering will do. Consequently, it makes no sense to ask "how much more is A preferred than B?" since that question has no unique answer. Surveys that ask people to rank their "happiness" on a scale of 1 to 10 could just as well use a scale of 7 to 1,000,000. About all that can be hoped for is that a person who reports he or she is a "6" on the scale one day and a "7" on the next day is indeed happier on the second day. Utility rankings are therefore like the ordinal rankings of restaurants or movies using one, two, three, or four stars. They simply record the relative desirability of commodity bundles.

This lack of uniqueness in the assignment of utility numbers also shows why it is not possible to compare utilities between people. If one person reports that a steak dinner provides a utility of "5" and another reports that the same dinner offers a utility of "100," we cannot say which individual values the dinner more because they could be using very different scales. Similarly, we have no way of measuring whether a move from situation A to situation B provides more utility to one person or to another. Nonetheless, as we will see, economists can say quite a bit about utility rankings by examining what people voluntarily choose to do.

---

[1] These properties and their connection to representation of preferences by a utility function are discussed in detail in Andreu Mas-Colell, Michael D. Whinston, and Jerry R. Green, *Microeconomic Theory* (New York: Oxford University Press, 1995).

[2] J. Bentham, *Introduction to the Principles of Morals and Legislation* (London: Hafner, 1848).

[3] We can denote this idea mathematically by saying that any numerical utility ranking *(U)* can be transformed into another set of numbers by the function F providing that $F(U)$ is order preserving. This can be ensured if $F'(U) > 0$. For example, the transformation $F(U) = U^2$ is order preserving as is the transformation $F(U) = \ln U$. At some places in the text and problems, we may find it convenient to make such transformations in order to make a particular utility ranking easier to analyze.

The ceteris paribus assumption

Because *utility* refers to overall satisfaction, such a measure clearly is affected by a variety of factors. A person's utility is affected not only by his or her consumption of physical commodities, but also by psychological attitudes, peer group pressures, personal experiences, and the general cultural environment. Although economists do have a general interest in examining such influences, usually a narrowing of focus is necessary. Consequently, a common practice is to devote attention exclusively to choices among quantifiable options (for example, the relative quantities of food and shelter bought, the number of hours worked per week, or votes among specific taxing formulas) while holding constant the other things that affect behavior. This ceteris paribus (other things being equal) assumption is invoked in all economic analyses of utility-maximizing choices so as to make the analysis of choices manageable within a simplified setting.

Utility from consumption of goods

As an important example of the ceteris paribus assumption, consider the individual's problem of choosing, at a single point in time, among n consumption goods $x_1, x_2, \ldots, x_n$. We shall assume that the individual's ranking of these goods can be represented by a utility function of the form

$$\text{utility} = U(x_1, x_2, \ldots, x_n; \text{other things}), \tag{3.1}$$

where the x's refer to the quantities of the goods that might be chosen and the "other things" notation is used as a reminder that many aspects of individual welfare are being held constant in the analysis.

Quite often it is easier to write Equation 3.1 as

$$\text{utility} = U(x_1, x_2, \ldots, x_n) \tag{3.2}$$

or, if only two goods are being considered,

$$\text{utility} = U(x, y), \tag{3.2'}$$

where it is clear that everything is being held constant (that is, outside the frame of analysis) except the goods actually referred to in the utility function. It would be tedious to remind you at each step what is being held constant in the analysis, but it should be remembered that some form of the ceteris paribus assumption will always be in effect.

Arguments of utility functions

The utility function notation is used to indicate how an individual ranks the particular arguments of the function being considered. In the most common case, the utility function (Equation 3.2) will be used to represent how an individual ranks certain bundles of goods that might be purchased at one point in time. On occasion we will use other arguments in the utility function, and it is best to clear up certain conventions at the outset. For example, it may be useful to talk about the utility an individual receives from real wealth (W). Therefore we shall use the notation

$$\text{utility} = U(W). \tag{3.3}$$

Unless the individual is a rather peculiar Scrooge-type of person, wealth in its own right gives no direct utility. Rather, it is only when wealth is spent on consumption goods that any utility results. For this reason Equation 3.3 will be taken to mean that the utility from wealth is in fact derived by spending that wealth in such a way as to yield as much utility as possible.

Two other arguments of utility functions will be used in later chapters. In Chapter 16 we will be concerned with the individual's labor-leisure choice and will therefore have to consider the presence of leisure in the utility function. A function of the form

$$\text{utility} = U(c, h) \tag{3.4}$$

will be used. Here c represents consumption and h represents hours of nonwork time (that is, leisure) during a particular time period.

In Chapter 17 we will be interested in the individual's consumption decisions in different time periods. In that chapter we will use a utility function of the form

$$\text{utility} = U(c_1, c_2), \tag{3.5}$$

where c_1 is consumption in this period and c_2 is consumption in the next period. By changing the arguments of the utility function, therefore, we will be able to focus on specific aspects of an individual's choices in a variety of simplified settings.

In summary then, we start our examination of individual behavior with the following definition:

DEFINITION

Utility. Individuals' preferences are assumed to be represented by a utility function of the form

$$U(x_1, x_2, \ldots, x_n), \tag{3.6}$$

where $x_1, x_2, \ldots, x_n$ are the quantities of each of n goods that might be consumed in a period. This function is unique only up to an order-preserving transformation.

Economic goods

In this representation the variables are taken to be "goods"—that is, whatever economic quantities they represent, we assume that more of any particular x_i during some period is preferred to less. We assume this is true of every good, be it a simple consumption item such as a hot dog or a complex aggregate such as wealth or leisure. We have pictured this convention for a two-good utility function in Figure 3.1. There, all consumption bundles in the shaded area are preferred to the bundle x^*, y^* because any bundle in the shaded area provides more of at least one of the goods. By our definition of "goods," then, bundles of goods in the shaded area are ranked more highly than x^*, y^*. Similarly, bundles in the area marked "worse" are clearly inferior to x^*, y^* since they contain less of at least one of the goods and no more of the other. Bundles in the two areas indicated by question marks are difficult to compare to x^*, y^* because they contain more of one of the goods and less of the other. Movements into these areas involve trade-offs between the two goods.

Trades and substitution

Most economic activity involves voluntary trading between individuals. When someone buys, say, a loaf of bread, he or she is voluntarily giving up one thing (money) for something else (bread) that is of greater value. To examine this kind of voluntary transaction, we need to develop a formal apparatus for illustrating trades in the utility function context.

FIGURE 3.1   **More of a Good Is Preferred to Less**

The shaded area represents those combinations of x and y that are unambiguously preferred to the combination x^*, y^*. Ceteris paribus, individuals prefer more of any good rather than less. Combinations identified by "?" involve ambiguous changes in welfare because they contain more of one good and less of the other.

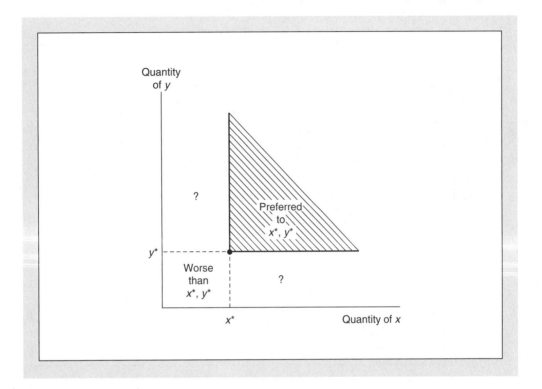

Indifference curves and the marginal rate of substitution

To discuss such voluntary trades, we develop the idea of an *indifference curve*. In Figure 3.2 the curve U_1 represents all the alternative combinations of x and y for which an individual is equally well off (remember again that all other arguments of the utility function are being held constant). This person is equally happy consuming, for example, either the combination of goods x_1, y_1 or the combination x_2, y_2. This curve representing all the consumption bundles that the individual ranks equally is called an *indifference curve*:

DEFINITION

Indifference curve. An *indifference curve* (or, in many dimensions, indifference surface) shows a set of consumption bundles among which the individual is indifferent. That is, the bundles all provide the same level of utility.

The slope of the indifference curve in Figure 3.2 is negative, showing that if the individual is forced to give up some y, he or she must be compensated by an additional amount of x to remain indifferent between the two bundles of goods. The curve is also drawn so that the slope increases as x increases (that is, the slope starts at negative infinity and increases toward zero). This is a graphical representation of the assumption that people become

FIGURE 3.2   **A Single Indifference Curve**

The curve U_1 represents those combinations of x and y from which the individual derives the same utility. The slope of this curve represents the rate at which the individual is willing to trade x for y while remaining equally well off. This slope (or, more properly, the negative of the slope) is termed the *marginal rate of substitution*. In the figure the indifference curve is drawn on the assumption of a diminishing marginal rate of substitution.

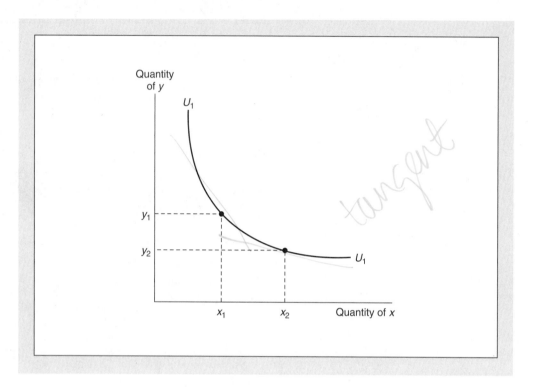

progressively less willing to trade away y to get more x. In mathematical terms, this slope diminishes as x increases. Hence, we have the following definition:

Marginal rate of substitution. The negative of the slope of an indifference curve (U_1) at some point is termed the *marginal rate of substitution* (*MRS*) at that point. That is,

$$MRS = -\frac{dy}{dx}\bigg|_{U = U_1} \tag{3.7}$$

where the notation indicates that the slope is to be calculated along the U_1 indifference curve.

The slope of U_1 and the *MRS* therefore tell us something about the trades this person will voluntarily make. At a point such as x_1, y_1, the person has quite a lot of y and is willing to trade away a significant amount to get one more x. The indifference curve at x_1, y_1 is therefore rather steep. This is a situation where the person has, say, many hamburgers (y) and little to drink with them (x). This person would gladly give up a few burgers (say, 5) to quench his or her thirst with one more drink.

At x_2, y_2, on the other hand, the indifference curve is flatter. Here this person has quite a few drinks and is willing to give up relatively few burgers (say, 1) to get another soft drink. Consequently, the *MRS* diminishes between x_1, y_1 and x_2, y_2. The changing slope of

FIGURE 3.3   **There Are Infinitely Many Indifference Curves in the *x-y* Plane**

There is an indifference curve passing through each point in the *x-y* plane. Each of these curves records combinations of *x* and *y* from which the individual receives a certain level of satisfaction. Movements in a northeast direction represent movements to higher levels of satisfaction.

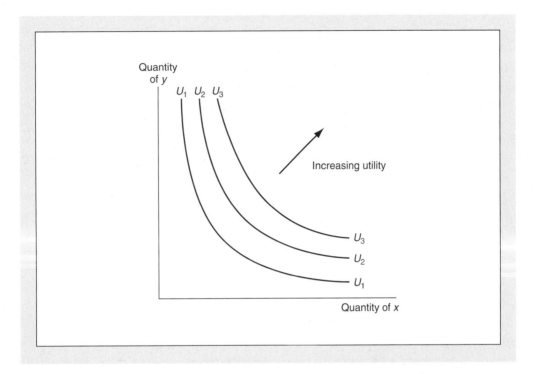

U_1 shows how the particular consumption bundle available influences the trades this person will freely make.

Indifference curve map

In Figure 3.2 only one indifference curve was drawn. The *x, y* quadrant, however, is densely packed with such curves, each corresponding to a different level of utility. Because every bundle of goods can be ranked and yields some level of utility, each point in Figure 3.2 must have an indifference curve passing through it. Indifference curves are similar to contour lines on a map in that they represent lines of equal "altitude" of utility. In Figure 3.3 several indifference curves are shown to indicate that there are infinitely many in the plane. The level of utility represented by these curves increases as we move in a northeast direction— the utility of curve U_1 is less than that of U_2, which is less than that of U_3. This is because of the assumption made in Figure 3.1: More of a good is preferred to less. As was discussed earlier, there is no unique way to assign numbers to these utility levels. All the curves show is that the combinations of goods on U_3 are preferred to those on U_2, which are preferred to those on U_1.

Indifference curves and transitivity

As an exercise in examining the relationship between consistent preferences and the representation of preferences by utility functions, consider the following question: Can any two of an individual's indifference curves intersect? Two such intersecting curves are shown in Figure 3.4. We wish to know if they violate our basic axioms of rationality. Using our map analogy, there would seem to be something wrong at point *E*—there, "altitude" is equal to two different numbers, U_1 and U_2. But no point can be both 100 and 200 feet above sea level.

FIGURE 3.4   Intersecting Indifference Curves Imply Inconsistent Preferences

Combinations A and D lie on the same indifference curve and therefore are equally desirable. But the axiom of transitivity can be used to show that A is preferred to D. Hence, intersecting indifference curves are not consistent with rational preferences.

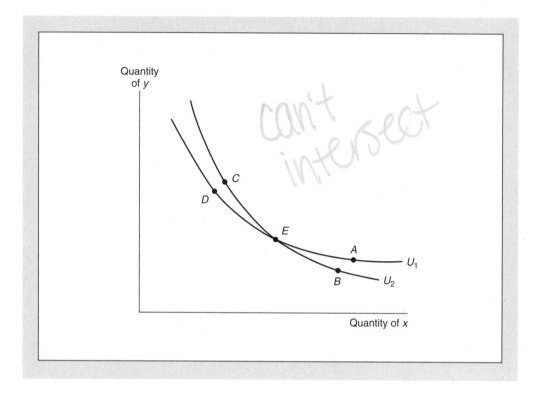

To proceed formally, let us analyze the bundles of goods represented by points A, B, C, and D. By the assumption of nonsatiation, "A is preferred to B" and "C is preferred to D." But this person is equally satisfied with either B or C (they lie on the same indifference curve), so the axiom of transitivity implies that A must be preferred to D. But that cannot be true, because A and D are on the same indifference curve and are by definition regarded as equally desirable. Hence, the axiom of transitivity shows that indifference curves cannot intersect. We therefore should always draw indifference curve maps as they appear in Figure 3.3.

Convexity of indifference curves

An alternative way of stating the principle of a diminishing marginal rate of substitution uses the mathematical notion of a convex set. A set of points is said to be *convex* if any two points within the set can be joined by a straight line that is contained completely within the set. The assumption of a diminishing *MRS* is equivalent to the assumption that all combinations of x and y, which are preferred to or indifferent to a particular combination x^*, y^*, form a convex set.[4] This is illustrated in Figure 3.5a, where all combinations preferred to or indif-

---

[4]This definition is equivalent to assuming that the utility function is quasi-concave. Such functions were discussed in Chapter 2, and we shall return to examine them in the next section. Sometimes the term *strict quasi-concavity* is used to rule out the possibility of indifference curves having linear segments. We generally will assume strict quasi-concavity, but in a few places will illustrate the complications posed by linear portions of indifference curves.

FIGURE 3.5   **The Notion of Convexity as an Alternative Definition of a Diminishing *MRS***

In (a) the indifference curve is *convex* (any line joining two points above U_1 is also above U_1). In (b) this is not the case, and the curve shown here does not everywhere have a diminishing *MRS*.

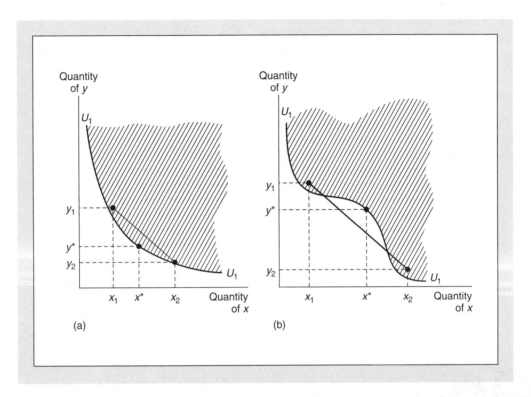

(a)   (b)

ferent to x^*, y^* are in the shaded area. Any two of these combinations—say, x_1, y_1 and x_2, y_2—can be joined by a straight line also contained in the shaded area. In Figure 3.5b this is not true. A line joining x_1, y_1 and x_2, y_2 passes outside the shaded area. Therefore, the indifference curve through x^*, y^* in Figure 3.5b does not obey the assumption of a diminishing *MRS*, because the set of points preferred or indifferent to x^*, y^* is not convex.

Convexity and balance in consumption

By using the notion of convexity, we can show that individuals prefer some balance in their consumption. Suppose that an individual is indifferent between the combination x_1, y_1 and x_2, y_2. If the indifference curve is strictly convex, then the combination $(x_1 + x_2)/2$, $(y_1 + y_2)/2$ will be preferred to either of the initial combinations.[5] Intuitively, "well-balanced" bundles of commodities are preferred to bundles that are heavily weighted toward one commodity. This is illustrated in Figure 3.6. Because the indifference curve is assumed to be convex, all points on the straight line joining (x_1, y_1) and (x_2, y_2) are preferred to these initial points. This therefore will be true of the point $(x_1 + x_2)/2$, $(y_1 + y_2)/2$, which lies at the midpoint of such a line. Indeed, any proportional combination of the two indifferent bundles of goods will be preferred to the initial bundles, because it will represent a more balanced combination. Thus, strict convexity is equivalent to the assumption of a diminishing *MRS*. Both assumptions rule out the possibility of an indifference curve being straight over any portion of its length.

[5]In the case in which the indifference curve has a linear segment, the individual will be indifferent among all three combinations.

FIGURE 3.6   Balanced Bundles of Goods Are Preferred to Extreme Bundles

If indifference curves are convex (if they obey the assumption of a diminishing *MRS*), then the line joining any two points that are indifferent will contain points preferred to either of the initial combinations. Intuitively, balanced bundles are preferred to unbalanced ones.

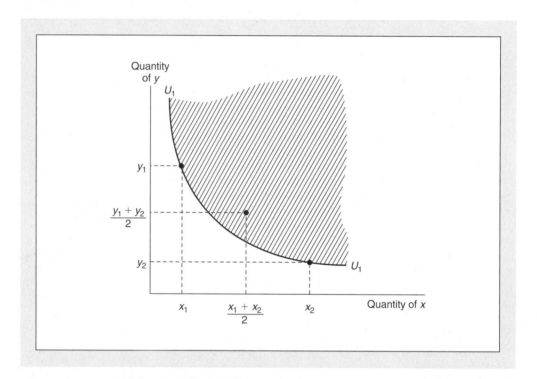

EXAMPLE 3.1

Utility and the *MRS*

Suppose a person's ranking of hamburgers *(y)* and soft drinks *(x)* could be represented by the utility function

$$\text{utility} = \sqrt{x \cdot y}. \tag{3.8}$$

An indifference curve for this function is found by identifying that set of combinations of *x* and *y* for which utility has the same value. Suppose we arbitrarily set utility equal to 10. Then the equation for this indifference curve is

$$\text{utility} = 10 = \sqrt{x \cdot y}. \tag{3.9}$$

Because squaring this function is order preserving, the indifference curve is also represented by

$$100 = x \cdot y, \tag{3.10}$$

which is easier to graph. In Figure 3.7 we show this indifference curve—it is a familiar rectangular hyperbola. One way to calculate the *MRS* is to solve Equation 3.10 for *y*,

$$y = 100/x, \tag{3.11}$$

and then use the definition (Equation 3.7):

$$MRS = -dy/dx \text{ (along } U_1) = 100/x^2. \tag{3.12}$$

Clearly this *MRS* declines as *x* increases. At a point such as *A* on the indifference curve with a lot of hamburgers (say, $x = 5$, $y = 20$), the slope is steep so the *MRS* is high:

$$MRS \text{ at } (5, 20) = 100/x^2 = 100/25 = 4. \qquad (3.13)$$

Here the person is willing to give up 4 hamburgers to get 1 more soft drink. On the other hand, at *B* where there are relatively few hamburgers (here $x = 20$, $y = 5$), the slope is flat and the *MRS* is low:

$$MRS \text{ at } (20, 5) = 100/x^2 = 100/400 = 0.25. \qquad (3.14)$$

Now he or she will only give up one quarter of a hamburger for another soft drink. Notice also how convexity of the indifference curve U_1 is illustrated by this numerical example. Point *C* is midway between points *A* and *B*—at *C* this person has 12.5 hamburgers and 12.5 soft drinks. Here utility is given by

$$\text{utility} = \sqrt{x \cdot y} = \sqrt{(12.5)^2} = 12.5, \qquad (3.15)$$

which clearly exceeds the utility along U_1 (which was assumed to be 10).

Query: From our derivation here, it appears that the *MRS* depends only on the quantity of *x* consumed. Why is this misleading? How does the quantity of *y* implicitly enter into Equations 3.13 and 3.14?

FIGURE 3.7   **Indifference Curve for Utility = $\sqrt{x \cdot y}$**

This indifference curve illustrates the function $10 = U = \sqrt{x \cdot y}$. At point *A* (5, 20), the *MRS* is 4, implying that this person is willing to trade 4*y* for an additional *x*. At point *B* (20, 5), however, the *MRS* is 0.25, implying a greatly reduced willingness to trade.

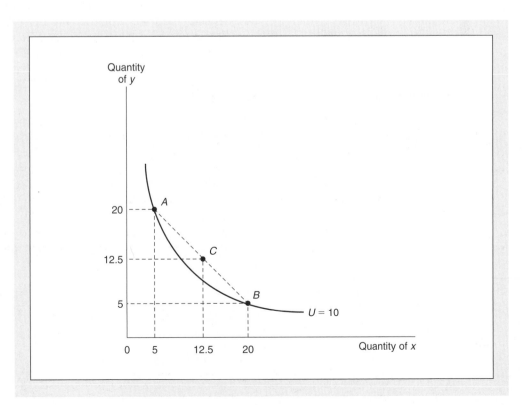

A mathematical derivation

A mathematical derivation of the *MRS* concept provides additional insights about the shape of indifference curves and the nature of preferences. In this section we provide such a derivation for the case of a utility function involving only two goods. This will allow us to compare the mathematics to the two-dimensional indifference curve map. The case of many goods will be taken up at the end of the chapter, but it will turn out that this more complicated analysis really adds very little.

The *MRS* and marginal utility

If the utility a person receives from two goods is represented by $U(x,y)$, we can write the total differential of this function as

$$dU = \frac{\partial U}{\partial x} \cdot dx + \frac{\partial U}{\partial y} \cdot dy. \qquad (3.16)$$

Along any particular indifference curve $dU = 0$, so a simple manipulation of Equation 3.16 yields

$$MRS = -\frac{dy}{dx}\Big|_{U=constant} = \frac{\dfrac{\partial U}{\partial x}}{\dfrac{\partial U}{\partial y}}. \qquad (3.17)$$

In words, the *MRS* of x for y is equal to the ratio of the marginal utility of x (that is, $\partial U/\partial x$) to the marginal utility of y ($\partial U/\partial y$). This result makes intuitive sense. Suppose for the moment that a person's utility were actually measurable in, say, units called "utils." Assume also that this person just consumes two goods, food (x) and clothing (y) and that each extra unit of food provides 6 utils whereas each extra unit of clothing provides 2 utils. Then Equation 3.17 would mean that the *MRS* is given by $MRS = \dfrac{dy}{dx}\Big|_{U=constant} = \dfrac{6\,utils}{2\,utils} = 3$, so this person is willing to trade away 3 units of clothing to get one more unit of food. This trade would result in no net change in utility because the gains and losses would be precisely offsetting. Notice that the units in which utility is measured (what we have, for lack of a better word, called "utils") cancel out in making this calculation. Although marginal utility is obviously affected by the units in which utility is measured, the *MRS* is independent of that choice.[6]

The convexity of indifference curves

In Chapter 1 we described how the assumption of diminishing marginal utility was used by Marshall to solve the water-diamond paradox. Marshall theorized that it is the marginal valuation that an individual places on a good that determines its value: It is the amount that an individual is willing to pay for one more pint of water that determines the price of water. Because it might be thought that this marginal value declines as the quantity of water that is consumed increases, Marshall showed why water has a low exchange value. Intuitively, it seems that the assumption of a decreasing marginal utility of a good is related to the assumption of a decreasing *MRS;* both concepts seem to refer to the same commonsense idea of an individual becoming relatively satiated with a good as more of it

---

[6]More formally, let $F(U)$ be any arbitrary order-preserving transformation of U (that is, $F'(U) > 0$). Then for the transformed utility function

$$MRS = \frac{\partial F/\partial x}{\partial F/\partial y} = \frac{F'(U)\partial U/\partial x}{F'(U)\partial U/\partial y}$$
$$= \frac{\partial U/\partial x}{\partial U/\partial y}$$

which is the *MRS* for the original function U—the fact that the $F'(U)$ terms cancel out shows that the *MRS* is independent of how utility is measured.

is consumed. Unfortunately, the two concepts are quite different. (See Problem 3.3.) Technically, the assumption of a diminishing *MRS* is equivalent to requiring that the utility function be quasi-concave. This requirement is related in a rather complex way to the assumption that each good encounters diminishing marginal utility (that is, that f_{ii} is negative for each good).[7] But that is to be expected because the concept of diminishing marginal utility is not independent of how utility itself is measured, whereas the convexity of indifference curves is indeed independent of such measurement.

 EXAMPLE 3.2

Showing Convexity of Indifference Curves

Calculation of the *MRS* for specific utility functions is frequently a good shortcut for showing convexity of indifference curves. In particular, the process can be much simpler than applying the definition of quasi-concavity, though it is more difficult to generalize to more than two goods. Here we look at how Equation 3.17 can be used for three different utility functions (for more practice, see Problem 3.1).

1. $U(x, y) = \sqrt{x \cdot y}$

This example just repeats the case illustrated in Example 3.1. One shortcut to applying Equation 3.17 that can simplify the algebra here is to take the logarithm of this utility function. Because taking logs is order-preserving, this will not alter the *MRS* to be calculated. So, let

$$U^*(x, y) = \ln[U(x, y)] = 0.5 \ln x + 0.5 \ln y. \qquad (3.18)$$

Applying Equation 3.17 yields

$$MRS = \frac{\dfrac{\partial U^*}{\partial x}}{\dfrac{\partial U^*}{\partial y}} = \frac{\dfrac{0.5}{x}}{\dfrac{0.5}{y}} = \frac{y}{x}. \qquad (3.19)$$

(continued)

---

[7] We have shown that if utility is given by $U = f(x, y)$, then

$$MRS = \frac{f_x}{f_y} = \frac{f_1}{f_2} = -\frac{dy}{dx}.$$

The assumption of a diminishing *MRS* means that $dMRS/dx < 0$, but

$$\frac{dMRS}{dx} = \frac{f_2(f_{11} + f_{12} \cdot dy/dx) - f_1(f_{21} + f_{22} \cdot dx/dy)}{f_2^2}.$$

Using the fact that $f_1/f_2 = -dy/dx$, we have

$$\frac{dMRS}{dx} = \frac{f_2[f_{11} - f_{12}(f_1/f_2)] - f_1[f_{21} - f_{22}(f_1/f_2)]}{f_2^2}.$$

Combining terms and recognizing that $f_{12} = f_{21}$ yields

$$\frac{dMRS}{dx} = \frac{f_2 f_{11} - 2f_1 f_{12} + (f_{22} f_1^2)/f_2}{f_2^2},$$

or, multiplying numerator and denominator by f_2,

$$\frac{dMRS}{dx} = \frac{f_2^2 f_{11} - 2f_1 f_2 f_{12} + f_1^2 f_{22}}{f_2^3}.$$

If we assume that $f_2 > 0$ (that marginal utility is positive), then the *MRS* will diminish provided that

$$f_2^2 f_{11} - 2f_1 f_2 f_{12} + f_1^2 f_{22} < 0.$$

Notice that diminishing marginal utility ($f_{11} < 0$ and $f_{22} < 0$) will not ensure this inequality. One must also be concerned with the f_{12} term. That is, one must know how decreases in *y* affect the marginal utility of *x*. In general it is not possible to predict the sign of that term.

  The condition required for a diminishing *MRS* is precisely that discussed in Chapter 2 to ensure that the function *f* is strictly quasi-concave. The condition shows that the necessary conditions for a maximum of *f* subject to a linear constraint are also sufficient. We will use this result in Chapter 4 and elsewhere.

EXAMPLE 3.2 CONTINUED

which seems to be a much simpler approach than we used previously.[8] Clearly this *MRS* is diminishing as x increases and y decreases. The indifference curves are therefore convex.

2. $U(x, y) = x + xy + y$

In this case there is no advantage to transforming this utility function. Applying Equation 3.17 yields

$$MRS = \frac{\frac{\partial U}{\partial x}}{\frac{\partial U}{\partial y}} = \frac{1 + y}{1 + x}. \tag{3.20}$$

Again, this ratio clearly decreases as x increases and y decreases so the indifference curves for this function are convex.

3. $U(x, y) = \sqrt{x^2 + y^2}$

For this example it is easier to use the transformation

$$U^*(x, y) = [U(x, y)]^2 = x^2 + y^2. \tag{3.21}$$

Because this is the equation for a circle, we should begin to suspect that there might be some problems with the indifference curves for this utility function. These suspicions are confirmed by again applying the definition of the *MRS* to yield

$$MRS = \frac{\frac{\partial U^*}{\partial x}}{\frac{\partial U^*}{\partial y}} = \frac{2x}{2y} = \frac{x}{y}. \tag{3.22}$$

For this function it is clear that, as x increases and y decreases, the *MRS increases!* Hence the curves are concave, not convex, and this is clearly not a quasi-concave function.

Query: Does a doubling of x and y change the *MRS* in each of these three examples? That is, does the *MRS* depend only on the ratio of x to y, not on the absolute scale of purchases? (See also Example 3.3).

Utility functions for specific preferences

Individuals' rankings of commodity bundles and the utility functions implied by these rankings are unobservable. All we can learn about people's preferences must come from the behavior we observe when they respond to changes in income, prices, and other factors. It is nevertheless useful to examine a few of the forms particular utility functions might take, both because such an examination may offer some insights into observed behavior and (more to the point) because understanding the properties of such functions can be of some help in solving problems. Here we will examine four specific examples of utility functions for two goods. Indifference curve maps for these functions are illustrated

---

[8]In Example 3.1 we looked at the $U = 10$ indifference curve. So, for that curve, $y = 100/x$ and the *MRS* in Equation 3.19 would be $MRS = 100/x^2$ as calculated before.

FIGURE 3.8   Examples of Utility Functions

The four indifference curve maps illustrate alternative degrees of substitutability of x for y. The Cobb-Douglas and CES functions (drawn here for relatively low substitutability) fall between the extremes of perfect substitution (panel b) and no substitution (panel c).

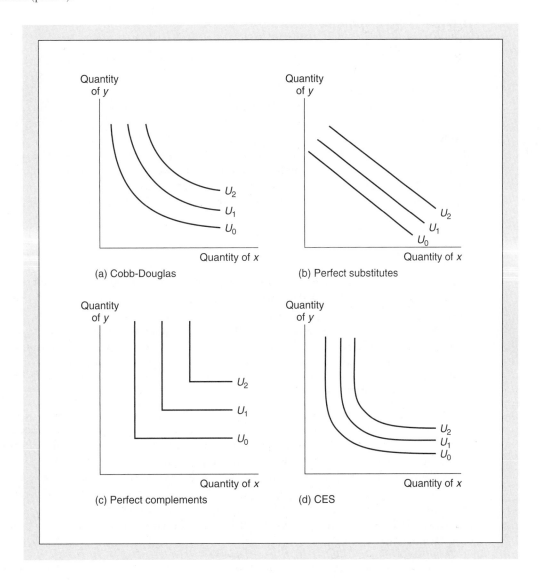

in the four panels of Figure 3.8. As should be visually apparent, these cover quite a few possible shapes. Even greater variety is possible once we move to functions for three or more goods, and some of these possibilities are mentioned in later chapters.

Cobb-Douglas utility

Figure 3.8a shows the familiar shape of an indifference curve. One commonly used utility function that generates such curves has the form

$$\text{utility} = U(x, y) = x^{\alpha} y^{\beta}, \tag{3.23}$$

where α and β are positive constants.

In Examples 3.1 and 3.2, we studied a particular case of this function for which $\alpha = \beta = 0.5$. The more general case presented in Equation 3.23 is termed a *Cobb-Douglas utility function* after two researchers who used such a function for their detailed study of production relationships in the U.S. economy (see Chapter 7). In general, the relative sizes of α and β indicate the relative importance of the two goods to this individual. Since utility is unique only up to a monotonic transformation, it is often convenient to normalize these parameters so that $\alpha + \beta = 1$.

Perfect substitutes

The linear indifference curves in Figure 3.8b are generated by a utility function of the form

$$\text{utility} = U(x, y) = \alpha x + \beta y, \tag{3.24}$$

where, again, α and β are positive constants. That the indifference curves for this function are straight lines should be readily apparent: any particular level curve can be calculated by setting $U(x, y)$ equal to a constant that, given the linear form of the function, clearly specifies a straight line. The linear nature of these indifference curves gave rise to the term *perfect substitutes* to describe the implied relationship between x and y. Because the *MRS* is constant (and equal to α/β) along the entire indifference curve, our previous notions of a diminishing *MRS* do not apply in this case. A person with these preferences would be willing to give up the same amount of y to get one more x no matter how much x was being consumed. Such a situation might describe the relationship between different brands of what is essentially the same product. For example, many people (including the author) don't care where they buy gasoline. A gallon of gas is a gallon of gas in spite of the best efforts of the Exxon and Shell advertising departments to convince me otherwise. Given this fact, I am always willing to give up 10 gallons of Exxon in exchange for 10 gallons of Shell because it doesn't matter to me which I use or where I got my last tankful. Indeed, as we will see in the next chapter, one implication of such a relationship is that I will buy all my gas from the least expensive seller. Because I don't experience a diminishing *MRS* of Exxon for Shell, I have no reason to seek a balance among the gasoline types I use.

Perfect complements

A situation directly opposite to the case of perfect substitutes is illustrated by the L-shaped indifference curves in Figure 3.8c. These preferences would apply to goods that "go together"—coffee and cream, peanut butter and jelly, and cream cheese and lox are familiar examples. The indifference curves shown in Figure 3.8c imply that these pairs of goods will be used in the fixed proportional relationship represented by the vertices of the curves. A person who prefers 1 ounce of cream with 8 ounces of coffee will want 2 ounces of cream with 16 ounces of coffee. Extra coffee without cream is of no value to this person, just as extra cream would be of no value without coffee. Only by choosing the goods together can utility be increased.

These concepts can be formalized by examining the mathematical form of the utility function that generates these L-shaped indifference curves:

$$\text{utility} = U(x, y) = \min(\alpha x, \beta y). \tag{3.25}$$

Here α and β are positive parameters, and the operator "min" means that utility is given by the smaller of the two terms in the parentheses. In the coffee-cream example, if we let ounces of coffee be represented by x and ounces of cream by y, utility would be given by

$$\text{utility} = U(x, y) = \min(x, 8y). \tag{3.26}$$

Now 8 ounces of coffee and 1 ounce of cream provide 8 units of utility. But 16 ounces of coffee and 1 ounce of cream still provide only 8 units of utility because min (16, 8) = 8. The extra coffee without cream is of no value, as shown by the horizontal section of the indifference curves for movement away from a vertex—utility does not increase when only *x* increases (with *y* constant). Only if coffee and cream are both doubled (to 16 and 2, respectively) will utility increase to 16.

More generally, neither of the two goods will be in excess only if

$$\alpha x = \beta y. \tag{3.27}$$

Hence,

$$y/x = \alpha/\beta, \tag{3.28}$$

which shows the fixed proportional relationship between the two goods that must occur if choices are to be at the vertices of the indifference curves.

CES utility

The three specific utility functions illustrated so far are special cases of the more general constant elasticity of substitution function (CES), which takes the form

$$\text{utility} = U(x, y) = \frac{x^\delta}{\delta} + \frac{y^\delta}{\delta} \tag{3.29}$$

where $\delta \leq 1$, $\delta \neq 0$, and

$$\text{utility} = U(x, y) = \ln x + \ln y \tag{3.30}$$

when $\delta = 0$. It is obvious that the case of perfect substitutes corresponds to the limiting case, $\delta = 1$ in Equation 3.29 and that the Cobb-Douglas[9] case corresponds to $\delta = 0$ in Equation 3.30. Less obvious is that the case of fixed proportions corresponds to $\delta = -\infty$ in Equation 3.29, but that result can also be shown using a limits argument.

The use of the term "elasticity of substitution" for this function derives from the notion that the possibilities illustrated in Figure 3.8 correspond to various values for the substitution parameter, σ, which for this function is given by $\sigma = 1/(1 - \delta)$. For perfect substitutes then $\sigma = \infty$, and the fixed proportions case has $\sigma = 0$.[10] Because the CES function allows us to explore all of these cases, and many cases in between, it will prove quite useful for illustrating the degree of substitutability present in various economic relationships.

The specific shape of the CES function illustrated in panel d of Figure 3.8 is for the case, $\delta = -1$: That is,

$$\text{utility} = -x^{-1} - y^{-1} = -\frac{1}{x} - \frac{1}{y}. \tag{3.31}$$

For this situation, $\sigma = \frac{1}{1 - \delta} = \frac{1}{2}$, and as the graph shows, these sharply curved indifference curves apparently fall between the Cobb-Douglas and fixed proportion cases. The negative signs in this utility function may seem strange, but the marginal utilities of both *x* and *y* are positive and diminishing, as would be expected. This explains why δ must appear in the denominators in Equation 3.29. In the particular case of Equation 3.31, utility increases from $-\infty$ (when $x = y = 0$) toward 0 as *x* and *y* increase. This is an odd utility scale, perhaps, but perfectly acceptable.

---

[9]The CES function could easily be generalized to allow for differing weights to be attached to the two goods. Since the main use of the function is to examine substitution questions, we will usually not make that generalization. In some of the applications of the CES function, we will also omit the denominators of the function because these constitute only a scale factor when δ is positive. For negative values of δ, however, the denominator is needed to ensure that marginal utility is positive.

[10]The elasticity of substitution concept is discussed in more detail in connection with production functions in Chapter 7.

EXAMPLE 3.3

Homothetic Preferences

All of the utility functions described in Figure 3.8 are homothetic (see Chapter 2)—that is, the marginal rate of substitution for these functions depends only on the *ratio* of the amounts of the two goods, not on the total quantities of the goods. This fact is obvious for the case of the perfect substitutes (when the *MRS* is the same at every point) and the case of perfect complements (where the *MRS* is infinite for $y/x > \alpha/\beta$, undefined when $y/x = \alpha/\beta$, and zero when $y/x, < \alpha/\beta$). For the general Cobb-Douglas function, the *MRS* can be found as

$$MRS = \frac{\dfrac{\partial U}{\partial x}}{\dfrac{\partial U}{\partial y}} = \frac{\alpha x^{\alpha-1} y^{\beta}}{\beta x^{\alpha} y^{\beta-1}} = \frac{\alpha}{\beta} \cdot \frac{y}{x} \qquad (3.32)$$

which clearly depends only on the ratio y/x. Showing that the CES function is also homothetic is left as an exercise (see Problem 3.10).

The importance of homothetic functions is that one indifference curve is much like another. Slopes of the curves depend only on the ratio y/x, not on how far the curve is from the origin. Indifference curves for higher utility are simple copies of those for lower utility. Hence, we can study the behavior of an individual who has homothetic preferences by looking only at one indifference curve or at a few nearby curves without fearing that our results would change dramatically at very different levels of utility.

Query: How might you define homothetic functions geometrically? What would the locus of all points with a particular *MRS* look like on an individual's indifference curve map?

EXAMPLE 3.4

Nonhomothetic Preferences

Although all of the indifference curve maps in Figure 3.8 exhibit homothetic preferences, this need not always be true. Consider the quasi-linear utility function

$$\text{utility} = U(x, y) = x + \ln y. \qquad (3.33)$$

For this function, good y exhibits diminishing marginal utility, but good x does not. The *MRS* can be computed as:

$$MRS = \frac{\dfrac{\partial U}{\partial x}}{\dfrac{\partial U}{\partial y}} = \frac{1}{\dfrac{1}{y}} = y \qquad (3.34)$$

The *MRS* diminishes as the quantity chosen of y decreases, but it is independent of the quantity of x consumed. Because x has a constant marginal utility, a person's willingness to give up y to get one more unit of x depends only on how much y he or she has. Contrary to the homothetic case, then, a doubling of both x and y doubles the *MRS* here rather than leaving it unchanged.

Query: What does the indifference curve map for the utility function in Equation 3.33 look like? Can you think of any situations that might be described by such a function?

The many-good case

All of the concepts we have studied so far for the case of two goods can be generalized to situations where utility is a function of arbitrarily many goods. In this section we will briefly explore those generalizations. Although this examination will not add very much to what we have already shown, considering peoples' preferences for many goods can be quite important in applied economies, as we will see in later chapters.

The *MRS* with many goods

Suppose utility is a function of n goods given by

$$\text{utility} = U(x_1, x_2, \cdots x_n). \tag{3.35}$$

The total differential of this expression is

$$dU = \frac{\partial U}{\partial x_1} dx_1 + \frac{\partial U}{\partial x_2} dx_2 + \cdots + \frac{\partial U}{\partial x_n} dx_n. \tag{3.36}$$

and, as before, we can find the *MRS* between any two goods by setting $dU = 0$. In this derivation we also hold constant quantities of all of the goods other than those that are of interest to us. Hence we have

$$dU = 0 = \frac{\partial U}{\partial x_i} dx_i + \frac{\partial U}{\partial x_j} dx_j \tag{3.37}$$

and, after some algebraic manipulation, we get

$$MRS(x_i \ for \ x_j) = -\frac{dx_j}{dx_i} = \frac{\dfrac{\partial U}{\partial x_i}}{\dfrac{\partial U}{\partial x_j}} \tag{3.38}$$

which is precisely what we got in Equation 3.17. Whether this concept is as useful as it is in two dimensions is open to question, however. With only two goods, asking how a person would trade one for the other is an interesting question—a transaction we might actually observe. With many goods, however, it seems unlikely that a person would simply trade one good for another while holding all other goods constant. Rather, it seems more likely that an event (such as a price increase) that caused a person to want to reduce, say, the quantity of cornflakes (x_i) consumed would also caused him or her to change the quantities consumed of many other goods such as milk, sugar, Cheerios, spoons, and so forth. As we shall see in Chapter 6, this entire reallocation process can best be studied by looking at the entire utility function as represented in Equation 3.35. Still, the notion of making trade-offs between only two goods will prove useful as a way of conceptualizing the utility maximization process that we will take up next.

Multigood indifference surfaces

Generalizing the concept of indifference curves to multiple dimensions poses no major mathematical difficulties. We simply define an indifference surface as being the set of points in n dimensions that satisfy the equation

$$U(x_1, x_2, \ldots x_n) = k \tag{3.39}$$

where k is any preassigned constant. If the utility function is quasi-concave, the set of points for which $U \geq k$ will be convex—that is, all of the points on a line joining any two points on the $U = k$ indifference surface will also have $U \geq k$. It is this property that we will find most useful in later applications. Unfortunately, however, the mathematical conditions that ensure quasi-concavity in many dimensions are not especially intuitive (see the Extensions to Chapter 2), and visualizing many dimensions is virtually impossible. Hence, when intuition is required, we will usually revert to two-good examples.

SUMMARY

In this chapter we have described the way in which economists formalize individuals' preferences about the goods they choose. We drew several conclusions about such preferences that will play a central role in our analysis of the theory of choice in the following chapters:

- If individuals obey certain basic behavioral postulates in their preferences among goods, they will be able to rank all commodity bundles, and that ranking can be represented by a utility function. In making choices, individuals will behave as if they were maximizing this function.

- Utility functions for two goods can be illustrated by an indifference curve map. Each indifference curve contour on this map shows all the commodity bundles that yield a given level of utility.

- The negative of the slope of an indifference curve is defined to be the marginal rate of substitution (MRS). This shows the rate at which an individual would willingly give up an amount of one good (y) if he or she were compensated by receiving one more unit of another good (x).

- The assumption that the MRS decreases as x is substituted for y in consumption is consistent with the notion that individuals prefer some balance in their consumption choices. If the MRS is always decreasing, individuals will have strictly convex indifference curves. That is, their utility function will be strictly quasi-concave.

- A few simple functional forms can capture important differences in individuals' preferences for two (or more) goods. Here we examined the Cobb-Douglas function, the linear function (perfect substitutes), the fixed proportions function (perfect complements), and the CES function (which includes the other three as special cases).

- It is a simple matter mathematically to generalize from two-good examples to many goods. And, as we shall see, studying peoples' choices among many goods can yield many insights. But the mathematics of many goods is not especially intuitive, so we will primarily rely on two-good cases to build such intuition.

PROBLEMS

3.1

Graph a typical indifference curve for the following utility functions and determine whether they have convex indifference curves (that is, whether the *MRS* declines as x increases).

a. $U(x, y) = 3x + y$

b. $U(x, y) = \sqrt{x \cdot y}$

c. $U(x, y) = \sqrt{x} + y$

d. $U(x, y) = \sqrt{x^2 - y^2}$

e. $U(x, y) = \dfrac{xy}{x + y}$

3.2

In footnote 7 of Chapter 3, we showed that in order for a utility function for two goods to have a strictly diminishing *MRS* (that is, to be strictly quasi-concave), the following condition must hold:

$$f_2^2 f_{11} - 2f_1 f_2 f_{12} + f_1^2 f_{22} < 0.$$

Use this condition to check the convexity of the indifference curves for each of the utility functions in Problem 3.1. Describe any shortcuts you discover in this process.

3.3

Consider the following utility functions:

a. $U(x, y) = xy$.

b. $U(x, y) = x^2 y^2$.

c. $U(x, y) = \ln x + \ln y$.

Show that each of these has a diminishing *MRS*, but that they exhibit constant, increasing, and decreasing marginal utility, respectively. What do you conclude?

3.4

As we saw in Figure 3.5, one way to show convexity of indifference curves is to show that, for any two points (x_1, y_1) and (x_2, y_2) on an indifference curve that promises $U = k$, the utility associated with the point $\left(\dfrac{x_1 + x_2}{2}, \dfrac{y_1 + y_2}{2} \right)$ is at least as great as k. Use this approach to discuss the convexity of the indifference curves for the following three functions. Be sure to graph your results.

a. $U(x,y) = Min\ (x,y)$

b. $U(x,y) = Max\ (x,y)$

c. $U(x,y) = x + y$.

3.5

The Phillie Phanatic always eats his ballpark franks in a special way—he uses a foot-long hot dog together with precisely half a bun, 1 oz. of mustard, and 2 oz. of pickle relish.

His utility is a function only of these four items and any extra amounts of a single item without the other constituents is worthless.

   a. What form does PP's utility function for these four goods have?

   b. How might we simplify matters by considering PP's utility to be a function of only one good? What is that good?

   c. Suppose foot-long hot dogs cost $1, buns cost $.50, mustard costs $.05 per oz, and pickle relish costs $.15 per oz. How much does the good defined in part b cost?

   d. If the price of foot-long hot dogs increases by 50 percent (to $1.50) what is the percentage increase in the price of the good?

   e. How would a 50 percent increase in the price of a bun affect the price of the good? Why is your answer different from part d?

   f. If the government wanted to raise $1 in taxes by taxing the goods that PP buys, how should it spread this tax over the four goods so as minimize the utility cost to PP?

3.6

Many advertising slogans seem to be asserting something about people's preferences. How would you capture the following slogans with a mathematical utility function?

   a. Promise margarine is just as good as butter.

   b. Things go better with Coke.

   c. You can't eat just one Pringle's potato chip.

   d. Krispy Kreme glazed doughnuts are just better than Dunkin'.

   e. Miller Brewing advises us to drink (beer) "responsibly." [What would "irresponsible" drinking be?]

3.7

Suppose that a person has initial amounts of the two goods that provide utility to him or her. These initial amounts are given by $\bar{x}$ and $\bar{y}$.

   a. Graph these initial amounts on this person's indifference curve map.

   b. If this person can trade x for y (or vice versa) with other people, what kinds of trades would he or she voluntarily make? What kinds would not be made? How do these trades relate to this person's *MRS* at the point $(\bar{x}, \bar{y})$?

   c. Suppose this person is relatively happy with the initial amounts in his or her possession and will only consider trades that increased utility by at least amount k. How would you illustrate this on the indifference curve map?

3.8

Example 3.3 shows that the *MRS* for the Cobb-Douglas function

$$U(x, y) = x^{\alpha}y^{\beta}$$

is given by

$$MRS = \frac{\alpha}{\beta}(y/x).$$

   a. Does this result depend on whether $\alpha + \beta = 1$? Does this sum have any relevance to the theory of choice?

b. For commodity bundles for which $y = x$, how does the *MRS* depend on the values of α and β? Develop an intuitive explanation of why if $\alpha > \beta$, $MRS > 1$. Illustrate your argument with a graph.

c. Suppose an individual obtains utility only from amounts of x and y that exceed minimal subsistence levels given by x_0, y_0. In this case,

$$U(x, y) = (x - x_0)^\alpha \, (y - y_0)^\beta.$$

Is this function homothetic? (For a further discussion, see the Extensions to Chapter 4.)

3.9

Two goods have independent marginal utilities if

$$\frac{\partial^2 U}{\partial y \partial x} = \frac{\partial^2 U}{\partial x \partial y} = 0.$$

Show that if we assume diminishing marginal utility for each good, then any utility function with independent marginal utilities will have a diminishing *MRS*. Provide an example to show that the converse of this statement is not true.

3.10

a. Show that the CES function

$$\alpha \frac{x^\delta}{\delta} + \beta \frac{y^\delta}{\delta}$$

is homothetic. How does the *MRS* depend on the ratio y/x?

b. Show that your results from part (a) agree with our discussion of the cases $\delta = 1$ (perfect substitutes) and $\delta = 0$ (Cobb-Douglas).

c. Show that the *MRS* is strictly diminishing for all values of $\delta < 1$.

d. Show that if $x = y$, the *MRS* for this function depends only on the relative sizes of α and β.

e. Calculate the *MRS* for this function when $y/x = .9$ and $y/x = 1.1$ for the two cases $\delta = .5$ and $\delta = -1$. What do you conclude about the extent to which the *MRS* changes in the vicinity of $x = y$? How would you interpret this geometrically?

SUGGESTIONS FOR FURTHER READING

Jehle, G. R., and P. J. Reny. *Advanced Microeconomic Theory, 2nd ed*. Boston: Addison Wesley-Longman, 2001.
  Chapter 2 has a good proof of the existence of utility functions when basic axioms of rationality hold.

Kreps, David M. *A Course in Microeconomic Theory*. Princeton, NJ: Princeton University Press, 1990.
  Chapter 1 covers preference theory in some detail. Good discussion of quasi-concavity.

Kreps, David M. *Notes on the Theory of Choice*. London: Westview Press, 1988.
  Good discussion of the foundations of preference theory. Most of the focus of the book is on utility in uncertain situations.

Marshall, A. *Principles of Economics*, 8th ed., Chaps. I–IV, book III. London: Macmillan, 1920.
  Early basic text. Still a very readable and interesting treatment of consumer theory.

Mas-Colell, Andrea, Michael D. Whinston, and Jerry R. Green. *Microeconomic Theory*. New York: Oxford University Press, 1995.
  Chapters 2 and 3 provide a detailed development of preference relations and their representation by utility functions.

Stigler, G. "The Development of Utility Theory." *Journal of Political Economy* 59, pts. 1–2 (August/October 1950): 307–27, 373–96.

A lucid and complete survey of the history of utility theory. Has many interesting insights and asides.

Special Preferences

The utility function concept is a quite general one that can be adapted to a large number of special circumstances. Discovery of ingenious functional forms that reflect the essential aspects of some problem can provide a number of insights that would not be readily apparent with a more literary approach. Here we look at three aspects of preferences that economists have tried to portray with special functional forms: (1) quality; (2) habits and addictions; and (3) second-party preferences.

E3.1 Quality

Because many consumption items differ widely in quality, economists have an interest in incorporating such differences into models of choice. One approach is simply to regard items of different quality as totally separate goods that are relatively close substitutes. But this approach can be unwieldy because of the large number of goods involved. An alternative approach focuses on quality as a direct item of choice. Utility might in this case be reflected by

$$\text{utility} = U(q, Q) \qquad (i)$$

where q is the quantity consumed and Q is the quality of that consumption. Although this approach permits some examination of quality-quantity trade-offs, it encounters difficulty when the quantity consumed of a commodity (e.g., wine) consists of a variety of qualities. Quality might then be defined as an average (see Theil,[1] 1982), but that approach may not be appropriate when the quality of new goods is changing rapidly (as in the case of personal computers, for example). A more general approach (originally suggested by Lancaster, 1971) focuses on a well-defined set of attributes of goods and assumes that those attributes provide utility. If a good q provides two such attributes, a_1 and a_2, then utility might be written as

$$\text{utility} = U[q, a_1(q), a_2(q)] \qquad (ii)$$

and utility improvements might arise either because this individual chooses a larger quantity of the good or because a given quantity yields a higher level of valuable attributes.

Personal computers

This is the practice followed by economists who study demand in such rapidly changing industries as personal computers. In this case it would be clearly incorrect to focus only on the quantity of personal computers purchased each year, since new machines are much better than old ones (and, presumably, provide more utility). For example, Berndt, Griliches, and Rappaport (1995) find that personal computer quality has been rising about 30 percent per year over a relatively long period of time primarily because of improved attributes such as faster processors or better hard drives. A person who spends, say, $2,000 for a personal computer today buys much more utility than did a similar consumer 5 years ago.

E3.2 Habits and addiction

Because consumption occurs over time, there is the possibility that decisions made in one period will affect utility in later periods. Habits are formed when individuals discover they enjoy using a commodity in one period and this increases their consumption in subsequent periods. An extreme case is addiction (be it to drugs, cigarettes, or Marx Brothers movies) where past consumption significantly increases the utility of present consumption. One way to portray these ideas mathematically is to assume that utility in period t depends on consumption in period t and on the total of all prior consumption of the habit-forming good (say X):

$$\text{utility} = U_t(x_t, y_t, s_t) \qquad (iii)$$

where $s_t = \sum_{i=1}^{\infty} x_{t-i}$.

In empirical applications, however, usually data on all past levels of consumption do not exist. It is therefore common to model habits using only data on current consumption (x_t) and on consumption in the previous period (x_{t-1}). A

---

[1]Theil also suggests measuring quality by looking at correlations between changes in consumption and the income elasticities of various goods.

common way to proceed is to assume that utility is given by

$$\text{utility} = U_t(x_t^*, y_t), \qquad (iv)$$

where x_t^* is some simple function of x_t and x_{t-1}, such as $x_t^* = x_t - x_{t-1}$ or $x_t^* = x_t / x_{t-1}$. Such functions imply that, ceteris paribus, the higher is x_{t-1}, the more x_t will be chosen in the current period.

Modeling habits

These approaches to modeling habits have been applied to a wide variety of topics. Stigler and Becker (1977) use such models to explain why people develop a "taste" for going to operas or playing golf. Becker, Grossman, and Murphy (1994) adapt the models to studying cigarette smoking and other addictive behavior. They show that reductions in smoking early in life can have very large effects on eventual cigarette consumption because of the dynamics in individuals' utility functions. Whether addictive behavior is "rational" has been extensively studied by economists. For example, Gruber and Koszegi (2001) show that smoking can be approached as a rational, though time-inconsistent,[2] choice.

E3.3 Second-party preferences

Individuals clearly care about the well-being of other individuals. Phenomena such as making charitable contributions or making bequests to children cannot be understood without recognizing the interdependence that exists among people. Second-party preferences can be incorporated into the utility function of person i, say, by

$$\text{utility} = U_i(x_i, y_i, U_j), \qquad (v)$$

where U_j is the utility of someone else.

If $\partial U_i / \partial U_j > 0$ this person will engage in altruistic behavior, whereas if $\partial U_i / \partial U_j < 0$ he or she will demonstrate the malevolent behavior associated with envy. The usual case of $\partial U_i / \partial U_j = 0$ is then simply a middle ground between these alternative preference types. Gary Becker has been a pioneer in the study of these possibilities and has written on a variety of topics, including the general theory of social interactions (1976) and the importance of altruism in the theory of the family (1981).

Evolutionary biology and genetics

Biologists have suggested a particular form for the utility function in Equation iv, drawn from the theory of genetics. In this case

$$\text{utility} = U_i(x_i, y_i) + \sum_j r_j U_j \qquad (vi)$$

where r_j measures closeness of the genetic relationship between person i and person j. For parents and children, for example, $r_j = .5$, whereas for cousins $r_j = .125$. Bergstrom (1996) describes a few of the conclusions about evolutionary behavior that biologists have drawn from this particular functional form.

References

Becker, Gary S. *The Economic Approach to Human Behavior.* Chicago: The University of Chicago Press, 1976.

———. *A Treatise on the Family.* Cambridge, MA: Harvard University Press, 1981.

Becker, Gary S., Michael Grossman, and Kevin M. Murphy. "An Empirical Analysis of Cigarette Addiction." *American Economic Review* (June 1994): 396–418.

Bergstrom, Theodore C. "Economics in a Family Way." *Journal of Economic Literature* (December 1996): 1903–34.

Berndt, Erst R., Zvi Griliches, and Neal J. Rappaport. "Econometric Estimates of Price Indexes for Personal Computers in the 1990s." *Journal of Econometrics* (July 1995): 243–68.

Gruber, Jonathan, and Botond Koszegi. "Is Addiction 'Rational' Theory and Evidence." *Quarterly Journal of Economics* (November 2001): 1261–1303.

Lancaster, Kelvin J. *Consumer Demand: A New Approach.* New York: Columbia University Press, 1971.

Stigler, George J., and Gary S. Becker. "De Gustibus Non Est Disputandum." *American Economic Review* (March 1977): 76–90.

Theil, Henri. "Qualities, Prices, and Budget Enquiries." *Review of Economic Studies* (April 1952): 129–47.

---

[2]For more on time inconsistency see Chapter 17.

Chapter 4

UTILITY MAXIMIZATION AND CHOICE

In this chapter we examine the basic model of choice that economists use to explain individuals' behavior. That model assumes that individuals who are constrained by limited incomes will behave as if they were using their purchasing power in such a way as to achieve the highest utility possible. That is, individuals are assumed to behave as if they maximized utility subject to a budget constraint. Although the specific applications of this model are quite varied, as we will show, all of them are based on the same fundamental mathematical model, and all arrive at the same general conclusion: To maximize utility, individuals will choose bundles of commodities for which the rate of trade-off between any two goods (the MRS) is equal to the ratio of the goods' market prices. Market prices convey information about opportunity costs to individuals, and this information plays an important role in affecting the choices actually made.

Utility maximization and lightning calculations

Before starting a formal study of the theory of choice, it may be appropriate to dispose of two complaints noneconomists often make about the approach we will take. First is the charge that no real person can make the kinds of "lightning calculations" required for utility maximization. According to this complaint, when moving down a supermarket aisle, people just grab what is available with no real pattern or purpose to their actions. Economists are not persuaded by this complaint. They doubt that people behave randomly (everyone, after all, is bound by some sort of budget constraint), and they view the lightning calculation charge as misplaced. Recall, again, Friedman's pool player. The pool player also cannot make the lightning calculations required to plan a shot according to the laws of physics, but those laws still predict the player's behavior. So too, as we shall see, the utility-maximization model predicts many aspects of behavior even though no one carries around a computer with his or her utility function programmed into it. To be precise, economists assume that people behave *as if* they made such calculations, so the complaint that the calculations cannot possibly be made is largely irrelevant.

Altruism and selfishness

A second complaint against our model of choice is that it appears to be extremely selfish—no one, according to this complaint, has such solely self-centered goals. Although economists are probably more ready to accept self-interest as a motivating force than are other, more Utopian thinkers (Adam Smith observed, "We are not ready to suspect any person of being deficient in selfishness"[1]), this charge is also misplaced. Nothing in the utility-maximization model prevents individuals from deriving satisfaction from philanthropy or generally "doing good." These activities also can be assumed to provide utility. Indeed, economists have used the utility-maximization model extensively to study such issues as donating time and money to charity, leaving bequests to children, or even giving blood. One need not take a position on whether such activities are selfish or selfless since economists doubt people would undertake them if they were against their own best interests, broadly conceived.

An initial survey

The general results of our examination of utility maximization can be stated succinctly:

OPTIMIZATION PRINCIPLE

Utility maximization. To maximize utility, given a fixed amount of income to spend, an individual will buy those quantities of goods that exhaust his or her total income and for which the psychic rate of trade-off between any two goods (the *MRS*) is equal to the rate at which the goods can be traded one for the other in the marketplace.

That spending all one's income is required for utility maximization is obvious. Because extra goods provide extra utility (there is no satiation) and because there is no other use for income, to leave any unspent would be to fail to maximize utility. Throwing money away is not a utility-maximizing activity.

The condition specifying equality of trade-off rates requires a bit more explanation. Because the rate at which one good can be traded for another in the market is given by the ratio of their prices, this result can be restated to say that the individual will equate the *MRS* (of *x* for *y*) to the ratio of the price of *x* to the price of *y* (p_x/p_y). This equating of a personal trade-off rate to a market-determined trade-off rate is a result common to all individual utility-maximization problems (and to many other types of maximization problems). It will occur again and again throughout this text.

A numerical illustration

To see the intuitive reasoning behind this result, assume that it were not true that an individual had equated the *MRS* to the ratio of the prices of goods. Specifically, suppose that the individual's *MRS* is equal to 1, that he or she is willing to trade 1 unit of *x* for 1 unit of *y* and remain equally well off. Assume also that the price of *x* is $2 per unit and of *y* is $1 per unit. It is easy to show in this case that this person can be made better off. Suppose this person reduces *x* consumption by one unit and trades it in the market for 2 units of *y*. Only 1 extra unit of *y* was needed to keep this person as happy as before the trade—the second unit of *y* is a net addition to well-being. Therefore, the individual's spending could not have been allocated optimally in the first place. A similar method of reasoning can be used whenever the *MRS* and the price ratio p_x/p_y differ. The condition for maximum utility must be the equality of these two magnitudes.

The two-good case: a graphical analysis

This discussion seems eminently reasonable, but it can hardly be called a proof. Rather, we must now show the result in a rigorous manner and, at the same time, illustrate several other important attributes of the maximization process. First we take a graphic analysis. Then we take a more mathematical approach.

---

[1]Adam Smith, *The Theory of Moral Sentiments* (1759; reprint, New Rochelle, NY: Arlington House, 1969), p. 446.

FIGURE 4.1   The Individual's Budget Constraint for Two Goods

Those combinations of x and y that the individual can afford are shown in the shaded triangle. If, as we usually assume, the individual prefers more rather than less of every good, the outer boundary of this triangle is the relevant constraint where all of the available funds are spent either on x or on y. The slope of this straight-line boundary is given by $-p_x/p_y$.

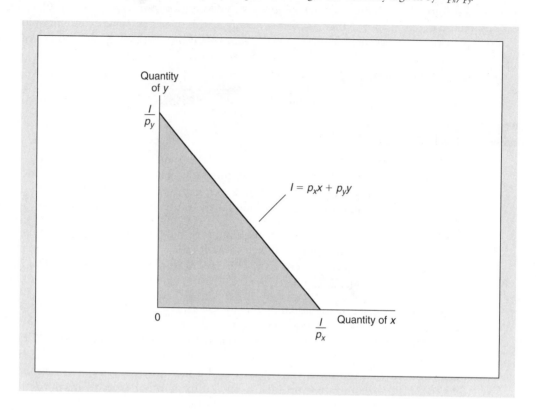

Budget constraint

Assume that the individual has I dollars to allocate between good x and good y. If p_x is the price of good x and p_y is the price of good y, then the individual is constrained by

$$p_x x + p_y y \leq I. \tag{4.1}$$

That is, no more than I can be spent on the two goods in question. This budget constraint is shown graphically in Figure 4.1. This person can afford to choose only combinations of x and y in the shaded triangle of the figure. If all of I is spent on good x, it will buy I/p_x units of x. Similarly, if all is spent on y, it will buy I/p_y units of y. The slope of the constraint is easily seen to be $-p_x/p_y$. This slope shows how y can be traded for x in the market. If $p_x = 2$ and $p_y = 1$, 2 units of y will trade for one unit of x.

First-order conditions for a maximum

This budget constraint can be imposed on this person's indifference curve map to show the utility-maximization process. Figure 4.2 illustrates this procedure. The individual would be irrational to choose a point such as A—he or she can get to a higher utility level just by spending some of the unspent portion of income. The assumption of nonsatiation implies that a person should spend all of his or her income in order to receive maximum utility from it. Similarly, by reallocating expenditures, the individual can do better than point B. Point D is out of the question because income is not large enough to purchase D. It is clear that the position of maximum utility is at point C, where the combination x^*, y^*

FIGURE 4.2	A Graphical Demonstration of Utility Maximization

Point C represents the highest utility level that can be reached by the individual, given the budget constraint. The combination x^*, y^* is therefore the rational way for the individual to allocate purchasing power. Only for this combination of goods will two conditions hold: All available funds will be spent; and the individual's psychic rate of trade-off *(MRS)* will be equal to the rate at which the goods can be traded in the market (p_x/p_y).

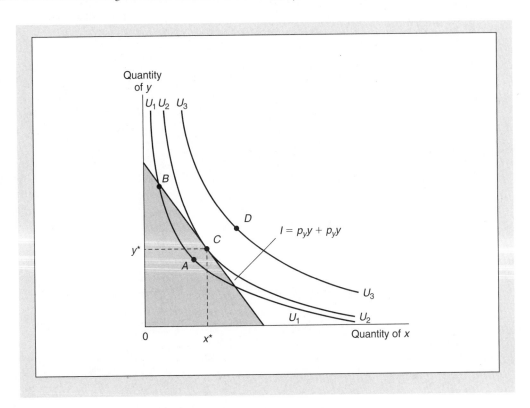

is chosen. This is the only point on indifference curve U_2 that can be bought with I dollars; no higher utility level can be bought. C is a point of tangency between the budget constraint and the indifference curve. Therefore at C,

$$\text{slope of budget constraint} = \frac{-p_x}{p_y} = \text{slope of indifference curve}$$

$$= \frac{dy}{dx}\bigg|_{U \,=\, \text{constant}} \qquad (4.2)$$

or

$$\frac{p_x}{p_y} = -\frac{dy}{dx}\bigg|_{U \,=\, \text{constant}} = MRS \,(\text{of } x \text{ for } y). \qquad (4.3)$$

Our intuitive result is proved—for a utility maximum, all income should be spent and the *MRS* should equal the ratio of the prices of the goods. It is obvious from the diagram that if this condition is not fulfilled, the individual could be made better off by reallocating expenditures.

Second-order conditions for a maximum

The tangency rule is only a necessary condition for a maximum. To see that it is not a sufficient condition, consider the indifference curve map shown in Figure 4.3. Here a point

FIGURE 4.3   Example of an Indifference Curve Map for Which the Tangency Condition Does Not Ensure a Maximum

If indifference curves do not obey the assumption of a diminishing *MRS*, not all points of tangency (points for which $MRS - p_x/p_y$) may truly be points of maximum utility. In this example tangency point *C* is inferior to many other points that can also be purchased with the available funds. In order that the necessary conditions for a maximum (that is, the tangency conditions) also be sufficient, one usually assumes that the *MRS* is diminishing; that is, the utility function is strictly quasi-concave.

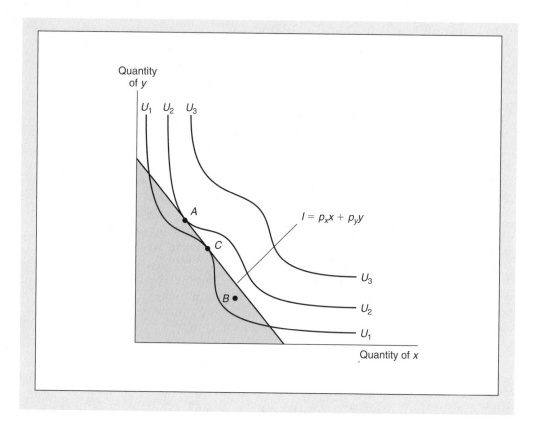

of tangency (*C*) is inferior to a point of nontangency (*B*). Indeed, the true maximum is at another point of tangency (*A*). The failure of the tangency condition to produce an unambiguous maximum can be attributed to the shape of the indifference curves in Figure 4.3. If the indifference curves are shaped like those in Figure 4.2, no such problem can arise. But we have already shown that "normally" shaped indifference curves result from the assumption of a diminishing *MRS*. Therefore, if the *MRS* is assumed to be diminishing, the condition of tangency is both a necessary and sufficient condition for a maximum.[2] Without this assumption one would have to be careful in applying the tangency rule.

Corner solutions

The utility-maximization problem illustrated in Figure 4.2 resulted in an "interior" maximum, in which positive amounts of both goods were consumed. In some situations individuals' preferences may be such that they can obtain maximum utility by choosing to

---

[2]In mathematical terms, because the assumption of a diminishing *MRS* is equivalent to assuming quasi-concavity, the necessary conditions for a maximum subject to a linear constraint are also sufficient, as we showed in Chapter 2.

| **FIGURE 4.4** | **Corner Solution for Utility Maximization** |

With the preferences represented by this set of indifference curves, utility maximization occurs at *E*, where 0 amounts of good *y* are consumed. The first-order conditions for a maximum must be modified somewhat to accommodate this possibility.

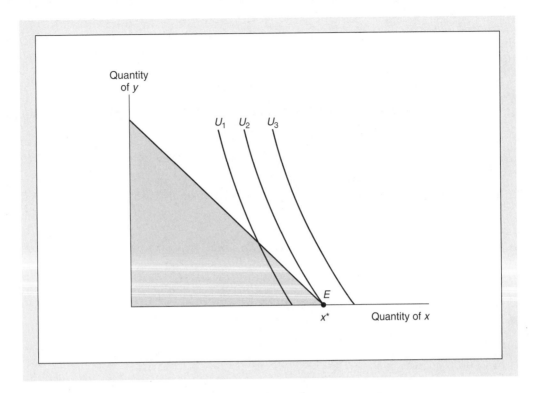

consume no amount of one of the goods. If someone does not like hamburgers very much, there is no reason to allocate any income to their purchase. This possibility is re-flected in Figure 4.4. There utility is maximized at *E*, where $x = x^*$ and $y = 0$—any point on the budget constraint where positive amounts of *y* are consumed yields a lower utility than does point *E*. Notice that at *E* the budget constraint is not precisely tangent to the indifference curve U_2. Instead, at the optimal point the budget constraint is flatter than U_2, indicating that the rate at which *x* can be traded for *y* in the market is lower than the individual's psychic trade-off rate (the *MRS*). At prevailing market prices the individual is more than willing to trade away *y* to get extra *x*. Because it is impossible in this problem to consume negative amounts of *y*, however, the physical limit for this process is the *X*-axis, along which purchases of *y* are 0. Hence, as this discussion makes clear, it is neces-sary to amend the first-order conditions for a utility maximum a bit to allow for corner so-lutions of the type shown in Figure 4.4. Following our discussion of the general *n*-good case, we will use the mathematics from Chapter 2 to show how this can be accomplished.

The *n*-good case

The results derived graphically in the case of two goods carry over directly to the case of *n* goods. Again it can be shown that for an interior utility maximum, the *MRS* between any two goods must equal the ratio of the prices of these goods. To study this more gen-eral case, however, it is best to use some mathematics.

First-order conditions

With n goods, the individual's objective is to maximize utility from these n goods:

$$\text{utility} = U(x_1, x_2, \ldots, x_n), \tag{4.4}$$

subject to the budget constraint:[3]

$$I = p_1x_1 + p_2x_2 + \cdots + p_nx_n \tag{4.5}$$

or

$$I - p_1x_1 - p_2x_2 - \cdots - p_nx_n = 0. \tag{4.6}$$

Following the techniques developed in Chapter 2 for maximizing a function subject to a constraint, we set up the Lagrangian expression

$$\mathscr{L} = U(x_1, x_2, \ldots, x_n) + \lambda(I - p_1x_1 - p_2x_2 - \cdots - p_nx_n). \tag{4.7}$$

Setting the partial derivatives of $\mathscr{L}$ (with respect to $x_1, x_2, \ldots, x_n$ and λ) equal to 0 yields $n + 1$ equations representing the necessary conditions for an interior maximum:

$$
\begin{aligned}
\frac{\partial \mathscr{L}}{\partial x_1} &= \frac{\partial U}{\partial x_1} - \lambda p_1 = 0 \\
\frac{\partial \mathscr{L}}{\partial x_2} &= \frac{\partial U}{\partial x_2} - \lambda p_2 = 0 \\
&\vdots \\
\frac{\partial \mathscr{L}}{\partial x_n} &= \frac{\partial U}{\partial x_n} - \lambda p_n = 0 \\
\frac{\partial \mathscr{L}}{\partial \lambda} &= I - p_1x_1 - p_2x_2 - \cdots - p_nx_x = 0.
\end{aligned}
\tag{4.8}
$$

These $n + 1$ equations can usually be solved for the optimal $x_1, x_2, \ldots, x_n$ and for λ (see Examples 4.1 and 4.2 to be convinced that such a solution is possible).

Equations 4.8 are necessary but not sufficient for a maximum. The second-order conditions that ensure a maximum are relatively complex and must be stated in matrix terms (see the Extension to Chapter 2). However, the assumption of strict quasi-concavity (a diminishing *MRS* in the two-good case) is sufficient to ensure that any point obeying Equations 4.8 is in fact a true maximum.

Implications of first-order conditions

The first-order conditions represented by Equations 4.8 can be rewritten in a variety of interesting ways. For example, for any two goods, x_i and x_j, we have

$$\frac{\partial U / \partial x_i}{\partial U / \partial x_j} = \frac{p_i}{p_j}. \tag{4.9}$$

In Chapter 3 we showed that the ratio of the marginal utilities of two goods is equal to the marginal rate of substitution between them. Therefore, the conditions for an optimal allocation of income become

$$MRS\,(x_i \text{ for } x_j) = \frac{p_i}{p_j}. \tag{4.10}$$

This is exactly the result derived graphically earlier in this chapter; to maximize utility, the individual should equate the psychic rate of trade-off to the market trade-off rate.

---

[3]Again, the budget constraint has been written as an equality here because, given the assumption of nonsatiation, it is clear that the individual will spend all available income.

Interpreting the Lagrangian multiplier

Another result can be derived by solving Equations 4.8 for λ:

$$\lambda = \frac{\partial U / \partial x_1}{p_1} = \frac{\partial U / \partial x_2}{p_2} = \cdots = \frac{\partial U / \partial x_n}{p_n} \tag{4.11}$$

or

$$\lambda = \frac{MU_{x_1}}{p_1} = \frac{MU_{x_2}}{p_2} = \cdots = \frac{MU_{x_n}}{p_n}.$$

This equation says that at the utility-maximizing point, each good purchased should yield the same marginal utility per dollar spent on that good. Each good therefore should have an identical (marginal) benefit to (marginal) cost ratio. If this were not true, one good would promise more "marginal enjoyment per dollar" than some other good, and funds would not be optimally allocated.

Although the reader is again warned against talking very confidently about marginal utility, what Equation 4.11 says is that an extra dollar should yield the same "additional utility" no matter which good it is spent on. The common value for this extra utility is given by the Lagrangian multiplier for the consumer's budget constraint (that is, by λ). Consequently, λ can be regarded as the marginal utility of an extra dollar of consumption expenditure (the marginal utility of "income").

One final way to rewrite the necessary conditions for a maximum is

$$p_i = \frac{MU_{x_i}}{\lambda} \tag{4.12}$$

for every good i that is bought. To interpret this equation, consider a situation where a person's marginal utility of income (λ) is constant over some range. Then variations in the price they must pay for good i (p_i) are directly proportional to the extra utility they get from that good. At the margin, therefore, the price of a good reflects an individual's willingness to pay for one more unit. This is a result of considerable importance in applied welfare economics because willingness to pay can be inferred from market reactions to prices. In Chapter 5 we will see how this insight can be used to evaluate the welfare effects of price changes and, in later chapters, we will use this idea to discuss a variety of questions about the efficiency of resource allocation.

Corner solutions

The first-order conditions of Equations 4.8 hold exactly only for interior maxima for which some positive amount of each good is purchased. As discussed in Chapter 2, when corner solutions (such as those illustrated in Figure 4.4) arise, the conditions have to be modified slightly.[4] In this case, Equations 4.8 become

$$\frac{\partial \mathscr{L}}{\partial x_i} = \frac{\partial U}{\partial x_i} - \lambda p_i \leq 0 \; (i = 1 \ldots n), \tag{4.13}$$

and, if

$$\frac{\partial \mathscr{L}}{\partial x_i} = \frac{\partial U}{\partial x_i} - \lambda p_i < 0, \tag{4.14}$$

then

$$x_i = 0. \tag{4.15}$$

---

[4]Formally, these conditions are called the "Kuhn-Tucker" conditions for nonlinear programming.

To interpret these conditions, we can rewrite Equation 4.14 as

$$p_i > \frac{\frac{\partial U}{\partial x_i}}{\lambda} = \frac{MU_{x_i}}{\lambda}. \tag{4.16}$$

Hence, the optimal conditions are as before, except that any good whose price (p_i) exceeds its marginal value to the consumer (MU_{x_i}/λ) will not be purchased ($x_i = 0$). Thus, the mathematical results conform to the commonsense idea that individuals will not purchase goods that they believe are not worth the money. Although corner solutions do not provide a major focus for our analysis in this book, the reader should keep in mind the possibilities for such solutions arising and the economic interpretation that can be attached to the optimal conditions in such cases.

 EXAMPLE 4.1

Cobb-Douglas Demand Functions

As we showed in Chapter 3, the Cobb-Douglas utility function is given by

$$U(x, y) = x^{\alpha} y^{\beta}, \tag{4.17}$$

where, for convenience,[5] we assume $\alpha + \beta = 1$. We can now solve for the utility-maximizing values of x and y for any prices (p_x, p_y) and income (I). Setting up the Lagrangian expression

$$\mathcal{L} = x^{\alpha} y^{\beta} + \lambda(I - p_x x - p_y y) \tag{4.18}$$

yields the first-order conditions

$$\frac{\partial \mathcal{L}}{\partial x} = \alpha x^{\alpha-1} y^{\beta} - \lambda p_x = 0$$

$$\frac{\partial \mathcal{L}}{\partial y} = \beta x^{\alpha} y^{\beta-1} - \lambda p_y = 0 \tag{4.19}$$

$$\frac{\partial \mathcal{L}}{\partial \lambda} = I - p_x x - p_y y = 0.$$

Taking the ratio of the first two terms shows that

$$\frac{\alpha y}{\beta x} = \frac{p_x}{p_y} \tag{4.20}$$

or

$$p_y y = \frac{\beta}{\alpha} p_x x = \frac{1 - \alpha}{\alpha} p_x x, \tag{4.21}$$

where the final equation follows because $\alpha + \beta = 1$. Substitution of this first-order condition in Equation 4.21 into the budget constraint gives

$$I = p_x x + p_y y = p_x x + \frac{1 - \alpha}{\alpha} p_x x = p_x x \left(1 + \frac{1 - \alpha}{\alpha}\right) = \frac{1}{\alpha} p_x x; \tag{4.22}$$

[5]Notice that the exponents in the Cobb-Douglas utility function can always be normalized to sum to 1 because $U^{1/(\alpha+\beta)}$ is a monotonic transformation.

solving for x yields

$$x^* = \frac{\alpha I}{p_x};$$
(4.23)

and a similar set of manipulations would give

$$y^* = \frac{\beta I}{p_y}.$$
(4.24)

These results show that an individual whose utility function is given by Equation 4.17 will always choose to allocate α percent of his or her income to buying good x (that is, $p_x x/I = \alpha$) and β percent to buying good y ($p_y y/I = \beta$). Although this feature of the Cobb-Douglas function often makes it very easy to work out simple problems, it does suggest that the function has limits in its ability to explain actual consumption behavior. Because the share of income devoted to particular goods often changes significantly in response to changing economic conditions, a more general functional form may provide insights not provided by the Cobb-Douglas function. We illustrate a few possibilities in Example 4.2, and the general topic of budget shares is taken up in more detail in the Extensions to this chapter.

Numerical example. First, however, let's look at a specific numerical example for the Cobb-Douglas case. Suppose that x sells for \$1 and y sells for \$4 and that total income is \$8. Succinctly then, assume that $p_x = 1$, $p_y = 4$, $I = 8$. Suppose also that $\alpha = \beta = 0.5$ so that this individual splits his or her income equally between these two goods. Now the demand Equations 4.23 and 4.24 imply

$$\textbf{x}^* = \alpha I/p_x = .5I/p_x = .5(8)/1 = 4$$
(4.25)
$$y^* = \beta I/p_y = .5I/p_y = .5(8)/4 = 1$$

and, at these optimal choices,

$$\textbf{Utility} = x^{.5}y^{.5} = (4)^{.5}(1)^{.5} = 2.$$
(4.26)

Notice also that we can compute the value for the Lagrangian multiplier associated with this income allocation by using Equation 4.19:

$$\lambda = \alpha x^{\alpha-1}y^{\beta}/p_x = .5(4)^{-.5}(1)^{.5}/1 = 0.25$$
(4.27)

This value implies that each small change in income will increase utility by about one-fourth of that amount. Suppose, for example that this person had one percent more income (\$8.08). In this case he or she would choose $x = 4.04$ and $y = 1.01$, and utility would be $4.04^{0.5} \cdot 1.01^{0.5} = 2.02$. Hence, a \$.08 increase in income increases utility by .02 as is predicted by the fact that $\lambda = 0.25$.

Query: Would a change in p_y affect the quantity of x demanded in Equation 4.23? Explain your answer mathematically. Also develop an intuitive explanation based on the notion that the share of income devoted to good y is given by the parameter of the utility function, β.

EXAMPLE 4.2

CES Demand

To illustrate cases in which budget shares are responsive to economic circumstances, let's look at three specific examples of the CES function.

Case 1. $\delta = 5$. In this case utility is

$$U(x, y) = x^{.5} + y^{.5}. \tag{4.28}$$

Setting up the Lagrangian expression

$$\mathcal{L} = x^{.5} + y^{.5} + \lambda\,(I - p_x x - p_y y) \tag{4.29}$$

yields the following first-order conditions for a maximum:

$$\partial\mathcal{L}/\partial x = .5x^{-.5} - \lambda p_x = 0 \tag{4.30}$$
$$\partial\mathcal{L}/\partial y = .5y^{-.5} - \lambda p_y = 0$$
$$\partial\mathcal{L}/\partial\lambda = I - p_x x - p_y y = 0.$$

Division of the first two of these shows that

$$(y/x)^{.5} = p_x/p_y. \tag{4.31}$$

By substituting this into the budget constraint and doing some messy algebraic manipulation, we can derive the demand functions associated with this utility function:

$$x^* = I/p_x[1 + (p_x/p_y)] \tag{4.32}$$
$$y^* = I/p_y[1 + (p_y/p_x)]. \tag{4.33}$$

Price responsiveness. In these demand functions notice that the share of income spent on, say, good x—that is, $p_x x/I = 1/[1 + (p_x/p_y)]$—is not a constant, it depends on the price ratio p_x/p_y. The higher is the relative price of x, the smaller will be the share of income spent on that good. In other words, the demand for x is so responsive to its own price that a rise in the price reduces total spending on x. That the demand for x is very price responsive can also be illustrated by comparing the implied exponent on p_x in the demand function given by Equation 4.32 (–2) to that from Equation 4.23 (–1). In Chapter 5 we will discuss this observation more fully when we examine the elasticity concept in detail.

Case 2. $\delta = -1$. Alternatively, let's look at a demand function with less substitutability[6] than the Cobb-Douglas. If $\delta = -1$, the utility function is given by

$$U(x, y) = -x^{-1} - y^{-1}, \tag{4.34}$$

and it is easy to show that the first-order conditions for a maximum require

$$y/x = (p_x/p_y)^{.5}. \tag{4.35}$$

Again, substitution of this condition into the budget constraint, together with some messy algebra, yields the demand functions

$$x^* = I/p_x\,[1 + (p_y/p_x)^{.5}]$$
$$y^* = I^{\cdot}/p_y[1 + (p_x/p_y)^{.5}]. \tag{4.36}$$

---

[6]One way to measure substitutability is by the elasticity of substitution, which for the CES function is given by $\sigma = 1/(1 - \delta)$. Here $\delta = .5$ implies $\sigma = 2$, $\delta = 0$ (the Cobb-Douglas) implies $\sigma = 1$, and $\delta = -1$ implies $\sigma = .5$. See also the discussion of the CES function in connection with the theory of production in Chapter 7.

That these demand functions are less price responsive can be seen in two ways. First, now the share of income spent on good x—$p_x x/I = 1/[1 + (p_y/p_x)^{.5}]$—responds positively to increases in p_x. As the price of x rises, this individual cuts back only modestly in good x, so total spending on that good rises. That the demand functions in Equations 4.36 are less price responsive than the Cobb-Douglas is also illustrated by the relatively small exponents of each good's own price ($-.5$).

Case 3. $\delta = -\infty$. This is the important case in which x and y must be consumed in fixed proportions. Suppose, for example, that each unit of y must be consumed together with exactly 4 units of x. The utility function that represents this situation is

$$U(x, y) = Min(x, 4y). \qquad (4.37)$$

In this situation, a utility-maximizing person will choose only combinations of the two goods for which $x = 4y$—that is, utility maximization implies that this person will choose to be at a vertex of his or her L-shaped indifference curves. Substituting this condition into the budget constraint yields

$$I = p_x x + p_y y = p_x x + p_y \frac{x}{4} = (p_x + 0.25p_y)x. \qquad (4.38)$$

Hence,

$$x^* = \frac{I}{p_x + 0.25p_y} \qquad (4.39)$$

and similar substitutions yield

$$y^* = \frac{I}{4p_x + p_y}. \qquad (4.40)$$

In this case, the share of a person's budget devoted to, say, good x rises rapidly as the price of x increases because x and y must be consumed in fixed proportions. For example, if we use the values assumed in Example 4.1 ($p_x = 1$, $p_y = 4$, $I = 8$), Equations 4.39 and 4.40 would predict $x^* = 4$, $y^* = 1$ and, as before, half of income would be spent on each good. If we use instead $p_x = 2$, $p_y = 4$, $I = 8$ we get $x^* = 8/3$, $y^* = 2/3$ and this person spends $2/3\left(= \frac{p_x x}{I} = \frac{2 \cdot 8/3}{8}\right)$ of his or her income on good x. Trying a few other numbers suggests that the share of income devoted to good x approaches 1 as the price of x gets larger.[7]

Query: Do changes in income affect expenditure shares in any of the CES functions discussed here? How is the behavior of expenditure shares related to the homothetic nature of this function?

---

[7]These relationships for the CES function are pursued in more detail in Problem 4.9 and in Extension E4.3.

Indirect utility function

Examples 4.1 and 4.2 illustrate the principle that it is often possible to manipulate the first-order conditions for a constrained utility-maximization problem to solve for the optimal values of $x_1, x_2, \ldots, x_n$. These optimal values in general will depend on the prices of all the goods and on the individual's income. That is,

$$x_1^* = x_1 (p_1, p_2, \ldots, p_n, I)$$
$$x_2^* = x_2 (p_1, p_2, \ldots, p_n, I) \qquad (4.41)$$
$$\vdots$$
$$x_n^* = x_n (p_1, p_2, \ldots, p_n, I).$$

In the next chapter we will analyze in more detail this set of *demand functions,* which show the dependence of the quantity of each x_i demanded on $p_1, p_2, \ldots, p_n$ and I. Here we use the optimal values of the x's from Equations 4.42 to substitute in the original utility function to yield

$$\textbf{maximum utility} = U(x_1^*, x_2^*, \ldots, x_n^*) \qquad (4.42)$$

$$= V(p_1, p_2, \ldots, p_n, I). \qquad (4.43)$$

In words, because of the individual's desire to maximize utility, given a budget constraint, the optimal level of utility obtainable will depend *indirectly* on the prices of the goods being bought and on the individual's income. This dependence is reflected by the indirect utility function V. If either prices or income were to change, the level of utility that can be attained would also be affected. Sometimes, in both consumer theory and in many other contexts, it is possible to use this indirect approach to study how changes in economic circumstances affect various kinds of outcomes, such as utility or (later in this book) firms' costs.

The lump sum principle

Many economic insights stem from the recognition that utility ultimately depends on the income of individuals and on the prices they face. One of the most important of these is the so-called lump sum principle that illustrates the superiority of taxes on a person's general purchasing power to taxes on specific goods. A related insight is that general income grants to low-income people will raise utility more than will a similar amount of money spent subsidizing specific goods. The intuition behind this result derives directly from the utility-maximization hypothesis—an income tax or subsidy leaves the individual free to decide how to allocate whatever final income he or she has. On the other hand, taxes or subsidies on specific goods both reduce a person's purchasing power and distort their choices because of the artificial prices incorporated in such schemes. Hence, general income taxes and subsidies are to be preferred if efficiency is an important criteria in social policy.

The lump sum principle as it applies to taxation is illustrated in Figure 4.5. Initially this person has an income of I and is choosing to consume the combination x^*, y^*. A tax on good x would raise its price, and the utility-maximizing choice would shift to combination x_1, y_1. Tax collections would be $t \cdot x_1$ (where t is the tax rate imposed on good x). Alternatively, an income tax that shifted the budget constraint inward to I' would also collect this same amount of revenue.[8] But the utility provided by the income tax (U_2) exceeds that provided by the tax on x alone (U_1). Hence, we have shown that the utility burden of the income tax is smaller. A similar argument can be used to illustrate the superiority of income grants to subsidies on specific goods.

---

[8]Because $I = (p_x + t)x_1 + p_y y_1$, we have $I' = I - tx_1 = p_x x_1 + p_y y_1$ which shows that the budget constraint with an equal size income tax also passes through the point x_1, y_1.

FIGURE 4.5	The Lump Sum Principle of Taxation

A tax on good *x* would shift the utility-maximizing choice from x^*, y^* to x_1, y_1. An income tax that collected the same amount would shift the budget constraint to I^1. Utility would be higher (U_2) with the income tax than with the tax on *x* alone (U_1).

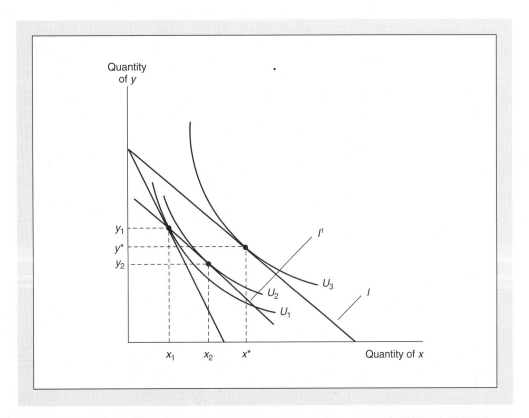

EXAMPLE 4.3

Indirect Utility and the Lump Sum Principle

In this example we use the notion of an indirect utility function to illustrate the lump sum principle as it applies to taxation. First we have to derive indirect utility functions for two illustrative cases.

Case 1. The Cobb-Douglas. In Example 4.1 we showed that for the Cobb-Douglas utility function with $\alpha = \beta = 0.5$ optimal purchases are

$$x^* = \frac{I}{2p_x}$$
$$y^* = \frac{I}{2p_y} \tag{4.44}$$

So the indirect utility function in this case is

$$V(p_x, p_y, I) = U(x^*, y^*) = (x^*)^{0.5}(y^*)^{0.5} = \frac{I}{2p_x^{0.5}p_y^{0.5}}. \tag{4.45}$$

Notice that when $p_x = 1$, $p_y = 4$, $I = 8$, we have $V = \frac{8}{2 \cdot 1 \cdot 2} = 2$ which is the utility that we calculated before for this situation.

(continued)

EXAMPLE 4.3 CONTINUED

Case 2. Fixed Proportions. In the third case of Example 4.2 we found that

$$x^* = \frac{I}{p_x + 0.25p_y}$$

$$y^* = \frac{I}{4p_x + p_y} \tag{4.46}$$

So, in this case indirect utility is given by

$$V(p_x, p_y, I) = Min(x^*, 4y^*) = x^* = \frac{I}{p_x + 0.25p_y} \tag{4.47}$$

$$= 4y^* = \frac{4}{4p_x + p_y} = \frac{I}{p_x + 0.25p_y}$$

and with $p_x = 1$, $p_y = 4$, $I = 8$ indirect utility is given by $V = 4$, which is what we calculated before.

The lump sum principle. Consider first using the Cobb-Douglas case to illustrate the lump sum principle. Suppose that a tax of $1 were imposed on good x. Equation 4.45 shows that indirect utility in this case would fall from 2 to 1.41 [= $8/(2 \cdot 2^{0.5} \cdot 2)$]. Because this person chooses $x^* = 2$ with the tax, total tax collections will be $2. An equal-revenue income tax would therefore reduce net income to $6, and indirect utility would be 1.5 [= $6/(2 \cdot 1 \cdot 2)$]. So the income tax is a clear improvement over the case where x alone is taxed. The tax on good x reduces utility for two reasons—it reduces a person's purchasing power and it biases his or her choices away from good x. With income taxation only the first effect is felt, so the tax is more efficient.[9]

The fixed-proportions case supports this intuition. In that case, a $1 tax on good x would reduce indirect utility from 4 to 8/3 [= $8/(2 + 1)$]. In this case $x^* = 8/3$ and tax collections would be $8/3. An income tax that collected $8/3 would leave this consumer with $16/3 in net income and that income would yield an indirect utility of $V = 8/3 \left[= \frac{16/3}{1+1} \right]$. Hence after-tax utility is the same under both the excise and income taxes. The reason the lump sum result does not appear in this case is that with fixed-proportions utility, the excise tax does not distort choices because preferences are so rigid.

Query: Both of the indirect utility functions illustrated here show that a doubling of income and all prices would leave indirect utility unchanged. Explain why you would expect this to be a property of all indirect utility functions.

---

[9]This discussion assumes that there are no incentive effects of income taxation—probably not a very good assumption.

Expenditure minimization

In Chapter 2 we pointed out that many constrained maximum problems have associated "dual" constrained minimum problems. For the case of utility maximization, the associated dual minimization problem concerns allocating income in such a way as to achieve a given utility level with the minimal expenditure. This problem is clearly analogus to the primary utility-maximization problem, but the goals and constraints of the problems have been reversed. Figure 4.6 illustrates this dual expenditure-minimization problem. There the individual must attain utility level U_2—this is now the constraint in the problem. Three possible expenditure amounts (E_1, E_2, and E_3) are shown as three "budget constraint" lines in the figure. Expenditure level E_1 is clearly too small to achieve U_2, hence it cannot solve the dual problem. With expenditures given by E_3, the individual can reach U_2 (at either of the two points B or C), but this is not the minimal expenditure level required. Rather, E_2 clearly provides just enough total expenditures to reach U_2 (at point A), and this is in fact the solution to the dual problem. By comparing Figures 4.2 and 4.6, it is obvious that both the primary utility-maximization approach and the dual expenditure-minimization approach yield the same solution (x^*, y^*)—they are simply alternative ways of

| FIGURE 4.6 | The Dual Expenditure-Minimization Problem |

The dual of the utility-maximization problem is to attain a given utility level (U_2) with minimal expenditures. An expenditure level of E_1 does not permit U_2 to be reached, whereas E_3 provides more spending power than is strictly necessary. With expenditure E_2 this person can just reach U_2 by consuming x^* and y^*.

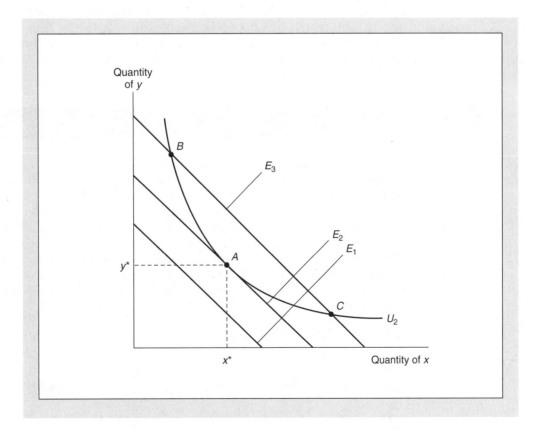

viewing the same process. Often the expenditure-minimization approach is more useful, however, because expenditures are directly observable, whereas utility is not.

A mathematical statement

More formally, the individual's dual expenditure-minimization problem is to choose x_1, x_2, . . . , x_n so as to minimize

$$\text{total expenditures} = E = p_1 x_1 + p_2 x_2 + . . . + p_n x_n, \qquad (4.48)$$

subject to the constraint

$$\text{utility} = \bar{U} = U(x_1, x_2, . . . , x_n). \qquad (4.49)$$

The optimal amounts of x_1, x_2, . . . , x_n chosen in this problem will depend on the prices of the various goods (p_1, p_2, . . . , p_n) and on the required utility level $\bar{U}_2$. If any of the prices were to change or if the individual had a different utility "target," another commodity bundle would be optimal. This dependence can be summarized by an *expenditure function*.

DEFINITION

Expenditure function. The individual's expenditure function shows the minimal expenditures necessary to achieve a given utility level for a particular set of prices. That is,

$$\text{minimal expenditures} = E(p_1, p_2, . . . , p_n, U). \qquad (4.50)$$

This definition shows that the expenditure function and the indirect utility function are inverse functions of one another (compare Equations 4.43 and 4.50). Both depend on market prices but involve different constraints (income or utility). In the next chapter we will see how this relationship is quite useful in allowing us to examine the theory of how individuals respond to price changes. First, however, let's look at two expenditure functions.

 EXAMPLE 4.4

Two Expenditure Functions

There are two ways one might compute an expenditure function. The first, most straightforward method would be to state the expenditure-minimization problem directly and apply the Lagrangian technique. Some of the problems at the end of this chapter ask you to do precisely that. Here, however, we will adopt a more streamlined procedure by taking advantage of the relationship between expenditure functions and indirect utility functions. Because these two functions are inverses of each other, calculation of one greatly facilitates the calculation of the other. But we have already calculated indirect utility functions for two important cases in Example 4.3. Retrieving the related expenditure functions is simple algebra.

Case 1. Cobb-Douglas utility. Equation 4.45 shows that the indirect utility function in the two-good, Cobb-Douglas case is

$$V(p_x, p_y, I) = \frac{I}{2 p_x^{0.5} p_y^{0.5}} \qquad (4.51)$$

If we now interchange the role of utility (which we will now treat as a constant denoted by U) and income (which we will now term "expenditures," E, and treat as a function of the parameters of this problem), we have the expenditure function:

$$E(p_x, p_y, U) = 2 p_x^{0.5} p_y^{0.5} U. \qquad (4.52)$$

Checking this against out former results, now we use a utility target of $U = 2$ with, again, $p_x = 1$, $p_y = 4$. With these parameters, Equation 4.52 predicts that the required minimal expenditures are \$8 (= $2 \cdot 1^{0.5} \cdot 4^{0.5} \cdot 2$). Not surprisingly both the primal utility-maximization problem and the dual expenditure-minimization problem are formally identical.

Case 2. Fixed proportions. For the fixed proportions case, Equation 4.47 gave the indirect utility function as

$$V(p_x, p_y, I) = \frac{I}{p_x + 0.25 p_y}. \qquad (4.53)$$

If we again switch the role of utility and expenditures, we quickly derive the expenditure function:

$$E(p_x, p_y, U) = (p_x + 0.25 \ p_y) U. \qquad (4.54)$$

A check of the hypothetical values used in Example 4.3 ($p_x = 1$, $p_y = 4$, $U = 4$) again shows that it would cost \$8 (= $(1 + 0.25 \cdot 4) \cdot 4$) to reach the utility target of 4.

Compensating for a price change. These expenditure functions allow us to investigate how a person might be compensated for a price change. Specifically, suppose that the price of good y were to rise from \$4 to \$5. This would clearly reduce a person's utility so we might ask what amount of monetary compensation would mitigate the harm. Because the expenditure function allows utility to be held constant, it provides a direct estimate of this amount. Specifically, in the Cobb-Douglas case, expenditures would have to be increased from \$8 to \$8.94 (= $2 \cdot 1 \cdot 5^{0.5} \cdot 2$) to provide enough extra purchasing power to precisely compensate for this price rise. With fixed-proportions, expenditures would have to be increased from \$8 to \$9 to compensate for the price increase. Hence, the compensations are about the same in these simple cases.

There is one important difference between the two examples, however. In the fixed-proportions case, the \$1 extra compensation simply permits this person to return to his or her prior consumption bundle ($x = 4$, $y = 1$). That is the only way to restore utility to $U = 4$ for this rigid person. In the Cobb-Douglas case, however, this person will not use the extra compensation to revert to his or her prior consumption bundle. Instead, utility maximization will require that the \$8.94 be allocated so that $x = 4.47$, $y = 0.894$. This will still provide a utility level of $U = 2$, but this person will economize on the now more expensive good y.

Query: How should a person be compensated for a price decline? What sort of compensation would be required if the price of good y fell from \$4 to \$3?

Properties of expenditure functions

Because expenditure functions are widely used in applied economics, it is useful to understand a few of the properties shared by all such functions. Here we look at three such properties. All of these follow directly from the fact that expenditure functions are based on individual utility maximization.

1. *Homogeneity:* For both of the functions illustrated in Example 4.4, a doubling of all prices will precisely double the value of required expenditures. Technically, these expenditure functions are "homogeneous of degree one" in all prices.[10] This is a quite

---

[10]As we described in Chapter 2, the function $f(x_1, x_2, \ldots x_n)$ is said to be homogeneous of degree k if $f(tx_1, tx_2, \ldots x_n) = t^k f(x_1, x_2, \ldots x_n)$. In this case, $k = 1$.

general property of expenditure functions. Because the individual's budget constraint is linear in prices, any proportional increase in both prices and purchasing power will permit the person to buy the same utility-maximizing commodity bundle that was chosen before the price rise. In Chapter 5 we will see that, for this reason, demand functions are homogenous of degree zero in all prices and income.

2. *Expenditure functions are nondecreasing in prices:* This property can be succinctly summarized by the mathematical statement

$$\frac{\partial E}{\partial p_i} \geq 0 \text{ for every good, } i. \tag{4.55}$$

This seems intuitively obvious. Because the expenditure function reports the minimum expenditure necessary to reach a given utility level, an increase in any price must increase this minimum. More formally, suppose p_1 takes on two values: p_1^a *and* p_1^b *with* $p_1^b > p_1^a$ with all other prices being unchanged between states a and b. Also, let x be the bundle of goods purchased in state a, and y the bundle purchased in state b. By the definition of the expenditure function, both of these bundles of goods must yield the same target utility. Clearly bundle y costs more with state b prices than it would with state a prices. But we know that bundle x is the lowest cost way to achieve the target utility level with state a prices. Hence, expenditures on bundle y must be greater than on bundle x. Similarly, a decline in a price must not increase expenditures.

3. *Expenditure functions are concave in prices:* In Chapter 2 we discussed concave functions as being functions that always lie below tangents to them. Although the technical mathematical conditions that describe such functions are complicated, it is relatively simple to show how the concept applies to expenditure functions by considering the variation in a single price. Figure 4.7 shows an individual's expenditures as a function of the single price, p_1. At the initial price, $p_1^\star$, this person's expenditures are given by $E(p_1^\star \ldots)$. Now consider prices higher or lower than $p_1^\star$. If this person continued to buy the same bundle of goods, expenditures would increase or decrease linearly as this price changed. This would give rise to the pseudo-expenditure function E^{pseudo} in the figure. This line shows a level of expenditures that would allow this person to buy the original bundle of goods despite the changing value of p_1. If, as seems more likely, this person adjusted his or her purchases as p_1 changes, we know (because of expenditure minimization) that actual expenditures will be less than these pseudo amounts. Hence, the actual expenditure function, E, will lie everywhere below E^{pseudo} and the function will be concave.[11] The concavity of the expenditure function is a useful property for a number of applications, especially those related to the construction of index numbers (see the Extensions to Chapter 5).

---

[11]One result of concavity is that $f_{ii} = \dfrac{\partial^2 E}{\partial p_i^2} \leq 0.$ This is precisely what Figure 4.7 shows.

FIGURE 4.7   **Expenditure Functions Are Concave in Prices**

At p_1^* this person spends $E(p_1^* \ldots)$. If he or she continues to buy the same set of goods as p_1 changes, expenditures would be given by E^{pseudo}. Because his or her consumption patterns will likely change as p_1 changes, actual expenditures will be less than this.

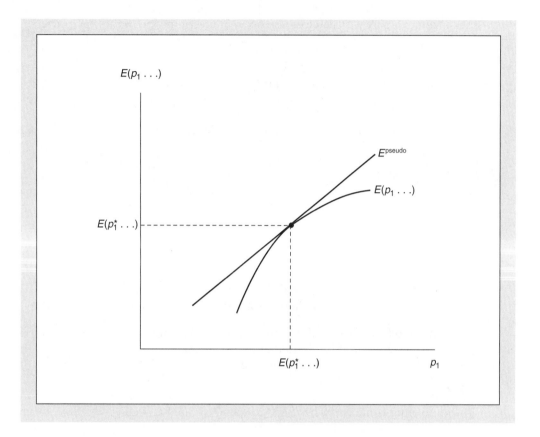

SUMMARY

In this chapter we explored the basic economic model of utility maximization subject to a budget constraint. Although we approached this problem in a variety of ways, all of these approaches lead to the same basic result:

- To reach a constrained maximum, an individual should spend all available income and should choose a commodity bundle such that the *MRS* between any two goods is equal to the ratio of those goods' market prices. This basic tangency will result in the individual equating the ratios of the marginal utility to market price for every good that is actually consumed. Such a result is common to most constrained optimization problems.

- The tangency conditions are only the first-order conditions for a unique constrained maximum, however. To ensure that these conditions are also sufficient, the individual's indifference curve map must exhibit a diminishing *MRS*. In formal terms, the utility function must be strictly quasi-concave.

- The tangency conditions must also be modified to allow for corner solutions in which the optimal level of consumption of some goods is zero. In this case, the ratio of marginal utility to price for such a good will be below the common marginal benefit–marginal cost ratio for goods actually bought.

- A consequence of the assumption of constrained utility maximization is that the individual's optimal choices will depend implicitly on the parameters of his or her budget constraint. That is, the choices observed will be implicit functions of all prices and income. Utility will therefore also be an indirect function of these parameters.

- The dual to the constrained utility-maximization problem is to minimize the expenditure required to reach a given utility target. Although this dual approach yields the same optimal solution as the primal constrained maximum problem, it also yields additional insight into the theory of choice. Specifically, this approach leads to expenditure functions in which the spending required to reach a given utility target depends on goods' market prices. Expenditure functions are therefore, in principle, measurable.

PROBLEMS

4.1

Each day Paul, who is in third grade, eats lunch at school. He likes only Twinkies (t) and soda (s), and these provide him a utility of

$$\text{utility} = U(t, s) = \sqrt{ts}.$$

a. If Twinkies cost $.10 each and soda costs $.25 per cup, how should Paul spend the $1 his mother gives him in order to maximize his utility?

b. If the school tries to discourage Twinkie consumption by raising the price to $.40, by how much will Paul's mother have to increase his lunch allowance to provide him with the same level of utility he received in part (a)?

4.2

a. A young connoisseur has $300 to spend to build a small wine cellar. She enjoys two vintages in particular: a 1997 French Bordeaux (w_F) at $20 per bottle and a less expensive 2002 California varietal wine (w_C) priced at $4. How much of each wine should she purchase if her utility is?

$$U(w_F, w_C) = w_F^{2/3} w_C^{1/3}$$

b. When she arrived at the wine store, our young oenologist discovered that the price of the French Bordeaux had fallen to $10 a bottle because of a decline in the value of the franc. If the price of the California wine remains stable at $4 per bottle, how much of each wine should our friend purchase to maximize utility under these altered conditions?

c. Explain why this wine-fancier is better off in part (b) than in part (a). How would you put a monetary value on this utility increase?

4.3

a. On a given evening J. P. enjoys the consumption of cigars (c) and brandy (b) according to the function

$$U(c, b) = 20c - c^2 + 18b - 3b^2.$$

How many cigars and glasses of brandy does he consume during an evening? (Cost is no object to J. P.)

b. Lately, however, J. P. has been advised by his doctors that he should limit the sum of brandy and cigars consumed to 5. How many glasses of brandy and cigars will he consume under these circumstances?

4.4

a. Mr. Odde Ball enjoys commodities x and y according to the utility function

$$U(x, y) = \sqrt{x^2 + y^2}.$$

Maximize Mr. Ball's utility if $p_x = \$3$, $p_y = \$4$, and he has $50 to spend.

Hint: It may be easier here to maximize U^2 rather than U. Why won't this alter your results?

b. Graph Mr. Ball's indifference curve and its point of tangency with his budget constraint. What does the graph say about Mr. Ball's behavior? Have you found a true maximum?

4.5

Mr. A derives utility from martinis (m) in proportion to the number he drinks:

$$U(m) = m.$$

Mr. A is very particular about his martinis, however: He only enjoys them made in the exact proportion of two parts gin (g) to one part vermouth (v). Hence, we can rewrite Mr. A's utility function as

$$U(m) = U(g, v) = \min\left(\frac{g}{2}, v\right).$$

a. Graph Mr. A's indifference curve in terms of g and v for various levels of utility. Show that regardless of the prices of the two ingredients, Mr. A will never alter the way he mixes martinis.

b. Calculate the demand functions for g and v.

c. Using the results from part (b), what is Mr. A's indirect utility function?

d. Calculate Mr. A's expenditure function; for each level of utility, show spending as a function of p_g and p_v.

Hint: Because this problem involves a fixed proportions utility function you cannot solve for utility-maximizing decisions by using calculus.

4.6

Suppose that a fast-food junkie derives utility from three goods: soft drinks (x), hamburgers (y), and ice cream sundaes (z) according to the Cobb-Douglas utility function

$$U(x, y, z) = x^{.5}\, y^{.5}\, (1 + z)^{.5}.$$

Suppose also that the prices for these goods are given by $p_x = .25$, $p_y = 1$, and $p_z = 2$ and that this consumer's income is given by $I = 2$.

a. Show that for $z = 0$, maximization of utility results in the same optimal choices as in Example 4.1. Show also that any choice that results in $z > 0$ (even for a fractional z) reduces utility from this optimum.

b. How do you explain the fact that $z = 0$ is optimal here?

c. How high would this individual's income have to be in order for any z to be purchased?

4.7

In Example 4.1 we looked at the Cobb-Douglas utility function $U(x, y) = x^{\alpha}y^{1-\alpha}$ where $0 \leq \alpha \leq 1$. This problem illustrates a few more attributes of that function.

a. Calculate the indirect utility function for this Cobb-Douglas case.

b. Calculate the expenditure function for this case.

c. Show explicitly how the compensation required to offset the effect of a rise in the price of x relates to the size of the exponent α.

4.8

The lump sum principle illustrated in Figure 4.5 applies to transfer policy as well as taxation. This problem examines this application of the principle.

a. Use a graph similar to Figure 4.5 to show that an income grant to a person provides more utility than does a subsidy on good x that costs the same amount to the government.

b. Use the Cobb-Douglas expenditure function presented in Equation 4.52 to calculate the extra purchasing power needed to raise this person's utility from $U = 2$ to $U = 3$.

c. Use Equation 4.52 again to estimate the degree to which good x must be subsidized to raise this person's utility from $U = 2$ to $U = 3$. How much would this subsidy cost the government? How would this cost compare to the cost calculated in part (b)?

d. Problem 4.7 asks you to compute an expenditure function for a more general Cobb-Douglas utility function than used in Example 4.4. Use that expenditure function to again answer parts (b) and (c) for the case where $\alpha = 0.3$—a figure close to the fraction of income that low-income people spend on food.

e. How would your calculations in this problem have changed if we had used the expenditure function for the fixed proportions case (Equation 4.54) instead?

4.9

The general CES utility function is given by

$$U(x, y) = \frac{x^{\delta}}{\delta} + \frac{y^{\delta}}{\delta}.$$

a. Show that the first-order conditions for a constrained utility maximum with this function require individuals to choose goods in the proportion

$$\frac{x}{y} = \left(\frac{p_x}{p_y}\right)^{\frac{1}{\delta-1}}.$$

b. Show that the result in part (a) implies that individuals will allocate their funds equally between x and y for the Cobb-Douglas case ($\delta = 0$), as we have shown before in several problems.

c. How does the ratio $p_x x / p_y y$ depend on the value of δ? Explain your results intuitively. (For further details on this function, see Extension E4.3.)

d. Use the Lagrangian technique to derive the expenditure function for this case.

4.10

Suppose individuals require a certain level of food (x) to remain alive. Let this amount be given by x_0. Once x_0 is purchased, individuals obtain utility from food and other goods (y) of the form

$$U(x, y) = (x - x_0)^\alpha\, y^\beta$$

where $\alpha + \beta = 1$.

a. Show that if $I > p_x x_0$ the individual will maximize utility by spending $\alpha(I - p_x x_0) + p_x x_0$ on good x and $\beta(I - p_x x_0)$ on good y. Interpret this result.

b. How do the ratios $p_x x/I$ and $p_y y/I$ change as income increases in this problem? (See also Extension E4.2.)

SUGGESTIONS FOR FURTHER READING

Barten, A. P., and Volker Böhm. "Consumer Theory." In K. J. Arrow and M. D. Intriligator, eds., *Handbook of Mathematical Economics,* vol. II. Amsterdam: North-Holland, 1982.
Sections 10 and 11 have compact summaries of many of the concepts covered in this chapter.

Deaton, A., and J. Muelbauer. *Economics and Consumer Behavior.* Cambridge: Cambridge University Press, 1980.
Section 2.5 provides a nice geometric treatment of duality concepts.

Dixit, A. K. *Optimization in Economic Theory.* Oxford: Oxford University Press, 1990.
Chapter 2 provides several Lagrangian analyses focusing on the Cobb-Douglas utility function.

Hicks, J. R. *Value and Capital.* Oxford: Clarendon Press, 1946.
Chapter II and the Mathematical Appendix provide some early suggestions of the importance of the expenditure function.

Mas-Colell, A., M. D. Whinston, and J. R. Green. *Microeconomic Theory.* Oxford: Oxford University Press, 1995.
Chapter 3 contains a thorough analysis of utility and expenditure functions.

Samuelson, Paul A. *Foundations of Economic Analysis.* Cambridge: Harvard University Press, 1947.
Chapter V and Appendix A provide a succinct analysis of the first-order conditions for a utility maximum. The appendix provides good coverage of second-order conditions.

Silberberg, E., and W. Suen. *The Stricture of Economics: A Mathematical Analysis,* 3rd ed. Boston: Irwin/McGraw-Hill, 2001.
A useful, though fairly difficult, treatment of duality in consumer theory.

Theil, H. *Theory and Measurement of Consumer Demand.* Amsterdam: North-Holland, 1975.
Good summary of basic theory of demand together with implications for empirical estimation.

EXTENSIONS

Budget Shares

The nineteenth-century economist Ernst Engel was one of the first social scientists to intensively study people's actual spending patterns. He focused specifically on food consumption. His finding that the fraction of income spent on food declines as income increases has come to be known as Engel's law and has been confirmed in many studies. Engel's law is such an empirical regularity that some economists have suggested measuring poverty by the fraction of income spent on food. Two other interesting applications are; (1) the study by Hayashi (1995) shows that the share of income devoted to foods favored by the elderly is much higher in two-generation households than in one-generation households; and (2) findings from less-developed countries by Behrman (1989) show that people's desires for a more varied diet as their incomes rise may in fact result in reducing the fraction of income spent on particular nutrients. In the remainder of this extension we look at some evidence on budget shares (denoted by $s_i = p_i x_i / I$) together with a bit more theory on the topic.

E4.1 The variability of budget shares

Table 4E.1 shows some recent budget share data from the United States. Engel's law is clearly visible in the table—as income rises families spend much less of their funds on food. Other important variations in the table include the declining share of income spent on healthcare needs and the much larger share of income devoted to retirement vehicles by higher-income people. Interestingly, the shares of income devoted to shelter and transportation are roughly constant over the range of income shown in the table—apparently high-income people buy bigger houses and cars as their incomes rise.

The variable income shares in Table E4.1 illustrate why the Cobb-Douglas utility function is not especially useful for detailed empirical studies of household behavior. When utility is given by $U(x, y) = x^{\alpha} y^{\beta}$ the implied demand equations are $x = \alpha I / p_x$ and $y = \beta I / p_y$. So,

$$s_x = p_x x / I = \alpha \text{ and}$$
$$s_y = p_y y / I = \beta \tag{i}$$

TABLE E4.1   Budget Shares of U.S. Households, 2001

	Annual Income		
	\$10,000–\$14,999	\$30,000–\$39,999	Over \$70,000
Expenditure Item			
Food	16.5	14.3	11.9
Shelter	19.8	17.6	18.3
Utilities, fuel, and public services	9.7	7.5	5.0
Transportation	17.1	21.3	18.2
Health insurance	4.1	3.1	1.7
Other health-care expenses	4.6	3.1	2.1
Entertainment (including alcohol)	4.9	5.5	6.1
Tobacco	1.3	1.0	0.4
Education	1.3	0.8	1.8
Insurance and pensions	3.4	8.4	15.2
Other (apparel, personal care, other housing expenses, and misc.)	17.3	17.2	19.2

SOURCE: *Consumer Expenditure Report*, 2001, Bureau of Labor Statistics website: http://www.bls.gov.

and budget shares are constant for all observed income levels and relative prices. Because of this shortcoming, economists have investigated a number of other possible forms for the utility function that permit more flexibility.

E4.2 Linear expenditure system

A generalization of the Cobb-Douglas function that incorporates the idea that certain minimal amounts of each good must be bought by an individual (x_0, y_0) is the utility function

$$U(x,y) = (x - x_0)^{\alpha}(y - y_0)^{\beta} \qquad \text{(ii)}$$

for values of $x \geq x_0$ and $y \geq y_0$ and again $\alpha + \beta = 1$.

Demand functions can be derived from this utility function in a way analogous to the Cobb-Douglas case by introducing the concept of supernumerary income (I^*), which represents the amount of purchasing power remaining after purchasing the minimum bundle

$$I^* = I - p_x x_0 - p_y y_0. \qquad \text{(iii)}$$

Using this notation, then, the demand functions are

$$x = (p_x x_0 + \alpha I^*)/p_x \qquad \text{(iv)}$$
$$y = (p_y y_0 + \beta I^*)/p_y$$

In this case, then, the individual spends a constant fraction of supernumerary income on each good once the minimum bundle has been purchased. Manipulation of Equation iv yields the share equations

$$s_x = \alpha + (\beta p_x x_0 - \alpha p_y y_0)/I \qquad \text{(v)}$$
$$s_y = \beta + (\alpha p_y y_0 - \beta p_x x_0)/I,$$

which show that this demand system is not homothetic. Inspection of Equation v shows the unsurprising result that the budget share of a good is positively related to the minimal amount of that good needed and negatively related to the minimal amount of the other good required. Because the notion of necessary purchases seems to accord well with real-world observation, this linear expenditure system (LES), which was first developed by Stone (1954), is widely used in empirical studies.

Traditional purchases

One of the most interesting uses of the LES is to examine how its notion of necessary purchases change as conditions change. For example, Oczkowski and Philip (1994) study how access to modern consumer goods may affect the share of income that individuals in transitional economies devote to traditional local items. They show that villagers of Papua, New Guinea reduce such shares significantly as outside goods become increasingly accessible. Hence, such improvements as better roads for moving goods provide one of the primary routes by which traditional cultural practices are undermined.

E4.3 CES utility

In Chapter 3 we introduced the CES utility function

$$U(x, y) = \frac{x^{\delta}}{\delta} + \frac{y^{\delta}}{\delta} \qquad \text{(vi)}$$

for $\delta \leq 1$, $\delta \neq 0$. The primary use of this function is to illustrate alternative substitution possibilities (as reflected in the value of the parameter δ). Budget shares implied by this utility function provide a number of such insights. Manipulation of the first-order conditions for a constrained utility maximum with the CES function yield the share equations

$$s_x = 1/[1 + (p_y/p_x)^K] \qquad \text{(vii)}$$
$$s_y = 1/[1 + (p_x/p_y)^K]$$

where $K = \delta/(\delta - 1)$.

The homothetic nature of the CES function is shown by the fact that these share expressions depend only on the price ratio, p_x/p_y. Behavior of the shares in response to changes in relative prices depends on the value of the parameter K. For the Cobb-Douglas case, $\delta = 0$ so $K = 0$ and $s_x = s_y = \frac{1}{2}$. When $\delta > 0$, substitution possibilities are great and $K < 0$. In this case Equation vii shows that s_x and p_x/p_y move in opposite directions. If p_x/p_y rises, the individual substitutes y for x to such an extent that s_x falls. Alternatively, if $\delta < 0$, substitution possibilities are limited, $K > 0$, and s_x and p_x/p_y move in the same direction. In this case an increase in p_x/p_y causes only minor substitution of y for x, and s_x actually rises because of the relatively higher price of good x.

North American Free Trade

CES demand functions are most often used in large-scale computer models of general equilibrium (see Chapter 12) that economists use to evaluate the impact of major economic changes. Because the CES model stresses that shares respond to changes in relative prices, it is particularly appropriate for looking at innovations such as changes in tax policy or in international trade restrictions where changes in relative prices are quite likely. One important recent area of such research has been on the impact of the North American Free Trade Agreement for Canada, Mexico, and the United States. In general, these models find that all of the countries involved might be expected to gain from the agreement, but that Mexico's gains may be the greatest because it is experiencing the greatest change in relative prices. Kehoe and Kehoe (1995) present a number of computable equilibrium models that economists have used in these examinations.[1]

References

Behrman, Jere R. "Is Variety the Spice of Life? Implications for Caloric Intake." *Review of Economics and Statistics* (November 1989): 666–72.

Green, H. A. *Consumer Theory*. London: The Macmillan Press, 1976.

Hyashi, Fumio. "Is the Japanese Extended Family Altruistically Linked? A Test Based on Engel Curves." *Journal of Political Economy* (June 1995): 661–74.

Kehoe, Patrick J., and Timothy J. Kehoe. *Modeling North American Economic Integration*. London: Klower Academic Publishers, 1995.

Oczkowski, E., and N. E. Philip. "Household Expenditure Patterns and Access to Consumer Goods in a Transitional Economy." *Journal of Economic Development* (June 1994): 165–83.

Stone, R. "Linear Expenditure Systems and Demand Analysis." *The Economic Journal* (September 1954): 511–27.

---

[1]The Research on the North American Free Trade Agreement is discussed in more detail in the Extensions to Chapter 12.

Chapter 5

INCOME AND SUBSTITUTION EFFECTS

In this chapter we will use the utility-maximization model to study how the quantity of a good that an individual chooses is affected by a change in that good's price. This examination will allow us to construct the individual's demand curve for the good. In the process we will provide a number of insights into the nature of this price response and into the kinds of assumptions that lie behind most analyses of demand.

Demand functions

As we pointed out in Chapter 4, in principle it will usually be possible to solve the necessary conditions of a utility maximum for the optimal levels of $x_1, x_2, \ldots, x_n$ (and λ, the Lagrangian multiplier) as functions of all prices and income. Mathematically, this can be expressed as n demand functions of the form

$$
\begin{aligned}
x_1^* &= x_1(p_1, p_2, \ldots p_n, I) \\
x_2^* &= x_2(p_1, p_2, \ldots p_n, I) \\
&\vdots \\
x_n^* &= x_n(p_1, p_2, \ldots p_n, I).
\end{aligned}
\tag{5.1}
$$

If there are only two goods (x and y—the case we will usually be concerned with), this notation can be simplified a bit as

$$
\begin{aligned}
x^* &= x(p_x, p_y, I) \\
y^* &= y(p_x, p_y, I).
\end{aligned}
\tag{5.2}
$$

Once we know the form of these demand functions and the values of all prices and income, these can be used to "predict" how much of each good this person will choose to buy. The notation stresses that prices and income are "exogenous" to this process—that is, these are parameters over which the individual has no control at this stage of the analysis. Changes in the parameters will, of course, shift the budget constraint and cause this person to make different choices. That is the question that is the focus of this chapter and the next. Specifically, in this chapter we will be looking at the partial derivatives $\partial x / \partial I$ and $\partial x / \partial p_x$ for any arbitrary good, x. Chapter 6 will carry the discussion further by looking at "cross-price" effects of the form $\partial x / \partial p_y$ for any arbitrary pair of goods, x and y.

Homogeneity

A first property of demand functions requires little mathematics. If we were to double all prices and income (indeed, if we were to multiply them all by any positive constant), the optimal quantities demanded would remain unchanged. Doubling all prices and income changes only the units by which we count, not the "real" quantity of goods demanded. This result can be seen in a number of ways, although perhaps the easiest is through a graphic approach. Referring back to Figures 4.1 and 4.2, it is clear that if we double p_x, p_y, and I, we do not affect the graph of the budget constraint. Hence, x^*, y^* will still be the combination that is chosen. $p_x x + p_y y = I$ is the same constraint as $2p_x x + 2p_y y = 2I$. Somewhat more technically, we can write this result as saying that for any good x_i,

$$x_i^* = x_i\,(p_1,\ p_2,\ \ldots\ p_n,\ I) = x_i\,(tp_1,\ tp_2,\ \ldots\ tp_n,\ tI) \qquad (5.3)$$

for any $t > 0$. Functions that obey the property illustrated in Equation 5.3 are said to be homogeneous of degree zero.[1] Hence, we have shown that individual *demand functions are homogeneous of degree zero in all prices and income.* Changing all prices and income in the same proportions will not affect the physical quantities of goods demanded. This result shows that (in theory) individuals' demands will not be affected by a "pure" inflation during which all prices and incomes rise proportionally. They will continue to demand the same bundle of goods. Of course, if an inflation were not pure (that is, if some prices rose more rapidly than others), this would not be the case.

    EXAMPLE 5.1

Homogeneity

Homogeneity of demand is a direct result of the utility-maximization assumption. Demand functions derived from utility maximization will be homogeneous and, conversely, demand functions that are not homogeneous cannot reflect utility maximization (unless prices enter directy into the utility function itself, as they might for goods with snob appeal). If, for example, an individual's utility for food (x) and housing (y) is given by

$$\text{utility} = U(x, y) = x^{.3}y^{.7}, \qquad (5.4)$$

it is a simple matter (following the procedure used in Example 4.1) to derive the demand functions

$$x^* = \frac{.3I}{p_x}$$
$$y^* = \frac{.7I}{p_y}. \qquad (5.5)$$

These functions obviously exhibit homogeneity—a doubling of all prices and income would leave x^* and y^* unaffected.

If the individual's preferences for x and y were reflected instead by the CES function:

$$U(x, y) = x^{.5} + y^{.5}, \qquad (5.6)$$

[1]More generally, as we saw in Chapter 2, a function $f(x_1, x_2, \ldots, x_n)$ is said to be homogeneous of degree k if $f(tx_1, tx_2, \ldots, tx_n) = t^k f(x_1, x_2, \ldots, x_n)$ for any $t > 0$. The most common cases of homogeneous functions are $k = 0$ and $k = 1$. If f is homogeneous of degree 0, doubling all of its arguments leaves f unchanged in value. If f is homogeneous of degree 1, doubling all its arguments will double the value of f.

we showed in Example 4.2 that the demand functions are given by

$$x^* = \left(\frac{1}{1 + p_x / p_y} \right) \cdot \frac{I}{p_x}$$

$$y^* = \left(\frac{1}{1 + p_y / p_x} \right) \cdot \frac{I}{p_y}.$$

(5.7)

As before, both these demand functions are homogeneous of degree zero—a doubling of p_x, p_y, and I would leave x^* and y^* unaffected.

Query: Do the demand functions derived in this example ensure that total spending on x and y will exhaust the individual's income for *any combination* of p_x, p_y, and I? Can you prove that this is the case?

Changes in income

As a person's purchasing power rises, it is natural to expect that the quantity of each good purchased will also increase. This situation is illustrated in Figure 5.1. As expenditures increase from I_1 to I_2 to I_3, the quantity of x demanded increases from x_1 to x_2 to x_3. Also, the quantity of y increases from y_1 to y_2 to y_3. Notice that the budget lines I_1, I_2, and I_3 are all parallel, reflecting the fact that only income is changing, not the relative prices of x and y. Because the ratio p_x / p_y stays constant, the utility-maximizing conditions also require that the *MRS* stay constant as the individual moves to higher levels of satisfaction. The *MRS* is therefore the same at point (x_3, y_3) as at (x_1, y_1).

Normal and inferior goods

In Figure 5.1, both x and y increase as income increases—$\partial x / \partial I$ and $\partial y / \partial I$ are both positive. This might be considered the usual situation, and goods that this property are called *normal goods* over the range of income change being observed.

For some goods, however, the quantity chosen may decrease as income increases in some ranges. Some examples of these goods might be rotgut whiskey, potatoes, and secondhand clothing. A good z for which $\partial z / \partial I$ is negative is called an *inferior good*. This phenomenon is illustrated in Figure 5.2 on page 125. In this diagram the good z is inferior because for increases in income in the range shown, less of z is actually chosen. Notice that indifference curves do not have to be "oddly" shaped to exhibit inferiority; the curves corresponding to goods y and z in Figure 5.2 continue to obey the assumption of a diminishing *MRS*. Good z is inferior because of the way it relates to the other goods available (good y here), not because of a peculiarity unique to it. Hence, we have developed the following definitions:

DEFINITION

Inferior and normal goods. A good x_i for which $\partial x_i / \partial I < 0$ over some range of income changes is an *inferior good* in that range. If $\partial x_i / \partial I \geq 0$ over some range of income variation, the good is a *normal*, or "noninferior," *good* in that range.

| FIGURE 5.1 | Effect of an Increase in Income on the Quantities of *x* and *y* Chosen |

As income increases from I_1 to I_2 to I_3, the optimal (utility-maximizing) choices of x and y are shown by the successively higher points of tangency. Notice that the budget constraint shifts in a parallel way because its slope (given by $-p_x/p_y$) does not change.

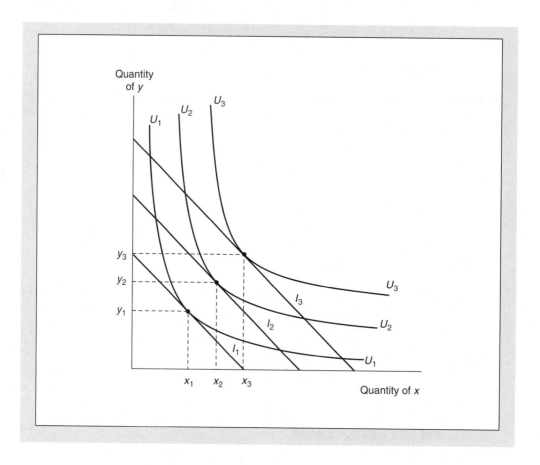

Changes in a good's price

The effect of a price change on the quantity of a good demanded is more complex to analyze than is the effect of a change in income. Geometrically, this is because changing a price involves changing not only the intercepts of the budget constraint, but also its slope. Consequently, moving to the new utility-maximizing choice entails not only moving to another indifference curve, but also changing the *MRS*. When a price changes, therefore, two analytically different effects come into play. One of these is a *substitution effect*—even if the individual were to stay on the *same* indifference curve, consumption patterns would be allocated so as to equate the *MRS* to the new price ratio. A second effect, the *income effect,* arises because a price change necessarily changes an individual's "real" income—the individual cannot stay on the initial indifference curve, but must move to a new one. We begin by analyzing these effects graphically. Then we will provide a mathematical development.

Graphical analysis of a fall in price

Income and substitution effects are illustrated in Figure 5.3 on page 126. This individual is initially maximizing utility (subject to total expenditures, I) by consuming the combination x^*, y^*. The initial budget constraint is $I = p_x^1 x + p_y y$. Now suppose that the price of x falls to p_x^2. The new budget constraint is given by the equation $I = p_x^2 x + p_y y$ in Figure 5.3.

FIGURE 5.2   **An Indifference Curve Map Exhibiting Inferiority**

In this diagram, good z is inferior because the quantity purchased actually declines as income increases. y is a normal good (as it must be if there are only two goods available), and purchases of y increase as total expenditures increase.

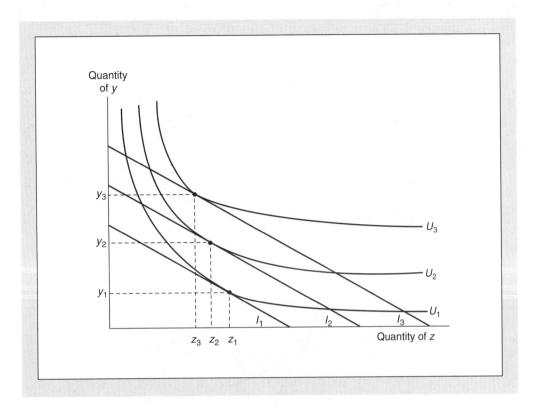

It is clear that the new position of maximum utility is at x^{**}, y^{**}, where the new budget line is tangent to the indifference curve U_2. The movement to this new point can be viewed as being composed of two effects. First, the change in the slope of the budget constraint would have motivated a move to point B, even if choices had been confined to those on the original indifference curve U_1. The dashed line in Figure 5.3 has the same slope as the new budget constraint $(I = p_x^2 x + p_y y)$, but is drawn to be tangent to U_1 because we are conceptually holding "real" income (that is, utility) constant. A relatively lower price for x causes a move from x^*, y^* to B if we do not allow this individual to be made better off as a result of the lower price. This movement is a graphic demonstration of the *substitution effect*. The further move from B to the optimal point x^{**}, y^{**} is analytically identical to the kind of change exhibited earlier for changes in income. Because the price of x has fallen, this person has a greater "real" income and can afford a utility level (U_2) that is greater than that which could previously be attained. If x is a normal good, more of it will be chosen in response to this increase in purchasing power. This observation explains the origin of the term *income effect* for the movement. Overall then, the result of the price decline is to cause more x to be demanded.

It is important to recognize that this person does not actually make a series of choices from x^*, y^* to B and then to x^{**}, y^{**}. We never observe point B; only the two optimal positions are reflected in observed behavior. However, the notion of income and substitution effects is analytically valuable because it shows that a price change affects the quantity of x that is demanded in two conceptually different ways. We will see how this separation offers major insights in the theory of demand.

FIGURE 5.3   **Demonstration of the Income and Substitution Effects of a Fall in the Price of *x***

When the price of *x* falls from p_x^1 to p_x^2, the utility-maximizing choice shifts from x^*, y^* to x^{**}, y^{**}. This movement can be broken down into two analytically different effects: first, the substitution effect, involving a movement along the initial in-difference curve to point *B*, where the *MRS* is equal to the new price ratio; and secondly, the income effect, entailing a movement to a higher level of utility, because real income has increased. In the diagram, both the substitution and income effects cause more *x* to be bought when its price declines. Notice that point I/p_y is the same as before the price change. This is because p_y has not changed. Point I/p_y therefore appears on both the old and new budget constraints.

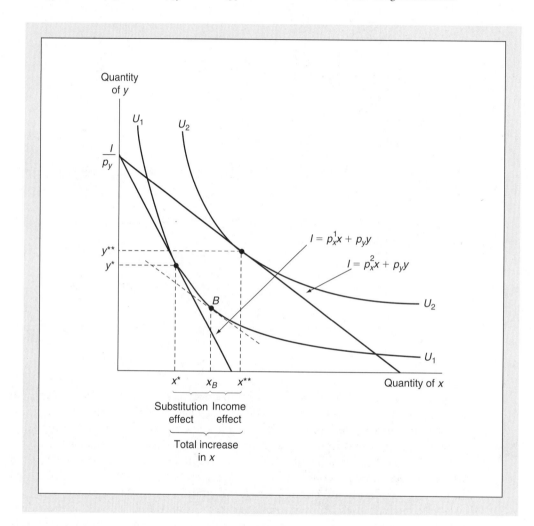

Graphical analysis of an increase in price

If the price of good *x* were to increase, a similar analysis would be used. In Figure 5.4 the budget line has been shifted inward because of an increase in the price of *x* from p_x^1 to p_x^2. The movement from the initial point of utility maximization (x^*, y^*) to the new point (x^{**}, y^{**}) can be decomposed into two effects. First, even if this person could stay on the initial indifference curve (U_2), there would still be an incentive to substitute *y* for *x* and move along U_2 to point *B*. However, because purchasing power has been reduced by the rise in the price of *x*, he or she must move to a lower level of utility. This movement is again called the income effect. Notice in Figure 5.4 that both the income and substitution effects work in the same direction and cause the quantity of *x* demanded to be reduced in response to an increase in its price.

FIGURE 5.4   **Demonstration of the Income and Substitution Effects of an Increase the Price of x**

When the price of x increases, the budget constraint shifts inward. The movement from the initial utility-maximizing point (x^*, y^*) to the new point (x^{**}, y^{**}) can be analyzed as two separate effects. The substitution effect would be depicted as a movement to point B on the initial indifference curve (U_2). The price increase, however, would create a loss of purchasing power and a consequent movement to a lower indifference curve. This is the income effect. In the diagram, both the income and substitution effects cause the quantity of x to fall as a result of the increase in its price. Again, the point I/p_y is not affected by the change in the price of x.

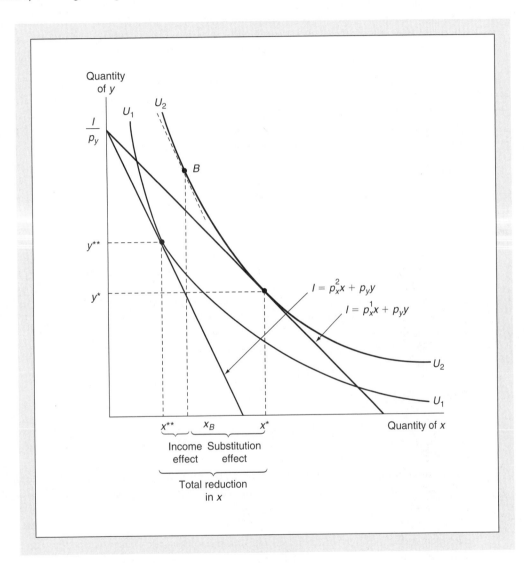

Effects of price changes for inferior goods

So far we have shown that substitution and income effects tend to reinforce one another. For a price decline, both cause more of the good to be demanded, whereas for a price increase, both cause less to be demanded. Although this analysis is accurate for the case of normal (noninferior) goods, the possibility of inferior goods complicates the story. In this case, income and substitution effects work in opposite directions, and the combined result of a price change is indeterminate. A fall price, for example, will always cause an individual to tend to consume more of a good because of the substitution effect. But if the good is inferior, the increase in purchasing power caused by the price decline may cause less of the good to be bought. The result is therefore indeterminate—the substitution effect tends to increase the quantity of the inferior good bought, whereas the (perverse) income effect tends to reduce this quantity. Unlike the situation for normal goods, it is not possible here to predict even the direction of the effect of a change in p_x on the quantity of x consumed.

Giffen's paradox

If the income effect of a price change is strong enough, the change in price and the resulting change in the quantity demanded could actually move in the same direction. Legend has it that the English economist Robert Giffen observed this paradox in nineteenth-century Ireland—when the price of potatoes rose, people reportedly consumed more of them. This peculiar result can be explained by looking at the size of the income effect of a change in the price of potatoes. Potatoes were not only inferior goods, but also used up a large portion of the Irish people's income. An increase in the price of potatoes therefore reduced real income substantially. The Irish were forced to cut back on other luxury food consumption in order to buy more potatoes. Even though this rendering of events is historically implausible, the possibility of an increase in the quantity demanded in response to an increase in the price of a good has come to be known as *Giffen's paradox*.[2] Later we will provide a mathematical analysis of how Giffen's paradox can occur.

A summary

Hence, our graphical analysis leads to the following conclusions:

OPTIMIZATION PRINCIPLE

Substitution and income effects. The utility-maximization hypothesis suggests that, for normal goods, a fall in the price of a good leads to an increase in quantity purchased because (1) the *substitution effect* causes more to be purchased as the individual moves *along* an indifference curve; and (2) the *income effect* causes more to be purchased because the price decline has increased purchasing power, thereby permitting movement to a *higher* indifference curve. When the price of a normal good rises, similar reasoning predicts a decline in the quantity purchased. For inferior goods, substitution and income effects work in opposite directions, and no definite predictions can be made.

The individual's demand curve

Frequently economists wish to graph demand functions. It will come as no surprise to you that these graphs are called "demand curves." Understanding how such widely used curves relate to underlying demand functions provides additional insights to even the most fundamental of economic arguments. To simplify the development, assume there are only two goods and that, as before, the demand function for good x is given by

$$x^* = x(p_x, p_y, I).$$

The demand curve derived from this function looks at the relationship between x and p_x while holding p_y, $\bar{I}$, and preferences constant. That is, it shows the relationship

$$x^* = x(p_x, \bar{p}_y, \bar{I}), \tag{5.8}$$

where the bars over p_y and I indicate that these determinants of demand are being held constant. This construction is shown in Figure 5.5. The graph shows utility-maximizing choices of x and y as this individual is presented with successively lower prices of good x

---

[2]A major problem with this explanation is that it disregards Marshall's observation that both supply and demand factors must be taken into account when analyzing price changes. If potato prices increased because of the potato blight in Ireland, then supply should have become smaller, so how could *more* potatoes possibly have been consumed? Also, since many Irish people were potato farmers, the potato price increase should have increased real income for them. For a detailed discussion of these and other fascinating bits of potato lore, see G. P. Dwyer and C. M. Lindsey, "Robert Giffen and the Irish Potato," *American Economic Review* (March 1984): 188–92.

FIGURE 5.5   **Construction of an Individual's Demand Curve**

In (a) the individual's utility-maximizing choices of x and y are shown for three different prices of x (p_x', p_x'', and p_x'''). In (b) this relationship between p_x and x is used to construct the demand curve for x. The demand curve is drawn on the assumption that p_y, I, and preferences remain constant as p_x varies.

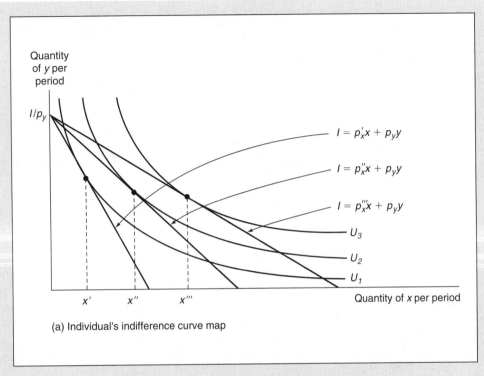

(a) Individual's indifference curve map

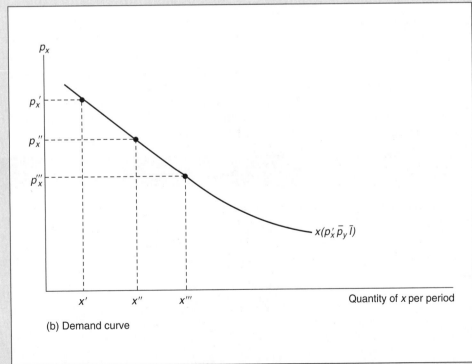

(b) Demand curve

(while holding p_y and I constant). We assume that the quantities of x chosen increase from x' to x'' to x''' as that good's price falls from p_x' to p_x'' to p_x'''. Such an assumption is in accord with our general conclusion that, except in the unusual case of Giffen's paradox, $\partial x / \partial p_x$ is negative.

In Figure 5.5b information about the utility-maximizing choices of good x is transferred to a *demand curve*, having p_x on the vertical axis and sharing the same horizontal axis as the figure above it. The negative slope of the curve again reflects the assumption that $\partial x / \partial p_x$ is negative. Hence, we may define an individual demand curve as follows:

Individual demand curve. An *individual demand curve* shows the relationship between the price of a good and the quantity of that good purchased by an individual assuming that all other determinants of demand are held constant.

The demand curve illustrated in Figure 5.5 stays in a fixed position only so long as all other determinants of demand remain unchanged. If one of these other factors were to change, the curve might shift to a new position, as we now describe.

Shifts in the demand curve

Three factors were held constant in deriving this demand curve: (1) income; (2) prices of other goods (say, p_y); and (3) the individual's preferences. If any of these were to change, the entire demand curve might shift to a new position. For example, if I were to increase, the curve would shift outward (provided that $\partial x / \partial I > 0$; that is, that the good is a "normal" good over this income range). More x would be demanded at *each* price. If another price, say, p_y, were to change, the curve would shift inward or outward, depending precisely on how x and y are related. In the next chapter we will examine that relationship in detail. Finally, the curve would shift if the individual's preferences for good x were to change. A sudden advertising blitz by the McDonald's Corporation might shift the demand for hamburgers outward, for example.

As this discussion makes clear, one must remember that the demand curve is only a two-dimensional representation of the true demand function (Equation 5.8) and that it is stable only if other things in fact stay constant. It is important to keep clearly in mind the difference between a movement along a given demand curve caused by a change in p_x and a shift in the entire curve caused by a change in income, in one of the other prices, or in preferences. Traditionally, the term *an increase in demand* is reserved for an outward shift in the demand curve, whereas the term *an increase in the quantity demanded* refers to a movement along a given curve caused by a change in p_x.

 EXAMPLE 5.2

Demand Functions and Demand Curves

To be able to graph a demand curve from a given demand function, we must assume that the preferences that generated the function remain stable and that we know the values of income and other relevant prices. In the first case studied in Example 5.1, we found that

$$x = \frac{.3I}{p_x} \qquad (5.9)$$

and

$$y = \frac{.7I}{p_y}.$$

If preferences do not change and if this individual's income is $100, these functions become

$$x = \frac{30}{p_x}$$

$$y = \frac{70}{p_y}$$

(5.10)

or

$$p_x x = 30$$

$$p_y y = 70,$$

which makes clear that the demand curves for these two goods are simple hyperbolas. A rise in income would shift both of the demand curves outward. Notice also, in this case, that the demand curve for x is not shifted by changes in p_y and vice versa.

For the second case examined in Example 5.1, the analysis is more complex. For good x, say, we know that

$$x = \left(\frac{1}{1 + p_x / p_y} \right) \cdot \frac{I}{p_x}$$

(5.11)

so to graph this in the $p_x - x$ plane we must know both I and p_y. If we again assume $I = 100$ and let $p_y = 1$, Equation 5.11 becomes

$$x = \frac{100}{p_x^2 + p_x},$$

(5.12)

which, when graphed, would also show a general hyperbolic relationship between price and quantity consumed. In this case the curve would be relatively flatter because substitution effects are larger than in the Cobb-Douglas case. From Equation 5.11 we also know that

$$\frac{\partial x}{\partial I} = \left(\frac{1}{1 + p_x / p_y} \right) \cdot \frac{1}{p_x} > 0$$

(5.13)

and

$$\frac{\partial x}{\partial p_y} = \frac{I}{(p_x + p_y)^2} > 0,$$

so increases in I or p_y would shift the demand curve for good x outward.

Query: How would the demand functions in Equations 5.10 change if this person spent half of income on each good? Show that these demand functions predict the same x consumption at the point $p_x = 1$, $p_y = 1$, $I = 100$ as does Equation 5.11. Use a numerical example to show that the CES demand function is more responsive to an increase in p_x than is the Cobb-Douglas demand function.

Compensated demand curves

In Figure 5.5, the level of utility this person gets varies along the demand curve. As p_x falls, he or she is made increasingly better off, as shown by the increase in utility from U_1 to U_2 to U_3. The reason this happens is that the demand curve is drawn on the assumption that *nominal* income and other prices are held constant; hence, a decline in p_x makes this person better off by increasing his or her real purchasing power. Although this is the most common way to impose the ceteris paribus assumption in developing a demand curve, it is not the only way. An alternative approach holds *real* income (or utility) constant while examining reactions to changes in p_x. The derivation is illustrated in Figure 5.6. There we hold utility constant (at U_2) while successively reducing p_x. As p_x falls, the individual's nominal income is effectively reduced, thus preventing any increase in utility. In other words, the effects of the price change on purchasing power are "compensated" so as to constrain the individual to remain on U_2. Reactions to changing prices include only substitution effects. If we were instead to examine effects of increases in p_x, income compensation would be positive: This individual's income would have to be in-

FIGURE 5.6   Construction of a Compensated Demand Curve

The curve h_x shows how the quantity of x demanded changes when p_x changes, holding p_y and *utility* constant. That is, the individual's income is "compensated" so as to keep utility constant. Hence, x^c reflects only substitution effects of changing prices.

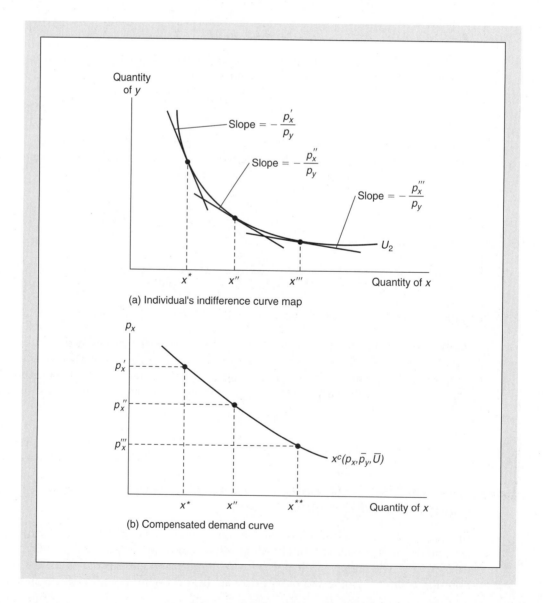

(a) Individual's indifference curve map

(b) Compensated demand curve

creased to permit him or her to stay on the U_2 indifference curve in response to the price rises. We can summarize these results as follows:

Compensated demand curve. A *compensated demand curve* shows the relationship between the price of a good and the quantity purchased on the assumption that other prices *and utility* are held constant. The curve (which is sometimes termed a "Hicksian" demand curve after the British economist John Hicks) therefore illustrates only substitution effects. Mathematically, the curve is a two-dimensional representation of the *compensated demand function*

$$x^* = x^c(p_x, p_y, U). \tag{5.14}$$

Relationship between compensated and uncompensated demand curves

This relationship between the two demand curve concepts we have developed is illustrated in Figure 5.7. At p_x'' the curves intersect, because at that price the individual's income is just sufficient to attain utility level U_2 (compare Figures 5.5 and 5.6). Hence, x'' is demanded under either demand concept. For prices below p_x'', however, the individual suffers a compensating reduction in income on the curve x^c to prevent an increase in utility from the lower price. Hence, assuming x is a normal good, less x is demanded at p_x'''

FIGURE 5.7   **Comparison of Compensated and Uncompensated Demand Curves**

The compensated (x^c) and uncompensated (x) demand curves intersect at p_x'' because x'' is demanded under each concept. For prices above p_x'', the individual's income is increased with the compensated demand curve, so more x is demanded than with the uncompensated curve. For prices below p_x'', income is reduced for the compensated curve, so less x is demanded than with the uncompensated curve. The standard demand curve is flatter because it incorporates both substitution and income effects whereas the curve x^c reflects only substitution effects.

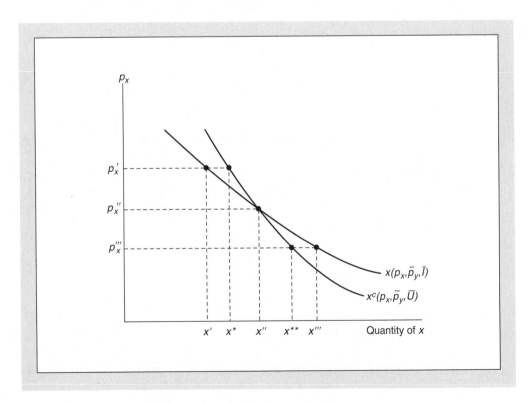

along x^c than along the uncompensated curve x. Alternatively, for a price above p_x'' (such as p_x'), income compensation is positive, because the individual needs some help to remain on U_2. Hence, again assuming x is a normal good, at p_x' more x is demanded along x^c than along x. In general then, for a normal good, the compensated demand curve is somewhat less responsive to price changes than is the uncompensated curve, because the latter reflects both substitution and income effects of price changes whereas the compensated curve reflects only substitution effects.

The choice between using compensated or uncompensated demand curves in economic analysis is largely a matter of convenience. In most empirical work uncompensated curves (which are sometimes called "Marshallian demand curves") are used because the data on prices and nominal incomes needed to estimate them are readily available. In the Extensions to Chapter 10 we will describe some of these estimates and show how they might be employed for practical policy purposes. For some theoretical purposes, however, compensated demand curves are a more appropriate concept, because the ability to hold utility constant offers some advantages. Our discussion of "consumer surplus" in the final section of this chapter offers one illustration of these advantages.

 EXAMPLE 5.3

Compensated Demand Functions

In Example 3.1, we assumed that the utility function for hamburgers (y) and soft drinks (x) was given by

$$\text{utility} = U(x, y) = x^{.5}y^{.5}, \qquad (5.15)$$

and in Example 4.1, we showed that we can calculate the Marshallian demand functions for such utility functions as

$$
\begin{aligned}
x &= \frac{\alpha I}{p_x} = \frac{I}{2p_x} \\
y &= \frac{\beta I}{p_y} = \frac{I}{2p_y}.
\end{aligned}
\qquad (5.16)
$$

Also, in Example 4.3, we calculated the indirect utility function by combining Equations 5.15 and 5.16 as

$$\text{utility} = V(I, p_x, p_y) = \frac{I}{2p_x^{.5}p_y^{.5}}. \qquad (5.17)$$

To obtain the compensated demand functions for x and y, we simply use Equation 5.17 to solve for I and then substitute this expression involving V into Equations 5.16. This permits us to interchange income and utility so we may hold the latter constant, as is required for the compensated demand concept. Making these substitutions yields

$$
\begin{aligned}
x &= \frac{Vp_y^{.5}}{p_x^{.5}} \\
y &= \frac{Vp_x^{.5}}{p_y^{.5}}.
\end{aligned}
\qquad (5.18)
$$

These are the compensated demand functions for x and y. Notice that now demand depends on utility (V) rather than on income. Holding utility constant, it is clear that increases in p_x reduce the demand for x—and this now reflects only the substitution effect (see Example 5.4 also).

Although p_y did not enter into the uncompensated demand function for good x, it does enter into the compensated function—increases in p_y shift the compensated demand curve for x outward. The two demand concepts agree at the assumed initial point $p_x = 1$, $p_y = 4$, $I = 8$, and $V = 2$—Equations 5.16 predict $x = 4$, $y = 1$ at this point as do Equations 5.18. For $p_x > 1$ or $p_x < 1$, the demands differ under the two concepts, however. If, say, $p_x = 4$, the uncompensated functions (Equations 5.16) predict $x = 1$, $y = 1$ whereas the compensated functions (Equations 5.18) predict $x = 2$, $y = 2$. The reduction in x resulting from the rise in its price is smaller with the compensated demand function than it is with the uncompensated function because the former concept adjusts for the negative effect on purchasing power that comes about from the price rise.

This example makes clear the different ceteris paribus assumptions inherent in the two demand concepts. With uncompensated demand, expenditures are held constant at $I = 2$ so the rise in p_x from 1 to 4 results in a loss of utility—in this case, utility falls from 2 to 1. In the compensated demand case, utility is held constant at $V = 2$. To keep utility constant, expenditures must rise to $E = 1(2) + 1(2) = 4$ in order to offset the effects of the price rise (see Equation 5.17).

Query: Are the compensated demand functions given in Equations 5.18 homogeneous of degree zero in p_x and p_y if utility is held constant? Would you expect that to be true for all compensated demand functions?

A mathematical development of response to price changes

Up to this point we have largely relied on graphical devices to describe how individuals respond to price changes. Additional insights are provided by a more mathematical approach. Our basic goal is to examine the partial derivative $\partial x / \partial p_x$; that is, how a ceteris paribus change in the price of a good affects its purchase. In the next chapter, we take up the question of how changes in the price of one commodity affect purchases of another commodity.

Direct approach

Our goal is to use the utility-maximization model to learn something about how the demand for good x changes when p_x changes; that is, we wish to calculate $\partial x / \partial p_x$. The direct approach to this problem makes use of the first-order conditions for utility maximization (Equations 4.8). Differentiation of these $n + 1$ equations yields a new system of $n + 1$ equations, which eventually can be solved for the derivative we seek.[3] Unfortunately, obtaining this solution is quite cumbersome and the steps required yield little in the way of economic insights. Hence, we will instead adopt an indirect approach that relies on the concept of duality. In the end, both approaches yield the same conclusion, but the indirect approach is much richer in terms of the economics it contains.

Indirect approach

To begin our indirect approach[4] we will assume (as before) there are only two goods (x and y) and focus on the compensated demand function, $x^c(p_x, p_y, U)$, introduced in Equation 5.14. We now wish to illustrate the connection between this demand function and the ordinary demand

[3]See, for example, Paul A. Samuelson, *Foundations of Economic Analysis* (Cambridge, MA: Harvard University Press, 1947), pp. 101–3.

[4]The following proof is adapted from Phillip J. Cook, "A 'One Line' Proof of the Slutsky Equation," *American Economic Review 62* (March 1972): 139.

function, $x(p_x, p_y, I)$. In Chapter 4 we introduced the expenditure function, which records the minimal expenditure necessary to attain a given utility level. If we denote this function by

$$\text{minimum expenditure} = E(p_x, p_y, U), \tag{5.19}$$

then by definition,

$$x^c(p_x, p_y, U) = x[p_x, p_y, E(p_x, p_y, U)]. \tag{5.20}$$

This conclusion was already introduced in connection with Figure 5.7, which showed that the quantity demanded is identical for the compensated and uncompensated demand functions when income is exactly what is needed to attain the required utility level. Equation 5.20 is obtained by inserting that expenditure level into the demand function, $x(p_x, p_y, I)$. Now we can proceed by partially differentiating Equation 5.20 with respect to p_x and recognizing that this variable enters into the ordinary demand function in two places. Hence,

$$\frac{\partial x^c}{\partial p_x} = \frac{\partial x}{\partial p_x} + \frac{\partial x}{\partial E} \cdot \frac{\partial E}{\partial p_x}, \tag{5.21}$$

and rearranging terms,

$$\frac{\partial x}{\partial p_x} = \frac{\partial x^c}{\partial p_x} - \frac{\partial x}{\partial E} \cdot \frac{\partial E}{\partial p_x}. \tag{5.22}$$

The substitution effect

Consequently, the derivative we seek has two terms. Interpretation of the first term is straightforward: It is the slope of the compensated demand curve. But that slope represents movement along a single indifference curve—it is in fact what we called the "substitution effect" earlier. The first term on the right of Equation 5.22 is a mathematical representation of that effect.

The income effect

The second term in Equation 5.22 reflects the way in which changes in p_x affect the demand for x through changes in necessary expenditure levels (that is, changes in purchasing power). This term therefore reflects the income effect. The negative sign in Equation 5.22 shows the direction of the effect. For example, an increase in p_x increases the expenditure level that would have been needed to keep utility constant (mathematically, $\partial E / \partial p_x > 0$). But because nominal income is in fact held constant in Marshallian demand, these extra expenditures are not available. Hence x (and y) must be reduced to meet this shortfall. The extent of the reduction in x is given by $\partial x / \partial E$. On the other hand, if p_x falls, the expenditure level required to attain a given utility falls too. The decline in x that would normally accompany such a fall in expenditures is precisely the amount that must be added back through the income effect. Notice that in this case the income effect works to increase x.

The Slutsky equation

The relationships embodied in Equation 5.22 were first discovered by the Russian economist Eugen Slutsky in the late nineteenth century. A slight change in notation is required to state the result the way Slutsky did. First, we write the substitution effect as

$$\text{substitution effect} = \frac{\partial x^c}{\partial p_x} = \frac{\partial x}{\partial p_x}\Big|_{U=\text{constant}} \tag{5.23}$$

to indicate movement along a single indifference curve. For the income effect we have

$$\text{income effect} = -\frac{\partial x}{\partial E} \cdot \frac{\partial E}{\partial p_x} = -\frac{\partial x}{\partial I} \cdot \frac{\partial E}{\partial p_x}, \tag{5.24}$$

because changes in income or expenditures amount to the same thing in the function $x(p_x, p_y, I)$.

It is a relatively easy matter to show that

$$\frac{\partial E}{\partial p_x} = x. \tag{5.25}$$

Intuitively, a \$1 increase in p_x raises necessary expenditures by x dollars, because \$1 extra must be paid for each unit of x purchased. A formal proof of this assertion, which relies on the envelope theorem (see Chapter 2), will be relegated to a footnote.[5]

By combining Equations 5.23–5.25 we can arrive at the following:

OPTIMIZATION PRINCIPLE

Slutsky equation. The utility-maximization hypothesis shows that the substitution and income effects arising from a price change can be represented by

$$\frac{\partial x}{\partial p_x} = \text{substitution effect} + \text{income effect}, \tag{5.26}$$

or

$$\frac{\partial x}{\partial p_x} = \frac{\partial x}{\partial p_x}\bigg|_{U=\text{constant}} - x\,\frac{\partial x}{\partial I}. \tag{5.27}$$

The Slutsky equation allows a more definitive treatment of the direction and size of substitution and income effects than was possible with only a graphic analysis. First, the substitution effect ($\partial x/\partial p_x |\, U = \text{constant}$) is always negative as long as the *MRS* is diminishing. A fall (rise) in p_x reduces (increases) p_x/p_y, and utility maximization requires that the *MRS* fall (rise) too. But this can only occur along an indifference curve if x increases (or, in the case of a rise in p_x, x decreases). Hence, insofar as the substitution effect is concerned, price and quantity always move in opposite directions. Equivalently, the slope of the compensated demand curve must be negative.[6] We will show this result in a somewhat different way in the final section to this chapter.

The sign of the income effect ($-x\partial x/\partial I$) depends on the sign of $\partial x/\partial I$. If x is a normal good, $\partial x/\partial I$ is positive and the entire income effect, like the substitution effect, is negative. Thus for normal goods, price and quantity always move in opposite directions. For example, a fall in p_x raises real income, and because x is a normal good, purchases of x rise. Similarly, a rise in p_x reduces real income and purchases of x fall. Overall then, as we described previously using a graphic analysis, substitution and income effects work in the same direction to yield a negatively sloped demand curve. In the case of an inferior good, $\partial x/\partial I < 0$ and the two terms in Equation 5.27 would have different signs. It is at least theoretically possible that in this case the second term could dominate the first, leading to Giffen's paradox ($\partial d_x/\partial p_x > 0$).

---

[5]Remember that the individual's dual problem is to minimize $E = p_x x + p_y y$, subject to $\bar{U} = U(x, y)$. The Lagrangian expression for this prolem is

$$\mathcal{L} = p_x x + p_y y + \lambda[\,\bar{U} - U(x,y)\,],$$

and the envelope theorem applied to constrained minimization problems states that at the optimal point,

$$\frac{\partial E}{\partial p_x} = \frac{\partial \mathcal{L}}{\partial p_x} = x.$$

This is the result in Equation 5.25. The result, and similar ones that we will encounter in the theory of firms' costs, is sometimes called *Shephard's lemma*. Its importance in empirical work is that the *demand function* for good x can be found directly from the expenditure function by simple partial differentiation. The demand functions generated in this way will depend on $\bar{U}$, so they should be interpreted as compensated demand functions. In Example 4.4 we found that the expenditure function was

$$E = 2\, V p_x^{.5} p_y^{.5}.$$

Partial differentiation of this expression with respect to p_x yields the compensated demand function in Equations 5.18. For a further discussion, see the Extensions to this chapter.

[6]It is possible that substitution effects would be 0 if indifference curves have an L-shape (implying that x and y are used in fixed proportions). Some examples are provided in the Chapter 5 problems.

EXAMPLE 5.4

A Slutsky Decomposition

The decomposition of a price effect that was first discovered by Slutsky can be nicely illustrated with the Cobb-Douglas example studied previously. In Example 5.3 we found that the Marshallian demand function for good x was

$$x(p_x, p_y, I) = \frac{0.5I}{p_x}, \tag{5.28}$$

and the Hicksian (compensated) demand function was

$$x^c(p_x, p_y, V) = \frac{Vp_y^{0.5}}{p_x^{0.5}}. \tag{5.29}$$

The overall effect of a price change on the demand for good x can be found by differentiating the Marshallian demand function:

$$\frac{\partial x}{\partial p_x} = \frac{-0.5I}{p_x^2}. \tag{5.30}$$

Now we wish to show that this effect is the sum of the two effects that Slutsky identified. As before, the substitution effect is found by differentiating the compensated demand function:

$$\textbf{substitution effect} = \frac{\partial x^c}{\partial p_x} = \frac{-0.5Vp_y^{0.5}}{p_x^{1.5}}. \tag{5.31}$$

We can eliminate indirect utility, V, by substitution from Equation 5.17:

$$\textbf{substitution effect} = \frac{-0.5(0.5Ip_x^{-0.5}p_y^{-0.5})p_y^{0.5}}{p_x^{1.5}} = \frac{-0.25I}{p_x^2}. \tag{5.32}$$

Calculation of the income effect in this example is considerably easier. Applying the results from Equation 5.27 we have

$$\textbf{income effect} = -x\frac{\partial x}{\partial I} = -\left[\frac{0.5I}{p_x}\right] \cdot \frac{0.5}{p_x} = -\frac{0.25I}{p_x^2}. \tag{5.33}$$

A comparison of Equations 5.30 with Equations 5.32 and 5.33 shows that we have indeed decomposed the price derivative of this demand function into substitution and income components. Interestingly, the substitution and income effects are of precisely the same size. This, as we will see in later examples, is one of the reasons that the Cobb-Douglas is a very special case.

The well-worn numerical example we have been using also demonstrates this decomposition. When the price of x rises from \$1 to \$4, the (uncompensated) demand for x falls from $x = 4$ to $x = 1$. But the compensated demand for x falls only from $x = 4$ to $x = 2$. That decline of 50 percent is the substitution effect. The further 50 percent fall from $x = 2$ to $x = 1$ represents reactions to the decline in purchasing power incorporated in Marshallian demand function. This income effect does not occur when the compensated demand notion is used.

Query: In this example the individual spends half his or her income on good x and half on good y. How would the relative sizes of the substitution and income effects be altered if the exponents of the Cobb-Douglas utility function were not equal?

Demand elasticities

So far in this chapter we have been examining how individuals respond to changes in prices and income by looking at the derivatives of the demand function. For many analytical questions this is a good way to proceed because calculus methods can be directly applied. However, as we pointed out in Chapter 2, focusing on derivatives has one major disadvantage for empirical work—the size of derivatives depends directly on how variables are measured. That can make comparisons among goods or across countries and time periods very difficult. For this reason, most empirical work in microeconomics uses some form of elasticity measure. In this section we introduce the three most common types of demand elasticities and explore some of the methematical relations among them. Again, for simplicity, we will look at a situation where the individual chooses between only two goods, though these ideas can be easily generalized.

Marshallian demand elasticities

Most of the commonly used demand elasticities are derived from the Marshallian demand function $x(p_x, p_y, I)$. Specifically, the following definitions are used:

DEFINITION

1. *Price elasticity of demand* (e_{x,p_x}): This measures the proportionate change in quantity demanded in response to a proportionate change in a good's own price. Mathematically,

$$e_{x,p_x} = \frac{\Delta x / x}{\Delta p_x / p_x} = \frac{\Delta x}{\Delta p_x} \cdot \frac{p_x}{x} = \frac{\partial x}{\partial p_x} \cdot \frac{p_x}{x}. \qquad (5.34)$$

2. *Income elasticity of demand* $(e_{x,I})$: This measures the proportionate change in quantity demanded in response to a proportionate change in income. In mathematical terms,

$$e_{x,I} = \frac{\Delta x / x}{\Delta I / I} = \frac{\Delta x}{\Delta I} \cdot \frac{I}{x} = \frac{\partial x}{\partial I} \cdot \frac{I}{x}. \qquad (5.35)$$

3. *Cross-price elasticity of demand* (e_{x,p_y}): This measures the proportionate change in the quantity of x demanded in response to a proportionate change in the price of some other good (y):

$$e_{x,p_y} = \frac{\Delta x / x}{\Delta p_y / p_y} = \frac{\Delta x}{\Delta p_y} \cdot \frac{p_y}{x} = \frac{\partial x}{\partial p_y} \cdot \frac{p_y}{x}. \qquad (5.36)$$

Notice that all of these definitions use partial derivatives thereby signifying that all other determinants of demand are to be held constant when examining the impact of a specific variable. In the remainder of this section we will explore the own price elasticity definition in some detail. Examining the cross-price elasticity of demand is the primary topic of Chapter 6.

Price elasticity of demand

The (own) price elasticity of demand is probably the most important elasticity concept in all of microeconomics. Not only does it provide a convenient way of summarizing how people respond to price changes for a wide variety of economic goods, but it is also a central concept in the theory of how firms react to the demand curves facing them. As you probably already learned in earlier economics courses, a distinction is usually made between cases of elastic demand (where price affects quantity significantly) and inelastic demand (where the effect of price is small). One mathematical complication in making these ideas precise is that the price elasticity of demand itself is negative[7] because, except in the

---

[7]Sometimes economists use the absolute value of the price elasticity of demand in their discussions. Although this is mathematically incorrect, such usage is quite common. For example, a study that finds that $e_{x,p_x} = -1.2$ may sometimes report the price elasticity of demand as "1.2."

unlikely case of Giffen's paradox, $\partial x/\partial p_x$ is negative. The dividing line between large and small responses is generally set at -1. If $e_{x,p_x} = -1$, changes in x and p_x are of the same proportionate size. That is, a 1 percent increase in price leads to a fall of 1 percent in quantity demanded. In this case demand is said to be "unit-elasic." Alternatively, if $e_{x,p_x} < -1$ quantity changes are proportionately larger than price changes and we say that demand is "elastic." For example, if $e_{x,p_x} = -3$, each 1 percent rise in price leads to a fall of 3 percent in quantity demanded. Finally, if $e_{x,p_x} > -1$, demand is inelastic—quantity changes are proportionately smaller than price changes. A value of $e_{x,p_x} = -0.3$, for example, means that a 1 percent increase in price leads to a fall in quantity demanded of 0.3 percent. In Chapters 10 and 11 we will see how aggregate data are used to estimate the typical individual's price elasticity of demand for a good and how such estimates are used in a variety of questions in applied microeconomics.

Price elasticity and total spending

The price elasticity of demand determines how a change in price, ceteris paribus, affects total spending on a good. The connection is most easily shown with calculus:

$$\frac{\partial(p_x \cdot x)}{\partial p_x} = p_x \cdot \frac{\partial x}{\partial p_x} + x = x[e_{x,p_x} + 1].$$ (5.37)

So, the sign of this derivative depends on whether e_{x,p_x} is larger or smaller than -1. If demand is inelastic $(0 > e_{x,p_x} > -1)$, the derivative is positive and price and total spending move in the same direction. Intuitively, if price does not affect quantity demanded very much, quantity stays relatively constant as price changes and total spending reflects mainly those price movements. This is the case, for example, for the demand for most agricultural products. Weather-induced changes in price for specific crops usually cause total spending on those crops to move in the same direction. On the other hand, if demand is elastic $(e_{x,p_x} < -1)$ reaction to a price change are so large that the effect on total spending is reversed—a rise in price causes total spending to fall (because quantity falls a lot) and a fall in price causes total spending to rise (quantity increases significantly). For the unit-elastic case $(e_{x,p_x} = -1)$ total spending is constant no matter how price changes.

Compensated price elasticities

Because some microeconomic analyses focus on the compensated demand function, it is also useful to define elasticities based on that concept. Such definitions follow directly from their Marshallian counterparts:

DEFINITION

If the compensated demand function is given by $x^c(p_x, p_y, U)$ we define:

1. *Compensated own price elasticity of demand* (e_{x^c,p_x}): This elasticity measures the proportionate compensated change in quantity demanded in response to a proportionate change in a good's own price:

$$e_{x^c,p_x} = \frac{\Delta x^c / x^c}{\Delta p_x / p_x} = \frac{\Delta x^c}{\Delta p_x} \cdot \frac{p_x}{x^c} = \frac{\partial x^c}{\partial p_x} \cdot \frac{p_x}{x^c}.$$ (5.38)

2. *Compensated cross-price elasticity of demand* (e_{x^c,p_x}): This measures the proportionate compensated change in quantity demanded in response to a proportionate change in the price of another good:

$$e_{x^c,p_y} = \frac{\Delta x^c / x^c}{\Delta p_y / p_y} = \frac{\Delta x^c}{\Delta p_y} \cdot \frac{p_y}{x^c} = \frac{\partial x^c}{\partial p_y} \cdot \frac{p_y}{x^c}.$$ (5.39)

Whether these price elasticities differ very much from their Marshallian counterparts depends on the importance of income compensation in the overall demand for good x. The precise connection between the two can be shown by multiplying the Slutsky result from Equation 5.27 by the factor p_x/x:

$$\frac{p_x}{x} \cdot \frac{\partial x}{\partial p_x} = e_{x,p_x} = \frac{p_x}{x} \cdot \frac{\partial x^c}{\partial p_x} - \frac{p_x}{x} \cdot x \cdot \frac{\partial x}{\partial I} = e_{x^c,p_x} - s_x e_{x,I}, \qquad (5.40)$$

where $s_x = \frac{p_x x}{I}$ is the share of total income devoted to the purchase of good x.

Equation 5.40 therefore shows that compensated and uncompensated own price elasticities of demand will be similar if either of two conditions hold: (1) The share of income devoted to good x (s_x) is small; or (2) The income elasticity of demand for good x ($e_{x,I}$) is small. Either of these conditions serves to reduce the importance of the income compensation employed in the construction of the compensated demand function. If good x is unimportant in a person's budget, the amount of income compensation required to offset a price change will be small. Even if a good is important in the budget, if a person does not react very strongly to compensating changes in income, results of either demand concept will be similar. Hence, there will be many circumstances where one can use the two price elasticity concepts more or less interchangeably. Put another way, there are many economic circumstances in which substitution effects constitute the most important component of price responses.

Relationships among demand elasticities

There are a number of relationships among the elasticity concepts that have been developed in this section. All of these are derived from the underlying model of utility maximization. Here we look at three such relationships that provide further insight on the nature of individual demand.

Homogeneity. The homogeneity of demand functions can also be expressed in elasticity terms. Because any proportional increase in all prices and income leaves quantity demanded unchanged, the net sum of all price elasticities together with the income elasticity for a particular good must sum to zero. A formal proof of this property relies on Euler's theorem (see Chapter 2). Applying that theorem to the demand function $x(p_x, p_y, I)$ and remembering that this function is homogeneous of degree zero yields

$$0 = p_x \cdot \frac{\partial x}{\partial p_x} + p_y \cdot \frac{\partial x}{\partial p_y} + I \cdot \frac{\partial x}{\partial I}. \qquad (5.41)$$

If we simply divide Equation 5.41 by x we get

$$0 = e_{x,p_x} + e_{x,p_y} + e_{x,I} \qquad (5.42)$$

as intuition suggests. This result shows that the elasticities of demand for any good can not follow a completely flexible pattern. They must exhibit a sort of internal consistency that reflects the basic utility-maximizing approach on which the theory of demand is based.

Engel aggregation

In the Extensions to Chapter 4 we discussed the empirical analysis of market shares and took special note of Engel's law—that the share of income devoted to food declines as income increases. From an elasticity perspective, Engel's law is a statement of the empirical regularity that the income elasticity of demand for food is generally found to be considerably less than one. Because of this, it must be the case that the income elasticity of all nonfood items must be greater than one. If an individual experiences an increase in his or her income we would expect food expenditures to increase by a smaller proportional amount, but the income must be spent somewhere. In the aggregate, these other expenditures must increase proportionally faster than income.

A more formal statement of this property of income elasticities can be derived by differentiating the individual's budget constraint ($I = p_x x + p_y y$) with respect to income while treating the prices as constants:

$$1 = p_x \cdot \frac{\partial x}{\partial I} + p_y \cdot \frac{\partial y}{\partial I}. \tag{5.43}$$

A bit of algebraic manipulation of this expression yields

$$1 = p_x \cdot \frac{\partial x}{\partial I} \cdot \frac{xI}{xI} + p_y \cdot \frac{\partial y}{\partial I} \cdot \frac{yI}{yI} = s_x e_{x,I} + s_y e_{y,I}, \tag{5.44}$$

where, as before, s_i represents the share of income spent on good i. Equation 5.44 shows that the weighted average on income elasticities for all goods that a person buys must be one. If we knew, say, that a person spent one-fourth of income on food and the income elasticity of demand for food were 0.5, the income elasticity of demand for everything else must be approximately 1.17 [= (1 − 0.25 · 0.5)/0.75]. Because food is an important "necessity," everything else is in some sense a "luxury."

Cournot aggregation. The eighteenth-century French economist Antoine Cournot provided one of the first mathematical analyses of price changes using calculus. His most important discovery was the concept of marginal revenue—a concept central to the profit-maximization hypothesis for firms. Cournot was also concerned with how the change in a single price might affect the demand for all goods. Our final relationship shows that there is indeed a connection among all of the reactions to the change in a single price. We begin by differentiating the budget constraint again, this time with respect to, say, p_x:

$$\frac{\partial I}{\partial p_x} = 0 = p_x \cdot \frac{\partial x}{\partial p_x} + x + p_y \cdot \frac{\partial y}{\partial p_x}.$$

Multiplication of this equation by p_x/I yields

$$0 = p_x \cdot \frac{\partial x}{\partial p_x} \cdot \frac{p_x}{I} \cdot \frac{x}{x} + x \cdot \frac{p_x}{I} + p_y \cdot \frac{\partial y}{\partial p_x} \cdot \frac{p_x}{I} \cdot \frac{y}{y} \tag{5.45}$$

$$0 = s_x e_{x,p_x} + s_x + s_y e_{y,p_x},$$

so the final Cournot result is

$$s_x e_{x,p_x} + s_y e_{y,p_x} = -s_x. \tag{5.46}$$

This equation shows that the size of the cross-price effect of a change in the price of x on the quantity of y consumed is restricted because of the budget constraint. Direct, own price effects cannot be totally overwhelmed by cross-price effects. This is the first of many connections among the demands for goods that we will study more intensively in the next chapter.

Generalizations. Although we have shown these aggregation results only for the case of two goods, they are in fact easily generalized to the case of many goods. You are asked to do just that in Problem 5.9. A more difficult issue is whether these results should be expected to hold in typical economic data in which the demands of many people are combined. Often economists treat aggregate demand relationships as describing the behavior of a "typical person," and these relationships should in fact hold for such a person. But the situation may not be quite that simple, as we will show when we discuss aggregation later in this book.

EXAMPLE 5.5

Demand Elasticities: The Importance of Substitution Effects

In this example we calculate the demand elasticities implied by three of the utility functions we have been using. Although the possibilities incorporated in these functions are too simple to reflect how economists actually study demand empirically, they do show how elasticities ultimately reflect peoples' preferences. One especially important lesson is to show why most of the variation in demand elasticities among goods probably arises because of differences in the size of substitution effects.

Case 1. Cobb-Douglas ($\sigma = 1$): $U(x, y) = x^\alpha y^\beta$ where $\alpha + \beta = 1$.

The demand functions derived from this utility function are

$$x(p_x, p_y, I) = \frac{\alpha I}{p_x}$$

$$y(p_x, p_y, I) = \frac{\beta I}{p_y} = \frac{(1 - \alpha)I}{p_y}$$

Application of the elasticity definitions shows that

$$e_{x,p_x} = \frac{\partial x}{\partial p_x} \cdot \frac{p_x}{x} = \frac{-\alpha I}{p_x^2} \cdot \frac{p_x}{\frac{\alpha I}{p_x}} = -1$$

$$e_{x,p_y} = \frac{\partial x}{\partial p_y} \cdot \frac{p_y}{x} = 0 \cdot \frac{p_y}{x} = 0 \qquad\qquad (5.47)$$

$$e_{x,I} = \frac{\partial x}{\partial I} \cdot \frac{I}{x} = \frac{\alpha}{p_x} \cdot \frac{I}{\frac{\alpha I}{p_x}} = 1.$$

The elasticities for good y take on analogous values. Hence, the elasticities associated with the Cobb-Douglas utility function are constant over all ranges of prices and income and take on especially simple values. That these obey the three relationships shown in the previous section can be easily demonstrated using the fact that here $s_x = \alpha$, $s_y = \beta$.

Homogeneity: $e_{x,p_x} + e_{x,p_y} + e_{x,I} = -1 + 0 + 1 = 0$.

Engel Aggregation: $s_x e_{x,I} + s_y e_{y,I} = \alpha \cdot 1 + \beta \cdot 1 = \alpha + \beta = 1$.

Cournot Aggregation: $s_x e_{x,p_x} + s_y e_{y,p_x} = \alpha(-1) + \beta \cdot 0 = -\alpha = -s_x$.

We can also use the Slutsky equation in elasticity form (Equation 5.40) to derive the compensated price elasticity in this example:

$$e_{x^c,p_x} = e_{x,p_x} + s_x e_{x,I} = -1 + \alpha(1) = \alpha - 1 = -\beta. \qquad (5.48)$$

So here the compensated price elasticity for x depends on how important other goods (y) are in the utility function.

(continued)

EXAMPLE 5.5 CONTINUED

Case 2. CES ($\sigma = 2$; $\delta = 0.5$): $U(x, y) = x^{0.5} + y^{0.5}$

In Example 4.2 we showed that the demand functions that can be derived from this utility function are

$$x(p_x, p_y, I) = \frac{I}{p_x(1 + p_x p_y^{-1})}$$

$$y(p_x, p_y, I) = \frac{I}{p_y(1 + p_x^{-1} p_y)}.$$

As you might imagine, calculating elasticities directly from these functions can take some time. Here we focus only on the own price elasticity and make use of the result (from Problem 5.6) that the "share elasticity" of any good is given by

$$e_{s_x, p_x} = \frac{\partial s_x}{\partial p_x} \cdot \frac{p_x}{s_x} = 1 + e_{x, p_x}. \tag{5.49}$$

In this case,

$$s_x = \frac{p_x x}{I} = \frac{1}{1 + p_x p_y^{-1}},$$

so the share elasticity is more easily calculated and is given by

$$e_{s_x, p_x} = \frac{\partial s_x}{\partial p_x} \cdot \frac{p_x}{s_x} = \frac{-p_y^{-1}}{(1 + p_x p_y^{-1})^2} \cdot \frac{p_x}{(1 + p_x p_y^{-1})^{-1}} = \frac{-p_x p_y^{-1}}{1 + p_x p_y^{-1}}. \tag{5.50}$$

Because the units in which goods are measured are rather arbitrary in utility theory, we might as well define them so that initially $p_x = p_y$, in which case[8] we get

$$e_{x, p_x} = e_{s_x, p_x} - 1 = \frac{-1}{1 + 1} - 1 = -1.5. \tag{5.51}$$

So, demand is more elastic in this case than in the Cobb-Douglas example. The reason for this is that the substitution effect is larger for this version of the CES utility function. This can be shown by again applying the Slutsky equation (and using the facts that $e_{x, I} = 1$ and $s_x = 0.5$):

$$e_{x^c, p_x} = e_{x, p_x} + s_x e_{x, I} = -1.5 + 0.5(1) = -1, \tag{5.52}$$

which is twice the size of the substitution effect for the Cobb-Douglas.

Case 3. CES ($\sigma = 0.5$; $\delta = -1$): $U(x, y) = -x^{-1} - y^{-1}$

Referring back to Example 4.2 we can see that the share of good x implied by this utility function is given by

$$s_x = \frac{1}{1 + p_y^{0.5} p_x^{-0.5}},$$

so the share elasticity is given by

$$e_{s_x, p_x} = \frac{\partial s_x}{\partial p_x} \cdot \frac{p_x}{s_x} = \frac{0.5 p_y^{0.5} p_x^{-1.5}}{(1 + p_y^{0.5} p_x^{-0.5})^2} \cdot \frac{p_x}{(1 + p_y^{0.5} p_x^{-0.5})^{-1}} = \frac{0.5 p_y^{0.5} p_x^{-0.5}}{1 + p_y^{0.5} p_x^{-0.5}}. \tag{5.53}$$

---

[8]Notice that making this substitution must be done after differentiation because the definition of elasticity requires that we change only p_x while holding p_y constant.

If we again adopt the simplification of equal prices, we can compute the own price elasticity as

$$e_{x,p_x} = e_{s_x,p_x} - 1 = \frac{0.5}{2} - 1 = -0.75 \qquad (5.54)$$

and the compensated price elasticity as

$$e_{x^c,p_x} = e_{x,p_x} + s_x e_{x,I} = -0.75 + 0.5(1) = -0.25. \qquad (5.55)$$

So, for this version of the CES utility function, the own price elasticity is smaller than in the cases 1 and 2 because the substitution effect is smaller. Hence, the main variation among the cases is indeed caused by differences in the size of the substitution effect.

If you never want to work out this kind of elasticity again, it may be helpful to make use of the quite general result that

$$e_{x^c,p_x} = -(1 - s_x)\sigma. \qquad (5.56)$$

You may wish to check out that this formula works in these three examples (with $s_x = 0.5$ and $\sigma = 1, 2, 0.5$ respectively), and Problem 5.6 asks you to show that this result is generally true. Because all of these cases based on the CES utility function have a unitary income elasticity, the own price elasticity can be computed from the compensated price elasticity by simply adding $-s_x$ to the figure computed in Equation 5.56.

Query: Why is it that the budget share for goods other than x enters into the compensated own price elasticities in this example?

Consumer surplus

An important problem in applied welfare economics is to devise a monetary measure of the gains and losses that individuals experience when prices change. One use for such a measure is to place a dollar value on the welfare loss that people experience when a market is monopolized with prices exceeding marginal costs. Another application concerns measuring the welfare gains the people experience when technical progress reduces the prices they pay for goods. Related applications occur in environmental economics (measuring the welfare costs of incorrectly priced resources), law and economics (evaluating the welfare costs of excess protections taken in fear of lawsuits), and public economics (measuring the excess burden of a tax). In order to make such calculations, economists use empirical data from studies of market demand in combination with the theory that underlies that demand. In this section we will examine the primary tools used in that process.

Consumer welfare and the expenditure function

The expenditure function that we developed in Chapter 4 provides the first component for the study of the price/welfare connection. Suppose that we wished to measure the change in welfare that an individual experiences if the price of good x rises from p_x^0 to p_x^1. Initially this person requires expenditures of $E(p_x^0, p_y, U_0)$ to reach a utility of U_0. To achieve the same utility once the price of x rises, he or she would require spending of at least $E(p_x^1, p_y, U_0)$. In order to compensate for the price rise, therefore, this person would require a compensation (formally called a *compensating variation—CV*) of

$$CV = E(p_x^1, p_y, U_0) - E(p_x^0, p_y, U_0). \qquad (5.57)$$

This situation is shown graphically in the top panel of Figure 5.8. Initially this person consumes the combination x_0, y_0 and obtains utility of U_0. When the price of x rises, he or

FIGURE 5.8   **Showing Compensating Variation**

If the price of x rises from p_x^0 to p_x^1 this person needs extra expenditures of CV to remain on the U_0 indifference curve. Integration shows that CV can also be represented by the shaded area below the compensated demand curve in panel (b).

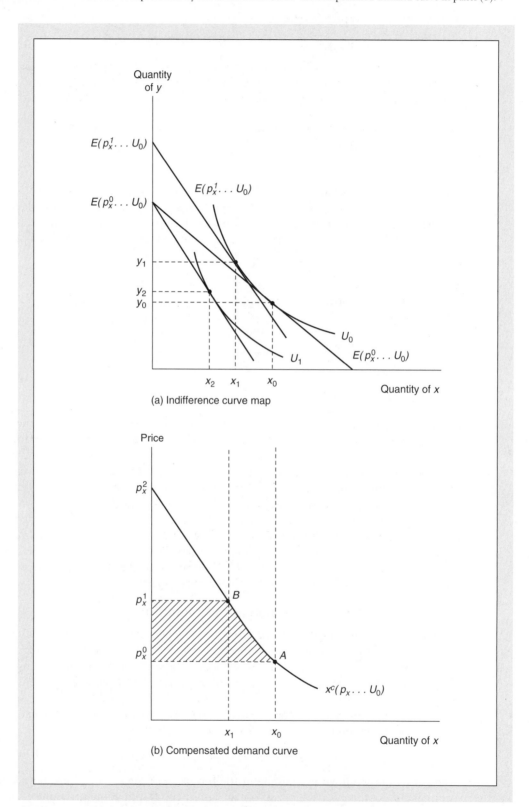

(a) Indifference curve map

(b) Compensated demand curve

she would be forced to move to combination x_2, y_2 and suffer a loss in utility. If he or she were compensated with extra purchasing power of amount CV, he or she could afford to remain on the U_0 indifference curve despite the price rise by choosing combination x_1, y_1. The distance CV, therefore, provides a monetary measure of how much this person needs if he or she is to be compensated for the price rise.

Using the compensated demand curve to show CV

Unfortunately, individuals' utility functions and their associated indifference curve maps are not directly observable. But we can make some headway on empirical measurement by determining how the CV amount can be shown on the compensated demand curve in the bottom panel of Figure 5.8. In footnote 5 of this chapter we described Shephard's lemma which uses the envelope theorem to show that the compensated demand function for a good can be found directly from the expenditure function by differentiation:

$$x^c(p_x, p_y, U) = \frac{\partial E(p_x, p_y, U)}{\partial p_x}. \tag{5.58}$$

Hence, the compensation described in Equation 5.57 can be found by integrating across a sequence of small increments to price from p_x^0 to p_x^1:

$$CV = \int_{p_x^0}^{p_x^1} dE = \int_{p_x^0}^{p_x^1} x^c(p_x, p_y, U_0) dp_x \tag{5.59}$$

while holding p_y and utility constant. The integral defined in Equation 5.59 has a geometric interpretation than can be shown in the lower panel of Figure 5.9—it is the shaded area to the left of the compensated demand curve and bounded by p_x^0 and p_x^1. So the welfare cost of this price increase can also be illustrated using areas below the compensated demand curve.

The consumer surplus concept

There is another way to look at this issue. We can ask how much this person would be willing to pay for the right to consume all of this good that he or she wanted at the market price of p_x^0 rather than doing without the good completely. The compensated demand curve in the bottom panel of Figure 5.8 shows that if the price of x rose to p_x^2 this person's consumption would fall to zero and he or she would require an amount of compensation equal to area $p_x^2 A p_x^0$ in order to accept the change voluntarily. The right to consume x_0 at a price of p_x^0 is therefore worth this amount to this individual. It is the extra benefit that this person receives by being able to make market transactions at the prevailing market price. This value, given by the area below the compensated demand curve and above the market price is termed *consumer surplus*. Looked at in this way, the welfare problem caused by a rise in the price of x can be described as a loss in consumer surplus. When the price rises from p_x^0 to p_x^1 the consumer surplus "triangle" declines in value from $p_x^2 A p_x^0$ to $p_x^2 B p_x^1$. As the figure makes clear, that is simply another way of describing the welfare loss represented in Equation 5.59.

Welfare changes and the Marshallian demand curve

So far our analysis of the welfare effects of price changes has focused on the compensated demand curve. This is in some ways unfortunate because most empirical work on demand actually estimates ordinary (Marshallian) demand curves. In this section we will show that studying changes in the area below such a demand curve may in fact be quite a good way to measure welfare losses.

Consider the Marshallian demand curve $x(p_x \ldots)$ illustrated in Figure 5.9. Initially this consumer faces the price p_x^0 and chooses to consume x_0. This consumption yields a utility level of U_0, and the initial compensated demand curve for x [that is, $x^c(p_x, p_y, U_0)$] also passes through the point x_0, p_x^0 (which we have labeled point A). When price rises to p_x^1, the Marshallian demand for good x falls to x_1 (point C on the demand curve) and this

FIGURE 5.9	Welfare Effects of Price Changes and the Marshallian Demand Curve

$x(p_x \ldots)$ is the usual Marshallian (nominal income constant) demand curve for good x. $x^c(\ldots U_0)$ and $x^c(\ldots U_1)$ denote the compensated demand curves associated with the utility levels experienced when p_x^0 and p_x^1, respectively, prevail. The area to the left of $x(p_x \ldots)$ between p_x^0 and p_x^1 is bounded by the similar areas to the left of the compensated demand curves. Hence, for small changes in price, the area to the left of the Marshallian demand curve is a good measure of welfare loss.

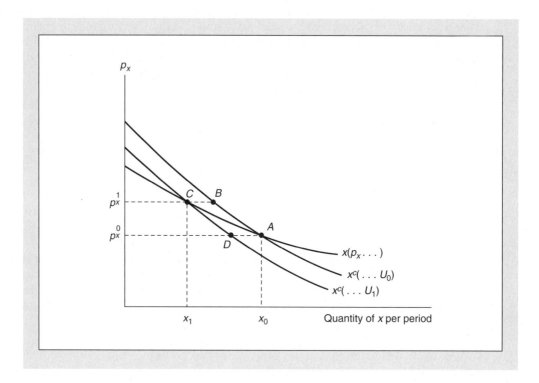

person's utility also falls to, say, U_1. There is another compensated demand curve associated with this lower level of utility, and it also is shown in Figure 5.9. Both the Marshallian demand curve and this new compensated demand curve pass through point C.

The presence of a second compensated demand curve in Figure 5.9 raises an intriguing conceptual question. Should we measure the welfare loss from the price rise as we did in Figure 5.8 using the compensating variation (CV) associated with the initial compensated demand curve (area $p_x^1 BA p_x^0$) or should we, perhaps, use this new compensated demand curve and measure the welfare loss as area $p_x^1 CD p_x^0$? A potential rationale for using the area under the second curve would be to focus on the individual's situation after the price rise (with utility level U_1). We might then ask how much he or she would be willing to pay to see the price return back to its old, lower levels.[9] The answer to this would be given by area $p_x^1 CD p_x^0$. The choice between which compensated demand curve to use therefore boils down to choosing which level of utility one regards as the appropriate target.

Luckily, the Marshallian demand curve provides a convenient compromise between these two positions. Because the size of the area between the two prices and below the Marshallian curve (area $p_x^1 CA p_x^0$) is smaller than that below the compensated demand curve based on U_0 but larger than that below the curve based on U_1, it does seem an attractive middle ground. Hence, this is the measure of welfare losses we will use throughout the remainder of the book.

---

[9]This alternative measure of compensation is sometimes termed the "equivalent variation" (EV).

DEFINITION

Consumer surplus. Consumer surplus is the area below the Marshallian demand curve and above market price. It shows what an individual would pay for the right to make voluntary transactions at this price. Changes in consumer surplus can be used to measure the welfare effects of price changes.

We should point out that some economists use either CV or EV to compute the welfare effects of price changes. Indeed, economists are often not very clear about which measure of welfare change they are using. Our discussion in the previous section shows that if income effects are small, it really does not make much difference in any case.

 EXAMPLE 5.6

Welfare Loss from a Price Increase

These ideas can be illustrated numerically by returning to our old hamburger/soft drink example. Let's look at the welfare consequences of an unconscionable price rise for soft drinks (good x) from \$1 to \$4. In Example 5.3 we found that the compensated demand for good x was given by

$$x^c(p_x, p_y, V) = \frac{V p_y^{0.5}}{p_x^{0.5}}. \tag{5.60}$$

Hence, the welfare cost of the price increase is given by

$$CV = \int_1^4 x^c(p_x, p_y, V)\,dp_x = \int_1^4 V p_y^{0.5} p_x^{-0.5}\,dp_x = 2 V p_y^{0.5} p_x^{0.5} \Big|_{p_x=1}^{p_x=4}. \tag{5.61}$$

If we use the values we have been assuming throughout this gastronomic feast ($V = 2$, $p_y = 4$) we get

$$CV = 2 \cdot 2 \cdot 2 \cdot (4)^{0.5} - 2 \cdot 2 \cdot 2 \cdot (1)^{0.5} = 8. \tag{5.62}$$

This figure would be cut in half (to 4) if we believed that the utility level after the price rise ($V = 1$) were the more appropriate utility target for measuring compensation. If instead we had used the Marshallian demand function

$$x(p_x, p_y, I) = 0.5 I p_x^{-1}$$

the loss would be calculated as

$$Loss = \int_1^4 x(p_x, p_y, I)\,dp_x = \int_1^4 0.5 I p_x^{-1}\,dp_x = 0.5 I \ln p_x \Big|_1^4. \tag{5.63}$$

So, with $I = 8$ this loss is

$$Loss = 4 \ln(4) - 4 \ln(1) = 4 \ln(4) = 4(1.39) = 5.55, \tag{5.64}$$

which seems a reasonable compromise between the two alternative measures based on compensated demand curves.

Query: In this problem, none of the demand curves has a finite price at which demand goes to precisely zero. How does this affect the computation of total consumer surplus? Does this affect the types of welfare calculations made here?

Revealed preference and the substitution effect

The principal unambiguous prediction that can be derived from the utility-maximization model is that the slope (or price elasticity) of the compensated demand curve is negative. The proof of this assertion relies on the assumption of a diminishing *MRS* and the related observation that with a diminishing *MRS* the necessary conditions for a utility maximum are also sufficient. To some economists, the reliance on a hypothesis about an unobservable utility function represented a weak foundation indeed on which to base a theory of demand. An alternative approach, which leads to the same result, was first proposed by Paul Samuelson in the late 1940s.[10] This approach, which Samuelson termed the *theory of revealed preference,* defines a principle of rationality that is based on observed behavior and then uses this principle to approximate an individual's utility function. In this sense, a person who follows Samuelson's principle of rationality behaves *as if* he or she were maximizing a proper utility function and exhibits a negative substitution effect. Because Samuelson's approach provides additional insights into our model of consumer choice, we will briefly examine it here.

Graphical approach

The principle of rationality in the theory of revealed preference is as follows: Consider two bundles of goods, *A* and *B.* If at some prices and income level, the individual can afford both *A* and *B* but chooses *A*, we say that *A* has been "revealed preferred" to *B.* The principle of rationality states that under any different price-income arrangement, *B* can never be revealed preferred to *A.* If *B* is in fact chosen at another price-income configuration, it must be because the individual could not afford *A.* The principle is illustrated in Figure 5.10. Suppose that when the budget constraint is given by I_1, point *A* is chosen, even though *B* also could have been purchased. *A* then has been revealed preferred to *B.* If for some other budget constraint, *B* is in fact chosen, it must be a case such as that represented by I_2—where *A* could not have been bought. If *B* were chosen when the budget constraint is I_3, this would be a violation of the principle of rationality, because with I_3 both *A* and *B* can be bought. With budget constraint I_3 it is likely that some point other than either *A* or *B*, say, *C*, will be bought. Notice how this principle uses observable reactions to alternative budget constraints to rank commodities rather than assuming the existence of a utility function itself.

Negativity of the substitution effect

Using the principle of rationality, we can now show why the substitution effect must be negative (or zero). Suppose that an individual is *indifferent* between two bundles, *C* (composed of x_C and y_C) and *D* (composed of x_D and y_D). Let p_x^C, p_y^C be the prices at which bundle *C* is chosen and p_x^D, p_y^D be the prices at which bundle *D* is chosen.

Because the individual is indifferent between *C* and *D*, it must be the case that when *C* was chosen, *D* cost at least as much as *C*:

$$p_x^C x_C + p_y^C y_C \leq p_x^C x_D + p_y^C y_D. \tag{5.65}$$

A similar statement holds when *D* is chosen:

$$p_x^D x_D + p_y^D y_D \leq p_x^D x_C + p_y^D y_C. \tag{5.66}$$

Rewriting these equations gives

$$p_x^C(x_C - x_D) + p_y^C(y_C - y_D) \leq 0 \tag{5.67}$$

$$p_x^D(x_D - x_C) + p_y^D(y_D - y_C) \leq 0. \tag{5.68}$$

---

[10]Paul A. Samuelson, *Foundations of Economic Analysis* (Cambridge, MA: Harvard University Press, 1947).

FIGURE 5.10 | **Demonstration of the Principle of Rationality in the Theory of Revealed Preference**

With income I_1 the individual can afford both points A and B. If A is selected, A is revealed preferred to B. It would be irrational for B to be revealed preferred to A in some other price-income configuration.

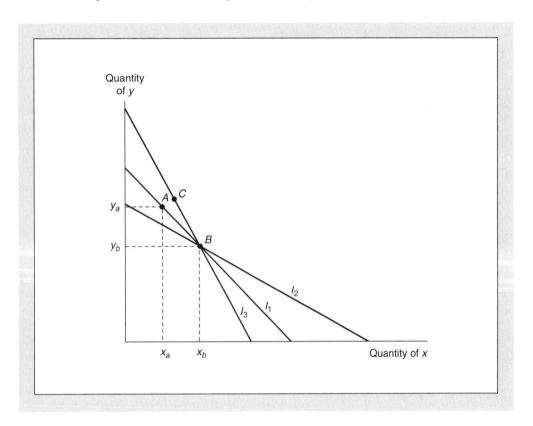

Adding these together we get

$$(p_x^C - p_x^D)(x_C - x_D) + (p_y^C - p_y^D)(y_C - y_D) \leq 0. \quad (5.69)$$

Now suppose that only the price of x changes; assume that $p_y^C = p_y^D$. Then

$$(p_x^C - p_x^D)(x_C - x_D) \leq 0. \quad (5.70)$$

But Equation 5.70 says that price and quantity move in the opposite direction when utility is held constant (remember, bundles C and D are equally attractive). This is precisely a statement about the nonpositive nature of the substitution effect:

$$\frac{\partial x^c(p_x, p_y, V)}{\partial p_x} = \left.\frac{\partial x}{\partial p_x}\right|_{U\,=\,\text{constant}} \leq 0. \quad (5.71)$$

We have arrived at the result by an approach that requires neither the existence of a utility function nor the assumption of a diminishing *MRS*.

Mathematical generalization

Generalizing the revealed preference idea to n goods is straightforward. If at prices p_i^0, bundle x_i^0 is chosen instead of x_i^1 and bundle x_i^1 is also affordable, then

$$\sum_{i=1}^{n} p_i^0 x_i^0 \geq s \sum_{i=1}^{n} p_i^0 x_i^1; \quad (5.72)$$

that is, bundle 0 has been "revealed preferred" to bundle 1. Consequently, at the prices that prevail when bundle 1 is bought (say, p_i^1), it must be the case that x_i^0 is more expensive:

$$\sum_{i=1}^{n} p_i^1 x_i^0 > \sum_{i=1}^{n} p_i^1 x_i^1. \tag{5.73}$$

Although this initial definition of revealed preference focuses on the relationship between two bundles of goods, the most often used version of the basic principle requires a degree of transitivity for preferences among an arbitrarily large number of bundles. This is summarized by the following "strong" axiom:

DEFINITION

Strong axiom of revealed preference. The *strong axiom of revealed preference* states that if commodity bundle 0 is revealed preferred to bundle 1, and if bundle 1 is revealed preferred to bundle 2, and if bundle 2 is revealed preferred to bundle 3, . . . , and if bundle $K - 1$ is revealed preferred to bundle K, *then* bundle K cannot be revealed preferred to bundle 0 (where K is any arbitrary number of commodity bundles).

Most other properties that we have developed using the concept of utility can be proved using this revealed preference axiom instead. For example, it is an easy matter to show that demand functions are homogeneous of degree zero in all prices and income. It therefore is apparent that the revealed preference axiom and the existence of "well-behaved" utility functions are somehow equivalent conditions. That this is in fact the case was first shown by H. S. Houthakker in 1950. Houthakker showed that a set of indifference curves can always be derived for an individual who obeys the strong axiom of revealed preference.[11] Hence, this axiom provides a quite general and believable foundation for utility theory based on simple comparisons among alternative budget constraints. This approach is widely used in the construction of price indices and for a variety of other applied purposes.

SUMMARY

In this chapter we have used the utility-maximization model to study how the quantity of a good that an individual chooses responds to changes in income or to changes in that good's price. The final result of this examination is the derivation of the familiar downward-sloping demand curve. In arriving at that result, however, we have drawn a wide variety of insights from the general economic theory of choice:

- Proportional changes in all prices and income do not shift the individual's budget constraint and therefore do not change the quantities of goods chosen. In formal terms, demand functions are homogeneous of degree zero in all prices and income.

- When purchasing power changes (that is, when income increases with prices remaining unchanged), budget constraints shift and individuals will choose new commodity bundles. For normal goods an increase in purchasing power causes more to be chosen. In the case of inferior goods, however, an increase in purchasing power causes less to be purchased. Hence, the sign of $\partial x_i / \partial I$ could be either positive or negative, although $\partial x_i / \partial I \geq 0$ is the most common case.

- A fall in the price of a good causes substitution and income effects that, for a normal good, cause more of the good to be purchased. For inferior goods, however, substi-

---

[11]H. S. Houthakker, "Revealed Preference and the Utility Function," *Economica 17* (May 1950): 159–74.

tution and income effects work in opposite directions and no unambiguous prediction is possible.

- Similarly, a rise in price induces both substitution and income effects that, in the normal case, cause less to be demanded. For inferior goods the net result is again ambiguous.

- The Marshallian demand curve summarizes the total quantity of a good demanded at each possible price. Changes in price induce both substitution and income effects that prompt movements along the curve. For a normal good, $\partial x_i / \partial p_i \leq 0$ along this curve. If income, prices of other goods, or preferences change, the curve may shift to a new location.

- Compensated demand curves illustrate movements along a given indifference curve for alternative prices. They are constructed by holding utility constant and exhibit only the substitution effects from a price change. Hence, their slope is unambiguously negative (or zero).

- Demand elasticities are often used in empirical work to summarize how individuals react to changes in prices and income. The most important such elasticity is the (own) price elasticity of demand, e_{x,p_x}. This measures the proportionate change in quantity in response to a 1 percent change in price. A similar elasticity can be defined for movements along the compensated demand curve.

- There are many relationships among demand elasticities. Some of the more important ones are: (1) own-price elasticities determine how a price change affects total spending on a good; (2) substitution and income effects can be summarized by the Slutsky equation in elasticity form; and (3) various aggregation relations hold among elasticities—these show how the demands for different goods are related.

- Welfare effects of price changes can be measured by changing areas below either compensated or ordinary demand curves. Such changes affect the size of the consumer surplus that individuals receive by being able to make market transactions.

- The negativity of the substitution effect is one of the most basic findings of demand theory. This result can be shown using revealed preference theory and does not necessarily require assuming the existence of a utility function.

PROBLEMS

5.1

Thirsty Ed drinks only pure spring water, but he can purchase it in two different-sized containers—.75 liter and 2 liter. Because the water itself is identical, he regards these two "goods" as perfect substitutes.

a. Assuming Ed's utility depends only on the quantity of water consumed and that the containers themselves yield no utility, express this utility function in terms of quantities of .75L containers (x) and 2L containers (y).

b. State Ed's demand function for x in terms of p_x, p_y, and I.

c. Graph the demand curve for x, holding I and p_y constant.

d. How do changes in I and p_y shift the demand curve for x?

e. What would the compensated demand curve for x look like in this situation?

5.2

David N. gets $3 per week as an allowance to spend any way he pleases. Because he likes only peanut butter and jelly sandwiches, he spends the entire amount on peanut butter (at $.05 per ounce) and jelly (at $.10 per ounce). Bread is provided free of charge by a concerned neighbor. David is a particular eater and makes his sandwiches with exactly 1 ounce of jelly and 2 ounces of peanut butter. He is set in his ways and will never change these proportions.

a. How much peanut butter and jelly will David buy with his $3 allowance in a week?

b. Suppose the price of jelly were to rise to $.15 an ounce. How much of each commodity would be bought?

c. By how much should David's allowance be increased to compensate for the rise in the price of jelly in part (b)?

d. Graph your results in parts (a) to (c).

e. In what sense does this problem involve only a single commodity, peanut butter and jelly sandwiches? Graph the demand curve for this single commodity.

f. Discuss the results of this problem in terms of the income and substitution effects involved in the demand for jelly.

5.3

As defined in Chapter 3, a utility function is homothetic if any straight line through the origin cuts all indifference curves at points of equal slope: The *MRS* depends on the ratio y/x.

a. Prove that in this case $\partial x/\partial I$ is constant.

b. Prove that if an individual's tastes can be represented by a homothetic indifference map, price and quantity must move in opposite directions; that is, prove that Giffen's paradox cannot occur.

5.4

As in Example 5.1, assume that utility is given by

$$\text{utility} = U(x, y) = x^{.3}y^{.7}.$$

a. Use the uncompensated demand functions given in Example 5.1 to compute the indirect utility function and the expenditure function for this case.

b. Use the expenditure function calculated in part (a) together with Shephard's lemma (footnote 5) to compute the compensated demand function for good x.

c. Use the results from part (b) together with the uncompensated demand function for good x to show that the Slutsky equation holds for this case.

5.5

Suppose the utility function for goods x and y is given by

$$\text{utility} = U(x, y) = xy + y.$$

a. Calculate the uncompensated (Marshallian) demand functions for x and y and describe how the demand curves for x and y are shifted by changes in I or in the price of the other good.

b. Calculate the expenditure function for x and y.

c. Use the expenditure function calculated in part (b) to compute the compensated demand functions for goods x and y. Describe how the compensated demand curves for x and y are shifted by changes in income or by changes in the price of the other good.

5.6

In the Extensions to Chapter 4 we showed that most empirical work in demand theory focuses on income shares. For any good, x, the income share is defined as $s_x = \frac{p_x x}{I}$. In this problem we show that most demand elasticities can be derived from corresponding share elasticities.

a. Show that the elasticity of a good's budget share with respect to income $(e_{s_x,I} = \frac{\partial s_x}{\partial I} \cdot \frac{I}{s_x})$ is equal to $e_{x,I} - 1$. Interpret this conclusion with a few numerical examples.

b. Show that the elasticity of a good's budget share with respect to its own price $(e_{s_x,p_x} = \frac{\partial s_x}{\partial p_x} \cdot \frac{p_x}{s_x})$ is equal to $e_{x,p_x} + 1$. Again, interpret this finding with a few numerical examples.

c. Use your results from part (b) to show that the "expenditure elasticity" of good x with respect to its own price $(e_{x \cdot p_x, p_x} = \frac{\partial(p_x \cdot x)}{\partial p_x} \cdot \frac{1}{x})$ is also equal to $e_{x,p_x} + 1$.

d. Show that the elasticity of a good's budget share with respect to a change in the price of some other good $(e_{s_x,p_y} = \frac{\partial s_x}{\partial p_y} \cdot \frac{p_y}{s_x})$ is equal to e_{x,p_y}.

e. In the Extensions to Chapter 4 we showed that with a CES utility function, the share of income devoted to good x is given by $s_x = \frac{1}{1 + p_y^k p_x^{-k}}$ where $k = \frac{\delta}{\delta - 1} = 1 - \sigma$.

Use this share equation to prove Equation 5.56: $e_{x^c,p_x} = -(1 - s_x)\sigma$.

Hint: This problem can be simplified by assuming $p_x = p_y$ in which case $s_x = 0.5$.

5.7

Suppose that a person regards ham and cheese as pure complements—he or she will always use one slice of ham in combination with one slice of cheese to make a ham and cheese sandwich. Suppose also that ham and cheese are the only goods that this person buys and that bread is free. Show:

a. That if the price of ham is equal to the price of cheese, the own price elasticity of demand for ham is −0.5 and that the cross-price elasticity of demand for ham with respect to the price of cheese is also −0.5.

b. Explain why the results from part (a) reflect only income effects not substitution effects. What are the compensated price elasticities in this problem?

c. Use the results from part (b) to show how your answers to part (a) would change if a slice of ham cost twice the price of a slice of cheese.

d. Explain how this problem could be solved intuitively by assuming this person consumes only one good—a ham-and-cheese sandwich.

5.8

Part (e) of Problem 5.6 has a number of useful applications because it shows how price responses depend ultimately on the underlying parameters of the utility function. Specifically, use that result together with the Slutsky equation is elasticity terms to show:

a. In the Cobb-Douglas case ($\sigma = 1$) the following relationship holds between the own-price elasticities of x and y: $e_{x,p_x} + e_{y,p_y} = -2$.

b. If $\sigma > 1$, $e_{x,p_x} + e_{y,p_x} < -2$ and if $\sigma < 1$, $e_{x,p_x} + e_{y,p_y} > -2$. Provide an intuitive explanation for this result.

c. How would you generalize this result to cases of more than two goods? Discuss whether such a generalization would be especially meaningful.

5.9

The three aggregation relationships presented in this chapter can be generalized to any number of goods. This problem asks you to do so. We assume that there are n goods and that the share of income devoted to good i is denoted by s_i. We also define the following elasticities:

$$e_{i,I} = \frac{\partial x_i}{\partial I} \cdot \frac{I}{x_i}$$

$$e_{i,j} = \frac{\partial x_i}{\partial p_j} \cdot \frac{p_j}{x_i}.$$

use this notation to show:

a. Homogeneity: $\sum_{j=1}^{n} e_{i,j} + e_{i,I} = 0$.

b. Engel aggregation: $\sum_{i=1}^{n} s_i e_{i,I} = 1$.

c. Cournot aggregation: $\sum_{i=1}^{n} s_i e_{i,j} = -s_j$.

5.10

Over a three-year period, an individual exhibits the following consumption behavior:

	p_x	p_y	x	y
Year 1	3	3	7	4
Year 2	4	2	6	6
Year 3	5	1	7	3

Is this behavior consistent with the strong axiom of revealed preference?

SUGGESTIONS FOR FURTHER READING

Cook, P. J. "A 'One Line' Proof of the Slutsky Equation." *American Economic Review 62* (March 1972): 139.

Clever use of duality to derive the Slutsky equation; uses the same method as in Chapter 5 but with rather complex notation.

Fisher, F. M., and K. Shell. *The Economic Theory of Price Indices*. New York: Academic Press, 1972.
Complete, technical discussion of the economic properties of various price indexes; describes "ideal" indexes based on utility-maximizing models in detail.

Mas-Colell, Andreu, Michael D. Whinston, and Jerry R. Green. *Microeconomic Theory*. New York: Oxford University Press, 1995.
Chapter 3 covers much of the material in this chapter at a somewhat higher level. Section I on measurement of the welfare effects of price changes is especially recommended.

Samuelson, Paul A. *Foundations of Economic Analysis*, Chap. V. Cambridge, MA: Harvard University Press, 1947.
Provides a complete analysis of substitution and income effects. Also develops the revealed preference notion.

Silberberg, E. and W. Suen *The Structure of Economics: A Mathematical Analysis*, 3rd ed. Boston: Irwin/McGraw-Hill, 2001.
Provides an extensive derivation of the Slutsky equation and a lengthy presentation of elasticity concepts.

Sydsaetter, K., A. Strom, and P. Berck *Economist's Mathematical Manual*, 2003 ed. Berlin: Springer-Verlag, 2003.
Provides a compact summary of elasticity concepts. The coverage of elasticity of substitution notions is especially complete.

Varian, H. *Microeconomic Analysis*, 3rd ed. New York: W. W. Norton, 1992.
Formal development of preference notions. Extensive use of expenditure functions and their relationship to the Slutsky equation. Also contains a nice proof of Roy's identity.

Demand Concepts and the Evaluation of Price Indices

In Chapters 4 and 5 we introduced a number of related demand concepts, all of which were derived from the underlying model of utility maximization. Relationships among these various concepts are summarized in Figure E5.1. We have already looked at most of the links in the table formally. We have not yet discussed the mathematical relationship between indirect utility functions and Marshallian demand functions (Roy's identity), and we will do that below. All of the entries in the table make clear that there are many ways to learn something about the relationship between individuals' welfare and the prices they face. In this extension we will explore

some of these approaches. Specifically, we will look at how the concepts can shed light on accuracy of the consumer price index (CPI), the primary measure of inflation in the United States. Similar cost-of-living measures are used throughout the world.

The CPI is a "marked basket" index of the cost of living. Researchers measure the amounts that people consume of a set of goods in some base period (in the two-good case these base-period consumption levels might be denoted by x_0 and y_0) and then use current price data to compute the changing price of this market basket. Using these procedure, the cost of the

| **FIGURE E5.1** | **Relationship Among Demand Concepts** |

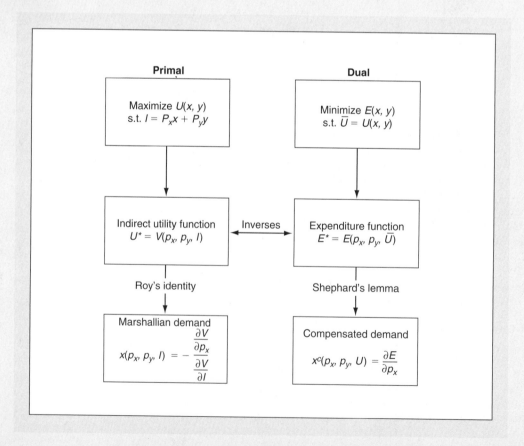

market basket initially would be $I_0 = p_x^0 x_0 + p_y^0 y_0$ and the cost in period 1 would be $I_1 = p_x^1 x_0 + p_y^1 y_0$. The change in the cost of living between these two periods would then be measured by I_1/I_0. Although this procedure is an intuitively plausible way of measuring inflation and market basket price indices are widely used, such indices have many shortcomings. These can be illustrated using various demand concepts.

E5.1: Expenditure functions and substitution bias

Market-basket price indices suffer from "substitution bias." Because they do not permit individuals to make substitutions in the market basket in response to changes in relative prices, they will tend to overstate the welfare losses that people incur from rising prices. This exaggeration is illustrated in Figure E5.2. To achieve the utility level U_0 initially requires expenditures of E_0 resulting in a purchase of the basket x_0, y_0. If p_x/p_y falls, the initial utility level can now be obtained with expenditures of E_1 by altering the consumption bundle to x_1, y_1. Computing the expenditure level needed to continue consuming x_0, y_0 exaggerates how much extra purchasing power this person needs to restore his or her level of well-being. Economics have extensively studied the extent of this substitution bias. Aizcorbe and Jackman (1993), for example, find that this difficulty with a market basket index may exaggerate the level of inflation shown by the CPI by about 0.2 percent per year.

FIGURE E5.2   **Substitution Bias in the CPI**

Initially expenditures are given by E_0 and this individual buys x_0, y_0. If p_x/p_y falls, utility level U_0 can be reached most cheaply by consuming x_1, y_1 and spending E_1. Purchasing x_0, y_0 at the new prices would cost more than E_1. Hence, holding the consumption bundle constant imparts an upward bias to CPI-type computations.

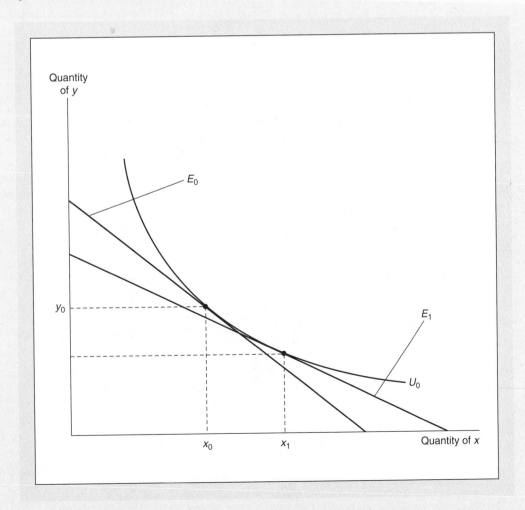

E5.2: Roy's identity and new goods bias

When new goods are introduced, it takes some time for them to be integrated into the CPI. For example, Hausman (1999, 2003) states that it took more than 15 years for cell phones to appear in the index. The problem with this delay is that market-basket indices will fail to reflect the welfare gains that people experience from using new goods. To measure these costs, Hausman sought to measure a "virtual" price (p^*) at which he demand for, say, cell phones would be zero and then to argue that the introduction of the good at its market price represented a change in consumer surplus that could be measured. Hence, the author was faced with the problem of how to get from the Marshallian demand function for cell phones (which he estimated econometrically) to the expenditure function. To do so he used Roy's identity (see Roy, 1942). Remember that the consumer's utility-maximizing problem can be represented by the Lagrangian expression $\mathscr{L} = U(x,y) + \lambda(I - p_x x - p_y y)$. If we apply the envelope theorem to this expression, we know that

$$\frac{\partial U^*}{\partial p_x} = \frac{\partial \mathscr{L}}{\partial p_x} = -\lambda x(p_x, p_y, I)$$

and   **(i)**

$$\frac{\partial U^*}{\partial I} = \frac{\partial \mathscr{L}}{\partial I} = \lambda.$$

Hence the Marshallian demand function is given by

$$x(p_x p_y, I) = \frac{-\partial U^*/\partial p_x}{\partial U^*/\partial I}.$$
(ii)

Using his estimates of the Marshallian demand function, Hausman then integrated Equation ii to obtain the implied indirect utility function and then calculated its inverse, the expenditure function (check Figure E5.1 to see the logic of the process). Though this certainly is a round-about scheme, it did yield very large estimates for the gain in consumer welfare from cell phones—a present value in 1999 of more than $100 billion per year. Delays in the inclusion of such goods into the CPI can therefore result in a misleading measure of consumer welfare.

E5.3: Other complaints about the CPI

Researchers have found several other faults with the CPI as currently constructed. Most of these focus on the consequences of using incorrect prices to compute the index. For example, when the quality of a good improves, people are made better off, though this may not show up in the good's price. Throughout the 1970s and 1980s the reliability of color television sets improved dramatically, but the price of a set did not change very much. A market basket that included "one color television set" would miss this source of improved welfare. Similarly, the opening of "big box" retailers such as Costco and Home Depot during the 1990s undoubtedly reduced the prices that consumers paid for various goods. But including these new retail outlets into the sample scheme for the CPI took several years, so the index misrepresented what people were actually paying. Assessing the magnitude of error introduced by these cases where incorrect prices are used in the CPI can also be accomplished by using the various demand concepts in Figure E5.1. For a summary of this research, see Moulton (1996).

References

Aizcorbe, Ana M., and Patrick C. Jackman. "The Commodity Substitution Effect in CPI Data, 1982–91." *Monthly Labor Review* (December 1993): 25–33.

Hausman, Jerry. "Cellular Telephone, New Products, and the CPI." *Journal of Business and Economic Statistics* (April 1999): 188–94.

Hausman, Jerry. "Sources of Bias and Solutions to Bias in the Consumer Price Index." *Journal of Economic Perspectives* (Winter 2003): 23–44.

Moulton, Brent R. "Bias in the Consumer Price Index: What Is the Evidence." *Journal of Economic Perspectives* (Fall 1996): 159–77.

Roy, R. *De l'utilité, contribution à la théorie des choix.* Paris: Hermann, 1942.

Chapter 6

DEMAND RELATIONSHIPS AMONG GOODS

In Chapter 5 we examined how changes in the price of a particular good (say, good x) affect the quantity of that good chosen. Throughout the discussion we held the prices of all other goods constant. It should be clear, however, that a change in one of these other prices could also affect the quantity of x chosen. For example, if x were taken to represent the quantity of automobile miles that an individual drives, this quantity might be expected to decline when the price of gasoline rises or to increase when air and bus fares rise. In this chapter we will use the utility-maximization model to study such relationships.

The two-good case

We begin our study of the demand relationship among goods with the two-good case. Unfortunately, this case proves to be rather uninteresting because the types of relationships that can occur when there are only two goods are quite limited. Still, the two-good case is useful because it can be illustrated with two-dimensional graphs. Figure 6.1 starts our examination by showing two examples of how the quantity of x chosen might be affected by a change in the price of y. In both panels of the figure, p_y has fallen. This has the result of shifting the budget constraint outward from I_0 to I_1. In both cases also the quantity of good y chosen has increased from y_0 to y_1 as a result of the decline in p_y, as would be expected if y is a normal good. For good x, however, the results shown in the two panels differ. In (a) the indifference curves are nearly L-shaped, implying a fairly small substitution effect. A decline in p_y does not induce a very large move along U_0 as y is substituted for x. That is, x drops relatively little as a result of the substitution. The income effect, however, reflects the greater purchasing power now available, and this causes the total quantity of x chosen to increase. Hence, $\partial x/\partial p_y$ is negative (x and p_y move in opposite directions).

In Figure 6.1b this situation is reversed—there $\partial x/\partial p_y$ is positive. The relatively flat indifference curves in Figure 6.1b result in a large substitution effect from the fall in p_y. The quantity of x declines sharply as y is substituted for x along U_0. As in Figure 6.1a, the increased purchasing power from the decline in p_y causes more x to be bought, but now the substitution effect dominates and the quantity of x declines to x_1. In this case, then, x and p_y move in the same direction.

FIGURE 6.1   **Differing Directions of Cross-Price Effects**

In both panels the price of *y* has fallen. In (a) substitution effects are small so the quantity of *x* consumed increases along with *y*. Because $\partial x/\partial p_y < 0$, *x* and *y* are gross complements. In (b) substitution effects are large so the quantity of *x* chosen falls. Because $\partial x/\partial p_y > 0$, *x* and *y* would be termed *gross substitutes*.

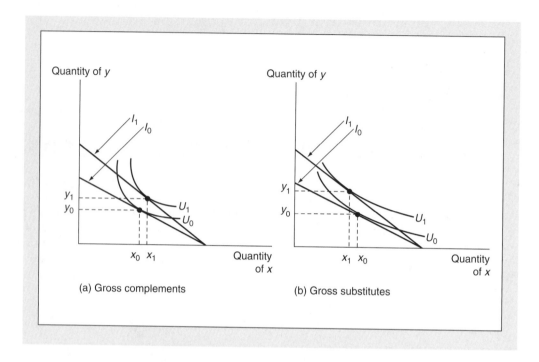

(a) Gross complements   (b) Gross substitutes

A mathematical treatment

The ambiguity in the effect of changes in p_y can be further illustrated by a Slutsky-type equation. By using procedures similar to those in Chapter 5, it is fairly simple to show that

$$\frac{\partial x(p_x, p_y, I)}{\partial p_y} = \text{Substitution Effect} + \text{Income Effect} = \frac{\partial x}{\partial p_y}\Big|_{U=\text{constant}} - y \cdot \frac{\partial x}{\partial I}, \quad (6.1)$$

or, in elasticity terms,

$$e_{x,p_y} = e_{x^c,p_y} - s_y e_{x,I}. \quad (6.2)$$

Notice that the size of the income effect is determined by the share of good *y* in this person's purchases. The impact that a change in p_y on purchasing power is determined by how important *y* is to this person.

For the two-good case, the terms on the right side of Equations 6.1 and 6.2 have different signs. Assuming that indifference curves are convex, the substitution effect $\partial x/\partial p_y|U = \text{constant}$ is positive. If we confine ourselves to moves along one indifference curve, increases in p_y increase *x* and decreases in p_y decrease the quantity of *x* chosen. But, assuming *x* is a normal good, the income effect ($-y\partial x/\partial I$ or $-s_y e_{x,I}$) is clearly negative. Hence, the combined effect is ambiguous; $\partial x/\partial p_y$ could be either positive or negative. Even in the two-good case, the demand relationship between *x* and p_y is rather complex.

EXAMPLE 6.1

Another Slutsky Decomposition for Cross-Price Effects

In Example 5.4 we examined the Slutsky decomposition for the effect of a change in the price of x. Now let's look at the cross-price effect of a change in y prices on x purchases. Remember that the uncompensated and compensated demand functions for x are given by

$$x(p_x, p_y, I) = \frac{0.5I}{p_x} \qquad (6.3)$$

and

$$x^c(p_x, p_y, V) = Vp_y^{0.5}p_x^{-0.5}. \qquad (6.4)$$

As we have pointed out before, the Marshallian demand function in this case yields $\frac{\partial x}{\partial p_y} = 0$—that is, changes in the price of y do not affect x purchases. Now we show that this occurs because the substitution and income effects of a price change are precisely counterbalancing. The substitution effect in this case is given by

$$\frac{\partial x}{\partial p_y}\Big|_{U=\text{constant}} = \frac{\partial x^c}{\partial p_y} = 0.5Vp_y^{-0.5}p_x^{-0.5}. \qquad (6.5)$$

Substituting for V from the indirect utility function ($V = 0.5Ip_y^{-0.5}p_x^{-0.5}$) gives a final statement for the substitution effect:

$$\frac{\partial x}{\partial p_y}\Big|_{U=\text{constant}} = 0.25Ip_y^{-1}p_x^{-1}. \qquad (6.6)$$

Returning to the Marshallian demand function for y ($y = 0.5Ip_y^{-1}$) to calculate the income effect yields

$$-y\frac{\partial x}{\partial I} = -[0.5Ip_y^{-1}] \cdot [0.5p_x^{-1}] = -0.25Ip_y^{-1}p_x^{-1}, \qquad (6.7)$$

and so the total effect of the change in the price of y is

$$\frac{\partial x}{\partial p_y} = 0.25Ip_y^{-1}p_x^{-1} - 0.25Ip_y^{-1}p_x^{-1} = 0. \qquad (6.8)$$

This makes clear that the reason that changes in the price of y have no effect on x purchases in the Cobb-Douglas case is that the substitution and income effects from such a change are precisely offsetting—neither of the effects alone, however, is zero.

Returning to our numerical example ($p_x = 1$, $p_y = 4$, $I = 8$, $V = 2$), suppose now that p_y falls to 2. This should have no effect on the Marshallian demand for good x. The compensated demand function in Equation 6.4 shows that the price change would cause the quantity of x demanded to decline from 4 to 2.83 (= $2\sqrt{2}$) as y is substituted for x with utility unchanged. However, the increased purchasing power arising from the price decline precisely reverses this effect.

Query: Why would it be incorrect to argue that if $\partial x/\partial p_y = 0$, x and y have no substitution possibilities—that is, they must be consumed in fixed proportions? Is there any case in which such a conclusion could be drawn?

Substitutes and complements

With many goods there is much more room for interesting relations among goods. It is relatively easy to generalize the Slutsky equation for any two goods, x_i, x_j, as

$$\frac{\partial x_i(p_1 \cdots p_n, I)}{\partial p_j} = \frac{\partial x_i}{\partial p_j}\Big|_{U=\text{constant}} - x_j \frac{\partial x_i}{\partial I}, \tag{6.9}$$

and, again, this can be readily translated into an elasticity relation:

$$e_{i,j} = e^c_{i,j} - s_j e_{i,x}. \tag{6.10}$$

This says that the change in the price of any good (here good j) induces income and substitution effects that may change the quantity of every good demanded. Equations 6.9 and 6.10 can be used to discuss the idea of substitutes and complements. Intuitively, these ideas are rather simple. Two goods are *substitutes* if one good may, as a result of changed conditions, replace the other in use. Some examples are tea and coffee, hamburgers and hot dogs, and butter and margarine. *Complements,* on the other hand, are goods that "go together," such as coffee and cream, fish and chips, or brandy and cigars. In some sense "substitutes" substitute for one another in the utility function, whereas "complements" complement each other.

There are two different ways to make these intuitive ideas precise. One of these focuses on the "gross" effects of price changes by including both income and substitution effects, while the other looks at substitution effects alone. Because both definitions are used, we will examine each in detail.

Gross substitutes and complements

Substitute and complementary relationships can be defined by referring to observed price reactions as:

DEFINITION

> **Gross substitutes and complements.** Two goods, x_i and x_j, are said to be gross substitutes if
>
> $$\frac{\partial x_i}{\partial p_j} > 0 \tag{6.11}$$
>
> and gross complements if
>
> $$\frac{\partial x_i}{\partial p_j} < 0. \tag{6.12}$$

That is, two goods are gross substitutes if a rise in the price of one good causes *more* of the other good to be bought. They are gross complements if a rise in the price of one good causes *less* of the other good to be purchased. For example, if the price of coffee rises, the demand for tea might be expected to increase (they are substitutes), whereas the demand for cream might decrease (coffee and cream are complements). Equation 6.9 makes it clear that this definition is a "gross" definition in that it includes both income and substitution effects that arise from price changes. Because these effects are in fact combined in any real-world observation we can make, it might be reasonable always to speak only of "gross" substitutes and "gross" complements.

Asymmetry of the gross definitions

There are, however, several things that are undesirable about the gross definitions of substitutes and complements. The most important of these is that the definitions are not symmetric. It is possible, by the definitions, for x_1 to be a substitute for x_2 and at the same time for x_2 to be a complement of x_1. The presence of income effects can produce paradoxical results. Let's look at a specific example:

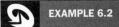

EXAMPLE 6.2

Asymmetry in Cross-Price Effects

Suppose the utility function for two goods (x and y) is given by

$$U(x, y) = \ln x + y. \qquad (6.13)$$

Setting up the Lagrangian expression

$$\mathscr{L} = \ln x + y + \lambda \, (I - p_x x - p_y y) \qquad (6.14)$$

yields the following first-order conditions:

$$\frac{\partial \mathscr{L}}{\partial x} = \frac{1}{x} - \lambda p_x = 0$$

$$\frac{\partial \mathscr{L}}{\partial y} = 1 - \lambda p_y = 0 \qquad (6.15)$$

$$\frac{\partial \mathscr{L}}{\partial \lambda} = I - p_x x - p_y y = 0.$$

Moving the terms in λ to the right and dividing the first equation by the second yields

$$\frac{1}{x} = \frac{p_x}{p_y} \qquad (6.16)$$

$$p_x x = p_y. \qquad (6.17)$$

Substitution into the budget constraint now permits us to solve for the Marshallian demand function for y:

$$I = p_x x + p_y y = p_y + p_y y. \qquad (6.18)$$

Hence,

$$y = \frac{I - p_y}{p_y} \qquad (6.19)$$

This equation shows that an increase in p_y must decrease spending on good y (that is, $p_y y$). Therefore, since p_x and I are unchanged, spending on x must rise. So

$$\frac{\partial x}{\partial p_y} > 0, \qquad (6.20)$$

and we would term x and y gross substitutes. On the other hand, Equation 6.19 shows that spending on y is independent of p_x. Consequently,

$$\frac{\partial y}{\partial p_x} = 0 \qquad (6.21)$$

and, looked at in this way, x and y would be said to be independent of each other—they are neither gross substitutes nor gross complements. Relying on gross market-based responses to define the relationship between x and y would therefore run into ambiguity.

Query: In Example 3.4 we showed that a utility function of the form given by Equation 6.13 is homothetic—the *MRS* does not depend only on the ratio of x to y. Can asymmetry arise in the homothetic case?

Net substitutes and complements

Because of the possible asymmetries involved in the definition of gross substitutes and complements, an alternative definition that focuses only on substitution effects is often used:

DEFINITION

Net substitutes and complements.[1] x_i and x_j are said to be net substitutes if

$$\frac{\partial x_i}{\partial p_j}\bigg|_{U = \text{constant}} > 0 \qquad (6.22)$$

and net complements if

$$\frac{\partial x_i}{\partial p_j}\bigg|_{U = \text{constant}} < 0 \qquad (6.23)$$

These definitions, then, look only at the substitution terms to determine whether two goods are substitutes or complements. This definition is both intuitively appealing (because it looks only at the shape of an indifference curve) and theoretically desirable (because it is unambiguous). Once x_i and x_j have been discovered to be substitutes, they stay substitutes, no matter in which direction the definition is applied. As a matter of fact the definitions are perfectly symmetric:

$$\frac{\partial x_i}{\partial p_j}\bigg|_{U = \text{constant}} = \frac{\partial x_j}{\partial p_i}\bigg|_{U = \text{constant}}. \qquad (6.24)$$

The substitution effect of a change in p_i on good x_j is identical to the substitution effect of a change in p_j on the quantity of x_i chosen. This symmetry is important in both theoretical and empirical work.[2]

The differences between the two definitions of substitutes and complements are easily demonstrated in Figure 6.1a. In this figure x and y are gross complements, but they are net substitutes. The derivative $\partial x / \partial p_y$ turns out to be negative (x and y are gross complements) because the (positive) substitution effect is outweighed by the (negative) income effect (a fall in the price of y causes real income to increase greatly and, consequently, actual purchases of x increase). However, as the figure makes clear, if there are only two goods from which to choose, they must net substitutes, although they may be either gross substitutes or gross complements. Because we have assumed a diminishing *MRS,* the own-price substitution effect must be negative and, consequently, the cross-price substitution effect must be positive.

---

[1]Sometimes these are called "Hicksian" substitutes and complements, named after the British economist John Hicks, who originally developed the definitions.

[2]This symmetry is easily shown using Shephard's lemma which was introduced in footnote 5 of Chapter 5. There we showed the compensated demand functions can be calculated from expenditure functions by differentiation:

$$x_i^c(p_1 \cdots p_n, V) = \frac{\partial E(p_1 \cdots p_n, V)}{\partial p_i}. \qquad [\text{i}]$$

Hence, the substitution effect is given by

$$\frac{\partial x_i}{\partial p_j}\bigg|_{U=\text{constant}} = \frac{\partial x_i^c}{\partial p_j} = \frac{\partial^2 E}{\partial p_j \partial p_i} = E_{ij}. \qquad [\text{ii}]$$

But now we can apply Young's theorem to the expenditure function:

$$E_{ij} = E_{ji} = \frac{\partial x_j^c}{\partial p_i} = \frac{\partial x_j}{\partial p_i}\bigg|_{U=\text{constant}}, \qquad [\text{iii}]$$

which proves the symmetry.

Substitutability with many goods

Once the utility-maximizing model is extended to many goods, a wide variety of demand patterns become possible. Whether a particular pair of goods are net substitutes or net complements is basically a question of a person's preferences, so one might observe all sorts of odd relationships. A major theoretical question that has concerned economists is whether substitutability or complementarity is more prevalent. In most discussions we tend to regard goods as substitutes (a price rise in one market tends to increase demand in most other markets). It would be nice to know whether this intuition is justified.

The British economist John Hicks studied this issue in some detail about 50 years ago and reached the conclusion that "most" goods must be substitutes. The result is summarized in what has come to be called[3] "Hicks' second law of demand." A modern proof starts with the compensated demand function for a particular good—$x_i^c (p_1 \ldots p_n, V)$. This function is homogeneous of degree zero in all prices (if utility is held constant and prices double, quantities demanded do not change because the utility-maximizing tangencies do not change). Applying Euler's theorem to the function yields

$$p_1 \cdot \frac{\partial x_i^c}{\partial p_1} + p_2 \cdot \frac{\partial x_i^c}{\partial p_2} + \cdots + p_n \cdot \frac{\partial x_i^c}{\partial p_n} \equiv 0. \qquad (6.25)$$

We can put this result into elasticity terms by dividing Equation 6.25 by x_i:

$$e_{i1}^c + e_{i2}^c + \ldots + e_{in}^c \equiv 0. \qquad (6.26)$$

But we know that $e_{ii}^c \leq 0$ because of the negativity of the own substitution effect. Hence it must be the case that

$$\sum_{j \neq i} e_{ij}^c \geq 0. \qquad (6.27)$$

In words this says that the sum of all the compensated cross-price elasticities for a particular goods must be positive (or zero). This is the sense that "most" goods are substitutes. Empirical evidence seems generally consistent with this theoretical finding—instances of net complementarity between goods are encountered relatively infrequently in empirical studies of demand.

Composite commodities

Our discussion in the previous section showed that the demand relationships among goods can be quite complicated. In the most general case, an individual who consumes n goods will have demand functions that reflect $n(n + 1)/2$ different substitution effects.[4] When n is very large (as it surely is for all the specific goods that individuals actually consume), this general case can be unmanageable. It is often far more convenient to group goods into larger aggregates such as food, clothing, shelter, and so forth. At the most extreme level of aggregates, we might wish to examine one specific good (say, gasoline, which we might call x) and its relationship to "all other goods," which we might call y.

---

[3]See John Hicks, *Value and Capital* (Oxford: Oxford University Press, 1939), mathematical appendices. There is some debate about whether this result should be called Hick's "second" or "third" law. In fact, two other laws that we have already seen are listed by Hicks: (1) $\frac{\partial x_i^c}{\partial p_i} \leq 0$ (negativity of the own substitution effect); and (2) $\frac{\partial x_i^c}{\partial p_j} = \frac{\partial x_j^c}{\partial p_i}$ (symmetry of cross-substitution effects). But he refers explicitly only to two "properties" in his written summary of his results.

[4]To see this, notice that all substitution effects, s_{ij}, could be recorded in an $n \times n$ matrix. However, symmetry of the effects ($s_{ij} = s_{ji}$) implies that only those terms on and below the principal diagonal of this matrix may be distinctly different from each other. This amounts to half the terms in the matrix $\left(\frac{1}{2}n^2\right)$ plus the remaining half of the terms on the main diagonal of the matrix $\left(\frac{1}{2}n\right)$.

This is the procedure we have been using in some of our two-dimensional graphs, and we will continue to do so at many other places in this book. In this section we show the conditions under which this procedure can be defended. In the Extension to this chapter, we explore more general issues involved in aggregating goods into larger groupings.

Composite commodity theorem

Suppose consumers choose among n goods, but that we are only interested specifically in one of them, say, x_1. In general, the demand for x_1 will depend on the individual prices of the other $n - 1$ commodities. But if all these prices move together, it may make sense to lump them into a single "composite commodity," y. Formally, if we let $p_2^0 \ldots p_n^0$ represent the initial prices of these goods, then we assume that these prices can only vary together. They might all double, or all decline by 50 percent, but the relative prices of $x_2 \ldots x_n$ would not change. Now we define the composite commodity y to be total expenditures on $x_2 \ldots x_n$, using the initial prices $p_2^0 \ldots p_n^0$:

$$y = p_2^0 x_2 + p_3^0 x_3 + \ldots + p_n^0 x_n. \tag{6.28}$$

This person's initial budget constraint is given by

$$I = p_1 x_1 + p_2^0 x_2 + \ldots + p_n^0 x_n = p_1 x_1 + y. \tag{6.29}$$

By assumption, all of the prices $p_2 \ldots p_n$ change in unison. Assume all of these prices change by a factor of $t\,(t > 0)$. Now the budget constraint is

$$I = p_1 x_1 + t p_2^0 y_2 + \ldots + t p_n^0 x_n = p_1 x_1 + ty. \tag{6.30}$$

Consequently, the factor of proportionality, t, plays the same role in this person's budget constraint as did the price of $y\ (p_y)$ in our earlier two-good analysis. Changes in p_1 or in t induce the same kinds of substitution effects we have been analyzing. So long as $p_2 \ldots p_n$ move together, we can therefore confine our examination of demand to choices between buying x_1 or buying "everything else."[5] Simplified graphs that show these two goods on their axes can therefore be defended rigorously so long as the conditions of this "composite commodity theorem" (that all other prices move together) are satisfied. Notice, however, that the theorem makes no predictions about how choices of $x_2 \ldots x_n$ behave—they need not move in unison. The theorem focuses only on total spending on $x_2 \ldots x_n$, not on how that spending is allocated among specific items (although this allocation is assumed to be done in a utility-maximizing way).

Generalizations and limitations

The composite commodity theorem applies to any group of commodities whose relative prices all move together. It is possible to have more than one such commodity if there are several groupings that obey the theorem (i.e., expenditures on "food," "clothing," and so forth). Hence, we have developed the following:

DEFINITION

Composite commodity. A composite commodity is a group of goods for which all prices move together. These goods can be treated as a single "commodity" in that the individual behaves as if he or she were choosing between other goods and total spending on the entire composite group.

This definition and the related theorem are very powerful results. They help simplify many problems that would otherwise be intractable. Still, one must be rather careful in

---

[5]The idea of a "composite commodity" was also introduced by J. R. Hicks in *Value and Capital,* 2nd ed. (Oxford: Oxford University Press, 1946), pp. 312–13. Proof of the theorem relies on the notion that to achieve maximum utility, the ratio of the marginal utilities for $x_2 \ldots x_n$ must remain unchanged when $p_2 \ldots p_n$ all move together. Hence, the n-good problem can be reduced to the two-dimensional problem of equating the ratio of the marginal utility from x to that from y to the "price ratio" p_1/t.

applying the theorem to the real world because its conditions are stringent. Finding a set of commodities whose prices move together may be rare. Slight departures from strict proportionality may negate the composite commodity theorem if cross-substitution effects are large. In the Extension to this chapter, we look at ways to simplify situations where prices move independently.

 EXAMPLE 6.3

Housing Costs as a Composite Commodity

Suppose that an individual receives utility from three goods: food (x), housing services (y) measured in hundreds of square feet, and household operations as measured by electricity use (z).

If the individual's utility is given by the three-good CES function

$$\text{utility} = U(x, y, z) = -\frac{1}{x} - \frac{1}{y} - \frac{1}{z}, \qquad (6.31)$$

the Lagrangian technique can be used to calculate Marshallian demand functions for these goods as

$$x = \frac{1}{p_x + \sqrt{p_x p_y} + \sqrt{p_x p_z}}$$

$$y = \frac{1}{p_y + \sqrt{p_y p_x} + \sqrt{p_y p_z}} \qquad (6.32)$$

$$z = \frac{1}{p_z + \sqrt{p_z p_x} + \sqrt{p_z p_y}}.$$

If initially $I = 100$, $p_x = 1$, $p_y = 4$, and $p_z = 1$, then the demand functions predict

$$\begin{aligned} x^* &= 25 \\ y^* &= 12.5 \qquad (6.33) \\ z^* &= 25. \end{aligned}$$

Hence, 25 is spent on food and a total of 75 is spent on housing-related needs. If we assume that housing service prices (p_y) and household operation prices (p_z) always move together, we can use their initial prices to define the "composite commodity" housing (h):

$$h = 4y + 1z. \qquad (6.34)$$

Here we also (arbitrarily) define the initial price of housing (p_h) to be 1. The initial quantity of housing is simply total dollars spent on h:

$$h = 4(12.5) + 1(25) = 75. \qquad (6.35)$$

Furthermore, because p_y and p_z always move together, p_h will always be related to these prices by

$$p_h = p_z = .25 p_y. \qquad (6.36)$$

Using this information, we can recalculate the demand function for x as a function of I, p_x, and p_h:

$$\begin{aligned} x &= \frac{1}{p_x + \sqrt{4 p_x p_h} + \sqrt{p_x p_h}} \\ &= \frac{1}{p_y + 3\sqrt{p_x p_h}}. \end{aligned} \qquad (6.37)$$

(continued)

EXAMPLE 6.3 CONTINUED

As before, initially $I = 100$, $p_x = 1$, and $p_h = 1$, so $x^* = 25$. Spending on housing can be most easily calculated from the budget constraint as $h^* = 75$, because here spending on housing represents "everything" other than food.

An increase in housing costs. If the prices of y and z were to rise proportionally to $p_y = 16$, $P_z = 4$ (with p_x remaining at 1), p_h would also rise to $p_h = 4$. Equation 6.37 now predicts that the demand for x would fall to

$$x^* = \frac{100}{1 + 3\sqrt{4}} = \frac{100}{7} \qquad (6.38)$$

and that housing purchases would be given by

$$p_h h^* = 100 - \frac{100}{7} = \frac{600}{7}, \qquad (6.39)$$

or, because $p_h = 4$,

$$h^* = 150/7. \qquad (6.40)$$

Notice that this is precisely the level of housing purchases predicted by the original demand functions for three goods in Equations 6.32. With $I = 100$, $p_x = 1$, $p_y = 16$, and $p_z = 4$, these equations can be solved as

$$x^* = 100/7 \qquad (6.41)$$
$$y^* = 100/28$$
$$z^* = 100/14,$$

so the total amount of the composite good "housing" consumed (according to Equation 6.34) is given by

$$h^* = 4y^* + 1z^* = 150/7. \qquad (6.42)$$

Hence, we obtained the same responses to price changes regardless of whether we chose to examine demands for the three goods x, y, and z or to look only at choices between x and the composite good h.

Query: How do we know that the demand function for x in Equation 6.37 continues to ensure utility maximization? Why is the Lagrangian constrained maximization problem unchanged by making the substitutions represented by Equation 6.36?

Home production attributes of goods and implicit prices

So far in this chapter we have focused on what economists can learn about the relationships among goods by observing individuals' changing consumption of these goods in reaction to changes in market prices. In some ways this analysis skirts the central question of *why* coffee and cream go together or *why* fish and chicken may substitute for each other in a person's diet. To develop a deeper understanding of such questions, economists have begun to explore activities within individuals' households. That is, they have sought to model nonmarket types of activities such as parental child care, meal preparation, or do-it-yourself construction to understand how such activities ultimately result in demands for goods in the market. In this section we briefly review some of these models. Our primary goal is to illustrate some of the implications of this approach for the traditional theory of choice that we have been examining.

Household production model

The starting point for most models of household production is to assume that individuals do not receive utility directly from goods they purchase in the market (as we have been assuming so far). Instead, it is only when market goods are combined with time inputs by the individual that utility-providing outputs are produced. In this view, then, raw beef and uncooked potatoes yield no utility until they are cooked together to produce stew. Similarly, market purchases of beef and potatoes can be understood only by examining the individual's preferences for stew and the underlying technology through which it is produced.

In formal terms, assume as before that there are three goods that a person might purchase in the market: x, y, and z. Purchasing these goods provides no direct utility, but the goods can be combined by the individual to produce either of two home-produced goods: a_1 or a_2. The technology of this household production can be represented by the production functions f_1 and f_2 (see Chapter 7 for a more complete discussion of the production function concept). Therefore,

$$a_1 = f_1(x, y, z)$$
$$a_2 = f_2(x, y, z)$$

(6.43)

and

$$\text{utility} = U(a_1, a_2).$$

(6.44)

The individual's goal is to choose x, y, z so as to maximize utility subject to the production constraints and to a financial budget constraint:[6]

$$p_x x + p_y y + p_z z = I.$$

(6.45)

Although we will not examine in detail the results that can be derived from this general model, two insights that can be drawn from it might be mentioned. First, the model may help clarify the nature of market relationships among goods. Because the production functions in Equations 6.43 are in principle measurable using detailed data on household operations, households can be treated as "multi-product" firms and studied using many of the techniques economists use to study production.

A second insight provided by the household production approach is the notion of the "implicit" or "shadow" prices associated with the home-produced goods: a_1 and a_2. Because consuming more a_1, say, requires the use of more of the "ingredients" x, y, and z, this activity obviously has an opportunity cost in terms of the quantity of a_2 that can be produced. To produce more bread, say, a person must not only divert some flour, milk, and eggs from using them to make cupcakes, but may also have to alter the relative quantities of these goods purchased because he or she is bound by an overall budget constraint. Hence, bread will have an implicit price in terms of the number of cupcakes that must be forgone in order to be able to consume one more loaf. That implicit price will reflect not only the market prices of bread ingredients, but also the available household production technology and, in more complex models, the relative time inputs required to produce the two goods. As a starting point, however, the notion of implicit prices can be best illustrated with a very simple model.

---

[6]Often household production theory also focuses on the individual's allocation of time to producing a_1 and a_2 or to working in the market. In Chapter 16 we look at a few simple models of this type.

The linear attributes model

A particularly simple form of the household production model was first developed by K. J. Lancaster to examine the underlying "attributes" of goods.[7] In this model it is the attributes of goods that provide utility to individuals, and each specific good contains a fixed set of attributes. If, for example, we focus only on the calories (a_1) and vitamins (a_2) that various foods provide, Lancaster's model assumes that utility is a function of these attributes and that individual's purchase various foods only for the purpose of obtaining the calories and vitamins they offer. In a mathematical terms, the model assumes that the "production" equations have the simple form

$$a_1 = a_x^1 x + a_y^1 y + a_z^1 z$$
$$a_2 = a_x^2 x + a_y^2 y + a_z^2 z, \tag{6.46}$$

where a_x^1 represents the number of calories per unit of food x, a_x^2 represents the number of vitamins per unit of food x, and so forth. In this form of the model, then, there is no actual "production" in the home. Rather the decision problem is how to choose a diet that provides the optimal mix of calories and vitamins given the available food budget.

Illustrating the budget constraints

To begin our examination of the theory of choice under the attributes model, we first illustrate the budget constraint. In Figure 6.2 the ray $0x$ records the various combinations of a_1 and a_2 available from successively larger amounts of good x. Because of the linear production technology assumed in the attributes model, these combinations of a_1 and a_2 lie along such a straight line, though in more complex models of home production that might not be the case. Similarly, rays of $0y$ and $0z$ show the quantities of the attributes a_1 and a_2 provided by various amounts of goods y and z that might be purchased.

If this person spends all of his or her income on good x, the budget constraint (Equation 6.45) allows the purchase of

$$x^* = \frac{I}{p_x}, \tag{6.47}$$

and that will yield

$$a_1^* = a_x^1 x^* = \frac{a_x^1 I}{p_x}$$

and

$$a_2^* = a_x^2 x^* = \frac{a_x^2 I}{p_x}. \tag{6.48}$$

This point is recorded as point x^* on the $0x$ ray in Figure 6.2. Similarly, the points y^* and z^* represent the combinations of a_1 and a_2 that would be obtained if all income were spent on good y or good z, respectively.

Bundles of a_1 and a_2 that are obtainable by purchasing both x and y, respectively (with a fixed budget), are represented by the line joining x^* and y^* in Figure 6.2.[8] Similarly, the line x^*z^* represents the combinations of a_1 and a_2 available from x and z, and the line

---

[7]See K. J. Lancaster, "A New Approach to Consumer Theory," *Journal of Political Economy 74* (April 1966): 132–57.

[8]Mathematically, suppose a fraction of α of the budget is spent on x and $(1 - \alpha)$ on y, then

$$a_1 = \alpha a_x^1 x^* + (1 - \alpha) a_y^1 y^*$$
$$a_2 = \alpha a_x^2 x^* + (1 - \alpha) a_y^2 y^*.$$

The line x^*y^* is traced out by allowing α to vary between 0 and 1. The lines x^*z^* and y^*z^* are traced out in a similar way, as is the triangular area $x^*y^*z^*$.

FIGURE 6.2   **Utility Maximization in the Attributes Model**

The points x^*, y^*, and z^* show the amounts of attributes a_1 and a_2 that can be purchased by buying only x, y, or z, respectively. The shaded area shows all combinations that can be bought with mixed bundles. Some individuals may maximize utility at E, others at E'.

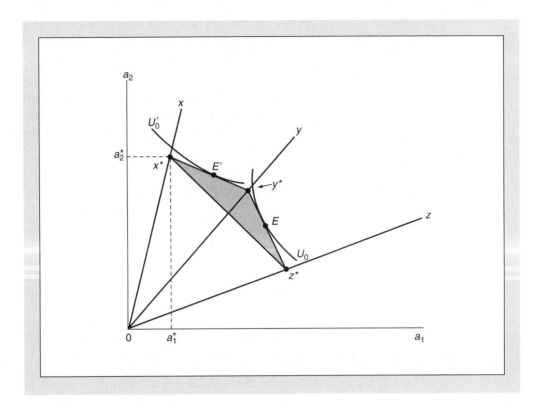

y^*z^* shows combinations available from mixing y and z. All possible combinations from mixing the three market goods are represented by the shaded triangular area $x^*y^*z^*$.

Corner solutions

One fact is immediately apparent from Figure 6.2—a utility-maximizing individual would never consume positive quantities of all three of these goods. Only the northeast perimeter of the $x^*y^*z^*$ triangle represents the maximal amounts of a_1 and a_2 available to this person given his or her income and the prices of the market goods. Individuals with a preference toward a_1 will have indifference curves similar to U_0 and will maximize utility by choosing a point such as E. The combination of a_1 and a_2 specified by that point can be obtained by consuming only goods y and z. Similarly, a person with preferences represented by the indifference curve U_0' will choose point E' and consume only goods x and y. The attributes model therefore predicts that corner solutions at which individuals consume zero amounts of some commodities will be relatively common, especially in cases where individuals attach value to fewer attributes (here, two) than there are market goods to choose from (three). If income, prices, or preferences change, consumption patterns may also change abruptly. Goods that were previously consumed may cease to be bought and goods previously neglected may experience a significant increase in purchases. This is a direct result of the linear assumptions inherent in the production functions assumed here. In household production models with greater substitutability assumptions, such discontinuous reactions are less likely.

SUMMARY

In this chapter we used the utility-maximizing model of choice to examine relationships among consumer goods. Although these relationships may be complex, the analysis presented here provided a number of ways of categorizing and simplifying them:

- When there are only two goods, the income and substitution effects from the change in the price of one good (say, p_y) on the demand for another good (x) usually work in opposite directions. The sign of $\partial x/\partial p_y$ is therefore ambiguous—its substitution effect is positive whereas its income effect is negative.

- In cases of more than two goods, demand relationships can be specified in two ways: Two goods (x_i and x_j) are "gross substitutes" if $\partial x_i/\partial p_j > 0$ and "gross complements" if $\partial x_i/\partial p_j < 0$. Unfortunately, because these price effects include income effects, they need not be symmetric. That is, $\partial x_i/\partial p_j$ does not necessarily equal $\partial x_j/\partial p_i$.

- Focusing only on the substitution effects from price changes eliminates this ambiguity because substitution effects are symmetric—that is, $\dfrac{\partial x_i^c}{\partial p_j} = \dfrac{\partial x_j^c}{\partial p_i}$. Now two goods are defined as net (or Hicksian) substitutes if $\dfrac{\partial x_i^c}{\partial p_j} > 0$ and net complements if $\dfrac{\partial x_i^c}{\partial p_j} < 0$. Hicks' "second law of demand" shows that net substitute are more prevalent.

- If a group of goods has prices that always move in unison, expenditures on these goods can be treated as a "composite commodity" whose "price" is given by the size of the proportional change in the composite goods' prices.

- An alternative way to develop the theory of choice among market goods is to focus on the ways in which market goods are used in household production to yield utility-providing attributes. This may provide additional insights into relationships among goods.

PROBLEMS

6.1

Heidi receives utility from two goods, goat's milk (m) and strudel (s), according to the utility function

$$U(m, s) = m \cdot s.$$

a. Show that increases in the price of goat's milk will not affect the quantity of strudel Heidi buys—that is, show that $\partial s/\partial p_m = 0$.

b. Show also that $\partial m/\partial p_s = 0$.

c. Use the Slutsky equation and the symmetry of net substitution effects to prove that the income effects involved with the derivatives in parts (a) and (b) are identical.

d. Prove part (c) explicitly using the Marshallian demand functions for m and s.

6.2

Hard Times Burt buys only rotgut whiskey and jelly donuts to sustain him. For Burt, rotgut whiskey is an inferior good that exhibits Giffen's paradox, although rotgut whiskey and jelly donuts are Hicksian substitutes in the customary sense. Develop an intuitive explanation to suggest why a rise in the price of rotgut must cause fewer jelly donuts to be bought. That is, the goods must also be gross complements.

6.3

Donald, a frugal graduate student, consumes only coffee (c) and buttered toast (bt). He buys these items at the university cafeteria and always uses two pats of butter for each piece of toast. Donald spends exactly half of his meager stipend on coffee and the other half on buttered toast.

   a. In this problem, buttered toast can be treated as a composite commodity. What is its price in terms of the prices of butter (p_b) and toast (p_t)?

   b. Explain why $\partial c / \partial p_{bt} = 0$.

   c. Is it also true here that $\partial c / \partial p_b$ and $\partial c / \partial p_t$ are equal to zero?

6.4

Ms. Sarah Traveler does not own a car and travels only by bus, train, or plane. Her utility function is given by

$$\text{utility} = b \cdot t \cdot p,$$

where each letter stands for miles traveled by a specific mode. Suppose that the ratio of the price of train travel to that of bus travel (p_t / p_b) never changes.

   a. How might one define a composite commodity for ground transportation?

   b. Phrase Sarah's optimization problem as one of choosing between ground (g) and air (p) transportation.

   c. What are Sarah's demand functions for g and p?

   d. Once Sarah decides how much to spend on g, how will she allocate those expenditures between b and t?

6.5

Suppose that an individual consumes three goods, x_1, x_2, and x_3, and that x_2 and x_3 are similar commodities (i.e., cheap and expensive restaurant meals) with $p_2 = kp_3$ where $k < 1$—that is, the goods' prices have a constant relationship to one another.

   a. Show that x_2 and x_3 can be treated as a composite commodity.

   b. Suppose both x_2 and x_3 are subject to a transaction cost of t per unit (for some examples, see Problem 6.6). How will this transaction cost affect the price of x_2 relative to that of x_3? How will this effect vary with the value of t?

   c. Can you predict how an income-compensated increase in t will affect expenditures on the composite commodity x_2 and x_3? Does the composite commodity theorem strictly apply to this case?

   d. How will an income-compensated increase in t affect how total spending on the composite commodity is allocated between x_2 and x_3?

   (For a further discussion of the complications involved in this problem, see T. E. Borcherding and E. Silberberg, "Shipping the Good Apples Out: The Alchian-Allen Theorem Reconsidered," *Journal of Political Economy* [February 1978]: 131–38.)

6.6

Apply the results of Problem 6.5 to explain the following observations:

a. It is difficult to find high-quality applies to buy in Washington State or good fresh oranges in Florida.

b. People with significant baby-sitting expenses are more likely to have meals out at expensive (rather than cheap) restaurants than are those without such expenses.

c. Individuals with a high value of time are more likely to fly the Concorde than those with a lower value of time.

d. Individuals are more likely to search for bargains for expensive items than for cheap ones. (*Note:* Observations (b) and (d) form the bases for perhaps the only two murder mysteries in which an economist solves the crime. See Marshall Jevons, *Murder at the Margin* and *The Fatal Equilibrium*.)

6.7

In general, uncompensated cross-price effects are not equal. That is,

$$\frac{\partial x_i}{\partial p_j} \neq \frac{\partial x_j}{\partial p_i}.$$

Use the Slutsky equation to show that these effects are equal if the individual spends a constant fraction of income on each good regardless of relative prices. (This is a generalization of Problem 6.1.)

6.8

In Chapter 5 we showed how the welfare costs of changes in a single price can be measured using expenditure functions and compensated demand curves. This problem asks you to generalize this to price changes in two (or many) goods.

a. Suppose that an individual consumes n goods and that the prices of two of those goods (say, p_1 and p_2) rise. How would you use the expenditure function to measure the compensating variation (CV) for this person of such a price rise?

b. A way to show these welfare costs graphically would be to use the compensated demand curves for goods x_1 and x_2 by assuming that one price rose before the other. Illustrate this approach.

c. In your answer to part (b), would it matter which order you considered the price changes? Explain.

d. In general, would you think that the CV for a price rise of these two goods would be greater if the goods were net substitutes or net complements? Or would the relationship between the goods have no bearing on the welfare costs?

6.9

A utility function is termed *separable* if it can be written as

$$U(x, y) = U_1(x) + U_2(y),$$

where $U_i' > 0$, $U_i'' < 0$, and U_1, U_2 need not be the same function.

a. What does separability assume about the cross-partial derivative U_{xy}? Give an intuitive discussion of what word this condition means and in what situations it might be plausible.

b. Show that if utility is separable, neither good can be inferior.

c. Does the assumption of separability allow you to conclude definitively whether x and y are gross substitutes or gross complements? Explain.

d. Use the Cobb-Douglas utility function to show that separability is not invariant with respect to monotonic transformations.

   Note: Separable functions are examined in more detail in the Extensions to this chapter.

6.10

Example 6.3 computes the demand functions implied by the three-good CES utility function

$$U(x, y, z) = -\frac{1}{x} - \frac{1}{y} - \frac{1}{z}$$

a. Use the demand function for x in Equation 6.32 to determine whether x and y or x and z are gross substitutes or gross complements.

b. How would you determine whether x and y or x and z are net substitutes or net complements?

SUGGESTIONS FOR FURTHER READING

Borcherding, T. E., and E. Silberberg, "Shipping the Good Apples Out—The Alchian-Allen Theorem Reconsidered," *Journal of Political Economy* (February 1978): 131–138.
   Good discussion of the relationships among three goods in demand theory. See also Problems 6.5 and 6.6.

Hicks, J. R. *Value and Capital,* 2nd ed. Oxford: Oxford University Press, 1946. See Chaps. I–III and related appendices.
   Proof of the composite commodity theorem. Also has one of the first treatments of net substitutes and complements.

Mas-Colell, A., M. D. Whinston, and J. R. Green. *Microeconomic Theory.* New York Oxford University Press, 1995.
   Explores the consequences of the symmetry of compensated cross-price effects for various aspects of demand theory.

Rosen, S. "Hedonic Prices and Implicit Markets." *Journal of Political Economy* (January/February 1974): 34–55.
   Nice graphical and mathematical treatment of the attribute approach to consumer theory and of the concept of "markets" for attributes.

Samuelson, P. A. "Complementarity—An Essay on the 40th Anniversary of the Hicks-Allen Revolution in Demand Theory." *Journal of Economic Literature* (December 1977): 1255–89.
   Reviews a number of definitions of complementarity and shows the connections among them. Contains an intuitive, graphical discussion and a detailed mathematical appendix.

Silberberg, E., and W. Suen. *The Structure of Economics: A Mathematical Analysis,* 3rd ed. Boston: Irwin-McGraw-Hill, 2001.
   Good discussion of expenditure functions and the use of indirect utility functions to illustrate the composite commodity theorem and other results.

Simplifying Demand and Two-Stage Budgeting

In Chapter 6 we saw that the theory of utility maximization in its full generality imposes rather few restrictions on what might happen. Other than the fact that net cross-substitution effects are symmetric, practically any type of relationship among goods is consistent with the underlying theory. This situation poses problems for economists who wish to study consumption behavior in the real world—theory just does not provide very much guidance when there are many thousands of goods potentially available for study.

There are two general ways in which simplifications are made. The first uses the composite commodity theorem from Chapter 6 to aggregate goods into categories within which relative prices move together. For situations where economists are specifically interested in changes in relatives prices within a category of spending (such as changes in the relative prices of various forms of energy) this process will not do, however. An alternative is to assume that consumers engage in a two-stage process in their consumption decisions. First they allocate income to various broad grouping of goods (food, clothing, and so forth) and then, given these expenditure constraints, they maximize utility within each of the subcategories of goods using only information about those goods' relatives prices. In that way, decisions can be studied in a simplified setting by looking only at one category at a time. This process is called "two-stage" budgeting. In these extensions we first look at the general theory of two-stage budgeting and then turn to examine some actual empirical examples.

E6.1 Theory of two-stage budgeting

The issue that arises in two-stage budgeting can be stated succinctly: Does there exist a partition of goods into m nonoverlapping groups (denoted by $r = l, m$) and a separate budget (l_r) devoted to each category such that the demand functions for the goods within any one category depend only on the prices of goods within the category and on the category's budget allocation? That is, can we partition goods so that demand is given by

$$x_i (p_1 \ldots p_n, I) = x_{i \in r} (p_{i \in r}, I_r)$$
$$for \ r = 1, m \ ? \qquad \text{(i)}$$

That it might be possible to do this is suggested by comparing the following two-stage maximization problem,

$$V^* (p_1, \cdots p_n, I_1, \cdots I_m)$$

$$= \underset{x_1, \cdots x_n}{Max} [U(x_1, \cdots x_n) s.t. \sum_{i \in r} p_i x_i \leq I_r, r = 1, m] \qquad \text{(ii)}$$

and

$$\underset{I_1, \cdots I_m}{Max} V^* \ s.t. \sum_{r=1}^{m} I_r = I,$$

to the utility-maximization problem we have been studying,

$$\underset{x_i}{Max} U(x_1, \cdots x_n) \ s.t. \sum_{i=1}^{n} p_i x_i \leq I. \qquad \text{(iii)}$$

Without any further restrictions, these two maximization processes will yield the same result—that is, Equation (ii) is just a more complicated way of stating Equation (iii). So, some restrictions have to be placed on the utility function to ensure that the demand functions that result from solving the two-stage process will be of the form specified in Equation (i). Intuitively it seems that such a categorization of goods should work providing that changes in the price of a good in one category do not affect the allocation of spending for goods in any category other than its own. In Problem 6.9 we showed a case where this is true for an "additively separable" utility function. Unfortunately, this proves to be a very special case. The more general mathematical restrictions that must be placed on the utility function to justify two-stage budgeting have been derived (see Blackorby, Primont, and Russell, 1978), but these are not especially intuitive. Of course, economists who wish to study decentralized decisions by consumers (or, perhaps more importantly, by firms that operate many divisions) must do something to simplify matters. Now we look at a few applied examples.

E6.2 Relation to the composition commodity theorem

Unfortunately, neither of the two available theoretical approaches to demand simplification is completely satisfying. The composite commodity theorem requires that the relative prices for goods within one group remain constant over time—an assumption that has been rejected during many different historical periods. On the other hand, the kind of separability and two-stage budgeting indicated by the utility function in Equation (i) also requires very strong assumptions about how changes in prices for a good in one group affect spending on goods in any other group. These assumptions appear to be rejected by the data (see Diewert and Wales, 1995).

Economists have tried to devise even more elaborate, hybrid methods of aggregation among goods. For example, Lewbel (1996) shows how the composite commodity theorem might be generalized to cases where within-group relative prices exhibit considerable variability. He uses this generalization for aggregating U.S. consumer expenditures into six large groups (food, clothing, household operation, medical care, transportation, and recreation). Using these aggregates, he concludes that his procedure is much more accurate than assuming two-stage budgeting among these expenditure categories.

E6.3 Homothetic functions and energy demand

One way to simplify the study of demand when there are many commodities is to assume that utility for certain subcategories of goods is homothetic and may be separated from the demand for other commodities. That is the procedure followed by Jorgenson, Slesnick, and Stoker (1997) in their study of energy demand by U.S. consumers. By assuming that demand functions for specific types of energy are proportional to total spending on energy, the authors were able to concentrate their empirical study on the topic that is of most interest to them—estimating the price elasticities of demand for various types of energy. They conclude that most types of energy (that is, electricity, natural gas, gasoline, and so forth) have fairly elastic demand functions. Demand appears to be most responsive to price for electricity.

References

Blackorby, Charles, Daniel Primont, and R. Robert Russell. *Duality, Separability and Functional Structure: Theory and Economic Applications.* New York: North Holland, 1978.

Diewert, W. Erwin, and Terrence J. Wales. "Flexible Functional Forms and Tests of Homogeneous Separability." *Journal of Econometrics* (June 1995): 259–302.

Jorgenson, Dale W., Daniel T. Slesnick, and Thomas M. Stoker. "Two-Stage Budgeting and Consumer Demand for Energy." In Dale W. Jorgenson, ed., *Welfare, Volume 1: Aggregate Consumer Behavior,* p. 475–510. Cambridge (MA): MIT Press, 1997.

Lewbel, Arthur. "Aggregation Without Separability: A Standardized Composite Commodity Theorem." *American Economic Review* (June 1996): 524–43.

Part 3

PRODUCTION AND SUPPLY

CHAPTER 7   **PRODUCTION FUNCTIONS**
CHAPTER 8   **COST FUNCTIONS**
CHAPTER 9   **PROFIT MAXIMIZATION**

In this part we examine the production and supply of economic goods. Institutions that coordinate the transformation of inputs into outputs are called firms. *They may be large institutions (such as General Motors, IBM, or the U.S. Department of Defense) or small ones (such as "Mom and Pop" stores or self-employed individuals). Although they may pursue different goals (IBM may seek maximum profits, whereas an Israeli kibbutz may try to make members of the kibbutz as well off as possible), all firms must make certain basic choices in the production process. The purpose of Part 3 is to develop some methods of analyzing those choices.*

In Chapter 7 we examine ways of modeling the physical relationship between inputs and outputs. We introduce the concept of a production function, *a useful abstraction from the complexities of real-world production processes. Two measurable aspects of the production function are stressed: its returns to scale (that is, how output expands when all inputs are increased) and its elasticity of substitution (that is, how easily one input may be replaced by another while maintaining the same level of output). We also briefly describe how technical improvements are reflected in production functions.*

The production function concept is then used in Chapter 8 to discuss costs of production. We assume that all firms seek to produce their output at the lowest possible cost, an assumption that permits the development of cost functions for the firm. Chapter 8 also focuses on how costs may differ between the short run and the long run.

In Chapter 9 we investigate the firm's supply decision. To do so, we assume that the firm's manager will make input and output choices so as to maximize profits. The chapter concludes with the fundamental model of supply behavior by profit-maximizing firms that we will use in many subsequent chapters.

Chapter 7

PRODUCTION FUNCTIONS

The principal activity of any firm is to turn inputs into outputs. Because economists are interested in the choices the firm makes in accomplishing this goal, but wish to avoid discussing many of the engineering intricacies involved, they have chosen to construct an abstract model of production. In this model the relationship between inputs and outputs is formalized by a production function *of the form*

$$q = f(k, l, m, \ldots), \tag{7.1}$$

where q represents the firm's output of a particular good during a period,[1] *k represents the machine (that is, capital) usage during the period, l represents hours of labor input, m represents raw materials used,*[2] *and the notation indicates the possibility of other variables affecting the production process. Equation 7.1 is assumed to provide, for any conceivable set of inputs, the engineer's solution to the problem of how best to combine those inputs to get output.*

Marginal productivity

In this section we shall study the change in output brought about by a change in one of the productive inputs. For the purposes of this examination (and indeed for most of the purposes of this book), it will be more convenient to use a simplified production function defined as follows:

DEFINITION

Production function. The firm's *production function* for a particular good, q,

$$q = f(k, l), \tag{7.2}$$

shows the maximum amount of the good that can be produced using alternative combinations of capital (k) and labor (l).

---

[1]Here we use a lowercase q to represent one firm's output. We reserve the uppercase Q to represent total output in a market. Generally, we assume that a firm produces only one output. Issues that arise in multiproduct firms are discussed in a few footnotes and problems.

[2]In empirical work raw material inputs often are disregarded and output, q, is measured in terms of "value added."

Of course, most of our analysis will hold for any two inputs to the production process we might wish to examine. The terms *capital* and *labor* are used only for convenience. Similarly, it would be a simple matter to generalize our discussion to cases involving more than two inputs; occasionally, we will do so. For the most part, however, limiting the discussion to two inputs will be quite helpful because we can show these inputs on two-dimensional graphs.

Marginal physical product

To study variation in a single input, we define marginal physical product as follows:

DEFINITION

Marginal physical product. The *marginal physical product* of an input is the additional output that can be produced by employing one more unit of that input while holding all other inputs constant. Mathematically,

$$\text{marginal physical product of capital} = MP_k = \frac{\partial q}{\partial k} = f_k$$

$$\text{marginal physical product of labor} = MP_l = \frac{\partial q}{\partial l} = f_l. \tag{7.3}$$

Notice that the mathematical definitions of marginal product use partial derivatives, thereby properly reflecting the fact that all other input usage is held constant while the input of interest is being varied. For an example, consider a farmer hiring one more laborer to harvest the crop but holding all other inputs constant. The extra output this laborer produces is that farmhand's marginal physical product, measured in physical quantities, such as bushels of wheat, crates of oranges, or heads of lettuce. We might observe, for example, that 50 workers on a farm are able to produce 100 bushels of wheat per year, whereas 51 workers, with the same land and equipment, can produce 102 bushels. The marginal physical product of the 51st worker is then 2 bushels per year.

Diminishing marginal productivity

We might expect that the marginal physical product of an input depends on how much of that input is used. Labor, for example, cannot be added indefinitely to a given field (while keeping the amount of equipment, fertilizer, and so forth fixed) without eventually exhibiting some deterioration in its productivity. Mathematically, the assumption of diminishing marginal physical productivity is an assumption about the second-order partial derivatives of the production function:

$$\frac{\partial MP_k}{\partial k} = \frac{\partial^2 f}{\partial k^2} = f_{kk} = f_{11} < 0$$

$$\frac{\partial MP_l}{\partial l} = \frac{\partial^2 f}{\partial l^2} = f_{ll} = f_{22} < 0. \tag{7.4}$$

The assumption of diminishing marginal productivity was originally proposed by the nineteenth-century economist Thomas Malthus, who worried that rapid increases in population would result in lower labor productivity. His gloomy predictions for the future of humanity led economics to be called the "dismal science." But the mathematics of the production function suggests that such gloom may be misplaced. Changes in the marginal productivity of labor over time depend not only on how labor input is growing, but also on changes in other inputs, such as capital. That is, we must also be concerned with $\partial MP_l / \partial k = f_{lk}$. In most cases, $f_{lk} > 0$, so declining labor productivity as *both l and k increase* is not a foregone conclusion. Indeed, it appears that labor productivity has risen significantly since Malthus' time primarily because increases in capital inputs have offset the impact of diminishing marginal productivity alone.

Average physical productivity

In common usage the term *labor productivity* often means *average productivity*. When it is said that a certain industry has experienced productivity increases, this is taken to mean that output per unit of labor input has increased. Although the concept of average productivity is not nearly as important in theoretical economic discussions as marginal productivity is, it receives a great deal of attention in empirical discussions. Because average productivity is easily measured (say, as so many bushels of wheat per labor-hour input), it is often used as a measure of efficiency. We define the average product of labor (AP_l) to be

$$AP_l = \frac{\text{output}}{\text{labor input}} = \frac{q}{l} = \frac{f(k, l)}{l}. \tag{7.5}$$

Notice that AP_l also depends on the level of capital employed. This observation will prove to be quite important when we examine the measurement of technical progress at the end of this chapter.

 EXAMPLE 7.1

A Two-Input Production Function

Suppose the production function for flyswatters during a particular period can be represented by

$$q = f(k, l) = 600 \, k^2 l^2 - k^3 l^3. \tag{7.6}$$

To construct the marginal and average productivity functions of labor (l) for this function, we must assume a particular value for the other input, capital (k). Suppose $k = 10$. Then the production function is given by

$$q = 60{,}000 l^2 - 1000 l^3. \tag{7.7}$$

Marginal product. The marginal productivity function is given by

$$MP_l = \frac{\partial q}{\partial l} = 120{,}000 l - 3000 l^2, \tag{7.8}$$

which diminishes as l increases, eventually becoming negative. This implies that q reaches a maximum value. Setting MP_l equal to 0,

$$120{,}000 l - 3000 l^2 = 0 \tag{7.9}$$

yields

$$40 l = l^2 \tag{7.10}$$

or

$$l = 40 \tag{7.11}$$

as the point at which q reaches its maximum value. Labor input beyond 40 units per period actually reduces total output. For example, when $l = 40$, Equation 7.7 shows that $q = 32$ million flyswatters, whereas when $l = 50$, production of flyswatters amounts to only 25 million.

Average product. To find the average productivity of labor in flyswatter production, we divide q by l, still holding $k = 10$:

$$AP_l = \frac{q}{l} = 60{,}000 l - 1000 l^2. \tag{7.12}$$

(continued)

EXAMPLE 7.1 CONTINUED

Again, this is an inverted parabola that reaches its maximum value when

$$\frac{\partial AP_l}{\partial l} = 60{,}000 - 2000l = 0, \tag{7.13}$$

which occurs when $l = 30$. At this value for labor input, Equation 7.12 shows that $AP_l = 900{,}000$, and Equation 7.8 shows that MP_l is also 900,000. When AP_l is at a maximum, average and marginal productivities of labor are equal.[3]

Notice the relationship between total output and average productivity that is illustrated by this example. Even though total production of flyswatters is greater with 40 workers (32 million) than with 30 workers (27 million), output per worker is higher in the second case. With 40 workers, each worker produces 800,000 flyswatters per period, whereas with 30 workers each worker produces 900,000. Because capital input (flyswatter presses) is held constant in this definition of productivity, the diminishing marginal productivity of labor eventually results in a declining level of output per worker.

Query: How would an increase in k from 10 to 11 affect the MP_l and AP_l functions here? Explain your results intuitively.

Isoquant maps and the rate of technical substitution

To illustrate possible substitution of one input for another in a production function, we use its *isoquant map*. Again, we study a production function of the form $q = f(k, l)$, with the understanding that "capital" and "labor" are simply convenient examples of any two inputs that might happen to be of interest. An isoquant (from *iso*, meaning "equal") records those combinations of k and l that are able to produce a given quantity of output. For example, all those combinations of k and l that fall on the curve labeled "$q = 10$" in Figure 7.1 are capable of producing ten units of output per period. This isoquant then records the fact that there are many alternative ways of producing ten units of output. One way might be represented by point A: We would use l_A and k_A to produce ten units of output. Alternatively, we might prefer to use relatively less capital and more labor and therefore would choose a point such as B. Hence, we may define an isoquant as follows:

DEFINITION

> **Isoquant.** An *isoquant* shows those combinations of k and l that can produce a given level of output (say, q_0). Mathematically, an isoquant records the set of k and l that satisfies
>
> $$f(k, l) = q_0. \tag{7.14}$$

As was the case for indifference curves, there are infinitely many isoquants in the $k - l$ plane. Each isoquant represents a different level of output. Isoquants record successively higher levels of output as we move in a northeasterly direction. Presumably, using more of

---

[3]This result is quite general. Because

$$\frac{\partial AP_l}{\partial l} = \frac{l \cdot MP_l - q}{l^2},$$

at a maximum $l \cdot MP_l = q$ or $MP_l = AP_l$.

FIGURE 7.1   **An Isoquant Map**

Isoquants record the alternative combinations of inputs that can be used to produce a given level of output. The slope of these curves shows the rate at which l can be substituted for k while keeping output constant. The negative of this slope is called the (marginal) *rate of technical substitution* (*RTS*). In the figure, the *RTS* is positive and diminishing for increasing inputs of labor.

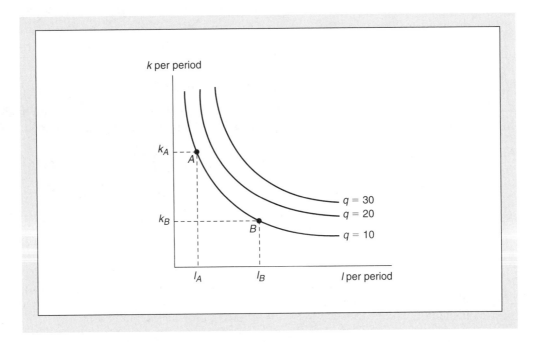

each of the inputs will permit output to increase. Two other isoquants (for $q = 20$ and $q = 30$) are shown in Figure 7.1. You will notice the similarity between an isoquant map and the individual's indifference curve map discussed in Part 2. They are indeed similar concepts, because both represent "contour" maps of a particular function. For isoquants, however, the labeling of the curves is measurable—an output of 10 units per period has a quantifiable meaning. Economists are therefore more interested in studying the shape of production functions than in examining the exact shape of utility functions.

The marginal rate of technical substitution (RTS)

The slope of an isoquant shows how one input can be traded for another while holding output constant. Examining the slope provides information about the technical possibility of substituting labor for capital. A formal definition is provided by:

Marginal rate of technical substitution. The *marginal rate of technical substitution* (*RTS*) shows the rate at which labor can be substituted for capital while holding output constant along an isoquant. In mathematical terms,

$$RTS \ (l \text{ for } k) = \frac{-dk}{dl}\bigg|_{q \, = \, q_0}. \qquad (7.15)$$

In this definition, the notation is intended as a reminder that output is to be held constant as l is substituted for k. The particular value of this trade-off rate will depend not only on the level of output but also on the quantities of capital and labor being used. Its value depends on the point on the isoquant map at which the slope is to be measured.

RTS and marginal productivities

To examine the shape of production function isoquants, it is useful to prove the following result: the *RTS* (of *l* for *k*) is equal to the ratio of the marginal physical productivity of labor (MP_l) to the marginal physical productivity of capital (MP_k). We begin by setting up the total differential of the production function:

$$dq = \frac{\partial f}{\partial l} \cdot dl + \frac{\partial f}{\partial k} \cdot dk = MP_l \cdot dl + MP_k \cdot dk, \qquad (7.16)$$

which records how small changes in *l* and *k* affect output. Along an isoquant, $dq = 0$ (output is constant), so

$$MP_l \cdot dl = -MP_k \cdot dk. \qquad (7.17)$$

This says that along an isoquant, the gain in output from increasing *l* slightly is exactly balanced by the loss in output from suitably decreasing *k*. Rearranging terms a bit gives

$$-\frac{dk}{dl}\bigg|_{q = q_0} = RTS \ (l \text{ for } k) = \frac{MP_l}{MP_k}. \qquad (7.18)$$

Hence the *RTS* is given by the ratio of the inputs' marginal productivities.

Equation 7.18 shows that those isoquants that we actually observe must be negatively sloped. Because both MP_l and MP_k will be nonnegative (no firm would choose to use a costly input that reduced output), the *RTS* also will be positive (or perhaps zero). Because the slope of an isoquant is the negative of the *RTS*, any firm we observe will not be operating on the positively sloped portion of an isoquant. Although it is mathematically possible to devise production functions whose isoquants have positive slopes at some points, it would not make economic sense for a firm to opt for such input choices.

Reasons for a diminishing RTS

The isoquants in Figure 7.1 are drawn not only with a negative slope (as they should be) but also as convex curves. Along any one of the curves, the *RTS* is *diminishing*. For high ratios of *k* to *l*, the *RTS* is a large positive number, indicating that a great deal of capital can be given up if one more unit of labor becomes available. On the other hand, when a lot of labor is already being used, the *RTS* is low, signifying that only a small amount of capital can be traded for an additional unit of labor if output is to be held constant. This assumption would seem to have some relationship to the assumption of diminishing marginal productivity. A hasty use of Equation 7.18 might lead one to conclude that a rise in *l* accompanied by a fall in *k* would result in a rise in MP_k, a fall in MP_l, and, therefore, a fall in the *RTS*. The problem with this quick "proof" is that the marginal productivity of an input depends on the level of *both* inputs—changes in *l* affect MP_k and vice versa. It is generally not possible to derive a diminishing *RTS* from the assumption of diminishing marginal productivity alone.

To see why this is so mathematically, assume that $q = f(k, l)$ and that f_k and f_l are positive (that is, the marginal productivities are positive). Assume also that $f_{kk} < 0$ and $f_{ll} < 0$ (that the marginal productivities are diminishing). To show that isoquants are convex, we would like to show that $d(RTS)/dl < 0$. Since $RTS = f_l/f_k$, we have

$$\frac{dRTS}{dl} = \frac{d(f_l / f_k)}{dl}. \qquad (7.19)$$

Because f_l and f_k are functions of both *k* and *l*, we must be careful in taking the derivative of this expression:

$$\frac{dRTS}{dl} = \frac{[f_k(f_{ll} + f_{lk} \cdot dk/dl) - f_l(f_{kl} + f_{kk} \cdot dk/dl)]}{(f_k)^2}. \qquad (7.20)$$

Using the fact that $dk/dl = -f_l/f_k$ along an isoquant and Young's theorem ($f_{kl} = f_{lk}$), we have

$$\frac{dRTS}{dl} = \frac{(f_k^2 f_{ll} - 2f_k f_l f_{kl} + f_l^2 f_{kk})}{(f_k)^3}. \tag{7.21}$$

Because we have assumed $f_k > 0$, the denominator of this function is positive. Hence the whole fraction will be negative if the numerator is negative. Because f_{ll} and f_{kk} are both assumed to be negative, the numerator definitely will be negative if f_{kl} is positive. If we can assume this, we have shown that $dRTS/dl < 0$ (that the isoquants are convex).[4]

Importance of cross-productivity effects

Intuitively, it seems reasonable that the cross-partial derivative $f_{kl} = f_{lk}$ should be positive. If workers had more capital, they would have higher marginal productivities. But, although this is probably the most prevalent case, it does not necessarily have to be so. Some production functions have $f_{kl} < 0$, at least for a range of input values. When we assume a diminishing RTS (as we will throughout most of our discussion), we are therefore making a stronger assumption than simply diminishing marginal productivities for each input—specifically, we are assuming that marginal productivities diminish "rapidly enough" to compensate for any possible negative cross-productivity effects.

 EXAMPLE 7.2

A Diminishing *RTS*

In Example 7.1, the production function for flyswatters was given by

$$q = f(k, l) = 600k^2l^2 - k^3l^3. \tag{7.22}$$

General marginal productivity functions for this production function are

$$MP_l = f_l = \frac{\partial q}{\partial l} = 1200k^2l - 3k^3l^2$$

$$MP_k = f_k = \frac{\partial q}{\partial k} = 1200kl^2 - 3k^2l^3. \tag{7.23}$$

Notice that each of these depends on the values of both inputs. Simple factoring shows that these marginal productivities will be positive for values of k and l for which $kl < 400$.

Because

$$f_{ll} = 1200k^2 - 6k^3l$$

and

$$f_{kk} = 1200l^2 - 6kl^3, \tag{7.24}$$

it is clear that this function exhibits diminishing marginal productivities for sufficiently large values of k and l. Indeed, again by factoring each expression, it is easy to show that $f_{ll}, f_{kk} < 0$ if $kl > 200$. Even within the range $200 < kl < 400$ where the marginal productivity relations for this function behave "normally," however, this production function may not necessarily have a diminishing RTS. Cross-differentiation of either of the marginal productivity functions (Equation 7.23) yields

$$f_{kl} = f_{lk} = 2400kl - 9k^2l^2, \tag{7.25}$$

which is positive only for $kl < 266$.

(continued)

---

[4]As we pointed out in Chapter 2, functions for which the numerator in Equation 7.21 is negative are called (strictly) *quasi-concave functions*.

EXAMPLE 7.2 CONTINUED

The numerator of Equation 7.21 will therefore definitely be negative for $200 < kl < 266$, but for larger scale flyswatter factories the case is not so clear, because f_{kl} is negative. When f_{kl} is negative, increases in labor input reduce the marginal productivity of capital. Hence, the intuitive argument that the assumption of diminishing marginal productivities yields an unambiguous prediction about what will happen to the RTS ($= f_l/f_k$) as l increases and k falls is incorrect. It all depends on the relative effects on marginal productivities of diminishing marginal productivities (which tend to reduce f_l and increase f_k) and the contrary effects of cross-marginal productivities (which tend to increase f_l and reduce f_k). Still, for this flyswatter case, it is true that the RTS is diminishing throughout the range of k and l, where marginal productivities are positive. For cases where $266 < kl < 400$, the diminishing marginal productivities exhibited by the function are sufficient to overcome the influence of a negative value for f_{kl} on the convexity of isoquants.

Query: For cases where $k = l$, what can be said about the marginal productivities of this production function? How would this simplify the numerator for Equation 7.21? How does this permit you to more easily evaluate this expression for some larger values of k and l?

Returns to scale

We now proceed to characterize production functions. A first question that might be asked about them is how output responds to increases in all inputs together. For example, suppose that all inputs were doubled: Would output double or would the relationship not be quite so simple? This is a question of the *returns to scale* exhibited by the production function that has been of interest to economists ever since Adam Smith intensively studied the production of pins. Smith identified two forces that came into operation when the conceptual experiment of doubling all inputs was performed. First, a doubling of scale permits a greater division of labor and specialization of function. Hence, there is some presumption that efficiency might increase—production might more than double. Second, doubling of the inputs also entails some loss in efficiency because managerial overseeing may become more difficult given the larger scale of the firm. Which of these two tendencies will have a greater effect is an important empirical question.

Presenting a technical definition of these concepts is misleadingly simple:

DEFINITION

Returns to scale. If the production function is given by $q = f(k, l)$ and all inputs are multiplied by the same positive constant, t (where $t > 1$), we classify the *returns to scale* of the production function by

Effect on Output	Returns to Scale
I. $f(tk, tl) = tf(k, l) = tq$	Constant
II. $f(tk, tl) < tf(k, l) = tq$	Decreasing
III. $f(tk, tl) > tf(k, l) = tq$	Increasing

In intuitive terms, if a proportionate increase in inputs increases output by the same proportion, the production function exhibits constant returns to scale. If output increases less than proportionately, the function exhibits diminishing returns to scale. And if output increases more than proportionately, there are increasing returns to scale. As we shall see, it is theoretically possible for a function to exhibit constant returns to scale for some levels of input usage and increasing or decreasing returns for other levels.[5] Often, however, economists refer to *the* degree of returns to scale of a production function with the implicit notion that only a fairly narrow range of variation in input usage and the related level of output is being considered.

Constant returns to scale

There are economic reasons why a firm's production function might exhibit constant returns to scale. If the firm operates many identical plants, it may increase or decrease production simply by varying the number of them in current operation. That is, the firm can double output by doubling the number of plants it operates, and that will require it to employ precisely twice as many inputs. Alternatively, if one were modeling the behavior of an entire industry composed of many firms, the constant returns-to-scale assumption might make sense because the industry can expand or contract by adding or dropping an arbitrary number of identical firms (see Chapter 10). Finally, studies of the entire U.S. economy have found that constant returns to scale is a reasonably good approximation to use for an "aggregate" production function. For all of these reasons, then, the constant returns-to-scale case seems worth examining in somewhat more detail.

When a production function exhibits constant returns to scale, it meets the definition of "homogeneity" that we introduced in Chapter 2. That is, the production is homogeneous of degree one in its inputs because

$$f(tk, tl) = t^1 f(k, l) = tq. \tag{7.26}$$

In Chapter 2 we showed that if a function is homogeneous of degree k, its derivatives are homogeneous of degree $k - 1$. In this context this implies that the marginal productivity functions derived from a constant returns-to-scale production function are homogeneous of degree zero. That is,

$$
\begin{aligned}
MP_k &= \frac{\partial f(k, l)}{\partial k} = \frac{\partial f(tk, tl)}{\partial k} \\
MP_l &= \frac{\partial f(k, l)}{\partial l} = \frac{\partial f(tk, tl)}{\partial l}
\end{aligned}
\tag{7.27}
$$

for any $t > 0$. In particular, we can let $t = \dfrac{1}{l}$ in Equations 7.27 and get

$$
\begin{aligned}
MP_k &= \frac{\partial f\left(\dfrac{k}{l}, 1\right)}{\partial k} \\
MP_l &= \frac{\partial f\left(\dfrac{k}{l}, 1\right)}{\partial l}.
\end{aligned}
\tag{7.28}
$$

That is, the marginal productivity of any input depends only on the ratio of capital to labor input, not on the absolute levels of these inputs. This fact is especially important, for example, in explaining differences in productivity among industries or across countries.

---

[5]A local measure of returns to scale is provided by the scale elasticity, defined as

$$e_{q,t} = \frac{\partial f(tk, tl)}{\partial t} \cdot \frac{t}{f(tk, tl)},$$

where this expression is to be evaluated at $t = 1$. This parameter can, in principle, take on different values depending on the level of input usage. For some examples using this concept, see Problems 7.4 and 7.5.

Homothetic production functions

One consequence of Equations 7.28 is that the RTS ($= MP_l / MP_k$) for any constant returns-to-scale production function will depend only on the ratio of the inputs, not on their absolute levels. That is, such a function will be homothetic (see Chapter 2)—its isoquants will be radial expansions of one another. This situation is shown in Figure 7.2. Along any ray through the origin (where the ratio k/l does not change), the slopes of successively higher isoquants are identical. This property of the isoquant map will be very useful to us on several occasions.

A simple numerical example may provide some intuition about this result. Suppose a roof can be installed in one day by three workers with one hammer each or by two workers with two hammers each (these workers are ambidextrous). The RTS of hammers for workers is therefore one for one—one extra hammer can be substituted for one worker. If this production process exhibits constant returns to scale, two roofs can be installed in one day either by six workers with six hammers or by four workers with eight hammers. In this latter case, two hammers are substituted for two workers, so again the RTS is one for one. In constant returns-to-scale cases, expanding the level of production does not alter trade-offs among inputs, so production functions are homothetic.

As production function can have a homothetic indifference curve map even if it does not exhibit constant returns to scale. As we showed in Chapter 2, this property of homotheticity is retained by any monotonic transformation of a homogeneous function. Hence, increasing or decreasing returns to scale can be incorporated into a constant returns-to-scale function through an appropriate transformation. Perhaps the most common such transformation is exponential. So, if $f(k, l)$ is a constant returns-to-scale producton function, we can let

$$F(k, l) = [f(k, l)]^\gamma, \qquad (7.29)$$

FIGURE 7.2   **Isoquant Map for a Constant Returns-to-Scale Production Function**

For a constant returns-to-scale production function, the RTS depends only on the ratio of k to l, not on the scale of production. Consequently, each isoquant will be a radial blowup of the unit isoquant. Along any ray through the origin (a ray of constant k/l), the RTS will be the same on all isoquants.

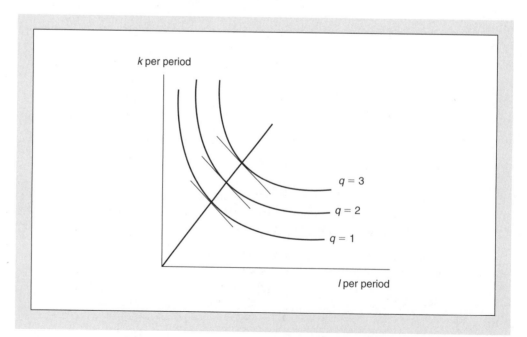

where γ is any positive exponent. If $\gamma > 1$ we have

$$F(tk, tl) = [f(tk, tl)]^\gamma = [tf(k, l)]^\gamma = t^\gamma [f(k, l)]^\gamma = t^\gamma F(k, l) > tF(k, l) \quad (7.30)$$

for any $t > 1$. Hence, this transformed production function exhibits increasing returns to scale. An identical proof shows that the function F exhibits decreasing returns to scale for $\gamma < 1$. Because this function remains homothetic through all such transformations, we have shown that there are important cases where the issue of returns to scale can be separated from issues involving the shape of an isoquant. In the next section we will look at how shapes of isoquants can be described.

The *n*-input case

The definition of returns to scale can be easily generalized to a production function with n inputs. If that production function is given by

$$q = f(x_1, x_2, \ldots, x_n), \quad (7.31)$$

and all inputs are multiplied by $t > 1$, we have

$$f(tx_1, tx_2, \ldots, tx_n) = t^k f(x_1, x_2, \ldots, x_n) = t^k q \quad (7.32)$$

for some constant k. If $k = 1$, the production function exhibits constant returns to scale. Diminishing and increasing returns to scale correspond to the cases $k < 1$ and $k > 1$, respectively.

The crucial part of this mathematical definition is the requirement that all inputs be increased by the same proportion, t. In many real-world production processes, this provision may make little economic sense. For example, a firm may have only one "boss," and that number would not necessarily be doubled even if all other inputs were. Or the output of a farm may depend on the fertility of the soil. It may not be literally possible to double the acres planted while maintaining fertility, because the new land may not be as good as that already under cultivation. Hence, some inputs may have to be fixed (or at least imperfectly variable) for most practical purposes. In such cases, some degree of diminishing productivity (a result of increasing employment of variable inputs) seems likely, although this cannot properly be called "diminishing returns to scale" because of the presence of inputs that are held fixed.

The elasticity of substitution

Another important characteristic of the production function is how "easy" it is to substitute one input for another. This is a question about the shape of a single isoquant rather than about the whole isoquant map. Along one isoquant the rate of technical substitution will decrease as the capital-labor ratio decreases (that is, as k/l decreases); now we wish to define some parameter that measures this degree of responsiveness. If the *RTS* does not change at all for changes in k/l, we might say that substitution is easy, because the ratio of the marginal productivities of the two inputs does not change as the input mix changes. Alternatively, if the *RTS* changes rapidly for small changes in k/l, we would say that substitution is difficult, because minor variations in the input mix will have a substantial effect on the inputs' relative productivities. A scale-free measure of this responsiveness is provided by the *elasticity of substitution*, a concept we encountered in Part 2. Now we can provide a formal definition:

DEFINITION

Elasticity of substitution. For the production function $q = f(k, l)$, the *elasticity of substitution* (σ) measures the proportionate change in k/l relative to the proportionate change in the *RTS* along an isoquant. That is,

$$\sigma = \frac{\text{percent } \Delta(k/l)}{\text{percent } \Delta RTS} = \frac{d(k/l)}{dRTS} \cdot \frac{RTS}{k/l} = \frac{\partial \ln k/l}{\partial \ln RTS} = \frac{\partial \ln k/l}{\partial \ln f_l/f_k}. \quad (7.33)$$

| FIGURE 7.3 | Graphic Description of the Elasticity of Substitution |

In moving from point A to point B on the $q = q_0$ isoquant, both the capital-labor ratio (k/l) and the RTS will change. The elasticity of substitution (σ) is defined to be the ratio of these proportional changes. It is a measure of how curved the isoquant is.

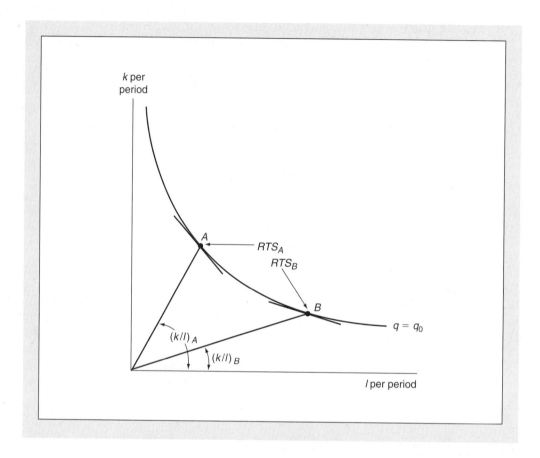

Because along an isoquant, k/l and RTS move in the same direction, the value of σ is always positive. Graphically, this concept is illustrated in Figure 7.3 as a movement from point A to point B on an isoquant. In this movement, both the RTS and the ratio k/l will change; we are interested in the relative magnitude of these changes. If σ is high, the RTS will not change much relative to k/l, and the isoquant will be relatively flat. On the other hand, a low value of σ implies a rather sharply curved isoquant; the RTS will change by a substantial amount as k/l changes. In general, it is possible that the elasticity of substitution will vary as one moves along an isoquant and as the scale of production changes. Often, however, it is convenient to assume that σ is constant along an isoquant. If the production function is also homothetic, then, because all the isoquants are merely radial blowups, σ will be the same along all isoquants. Later in this chapter and in many of its problems we will encounter such functions.[6]

---

[6]The elasticity of substitution can be phrased directly in terms of the production function and its derivatives in the constant returns-to-scale case as

$$\sigma = \frac{f_k \cdot f_l}{f \cdot f_{k,l}}.$$

But this form is quite cumbersome. Hence usually the logarithmic definition in Equation 7.33 is easiest to apply. For a compact summary, see P. Berck and K. Sydsaeter, *Economist's Mathematical Manual* (Berlin: Springer-Verlag, 1999), Chapter 5.

The *n*-input case

Generalizing the elasticity of substitution to the many-input case raises several complications. One approach is to adopt a definition analogous to Equation 7.33; that is, to define the elasticity of substitution between two inputs to be the proportionate change in the ratio of the two inputs to the proportionate change in the *RTS* between them while holding output constant.[7] To make this definition complete, it is necessary to require that all inputs other than the two being examined be held constant. However, this latter requirement (which is not relevant when there are only two inputs) restricts the value of this potential definition. In real-world production processes, it is likely that any change in the ratio of two inputs will also be accompanied by changes in the levels of other inputs. Some of these other inputs may be complementary with the ones being changed, whereas others may be substitutes, and to hold them constant creates a rather artificial restriction. For this reason, an alternative definition of the elasticity of substitution that permits such complementarity and substitutability in the firm's cost function is generally used in the *n*-good case. We will describe this alternative concept in the next chapter.

Four simple production functions

In this section we illustrate four simple production functions, each characterized by a different elasticity of substitution. These are shown only for the case of two inputs, but generalization to many inputs is easily accomplished (see the Extensions for this chapter).

Case 1: Linear ($\sigma = \infty$)

Suppose that the production function is given by

$$q = f(k, l) = ak + bl. \tag{7.34}$$

It is easy to show that this production function exhibits constant returns to scale: For any $t > 1$,

$$f(tk, tl) = atk + btl = t(ak + bl) = tf(k, l). \tag{7.35}$$

All isoquants for this production function are parallel straight lines with slope $-b/a$. Such an isoquant map is pictured in panel (a) of Figure 7.4. Because, along any straight-line isoquant, the *RTS* is constant, the denominator in the definition of σ (Equation 7.33) is equal to 0, and hence σ is infinite. Although this linear production function is a useful example, it is rarely encountered in practice because few production processes are characterized by such ease of substitution. Indeed, in this case capital and labor can be thought of as perfect substitutes for each other. An industry characterized by such a production function could use *only* capital or *only* labor, depending on these inputs' prices. It is hard to envision such a production process: Every machine needs someone to press its buttons, and every laborer requires some capital equipment, however modest.

Case 2: Fixed proportions ($\sigma = 0$)

The production function characterized by $\sigma = 0$ is the important case of a *fixed-proportions production function*. Capital and labor must always be used in a fixed ratio. The isoquants for this production function are L-shaped and are pictured in panel (b) of

---

[7]That is, the elasticity of substitution between input *i* and input *j* might be defined as

$$\sigma_{ij} = \frac{\partial \ln\left(\dfrac{x_i}{x_j}\right)}{\partial \ln\left(\dfrac{f_j}{f_i}\right)}$$

for movements along $f(x_1, x_2, \ldots x_n) = c$. Notice that the use of partial derivatives in this definition effectively requires that all inputs other than *i* and *j* be held constant when considering movements along the *c* isoquant.

FIGURE 7.4   **Isoquant Maps for Simple Production Functions with Various Values for σ**

Three possible values for the elasticity of substitution are illustrated in these figures. In (a), capital and labor are perfect substitutes. In this case the *RTS* will not change as the capital-labor ratio changes. In (b), the fixed-proportions case, no substitution is possible. The capital-labor ratio is fixed at *b/a*. A case of limited substitutability is illustrated in (c).

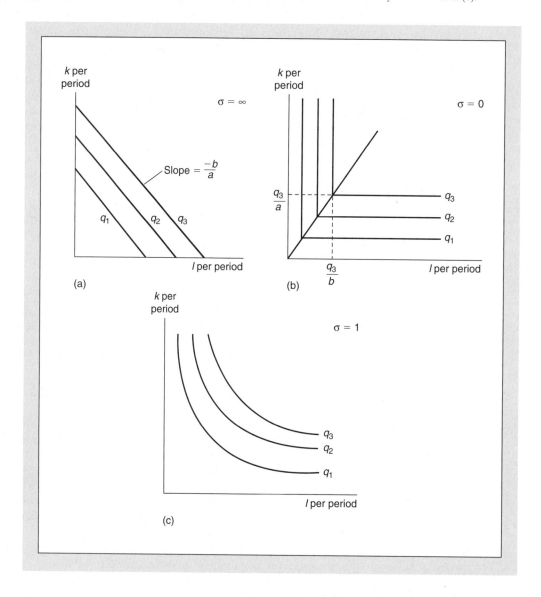

Figure 7.4. A firm characterized by this production function will always operate along the ray where the ratio *k/l* is constant. To operate at some point other than at the vertex of the isoquants would be inefficient, because the same output could be produced with fewer inputs by moving along the isoquant toward the vertex. Because *k/l* is a constant, it is easy to see from the definition of the elasticity of substitution that σ must equal 0.

The mathematical form of the fixed-proportions production function is given by

$$q = \min \, (ak, \, bl) \quad a, \, b > 0, \tag{7.36}$$

where the operator "min" means that *q* is given by the smaller of the two values in parentheses. For example, suppose that *ak < bl*; then *q = ak*, and we would say that capital is the binding constraint in this production process. The employment of more labor would not raise output, and hence the marginal product of labor is zero; additional labor is superfluous in this case. Similarly, if $ak > bl$, labor is the binding constraint on output and additional capital is superfluous. When $ak = bl$, both inputs are fully utilized. When this happens, $k/l = b/a$, and production takes place at a vertex on the isoquant map. If both inputs are costly, this is the only cost-minimizing place to operate. The locus of all such vertices is a straight line through the origin with a slope given by b/a.

The fixed-proportions production function has a wide range of applications.[8] Many machines, for example, require a certain number of people to run them, but any excess labor is superfluous. Consider combining capital (a lawn mower) and labor to mow a lawn. It will always take one person to run the mower, and either input without the other is not able to produce any output at all. It may be that many machines are of this type and require a fixed complement of workers per machine.[9]

Case 3: Cobb-Douglas ($\sigma = 1$)

The production function for which $\sigma = 1$, called a *Cobb-Douglas production function*[10] provides a middle ground between the two polar cases previously discussed. Isoquants for the Cobb-Douglas case have the "normal" convex shape and are shown in panel (c) of Figure 7.4. The mathematical form of the Cobb-Douglas production function is given by

$$q = f(k, l) = ak^a l^b, \qquad (7.37)$$

where A, a, and b are all positive constants.

The Cobb-Douglas function can exhibit any degree of returns to scale, depending on the values of a and b. Suppose all inputs were increased by a factor of t. Then

$$f(tk, tl) = A(tk)^a(tl)^b = at^{a+b}k^a l^b$$
$$= t^{a+b}f(k, l). \qquad (7.38)$$

Hence, if $a + b = 1$, the Cobb-Douglas function exhibits constant returns to scale, because output also increases by a factor of t. If $a + b > 1$, the function exhibits increasing returns to scale, whereas $a + b < 1$ corresponds to the decreasing returns-to-scale case. It is a simple matter to show that the elasticity of substitution is 1 for the Cobb-Douglas function.[11] This fact has led researchers to use the constant-returns-to-scale version of the function for a general description of aggregate production relationships in many countries.

---

[8]With the form reflected by Equation 7.35, the fixed-proportions production function exhibits constant returns to scale, because

$$f(tk, tl) = \min(atk, btl) = t \cdot \min(ak, bl) = tf(k, l)$$

for any $t > 1$. As before, increasing or decreasing returns can be easily incorporated into the functions by using a nonlinear transformation of this functional form, such as $[f(k, l)]^\gamma$ where γ may be greater than or less than one.

[9]The lawn mower example points up another possibility, however. Presumably there is some leeway in choosing what size of lawn mower to buy. Hence, prior to the actual purchase, the capital-labor ratio in lawn mowing can be considered variable: Any device, from a pair of clippers to a gang mower, might be chosen. Once the mower is purchased, however, the capital-labor ratio becomes fixed.

[10]Named after C. W. Cobb and P. H. Douglas. See P. H. Douglas, *The Theory of Wages* (New York: Macmillan Co., 1934), pp. 132–35.

[11]For the Cobb-Douglas,

$$RTS = \frac{f_l}{f_k} = \frac{bAk^a l^{b-1}}{aAk^{a-1}l^b} = \frac{b}{a}\frac{k}{l}$$

or

$$\ln RTS = \ln\left(\frac{b}{a}\right) + \ln\left(\frac{k}{l}\right).$$

Hence:

$$\sigma = \frac{\partial \ln k/l}{\partial \ln RTS} = 1.$$

The Cobb-Douglas function has also proved to be quite useful in many applications because it is linear in logarithms:

$$\ln q = \ln A + a \ln k + b \ln l. \tag{7.39}$$

The constant a is then the elasticity of output with respect to capital input, and b is the elasticity of output with respect to labor input.[12] These constants can sometimes be estimated from actual data, and such estimates may be used to measure returns to scale (by examining the sum $a + b$) and for other purposes.

Case 4: CES production function

A functional form that incorporates all of the three previous cases and allows σ to take on other values as well is the constant elasticity of substitution (CES) production function first introduced by Arrow et al. in 1961.[13] This function is given by

$$q = f(k, l) = [k^\rho + l^\rho]^{\gamma/\rho} \tag{7.40}$$

for $\rho \leq 1$, $\rho \neq 0$, and $\gamma > 0$. This function closely resembles the CES utility function discussed in Chapter 3, though now we have added the exponent γ/ρ to permit explicit introduction of returns-to-scale factors. For $\gamma > 1$ the function exhibits increasing returns to scale, whereas for $\gamma < 1$ it exhibits diminishing returns.

Direct application of the definition of σ to this function[14] gives the important result that

$$\sigma = \frac{1}{1 - \rho}. \tag{7.41}$$

Hence, the linear, fixed proportions and Cobb-Douglas cases correspond to $\rho = 1$, $\rho = -\infty$, and $\rho = 0$, respectively. Proof of this result for the fixed proportions and Cobb-Douglas cases requires a limit argument.

Often the CES function is used with a distributional weight, β $(0 \leq \beta \leq 1)$, to indicate the relative significance of the inputs:

$$q = f(k, l) = [\beta k^\rho + (1 - \beta)l^\rho]^{\gamma/\rho}. \tag{7.42}$$

With constant returns to scale and $\rho = 0$, this function converges to the Cobb-Douglas form

$$q = f(k, l) = k^\beta l^{1-\beta}. \tag{7.43}$$

---

[12]See Problem 7.5.

[13]K. J. Arrow, H. B. Chenery, B. S. Minhas, and R. M. Solow, "Capital-Labor Substitution and Economic Efficiency," *Review of Economics and Statistics* (August 1961): 225–50.

[14]For the CES function we have

$$RTS = \frac{f_l}{f_k} = \frac{\dfrac{\gamma}{\rho} \cdot q^{(\gamma-\rho)/\gamma} \cdot \rho l^{\rho-1}}{\dfrac{\gamma}{\rho} \cdot q^{(\gamma-\rho)/\gamma} \cdot \rho k^{\rho-1}} = \left(\frac{l}{k}\right)^{\rho-1} = \left(\frac{k}{l}\right)^{1-\rho}.$$

So, applying the definition of the elasticity of substitution yields

$$\sigma = \frac{\partial \ln(k/l)}{\partial \ln RTS} = \frac{1}{1-\rho}.$$

Notice in this computation that the factor ρ cancels out of the marginal productivity functions, thereby ensuring that these marginal productivities are positive even when ρ is negative (as it is in many cases). This explains why ρ appears in two different places in the definition of the CES function.

EXAMPLE 7.3

A Generalized Leontief Production Function

Suppose that the production function for a good is given by

$$q = f(k, l) = k + l + 2\sqrt{k \cdot l}. \qquad (7.44)$$

This function is a special case of a class of functions named for the Russian American economist Wassily Leontief.[15] The function clearly exhibits constant returns to scale because

$$f(tk, tl) = tk + tl + 2t\sqrt{kl} = tf(k,l). \qquad (7.45)$$

Marginal productivities for the Leontief function are

$$f_k = 1 + (k/l)^{-0.5}$$
$$f_l = 1 + (k/l)^{0.5}. \qquad (7.46)$$

Hence, marginal productivities are positive and diminishing. As would be expected (because this function exhibits constant returns to scale) the RTS here depends only on the ratio of the two inputs

$$RTS = \frac{f_l}{f_k} = \frac{1 + (k/l)^{0.5}}{1 + (k/l)^{-0.5}}. \qquad (7.47)$$

This RTS diminishes as k/l falls, so the isoquants have the usual convex shape.

There are two ways you might calculate the elasticity of substitution for this production function. First, you might notice that in this special case the function can be factored as

$$q = k + l + \sqrt{kl} = (\sqrt{k} + \sqrt{l})^2 = (k^{0.5} + l^{0.5})^2, \qquad (7.48)$$

which makes clear that this function has a CES form with $\rho = 0.5$, $\gamma = 1$. Hence the elasticity of substitution here is $\sigma = 1/(1 - \rho) = 2$.

Of course, in most cases it is not possible to do such a simple factorization. A more exhausting approach is to apply the definition of the elasticity of substitution given in footnote 6 of this chapter:

$$\sigma = \frac{f_k f_l}{f \cdot f_{kl}} = \frac{[1 + (k/l)^{0.5}][1 + (k/l)^{-0.5}]}{q \cdot (0.5/\sqrt{kl})}$$
$$= \frac{2 + (k/l)^{0.5} + (k/l)^{-0.5}}{1 + 0.5(k/l)^{0.5} + 0.5(k/l)^{-0.5}} = 2. \qquad (7.49)$$

Notice that in this calculation the input ratio (k/l) drops out, leaving a very simple result. In other applications one might doubt that such a fortuitous result would occur and therefore that the elasticity of substitution might not be constant along an isoquant (see Problem 7.7). But here the result that $\sigma = 2$ is intuitively reasonable because that value represents a compromise between the elasticity of substitution for this production function's linear part ($q = k + l$, $\sigma = \infty$) and its Cobb-Douglas part $q = 2k^{0.5}l^{0.5}$, $\sigma = 1$.

Query: What can you learn about this production function by graphing the $q = 4$ isoquant? Why does this function generalize the fixed proportions case?

---

[15]Lenotief was a pioneer in the development of input-output analysis. In input-output analysis, production is assumed to take place with a fixed-proportions technology. The Leontief production function generalizes the fixed-proportions case. For more details see the discussion of Leontief production functions in the Extensions to this chapter.

FIGURE 7.5   **Technical Progress**

Technical progress shifts the q_0 isoquant toward the origin. The new q_0 isoquant, q_0', shows that a given level of output can now be produced with less input. For example, with k_1 units of capital, it now only takes l_1 units of labor to produce q_0, whereas before the technical advance, it took l_2 units of labor.

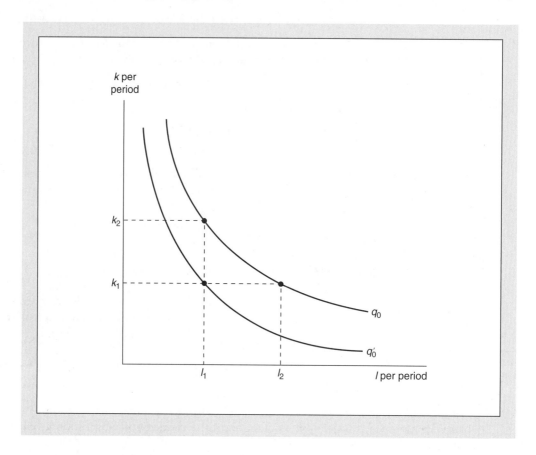

Technical progress

Methods of production improve over time, and it is important to be able to capture these improvements with the production function concept. A simplified view of such progress is provided by Figure 7.5. Initially, isoquant q_0 records those combinations of capital and labor that can be used to produce an output level of q_0. Following the development of superior production techniques, this isoquant shifts to q_0'. Now the same level of output can be produced with fewer inputs. One way to measure this improvement is by noting that with a level of capital input of, say, k_1, it previously took l_2 units of labor to produce q_0, whereas now it takes only l_1. Output per worker has risen from q_0/l_2 to q_0/l_1. But one must be careful in this type of calculation. An increase in capital input to k_2 would also have permitted a reduction in labor input to l_1 along the original q_0 isoquant. In this case, output for workers would also rise, although there would have been no true technical progress. Use of the production function concept can help to differentiate between these two concepts and therefore allow economists to obtain an accurate estimate of the rate of technical change.

Measuring technical progress

The first observation to be made about technical progress is that historically the rate of growth of output over time has exceeded the growth rate that can be attributed to the growth in conventionally defined inputs. Suppose that we let

$$q = A(t) f(k, l) \tag{7.50}$$

be the production function for some good (or perhaps for society's output as a whole). The term $A(t)$ in the function represents all the influences that go into determining q other than k (machine-hours) and l (labor-hours). Changes in A over time represent technical progress. For this reason, A is shown as a function of time. Presumably $dA/dt > 0$; particular levels of input of labor and capital become more productive over time.

Differentiating Equation 7.50 with respect to time gives

$$\begin{aligned}
\frac{dq}{dt} &= \frac{dA}{dt} \cdot f(k, l) + A \cdot \frac{df(k, l)}{dt} \\
&= \frac{dA}{dt} \cdot \frac{q}{A} + \frac{q}{f(k, l)} \left[\frac{\partial f}{\partial k} \cdot \frac{dk}{dt} + \frac{\partial f}{\partial l} \cdot \frac{dl}{dt} \right].
\end{aligned} \tag{7.51}$$

Dividing by q gives

$$\frac{dq/dt}{q} = \frac{dA/dt}{A} + \frac{\partial f/\partial k}{f(k, l)} \cdot \frac{dk}{dt} + \frac{\partial f/\partial l}{f(k, l)} \cdot \frac{dl}{dt} \tag{7.52}$$

or

$$\frac{dq/dt}{q} = \frac{dA/dt}{A} + \frac{\partial f}{\partial k} \cdot \frac{k}{f(k, l)} \cdot \frac{dk/dt}{k} + \frac{\partial f}{\partial l} \cdot \frac{l}{f(k, l)} \cdot \frac{dl/dt}{l}. \tag{7.53}$$

Now, for any variable x, $(dx/dt)/x$ is the proportional rate of growth of x per unit of time. We shall denote this by G_x.[16] Hence, Equation 7.53 can be written in terms of growth rates as

$$G_q = G_A + \frac{\partial f}{\partial k} \cdot \frac{k}{f(k, l)} \cdot G_k + \frac{\partial f}{\partial l} \cdot \frac{l}{f(k, l)} \cdot G_l, \tag{7.54}$$

but

$$\frac{\partial f}{\partial k} \cdot \frac{k}{f(k, l)} = \frac{\partial q}{\partial k} \cdot \frac{k}{q} = \text{elasticity of output with respect to capital input}$$

$$= e_{q,k}$$

and

$$\frac{\partial f}{\partial l} \cdot \frac{l}{f(k, l)} = \frac{\partial q}{\partial l} \cdot \frac{l}{q} = \text{elasticity of output with respect to labor input}$$

$$= e_{q,l}.$$

---

[16]Two useful features of this definition are: (1) $G_{x \cdot y} = G_x + G_y$—that is, the growth rate of a product of two variables is the sum of each one's growth rate; and (2) $G_{x/y} = G_x - G_y$.

Growth accounting

Therefore our growth equation finally becomes

$$G_q = G_A + e_{q,k}G_x + e_{q,l}G_l. \tag{7.55}$$

This shows that the rate of growth in output can be broken down into the sum of two components: growth attributed to changes in inputs (k and l) and other "residual" growth (that is, changes in A) that represents technical progress.

Equation 7.55 provides a way of estimating the relative importance of technical progress (G_A) in determining the growth of output. For example, in a pioneering study of the entire U.S. economy between the years 1909 and 1949, R. M. Solow recorded the following values for the terms in the equation:[17]

$$G_q = 2.75 \text{ percent per year}$$
$$G_l = 1.00 \text{ percent per year}$$
$$G_k = 1.75 \text{ percent per year}$$
$$e_{q,l} = 0.65$$
$$e_{q,k} = 0.35.$$

Consequently,

$$\begin{aligned} G_A &= G_q - e_{q,l}G_l - e_{q,k}G_k \\ &= 2.75 - 0.65(1.00) - 0.35(1.75) \\ &= 2.75 - 0.65 - 0.60 \\ &= 1.50. \end{aligned} \tag{7.56}$$

The conclusion Solow reached, then, was that technology advanced at a rate of 1.5 percent per year from 1909 to 1949. More than one-half of the growth in real output could be attributed to technical change rather than to growth in the physical quantities of the factors of production. More recent evidence has tended to confirm Solow's conclusions about the relative importance of technical change. Considerable uncertainty remains, however, about the precise causes of such change.

 EXAMPLE 7.4

Technical Progress in the Cobb-Douglas Production Function

The Cobb-Douglas production function provides an especially easy avenue for illustrating technical progress. Assuming constant returns to scale, such a production function with technical progress might be represented by

$$q = A(t)f(k,l) = A(t)k^{\alpha}l^{1-\alpha}. \tag{7.57}$$

If we also assume that technical progress occurs at a constant exponential (θ) we can write $A(t) = Ae^{\theta t}$ and the production function becomes

$$q = Ae^{\theta t}k^{\alpha}l^{1-\alpha}. \tag{7.58}$$

A particularly easy way to study the properties of this type of function over time is to use "logarithmic differentiation":

$$\frac{\partial \ln q}{\partial t} = \frac{\partial \ln q}{\partial q} \cdot \frac{\partial q}{\partial t} = \frac{\partial q/\partial t}{q} = G_q = \frac{\partial(\ln A + \theta t + \alpha \ln k + (1-\alpha)\ln l)}{\partial t}$$

$$= \theta + \alpha \cdot \frac{\partial \ln k}{\partial t} + (1-\alpha) \cdot \frac{\partial \ln l}{\partial t} = \theta + \alpha G_k + (1-\alpha)G_l. \tag{7.59}$$

[17]R. M. Solow, "Technical Progress and the Aggregate Production Function," *Review of Economics and Statistics 39* (August 1957): 312–20.

So this derivation just repeats Equation 7.55 for the Cobb-Douglas case. Here the technical change factor is explicitly modeled and the output elasticities are given by the values of the exponents in the Cobb-Douglas.

The importance of technical progress can be illustrated numerically with this function. Suppose $A = 10$, $\theta = .03$, $\alpha = 0.5$ and that a firm uses an input mix of $k = l = 4$. Then at $t = 0$, output is 40 ($= 10 \cdot 4^{0.5} \cdot 4^{0.5}$). After 20 years ($t = 20$), the production function becomes

$$q = 10e^{.03 \cdot 20}k^{0.5}l^{0.5} = 10 \cdot (1.82)k^{0.5}l^{0.5} = 18.2k^{0.5}l^{0.5}. \qquad (7.60)$$

In year 20 the original input mix now yields $q = 72.8$. Of course, one could also have produced $q = 72.8$ in year 0, but it would have taken a lot more inputs. For example, with $k = 13.25$, $l = 4$, output is indeed 72.8, but much more capital is used. Output per unit of labor input would rise from 10 ($q/l = 40/4$) to 18.2 ($= 72.8/4$) in either circumstance, but only the first case would have been true technical progress.

Input-augmenting technical progress. It is tempting to attribute the increase in the average productivity of labor in this example to, say, improved worker skills, but that would be misleading in the Cobb-Douglas case. One might just as well have said that output per unit of capital rose from 10 to 18.2 over the 20 years and attribute this rise to improved machinery. A plausible approach to modeling improvements in labor and capital separately is to assume that the production function is

$$q = A(e^{\phi t}k)^{\alpha} (e^{\varepsilon t}l)^{1-\alpha}, \qquad (7.61)$$

where ϕ represents the annual rate of improvement in capital input and ε represents the annual rate of improvement in labor input. But, because of the exponential nature of the Cobb-Douglas function, this would be indistinguishable from our original example:

$$q = Ae^{[\alpha\phi+(1-\alpha)\varepsilon]t}k^{\alpha}l^{1-\alpha} = Ae^{\theta t}k^{\alpha}l^{1-\alpha}, \qquad (7.62)$$

where $\theta = \alpha \phi + (1 - \alpha)\varepsilon$. Hence, to study technical progress in individual inputs it is necessary either to adopt a more complex way of measuring inputs that allows for improving quality or (what amounts to the same thing) use a multi-input production function.

Query: Actual studies of production using the Cobb-Douglas tend to find $\alpha \approx 0.3$. Use this finding together with Equation 7.62 to discuss the relative importance of improving capital and labor quality to the overall rate of technical progress.

SUMMARY

In this chapter we illustrated the ways in which economists conceptualize the production process of turning inputs into outputs. The fundamental tool is the production function, which, in its simplest form, assumes that output per period (q) is a simple function of capital and labor inputs during that period, $q = f(k, l)$. Using this starting point, we developed several basic results for the theory of production:

- If all but one of the inputs are held constant, a relationship between the single variable input and output can be derived. From this relationship, one can derive the marginal physical productivity (*MP*) of the input as the change in output resulting from a one-unit increase in the use of the input. The marginal physical productivity of an input is assumed to decline as use of the input increases.

- The entire production function can be illustrated by its isoquant map. The (negative of the) slope of an isoquant is termed the *marginal rate of technical substitution* (*RTS*), because it shows how one input can be substituted for another while holding output constant. The *RTS* is the ratio of the marginal physical productivities of the two inputs.

- Isoquants are usually assumed to be convex—they obey the assumption of a diminishing *RTS*. This assumption cannot be derived exclusively from the assumption of diminishing marginal physical productivities. One must also be concerned with the effect of changes in one input on the marginal productivity of other inputs.

- The returns to scale exhibited by a production function record how output responds to proportionate increases in all inputs. If output increases proportionately with input use, there are constant returns to scale. If there are greater than proportionate increases in output, there are increasing returns to scale, whereas if there are less than proportionate increases in output, there are decreasing returns to scale.

- The elasticity of substitution (σ) provides a measure of how easy it is to substitute one input for another in production. A high σ implies nearly straight isoquants, whereas a low σ implies that isoquants are nearly L-shaped.

- Technical progress shifts the entire production function and its related isoquant map. Technical improvements may arise from the use of improved, more-productive inputs, or from better methods of economic organization.

PROBLEMS

7.1

Power Goat Lawn Company uses two sizes of mowers to cut lawns. The smaller mowers have a 24-inch blade and are used on lawns with many trees and obstacles. The larger mowers are exactly twice as big as the smaller mowers and are used on open lawns where maneuverability is not so difficult. The two production functions available to Power Goat are:

	Output per Hour (Square Feet)	Capital Input (# of 24″ Mowers)	Labor Input
Large mowers	8000	2	1
Small mowers	5000	1	1

a. Graph the $q = 40,000$ square feet isoquant for the first production function. How much k and l would be used if these factors were combined without waste?

b. Answer part (a) for the second function.

c. How much k and l would be used without waste if half of the 40,000-square-foot lawn were cut by the method of the first production function and half by the method of the second? How much k and l would be used if three-fourths of the lawn were cut by the first method and one-fourth by the second? What does it mean to speak of fractions of k and l?

d. On the basis of your observations in part (c), draw a $q = 40,000$ isoquant for the combined production functions.

7.2

Suppose the production function for widgets is given by

$$q = kl - .8k^2 - .2l^2,$$

where q represents the annual quantity of widgets produced, k represents annual capital input, and l represents annual labor input.

    a. Suppose $k = 10$; graph the total and average productivity of labor curves. At what level of labor input does this average productivity reach a maximum? How many widgets are produced at that point?

    b. Again assuming that $k = 10$, graph the MP_l curve. At what level of labor input does $MP_l = 0$?

    c. Suppose capital inputs were increased to $k = 20$. How would your answers to parts (a) and (b) change?

    d. Does the widget production function exhibit constant, increasing, or decreasing returns to scale?

7.3

    Sam Malone is considering renovating the bar stools at Cheers. The production function for new bar stools is given by

$$q = 0.1k^{0.2}l^{0.8},$$

where q is the number of bar stools produced during the renovation week, k represents the number of hours of bar stool lathes used during the week, and l represents the number of worker hours employed during the period. Sam would like to provide 10 new bar stools, and he has allocated a budget of \$10,000 for the project.

    a. Sam reasons that because bar stool lathes and skilled bar stool workers both cost the same amount (\$50 per hour), he might as well hire these two inputs in equal amounts. If Sam proceeds in this way, how much of each input will he hire and how much will the renovation project cost?

    b. Norm (who knows something about bar stools) argues that once again Sam has forgotten his microeconomics. He asserts that Sam should choose quantities of inputs so that their marginal (not average) productivities are equal. If Sam opts for this plan instead, how much of each input will he hire and how much will the renovation project cost?

    c. Upon hearing that Norm's plan will save money, Cliff argues that Sam should put the savings into more bar stools in order to provide seating to more of his USPS colleagues. How many more bar stools can Sam get for his budget if he follows Norm's plan?

    d. Carla worries that Cliff's suggestion will just mean more work for her in delivering food to bar patrons. How might she convince Sam to stick to his original 10–bar stool plan?

7.4

    A local measure of the returns to scale incorporated in a production function is given by the scale elasticity $e_{q,t} = \dfrac{\partial f(tk, tl)}{\partial t} \cdot \dfrac{t}{q}$ evaluated at $t = 1$.

    a. Show that if the production function exhibits constant returns to scale, $e_{q,t} = 1$.

b. We can define the output elasticities of the inputs k and l as

$$e_{q,k} = \frac{\partial f(k,l)}{\partial k} \cdot \frac{k}{q}$$

$$e_{q,l} = \frac{\partial f(k,l)}{\partial l} \cdot \frac{l}{q}.$$

Show that $e_{q,t} = e_{q,k} + e_{q,l}$.

c. A function that exhibits variable scale elasticity is

$$q = (1 + k^{-1}l^{-1})^{-1}.$$

Show that for this function $e_{q,t} > 1$ for $q < 0.5$ and that $e_{q,t} < 1$ for $q > 0.5$.

d. Explain your results from part (c) intuitively. (*Hint:* Does q have an upper bound for this production function?)

7.5

As we have seen in many places, the general Cobb-Douglas production function for two inputs is given by

$$q = f(k,l) = Ak^{\alpha}l^{\beta},$$

where $0 < \alpha < 1$ and $0 < \beta < 1$. For this production function:

a. Show that $f_k > 0$, $f_l > 0$, $f_{kk} < 0$, $f_{ll} < 0$, $f_{kl} = f_{lk} > 0$.

b. Show that $e_{q,k} = \alpha$, $e_{q,l} = \beta$.

c. The results from part (b) suggest that for this function, $e_{q,t} = \alpha + \beta$. Show that this is correct by using a direct application of the definition for scale elasticity (see Problem 7.4).

d. Show that this function is quasi-concave.

e. Show that the function is concave for $\alpha + \beta \le 1$, but not concave for $\alpha + \beta > 1$.

7.6

Show that for the constant returns-to-scale CES production function

$$q = [k^{\rho} + l^{\rho}]^{1/\rho},$$

a. $MP_k = \left(\frac{q}{k}\right)^{1-\rho}$ and $MP_l = \left(\frac{q}{l}\right)^{1-\rho}$

b. $RTS = \left(\frac{l}{k}\right)^{1-\rho}$. Use this to show that $\sigma = 1/(1-\rho)$.

c. Determine the output elasticities for k and l. Show that their sum equals 1.

d. Prove that

$$\frac{q}{l} = \left(\frac{\partial q}{\partial l}\right)^{\sigma}.$$

Hence, show

$$\ln\left(\frac{q}{l}\right) = \sigma \ln\left(\frac{\partial q}{\partial l}\right).$$

Note: The latter equality is useful in empirical work, because we may approximate $\partial q/\partial l$ by the competitively determined wage rate. Hence, σ can be estimated from a regression of $\ln(q/l)$ on $\ln w$.

7.7

Consider a generalization of the production function in Example 7.3:

$$q = \beta_0 + \beta_1 \sqrt{kl} + \beta_2 k + \beta_3 l,$$

where

$$0 \leq \beta_i \leq 1 \qquad i = 0 \ldots 3.$$

a. If this function is to exhibit constant returns to scale, what restrictions should be placed on the parameters $\beta_0 \ldots \beta_3$?

b. Show that in the constant returns-to-scale case this function exhibits diminishing marginal productivities and that the marginal productivity functions are homogeneous of degree zero.

c. Calculate σ in this case. Although σ is not in general constant, for what values of the β's does $\sigma = 0$, 1, or ∞?

7.8

Show that Euler's theorem implies that for a constant returns-to-scale production function $[q = f(k, l)]$,

$$q = f_k \cdot k + f_l \cdot l.$$

Use this result to show that for such a production function, if $MP_l > AP_l$, MP_k must be negative. What does this imply about where production must take place? Can a firm ever produce at a point where AP_l is increasing?

7.9

As in Problem 7.8, again use Euler's theorem to prove that for a constant returns-to-scale production function with only two inputs (k and l), f_{kl} must be positive. Interpret this result. Is there any similar constraint on a production function with many inputs?

7.10

Although much of our discussion of measuring the elasticity of substitution for various production functions has assumed constant returns to scale, often that assumption is not necessary. This problem illustrates some of these cases.

a. In footnote 6 we showed that, in the constant returns-to-scale case, the elasticity of substitution for a two-input production function is given by

$$\sigma = \frac{f_k f_l}{f \cdot f_{kl}}.$$

Suppose now that we define the homothetic production function, F, as

$$F(k,l) = [f(k,l)]^\gamma,$$

where $f(k,l)$ is a constant returns-to-scale production function and γ is a positive exponent. Show that the elasticity of substitution for this production function is the same as the elasticity of substitution for the function f.

b. Show how this result can be applied to both the Cobb-Douglas and CES production functions.

SUGGESTIONS FOR FURTHER READING

Clark, J. M. "Diminishing Returns." In *Encyclopaedia of the Social Sciences*, vol. 5. New York: Crowell-Collier and Macmillan, 1931, pp. 144–46.
Lucid discussion of the historical development of the diminishing returns concept.

Douglas, P. H. "Are There Laws of Production?" *American Economic Review 38* (March 1948): 1–41.
A nice methodological analysis of the uses and misuses of production functions.

Ferguson, C. E. *The Neoclassical Theory of Production and Distribution*. New York: Cambridge University Press, 1969.
A thorough discussion of production function theory (as of 1970). Good use of three-dimensional graphs.

Fuss, M., and D. McFadden. *Production Economics: A Dual Approach to Theory and Application*. Amsterdam: North-Holland, 1980.
An approach with a heavy emphasis on the use of duality.

Mas-Collell, A., M. D. Whinston, and J. R. Green, *Microeconomic Theory*. New York: Oxford University Press, 1995.
Chapter 5 provides a sophisticated, if somewhat spare, review of production theory. The use of the profit function (see the Extensions to Chapter 9) is quite sophisticated and illuminating.

Shephard, R. W. *Theory of Cost and Production Functions*. Princeton, NJ: Princeton University Press, 1978.
Extended analysis of the dual relationship between production and cost functions.

Silberberg, E., and W. Suen. *The Structure of Economics: A Mathematical Analysis*, 3rd ed. Boston: Irwin, McGraw-Hill, 2001.
Thorough analysis of the duality between production functions and cost curves. Provides a proof that the elasticity of substitution can be derived as shown in footnote 6 of this chapter.

Stigler, G. J. "The Division of Labor Is Limited by the Extent of the Market." *Journal of Political Economy 59* (June 1951): 185–93.
Careful tracing of the evolution of Smith's ideas about economies of scale.

EXTENSIONS

Many-Input Production Functions

Most of the production functions illustrated in Chapter 7 can be easily generalized to many-input cases. Here we show this for the Cobb-Douglas and CES cases and then examine two, quite flexible forms that such production functions might take. In all of these examples, the β's are nonnegative parameters, and the n inputs are represented by $x_1 \ldots x_n$.

E7.1 Cobb-Douglas

The many-input Cobb-Douglas production function is given by

$$q = \prod_{i=1}^{n} x_i^{\beta_i}. \qquad \text{(i)}$$

a. This function exhibits constant returns to scale if

$$\sum_{i=1}^{n} \beta i = 1. \qquad \text{(ii)}$$

b. In the constant-returns-to-scale Cobb-Douglas function, β_i is the elasticity of q with respect to input x_i. Because $0 \leq \beta_i < 1$, each input exhibits diminishing marginal productivity.

c. Any degree of increasing returns to scale can be incorporated into this function, depending on

$$\in = \sum_{i=1}^{n} \beta_i. $$

E7.2 The Solow growth model

The many-input Cobb-Douglas production function is a primary feature of many models of economic growth. For example, Solow's (1956) pioneering model of equilibrium growth can be most easily derived using a two-input constant-returns-to-scale Cobb-Douglas function of the form

$$\Upsilon = A K^{\alpha} L^{1-\alpha}, \qquad \text{(iii)}$$

where A is a technical change factor that can be represented by exponential growth of the form

$$A = e^{at}. \qquad \text{(iv)}$$

Dividing both sides of equation iii by L yields

$$y = e^{at} k^{\alpha}, \qquad \text{(v)}$$

where

$$y = \Upsilon/L, k = K/L.$$

Solow shows that economies will evolve toward an equilibrium value of k (the capital-labor ratio). Hence cross-country differences in growth rates can be accounted for only by differences in the technical change factor, a.

Two features of Equation v argue for including more inputs in the Solow model. First, the equation as it stands is incapable of explaining the large differences in per capita output (y) that are observed around the world. Assuming $\alpha = .3$, say, (a figure consistent with many empirical studies), it would take cross-country differences in K/L of as much as 4,000,000-to-1 to explain the 100-to-1 differences in per capita income observed—a clearly unreasonable magnitude. By introducing additional inputs, such as human capital, these differences become more explainable.

A second shortcoming of the simple Cobb-Douglas formulation of the Solow model is that it offers no explanation of the technical change parameter, a—its value is determined "exogenously." By adding additional factors it becomes easier to understand how the parameter a may respond to economic incentives. This is the key insight of recent literature on "endogenous" growth theory (for a summary, see Romer, 1996).

E7.3 CES

The many-input constant elasticity of substitution (CES) production function is given by

$$q = [\Sigma \beta_i \, x_i^{\rho}]^{\epsilon/\rho}, \rho \leq 1. \qquad \text{(vi)}$$

a. By substituting $m x_i$ for each output, it is easy to show that this function exhibits constant returns to scale for $\in = 1$. For $\in > 1$, the function exhibits increasing returns to scale.

b. The production function exhibits diminishing marginal productivities for each input because $\rho \leq 1$.

c. As in the two-input case, the elasticity of substitution here is given by

$$\sigma = \frac{1}{1-\rho}, \qquad \text{(vii)}$$

and this elasticity applies to substitution between any two of the inputs.

Checking the Cobb-Douglas in the Soviet Union

One way in which the multi-input CES function is used is to determine whether the estimated substitution parameter (ρ) is consistent with the value implied by the Cobb-Douglas ($\rho = 0$, $\sigma = 1$). For example, in a study of five major industries in the former Soviet Union, E. Bairam (1991) finds that the Cobb-Douglas provides a relatively good explanation of changes in output in most major manufacturing sectors. Only for food processing does a lower value for σ seem appropriate.

The next two examples illustrate flexible-form production functions that may approximate any general function of n inputs. In the Chapter 8 extensions, we examine the cost function analogues to some of these functions, which are more widely used than the production functions themselves.

E7.4 Generalized Leontief

$$q = \sum_{i=1}^{n} \sum_{j=1}^{n} \beta_{ij} \sqrt{x_i x_j},$$

where $\beta_{ij} = \beta_{ji}$

a. The function considered in Problem 7.7 is a simple case of this function for the case $n = 2$. For $n = 3$, the function would have linear terms in the three inputs together with three radical terms representing all possible cross-products of the inputs.

b. The function exhibits constant returns to scale as can be shown by using mx_i. Increasing returns to scale can be incorporated into the function by using the transformation

$$q' = q^\epsilon, \epsilon > 1.$$

c. Because each input appears both linearly and under the radical, the function exhibits diminishing marginal productivities to all inputs.

d. The restriction $\beta_{ij} = \beta_{ji}$ is used to ensure symmetry of the second-order partial derivatives.

E7.5 Translog

$$\ln q = \beta_0 + \sum_{i=1}^{n} \beta_i \ln x_i$$

$$+ 0.5 \sum_{i=1}^{n} \sum_{j=1}^{n} \beta_{ij} \ln x_i \ln x_j,$$

$$\beta_{ij} = \beta_{ji}$$

a. Note that the Cobb-Douglas function is a special case of this function where $\beta_0 = \beta_{ij} = 0$ for all i, j.

b. As for the Cobb-Douglas, this function may assume any degree of returns to scale. If

$$\sum_{i=1}^{n} \beta_i = 1$$

and

$$\sum_{j=1}^{n} \beta_{ij} = 0$$

for all i, this function exhibits constant returns to scale. The proof requires some care in dealing with the double summation sign.

c. Again, the condition $\beta_{ij} = \beta_{ji}$ is required to ensure equality of the cross-partial derivatives.

Immigration

Because the translog production function incorporates a large number of substitution possibilities among various inputs, it has been widely used to study the ways in which newly arrived workers may substitute for existing workers. Of particular interest is the way in which the skill level of immigrants may lead to differing reactions in the demand for skilled and unskilled workers in the domestic economy. Studies of the United States and many other countries (Canada, Germany, France, and so forth) have suggested that the overall size of such effects is modest, especially given relatively small immigration flows. But there is some evidence that unskilled immigrant workers may act as substitutes for unskilled domestic workers but complements to skilled domestic workers. Hence increased immigration flows may exacerbate trends toward rising wage differentials. For a summary, see Borjas (1994).

References

Bairam, Erkin. "Elasticity of Substitution, Technical Progress and Returns to Scale in Branches of Soviet Industry: A New CES Production Function Approach." *Journal of Applied Economics* (January–March 1991): 91–96.

Borjas, G. J. "The Economics of Immigration." *Journal of Economic Literature* (December 1994): 1667–1717.

Christenson, L. R., D. W. Jorgenson, and L. J. Lau. "Transcendental Logarithmic Production Frontiers." *Review of Economics and Statistics* (February 1973): 28–45.

Fuss, M., and D. McFadden, eds. *Production Economics: A Dual Approach to Theory and Applications.* Amsterdam: North-Holland, 1978. See especially Chap. I.1, "Cost Revenue and Profit Functions," and Chap. II.1, "A Survey of Functional Forms in the Economic Analysis of Production."

Romer, David. *Advanced Macroeconomics.* New York: McGraw-Hill, 1996.

Solow, R. M. "A Contribution to the Theory of Economic Growth." *Quarterly Journal of Economics* (1956): 65–94.

Chapter 8

COST FUNCTIONS

In this chapter we illustrate the costs that a firm incurs when it produces output. In Chapter 9, we will pursue this topic further by showing how firms make profit-maximizing input and output decisions.

Definitions of costs

Before we can discuss the theory of costs, some difficulties about the proper definition of "costs" must be cleared up. Specifically, we must differentiate between (1) accounting cost and (2) economic cost. The accountant's view of cost stresses out-of-pocket expenses, historical costs, depreciation, and other bookkeeping entries. The economist's definition of cost (which in obvious ways draws on the fundamental opportunity-cost notion) is that the cost of any input is given by the size of the payment necessary to keep the resource in its present employment. Alternatively, the economic cost of using an input is what that input would be paid in its next best use. One way to distinguish between these two views is to consider how the costs of various inputs (labor, capital, and entrepreneurial services) are defined under each system.

Labor costs

Economists and accountants regard labor costs in much the same way. To accountants, expenditures on labor are current expenses and hence costs of production. For economists, labor is an *explicit* cost. Labor services (labor-hours) are contracted at some hourly wage rate (w), and it is usually assumed that this is also what the labor services would earn in their best alternative employment. The hourly wage, of course, includes costs of fringe benefits provided to employees.

Capital costs

In the case of capital services (machine-hours), the two concepts of cost differ. In calculating capital costs, accountants use the historical price of the particular machine under investigation and apply some more-or-less arbitrary depreciation rule to determine how much of that machine's original price to charge to current costs. Economists regard the historical price of a machine as a "sunk cost," which is irrelevant to output decisions. They instead regard the *implicit* cost of the machine to be what someone else would be willing to pay for its use. Thus the cost of one machine-hour is the *rental rate* for that machine in its best alternative use. By continuing to use the machine itself, the firm is implicitly forgoing what someone else would be willing to pay to use it. This rental rate for one machine-hour will be denoted by v.[1]

Costs of entrepreneurial services

The owner of a firm is a residual claimant who is entitled to whatever extra revenues or losses are left after paying other input costs. To an accountant, these would be called *profits* (which might be either positive or negative). Economists, however, ask whether owners (or entrepreneurs) also encounter opportunity costs by working at a particular firm or devoting some of their funds to its operation. If so, these services should be considered an input and some cost should be imputed to them. For example, suppose a highly skilled computer programmer starts a software firm with the idea of keeping any (accounting) profits that might be generated. The programmer's time is clearly an input to the firm, and a cost should be imputed for it. Perhaps the wage that the programmer might command if he or she worked for someone else could be used for that purpose. Hence some part of the accounting profits generated by the firm would be categorized as entrepreneurial costs by economists. Economic profits would be smaller than accounting profits and might be negative if the programmer's opportunity costs exceeded the accounting profits being earned by the business. Similar arguments apply to the capital that an entrepreneur provides to the firm.

Economic costs

In this book, not surprisingly, we use economists' definition of cost:

DEFINITION

Economic cost. The *economic cost* of any input is the payment required to keep that input in its present employment. Equivalently, the economic cost of an input is the remuneration the input would receive in its best alternative employment.

Use of this definition is not meant to imply that accountants' concepts are irrelevant to economic behavior. Indeed, accounting procedures are integrally important to any manager's decision-making process because they can greatly affect the rate of taxation to be applied against profits. Accounting data are also readily available, whereas data on economic costs must often be developed separately. Economists' definitions, however, do have the desirable features of being broadly applicable to all firms and of forming a conceptually consistent system. They therefore are best suited for a general theoretical analysis.

Two simplifying assumptions

As a start, we will make two simplifications about the inputs a firm uses. First, we will assume that there are only two inputs: homogeneous labor (l, measured in labor-hours) and homogeneous capital (k, measured in machine-hours). Entrepreneurial costs are included in capital costs. That is, we assume that the primary opportunity costs faced by a firm's owner are those associated with the capital that the owner provides.

Second, we assume that inputs are hired in perfectly competitive markets. Firms can buy (or sell) all the labor or capital services they want at the prevailing rental rates (w and v). In graphic terms the supply curve for these resources is horizontal at the prevailing factor prices. Both w and v are treated as "parameters" in the firm's decisions; there is nothing the firm can do to affect them. These conditions will be relaxed in later chapters (notably Chapter 16), but for the moment the perfectly competitive assumption is a convenient and useful one to make.

---

[1]Sometimes the symbol r is chosen to represent the rental rate on capital. Because this variable is often confused with the related though distinct concept of the market interest rate, an alternative symbol was chosen here. The exact relationship between v and the interest rate is examined in Chapter 17.

Economic profits and cost minimization

Total costs for the firm during a period are therefore given by

$$\text{total costs} = C = wl + vk, \tag{8.1}$$

where, as before, l and k represent input usage during the period. Assuming the firm produces only one output, its total revenues are given by the price of its product (p) times its total output [$q = f(k, l)$ where $f(k, l)$ is the firm's production function]. Economic profits (π) are then the difference between total revenues and total economic costs:

DEFINITION

Economic profits. *Economic profits* (π) the difference between a firm's total revenues and its total costs:

$$\pi = \text{total revenue} - \text{total cost} = pq - wl - vk$$
$$= pf(k, l) - wl - vk \tag{8.2}$$

Equation 8.2 shows that the economic profits obtained by a firm are a function of the amount of capital and labor employed. If, as we will assume in many places in this book, the firm seeks maximum profits, we might study its behavior by examining how k and l are chosen so as to maximize Equation 8.2. This would, in turn, lead to a theory of supply and to a theory of the "derived demand" for capital and labor inputs. In the next chapter we will take up those subjects in detail. Here, however, we wish to develop a theory of costs that is somewhat more general and might apply to firms that are not necessarily profit maximizers. Hence, we begin the study of costs by finessing, for the moment, a discussion of output choice. That is, we assume that for some reason the firm has decided to produce a particular output level (say, q_0). The firm's revenues are therefore fixed at pq_0. Now we wish to examine how the firm can produce q_0 at minimal costs.

Cost-minimizing input choices

Mathematically, this is a constrained minimization problem. But before proceeding with a rigorous solution, it is useful to state the result to be derived with an intuitive argument. To minimize the cost of producing a given level of output, a firm should choose that point on the q_0 isoquant at which the rate of technical substitution of l for k is equal to the ratio w/v: It should equate the rate at which k can be traded for l in production to the rate at which they can be traded in the marketplace. Suppose that this were not true. In particular, suppose that the firm were producing output level q_0 using $k = 10$, $l = 10$, and assume that the RTS was 2 at this point. Assume also that $w = \$1$, $v = \$1$, and hence that $w/v = 1$ (which is unequal to 2). At this input combination, the cost of producing q_0 is \$20. It is easy to show this is not the minimal input cost. q_0 can also be produced using $k = 8$ and $l = 11$; we can give up two units of k and keep output constant at q_0 by adding one unit of l. But at this input combination the cost of producing q_0 is \$19, and hence the initial input combination was not optimal. A proof similar to this one can be demonstrated whenever the RTS and the ratio of the input costs differ.

Mathematical analysis

Mathematically, we seek to minimize total costs, given $q = f(k, l) = q_0$. Setting up the Lagrangian expression

$$\mathscr{L} = wl + vk + \lambda[q_0 - f(k, l)], \tag{8.3}$$

the first-order conditions for a constrained minimum are

$$\frac{\partial \mathscr{L}}{\partial l} = w - \lambda \frac{\partial f}{\partial l} = 0$$

$$\frac{\partial \mathscr{L}}{\partial k} = v - \lambda \frac{\partial f}{\partial k} = 0 \qquad\qquad (8.4)$$

$$\frac{\partial \mathscr{L}}{\partial \lambda} = q_0 - f(k, l) = 0$$

or, dividing the first two equations,

$$\frac{w}{v} = \frac{\partial f/\partial l}{\partial f/\partial k} = RTS(l \text{ for } k). \qquad\qquad (8.5)$$

This says that the cost-minimizing firm should equate the *RTS* for the two inputs to the ratio of their prices.

Further interpretations

These first-order conditions for minimal costs can be manipulated in several different ways to yield interesting results. For example, cross-multiplying Equation 8.5 gives

$$\frac{f_k}{v} = \frac{f_l}{w}. \qquad\qquad (8.6)$$

That is, for costs to be minimized the marginal productivity per dollar spent should be the same for all inputs. If increasing one input promised to increase output by a greater amount per dollar spent than did another input, costs would not be minimal—the firm should hire more of the input that promises a bigger "bang per buck" and less of the more costly (in terms of productivity) input. Any input that cannot meet the common benefit-cost ratio defined in Equation 8.6 should not be hired at all.

Equation 8.6 can, of course, also be derived from Equation 8.4, but it is more instructive to derive its inverse:

$$\frac{w}{f_l} = \frac{v}{f_k} = \lambda. \qquad\qquad (8.7)$$

This equation reports the extra cost of obtaining an extra unit of output by hiring either added labor or added capital input. Because of cost minimization this marginal cost is the same no matter which input is hired. This common marginal cost is also measured by the Lagrangian multiplier from the cost-minimization problem. As is the case for all constrained optimization problems, here the Lagrangian multiplier shows how much in extra costs would be incurred by increasing the output constraint slightly. Because marginal cost plays an important role in a firm's supply decisions, we will return to this feature of cost minimization frequently.

Graphical analysis

Cost minimization is shown graphically in Figure 8.1. Given the output isoquant q_0, we wish to find the least costly point on the isoquant. Lines showing equal cost are parallel straight lines with slopes—w/v. Three lines of equal total cost shown in Figure 8.1. $C_1 < C_2 < C_3$. It is clear from the figure that the minimum total cost for producing q_0 is given by C_1, where the total cost curve is just tangent to the isoquant. The cost-minimizing input combination is l^*, k^*. This combination will be a true minimum if the

| FIGURE 8.1 | Minimization of Costs Given $q = q_0$ |

A firm is assumed to choose k and l to minimize total costs. The condition for this minimization is that the rate at which k and l can be traded technically (while keeping $q = q_0$) should be equal to the rate at which these inputs can be traded in the market. In other words, the RTS (of l for k) should be set equal to the price ratio w/v. This tangency is shown in the figure; costs are minimized at C_1 by choosing inputs k^* and l^*.

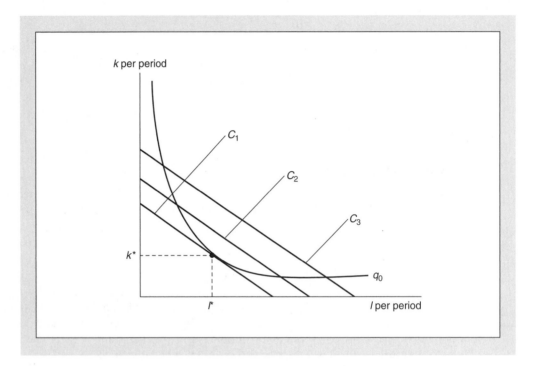

isoquant is convex (if the RTS diminishes for decreases in k/l). The mathematical and graphic analyses arrive at the same conclusion:

OPTIMIZATION PRINCIPLE

Cost minimization. In order to minimize the cost of any given level of input (q_0), the firm should produce at that point on the q_0 isoquant for which the RTS (of l for k) is equal to the ratio of the inputs' rental prices (w/v).

Contingent demand for inputs

Figure 8.1 exhibits the formal similarity between the firm's cost-minimization problem and the individual's expenditure-minimization problem studied in Chapter 4 (see Figure 4.6). In both problems, the economic actor seeks to achieve his or her target (output or utility) at minimal cost. In Chapter 5 we showed how this process is used to construct a theory of compensated demand for a good. In the present case, cost minimization leads to a demand for capital and labor input that is contingent on the level of output being produced. This is not, therefore, the complete story of a firm's demand for the inputs it uses because it does not address the issue of output choice. But studying the contingent demand for inputs provides an important building block for analyzing the firm's overall demand for inputs, and we will take up this topic in more detail later in this chapter.

The firm's expansion path

A firm can follow the cost-minimization process for each level of output: For each q it finds the input choice that minimizes the cost of producing it. If input costs (w and v) re-

FIGURE 8.2   The Firm's Expansion Path

The firm's expansion path is the locus of cost-minimizing tangencies. Assuming fixed input prices, the curve shows how inputs increase as output increases.

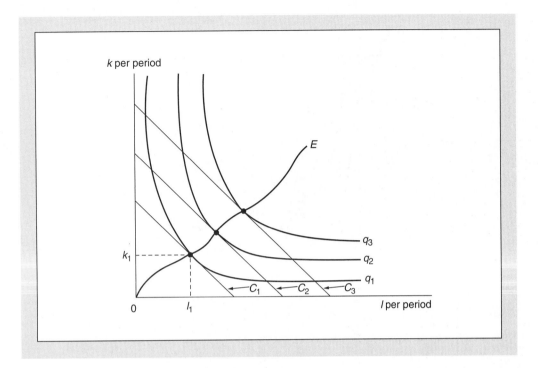

main constant for all amounts the firm may demand, we can easily trace this locus of cost-minimizing choices. This procedure is shown in Figure 8.2. The line $0E$ records the cost-minimizing tangencies for successively higher levels of output. For example, the minimum cost for producing output level q_1 is given by C_1, and inputs k_1 and l_1 are used. Other tangencies in the figure can be interpreted in a similar way. The locus of these tangencies is called the firm's *expansion path,* because it records how input expands as output expands while holding the prices of the inputs constant.

As Figure 8.2 shows, the expansion path need not be a straight line. The use of some inputs may increase faster than others as output expands. Which inputs expand more rapidly will depend on the shape of the production isoquants. Because cost minimization requires that the RTS always be set equal to the ratio w/v, and because the w/v ratio is assumed to be constant, the shape of the expansion path will be determined by where a particular RTS occurs on successively higher isoquants. If the production function exhibits constant returns to scale (or, more generally, if it is homothetic), the expansion path will be a straight line, because, in that case, the RTS depends only on the ratio of k to l. That ratio would be constant along such a linear expansion path.

It would seem reasonable to assume that the expansion path will be positively sloped; that is, successively higher output levels will require more of both inputs. This need not be the case, however, as Figure 8.3 illustrates. Increases of output beyond q_2 actually cause the quantity of labor used to decrease. In this range, labor would be said to be an *inferior input.* The occurrence of inferior inputs is then a theoretical possibility that may happen, even when isoquants have their usual convex shape.

Much theoretical discussion has centered on the analysis of factor inferiority. Whether inferiority is likely to occur in real-world production functions is a difficult empirical

FIGURE 8.3   Input Inferiority

With this particular set of isoquants, labor is an inferior input, because less l is chosen as output expands beyond q_2.

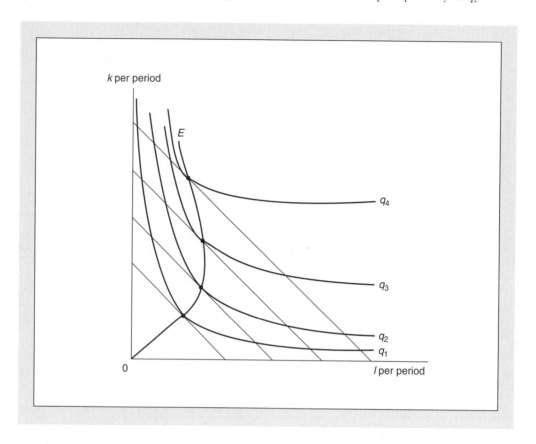

question to answer. It seems unlikely that such comprehensive magnitudes as "capital" and "labor" could be inferior, but a finer classification of inputs may bring inferiority to light. For example, the use of shovels may decline as production of building foundations (and the use of backhoes) increases. In this book we shall not be particularly concerned with the analytical issues raised by this possibility, although complications raised by inferior inputs will be mentioned in a few places.

    EXAMPLE 8.1

Cost Minimization

The cost-minimization process can be readily illustrated with two of the production functions we encountered in the last chapter.

a. Cobb-Douglas: $q = f(k, l) = k^\alpha l^\beta$

For this case the relevant Lagrangian expression for minimizing the cost of producing, say, q_0 is

$$\mathcal{L} = vk + wl + \lambda(q_0 - k^\alpha l^\beta), \tag{8.8}$$

and the first-order conditions for a minimum are

$$\frac{\partial \mathscr{L}}{\partial k} = v - \lambda \alpha k^{\alpha-1} l^{\beta} = 0$$

$$\frac{\partial \mathscr{L}}{\partial l} = w - \lambda \beta k^{\alpha} l^{\beta-1} = 0 \tag{8.9}$$

$$\frac{\partial \mathscr{L}}{\partial \lambda} = q_0 - k^{\alpha} l^{\beta} = 0.$$

Dividing the second of these by the first yields

$$\frac{w}{v} = \frac{\beta k^{\alpha} l^{\beta-1}}{\alpha k^{\alpha-1} l^{\beta}} = \frac{\beta}{\alpha} \cdot \frac{k}{l}, \tag{8.10}$$

which again shows that costs are minimized when the ratio of the inputs' prices is equal to the *RTS*. Because the Cobb-Douglas function is homothetic, the *RTS* depends only on the ratio of the two inputs. If the ratio of input costs does not change, the firms will use the same input ratio no matter how much it produces—that is, the expansion path will be a straight line through the origin.

As a numerical example, suppose $\alpha = \beta = 0.5$, $w = 12$, $v = 3$ and that the firm wishes to produce $q_0 = 40$. The first-order condition for a minimum requires that $k = 4l$. Inserting that into the production function (the final requirement in Equation 8.9) we have $q_0 = 40 = k^{0.5} l^{0.5} = 2l$. So the cost minimizing input combination is $l = 20$, $k = 80$ and total costs are given by $vk + wl = 3(80) + 12(20) = 480$. That this is a true cost minimum is suggested by looking at a few other input combinations that also are capable of producing 40 units of output:

$$k = 40, \ l = 40, \ C = 600$$
$$k = 10, \ l = 160, \ C = 2220 \tag{8.11}$$
$$k = 160, \ l = 10, \ C = 600.$$

Any other input combination able to produce 40 units of output will also cost more than 480. Cost minimization is also suggested by considering marginal productivities. At the optimal point

$$MP_k = f_k = 0.5 k^{-0.5} l^{0.5} = 0.5(20/80)^{0.5} = 0.25$$
$$MP_l = f_l = 0.5 k^{0.5} l^{-0.5} = 0.5(80/20)^{0.5} = 1.0, \tag{8.12}$$

so at the margin labor is four times as productive as capital, and this extra productivity precisely compensates for the higher unit price of labor input.

b. CES: $q = f(k, l) = (k^{\rho} + l^{\rho})^{\gamma/\rho}$

Again we set up the Lagrangian expression

$$\mathscr{L} = vk + wl + \lambda[q_0 - (k^{\rho} + l^{\rho})^{\gamma/\rho}], \tag{8.13}$$

and the first-order conditions for a minimum are

$$\frac{\partial \mathscr{L}}{\partial k} = v - \lambda(\gamma/\rho)(k^{\rho} + l^{\rho})^{(\gamma-\rho)/\rho}(\rho)k^{\rho-1} = 0$$

$$\frac{\partial \mathscr{L}}{\partial l} = w - \lambda(\gamma/\rho)(k^{\rho} + l^{\rho})^{(\gamma-\rho)/\rho}(\rho)l^{\rho-1} = 0 \tag{8.14}$$

$$\frac{\partial \mathscr{L}}{\partial \lambda} = q_0 - (k^{\rho} + l^{\rho})^{\gamma/\rho} = 0.$$

(continued)

EXAMPLE 8.1   CONTINUED

Dividing the first two of these equations causes a lot of this mass of symbols to drop out, leaving

$$\frac{w}{v} = \left(\frac{l}{k}\right)^{\rho-1} = \left(\frac{k}{l}\right)^{1-\rho} = \left(\frac{k}{l}\right)^{1/\sigma}, \text{ or, } \frac{k}{l} = \left(\frac{w}{v}\right)^{\sigma}. \qquad (8.15)$$

Because the CES function is also homothetic, the cost-minimizing input ratio is independent of the absolute level of production. The result in Equation 8.15 is a simple generalization of the Cobb-Douglas result (when $\sigma = 1$). With the Cobb-Douglas the cost-minimizing capital-labor ratio changes directly in proportion with changes in the ratio of wages to capital rental rates. In cases with greater substitutability ($\sigma > 1$), changes in the ratio of wages to rental rates cause a greater than proportional increase in the cost-minimizing capital-labor ratio. With less substitutability ($\sigma < 1$) the response is proportionally smaller.

Query: In the Cobb-Douglas numerical example with $w/v = 4$ we found that the cost-minimizing input ratio for producing 40 units of output was $k/l = 80/20 = 4$. How would this value change for $\sigma = 2$ or $\sigma = 0.5$? What actual input combinations would be used? What would total costs be?

Cost functions

We are now in a position to examine the firm's overall cost structure. To do so it will be convenient to use the expansion path solutions to derive the total cost function.

Total cost function. The *total cost function* shows that for any set of input costs and for any output level, the minimum total cost incurred by the firm is

$$C = C(v, w, q). \qquad (8.16)$$

Figure 8.2 makes clear that total costs increase as output, q, increases. We will begin by analyzing this relationship between total cost and output while holding input prices fixed. Then we will consider how a change in an input price shifts the expansion path and its related cost functions.

Average and marginal cost functions

Although the total cost function provides complete information about the output-cost relationship, it is often convenient to analyze costs on a per unit of output basis, because that approach corresponds more closely to the analysis of demand, which focused on the price per unit of a commodity. Two different unit cost measures are widely used in economics: (1) average cost, which is the cost per unit of output; and (2) marginal cost, which is the cost of one more unit of output. The relationship of these concepts to the total cost function is described in the following definitions:

Average and marginal cost functions. The *average cost function* (AC) is found by computing total costs per unit of output:

$$\text{average cost} = AC(v, w, q) = \frac{C(v, w, q)}{q}. \qquad (8.17)$$

The *marginal cost function* (MC) is found by computing the change in total costs for a change in output produced:

$$\text{marginal cost} = MC(v, w, q) = \frac{\partial C(v, w, q)}{\partial q}. \qquad (8.18)$$

Notice that in these definitions, average and marginal costs depend both on the level of output being produced and on the prices of inputs. In many places throughout this book, we will graph simple two-dimensional relationships between costs and output. As the definitions make clear, all such graphs are drawn on the assumption that the prices of inputs remain constant and that technology does not change. If input prices change or if technology advances, cost curves generally will shift to new positions. Later in this chapter we will explore the likely direction and size of such shifts when we study the entire cost function in detail.

Graphical analysis of total costs

Figures 8.4a and 8.5a illustrate two possible shapes for the relationship between total cost and the level of the firm's output. In Figure 8.4a, total cost is simply proportional to output. Such a situation would arise if the underlying production function exhibits constant returns to scale. In that case, suppose k_1 units of capital input and l_1 units of labor input are required to produce one unit of output. Then

$$C(q = 1) = vk_1 + wl_1. \qquad (8.19)$$

To produce m units of output, then, requires mk_1 units of capital and ml_1 units of labor because of the constant returns-to-scale assumption.[2] Hence

$$\begin{aligned} C(q = m) &= vmk_1 + wml_1 = m(vk_1 + wl_1) \\ &= m \cdot C(q = 1), \end{aligned} \qquad (8.20)$$

and the proportionality between output and cost is established.

The situation in Figure 8.5a is more complicated. There it is assumed that initially the total cost curve is concave; although initially costs rise rapidly for increases in output, that rate of increase slows as output expands into the midrange of output. Beyond this middle range, however, the total cost curve becomes convex, and costs begin to rise progressively more rapidly. One possible reason for such a shape for the total cost curve is that there is some third factor of production (say, the services of an entrepreneur) that is fixed as capital and labor usage expands. In this case the initial concave section of the curve might be explained by the increasingly optimal usage of the entrepreneur's services—he or she needs a moderate level of production to utilize his or her skills fully. Beyond the point of inflection, however, the entrepreneur becomes overworked in attempting to coordinate production, and diminishing returns set in. Hence, total costs rise rapidly.

A variety of other explanations have been offered for the cubic-type total cost curve in Figure 8.5a, but we will not examine them here. Ultimately, the shape of the total cost curve is an empirical question that can only be determined by examining real-world data. In the extensions to this chapter we illustrate some of the literature on cost functions.

---

[2]The input combination ml_1, mk_1 minimizes the cost of producing m units of output because the ratio of the inputs is still k_1/l_1 and the *RTS* for a constant returns-to-scale production function depends only on that ratio.

| FIGURE 8.4 | Total, Average, and Marginal Cost Curves for the Constant Returns-to-Scale Case |

In (a) total costs are proportional to output level. Average and marginal costs, as shown in (b), are equal and constant for all output levels.

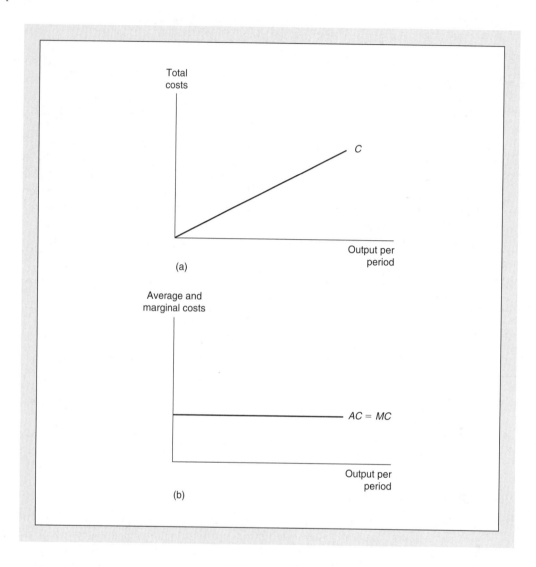

Graphical analysis of average and marginal costs

Information from the total cost curves can be used to construct the average and marginal cost curves shown in Figures 8.4b and 8.5b. For the constant returns-to-scale case (Figure 8.4), this is quite simple. Because total costs are proportional to output, average and marginal costs are constant and equal for all levels of output.[3] These costs are shown by the horizontal line $AC = MC$ in Figure 8.4b.

For the cubic total cost curve case (Figure 8.5), computation of the average and marginal cost curves requires some geometric intuition. As the definition in Equation 8.18 makes clear, marginal cost is simply the slope of the total cost curve. Hence, because of

---

[3]Mathematically, because $C = aq$ (where a is the cost of 1 unit of output),

$$AC = \frac{C}{q} = a = \frac{\partial C}{\partial q} = MC.$$

FIGURE 8.5   Total, Average, and Marginal Cost Curves for the Cubic Total Cost Curve Case

If the total cost curve has the cubic shape shown in (a), average and marginal cost curves will be U-shaped. In (b) the marginal cost curve passes through the low point of the average cost curve at output level q^*.

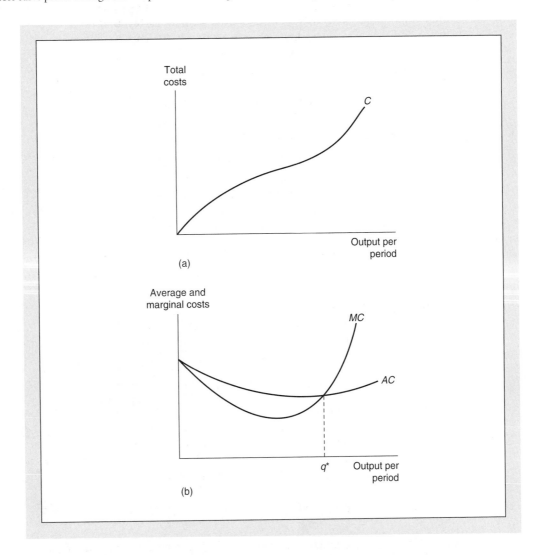

the assumed shape of the curve, the *MC* curve is U-shaped, with *MC* falling over the concave portion of the total cost curve and rising beyond the point of inflection. Because the slope is always positive, however, *MC* is always greater than zero. Average costs (*AC*) start out being equal to marginal cost for the "first" unit of output.[4] As output expands, however, *AC* exceeds *MC*, because *AC* reflects both the marginal cost of the last unit

---

[4]Technically, $AC = MC$ at $q = 0$. This can be shown by L'Hopital's rule, which states that if $f(a) = g(a) = 0$,

$$\lim_{x \to a} \frac{f(x)}{g(x)} = \lim_{x \to a} \frac{f'(x)}{g'(x)}.$$

In this case, $C = 0$ at $q = 0$, so

$$\lim_{q \to 0} AC = \lim_{q \to 0} \frac{C}{q} = \lim_{q \to 0} \frac{\partial C / \partial q}{1} = \lim_{q \to 0} MC$$

or

$$AC = MC \text{ at } q = 0,$$

which was to be shown.

produced and the higher marginal costs of the previously produced units. So long as $AC > MC$, average costs must be falling. Because the lower costs of the newly produced units are below average cost, they continue to pull average costs downward. Marginal costs rise, however, and eventually (at q^*) equal average cost. Beyond this point, $MC > AC$, and average costs will be rising because they are being pulled upward by increasingly higher marginal costs. Consequently, we have shown that the AC curve also has a U-shape and that it reaches a low point at q^*, where AC and MC intersect.[5] In empirical studies of cost functions, there is considerable interest in this point of minimum average cost. It reflects the "minimum efficient scale" (*MES*) for the particular production process being examined. The point is also theoretically important because of the role it plays in perfectly competitive price determination in the long run (see Chapter 10).

Cost functions and shifts in cost curves

The cost curves illustrated in Figures 8.4 and 8.5 show the relationship between costs and quantity produced on the assumption that all other factors are held constant. Specifically, construction of the curves assumes that input prices and the level of technology do not change.[6] If these factors do change, the cost curves will shift. In this section we delve further into the mathematics of cost functions as a way of studying these shifts. We begin with same examples.

 EXAMPLE 8.2

Some Illustrative Cost Functions

In this example we calculate the cost functions associated with three different production functions. Later we will use these examples to illustrate some of the general properties of cost functions.

a. Fixed Proportions: $q = f(k, l) = \min(ak, bl)$.

The calculation of cost functions from their underlying production functions is one of the more frustrating tasks for economics students. So, let's start with a very simple example. What we wish to do is show how total costs depend on input costs and on quantity produced. In the fixed-proportions case we know that production will occur at a vertex of the L-shaped isoquants where $q = ak = bl$. Hence, total costs are

$$\text{Total Costs} = C(v, w, q) = vk + wl = v(q/a) + w(q/b) = q\left(\frac{v}{a} + \frac{w}{b}\right). \quad (8.21)$$

This is indeed the sort of function we want because it states total costs as a function of v, w, and q only together with some parameters of the underlying production function. Because of the constant returns-to-scale nature of this production function, it takes the special form

$$C(v,w,q) = qC(v,w,1). \quad (8.22)$$

---

[5]Mathematically, we can find the minimum AC by setting its derivative equal to 0:

$$\frac{\partial AC}{\partial q} = \frac{\partial \frac{C}{q}}{\partial q} = \frac{q \cdot \frac{\partial C}{\partial q} - C \cdot 1}{q^2} = \frac{q \cdot MC - C}{q^2} = 0$$

or

$$q \cdot MC - C = 0 \text{ or } MC = C/q = AC.$$

[6]For multiproduct firms, an additional complication must be considered. For such firms it is possible that the costs associated with producing one output (say q_1) are also affected by the amount of some other output being produced (q_2). In this case the firm is said to exhibit "economies of scope," and the total cost function will be of the form $C(q_1, q_2, w, v)$. Hence, q_2 must also be held constant in constructing the q_1 cost curves. Presumably increases in q_2 shift the q_1 cost curves downward. Although we will not be concerned with multiproduct firms in this chapter, the concept of economies of scope is addressed briefly in Problem 12.2 and in the Extensions to this chapter.

That is, total costs are given by output times the cost of producing one unit. Increases in input prices clearly increase total costs with this function, and technical improvements that take the form of increasing the parameters a and b reduce costs.

b. Cobb-Douglas: $q = f(k, l) = k^{\alpha}l^{\beta}$.

This is our first example of burdensome computation, but being clear that the final goal is to use the results of cost minimization to replace the inputs in the production function with costs can clarify the process. From Example 8.1 we know that cost minimization requires that

$$\frac{w}{v} = \frac{\beta}{\alpha} \cdot \frac{k}{l} \quad \text{so} \quad k = \frac{\alpha}{\beta} \cdot \frac{w}{v} \cdot l.$$

Substitution into the production function permits a solution for labor input in terms of q, v, and w as

$$q = k^{\alpha}l^{\beta} = \left(\frac{\alpha}{\beta} \cdot \frac{w}{v}\right)^{\alpha} l^{\alpha+\beta} \quad \text{or} \quad l = q^{1/\alpha+\beta}\left(\frac{\beta}{\alpha}\right)^{\alpha/\alpha+\beta} w^{-\alpha/\alpha+\beta}v^{\alpha/\alpha+\beta}. \quad (8.23)$$

A similar set of manipulations gives

$$k = q^{1/\alpha+\beta}\left(\frac{\alpha}{\beta}\right)^{\beta/\alpha+\beta} w^{\beta/\alpha+\beta}v^{-\beta/\alpha+\beta}. \quad (8.24)$$

Now we are ready to derive total costs as

$$C(v,w,q) = vk + wl = q^{1/\alpha+\beta}Bv^{\alpha/\alpha+\beta}w^{\beta/\alpha+\beta}, \quad (8.25)$$

where $B = (\alpha + \beta)\,\alpha^{-\alpha/\alpha+\beta}\,\beta^{-\beta/\alpha+\beta}$—a constant that involves only the parameters α and β. Although this derivation was a bit messy, several interesting aspects of this Cobb-Douglas cost function are readily apparent. First, whether the function is a convex, linear, or concave function of output depends on whether there are decreasing returns to scale ($\alpha + \beta < 1$), constant returns to scale ($\alpha + \beta = 1$), or increasing returns to scale ($\alpha + \beta > 1$). Second, an increase in any input price increases costs, with the extent of the increase being determined by the relative importance of the input as reflected by the size of its exponent in the production function. Finally, the cost function is homogeneous of degree one in the input costs—a general feature of all cost functions, as we shall show shortly.

c. CES: $q = f(k, l) = (k^{\rho} + l^{\rho})^{\gamma/\rho}$

For this case your author will mercifully spare you the algebra. To derive the total cost function we use the cost-minimization condition specified in Equation 8.15, solve for each input individually, and eventually get

$$C(v, w, q) = vk + wl = q^{1/\gamma}(v^{\rho/\rho-1} + w^{\rho/\rho-1})^{(\rho-1)/\rho}$$
$$= q^{1/\gamma}(v^{1-\sigma} + w^{1-\sigma})^{1/1-\sigma}, \quad (8.26)$$

where the elasticity of substitution is given by $\sigma = 1/(1 - \rho)$. Once again the shape of the total cost is determined by the scale parameter (γ) for this production function, and the cost function is increasing in both of the input prices. The function is also homogeneous of degree one in those prices. One limiting feature of this form of the CES function is that the inputs are given equal weights—hence their prices are equally important in the cost function. This feature of the CES is easily generalized, however (see Problem 8.7).

Query: How are the various substitution possibilities inherent in the CES function reflected in the CES cost function in Equation 8.26.

Properties of cost functions

These examples illustrate some properties of total cost functions that are quite general. They include:

1. *Homogeneity:* The total cost functions in Example 8.3 are all homogeneous of degree one in the input prices. That is, a doubling of input prices will precisely double the cost of producing any given output level (you might check this out for yourself). This is a property of all proper cost functions. When all input prices double (or are increased by any uniform proportion), the ratio of any two input prices will not change. Because cost minimization requires that the ratio of input prices be set equal to the *RTS* along a given isoquant, the cost-minimizing input combination also will not change. Hence, the firm will buy exactly the same set of inputs and pay precisely twice as much for them. One implication of this result is that a pure, uniform inflation in all input costs will not change a firm's input decisions, and its cost curves will shift upward in direct correspondence to the rate of inflation.

2. *Total cost functions are nondecreasing in q, v, and w:* This property seems obvious, but it is worth dwelling on it a bit. Because cost functions are derived from a cost-minimization process, any decline in costs from an increase in one of the function's arguments would lead to a contradiction. For example, if an increase in output from q_1 to q_2 caused total costs to decline, it must be the case that the firm was not minimizing costs in the first place. It could have produce q_2 and thrown away an output of $q_2 - q_1$, thereby producing q_1 at a lower cost. Similarly, if an increase in the price of an input ever reduced total cost, the firm could not have been minimizing its costs in the first place. To see this, suppose the firm was using the input combination k_1, l_1 and that w increases. Clearly that will increase the cost of the initial input combination. But if changes in input choices actually caused total costs to decline, that must imply that there was a lower cost input mix than k_1, l_1 initially. Hence, we have a contradiction and this property of cost functions is established.[7]

3. *Total cost functions are concave in input prices:* It is probably easiest to illustrate this property with a graph. Figure 8.6 shows total costs for various values of an input price, say w, holding q and v constant. Suppose that initially a wage rate of w_1 prevails and that the total costs associated with producing q_1 are given by $C(v, w_1, q_1)$. If the firm did not change its input mix in response to changes in wages, its total cost curve would be linear as reflected by the line $C_{PSEUDO}(v, w, q_1)$ in the figure. But a cost-minimizing firm probably would change its input mix used to produce q_1 when wages change and these actual cost $[C(v, w, q_1)]$ would fall below the "pseudo" costs. Hence, the total cost function must have the concave shape shown in the Figure 8.6. One implication of this finding is that costs will be lower when a firm faces input prices that fluctuate around a given level than when they remain constant at that level. With fluctuating input prices the firm can adapt its input mix to take advantage of such fluctuations by using a lot of, say, labor when its price is low and economizing on that input when its price is high.

---

[7]A formal proof could also be based on the envelope theorem as applied to constrained minimization problems. Consider the Lagrangian expression in Equation 8.3. As was pointed out in Chapter 2, we can calculate the change in the objective in such an expression (here total cost) with respect to a change in a variable by differentiating the Lagrangian expression. Performing this differentiation yields

$$\frac{\partial C^*}{\partial q} = \frac{\partial \mathcal{L}}{\partial q} = \lambda \quad (= MC) \geq 0$$
$$\frac{\partial C^*}{\partial v} = \frac{\partial \mathcal{L}}{\partial v} = k \geq 0$$
$$\frac{\partial C^*}{\partial w} = \frac{\partial \mathcal{L}}{\partial w} = l \geq 0$$

Not only do these envelope results prove this property of cost functions, but they also are quite useful in their own right as we will show later in this chapter.

FIGURE 8.6   **Cost Functions Are Concave in Input Prices**

With a wage rate of w_1 total costs of producing q_1 are (v, w_1, q_1). If the firm does not change its input mix, costs of producing q_1 would follow the straight line C_{PSEUDO}. With input substitution, actual costs, $C(v, w, q_1)$, will fall below this line, and hence the cost function is concave in w.

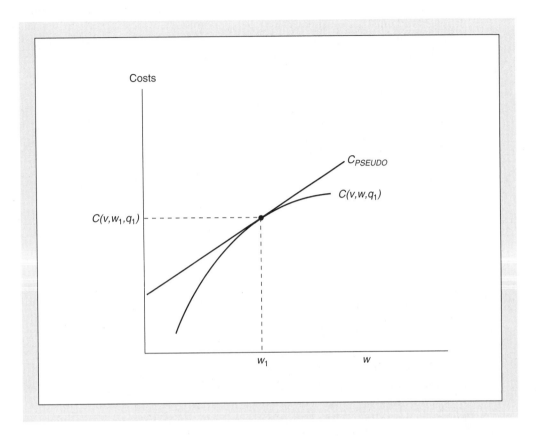

4. *Average and marginal costs:* Some, but not all, of these properties of total-cost functions carry over to their related average and marginal cost functions. Homogeneity is one property that carries over directly. Because $C(tv, tw, q) = tC(v, w, q)$ we have

$$AC(tv, tw, q) = \frac{C(tv, tw, q)}{q} = \frac{tC(v, w, q)}{q} = tAC(v, w, q) \quad (8.27)$$

and,[8]

$$MC(tv, tw, q) = \frac{\partial C(tv, tw, q)}{\partial q} = \frac{t\partial C(v, w, q)}{\partial q} = tMC(v, w, q). \quad (8.28)$$

The effects of changes in q, v, and w on average and marginal costs are sometimes ambiguous, however. We have already shown that average and marginal cost curves may have negatively sloped segments, so neither AC nor MC is nondecreasing in q. Because total costs must not decrease when an input price rises, it is clear that average cost is increasing in w and v. But the case of marginal cost is more complex. The main complication arises because of the possibility of input inferiority. In that (admittedly rare) case, an increase in an inferior input's price will actually cause marginal cost to decline. Although the proof of this is relatively

---

[8]This result does not violate the theorem that the derivative of a function that is homogeneous of degree k is homogeneous of degree $k - 1$ because we are differentiating with respect to q and total costs are homogeneous with respect to input prices only.

straightforward,[9] an intuitive explanation for it is elusive. Still, in most cases, it seems clear that the increase in the price of an input will increase marginal cost as well.

Input substitution

A change in the price of an input will cause the firm to alter its input mix. Hence a full study of how cost curves shift when input prices change must also include an examination of substitution among inputs. To study this process economists have developed a somewhat different measure of the elasticity of substitution than the one we encountered in the theory of production. Specifically, we wish to examine how the ratio of input usage (k/l) changes in response to a change in w/v, while holding q constant. That is, we wish to examine the derivative

$$\frac{\partial\left(\dfrac{k}{l}\right)}{\partial\left(\dfrac{w}{v}\right)} \tag{8.29}$$

along an isoquant.

Putting this in proportional terms as

$$s = \frac{\partial k/l}{\partial w/v} \cdot \frac{w/v}{k/l} = \frac{\partial \ln k/l}{\partial \ln w/v} \tag{8.30}$$

gives an alternative and more intuitive definition of the elasticity of substitution.[10] In the two-input case, s must be nonnegative; an increase in w/v will be met by an increase in k/l (or, in the limiting fixed-proportions case, k/l will stay constant). Large values of s indicate that firms change their input proportions significantly in response to changes in input prices, whereas low values indicate that changes in input prices have relatively little effect.

Partial elasticity of substitution

When there are only two inputs, the substitution elasticity defined in Equation 8.30 is identical to that defined in Chapter 7 (see Equation 7.32). This can be shown by remembering that a cost-minimizing[11] firm will equate its RTS (of l for k) to the input price ratio w/v. The great advantage of the definition given in Equation 8.30 is that it can be more easily generalized to the many-input case than can the definition of the previous chapter. Specifically, we have the following definition:

DEFINITION

Partial elasticity of substitution (s_{ij}). The *partial elasticity of substitution* between two inputs (x_i and x_j) with prices w_i and w_j is given by

$$s_{ij} = \frac{\partial x_i/x_j}{\partial w_j/w_i} \cdot \frac{w_j/w_i}{x_i/x_j} = \frac{\partial \ln(x_i/x_j)}{\partial \ln(w_i/w_j)}, \tag{8.31}$$

where output and all other input prices are held constant.

---

[9]The proof follows the envelope theorem results presented in footnote 7. Because the MC function can be derived by differentiation from the Lagrangian for cost minimization, we can use Young's theorem to show

$$\frac{\partial MC}{\partial v} = \frac{\partial(\partial \mathcal{L}/\partial q)}{\partial v} = \frac{\partial^2 \mathcal{L}}{\partial v \partial q} = \frac{\partial^2 \mathcal{L}}{\partial q \partial v} = \frac{\partial k}{\partial q}.$$

Hence, if capital is a normal input, an increase in v will raise MC whereas, if capital is inferior, an increase in v will actually reduce MC.

[10]This definition is usually attributed to R. G. D. Allen, who developed it in an alternative form in his *Mathematical Analysis for Economists* (New York: St. Martin's Press, 1938), pp. 504–9.

[11]In Example 8.1 we found that, for the CES production function, cost minimization requires that $\dfrac{k}{l} = \left(\dfrac{w}{v}\right)^{\sigma}$ so $\ln(k/l) = \sigma \ln(w/v)$ and therefore $s_{k,l} = \dfrac{\partial \ln(k/l)}{\partial \ln(w/v)} = \sigma.$

The word *partial* is used in this definition to differentiate the concept from the production function–based definition. In fact, s_{ij} is a more flexible concept because it permits the firm to alter the usage of inputs other than x_i or x_j when input prices change, whereas other input usage was held constant in the definition in Chapter 7. Suppose, for example, that energy prices rise and we wish to know how this affects the ratio of energy to capital input while holding output constant. Although we would expect energy input to fall, it is possible that the firm will substitute a third input, say, labor, for *both* energy and capital, so capital input may fall too. Hence, depending on the specific sizes of these changes, it is possible that the energy-capital ratio may in fact rise. In such a case, we might call energy and capital *complements,* because of the way their joint usage relates to labor input. Although we will not examine the implications of these possibilities for production and cost theory here, the extensions in this chapter show how s_{ij} can be calculated if the cost function is known.

Quantitative size of shifts in cost curves

We have already shown that increases in an input price will raise total, average, and (except in the inferior input case) marginal costs. We are now in a position to judge the extent of such increases. First, and most obviously, the increase in costs will be influenced importantly by the relative significance of the input in the production process. If an input constitutes a large fraction of total costs, an increase in its price will raise costs significantly. A rise in the wage rate would sharply increase home-builders' costs because labor is a major input in construction. On the other hand, a price rise for a relatively minor input will have a small cost impact. An increase in nail prices will not raise home costs very much.

A less obvious determinant of the extent of cost increases is input substitutability. If firms can easily substitute another input for the one that has risen in price, there may be little increase in costs. Increases in copper prices in the late 1960s, for example, had little impact on electric utilities' costs of distributing electricity because they found they could easily substitute aluminum for copper cables. Alternatively, if the firm finds it difficult or impossible to substitute for the input that has become more costly, costs may rise rapidly. The cost of gold jewelry, along with the price of gold, rose rapidly during the early 1970s because there was simply no substitute for the raw input.

It is possible to give a precise mathematical statement of the quantitative sizes of all of these effects by using the partial elasticity of substitution. To do so, however, would risk further cluttering the book with symbols.[12] For our purposes, it is sufficient to rely on the previous intuitive discussion. This should serve as a reminder that changes in the price of an input will have the effect of shifting firms' cost curves, with the size of the shift depending on the relative importance of the input and on the substitution possibilities that are available.

Technical progress

Technical improvements allow the firm to produce a given output with fewer inputs. So, such improvements obviously shift total costs downward (if input prices stay constant). Although the actual way in which technical change affects the mathematical form of the total cost curve can be complex, there are cases where one may draw simple conclusions. Suppose, for example, that the production function exhibits constant returns to scale and that technical change enters that function in the way we described in Chapter 7 (that is, $q = A(t)f(k, l)$ where $A(0) = 1$). In this case, total costs in the initial period are given by

$$C_0 = C_0(v, w, q) = qC_0(v, w, 1). \qquad (8.32)$$

Because the same inputs that produced one unit of output in period zero will produce $A(t)$ units of output in period t, we know that

$$C_t(v, w, A(t)) = A(t)C_t(v, w, 1) = C_0(v, w, 1); \qquad (8.33)$$

---

[12]For a complete statement, see Ferguson, *Neoclassical Theory of Production and Distribution,* (Cambridge: Cambridge University Press, 1969), pp. 154–60.

therefore we can compute the total-cost function in period t as

$$C_t(v, w, q) = qC_t(v, w, 1) = qC_0(v, w, 1)/A(t) = C_0(v, w, q)/A(t). \quad (8.34)$$

Hence, total costs fall over time at the rate of technical change. Note that in this case technical change is "neutral" in that it does not affect the firm's input choices (so long as input prices stay constant). This neutrality result might not hold in cases where technical progress takes a more complex form or where there are variable returns to scale. Even in these more complex cases, however, technical improvements will cause total costs to fall.

 EXAMPLE 8.3

Shifting the Cobb-Douglas Cost Function

In Example 8.2 we computed the Cobb-Douglas cost function as

$$C(v, w, q) = q^{1/\alpha+\beta} \, Bv^{\alpha/\alpha+\beta} \, w^{\beta/\alpha+\beta}, \quad (8.35)$$

where $B = (\alpha + \beta)\alpha^{-\alpha/\alpha+\beta} \beta^{-\beta/\alpha+\beta}$. As in the numerical illustration in Example 8.1, let's assume that $\alpha = \beta = 0.5$, in which case the total-cost function is greatly simplified:

$$C(v, w, q) = 2qv^{0.5} \, w^{0.5}. \quad (8.36)$$

This function will yield a total cost curve relating total costs and output if we specify particular values for the input prices. If, as before, we assume $v = 3$ and $w = 12$, the relationship is

$$C(3, 12, q) = 2q\sqrt{36} = 12q, \quad (8.37)$$

and, as in Example 8.1, it costs 480 to produce 40 units of output. Here average and marginal costs are easily computed as

$$AC = \frac{C}{q} = 12$$

$$MC = \frac{\partial C}{\partial q} = 12. \quad (8.38)$$

As should have been expected, average and marginal costs are constant and equal to each other for this constant returns-to-scale production function.

Changes in input prices. If either input price were to change, all of these costs would change also. For example, if wages were to increase to 27 (an easy number with which to work), costs would become

$$C(3, 27, q) = 2q\sqrt{81} = 18q$$
$$AC = 18 \quad (8.39)$$
$$MC = 18.$$

Notice that an increase in wages of 125 percent raised costs by only 50 percent here, both because labor represents only 50 percent of all costs and because the change in input prices encouraged the firm to substitute capital for labor. The total-cost function, because it is derived from the cost-minimization assumption, accomplishes this substitution "behind the scenes," reporting only the final impact on total costs.

Technical progress. Let's look now at the impact the technical progress can have on costs. Specifically, assume that the Cobb-Douglas production function is

$$q = A(t)k^{0.5}l^{0.5} = e^{.03t}k^{0.5}l^{0.5}. \quad (8.40)$$

That is, we assume that technical change takes an exponential form and that the rate of technical change is 3 percent per year. Using the results of the previous section (Equation 8.34) yields

$$C_t(v, w, q) = C_0(v, w, q)/A(t) = 2qv^{0.5}w^{0.5}e^{-.03t} \qquad (8.41)$$

So, if input prices remain the same, total costs fall at the rate of technical improvement—that is, at 3 percent per year. After, say, 20 years, costs will be (with $v = 3$, $w = 12$)

$$C_{20}(3, 12, q) = 2q\sqrt{36} \cdot e^{-.60} = 12q \cdot (0.55) = 6.6q$$
$$AC_{20} = 6.6 \qquad\qquad\qquad (8.42)$$
$$MC_{20} = 6.6.$$

Consequently, costs will have fallen by nearly 50 percent as a result of the technical change. This would, for example, more than have offset the wage rise illustrated previously.

Query: In this example what are the elasticities of total costs with respect to changes in input costs? Is the size of these elasticities affected by technical change?

Contingent demand for inputs and Shephard's lemma

As we described earlier, the process of cost minimization creates an implicit demand for inputs. Because that process holds quantity produced constant, this demand for inputs will also be "contingent" on the quantity being produced. This relationship is fully reflected in the firm's total-cost function and, perhaps surprisingly, contingent demand functions for all of the firm's inputs can be easily derived from that function. The process involves what has come to be called Shephard's lemma[13] which states that the contingent demand function for any input is given by the partial derivative of the total-cost function with respect to that input's price. Because Shephard's lemma is widely used in many areas of economic research, we will provide a relatively detailed examination of it.

The intuition behind Shephard's lemma is straightforward. Suppose that the price of labor (w) were to increase slightly. How would this impact total costs? If nothing else changed, it seems that costs would rise by approximately the amount of labor (l) that the firm was currently hiring. Roughly speaking, then, $\partial C/\partial w = l$, and that is what Shephard's lemma claims. Figure 8.6 makes roughly the same point graphically. Along the "pseudo" cost function all inputs are held constant, so an increase in the wage increases costs in direct proportion to the amount of labor used. Because the true cost function is tangent to the pseudo-function at the current wage, its slope (that is, its partial derivative) also will show the current amount of labor input demanded.

Technically, Shephard's lemma is one result of the envelope theorem that was first discussed in Chapter 2. There we showed that the change in the optimal value in a constrained optimization problem with respect to one of the parameters of the problem can be found by differentiating the Lagrangian expression for that optimization problem with respect to this changing parameter. In the cost-minimization case, the Lagrangian expression is

$$\mathscr{L} = vk + wl + \lambda[\bar{q} - f(k,l)] \qquad (8.43)$$

---

[13]Named for R. W. Shephard who highlighted the important relationship between cost functions and input demand functions in his *Cost and Production Functions* (Princeton: Princeton University Press, 1970).

and the envelope theorem applied to either input is

$$\frac{\partial C(v, w, q)}{\partial v} = \frac{\partial \mathscr{L}(v, w, q, \lambda)}{\partial v} = k^c(v, w, q)$$

$$\frac{\partial C(v, w, q)}{\partial w} = \frac{\partial \mathscr{L}(v, w, q, \lambda)}{\partial w} = l^c(v, w, q),$$

(8.44)

where the notation is intended to make clear that the resulting demand functions for capital and labor input depend on v, w, and q. Because quantity produced enters these functions, input demand is indeed contingent on that variable. This feature of the demand functions is also reflected by the "c" in the notation.[14] Hence, the demand relations in Equation 8.44 do not represent a complete picture of input demand because they still depend on a variable that is under the firm's control. In the next chapter we will complete the study of input demand by showing how the assumption of profit maximization allows us to effectively replace q in the input demand relationships with the market price of the firm's output, p.

 EXAMPLE 8.4

Contingent Input Demand Functions

In this example we will show how the total cost functions derived in Example 8.2 can be used to derive contingent demand functions for the inputs capital and labor.

a. Fixed Proportions: $C(v, w, q) = q\left(\dfrac{v}{a} + \dfrac{w}{b}\right)$.

For this cost function, contingent demand functions are quite simple:

$$k^c(v, w, q) = \frac{\partial C(v, w, q)}{\partial v} = \frac{q}{a}$$

$$l^c(v, w, q) = \frac{\partial C(v, w, q)}{\partial w} = \frac{q}{b}.$$

(8.45)

In order to produce any particular output with a fixed proportions production function at minimal cost, the firm must produce at the vertex of its isoquants no matter what the inputs' prices are. Hence, the demand for inputs depends only on the level of output, and v and w do not enter the contingent input demand functions. Input prices may, however, affect total input demands in the fixed proportions case because they may affect how much the firm can sell.

b. Cobb-Douglas: $C(v, w, q) = q^{1/\alpha+\beta} B v^{\alpha/\alpha+\beta} w^{\beta/\alpha+\beta}$.

In this case, the derivation is messier, but also more instructive:

$$k^c(v, w, q) = \frac{\partial C}{\partial v} = \frac{\alpha}{\alpha+\beta} \cdot q^{1/\alpha+\beta} B v^{-\beta/\alpha+\beta} w^{\beta/\alpha+\beta}$$

$$= \frac{\alpha}{\alpha+\beta} \cdot q^{1/\alpha+\beta} B \left(\frac{w}{v}\right)^{\beta/\alpha+\beta}$$

$$l^c(v, w, q) = \frac{\partial C}{\partial w} = \frac{\beta}{\alpha+\beta} \cdot q^{1/\alpha+\beta} B v^{\alpha/\alpha+\beta} w^{-\alpha/\alpha+\beta}$$

$$= \frac{\beta}{\alpha+\beta} \cdot q^{1/\alpha+\beta} B \left(\frac{w}{v}\right)^{-\alpha/\alpha+\beta}.$$

(8.46)

---

[14]The notation mirrors that used for compensated demand curves in Chapter 5 (which were derived from the expenditure function). In that case, such demand functions were contingent on the utility target assumed.

Consequently the contingent demands for inputs depend on both inputs' prices. If we assume $\alpha = \beta = 0.5$ (so, $B = 2$), these reduce to

$$k^c(v, w, q) = 0.5 \cdot q \cdot 2 \cdot \left(\frac{w}{v}\right)^{0.5} = q\left(\frac{w}{v}\right)^{0.5}$$

$$l^c(v, w, q) = 0.5 \cdot q \cdot 2 \cdot \left(\frac{w}{v}\right)^{-0.5} = q\left(\frac{w}{v}\right)^{-0.5}. \tag{8.47}$$

With $v = 3$, $w = 12$, and $q = 40$ these yield the result we got previously—that the firm should choose the input combination $k = 80$, $l = 20$ to minimize the cost of producing 40 units of output. If the wage were to rise to, say, 27, the firm would choose the input combination $k = 120$, $l = 40/3$ to produce 40 units of output. Total costs would rise from 480 to 520, but the ability of the firm to substitute capital for the now more expensive labor does save considerably. For example, the initial input combination now costs 780.

c. CES: $C(v, w, q) = q^{1/\gamma}(v^{1-\sigma} + w^{1-\sigma})^{1/1-\sigma}$

The importance of input substitution is shown even more clearly with the contingent demand functions derived from the CES function. For that function,

$$k^c(v, w, q) = \frac{\partial C}{\partial v} = \frac{1}{1-\sigma} \cdot q^{1/\gamma}(v^{1-\sigma} + w^{1-\sigma})^{\sigma/1-\sigma}(1-\sigma)v^{-\sigma}$$

$$= q^{1/\gamma}(v^{1-\sigma} + w^{1-\sigma})^{\sigma/1-\sigma}v^{-\sigma}$$

$$l^c(v, w, q) = \frac{\partial C}{\partial w} = \frac{1}{1-\sigma} \cdot q^{1/\gamma}(v^{1-\sigma} + w^{1-\sigma})^{\sigma/1-\sigma}(1-\sigma)w^{-\sigma} \tag{8.48}$$

$$= q^{1/\gamma}(v^{1-\sigma} + w^{1-\sigma})^{\sigma/1-\sigma}w^{-\sigma}.$$

These functions collapse when $\sigma = 1$ (the Cobb-Douglas case), but we can study examples with either more ($\sigma = 2$) or less ($\sigma = 0.5$) substitutability and use case b as the middle ground. If we assume constant returns to scale ($\gamma = 1$) and $v = 3$, $w = 12$, and $q = 40$, contingent demands for the inputs when $\sigma = 2$ are

$$k^c(3, 12, 40) = 40(3^{-1} + 12^{-1})^{-2} \cdot 3^{-2} = 25.6$$
$$l^c(3, 12, 40) = 40(3^{-1} + 12^{-1})^{-2} \cdot 12^{-2} = 1.6. \tag{8.49}$$

That is, the level of capital input is 16 times the amount of labor input. With less substitutability ($\sigma = 0.5$), contingent input demands are

$$k^c(3, 12, 40) = 40(3^{0.5} + 12^{0.5})^1 \cdot 3^{-0.5} = 120$$
$$l^c(3, 12, 40) = 40(3^{0.5} + 12^{0.5})^1 \cdot 12^{-0.5} = 60. \tag{8.50}$$

So, in this case capital input is only twice as large as labor input. Although these various cases cannot be compared directly because different values for σ scale output differently, we can, an example, look at the consequence of a rise in w to 27 in the low substitutability case. With $w = 27$, the firm will choose $k = 160$, $l = 53.3$. In this case the cost savings from substitution can be calculated by comparing total costs when using the initial input combination ($= 120(3) + 27(60) = 1980$) to total costs with the optimal combination ($= 160(3) + 27(53.3) = 1919$). Hence, moving to the optimal input combination reduces total costs by only about 3 percent. In the Cobb-Douglas case, cost savings are over 20 percent.

Query: How would total costs change if w increased from 12 to 27 and the production function took the simple linear form $q = k + 4l$? What light does this result shed on the other cases in this example?

Short-run, long-run distinction

It is customary in economics to make a distinction between the "short run" and the "long run." Although no very precise temporal definition can be provided for these terms, the general purpose of the distinction is to differentiate between a short period during which economic actors have only limited flexibility in their actions and a longer period that provides greater freedom. One area of study in which this distinction is quite important is in the theory of the firm and its costs, because economists are interested in examining supply reactions during different potential time intervals. In the remainder of this chapter, we will examine the implications of such differential response periods.

To illustrate why short-run and long-run reactions might differ, we assume that capital input is held fixed at a level of k_1, and that (in the short run) the firm is free to vary only its labor input.[15] Implicitly, we are assuming that alterations in the level of capital input are infinitely costly in the short run. As a result of this assumption, we may write the short-run production function as

$$q = f(k_1, l), \tag{8.51}$$

where this notation explicitly shows that capital inputs may not vary. Of course, the level of output still may be changed if the firm alters its use of labor.

Short-run total costs

Total cost for the firm continues to be defined as

$$C = vk + wl \tag{8.52}$$

for our short-run analysis, but now capital input is fixed at k_1. To denote this fact, we will write

$$SC = vk_1 + wl, \tag{8.53}$$

where the S indicates that we are analyzing short-run costs with the level of capital input fixed. Throughout our analysis, we will use this method to indicate short-run costs, whereas long-run costs will be denoted by C, AC, and MC. Usually we will not denote the level of capital input explicitly, but it is understood that this input is fixed.

Fixed and variable costs

The two types of input costs in Equation 8.53 are given special names. The term vk_1 is referred to as (short-run) *fixed costs;* because k_1 is constant, these costs will not change in the short run. The term wl is referred to as (short-run) *variable costs*—labor input can indeed be varied in the short run. Hence we have the following definitions:

Short-run fixed and variable costs. *Short-run fixed costs* are costs associated with inputs that cannot be varied in the short run. *Short-run variable costs* are costs of those inputs that can be varied in order to change the firm's output level.

The importance of this distinction is to differentiate between variable costs that the firm can avoid by producing nothing in the short run and costs that are fixed and must be paid regardless of the output level chosen (even zero).

Nonoptimality of short-run costs

It is important to understand that total short-run costs are not the minimal costs for producing the various output levels. Because we are holding capital fixed in the short run,

---

[15]Of course, this approach is for illustrative purposes only. In many actual situations labor input may be less flexible in the short run than is capital input.

FIGURE 8.7   **"Nonoptional" Input Choices Must Be Made in the Short Run**

Because capital input is fixed at k_1 in the short run, the firm cannot bring its RTS into equality with the ratio of input prices. Given the input prices, q_0 should be produced with more labor and less capital than it will be in the short run, whereas q_2 should be produced with more capital and less labor than it will be.

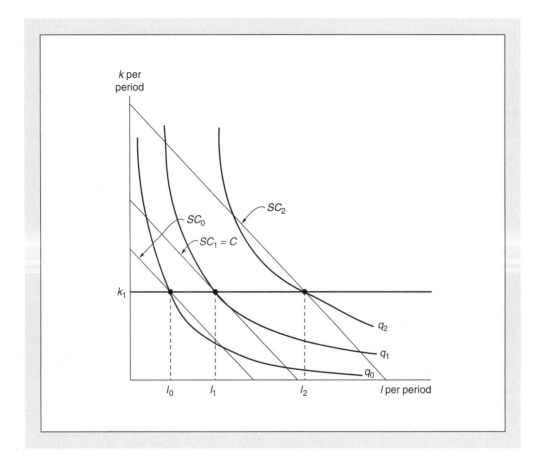

the firm does not have the flexibility of input choice that we assumed when we discussed cost minimization earlier in this chapter. Rather, to vary its output level in the short run, the firm will be forced to use "nonoptimal" input combinations: The RTS will not be equal to the ratio of the input prices. This is shown in Figure 8.7. In the short run, the firm is constrained to use k_1 units of capital. To produce output level q_0, it therefore will use l_0 units of labor. Similarly, it will use l_1 units of labor to produce q_1, and l_2 units to produce q_2. The total costs of these input combinations are given by SC_0, SC_1, and SC_2, respectively. Only for the input combination k_1, l_1 is output being produced at minimal cost. Only at that point is the RTS equal to the ratio of the input prices. From Figure 8.7 it is clear that q_0 is being produced with "too much" capital in this short-run situation. Cost minimization should suggest a southeasterly movement along the q_0 isoquant, indicating a substitution of labor for capital in production. Similarly, q_2 is being produced with "too little" capital, and costs could be reduced by substituting capital for labor. Neither of these substitutions is possible in the short run. Over a longer period, however, the firm will be able to change its level of capital input and will adjust its input usage to the cost-minimizing combinations. We have already discussed this flexible case earlier in this chapter and shall return to it to illustrate the connection between long-run and short-run cost curves.

Short-run marginal and average costs

Frequently, it is more useful to analyze short-run costs on a per-unit of output basis rather than on a total basis. The two most important per-unit concepts that can be derived from the short-run total cost function are the *short-run average total cost function* (*SAC*) and the *short-run marginal cost function* (*SMC*). These concepts are defined as

$$SAC = \frac{\text{total costs}}{\text{total output}} = \frac{SC}{q}$$
$$SMC = \frac{\text{change in total costs}}{\text{change in output}} = \frac{\partial SC}{\partial q}, \tag{8.54}$$

where, again, these are defined for a specified level of capital input. These definitions for average and marginal costs are identical to those developed previously for the long-run, fully flexible case, and the derivation of cost curves from the total cost function proceeds in exactly the same way. Because the short-run total cost curve has the same general type of cubic shape as did the total cost curve in Figure 8.5, these short-run average and marginal cost curves will also be U-shaped.

Relationship between short-run and long-run cost curves

By considering all possible variations in capital input, we can establish the relationship between the short-run costs and the fully flexible long-run costs that were derived previously in this chapter. Figure 8.8 shows this relationship for both the constant returns-to-scale and cubic total cost curve cases. Short-run total costs for three levels of capital input are shown, although of course it would be possible to show many more such short-run curves. The figures show that long-run total costs (*C*) are always less than short-run total costs, except at that output level for which the assumed fixed capital input is appropriate to long-run cost minimization. For example, as in Figure 8.7, with capital input of k_1, the firm can obtain full cost minimization when q_1 is produced. Hence, short-run and long-run total costs are equal at this point. For output levels other than q_1, however, $SC > C$, as was the case in Figure 8.7.

Technically, the long-run total cost curves in Figure 8.8 are said to be an "envelope" of their respective short-run curves. These short-run total cost curves can be represented parametrically by

$$\text{Short-run total cost} = SC(v,w,q,k), \tag{8.55}$$

and the family of short-run total cost curves is generated by allowing k to vary while holding v and w constant. The long-run total cost curve C must obey the short-run relationship in Equation 8.55 and the further condition that k must be chosen to be cost minimizing for any level of output. A first-order condition for this minimization is that

$$\frac{\partial SC(v, w, q, k)}{\partial km} = 0. \tag{8.56}$$

Solving Equations 8.55 and 8.56 simultaneously then generates the long-run total cost function. Although this is a different approach to deriving the total-cost function, it should give precisely the same results as we got earlier in this chapter—as the next example illustrates.

FIGURE 8.8   **Two Possible Shapes for Long-Run Total Cost Curves**

By considering all possible levels of capital input, the long-run total cost curve *(C)* can be traced. In (a) the underlying production function exhibits constant returns to scale—in the long run, though not in the short run, total costs are proportional to output. In (b) the long-run total cost curve has a cubic shape, as do the short-run curves. Diminishing returns set in more sharply for the short-run curves, however, because of the assumed fixed level of capital input.

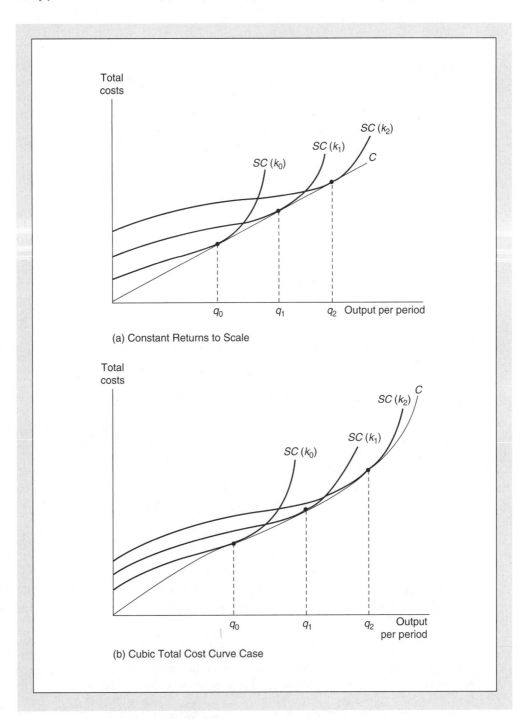

(a) Constant Returns to Scale

(b) Cubic Total Cost Curve Case

EXAMPLE 8.5

Envelope Relations and Cobb-Douglas cost functions

Again we start with the Cobb-Douglas production function $q = k^\alpha l^\beta$ but now we hold capital input constant at k_1. So, in the short run,

$$q = k_1^\alpha l^\beta \text{ or } l = q^{1/\beta} k_1^{-\alpha/\beta}, \tag{8.57}$$

and total costs are given by

$$SC(v, w, q, k_1) = vk_1 + wl = vk_1 + wq^{1/\beta} k_1^{-\alpha/\beta}. \tag{8.58}$$

Notice that the fixed level of capital enters into this short-run total cost function in two ways: (1) k_1 determines fixed costs; and (2) k_1 also in part determines variable costs because it determines how much of the variable input (labor) is required to produce various levels of output. To derive long-run costs, we require that k be chosen to minimize total costs:

$$\frac{\partial SC(v, w, q, k)}{\partial k} = v + \frac{-\alpha}{\beta} \cdot q^{1/\beta} k^{-(\alpha+\beta)/\beta} = 0. \tag{8.59}$$

Although the algebra is messy, this equation can be solved for k and substituted into Equation 8.58 to return us to the Cobb-Douglas cost function:

$$C(v, w, q) = Bq^{1/\alpha+\beta} v^{\alpha/\alpha+\beta} w^{\beta/\alpha+\beta}. \tag{8.60}$$

Numerical example. If we again let $\alpha = \beta = 0.5$, $v = 3$, $w = 12$, the short-run cost function is

$$SC(3, 12, q, k) = 3k_1 + 12q^2 k_1^{-1}. \tag{8.61}$$

In Example 8.1 we found that the cost-minimizing level of capital input for, say, $q = 40$ was $k = 80$. Equation 8.61 shows that short-run total costs for producing 40 units of output with $k = 80$ is

$$SC(3, 12, q, 80) = 3 \cdot 80 + 12 \cdot q^2 \cdot \frac{1}{80} = 240 + \frac{3q^2}{20} \tag{8.62}$$
$$= 240 + 240 = 480,$$

which is just what we found before. We can also use Equation 8.61 to show how costs differ in the short and long run. Table 8.1 shows that for output levels other than $q = 40$, short-run costs are larger than long-run costs and that this difference is proportionally larger the further one gets from the output level for which $k = 80$ is optimal.

It is also instructive to study differences between the long-run and short-run per unit costs in this situation. Here $AC = MC = 12$. We can compute the short-run equivalents (when $k = 80$) as

$$SAC = \frac{SC}{q} = \frac{240}{q} + \frac{3q}{20}$$
$$SMC = \frac{\partial SC}{\partial q} = \frac{6q}{20}. \tag{8.63}$$

Both of these short-run unit costs are equal to 12 when $q = 40$. However, as Table 8.2 shows, unit costs can differ significantly from this figure depending on the output level that the firm produces.

Notice in particular that short-run marginal cost increases rapidly as output expands beyond $q = 40$ because of diminishing returns to the variable input (labor). This conclusion plays an important role in the theory of short-run price determination.

Query: Explain why an increase in w will increase both short-run average cost and short-run marginal cost in this illustration, but an increase in v affects only short-run average cost.

TABLE 8.1	Difference Between Short-Run and Long-Run Total Cost with $k = 80$

q	$C = 12q$	$SC = 240 + \dfrac{3q_2}{20}$
10	120	255
20	240	300
30	360	375
40	480	480
50	600	615
60	720	780
70	840	975
80	960	1200

TABLE 8.2	Unit Costs in the Long Run and the Short Run when $k = 80$

q	AC	MC	SAC	SMC
10	12	12	25.5	3
20	12	12	15	6
30	12	12	12.5	9
40	12	12	12	12
50	12	12	12.3	15
60	12	12	13	18
70	12	12	13.9	21
80	12	12	15	24

Graphs of per-unit cost curves

The envelope total cost curve relationships exhibited in Figure 8.8 can be used to show geometric connections between short-run and long-run average and marginal cost curves. These are presented in Figure 8.9 for the cubic total cost curve case. In the figure, short-run and long-run average costs are equal at that output for which the (fixed) capital input is appropriate. At q_1, for example, $SAC(k_1) = AC$ because k_1 is used in producing q_1 at minimal costs. For movements away from q_1, short-run average costs exceed long-run average costs, thus reflecting the cost-minimizing nature of the long-run total cost curve.

Because the minimum point of the long-run average cost curve (AC) plays a major role in the theory of long-run price determination, it is important to note the various curves that pass through this point in Figure 8.9. First, as is always true for average and marginal cost curves, the MC curve passes through the low point of the AC curve. At q_1, long-run average and marginal costs are equal. Associated with q_1 is a certain level of capital input (say, k_1); the short-run average cost curve for this level of capital input is tangent to the AC curve at its minimum point. The SAC curve also reaches its minimum at output level q_1. For movements away from q_1, the AC curve is much flatter than the SAC curve, and this reflects the greater flexibility open to firms in the long run. Short-run costs rise rapidly because capital inputs are fixed. In the long run, such inputs are not fixed, and diminishing marginal productivities do not occur so abruptly. Finally, because the SAC curve

FIGURE 8.9   **Average and Marginal Cost Curves for the Cubic Cost Curve Case**

This set of curves is derived from the total cost curves shown in Figure 8.8. The *AC* and *MC* curves have the usual U-shapes, as do the short-run curves. At q_1, long-run average costs are minimized. The configuration of curves at this minimum point is quite important.

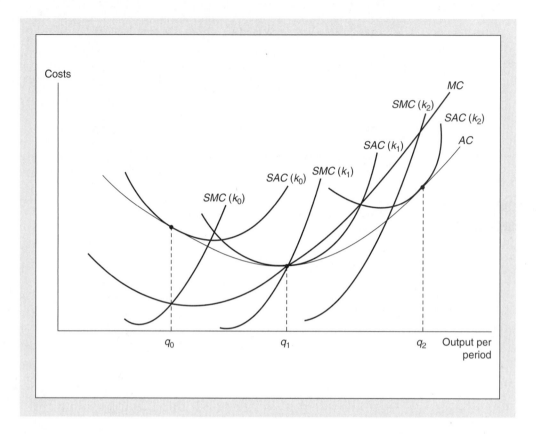

reaches its minimum at q_1, the short-run marginal cost curve [*SMC*] also passes through this point. The minimum point of the *AC* curve therefore brings together the four most important per-unit costs. At this point

$$AC = MC = SAC = SMC. \qquad (8.64)$$

For this reason, as we shall show in Chapter 10, the output level q_1 is an important equilibrium point for a competitive firm in the long run.

SUMMARY

In this chapter we examined the relationship between the level of output a firm produces and the input costs that level of production requires. The resulting cost curves should generally be familiar to you because they are widely used in most courses in introductory economics. Here we have shown how such curves reflect the firm's underlying production function and the firm's desire to minimize costs. By developing cost curves from these basic foundations, we were able to illustrate a number of important findings:

- A firm that wishes to minimize the economic costs of producing a particular level of output should choose that input combination for which the rate of technical substitution (*RTS*) is equal to the ratio of the inputs' rental prices.

- Repeated application of this minimization procedure yields the firm's expansion path. Because the expansion path shows how input usage expands with the level of output, it also shows the relationship between output level and total cost. That relationship is summarized by the total-cost function—$C(q, v, w)$—which shows production costs as a function of output levels and input prices.

- The firm's average cost ($AC = C/q$) and marginal cost ($MC = \partial C/\partial q$) functions can be derived directly from the total-cost function. If the total cost curve has a general cubic shape, the AC and MC curves will be U-shaped.

- All cost curves are drawn on the assumption that the input prices are held constant. When input prices change, cost curves will shift to new positions. The extent of the shifts will be determined by the overall importance of the input whose price has changed and by the ease with which the firm may substitute one input for another. Technical progress will also shift cost curves.

- Input demand functions can be derived from the firm's total-cost function through partial differentiation. These input demand functions will depend on the quantity of output that the firm chooses to produce and are therefore called "contingent" demand functions.

- In the short run, the firm may not be able to vary some inputs. It can then alter its level of production only by changing its employment of variable inputs. In so doing, it may have to use nonoptimal, higher-cost input combinations than it would choose if it were possible to vary all inputs.

PROBLEMS

8.1

In a famous article [J. Viner, "Cost Curves and Supply Curves," *Zeitschrift fur Nationalokonomie* 3 (September 1931): 23–46], Viner criticized his draftsman who could not draw a family of *SAC* curves whose points of tangency with the U-shaped *AC* curve were also the minimum points on each *SAC* curve. The draftsman protested that such a drawing was impossible to construct. Whom would you support in this debate?

8.2

Suppose that a firm produces two different outputs, the quantities of which are represented by q_1 and q_2. In general, the firm's total costs can be represented by $C(q_1, q_2)$. This function exhibits economies of scope if $C(q_1, 0) + C(0, q_2) > C(q_1, q_2)$ for all output levels of either good.

a. Explain in words why this mathematical formulation implies that costs will be lower in this multiproduct firm than in two single-product firms producing each good separately.

b. If the two outputs are actually the same good, we can define total output as $q = q_1 + q_2$. Suppose that in this case average cost ($= C/q$) falls as q increases. Show that this firm also enjoys economies of scope under the definition provided here.

8.3

Professor Smith and Professor Jones are going to produce a new introductory textbook. As true scientists, they have laid out the production function for the book as

$$q = S^{1/2}J^{1/2},$$

where q = the number of pages in the finished book, S = the number of working hours spent by Smith, and J = the number of hours spent working by Jones.

Smith values his labor as $3 per working hour. He has spent 900 hours preparing the first draft. Jones, whose labor is valued at $12 per working hour, will revise Smith's draft to complete the book.

a. How many hours will Jones have to spend to produce a finished book of 150 pages? Of 300 pages? Of 450 pages?

b. What is the marginal cost of the 150th page of the finished book? Of the 300th page? Of the 450th page?

8.4

Suppose that a firm's fixed proportion production function is given by

$$q = \min(5k, 10l),$$

and that the rental rates for capital and labor are given by $v = 1$, $w = 3$.

a. Calculate the firm's long-run total, average, and marginal cost curves.

b. Suppose that k is fixed at 10 in the short run. Calculate the firm's short-run total, average, and marginal cost curves. What is the marginal cost of the 10th unit? The 50th unit? The 100th unit?

8.5

A firm producing hockey sticks has a production function given by

$$q = 2\sqrt{k \cdot l}.$$

In the short run, the firm's amount of capital equipment is fixed at $k = 100$. The rental rate for k is $v = \$1$, and the wage rate for l is $w = \$4$.

a. Calculate the firm's short-run total cost curve. Calculate the short-run average cost curve.

b. What is the firm's short-run marginal cost function? What are the SC, SAC, and SMC for the firm if it produces 25 hockey sticks? Fifty hockey sticks? One hundred hockey sticks? Two hundred hockey sticks?

c. Graph the SAC and the SMC curves for the firm. Indicate the points found in part (b).

d. Where does the SMC curve intersect the SAC curve? Explain why the SMC curve will always intersect the SAC curve at its lowest point.

Suppose, now that capital used for producing hockey sticks is fixed at $\bar{k}$ in the short run.

e. Calculate the firm's total costs as a function of q, w, v, and $\bar{k}$.

f. Given q, w, and v, how should the capital stock be chosen to minimize total cost?

g. Use your results from part (f) to calculate the long-run total cost of hockey stick production.

h. For $w = \$4$, $v = \$1$, graph the long-run total cost curve for hockey stick production. Show that this is an envelope for the short-run curves computed in part (a) by examining values of $\bar{k}$ of 100, 200, and 400.

8.6

An enterprising entrepreneur purchases two firms to produce widgets. Each firm produces identical products, and each has a production function given by

$$q = \sqrt{k_i l_i} \quad i = 1, 2.$$

The firms differ, however, in the amount of capital equipment each has. In particular, firm 1 has $k_1 = 25$, whereas firm 2 has $k_2 = 100$, Rental rates for k and l are given by $w = v = \$1$.

a. If the entrepreneur wishes to minimize short-run total costs of widget production, how should output be allocated between the two firms?

b. Given that output is optimally allocated between the two firms, calculate the short-run total, average, and marginal cost curves. What is the marginal cost of the 100th widget? The 125th widget? The 200th widget?

c. How should the entrepreneur allocate widget production between the two firms in the long run? Calculate the long-run total, average, and marginal cost curves for widget production.

d. How would your answer to part (c) change if both firms exhibited diminishing returns to scale?

8.7

The CES production function can be generalized to permit weighting of the inputs. In the two-input case, this function is

$$q = f(k, l) = \left[(ak)^\rho + (bl)^\rho\right]^{\gamma/\rho}.$$

a. What is the total-cost function for a firm with this production function? (*Hint:* you can, of course, work this out from scratch. Easier, perhaps is to use the results from Example 8.2 and reason that the price for a unit of capital input in this production function is v/a and for a unit of labor input is w/b).

b. If $\gamma = 1$ and $a + b = 1$, it can be shown that this production function converges to the Cobb-Douglas form $q = k^a l^b$ as $\rho \to 0$. What is the total-cost function for this particular version of the CES function?

c. The relative labor cost share for a two-input production function is given by wl/vk. Show that this share is constant for the Cobb-Douglas function in part (b). How is the relative labor share affected by the parameters a and b?

d. Calculate the relative labor cost share for the general CES function introduced above. How is that share affected by changes in w/v? How is the direction of this effect determined by the elasticity of substitution, σ? How is it affected by the sizes of the parameters a and b?

8.8

The own-price elasticities of contingent input demand for labor and capital are defined as

$$e_{l^c,w} = \frac{\partial l^c}{\partial w} \cdot \frac{w}{l^c} \qquad e_{k^c,v} = \frac{\partial k^c}{\partial v} \cdot \frac{v}{k^c}.$$

a. Calculate $e_{l^c,w}$ and $e_{k^c,v}$ for each of the cost functions shown in Example 8.2.

b. Show that, in general, $e_{l^c,w} + e_{l^c,v} = 0$

c. Show that the cross-price derivatives of contingent demand functions are equal— that is, show that $\dfrac{\partial l^c}{\partial v} = \dfrac{\partial k^c}{\partial w}$. Use this fact to show that $s_l e_{l^c,v} = s_k e_{k^c,w}$ where s_l, s_k are, respectively, the share of labor in total cost (wl/C) and of capital in total cost (vk/C).

d. Use the results from part (b) and (c) to shown that $s_l e_{l^c,w} + s_k e_{k^c,w} = 0$.

e. Interpret these various eleasticity relationships in words and discuss their overall relevance to a general theory of input demand.

8.9

Suppose the total-cost function for a firm is given by

$$C = qw^{2/3}v^{1/3}.$$

a. Use Shephard's lemma to compute the constant output demand functions for inputs l and k.

b. Use your results from part (a) to calculate the underlying production function for q.

8.10

Suppose the total-cost function for a firm is given by

$$C = q(2 + v\sqrt{vw} + w).$$

a. Use Shephard's lemma to compute the constant output demand function for each input, k and l.

b. Use the results from part (a) to compute the underlying production function for q.

c. You can check the result by using results from Example 8.2 to show that the CES cost function with $\sigma = .5$, $\rho = -1$ generates this total-cost function.

SUGGESTIONS FOR FURTHER READING

Allen, R. G. D. *Mathematical Analysis for Economists*. New York: St. Martin's Press, 1938. Various pages—see index.
Complete mathematical analysis of substitution possibilities and cost functions. Notation somewhat difficult.

Ferguson, C. E. *The Neoclassical Theory of Production and Distribution*, Chap. 6. Cambridge: Cambridge University Press, 1969.
Nice development of cost curves, especially strong on graphic analysis.

Fuss, M., and D. McFadden. *Production Economics: A Dual Approach to Theory and Applications*. Amsterdam: North-Holland, 1978.
Difficult and quite complete treatment of the dual relationship between production and cost functions. Some discussion of empirical issues.

Knight, H. H. "Cost of Production and Price over Long and Short Periods." *Journal of Political Economics, 29 (April 1921); 304–35*
Class treatment of the short-run, long-run distinction.

Silberberg, E. and W. Suen. The Structure of Economics: A Mathematical Analysis, 3rd ed. Boston: Irwin/McGraw-Hill. 2001.
Chapter 7–9 have a great deal of material on cost functions. Especially recommended is the authors' discussions of "reciprocity effects" and their treatment of the short-run, long-run distinction as an application of the Le Chatelier principle from physics.

Sydsaeter, K., A Strom, and P. Berck. *Economists' Mathematical Manual,* 3rd ed. Berlin: Springer-Verlag, 2000.
Chapter 25 provides a succinct summary of the mathematical concepts in this chapter. A nice summary of many input cost functions though beware of typos.

The Translog Cost Function

The two cost functions studied in Chapter 8 (the Cobb-Douglas and the CES) are very restrictive in the substitution possibilities they permit. The Cobb-Douglas implicity assumes that $\sigma = 1$ between all inputs. The CES permits σ to take any value, but it requires that the elasticity of substitution be the same between any two inputs. Because empirical economists would prefer to let the data show what the actual substitution possibilities among inputs are, they have tried to find more flexible functional forms. One especially popular such form is the translog cost function, first made popular by Fuss and McFadden (1978). In this extension we will look at this function.

E8.1 The translog with two inputs

In Example 8.2 we calculated the Cobb-Douglas cost function in the two-input case as $C(q, v, w) = Bq^{1/\alpha+\beta} v^{\alpha/\alpha+\beta} w^{\beta/\alpha+\beta}$. If we take the natural logarithm of this we have

$$\ln C(q, v, w) = \ln B + [1/(\alpha + \beta)]\ln q \\ + [\alpha/(\alpha + \beta)] \ln v \\ + [\beta/(\alpha + \beta)] \ln w. \quad \text{(i)}$$

That is, the log of total costs is linear in the logs of output and the input prices. The translog function generalizes this by permitting second-order terms in input prices:

$$\ln C(q, v, w) = \ln q + \beta_0 + \beta_1 \ln v + \beta_2 \ln w \\ + \beta_3 (\ln v)^2 + \beta_4 (\ln w)^2 \\ + \beta_5 \ln v \ln w, \quad \text{(ii)}$$

where this function implicitly assumes constant returns to scale (because the coefficient of $\ln q$ is 1.0), but that need not be the case.

Some of the properties of this function are:

- For the function to be homogeneous of degree one in input prices it must be the case that $\beta_1 + \beta_2 = 1$ and $\beta_3 + \beta_4 + \beta_5 = 0$.

- This function includes the Cobb-Douglas as the special case $\beta_3 = \beta_4 = \beta_5 = 0$. Hence, the function can be used to test statistically whether the Cobb-Douglas is appropriate.

- Shephard's lemma can be used to calculate the contingent input demand functions for the translog as

$$k^c = \frac{\partial C}{\partial v} = \frac{\partial C}{\partial \ln C} \cdot \frac{\partial \ln C}{\partial \ln v} \cdot \frac{\partial \ln v}{\partial v}$$
$$= \frac{C}{v} \cdot [\beta_1 + 2\beta_3 \ln v + \beta_5 \ln w]$$
$$l^c = \frac{\partial C}{\partial w} = \frac{\partial C}{\partial \ln C} \cdot \frac{\partial \ln C}{\partial \ln w} \cdot \frac{\partial \ln w}{\partial w} \quad \text{(iii)}$$
$$= \frac{C}{w} \cdot [\beta_2 + 2\beta_4 \ln w + \beta_5 \ln v],$$

and the input shares are given by

$$s_k = \frac{vk}{C} = \beta_1 + 2\beta_3 \ln v + \beta_5 \ln w$$
$$\quad \text{(iv)}$$
$$s_l = \frac{wl}{C} = \beta_2 + 2\beta_4 \ln w + \beta_5 \ln v.$$

This shows that, contrary to the Cobb-Douglas case, the input shares are not constant, but rather depend on the input prices. Because equations iv are especially simple, this is the way that the translog is typically estimated econometrically.

- The partial elasticity of substitution between capital and labor for this function is given by $s_{k,l} = (\beta_5 + s_k s_l)/s_k s_l$. So this parameter, too, is determined by the data. Notice that the key component of the parameter is the coefficient β_5 which represents the interaction term in v and w. If that coefficient is zero, we get the Cobb-Douglas result $s_{k,l} = 1$.

E8.2 The many input translog cost function

Most empirical studies include more than two inputs. The translog cost function is especially easy to generalize to these situations. If we assume there are n inputs, each with a price of w_i ($i = 1, n$), this function is

$$C(q, w_1 \cdots w_n) = \ln q$$
$$+ \beta_0 + \sum_{i=1}^{n} \beta_i \ln w_i$$
$$+ 0.5 \sum_{i=1}^{n} \sum_{j=1}^{n} \beta_{ij} \ln w_i \ln w_j, \tag{v}$$

where, again, we have assumed constant returns to scale. This function requires $\beta_{ij} = \beta_{ji}$ so each term for which $i \neq j$ appears twice in the final double sum (which explains the presence of the 0.5 in the expression). For this function to be homogeneous of degree one in the input prices, it must be the case that $\sum_{i=1}^{n} \beta_i = 1$ and $\sum_{j=1}^{n} \beta_{ij} = 0$. Two useful properties of this function are:

- Input shares take the linear form:

$$s_i = \beta_i + \sum_{j=1}^{n} \beta_{ij} \ln w_j. \tag{vi}$$

Again, this shows why the translog is usually estimated in a share form. Sometimes a term in $\ln q$ is also added to the share equations to allow for scale effects on the shares (see Sydsaeter, Strom, and Bercke, 2000).

- The partial elasticity of substitution between any two inputs in the translog function is given by

$$s_{i,j} = (\beta_{ij} + s_i s_j)/s_i s_j. \tag{vii}$$

Hence substitutability can again be judged directly from the parameters estimated for the translog function.

E8.3 Some applications

The translog cost function has become the main choice for empirical studies of production. Two factors account for this popularity. First, the function allows a fairly complete characterization of substitution patterns among inputs—it does not require that the data fit any prespecified pattern. Second, the function's format incorporates input prices in a very flexible way so that one can be reasonable sure that he or she has controlled for such prices in regression analysis. When such control is assured, measures of other aspects of

the cost function (such as its returns to scale) will be more reliable.

One example of using the translog function to study input substitution is the study by Westbrook and Buckley (1990) of the responses that shippers made to changing relative prices of moving goods that resulted from deregulation of the railroad and trucking industries in the United States. The authors look specifically at the shipping of fruits and vegetables from the western states to Chicago and New York. They find relatively high substitution elasticities among shipping options and conclude therefore that deregulation had significant welfare benefits. Doucouliagos and Hone (2000) provide a similar analysis of deregulation of dairy prices in Australia. They show that changes in the price of raw milk caused dairy processing firms to undertake significant changes in input usage. They also show that the industry adopted significant new technologies in response to the price change.

An interesting study that uses the translog primarily to judge returns to scale is Latzko's (1999) analysis of the U.S. mutual fund industry. He finds that the elasticity of total costs with respect to the total assets managed by the fund is significant less than one for all but the largest funds (those with more than \$4 billion in assets). Hence, the author concludes that money management exhibits substantial returns to scale. A number of other studies that use the translog to estimate economies of scale focus on municipal services. For example, Garcia and Thomas (2001) look at water supply systems in local French communities. They conclude that there are significant operating economies of scale in such systems and that some merging of systems would make sense. Yatchew (2000) reaches a similar conclusion about electricity distributing in small communities in Ontario, Canada. He finds that there are economies of scale for electricity distribution systems up to about 20,000 customers. Again, some efficiencies might be obtained from merging systems that are much smaller than this size.

References

Doucouliagos, H. and P. Hone. "Deregulation and Subequilibrium in the Australian Dairy Processing Industry." *Economic Record* (June 2000): 152–62.

Fuss, M. and D. McFadden, eds. *Production Economics: A Dual Approach to Theory and Applications*. Amsterdam: North Holland, 1978.

Garcia, S., and A. Thomas. "The Structure of Municipal Water Supply Costs: Application to a Panel of French Local Communities." *Journal of Productivity Analysis* (July 2001): 5–29.

Latzko, D. "Economies of Scale in Mutual Fund Administration." *Journal of Financial Research* (Fall 1999): 331–39.

Sato, R., and T. Koizumi. "On Elasticities of Substitution and Complementarity." *Oxford Economic Papers* (March 1973): 44–50.

Sydsaeter, K., A. Strom, and P. Berck. *Economists' Mathematical Manual*, 3rd ed. Berlin: Springer-Verlag, 2000.

Westbrook, M. D., and P. A. Buckley. "Flexible Functional Forms and Regularity: Assessing the Competitive Relationship Between Truck and Rail Transportation." *Review of Economics and Statistics* (November 1990): 623–30.

Yatchew, A. "Scale Economies in Electricity Distribution: A Semiparametric Analysis." *Journal of Applied Econometrics* (March–April 2000): 187–210.

Chapter 9

PROFIT MAXIMIZATION

In Chapter 8 we examined the way in which firms minimize costs for any level of output they may choose. In this chapter we will focus on how the level of output is chosen by profit-maximizing firms. Before investigating that decision, however, it is appropriate to discuss briefly the nature of firms and the ways in which their choices should be analyzed.

The nature and behavior of firms

As we pointed out at the beginning of our analysis of production, a firm is an association of individuals who have organized themselves for the purpose of turning inputs into outputs. Different individuals will provide different types of inputs, such as workers' skills and varieties of capital equipment, with the expectation of receiving some sort of reward for doing so.

Contractual relationships within firms

The nature of the contractual relationship between the providers of inputs to a firm may be quite complicated. Each provider agrees to devote his or her input to production activities under a set of understandings about how it is to be used and what benefit is to be expected from that use. In some cases these contracts are *explicit*. Workers often negotiate contracts that specify in considerable detail what hours are to be worked, what rules of work are to be followed, and what rate of pay is to be expected. Similarly, capital owners invest in a firm under a set of explicit legal principles about the ways in which that capital may be used, the compensation the owner can expect to receive, and whether the owner retains any profits or losses after all economic costs have been paid. Despite these formal arrangements, it is clear that many of the understandings between the providers of inputs to a firm are *implicit;* relationships between managers and workers follow certain procedures about who has the authority to do what in making production decisions. Among workers, numerous implicit understandings exist about how work tasks are to be shared; and capital owners may delegate much of their authority to managers and workers to make decisions on their behalf (General Motors' shareholders, for example, are never involved in how assembly-line equipment will be used, though technically they own it). All of these explicit and implicit relationships change in response to experiences and events external to the firm. Much as a basketball team will try out new plays and defensive strategies, so too firms will alter the nature of their internal organizations to achieve better long-term results.[1]

Modeling firms' behavior

Although some economists have adopted a "behavioral" approach to studying firms' decisions, most have found that approach too cumbersome for general purposes. Rather, they have adopted a "holistic" approach that treats the firm as a single decision-making unit and sweeps away all the complicated behavioral issues about relationships among input providers. Under this approach, it is often convenient to assume that a firm's decisions are made by a single dictatorial manager who rationally pursues some goal, usually profit-maximization. That is the approach we take here. In Chapter 19 we look at some of the informational issues that arise in intrafirm contracts.

Profit maximization

Most models of supply assume that the firm and its manager pursue the goal of achieving the largest economic profits possible. Hence we will use the following definition:

Profit-maximizing firm. A *profit-maximizing firm* chooses both its inputs and its outputs with the sole goal of achieving maximum economic profits. That is, the firm seeks to make the difference between its total revenues and its total economic costs as large as possible.

This assumption—that firms seek maximum economic profits—has a long history in economic literature. It has much to recommend it. It is plausible because firm owners may indeed seek to make their asset as valuable as possible, and competitive markets may punish firms that do not maximize profits. The assumption also yields interesting theoretical results that can explain actual firms' decisions.

Profit maximization and marginalism

If firms are strict profit maximizers, they will make decisions in a "marginal" way. The entrepreneur will perform the conceptual experiment of adjusting those variables that can be controlled until it is impossible to increase profits further. This involves, say, looking at the incremental, or "marginal," profit obtainable from producing one more unit of output, or at the additional profit available from hiring one more laborer. As long as this incremental profit is positive, the extra output will be produced or the extra laborer will be hired. When the incremental profit of an activity becomes zero, the entrepreneur has pushed that activity far enough, and it would not be profitable to go further. In this chapter, we will explore the consequences of this assumption using increasingly sophisticated mathematics.

Output choice

First we examine a topic that should be very familiar—what output level a firm will choose to produce in order to obtain maximum profits. A firm sells some level of output, q, at a market price of p per unit. Total revenues (R) are given by

$$R(q) = p(q) \cdot q, \tag{9.1}$$

where we have allowed for the possibility that the selling price the firm receives might be affected by how much it sells. In the production of q, certain *economic* costs are incurred and, as in Chapter 8, we will denote these by $C(q)$.

---

[1]The initial development of the theory of the firm from the notion of the contractual relationships involved can be found in R. H. Coase, "The Nature of the Firm," *Economica* (November 1937): 386–405.

The difference between revenues and costs is called *economic profits* (π). Because both revenues and costs depend on the quantity produced, economic profits will also. That is,

$$\pi(q) = p(q) \cdot q - C(q) = R(q) - C(q). \tag{9.2}$$

The necessary condition for choosing the value of q that maximizes profits is found by setting the derivative of Equation 9.2 with respect to q equal to 0:[2]

$$\frac{d\pi}{dq} = \pi'(q) = \frac{dR}{dq} - \frac{dC}{dq} = 0, \tag{9.3}$$

so the first-order condition for a maximum is that

$$\frac{dR}{dq} = \frac{dC}{dq}. \tag{9.4}$$

This is a mathematical statement of the marginal revenue equals marginal cost rule usually studied in introductory economics courses. Hence we have the following:

OPTIMIZATION PRINCIPLE

Profit maximization. To maximize economic profits, the firm should choose that output for which marginal revenue is equal to marginal cost. That is,

$$MR = \frac{dR}{dq} = \frac{dC}{dq} = MC. \tag{9.5}$$

Second-order conditions

Equation 9.4 or 9.5 is only a necessary condition for a profit maximum. For sufficiency, it is also required that

$$\left. \frac{d^2\pi}{dq^2} \right|_{q = q^*} = \left. \frac{d\pi'(q)}{dq} \right|_{q = q^*} < 0, \tag{9.6}$$

or that "marginal" profit must be decreasing at the optimal level of q. For q less than q^* (the optimal level of output), profit must be increasing [$\pi'(q) > 0$]; and for q greater than q^*, profit must be decreasing [$\pi'(q) < 0$]. Only if this condition holds has a true maximum been achieved.

Graphical analysis

These relationships are illustrated in Figure 9.1, where the top panel depicts typical cost and revenue functions. For low levels of output, costs exceed revenues and therefore economic profits are negative. In the middle ranges of output, revenues exceed costs; this means that profits are positive. Finally, at high levels of output, costs rise sharply and again exceed revenues. The vertical distance between the revenue and cost curves (that is, profits) is shown in Figure 9.1b. Here profits reach a maximum at q^*. At this level of output it is also true that the slope of the revenue curve (marginal revenue) is equal to the slope of the cost curve (marginal cost). It is clear from the figure that the sufficient conditions for a maximum are also satisfied at this point, because profits are increasing to the left of q^* and decreasing to the right of q^*. Output level q^* is therefore a true profit maximum. This is not so for output level q^{**}. Although marginal revenue is equal to marginal cost at this output, profits are in fact at a minimum there.

---

[2]Notice that this is an unconstrained maximization problem; the constraints in the problem are implicit in the revenue and cost functions. Specifically, the demand curve facing the firm determines the revenue function, and the firm's production function (together with input prices) determines its costs.

FIGURE 9.1   **Marginal Revenue Must Equal Marginal Cost for Profit Maximization**

Because profits are defined to be revenues (R) minus costs (C), it is clear that profits reach a maximum when the slope of the revenue function (marginal revenue) is equal to the slope of the cost function (marginal cost). This equality is only a necessary condition for a maximum, as may be seen by comparing points q^* (a true *maximum*) and q^{**} (a true *minimum*), for both of which marginal revenue equals marginal cost.

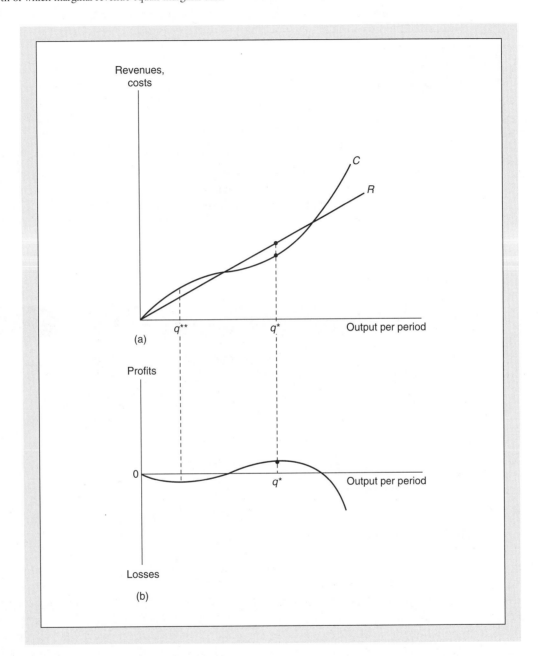

Marginal revenue

It is the revenue obtained from selling one more unit of output that is relevant to the profit-maximizing firm's output decision. If the firm can sell all it wishes without having any effect on market price, the market price will indeed be the extra revenue obtained from selling one more unit. Phrased in another way, if a firm's output decisions will not affect market price, marginal revenue is equal to the price at which a unit sells.

A firm may not always be able to sell all it wants at the prevailing market price, however. If it faces a downward-sloping demand curve for its product, more output can be sold only by reducing the good's price. In this case the revenue obtained from selling one more unit will be less than the price of that unit because, in order to get consumers to take the extra unit, the price of all other units must be lowered. This result can be easily demonstrated. As before, total revenue (R) is the product of the quantity sold (q) times the price at which it is sold (p), which may also depend on q. Marginal revenue (MR) is then defined to be the change in R resulting from a change in q:

DEFINITION

Marginal revenue.

$$\text{marginal revenue} = MR(q) = \frac{dR}{dq} = \frac{d[p(q) \cdot q]}{dq} = p + q \cdot \frac{dp}{dq} \quad (9.7)$$

Notice that the marginal revenues is a function of output. In general, MR will be different for different levels of q. From Equation 9.7 it is easy to see that if price does not change as quantity increases ($dp/dq = 0$), marginal revenue will be equal to price. In this case we say that the firm is a *price taker* because its decisions do not influence the price it receives. On the other hand, if price falls as quantity increases ($dp/dq < 0$), marginal revenue will be less than price. A profit-maximizing entrepreneur must know how increases in output will affect the price received before making an optimal output decision. If increases in q cause market price to fall, this must be taken into account.

  EXAMPLE 9.1

Marginal Revenue from a Linear Demand Function

Suppose a sub sandwich (also called grinders, torpedoes, or, in Philadelphia, hoagies) shop faces a linear demand curve for its daily output over period (q) of the form

$$q = 100 - 10p. \quad (9.8)$$

Solving for the price the shop receives, we have

$$p = -q/10 + 10, \quad (9.9)$$

and total revenues (as a function of q) are given by

$$R = pq = -q^2/10 + 10q. \quad (9.10)$$

The sub firm's marginal revenue function is

$$MR = \frac{dR}{dq} = \frac{-q}{5} + 10, \quad (9.11)$$

and, in this case, $MR < p$ for all values of q. If, for example, the firm produces 40 subs per day, Equation 9.9 shows that it will receive a price of $6 per sandwich. But at this level of output Equation 9.11 shows that MR is only $2. If the firm produces 40 subs per day, total revenue will be $240 (= $6 × 40), whereas, if it produced 39 subs, total revenue would be $238 (= $6.1 × 39) because price will rise slightly when less is produced. Hence the marginal revenue from the 40th unit sold is considerably less than its price. Indeed, for $q = 50$, marginal revenue is zero (total revenues are a maximum at $250 = $5 × 50), and any further expansion in daily sub output will actually result in a reduction in total revenue to the firm.

To determine the profit-maximizing level of sub output, we must know the firm's costs. If subs can be produced at a constant average and marginal cost of $4, Equation 9.11 shows that $MR = MC$ at a daily output of 30 subs. With this level of output, each sub will sell for $7 and profits are $90 [= ($7 − $4) · 30]. Although price exceeds average and marginal cost here by a substantial margin, it would not be in the firm's interest to expand output. With $q = 35$, for example, price will fall to $6.50 and profits will fall to $87.50 [= ($6.50 − $4.00) · 35]. Marginal revenue, not price, is the primary determinant of profit-maximizing behavior.

Query: How would an increase in the marginal cost of sub production to $5 affect the output decision of this firm? How would it affect the firm's profits?

Marginal revenue and elasticity

The concept of marginal revenue is directly related to the elasticity of the demand curve facing the firm. Remember that the elasticity of demand ($e_{q,p}$) is defined as the percentage change in quantity that results from a 1 percent change in price:

$$e_{q,p} = \frac{dq/q}{dp/p} = \frac{dq}{dp} \cdot \frac{p}{q}.$$

Now, this definition can be combined with Equation 9.7 to give

$$MR = p + \frac{qdp}{dq} = p\left(1 + \frac{q}{p} \cdot \frac{dp}{dq}\right) = p\left(1 + \frac{1}{e_{q,p}}\right). \qquad (9.12)$$

If the demand curve facing the firm is negatively sloped, $e_{q,p} < 0$ and marginal revenue will be less than price, as we have already shown. If demand is elastic ($e_{q,p} < -1$), marginal revenue will be positive. If demand is elastic, the sale of one more unit will not affect price "very much," and hence more revenue will be yielded by the sale. In fact, if demand facing the firm is infinitely elastic ($e_{q,p} = -\infty$), marginal revenue will equal price. The firm is, in this case, a price taker. However, if demand is inelastic ($e_{q,p} > -1$), marginal revenue will be negative. Increases in q can be obtained only through "large" declines in market price, and these declines will actually cause total revenue to decrease.

The relationship between marginal revenue and elasticity is summarized by Table 9.1.

TABLE 9.1	Relationship Between Elasticity and Marginal Revenue

$e_{q,p} < -1$	$MR > 0$
$e_{q,p} = -1$	$MR = 0$
$e_{q,p} > -1$	$MR < 0$

The inverse elasticity rule

If we assume the firm wishes to maximize profits, this analysis can be extended to illustrate the connection between price and marginal cost. Setting $MR = MC$ yields

$$MC = p\left(1 + \frac{1}{e_{q,p}}\right)$$

or

$$\frac{p - MC}{p} = -\frac{1}{e_{q,p}}. \tag{9.13}$$

That is, the gap between price and marginal cost will decrease as the demand curve facing the firm becomes more elastic. Indeed, in the case of a price-taking firm, $e_{q,p} = -\infty$ so $p = MR = MC$ and there is no gap. Because, as we shall see in later chapters, the gap between price and marginal cost is an important measure of inefficient resource allocation, Equation 9.13 is widely used in empirical studies of market organization. Notice also that Equation 9.13 makes sense only if the demand curve facing the firm is elastic ($e_{q,p} < -1$). If $e_{q,p}$ were greater than -1, Equation 9.13 would imply a negative marginal cost—an obvious impossibility. Hence profit-maximizing firms will choose to operate only at points on the demand curves facing them where demand is elastic. Of course, when there are many

---

FIGURE 9.2   **Market Demand Curve and Associated Marginal Revenue Curve**

Because the demand curve is negatively sloped, the marginal revenue curve will fall below the demand ("average revenue") curve. For output levels beyond q_1, MR is negative. At q_1, total revenues ($p_1 \times q_1$) are a maximum; beyond this point additional increases in q actually cause total revenues to fall because of the concomitant declines in price.

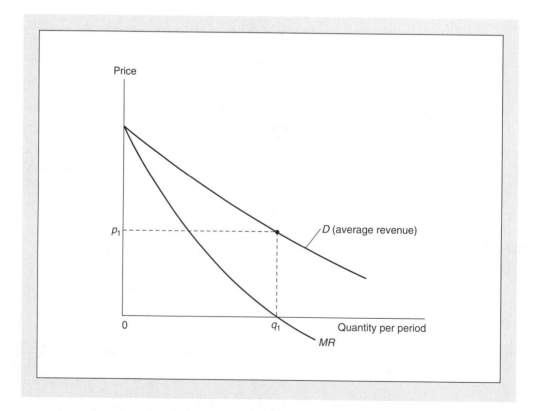

firms producing a single good, the demand curve facing one firm may be quite elastic even though the overall market demand curve may be relatively inelastic.

Marginal revenue curve

Any demand curve has a marginal revenue curve associated with it. If, as we sometimes assume, the firm must sell all its output at one price, it is convenient to think of the demand curve facing the firm as an *average revenue curve*. That is, the demand curve shows the revenue per unit (in other words, the price) yielded by alternative output choices. The marginal revenue curve, on the other hand, shows the extra revenue provided by the last unit sold. In the usual case of a downward-sloping demand curve, the marginal revenue curve will lie below the demand curve because, according to Equation 9.7, $MR < p$. In Figure 9.2 we have drawn such a curve, together with the demand curve from which it was derived. Notice that for output levels greater than q_1, marginal revenue is negative. As output increases from 0 to q_1, total revenues ($p \cdot q$) increase. However, at q_1 total revenues ($p_1 \cdot q_1$) are as large as possible; beyond this output level, price falls proportionately faster than output rises.

In Part 2 we talked in detail about the possibility of a demand curve's shifting because of changes in income, prices of other goods, or preferences. Whenever a demand curve does shift, its associated marginal revenue curve also shifts. This should be obvious, because a marginal revenue curve cannot be calculated without referring to a specific demand curve.

  EXAMPLE 9.2

The Constant Elasticity Case

In Chapter 5 we showed that a demand function of the form

$$q = ap^b \tag{9.14}$$

has a constant price elasticity of demand, and that this elasticity is given by the parameter b. To compute the marginal revenue function for this function first solve for p:

$$p = (1/a)^{1/b}q^{1/b} = kq^{1/b}, \tag{9.15}$$

where $k = (1/a)^{1/b}$. Hence

$$R = pq = kq^{(1+b)/b}$$

and

$$MR = dR/dq = [(1+b)/b]kq^{1/b} = [(1+b)/b]p. \tag{9.16}$$

For this particular function, then, MR is proportional to price. If, for example, $e_{q,p} = b = -2$, $MR = 0.5p$. For a more elastic case, suppose $b = -10$. Then $MR = 0.9p$. The MR curve approaches the demand curve as demand becomes more elastic. Again, if $b = -\infty$, $MR = p$; that is, in the case of infinitely elastic demand, the firm is a price taker. For inelastic demand, on the other hand, MR is negative (and profit maximization would be impossible).

Query: Suppose demand depended on other factors in addition to p. How would this change the analysis of this example? How would a change in one of these other factors shift the demand curve and its marginal revenue curve?

Short-run supply by a price-taking firm

We are now ready to study the supply decision of a profit-maximizing firm. In this chapter we will examine only the case in which the firm is a price taker. We will be looking at other cases in considerably more detail later on in Part 5. Also, we will focus only on supply decisions in the short run here. Long-run questions are the primary focus of the next chapter. The firm's set of short-run cost curves is therefore the appropriate model for our analysis.

Profit-maximizing decision

Figure 9.3 shows the firm's short-run decision. The market price[3] is given by P^*. The demand curve facing the firm is therefore a horizontal line through P^*. This line is labeled $P^* = MR$ as a reminder that an extra unit can always be sold by this price-taking firm without affecting the price it receives. Output level q^* provides maximum profits, because at q^* price is equal to short-run marginal cost. The fact that profits are positive can be seen by noting that at q^* price exceeds average costs. The firm earns a profit on each unit sold. If price were below average cost (as is the case for P^{***}), the firm would have a loss on each unit sold. If price and average cost were equal, profits would be zero. Notice that at q^* the marginal cost curve has a positive slope. This is required if profits are to be a true maximum. If $P = MC$ on a negatively sloped section of the marginal cost curve, this would not be a point of maximum profits, because increasing output would yield more in revenues (price times the amount produced) than this production would cost (marginal cost would decline if the MC curve has a negative slope). Consequently, profit maximization requires both that $P = MC$ and that marginal cost be increasing at this point.[4]

The firm's short-run supply curve

The positively sloped portion of the short-run marginal cost curve is the short-run supply curve for this price-taking firm. That curve shows how much the firm will produce for every possible market price. For example, as Figure 9.3 shows, at a higher price of P^{**} the firm will produce q^{**}, because it will find it in its interest to incur the higher marginal costs q^{**} entails. With a price of P^{***}, on the other hand, the firm opts to produce less (q^{***}), because only a lower output level will result in lower marginal costs to meet this lower price. By considering all possible prices the firm might face, we can see by the marginal cost curve how much output the firm should supply at each price.

For very low prices we have to be careful about this conclusion. Should market price fall below P_1, the profit-maximizing decision would be to produce nothing. As Figure 9.3 shows, prices less than P_1 do not cover average variable costs. There will be a loss on each unit produced in addition to the loss of all fixed costs. By shutting down production, the firm must pay fixed costs, but it avoids the losses incurred on each unit produced. Because, in the short run, the firm cannot close down and avoid all costs, its best decision is to produce no output. On the other hand, a price only slightly above P_1 means the firm should produce some output. Although profits may be negative (which they will be if price falls below short-run average total costs, the case at P^{***}), as long as variable costs are covered,

---

[3]We will usually use an uppercase italic P to denote market price for a single good here and in later chapters. When notation is complex, however, we will sometimes revert to using a lowercase P.

[4]Mathematically, because

$$\pi(q) = Pq - C(q),$$

profit maximization requires (the first-order condition)

$$\pi'(q) = P - MC(q) = 0$$

and (the second-order condition)

$$\pi''(q) = -MC'(q) < 0.$$

Hence it is required that $MC'(q) > 0$; marginal cost must be increasing.

FIGURE 9.3	Short-Run Supply Curve for a Price-Taking Firm

In the short run, a price-taking firm will produce the level of output for which $SMC = P$. At P^*, for example, the firm will produce q^*. The SMC curve also shows what will be produced at other prices. For prices below $SAVC$, however, the firm will choose to produce no output. The heavy lines in the figure represent the firm's short-run supply curve.

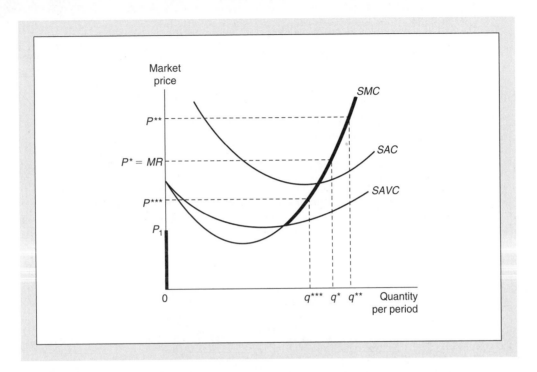

the profit-maximizing decision is to continue production. Fixed costs must be paid in any case, and any price that covers variable costs will provide revenue as an offset to the fixed costs.[5] Hence we have a complete description of this firm's supply decisions in response to alternative prices for its output. These are summarized in the following definition:

DEFINITION

Short-run supply curve. The firm's *short-run supply curve* shows how much it will produce at various possible output prices. For a profit-maximizing firm that takes the price of its output as given, this curve consists of the positively sloped segment of the firm's short-run marginal cost above the point of minimum average variable cost. For prices below this level, the firm's profit-maximizing decision is to shut down and produce no output.

Of course, any factor that shifts the firm's short-run marginal cost curve (such as changes in input prices or changes in the level of fixed inputs employed) will also shift the

---

[5]Some algebra may clarify matters. We know total costs equal the sum of fixed and variable costs:

$$SC = SFC + SVC,$$

and profits are given by

$$\pi = R - SC = P \cdot q - SFC - SVC.$$

If $q = 0$, variable costs and revenues are 0, so

$$\pi = -SFC.$$

The firm will produce something only if $\pi > -SFC$. But that means that

$$P \cdot q > SVC \quad \text{or} \quad P > SVC/q.$$

short-run supply curve. In Chapter 10 we will make extensive use of this type of analysis to study the operations of perfectly competitive markets.

 EXAMPLE 9.3

Short-Run Supply

In Example 8.5 we calculated the short-run total-cost function for the Cobb-Douglas production function as

$$SC(v, w, q, k) = vk_1 + wq^{1/\beta}k_1^{-\alpha/\beta}, \tag{9.17}$$

where k_1 is the level of capital input that is held constant in the short run.[6] Short-run marginal cost is easily computed as

$$SMC(v, w, q, k_1) = \frac{\partial SC}{\partial q} = \frac{w}{\beta} q^{(1-\beta)/\beta} k_1^{-\alpha/\beta}. \tag{9.18}$$

Notice that short-run marginal cost is increasing in output for all values of q. Short-run profit maximization for a price-taking firm requires that output be chosen so that market price (P) is equal to short-run marginal cost:

$$SMC = \frac{w}{\beta} q^{(1-\beta)/\beta} k_1^{-\alpha/\beta} = P \tag{9.19}$$

and we can solve for quantity supplied as

$$q = \left(\frac{w}{\beta}\right)^{-\beta/(1-\beta)} k_1^{\alpha/(1-\beta)} P^{\beta/(1-\beta)}. \tag{9.20}$$

This supply function provides a number of insights that should be familiar from earlier economics courses: (1) the supply curve is positively sloped—increases in P cause the firm to produce more because it is willing to incur a higher marginal cost;[7] (2) the supply curve is shifted to the left by increases in the wage rate, w—that is, for any given output price, less is supplied with a higher wage; (3) the supply curve is shifted outward by increases in capital input, k—with more capital in the short run the firm incurs a given level of short-run marginal cost at a higher output level; and (4) the rental rate of capital, v, is irrelevant to short-run supply decisions because it is only a component of fixed costs.

Numerical example. We can pursue once more the numerical example from Example 8.5, where $\alpha = \beta = 0.5$, $v = 3$, $w = 12$, $k_1 = 80$. For these specific parameters, the supply function is

$$q = \left(\frac{w}{0.5}\right)^{-1} \cdot (k_1)^1 \cdot P^1 = 40 \cdot \frac{P}{w} = \frac{40P}{12} = \frac{10P}{3}. \tag{9.21}$$

That this computation is correct can be checked by comparing the quantity supplied at various prices with the computation of short-run marginal cost in Table 8.2. For example, if $P = 12$, the supply function predicts that $q = 40$ will be supplied and Table 8.2 shows that this will agree with the $P = SMC$ rule. If price were to double to $P = 24$, an output level of 80 would be supplied and, again, Table 8.2 shows that when $q = 80$, $SMC = 24$. A lower price (say $P = 6$) would cause less to be produced ($q = 20$).

---

[6]Because capital input is held constant, the short-run cost function exhibits increasing marginal cost and this will therefore yield a unique profit-maximizing output level. If we had used a constant returns-to-scale production function in the long run, there would have been no such unique output level. We elaborate on this point later in this chapter and in Chapter 10.

[7]In fact, the short-run elasticity of supply can be read directly off Equation 9.20 as $\beta/(1 - \beta)$.

Before adopting Equation 9.21 as *the* supply curve in this situation, we should also check the firm's shutdown decision. Is there a price where it would be more profitable to produce $q = 0$ than to follow the $P = SMC$ rule? From Equation 9.17 we know that short-run variable costs are given by

$$SVC = wq^{1/\beta}k_1^{-\alpha/\beta}, \tag{9.22}$$

and so,

$$\frac{SVC}{q} = wq^{(1-\beta)/\beta}k_1^{-\alpha/\beta}. \tag{9.23}$$

A comparison of Equation 9.23 with Equation 9.18 shows that $SVC/q < SMC$ for all values of q providing that $\beta < 1$. So in this problem there is no price low enough that by following the $P = SMC$ the firm would lose more than if it produced nothing.

In our numerical example, consider the case $P = 3$. With such a low price the firm would opt for $q = 10$. Total revenue would be $R = 30$, and total short-run costs would be $SC = 255$ (see Table 8.1). Hence, profits would be $\pi = R - SC = -225$. Although the situation is dismal for the firm, it is better than opting for $q = 0$. If it produces nothing it avoids all variable (labor) costs, but it still loses 240 in fixed costs of capital. By producing 10 units of output, its revenues cover variable costs ($R - SVC = 30 - 15 = 15$) and contribute 15 to offset slightly the loss of fixed costs.

Query: How would you graph the short-run supply curve in Equation 9.21? How would the curve be shifted if w rose to 15? How would it be shifted if capital input increased to $k_1 = 100$? How would the short-run supply curve be shifted if v fell to 2? Would any of these changes alter the firm's determination to avoid shutting down in the short run?

Profit functions

Additional insights into the profit-maximization process for a price-taking firm[8] can be obtained by looking at the profit function. This function shows the firm's (maximized) profits as depending only on the prices that the firm faces. To understand the logic of its construction, remember that economic profits are defined as

$$\pi = Pq - C = Pf(k, l) - vk - wl. \tag{9.24}$$

Only the variables k and l (and also $q = f(k, l)$) are under the firm's control in this expression. The firm chooses levels of these inputs in order to maximize profits, treating the three prices, P, v, and w as fixed parameters in its decision. Looked at in this way, the firm's maximum profits ultimately depend only on these three exogenous prices, together with the form of the production function. We summarize this dependence by the *profit function:*

Profit function. The firm's profit function shows its maximal profits as a function of the prices that the firm faces:

$$\Pi(P, v, w) = \underset{k,l}{Max} \ \pi(k, l) = \underset{k,l}{Max}[Pf(k, l) - vk - wl]. \tag{9.25}$$

---

[8]Much of the analysis here would also apply to a firm that had some market power over the price it received for its product, but we will delay a discussion of that possibility until Part 5.

In this definition we use an upper case Π to indicate that the value given by the function is the maximum profits obtainable given the prices. This function implicitly incorporates the form of the firm's production function—a process we will illustrate shortly in Example 9.4. The profit function can refer to either long-run or short-run profit maximization, but in the latter case we would need also to specify the levels of any inputs that are fixed in the short run.

Properties of the profit function

As for the other optimized functions we have already looked at, the profit function has a number of properties that are very useful for economic analysis. These include:

1. *Homogeneity:* A doubling of all of the prices in the profit function will precisely double profits—that is, the profit function is homogeneous of degree one in all prices. We have already shown that marginal costs are homogeneous of degree one in input prices, hence a doubling of input prices and a doubling of the market price of a firm's output will not change the profit-maximizing quantity it decides to produce. But, because both revenues and costs have doubled, profits will double. This shows that with pure inflation (where all prices rise together) firms will not change their production plans and the levels of their profits will just keep up with that inflation.

2. *Profit functions are nondecreasing in output price, P:* This result seems obvious—a firm could always respond to a rise in the price of its output by not changing its input or output plans. Given the definition of profits, they must rise. Hence, if the firm changes its plans, it must be doing so in order to make even more profits. If profits were to decline, the firm would not be maximizing profits.

3. *Profit functions are nonincreasing in input prices, v, and w:* Again, this feature of the profit function seems obvious. A proof is similar to that used above in our discussion of output prices.

4. *Profit functions are convex in output prices:* This important feature of profit functions says that the profits obtainable by averaging those available from two different output prices will be at least as large as those obtainable from the average[9] of the two prices. Mathematically,

$$\frac{\Pi(P_1, v, w) + \Pi(P_2, v, w)}{2} \geq \Pi\left[\frac{P_1 + P_2}{2}, v, w\right]. \qquad (9.26)$$

The intuitive reason for this is that when firms are able to adapt their decisions to two different prices freely they can get better results than when they can make only one set of choices in response to the single average price. More formally, let $P_3 = (P_1 + P_2)/2$ and let q_i, k_i, l_i represent the profit-maximizing output and input choices for these various prices. Because of the profit-maximization assumption implicit in the function Π, we can write

$$\Pi(P_3, v, w) \equiv P_3 q_3 - v k_3 - w l_3 = \frac{P_1 q_3 - v k_3 - w l_3}{2} + \frac{P_2 q_3 - v k_3 - w l_3}{2}$$
$$\leq \frac{P_1 q_1 - v k_1 - w l_1}{2} + \frac{P_2 q_2 - v k_2 - w l_2}{2} \equiv \frac{\Pi(P_1, v, w) + \Pi(P_2, v, w)}{2}, \qquad (9.27)$$

which proves Equation 9.26. The convexity of the profit function has many applications to topics such as price stabilization. Some of these are discussed in the Extensions to this chapter.

---

[9]Although we only discuss a simple averaging of prices here, it is clear that with convexity a condition similar to Equation 9.26 holds for any weighted average price $\bar{P} = tP_1 + (1 - t)P_2$ where $0 \leq t \leq 1$.

Envelope results

Because the profit function reflects an underlying process of unconstrained maximization, we may also apply the envelope theorem to see how profits respond to changes in output and input prices. This application of the theorem yields a variety of very useful results. Specifically, using the definition of profits we have

$$\frac{\partial \Pi(P, v, w)}{\partial P} = q(P, v, w)$$

$$\frac{\partial \Pi(P, v, w)}{\partial v} = -k(P, v, w)$$

$$\frac{\partial \Pi(P, v, w)}{\partial w} = -l(P, v, w).$$

(9.28)

Again, these equations make intuitive sense—a small change in output price will increase profits in proportion to how much the firm is producing whereas a small increase in the price of an input will reduce profits in proportion to the amount of that input being employed. The first of these equations says that the firm's supply function can be calculated from its profit function by partial differentiation with respect to the output price.[10] The second and third equations show that input demand functions[11] can also be derived from the profit functions. Because the profit function itself is homogeneous of degree one, all of the functions described in Equations 9.28 are homogeneous of degree zero. That is, a doubling of both output and input prices will not change the input levels that the firm chooses, nor will this change the firm's profit-maximizing output level. All of the findings also have short-run analogues, as will be shown later with a specific example.

Producer surplus in the short run

In Chapter 5 we discussed the concept of "consumer surplus" and showed how areas below the demand curve can be used to measure the welfare costs to consumers of price changes. We also showed how such changes in welfare could be captured in the individual's expenditure function. The process of measuring the welfare effects of price changes for firms is very similar in short-run analysis. This is the topic we will pursue in this section. However, as we show in the next chapter, measuring the welfare impact of price changes for producers in the long run requires a very different approach because most such long-term effects are felt not by firms themselves, but rather by their input suppliers. In general it is this long-run approach that will prove more useful for our subsequent study of the welfare impacts of price changes.

Because the profit function is nondecreasing in output prices we know that if $P_2 > P_1$

$$\Pi(P_2, \ . \ . \ .) \geq \Pi(P_1, \ . \ . \ .),$$

and it would be natural to measure the welfare gain to the firm from the price change as

Welfare Gain = $\Pi(P_2, \ . \ . \ .) - \Pi(P_1, \ . \ . \ .)$. (9.29)

Figure 9.4 shows how this value can be measured graphically as the area bounded by the two prices and above the short-run supply curve. Intuitively, the supply curve shows the minimum price that the firm will accept for producing its output. Hence, when market price rises from P_1 to P_2, the firm is both able to sell its prior output level (q_1) at a higher price, and opts to sell additional output ($q_2 - q_1$) for which, at the margin, it also earns

---

[10]This relationship is sometimes referred to as "Hotelling's lemma" after the economist Harold Hotelling who discovered it in the 1930s.

[11]Unlike the input demand functions derived in Chapter 8, these input demand functions are not conditional on output levels. Rather, the firm's profit-maximizing output decision has already been taken into account in the functions. This demand concept is therefore more general than the one we introduced in Chapter 8, and we will have much more to say about it in the next section.

FIGURE 9.4   **Changes in Short-Run Producer Surplus Measure Firm Profits**

If price rises from P_1 to P_2 the increase in the firm's profits is given by area P_2ABP_1. At a price of P_1 the firm earns short-run producer surplus given by area P_0BP_1. This measures the increase in short-run profits for the firm when it produces q_1 rather than shutting down when price is P_0 or below.

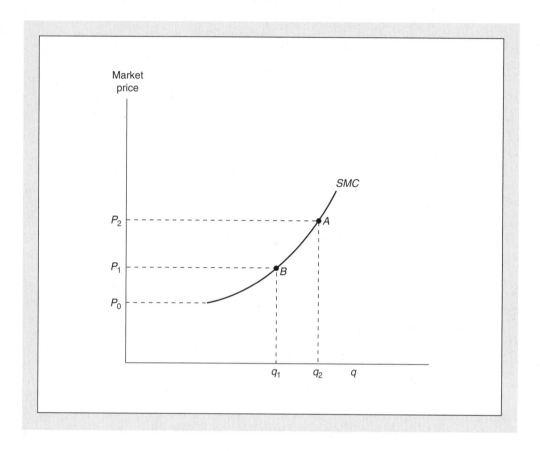

added profits on all but the final unit. Hence, the total gain in the firm's profits is given by area P_2ABP_1. Mathematically, we can make use of the envelope results from the previous section to derive

$$\textbf{Welfare Gain} = \int_{P_1}^{P_2} q(P)dP = \int_{P_1}^{P_2} (\partial\Pi/\partial P)dP = \Pi(P_2,\cdots) - \Pi(P_1,\cdots). \quad (9.30)$$

So, the geometric and mathematical measures of the welfare change agree.

Using this approach, we can also measure how much the firm values the right to produce at the prevailing market price relative to a situation where it would produce no output. If we denote the short-run shutdown price as P_0 (which might in fact be a price of zero, but not necessarily), then the extra profits available from facing a price of P_1 are defined to be producer surplus:

$$\textbf{Producer Surplus} = \Pi(P_1,\cdots) - \Pi(P_0,\cdots) = \int_{P_0}^{P_1} q(P)dP \quad (9.31)$$

This is shown as area P_1BP_0 in Figure 9.4 Hence we have a formal definition:

Producer surplus. Production surplus is the extra return that producers make by making transactions at the market price over and above what they would earn if nothing were produced. It is illustrated by the size of the area below the market price and above the supply curve.

In this definition we have made no distinction between the short run and the long run, though our development so far has involved only short-run analysis. In the next chapter we will see that the same definition can serve dual duty by describing producer surplus in the long run, so using this generic definition works for both concepts. Of course, as we will show, the meaning of long-run producer surplus is quite different from what we have studied here.

One more aspect of short-run producer surplus should be pointed out. Because the firm produces no output at its shutdown price, we know that $\Pi(P_0, \ldots) = -vk_1$—that is, profits at the shutdown price are solely made up of losses of all fixed costs. Hence:

$$\text{Producer Surplus} = \Pi(P_1, \ldots) - \Pi(P_0, \ldots)$$
$$= \Pi(P_1, \ldots) - (-vk_1) = \Pi(P_1, \ldots) + vk_1 \quad (9.32)$$

That is, producer surplus is given by current profits being earned *plus* short-run fixed costs. Further manipulation shows that magnitude can also be expressed as

$$\text{Producer Surplus} = \Pi(P_1, \ldots) - \Pi(P_0, \ldots)$$
$$= P_1 q_1 - vk_1 - wl_1 + vk_1 = P_1 q_1 - wl_1. \quad (9.33)$$

In words, a firm's short-run producer surplus is given by the extent to which its revenues exceed its variable costs—that is indeed what the firm gains by producing in the short run rather than shutting down and producing nothing.

 EXAMPLE 9.4

A Short-Run Profit Function

These various uses of the profit function can be illustrated with the Cobb-Douglas production function we have been using. Because $q = k^\alpha l^\beta$ and we treat capital as fixed at k_1 in the short run, profits are

$$\pi = Pk_1^\alpha l^\beta - vk_1 - wl. \quad (9.34)$$

To find the profit function we use the first-order conditions for a maximum to eliminate l from this expression:

$$\frac{\partial \pi}{\partial l} = \beta Pk_1^\alpha l^{\beta-1} - w = 0 \text{ so } l = \left(\frac{w}{\beta Pk_1^\alpha}\right)^{1/(\beta-1)}. \quad (9.35)$$

We can simplify the process of substituting this back into the profit equation by letting $A = (w/\beta Pk_1^\alpha)$. Making use of this shortcut, we have

$$\Pi(P, v, w, k_1) = Pk_1^\alpha A^{\beta/(\beta-1)} - vk_1 - wA^{1/(\beta-1)}$$
$$= wA^{1/(\beta-1)}[Pk_1^\alpha(A/w) - 1] - vk_1 \quad (9.36)$$
$$= wA^{1/(\beta-1)}[(1-\beta)/\beta] - vk_1.$$

Though admittedly messy, this solution is what was promised—the firm's maximal profits are expressed as a function of only the prices it faces and its technology. Notice that the firm's fixed costs (vk_1) enter this expression in a simple linear way. The prices the firm

(*continued*)

EXAMPLE 9.4 CONTINUED

faces determine the extent to which revenues exceed variable costs, then fixed costs are subtracted to obtain the final profit number.

Because it is always wise to check that one's algebra is correct, let's try out the numerical example we have been using. With $\alpha = \beta = 0.5$, $v = 3$, $w = 12$, $k_1 = 80$, we know that at a price of $P = 12$ the firm will produce 40 units of output and use labor input of $l = 20$. Hence profits will be $\pi = R - C = 12 \cdot 40 - 3 \cdot 80 - 12 \cdot 20 = 0$. The firm will just break even at a price of $P = 12$. Using the profit function yields

$$
\begin{aligned}
\Pi(P, v, w, k_1) &= \Pi(12, 3, 12, 80) \\
&= 12 \cdot [12/(0.5 \cdot 12 \cdot 80^{0.5})]^{-2}(1) - 3 \cdot 80 \\
&= 12 \cdot (80^{0.5}/2)^2 - 240 = 240 - 240 = 0. \qquad (9.37)
\end{aligned}
$$

So, at a price of 12, the firm earns 240 in profits on its variable costs, and these are precisely offset by fixed costs in arriving at the final total. With a higher price for its output, the firm earns positive profits. If the price falls below 12, however, the firm incurs short-run losses.[12]

Hotelling's Lemma: We can use the profit function in Equation 9.36 together with the envelope theorem to derive this firm's short-run supply function:

$$
\begin{aligned}
q(P, v, w, k_1) &= \frac{\partial \Pi}{\partial P} = \frac{-w}{\beta} \cdot A^{(2-\beta)/(\beta-1)} \cdot \left(\frac{-w}{\beta P^2 k_1^{\alpha}} \right) \\
&= \left(\frac{w}{\beta} \right)^{\beta/\beta-1} k_1^{\alpha/(1-\beta)} P^{\beta/(1-\beta)}, \qquad (9.38)
\end{aligned}
$$

which is precisely the short-run supply function that we calculated in Example 9.3 (see Equation 9.20).

Producer surplus: We can also use the supply function to calculate the firm's short-run producer surplus. To do so, we again return to our numerical example: $\alpha = \beta = 0.5$, $v = 3$, $w = 12$, $k_1 = 80$. With these parameters the short-run supply relationship is $q = 10P/3$ and the shutdown price is zero. Hence, at a price of $P = 12$, producer surplus is

$$
\text{Producer Surplus} = \int_{0}^{12} (10P/3)dP = \frac{10P^2}{6} \Big|_{0}^{12} = 240. \qquad (9.39)
$$

This is precisely short-run profits at a price of 12 ($\pi = 0$) plus short-run fixed costs ($= vk_1 = 3 \cdot 80 = 240$). If price were to rise to, say, 15, producer surplus would increase to 375 which would still consist of 240 in fixed costs plus total profits at the higher price ($\pi = 135$).

Query: How is the amount of short-run producer surplus here affected by changes in the rental rate for capital (v)? How is it affected by changes in the wage, w?

---

[12]In Table 8.2 we showed that if $q = 40$, $SAC = 12$. So zero profits are also indicated by $P = 12 = SAC$.

Profit maximization and input demand

Thus far, we have treated the firm's decision problem as one of choosing a profit-maximizing level of output. But our discussion throughout has made clear that the firm's output is, in fact, determined by the inputs it chooses to employ, a relationship that is summarized by the production function $q = f(k, l)$. Consequently, the firm's economic profits can also be expressed as a function of only the inputs it employs:

$$\pi\,(k, l) = Pq - C(q) = Pf(k, l) - (vk + wl). \qquad (9.40)$$

Viewed in this way, the profit-maximizing firm's decision problem becomes one of choosing the appropriate levels of capital and labor input.[13] The first-order conditions for a maximum are

$$\frac{\partial \pi}{\partial k} = P\frac{\partial f}{\partial k} - v = 0$$

$$\frac{\partial \pi}{\partial l} = P\frac{\partial f}{\partial l} - w = 0. \qquad (9.41)$$

These conditions make the intuitively appealing point that a profit maximizing firm should hire any input up to the point at which the input's marginal contribution to revenue is equal to the marginal cost of hiring the input. Because the firm is assumed to be a price-taker in its hiring, the marginal cost of hiring any input is equal to its market price. The input's marginal contribution to revenue is given by the extra output it produces (the marginal product) times that good's market price. This demand concept is given a special name:

Marginal revenue product. The extra revenue a firm receives when it employs one more unit of an input. In the price-taking[14] case, $MRP_l = Pf_l$, $MRP_k = Pf_k$.

Hence, profit maximization requires that the firm hire each input up to the point at which its marginal revenue product is equal to its market price. Notice also that the profit-maximizing Equations 9.41 also imply cost minimization because $RTS = f_l/f_k = w/v$.

Second-order conditions

Because the profit function in Equation 9.40 depends on two variables, k and l, the second-order conditions for a profit maximum are somewhat more complex than in the single-variable case we examined earlier. In Chapter 2, we showed that to ensure a true maximum it is required that the profit function be concave. That is,

$$\pi_{kk} = f_{kk} < 0 \qquad \pi_{ll} = f_{ll} < 0 \qquad (9.42)$$

and

$$\pi_{kk}\pi_{ll} - \pi^2_{kl} = f_{kk}\,f_{ll} - f^2_{kl} > 0.$$

So concavity of the profit relationship amounts to requiring that the production function itself be concave. Notice that diminishing marginal productivity for each input is not sufficient to ensure increasing marginal costs. Expanding output usually requires the firm to use more capital *and* more labor. Thus we must also ensure that increases in capital input do not raise the marginal productivity of labor (and thereby reduce marginal cost) by a

---

[13]Throughout our discussion in this section, we will assume that the firm is a price taker so the prices of its output and its inputs can be treated as fixed parameters. Results can be generalized fairly easily in the case where prices depend on quantity.

[14]If the firm is not a price-taker in the output market, this definition is generalized by using marginal revenue in place of price. That is, $MRP_l = \partial R/\partial l = \partial R/\partial q \cdot \partial q/\partial l = MR \cdot MP_l$. A similiar derivation holds for capital input.

large enough amount to reverse the effect of diminishing marginal productivity of labor itself. The second part of Equation 9.42 therefore requires that such cross-productivity effects be relatively small—that they be dominated by diminishing marginal productivities of the inputs. If these conditions are satisfied, marginal costs will be increasing at the profit-maximizing choices for k and l, and the first-order conditions will represent a local maximum.

Input demand functions

In principle the first-order conditions for hiring inputs in a profit-maximizing way can be manipulated to yield input demand functions that show how hiring depends on the prices that the firm faces. We will denote these demand functions by

$$\text{Capital Demand} = k(P, v, w)$$
$$\text{Labor Demand} = l(P, v, w).$$

$$(9.43)$$

Notice that, contrary to the input demand concepts discussed in Chapter 8, these demand functions are "unconditional"—that is, they implicitly permit the firm to adjust its output to changing prices. Hence, these demand functions provide a more complete picture of how prices affect input demand than did the contingent demand functions introduced in Chapter 8. We have already shown that these input demand functions can also be derived from the profit function through differentiation. In Example 9.5 we show that process explicitly. First, however, we will explore how changes in the price of an input might be expected to affect the demand for it. To simplify matters we look only at labor demand, but the analysis of the demand for any other input would be the same. In general, we conclude that the direction of this effect is unambiguous in all cases—that is, that $\partial l / \partial w \leq 0$ no matter how many inputs there are. To develop some intuition for this result, we begin with some simple cases.

Single-input case

One reason for expecting $\partial l / \partial w$ to be negative is based on the presumption that the marginal physical product of labor declines as the quantity of labor employed increases. A decrease in w means that more labor must be hired to bring about the equality $w = P \cdot MP_l$: A fall in w must be met by a fall in MP_l (because P is fixed), and this can be brought about by increasing l. That this argument is strictly correct for the case of one input can be shown as follows. Write the total differential of the profit-maximizing Equation 9.41 as

$$dw = P \cdot \frac{\partial f_l}{\partial l} \cdot \frac{\partial l}{\partial w} \cdot dw$$

or

$$1 = P \cdot f_{ll} \cdot \frac{\partial l}{\partial w}$$

$$(9.44)$$

or

$$\frac{\partial l}{\partial w} = \frac{1}{P \cdot f_{ll}} \leq 0,$$

where the final inequality holds because the marginal productivity of labor is assumed to be diminishing ($f_{ll} \leq 0$). Hence we have shown that, at least in the single input case, a ceteris paribus increase in the wage will cause less labor to be hired.

Two-input case

For the case of two (or more) inputs, the story is more complex. The assumption of a diminishing marginal physical product of labor can be misleading here. If w falls, there will not only be a change in l but also a change in k as a new cost-minimizing combination of inputs is chosen. When k changes, the entire f_l function changes (labor now has a different

FIGURE 9.5   **The Substitution and Output Effects of a Decrease in the Price of a Factor**

When the price of labor falls, two analytically different effects come into play. One of these, the substitution effect, would cause more labor to be purchased if output were held constant. This is shown as a movement from point A to point B in (a). At point B the cost-minimizing condition ($RTS = w/v$) is satisfied for the new, lower w. This change in w/v will also shift the firm's expansion path and its marginal cost curve. A normal situation might be for the MC curve to shift downward in response to a decrease in w as shown in (b). With this new curve (MC') a higher level of output (q_2) will be chosen. Consequently, the hiring of labor will increase (to l_2), also from this output effect.

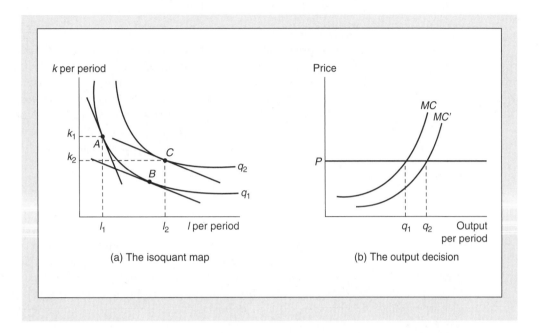

(a) The isoquant map   (b) The output decision

amount of capital to work with), and the simple argument we used above cannot be made. In the remainder of this section we will use a graphic approach to suggest why, even in the two-input case, $\partial l/\partial w$ must be negative. A more precise, mathematical analysis is presented in the next section.

Substitution effect

In some ways, analyzing the two-input case is similar to the analysis of the individual's response to a change in the price of a good that was presented in Chapter 5. When w falls, we can decompose the total effect on the quantity of l hired into two components. The first of these is called the *substitution effect*. If q is held constant at q_1, there will be a tendency to substitute l for k in the productive process. This effect is illustrated in Figure 9.5a. Because the condition for minimizing the cost of producing q_1 requires that $RTS = w/v$, a fall in w will necessitate a movement from input combination A to combination B. Because the isoquants exhibit a diminishing RTS, it is clear from the diagram that this substitution effect must be negative. A decrease in w will cause an increase in labor hired if output is held constant.

Output effect

It is not correct, however, to hold output constant. It is in considering a change in q (the *output effect*) that the analogy to the individual's utility-maximization problem breaks down. Consumers have budget constraints, but firms do not. Firms produce as much as the available demand allows. To investigate what happens to the quantity of output produced, we must investigate the firm's profit-maximizing output decision. A change in w, because it changes relative input costs, will shift the firm's expansion path. Consequently, all the firm's cost curves will be shifted, and probably some output level other than q_1 will be chosen. In Figure 9.5b what might be considered the "normal" case has been drawn. There the fall in w causes MC to shift downward to MC'. Consequently, the profit-maximizing level of output rises from q_1 to q_2. The profit-maximizing condition ($P = MC$) is now satisfied at a higher level of output. Returning to Figure 9.5a, this increase in output will cause even more l to be demanded, providing l is not an inferior input (see below). The result of both the substitution and output effects will be to move the input choice to point C on the firm's isoquant map. Both effects work to increase the quantity of labor hired in response to a decrease in the real wage.

The analysis provided in Figure 9.5 assumed that the market price (or marginal revenue, if this does not equal price) of the good being produced remained constant. This would be an appropriate assumption if only one firm in an industry experienced a fall in unit labor costs. However, if (as seems more likely) the decline were industrywide, a slightly different analysis would be required. In that case *all* firms' marginal cost curves would shift outward, and hence the industry supply curve would shift also. Assuming that demand is downward sloping, this will lead to a decline in product price. Output for the industry and for the typical firm will still increase and, as before, more labor will be hired.

Cross-price effects

We have shown that at least in simple cases, $\partial l/\partial w$ is unambiguously negative; substitution *and* output effects cause more labor to be hired when the wage rate falls. From Figure 9.5 it should be clear that no definite statement can be made about how capital usage responds to the wage change. That is, the sign of $\partial k/\partial w$ is indeterminate. In the simple two-input case, a fall in the wage will cause a substitution away from capital; that is, less capital will be used to produce a given output level. But the output effect will cause more capital to be demanded as part of the firm's increased production plan. So, substitution and output effects in this case work in opposite directions, and no definite conclusion about the sign of $\partial k/\partial w$ is possible.

A summary of substitution and output effects

The results of this discussion can be summarized by the following principle:

OPTIMIZATION PRINCIPLE

> **Substitution and output effects in input demand.** When the price of an input falls, two effects cause the quantity demanded of that input to rise:
>
> 1. The *substitution effect* causes any given output level to be produced using more of the input; and
>
> 2. The fall in costs causes more of the good to be sold, thereby creating an additional *output effect* that increases demand for the input.

For a rise in input price, both substitution and output effects cause the quantity of an input demanded to decline.

We now provide a more precise development of these concepts using a mathematical approach to the analysis.

A mathematical development

Our mathematical development of the substitution and output effects that arise from the change in an input price follows the method we used to study the effect of price changes in consumer theory. The end result is a Slutsky-style equation that resembles the one we derived in Chapter 5. However, the ambiguity provided by Giffen's paradox in the theory of consumption demand does not occur here.

We start with a reminder that we have two concepts of demand for any input (say, labor): (1) the conditional demand for labor, denoted by $l^c(v, w, q)$; and (2) the unconditional demand for labor, which is denoted by $l(P, v, w)$. At the profit-maximizing choice for labor input, these two concepts agree about the amount of labor hired:

$$l(P, v, w) = l^c(v, w, q). \qquad (9.45)$$

Differentiation of this identity with respect to the market wage yields

$$\frac{\partial l(P, v, w)}{\partial w} = \frac{\partial l^c(v, w, q)}{\partial w} + \frac{\partial l^c(v, w, q)}{\partial q} \cdot \frac{\partial q}{\partial w}. \qquad (9.46)$$

So, the total effect of a change in the wage on labor demanded can be decomposed into two components: (1) the change in contingent labor demand, holding q constant (the substitution effect); and (2) the change in contingent labor demand from a change in the level of output (the output effect). The first of these effects is obviously negative because of the convexity of the firm's isoquants. In order to study the sign of the second effect, consider the following quasi-mathematical analysis that shows precisely how a change in the wage affects output:

$$\textbf{Output Effect} = \frac{\partial l^c}{\partial q} \cdot \frac{\partial q}{\partial w} = \frac{\partial l^c}{\partial q} \cdot \frac{\partial q(P = MC)}{\partial MC} \cdot \frac{\partial MC}{\partial w}. \qquad (9.47)$$

Now $\partial q/\partial MC$ is clearly negative—for a given market price a shift upward in the marginal cost curve will cause less to be produced. For a normal good, both $\partial l^c/\partial q$ and $\partial MC/\partial w$ are positive, so the output effect will definitely be negative. But even in the pesky case of an inferior input, footnote 9 of Chapter 8 shows that both of these derivatives will be negative, so their product is positive. Hence even for inferior goods the output effect is negative.

Our mathematical development therefore supports the graphical analysis of Figure 9.5. The effect of an increase in an input price on the demand for that input is definitely negative. Because of the profit-maximization hypothesis, oddities such as Giffen's paradox cannot occur. The decomposition of input demand developed in Equation 9.46 also provides a useful way of studying the impact of changes in input prices, as the next example shows.

 EXAMPLE 9.5

Decomposing Input Demand into Substitution and Output Components

To study input demand we need to start with a production function that has two features: (1) the function must permit capital-labor substitution (because substitution is an important part of the story); and (2) the production function must exhibit increasing marginal costs (so that the second-order conditions for profit maximization are satisfied). One function that satisfies these conditions is a three-input Cobb-Douglas function when one of the inputs is held fixed. So, let $q = f(k, l, g) = k^{0.25}l^{0.25}g^{0.5}$, where k and l are the familiar capital and labor inputs and g is a third input (size of the factory) that is held fixed at $g = 16$ (square meters?) for all of our analysis. The short-run production function is therefore $q = 4k^{0.25}l^{0.25}$. We assume that the factory can be rented at a cost of r per square meter per period. To study the demand for, say, labor input, we need both the total-cost function and the profit function implied by this production function. Mercifully, your author has computed these functions for you as

$$C(v, w, r, q) = \frac{q^2 v^{0.5} w^{0.5}}{8} + 16r \qquad (9.48)$$

and

$$\Pi(P, v, w, r) = 2P^2 v^{-0.5} w^{-0.5} - 16r.$$

As expected, the costs of the fixed input (g) enter as a constant in these equations, and these costs will play very little role in our analysis.

(*continued*)

EXAMPLE 9.5 CONTINUED

Envelope Results

Labor-demand relationships can be derived from both of these functions through differentiation:

$$l^c(v, w, r, q) = \frac{\partial C}{\partial w} = \frac{q^2 v^{0.5} w^{-0.5}}{16} \qquad (9.49)$$

and

$$l(P, v, w, r) = -\frac{\partial \Pi}{\partial w} = P^2 v^{-0.5} w^{-1.5}.$$

These functions already suggest that a change in the wage has a larger effect on total labor demand than it does on contingent labor demand because the exponent of w is more negative in the total demand equation. That is, the output effect must also be playing a role here. To see that directly, we turn to some numbers.

Numerical example. Let's start again with the assumed values we have been using in several previous examples: $v = 3$, $w = 12$ and let $P = 60$. Let's first calculate what output the firm will choose in this situation. To do so, we need its supply function:

$$q(P, v, w, r) = \frac{\partial \Pi}{\partial P} = 4 P v^{-0.5} w^{-0.5}. \qquad (9.50)$$

With this function and the prices we have chosen, the firm's profit-maximizing output level is (surprise) $q = 40$. With these prices and an output level of 40 both of the demand functions in Equation 9.49 predict that the firm will hire $l = 50$. Because the RTS here is given by k/l, we also know that $k/l = w/v$, so at these prices $k = 200$.

Suppose now that the wage rate rises to $w = 27$ but that the other prices remain unchanged. The firm's supply function (Equation 9.50) shows that it will now produce $q = 26.67$. The rise in the wage shifts the firm's marginal cost curve upward and, with a constant output price, this causes the firm to produce less. To produce this output, either of the labor-demand functions can be used to show that the firm will hire $l = 14.8$. Hiring of capital will also fall to $k = 133.3$ because of the large reduction in output.

We can decompose the fall in labor hiring from $l = 50$ to $l = 14.8$ into substitution and output effects using the contingent demand function. If the firm had continued to produce $q = 40$ even though the wage rose, Equation 9.49 shows that it would have used $l = 33.33$. Capital input would have increased to $k = 300$. Because we are holding output constant at its initial level of $q = 40$, these changes represent the firm's substitution effects in response to the higher wage.

The decline in output needed to restore profit maximization causes the firm to cut back on its output. In doing so it reduces its input usage substantially. Notice in particular that in this example the rise in the wage not only caused labor usage to decline sharply, but it also caused capital usage to fall because of the large output effect.

Query: How would the calculations in this problem be affected if all firms had experienced the rise in wages? Would the decline in labor (and capital) demand be greater or smaller than found here?

SUMMARY

In this chapter we studied the supply decision of a profit-maximizing firm. Our general goal was to show how such a firm responds to price signals from the marketplace. In addressing that question, we developed a number of analytical results:

- In order to maximize profits, the firm should choose to produce that output level for which marginal revenue (the revenue from selling one more unit) is equal to marginal cost (the cost of producing one more unit).

- If a firm is a price taker, its output decisions to not affect the price of its output, so marginal revenue is given by this price. If the firm faces a downward-sloping demand for its output, however, it can sell more only at a lower price. In this case marginal revenue will be less than price and may even be negative.

- Marginal revenue and the price elasticity of demand are related by the formula

$$ MR = P\left(1 + \frac{1}{e_{q,p}}\right), $$

where P is the market price of the firm's output and $e_{q,p}$ is the price elasticity of demand for its product.

- The supply curve for a price-taking, profit-maximizing firm is given by the positively sloped portion of its marginal cost curve above the point of minimum average variable cost (AVC). If price falls below minimum AVC, the firm's profit-maximizing choice is to shut down and produce nothing.

- The firm's reactions to changes in the various prices it faces can be judged through use of its profit function, $\Pi(P, v, w)$. That function shows the maximum profits that the firm can achieve given the price for its output, the prices of its input, and its production technology. The profit function yields particularly useful envelope results. Differentiation with respect to market price yields the supply function whereas differentiation with respect to any input price yields (negative of) the demand function for that input.

- Short-run changes in market price result is changes in the firm's short-run profitability. These can be measured graphically by changes in the size of producer surplus. The profit function can also be used to calculate changes in producer surplus.

- Profit maximization provides a theory of the firm's derived demand for inputs. The firm will hire any input up to the point at which its marginal revenue product is just equal to its per-unit market price. Increases in the price of an input will induce substitution and output effects that cause the firm to reduce hiring of that input.

PROBLEMS

9.1

John's Lawn Moving Service is a small business that acts as a price taker (i.e., $MR = P$). The prevailing market price of lawn mowing is $20 per acre. John's costs are given by

$$ \text{total cost} = .1q^2 + 10q + 50, $$

where q = the number of acres John chooses to cut a day.

a. How many acres should John choose to cut in order to maximize profit?

b. Calculate John's maximum daily profit.

c. Graph these results and label John's supply curve.

9.2

Would a lump-sum profits tax affect the profit-maximizing quantity of output? How about a proportional tax on profits? How about a tax assessed on each unit of output? How about a tax on labor input?

9.3

This problem concerns the relationship between demand and marginal revenue curves for a few functional forms. Show that:

a. for a linear demand curve, the marginal revenue curve bisects the distance between the vertical axis and the demand curve for any price.

b. for any linear demand curve, the vertical distance between the demand and marginal revenue curves is $-1/b \cdot q$, where $b\, (<0)$ is the slope of the demand curve.

c. for a constant elasticity demand curve of the form $q = aP^b$, the vertical distance between the demand and marginal revenue curves is a constant ratio of the height of the demand curve, with this constant depending on the price elasticity of demand.

d. for any downward-sloping demand curve, the vertical distance between the demand and marginal revenue curves at any point can be found by using a linear approximation to the demand curve at that point and applying the procedure described in part (b).

e. Graph the results of parts (a) through (d) of this problem.

9.4

Universal Widget produces high-quality widgets at its plant in Gulch, Nevada, for sale throughout the world. The cost function for total widget production (q) is given by

$$\text{total cost} = .25q^2.$$

Widgets are demanded only in Australia (where the demand curve is given by $q = 100 - 2P$) and Lapland (where the demand curve is given by $q = 100 - 4P$). If Universal Widget can control the quantities supplied to each market, who many should it sell in each location in order to maximize total profits? What price will be charged in each location?

9.5

The production function for a firm in the business of calculator assembly is given by

$$q = 2\sqrt{l},$$

where q is finished calculator output and l represents hours of labor input. The firm is a price taker for both calculators (which sell for P) and workers (which can be hired at a wage rate of w per hour).

a. What is the total-cost function for this firm?

b. What is the profit function for this firm?

c. What is the supply function for assembled calculators $[q(P,w)]$?

d. What is this firm's demand for labor function $[l(P,w)]$?

9.6

The market for high-quality caviar is dependent on the weather. If the weather is good, there are many fancy parties and caviar sells for $30 per pound. In bad weather it sells for only $20 per pound. Caviar produced one week will not keep until the next week. A small caviar producer has a cost function given by

$$C = \tfrac{1}{2}q^2 + 5q + 100,$$

where q is weekly caviar production. Production decisions must be made before the weather (and the price of caviar) is known, but it is known that good weather and bad weather each occur with a probability of 0.5.

    a. How much caviar should this firm produce if it wishes to maximize the expected value of its profits?

    b. Suppose the owner of this firm has a utility function of the form

$$\text{utility} = \sqrt{\pi},$$

       where π is weekly profits. What is the expected utility associated with the output strategy defined in part (a)?

    c. Can this firm owner obtain a higher utility of profits by producing some output other than that specified in parts (a) and (b)? Explain.

    d. Suppose this firm could predict next week's price, but could not influence that price. What strategy would maximize expected profits in this case? What would expected profits be?

9.7

The Acme Heavy Equipment School teaches students how to drive construction machinery. The number of students the school can educate per week is given by $q = 10 \min(k, l)^\gamma$, where k is the number of backhoes the firm rents per week, l is the number of instructors hired each week, and γ is a parameter indicating the returns to scale in this production function.

    a. Explain why development of a profit-maximizing model here requires $0 < \gamma < 1$.

    b. Suppposing $\gamma = 0.5$, calculate the firm's total-cost and profit functions.

    c. If $v = 1000$, $w = 500$, and $P = 600$, how many students will Acme serve and what are its profits?

    d. If the price students are willing to pay rises to $P = 900$, how much will profits change?

    e. Graph Acme's supply curve for student slots, and show that the increase in profits calculated in part (d) can be shown on that graph.

9.8

How would you expect an increase in output price, P, to affect the demand for capital and labor inputs?

    a. Explain graphically why if neither input is inferior it seems clear that a rise in P must not reduce the demand for either factor.

    b. Show that the graphical presumption from part (a) is demonstrated by the input demand functions that can be derived in the Cobb-Douglas case.

    c. Use the profit function to show how the presence of inferior inputs would lead to ambiguity in the effect of P on input demand.

9.9

With a CES production function of the form $q = (k^\rho + l^\rho)^{\gamma/\rho}$ a lot of algebra can be used to compute the profit function as $\Pi(P, v, w) = KP^{1/(1-\gamma)} (v^{1-\sigma} + w^{1-\sigma})^{\gamma/(1-\sigma)(\gamma-1)}$, where $\sigma = 1/(1-\rho)$ and K is a constant.

    a. If you are a glutton for punishment (or if your instructor is), prove that the profit function takes this form—perhaps the easiest way to do so is to start from the CES cost function in Example 8.2.

b. Explain why this profit function provides a reasonable representation for a firm's behavior only for $0 < \gamma < 1$.

c. Explain the role of the elasticity of substitution (σ) in this profit function.

d. What is the supply function in this case? How does σ determine the extent to which that function shifts when input prices change?

e. Derive the input demand functions in this case. How are these functions affected by the size of σ?

9.10

Young's theorem can be used in combination with the envelope results in this chapter to derive some useful results.

a. Show that $\partial l(P, v, w)/\partial v = \partial k(P, v, w)/\partial w$. Interpret this result.

b. Use the result from part (a) to show how a unit tax on labor would be expected to affect capital input.

c. Show that $\partial q/\partial w = -\partial l/\partial P$. Interpret this result.

d. Use the result from part (c) to discuss how a unit tax on labor input would affect quantity supplied.

SUGGESTIONS FOR FURTHER READING

Ferguson, C. E. *The Neoclassical Theory of Production and Distribution.* Cambridge, UK: Cambridge University Press, 1969.
  Provides a complete analysis of the output effect in factor demand. Also shows how the degree of substitutability affects many of the results in this chapter.

Hicks, J. R. *Value and Capital,* 2nd ed. Oxford: Oxford University Press, 1947.
  The Appendix looks in detail at the notion of factor complementarity.

Mas-Colell, A., M. D. Whinston, and J.R. Green. *Microeconomic Theory.* New York: Oxford University Press, 1995.
  Provides a very elegant introduction to the theory of production using vector and matrix notation. This allows for any arbitrary number of inputs and outputs.

Samuelson, P. A. *Foundations of Economic Analysis.* Cambridge, MA: Harvard University Press, 1947.
  Early development of the profit function idea together with a very nice discussion of the consequences of constant returns to scale for market equilibrium.

Sydsaeter, K., A. Strom, and P. Berck. *Economists' Mathematical Manual,* 3rd ed. Berlin: Springer-Verlag, 2000.
  Chapter 25 offers formulas for a number of profit and factor demand functions.

Varian, H. R. *Microeconomic Analysis,* 3rd ed. New York: W.W. Norton, 1992.
  Offers an entire chapter on the profit function. Varian offers a novel approach for comparing short- and long-run responses using the LeChatelier principle.

EXTENSIONS

Applications of the Profit Function

In Chapter 9 we introduced the profit function. That function summarizes the firm's "bottom line" as it depends on the prices it faces for its outputs and inputs. In these extensions we show how some of the properties of the profit function have been used to assess important empirical and theoretical questions.

E9.1 Convexity and price stabilization

Convexity of the profit function implies that a single firm will generally prefer a fluctuating output price to one that is stabilized (say, through government intervention) at is mean value. The result runs contrary to the direction of economic policy in many less developed countries, which tends to stress the desirability of stabilization of commodity prices. Several factors may account for this seeming paradox. First, many plans to "stabilize" commodity prices are in reality plans to raise the average level of these prices. Cartels of producers often have this as their primary goal, for example. Second, the convexity result applies for a single, price-taking firm. From the perspective of the entire market, total revenues from stabilized or fluctuating prices will depend on the nature of the demand for the product.[1] A third complication that must be addressed in assessing price stabilization schemes is firms' expectation of future prices. When commodities can be stored, optimal production decisions in the presence of price stabilization schemes can be quite complex. Finally, the purpose of price stabilization schemes may in some situations be more focused on reducing risks for the consumers of basic commodities such as food, rather than on the welfare of producers. Still, this fundamental property of the profit function suggests caution in devising price stabilization schemes that have desirable long-run effects on producers. For an extended theoretical analysis of these issues, see Newbury and Stiglitz (1981).

E9.2 Producer surplus and the short-run costs of disease

Disease episodes can severely disrupt markets, leading to short-run losses in producer and consumer surplus. For firms, these losses can be computed as the short-run losses of profits from temporarily lower prices for their output or from the temporarily higher input prices they must pay. A particular extensive set of such calculations is provided by Harrington, Krupnick, and Spofford (1991) in their detailed study of a giardiasis outbreak in Pennsylvania in 1983. Although consumers suffered most of the losses associated with this outbreak, the authors also calculate substantial losses for restaurants and bars in the immediate area. Such losses arose both from reduced business for these firms and from the temporary need to use bottled water and other high-cost inputs in their operations. Quantitative calculations of these losses are based on profit functions described by the authors.

E9.3 Profit functions and productivity measurement

In Chapter 7 we showed that total factor productivity growth is usually measured as

$$G_A = G_q - s_k G_k - s_l G_l, \text{ where } G_x = \frac{dx/dt}{x} = \frac{d \ln x}{dt}$$

and s_k, s_l are the shares of capital and labor in total costs, respectively. One difficulty with making this calculation is that it requires measuring changes in input usage over time—a measurement that can be especially difficult for capital. The profit function provides an alternative way of measuring the same phenomenon without needing to estimate input usage directly. To understand the logic of this approach, consider the production function we wish to examine, $q = f(k, l, t)$. We want to know how output would change over time even if input levels were held constant. That is, we wish to measure $\partial \ln q / \partial t = f_t / f$. Notice the use of partial differentiation in this expression—in words, we want to know the proportionate change in f over time when other inputs are held constant. If the production function exhibits constant returns to scale and if the

---

[1]Specifically, for a constant elasticity demand function, total revenue will be a concave function of price if demand is inelastic, but convex if demand is elastic. Hence, in the elastic case, producers will obtain higher total revenues from a fluctuating price than from a price stabilized at its mean value.

firm is a price taker for both inputs and its output, if is fairly easy[2] to show that this partial derivative is the measure of changing total factor productivity we want—that is, $G_A = f_t/f$. Now consider the profit function, $\Pi(P, v, w, t)$. By definition profits are given by

$$\pi = Pq - vk - wl = Pf - vk - wl,$$

so

$$\frac{\partial \ln \Pi}{\partial t} = \frac{Pf_t}{\Pi}$$

and so,

$$G_A = \frac{f_t}{f} = \frac{\Pi}{Pf} \cdot \frac{\partial \ln \Pi}{\partial t} = \frac{\Pi}{Pq} \cdot \frac{\partial \ln \Pi}{\partial t}. \quad \text{(i)}$$

So, in this special case, changes in total factor productivity can be inferred from the share of profits in total revenue and the time derivative of the log of the profit function. But this conclusion can be readily generalized to cases of nonconstant returns to scale and even to firms that produce multiple outputs (see, for example, Kumbhakar, 2002). So, for situations where input and output prices are more readily available than input quantities, using the profit function is an attractive way to proceed.

Three examples of this use for the profit function might be mentioned. Karagiannis and Mergos (2000) reassess the major increases in total factor productivity that have been experienced by U.S. agriculture during the past 50 years using the profit function approach. They find results that are broadly consistent with those using more conventional measures. Huang (2000) adopts the same approach in a study of Taiwanese banking and finds significant increases in productivity that could not be detected using other methods. Finally, Coelli and Perelman (2000) use a modified profit function approach to measure the relative efficiency of European railroads. Perhaps not surprisingly, they find that Dutch railroads are the most efficient in Europe, whereas those in Italy are the least efficient.

References

Coelli, T., and S. Perelman. "Technical Efficiency of European Railways: A Distance Function Approach." *Applied Economics* (December 2000): 1967–76.

Harrington, W. A., J. Krupnick, and W. O. Spofford. *Economics and Episodic Disease: The Benefits of Preventing a Giardiasis Outbreak*. Baltimore: Johns Hopkins University Press, 1991.

Huang, T. "Estimating X-Efficiency in Taiwanese Banking Using a Translog Shadow Profit Function." *Journal of Productivity Analysis* (November 2000): 225–45.

Karagiannis, G., and G. J. Mergos. "Total Factor Productivity Growth and Technical Change in a Profit Function Framework." *Journal of Productivity Analysis* (July 2000): 31–51.

Kumbhakar, S. "Productivity Measurement: A Profit Function Approach." *Applied Economics Letters* (April 2002): 331–34.

Newbury, D. M. G., and J. E. Stiglitz. *The Theory of Commodity Price Stabilization*. Oxford: Oxford University Press, 1981.

---

[2]The proof proceeds by differentiating the production function logarithmically with respect to time as $G_q = d \ln q/dt = e_{q,k}G_k + e_{q,l}G_l + f_t/f$ and then recognizing that with constant returns to scale and price-taking behavior $e_{q,k} = S_k\ e_{q,l} = s_l$.

Part 4

COMPETITIVE MARKETS

In Parts 2 and 3 we developed models to explain the demand for goods by utility-maximizing individuals and the supply of goods by profit-maximizing firms. In this part we will bring these two strands of analysis together to describe the process by which prices are determined. We will focus on only one specific model of price determination, the perfectly competitive model. That model assumes a large enough number of demanders and suppliers of each good so that each must be a price taker. In Part 5 we will illustrate some of the models that result from relaxing the strict price-taking assumptions of the competitive case, but in this part we assume price-taking behavior throughout.

Chapter 10 develops the familiar partial equilibrium model of price determination in competitive markets. The principal result is the Marshallian "cross" diagram of supply and demand that we first discussed in Chapter 1. This model illustrates a "partial" equilibrium view of price determination because it focuses on only a single market.

Chapter 11 continues the analysis of partial equilibrium competitive models by examining some of the ways such models are applied. A specific focus of the chapter is on showing how the competitive model can be used to judge the welfare consequences for market participants of changes in market equilibria.

Although the partial equilibrium competitive model is quite useful for studying a single market in detail, it is inappropriate for examining relationships among markets. To capture such cross-market effects requires the development of "general" equilibrium models—a topic we take up in Chapter 12. There we show how an entire economy can be viewed as a system of interconnected competitive markets that determine all prices simultaneously. We also examine how the welfare consequences of perfect competition can be studied in this model.

Chapter 10

THE PARTIAL EQUILIBRIUM COMPETITIVE MODEL

In this chapter we describe the familiar model of price determination under perfect competition originally developed by Alfred Marshall in the late nineteenth century. That is, we provide a fairly complete analysis of the supply-demand mechanism as it applies to a single market. This is perhaps the most widely used model for the study of prices.

Market demand

In Part 2 we showed how to construct individual demand functions that illustrate changes in the quantity of a good that a utility-maximizing individual chooses as the market price and other factors change. With only two goods (x and y) we concluded that an individual's (Marshallian) demand function can be summarized as

$$\text{Quantity of } x \text{ demanded} = x(p_x, p_y, I). \qquad (10.1)$$

Now we wish to show how these demand functions can be added up to reflect the demand of all individuals in a marketplace. If we use a subscript i ($i = l, n$) to represent each person's demand function for good x we can define the total demand in the market as

$$\text{Market Demand for } X = \sum_{i=1}^{n} x_i(p_x, p_y, I_i). \qquad (10.2)$$

Notice three things about this summation. First, we assume that everyone in this marketplace faces the same prices for both goods. That is, p_x and p_y enter Equation 10.2 without person-specific subscripts. On the other hand, each person's income enters into his or her own specific demand function. Market demand depends not only on the total income of all market participants but also on how that income is distributed among consumers. Finally, notice that we have used an upper case X to refer to market demand—a notation we will soon modify slightly.

The market demand curve

Equation 10.2 makes clear that the total quantity of a good demanded depends not only on its own price, but also on the prices of other goods and on the income of each person. To construct the market demand curve for good X we allow p_x to vary while holding p_y and the

A market demand curve is the "horizontal sum" of each individual's demand curve. At each price the quantity demanded in the market is the sum of the amounts each individual demands. For example, at p_x^* the demand in the market is $x_1^* + x_2^* = x^*$.

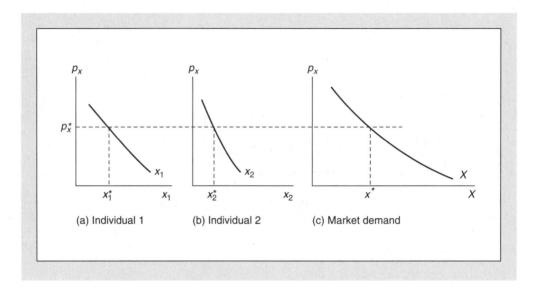

(a) Individual 1   (b) Individual 2   (c) Market demand

income of each person constant. Figure 10.1 shows this construction for the simple case where there are only two consumers in the market. For each potential price of x, the point on the market demand curve for X is found by adding up the quantities demanded by each person. For example, at a price of p_x^* person 1 demands x_1^* and person 2 demands x_2^*. The total quantity demanded in this two-person market is the sum of these two amounts ($X^* = x_1^* + x_2^*$). The point p_x^*, X^* is therefore one point on the market demand curve for X. Other points on the curve are derived in a similar way. The market demand curve is therefore a "horizontal sum" of each individual's demand curve.[1]

Shifts in the market demand curve

The market demand curve, then, summarizes the ceteris paribus relationship between X and p_x. It is important to keep in mind that the curve is in reality a two-dimensional representation of a many-variable function. Changes in p_x result in movements along this curve. But changes in any of the other determinants of the demand for X cause the curve to shift to a new position. A general rise in incomes would, for example, cause the demand curve to shift outward (assuming X is a normal good) because each individual would choose to buy more X at every price. Similarly, a rise in p_Y would shift the demand curve to X outward if individuals regarded X and Y as substitutes, but shift the demand curve for X inward if the goods were regarded as complements. Accounting for all such shifts may sometimes require returning to examine the individual demand functions that constitute the market relationship, especially when examining situations in which the distribution of income changes, thereby raising some incomes and reducing others. To keep matters straight, economists usually reserve the term *change in quantity demanded* for a movement along a fixed demand curve in response to a change in p_x. Alternatively, any shift in the position of the demand curve is referred to as a "change in demand."

---

[1]Compensated market demand curves can be constructed in exactly the same way by summing each individual's compensated demand. Such a compensated market demand curve would hold each person's utility constant.

EXAMPLE 10.1

Shifts in Market Demand

These ideas can be illustrated with a simple set of linear demand functions. Suppose individual 1's demand for oranges (x—measured in dozens per year) is given by[2]

$$x_1 = 10 - 2p_x + .1I_1 + .5p_y, \qquad (10.3)$$

where

p_x = price of oranges (dollars per dozen)

I_1 = individual 1's income (in thousands of dollars)

p_y = price of grapefruit (a gross substitute for oranges—dollars per dozen).

Individual 2's demand for oranges is given by

$$x_2 = 17 - p_x + .05I_2 + .5p_y. \qquad (10.4)$$

Hence the market demand function is

$$X(p_x, p_y, I_1, I_2) = x_1 + x_2 = 27 - 3p_x + .1I_1 + .05I_2 + p_y. \quad (10.5)$$

Here the coefficient for the price of oranges represents the sum of the two individuals' coefficients, as does the coefficient for grapefruit prices. This reflects the assumption that orange and grapefruit markets are characterized by the law of one price. Because the individuals have differing coefficients for income, however, the demand function depends on the distribution of income between them.

To graph Equation 10.5 as a market demand curve, we must assume values for I_1, I_2, and p_y (because the demand curve reflects only the two-dimensional relationship between x and p_x). If $I_1 = 40$, $I_2 = 20$, and $p_y = 4$, the market demand curve is given by

$$X = 27 - 3p_x + 4 + 1 + 4 = 36 - 3p_x, \qquad (10.6)$$

which is a simple linear demand curve. If the price of grapefruit were to rise to $p_y = 6$, the curve would, assuming incomes remain unchanged, shift outward to

$$X = 27 - 3p_x + 4 + 1 + 6 = 38 - 3p_x, \qquad (10.7)$$

whereas an income tax that took 10 (thousand dollars) from individual 1 and transferred it to individual 2 would shift the demand curve inward to

$$X = 27 - 3p_x + 3 + 1.5 + 4 = 35.5 - 3p_x \qquad (10.8)$$

because individual 1 has a larger marginal effect of income changes on orange purchases. All of these changes shift the demand curve in a parallel way because, in this linear case, none of them affects either individual's coefficient for p_x. In all cases, a rise in p_x of .10 (ten cents) would cause X to fall by .30 (dozen per year).

Query: For this linear case, when would it be possible to express market demand as a linear function of total income $(I_1 + I_2)$? Alternatively, suppose the individuals had differing coefficients for p_y. Would that change the analysis in any fundamental way?

[2]This linear form is used to illustrate some issues in aggregation. It is difficult to defend this form theoretically, however. For example, it is not homogeneous of degree zero in all prices and income.

Generalizations

Although our construction concerns only two goods and two individuals, it is easily generalized. Suppose there are n goods (denoted by x_i, $i = 1$, n) with prices p_i, $i = 1$, n. Assume also there are m individuals in society. Then the jth individual's demand for the ith good will depend on all prices and on I_j, the income of this person. This can be denoted by

$$x_{i,j} = x_{i,j}(p_1, \cdots p_n, I_j), \qquad (10.9)$$

where $i = 1$, n and $j = 1$, m.

Using these individual demand functions, market demand concepts are provided by the following definitions:

Market demand. The *market demand function* for a particular good (X_i) is the sum of each individual's demand for that good:

$$X_i = \sum_{j=1}^{m} x_{i,j}(p_1, \cdots p_n, I_j). \qquad (10.10)$$

The *market demand curve* for X_i is constructed from the demand function by varying p_i, while holding all other determinants of X_i constant. Assuming each individual's demand curve is downward sloping, this market demand curve will also be downward sloping.

Of course, this definition is just a generalization of our prior discussion, but three features warrant repetition. First, the functional representation of Equation 10.10 makes clear that the demand for X_i depends not only on p_i but also on the prices of all other goods. A change in one of those other prices would therefore be expected to shift the demand curve to a new position. Second, the functional notation indicates that the demand for X_i depends on the entire distribution of individuals' incomes. Although in many economic discussions it is customary to refer to the effect of changes in aggregate total purchasing power on the demand for a good, this approach may be a misleading simplification, because the actual effect of such a change on total demand will depend on precisely how the income changes are distributed among individuals. Finally, although they are obscured somewhat by the notation we have been using, the role of changes in preferences should be mentioned. We have constructed individuals' demand functions with the assumption that preferences (as represented by indifference curve maps) remain fixed. If preferences were to change, so would individual and market demand functions. Hence, market demand curves can clearly be shifted by changes in preferences. In many economic analyses, however, it is assumed that these changes occur so slowly that they may be implicitly held constant without misrepresenting the situation.

A word on notation

Often in this book we shall be looking at only one market. In order to simplify the notation, in these cases we shall use the letter Q_D to refer to the quantity of the particular good demanded in this market and P to denote its market price. As always, when we draw a demand curve in the Q–P plane, the ceteris paribus assumption is in effect. If any of the factors mentioned in the previous section (other prices, individuals' incomes, or preferences) should change, the Q–P demand curve will shift, and we should keep that possibility in mind. When we turn to consider relationships among two or more goods, however, we will return to the notation we have been using up until now (that is, denoting goods by x and y or by x_i).

Elasticity of market demand

When we use this notation for market demand, we will also use a compact notation for the price elasticity of the market demand function:

$$\text{Price Elasticity of Market Demand} = e_{Q,P} = \frac{\partial Q_D(P, P', I)}{\partial P} \cdot \frac{P}{Q_D}, \quad (10.11)$$

where the notation is intended as a reminder that the demand for Q depends on many factors other than its own price, such as the prices of other goods (P') and the incomes of all potential demanders (I). These other factors are held constant when computing the own-price elasticity of market demand. As in Chapter 5, this elasticity measures the proportionate response in quantity demanded to a one percent change in a good's price. Market demand is also characterized by whether demand is elastic ($e_{Q,P} < -1$) or inelastic ($0 > e_{Q,P} > -1$). Many of the other concepts examined in Chapter 5 such as the cross-price elasticity of demand or the income elasticity of demand also carry over directly into the market context:[3]

$$\text{Cross-Price Elasticity of Market Demand} = \frac{\partial Q_D(P, P', I)}{\partial P'} \cdot \frac{P'}{Q_D} \quad (10.12)$$

and

$$\text{Income Elasticity of Market Demand} = \frac{\partial Q_D(P, P', I)}{\partial I} \cdot \frac{I}{Q_D}.$$

Given these conventions about market demand, we now turn to an extended examination of supply and market equilibrium in the perfectly competitive model.

Timing of the supply response

In the analysis of competitive pricing, it is important to decide the length of time to be allowed for a *supply response* to changing demand conditions. The establishment of equilibrium prices will be different if we are talking about a very short period of time during which most inputs are fixed or if we are envisioning a very long-run process in which it is possible for new firms to enter an industry. For this reason, it has been traditional in economics to discuss pricing in three different time periods: (1) very short run, (2) short run, and (3) long run. Although it is not possible to give these terms an exact chronological definition, the essential distinction being made concerns the nature of the supply response that is assumed to be possible. In the *very short run*, there is no supply response: Quantity supplied is fixed and does not respond to changes in demand. In the *short run*, existing firms may change the quantity they are supplying, but no new firms can enter the industry. In the *long run*, new firms may enter an industry, thereby producing a very flexible supply response. In this chapter we will discuss each of these possibilities.

Pricing in the very short run

In the very short run, or the *market period,* there is no supply response. The goods are already "in" the marketplace and must be sold for whatever the market will bear. In this situation, price acts only as a device to ration demand. Price will adjust to clear the market of the quantity that must be sold during the period. Although the market price may act as a signal to producers in future periods, it does not perform such a function in the current period because current period output is fixed. Figure 10.2 depicts this situation. Market demand is represented by the curve D. Supply is fixed at Q^*, and the price that clears the

---

[3]In many applications market demand is modeled in *per capita* terms and treated as referring to the "typical person." In such applications it is also common to use many of the relationships among elasticities discussed in Chapter 5. Whether such aggregation across individuals is appropriate is discussed briefly in the Extensions to this chapter.

FIGURE 10.2   Pricing in the Very Short Run

When quantity is fixed in the very short run, price acts only as a device to ration demand. With quantity fixed at Q^*, price P_1 will prevail in the marketplace if D is the market demand curve. At this price, individuals are willing to consume exactly that quantity available. If demand should shift upward to D', the equilibrium market price would rise to P_2.

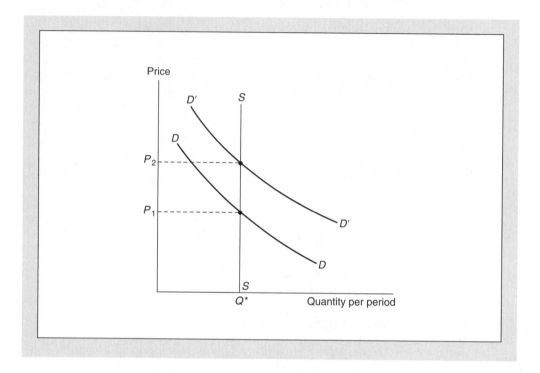

market is P_1. At P_1 individuals are willing to take all that is offered in the market. Sellers want to dispose of Q^* without regard to price (suppose that the good in question is perishable and will be worthless if it is not sold in the very short run). Hence, P_1, Q^* is an equilibrium price-quantity combination. If demand should shift to D', the equilibrium price would increase to P_2, but Q^* would stay fixed because no supply response is possible. The *supply curve* in this situation, then, is a vertical straight line at output Q^*.

The analysis of the very short run is not particularly useful for many markets. Such a theory may adequately represent some situations in which goods are perishable or must be sold on a given day, as is the case in auctions. Indeed, the study of auctions provides a number of insights about the informational problems involved in arriving at equilibrium prices, which we take up in Chapter 15. But auctions are unusual in that supply is fixed. The far more usual case involves some degree of supply response to changing demand. It is presumed that a rise in price will bring additional quantity into the market. In the remainder of this chapter, we will examine this process.

Before beginning our analysis, we should note that increases in quantity supplied need not come only from increased production. In a world in which some goods are durable (that is, last longer than a single period), current owners of these goods may supply them in increasing amounts to the market as price rises. For example, even though the supply of Rembrandts is fixed, we would not want to draw the market supply curve for these paintings as a vertical line, such as that shown in Figure 10.2. As the price of Rembrandts rises, individuals and museums will become increasingly willing to part with them. From a market point of view, therefore, the supply curve for Rembrandts will have an upward slope, even though no new production takes place. A similar analysis would follow for many types of durable goods, such as antiques, used cars, back issues of the *National Geo-*

graphic, or corporate shares, all of which are in nominally "fixed" supply. Because we are more interested in examining how demand and production are related, we will analyze those cases only briefly in Chapter 13.

Short-run price determination

In short-run analysis the number of firms in an industry is fixed. These firms are able to adjust the quantity they are producing in response to changing conditions. They will do this by altering levels of employment for those inputs that can be varied in the short run, and we shall investigate this supply decision here. Before beginning the analysis, we should perhaps state explicitly the assumptions of this perfectly competitive model:

DEFINITION

> **Perfect competition.** A *perfectly competitive industry* is one that obeys the following assumptions:
>
> 1. There are a large number of firms, each producing the same homogeneous product.
>
> 2. Each firm attempts to maximize profits.
>
> 3. Each firm is a price taker: It assumes that its actions have no effect on market price.
>
> 4. Prices are assumed to be known by all market participants—information is perfect.
>
> 5. Transactions are costless: Buyers and sellers incur no costs in making exchanges (for more on this and the previous assumption, see Chapter 19).

Now we will make use of these assumptions to study price determination in the short run.

Short-run market supply curve

In Chapter 9 we showed how to construct the short-run supply curve for a single profit-maximizing firm. To construct a market supply curve, we start by recognizing that the quantity of output supplied to the entire market in the short run is the sum of the quantities supplied by each firm. Because each firm uses the same market price to determine how much to produce, the total amount supplied to the market by all firms will obviously depend on price. This relationship between price and quantity supplied is called a *short-run market supply curve.* Figure 10.3 illustrates the construction of the curve. For simplicity assume there are only two firms, A and B. The short-run supply (that is, marginal cost) curves for firms A and B are shown in Figures 10.3a and 10.3b. The market supply curve shown in Figure 10.3c is the horizontal sum of these two curves. For example, at a price of P_1, firm A is willing to supply q_1^A, and firm B is willing to supply q_1^B. Therefore, at this price the total supply in the market is given by Q_1, which is equal to $q_1^A + q_1^B$. The other points on the curve are constructed in an identical way. Because each firm's supply curve has a positive slope, the market supply curve will also have a positive slope. The positive slope reflects the fact that short-run marginal costs increase as firms attempt to increase their outputs.

Short-run market supply

More generally, if we let $q_i (P, v, w)$ represent the short-run supply function for each of the n firms in the industry, we can define the short-run market supply function as follows:

DEFINITION

> **Short-run market supply function.** The *short-run market supply function* shows total quantity supplied by each firm to a market:
>
> $$Q_S(P, v, w) = \sum_{i=1}^{n} q_i(P, v, w). \qquad (10.13)$$

FIGURE 10.3   **Short-Run Market Supply Curve**

The supply (marginal cost) curves of two firms are shown in (a) and (b). The market supply curve (c) is the horizontal sum of these curves. For example, at P_1 firm A supplies q_1^A, firm B supplies q_1^B, and total market supply is given by $Q_1 = q_1^A + q_1^B$.

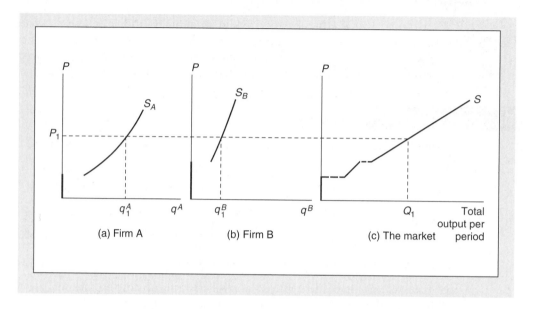

(a) Firm A   (b) Firm B   (c) The market

Notice that the firms in the industry are assumed to face the same market price and the same prices for inputs.[4] The *short-run market supply curve* shows the two-dimensional relationship between Q and P, holding v and w (and each firm's underlying technology) constant. The notation makes clear that if v, w, or technology were to change, the supply curve would shift to a new location.

Short-run supply elasticity

One way of summarizing the responsiveness of the output of firms in an industry to higher prices is by the *short-run supply elasticity*. This measure shows how proportional changes in market price are met by changes in total output. Consistent with the elasticity concepts developed in Chapter 5, this is defined as follows:

DEFINITION

Short-run elasticity of supply ($e_{S,P}$).

$$e_{S,P} = \frac{\text{percentage change in } Q \text{ supplied}}{\text{percentage change in } P} = \frac{\partial Q_S}{\partial P} \cdot \frac{P}{Q_S}. \quad (10.14)$$

Because quantity supplied is an increasing function of price ($\partial Q_S / \partial P > 0$), the supply elasticity is positive. High values for $e_{S,P}$ imply that small increases in market price lead to a relatively large supply response by firms, because marginal costs do not rise steeply and input price interaction effects are small. Alternatively, a low value for $e_{S,P}$ implies that it takes relatively large changes in price to induce firms to change their output levels, because marginal costs rise rapidly. Notice that, as for all elasticity notions, computation of $e_{S,P}$ requires that input prices and technology be held constant. To make sense as a market response, the concept also requires that all firms face the same price for their output. If firms sold their output at different prices, we would need to define a supply elasticity for each firm.

---

[4] Later in this chapter we show how this assumption can be relaxed.

EXAMPLE 10.2

A Short-Run Supply Function

In Example 9.3 we calculated the general short-run supply function for any single firm with a two-input Cobb-Douglas production function as

$$q_i(P, v, w) = \left(\frac{w}{\beta}\right)^{-\beta/(1-\beta)} k_1^{\alpha/(1-\beta)} P^{\beta/(1-\beta)}. \qquad (10.15)$$

If we let $\alpha = \beta = 0.5$, $v = 3$, $w = 12$, $k_1 = 80$, this yields the simple, single firm supply function

$$q_i(P, v, w = 12) = \frac{10P}{3}. \qquad (10.16)$$

Now assume that there are 100 identical such firms and that each firm faces the same market prices for both its output and its input hiring. Given these assumptions, the short-run market supply function is given by

$$Q_S(P, v, w = 12) = \sum_{i=1}^{100} q_i = \sum_{i=1}^{100} \frac{10P}{3} = \frac{1000P}{3}. \qquad (10.17)$$

So, at a price of, say, $P = 12$, total market supply will be 4,000, with each of the one hundred firms supplying 40 units. We can compute the short-run elasticity of supply in this situation as

$$e_{S,P} = \frac{\partial Q_S(P, v, w)}{\partial P} \cdot \frac{P}{Q_S} = \frac{1000}{3} \cdot \frac{P}{1000P/3} = 1 \quad (10.18)$$

as might have been expected given the exponent of P in the supply function.

Effect of an increase in w. If all of the firms in this marketplace experienced an increase in the wage they must pay for their labor input, the short-run supply curve would shift to a new position. To calculate the shift, we must return to the single firm's supply function (Equation 10.15) and now use a new wage, say $w = 15$. If none of the other parameters of the problem have changed (the firm's production function and the level of capital input it has in the short run), the supply function becomes

$$q_i(P, v, w = 15) = \frac{8P}{3} \qquad (10.19)$$

and the market supply function is

$$Q_S(P, v, w = 15) = \sum_{i=1}^{100} \frac{8P}{3} = \frac{800P}{3}. \qquad (10.20)$$

So, at a price of $P = 12$, now this industry will supply only $Q_S = 3200$, with each firm producing $q_i = 32$. In other words, the supply curve has shifted upward because of the increase in the wage. Notice, however, that the price elasticity of supply has not changed—it remains $e_{S,P} = 1$.

Query: How would the results of this example change by assuming different values for the weight of labor in the production function (that is, for α and β)?

| **FIGURE 10.4** | **Interactions of Many Individuals and Firms Determine Market Price in the Short Run** |

Market demand curves and market supply curves are each the horizontal sum of numerous components. These market curves are shown in (b). Once price is determined in the market, each firm and each individual treat this price as a fixed parameter in their decisions. Although individual firms and persons are important in determining price, their interaction as a whole is the sole determinant of price. This is illustrated by a shift in an individual's demand curve to *d'*. If only one individual reacts in this way, market price will not be affected. However, if everyone exhibits an increased demand, market demand will shift to *D'*; in the short run, price will rise to P_2.

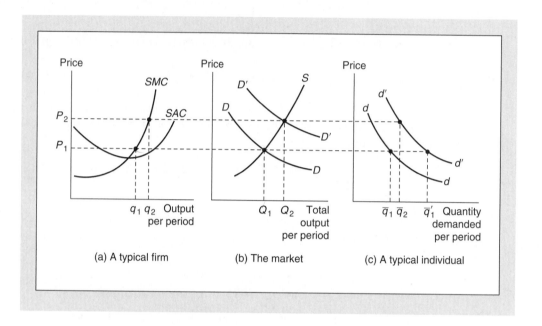

(a) A typical firm

(b) The market

(c) A typical individual

Equilibrium price determination

We can now combine demand and supply curves to demonstrate the establishment of equilibrium prices in the market. Figure 10.4 shows this process. Looking first at Figure 10.4b, we see the market demand curve D (ignore D' for the moment) and the short-run supply curve S. The two curves intersect at a price of P_1 and a quantity of Q_1. This price-quantity combination represents an *equilibrium* between the demands of individuals and the costs of firms. The equilibrium price P_1 serves two important functions. First, this price acts as a signal to producers by providing them with information with which to decide how much should be produced. In order to maximize profits, firms will produce that output level for which marginal costs are equal to P_1. In the aggregate, then, production will be Q_1. A second function of the price is to ration demand. Given the market price P_1, utility-maximizing individuals will decide how much of their limited incomes to devote to buying the particular good. At a price of P_1, total quantity demanded will be Q_1, and this is precisely the amount that will be produced. Hence we define equilibrium price as follows:

DEFINITION

Equilibrium price. An *equilibrium price* is one at which quantity demanded is equal to quantity supplied. At such a price, neither demanders nor suppliers have an incentive to alter their economic decisions. Mathematically, an equilibrium price, P^*, solves the equation:

$$Q_D(P^*, P', I) = Q_S(P^*, v, w) \qquad (10.21)$$

or, more compactly,

$$Q_D(P^*) = Q_S(P^*) \qquad (10.22)$$

The definition given in Equation 10.22 makes clear that an equilibrium price depends on the values of many exogenous factors, such as incomes or prices of other goods and of firms' inputs. As we will see in the next section, changes in any of these factors will likely result in a change in the equilibrium price required to equate quantity supplied to quantity demanded.

The implications of the equilibrium price (P_1) for a typical firm and a typical individual are shown in Figures 10.4a and 10.4c, respectively. For the typical firm the price P_1 will cause an output level of q_1 to be produced. The firm earns a small profit at this particular price because short-run average total costs are covered. The demand curve d (ignore d' for the moment) for a typical individual is shown in Figure 10.4c. At a price of P_1, this individual demands $\bar{q}_1$. By adding up the quantities that each individual demands at P_1 and the quantities that each firm supplies, we can see that the market is in equilibrium. The market supply and demand curves provide a convenient way of making such a summation.

Market reaction to a shift in demand

The three panels in Figure 10.4 can be used to show two important facts about short-run market equilibrium: the individual's "impotence" in the market and the nature of short-run supply response. First, suppose that a single individual's demand curve were to shift outward to d', as shown in Figure 10.4c. Because the competitive model assumes there are many demanders, this shift will have practically no effect on the market demand curve. Consequently, market price will be unaffected by the shift to d'; that is, price will remain at P_1. Of course, at this price, the person for whom the demand curve has shifted will consume slightly more ($\bar{q}_1'$) as shown in Figure 10.4c. But this amount is a tiny part of the market.

If many individuals experience shifts outward in their demand curves, the entire market demand curve may shift. Figure 10.4b shows the new demand curve D'. The new equilibrium point will be at P_2, Q_2: At this point, supply-demand balance is reestablished. Price has increased from P_1 to P_2 in response to the demand shift. Notice also that the quantity traded in the market has increased from Q_1 to Q_2. The rise in price has served two functions. First, as in our previous analysis of the very short run, it has acted to ration demand. Whereas at P_1 a typical individual demanded $\bar{q}_1'$, at P_2 only $\bar{q}_2$ is demanded. The rise in price has also acted as a signal to the typical firm to increase production. In Figure 10.4a the firm's profit-maximizing output level has increased from q_1 to q_2 in response to the price rise. That is what we mean by a *short-run supply response*: An increase in market price acts as an inducement to increase production. Firms are willing to increase production (and to incur higher marginal costs) because price has risen. If market price had not been permitted to rise (suppose that government price controls were in effect), firms would not have increased their outputs. At P_1 there would now be an excess (unfilled) demand for the good in question. If market price is allowed to rise, a supply-demand equilibrium can be reestablished so that what firms produce is again equal to what individuals demand at the prevailing market price. Notice also that at the new price P_2, the typical firm has increased its profits. This increasing profitability in the short run will be important to our discussion of long-run pricing later in this chapter.

Shifts in supply and demand curves: a graphical analysis

In previous chapters we established many reasons why either a demand curve or a supply curve might shift. These reasons are briefly summarized in Table 10.1. Although most of these merit little additional explanation, it is important to note that a change in the number of firms will shift the short-run market supply curve (because the sum in Equation 10.13 will be over a different number of firms). This observation allows us to tie together short-run and long-run analysis.

It seems likely that the types of changes described in Table 10.1 are constantly occurring in real-world markets. When either a supply curve or a demand curve does shift,

TABLE 10.1	Reasons for Shifts in Demand or Supply Curves

Demand Curves Shift Because	Supply Curves Shift Because
• Incomes change	• Input prices change
• Prices of substitutes or complements change	• Technology changes
• Preferences change	• Number of producers changes

FIGURE 10.5	Effect of a Shift in the Short-Run Supply Curve Depends on the Shape of the Demand Curve

In (a) the shift upward in the supply curve causes price to increase only slightly whereas quantity declines sharply. This results from the elastic shape of the demand curve. In (b) the demand curve is inelastic; price increases substantially, with only a slight decrease in quantity.

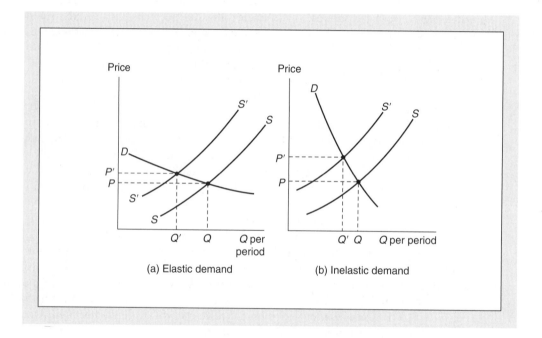

(a) Elastic demand   (b) Inelastic demand

equilibrium price and quantity will change. In this section we investigate graphically the relative magnitudes of such changes. In the next section we show the results mathematically.

Shifts in supply curves: importance of the shape of the demand curve

Consider first a shift inward in the short-run supply curve for a good. As in Example 10.2, such a shift might have resulted from an increase in the prices of inputs used by firms to produce the good. Whatever the cause of the shift, it is important to recognize that the effect of the shift on the equilibrium level of P and Q will depend on the shape of the demand curve for the product. Figure 10.5 illustrates two possible situations. The demand curve in Figure 10.5a is relatively price elastic; that is, a change in price substantially affects quantity demanded. For this case, a shift in the supply curve from S to S' will cause equilibrium price to rise only moderately (from P to P'), whereas quantity declines sharply (from Q to Q'). Rather than being "passed on" in higher prices, the increase in the firms' input costs is met primarily by a decrease in quantity (a movement down each firm's marginal cost curve) and only a slight increase in price.

FIGURE 10.6	Effect of a Shift in the Demand Curve Depends on the Shape of the Short-Run Supply Curve

In (a) supply is inelastic; a shift in demand causes price to increase greatly, with only a small concomitant increase in quantity. In (b), on the other hand, supply is elastic; price rises only slightly in response to a demand shift.

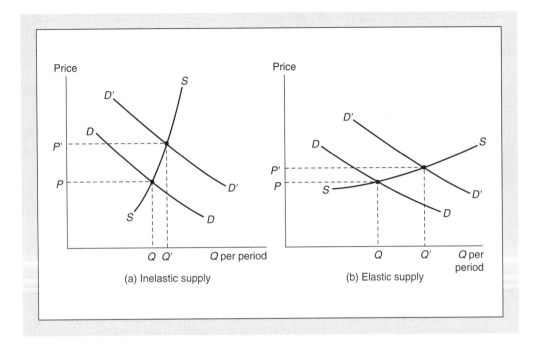

(a) Inelastic supply   (b) Elastic supply

This situation is reversed when the market demand curve is inelastic. In Figure 10.5b a shift in the supply curve causes equilibrium price to rise substantially, whereas quantity is little changed. The reason for this is that individuals do not reduce their demands very much if prices rise. Consequently, the shift upward in the supply curve is almost entirely passed on to demanders in the form of higher prices.

Shifts in demand curves: importance of the shape of the supply curve

Similarly, a shift in a market demand curve will have different implications for P and Q, depending on the shape of the short-run supply curve. Two illustrations are shown in Figure 10.6. In Figure 10.6a the supply curve for the good in question is inelastic. In this situation a shift outward in the market demand curve will cause price to increase substantially. On the other hand, the quantity traded increases only slightly. Intuitively, what has happened is that the increase in demand (and in Q) has caused firms to move up their steeply sloped marginal cost curves. The concomitant large increase in price serves to ration demand.

Figure 10.6b shows a relatively elastic short-run supply curve. Such a curve would occur for an industry in which marginal costs do not rise steeply in response to output increases. For this case an increase in demand produces a substantial increase in Q. However, because of the nature of the supply curve, this increase is not met by great cost increases. Consequently, price rises only moderately.

These examples again demonstrate Marshall's observation that demand and supply simultaneously determine price and quantity. Recall his analogy from Chapter 1: Just as it is impossible to say which blade of a scissors does the cutting, so too is it impossible to attribute price solely to demand or to supply characteristics. Rather, the effect that shifts in either a demand curve or a supply curve will have depends on the shapes of both of the curves. Example 10.3 illustrates some of these points.

EXAMPLE 10.3

Short-Run Market Equilibria

We can illustrate these various points numerically by using the short-run supply function from Example 10.2 and assuming that it applies to, say, Gucci beach towels. We also assume that the market demand function for these luxury beach towels takes the form

$$Q_D(P, P', I) = 4{,}000 - 500P + 200P' + 0.1I, \quad (10.23)$$

where P' represents the price of a Gucci towel substitute (say, Polo towels) and I represents average annual income for potential towel consumers. In order to study a specific supply-demand equilibrium in this market, we must assume values for the components of demand other than market price. So, initially, let $P' = 10$, $I = 40{,}000$. Hence the demand function becomes

$$Q_D = 4{,}000 + 200(10) + 0.1(40{,}000) - 500P = 10{,}000 - 500P. \quad (10.24)$$

Now, setting supply equal to demand yields

$$Q_S = 1{,}000P/3 = Q_D = 10{,}000 - 500P$$

or

$$2{,}500P = 30{,}000 \qquad (10.25)$$

so market equilibrium is given by

$$P^* = 12$$
$$Q^* = Q_D = Q_S = 4{,}000 \qquad (10.26)$$

and each firm produces 40 towels.

A shift in demand. An increase in the price of Polo towels (to $P' = 22.50$) would shift the demand for Gucci towels outward to $Q'_D = 12{,}500 - 500P$ and the new market equilibrium would be

$$Q_S = 1{,}000P/3 = Q'_D = 12{,}500 - 500P$$

or

$$P^* = 15, \ Q^* = 5{,}000. \qquad (10.27)$$

Hence, the increase in the price of the Polo substitute causes both the equilibrium price and equilibrium quantity of Gucci towels to rise. If price had remained at $P = 12$ there would have been an excess demand of $Q_D(P = 12) - Q_S(P = 12) = 6{,}500 - 4{,}000 = 2{,}500$. The rise in price from 12 to 15 both encourages firms to produce 1,000 more towels and reduces demand by 1,500 towels, thereby eliminating the excess demand.[5]

A shift in supply. An increase in, say, the wages of towel cutters would also disturb the initial market equilibrium calculated in Equation 10.26. If the wage were to increase to $w = 15$, we know from Example 10.2 that the short-run supply function would shift to $Q_S = 800P/3$ and, with the initial demand situation, market equilibrium would become

$$Q_S = 800P/3 = Q_D = 10{,}000 - 500P$$

so

$$P^* = 300/23 = 13.04, \ Q^* = 3{,}480. \qquad (10.28)$$

The shift upward in supply causes equilibrium price to rise and quantity to fall.

Query: How would you change the demand function in this problem so as to yield a smaller price increase and a larger decrease in quantity as a result of the shift in supply modeled in Equation 10.28?

---

[5]Notice that the results here confirm that the short-run elasticity of supply is 1. An increase in price of 25 percent has been met by an increase in quantity supplied of 25 percent.

Mathematical model of market equilibrium

A general mathematical model of the supply-demand process can further illuminate the comparative statics of changing equilibrium prices and quantities. Suppose that the demand function is represented by

$$Q_D = D(P, \alpha), \qquad (10.29)$$

where α is a parameter that allows us to shift the demand curve. It might represent consumer income, prices of other goods (this would permit the tying together of supply and demand in several related markets), or changing preferences. In general we expect $\partial D / \partial P = D_P < 0$, but $\partial D / \partial \alpha = D_\alpha$ may have any sign, depending precisely on what the parameter α means. Using this same procedure, we can write the supply relationship as

$$Q_S = S(P, \beta), \qquad (10.30)$$

where β is a parameter that shifts the supply curve and might include such factors as input prices, technical changes, or (for a multiproduct firm) prices of other potential outputs. Here $\partial S / \partial P = S_P > 0$, but $\partial S / \partial \beta = S_\beta$ may have any sign. The model is closed by requiring that in equilibrium,[6]

$$Q_D = Q_S. \qquad (10.31)$$

To analyze the comparative statics of this model of equilibrium, we write the total differentials of the demand and supply functions as

$$dQ_D = D_P dP + D_\alpha d\alpha \qquad (10.32)$$

and

$$dQ_S = S_P dP + S_\beta d\beta.$$

Because maintenance of equilibrium requires that

$$dQ_D = dQ_S, \qquad (10.33)$$

we can solve these equations for the change in equilibrium price for any combination of shifts in demand (α) or supply (β). For example, suppose the demand parameter α were to change while β remains constant. Then, using the equilibrium condition, we have

$$D_P dP + D_\alpha d\alpha = S_P dP, \qquad (10.34)$$

or, manipulating terms a bit,

$$\frac{\partial P}{\partial \alpha} = \frac{D_\alpha}{S_P - D_P}. \qquad (10.35)$$

Because the denominator of this expression is positive, the sign of $\partial P / \partial \alpha$ will be the same as the sign of D_α. If α represents consumer income (and the good in question is normal), D_α would be positive, and a rise in income would shift demand outward. This, as Equation 10.35 also indicates, would cause equilibrium price to rise, a result reflected graphically in Figure 10.6.

---

[6]The model could be further modified to show how the equilibrium quantity supplied is to be allocated among the firms in the industry. If, for example, the industry is composed of n identical firms, the output of any one of them would be given by

$$q = \frac{Q}{n}.$$

In the short run, with n fixed, this would add little to our analysis. In the long run, however, n must also be determined by the model, as we show later in this chapter.

An elasticity interpretation

Further algebraic manipulation of Equation 10.35 yields a more useful comparative statics result. Multiplying both sides of that equation by α/P gives

$$e_{P,\alpha} = \frac{\partial P}{\partial \alpha} \cdot \frac{\alpha}{P} = \frac{D_\alpha}{S_P - D_P} \cdot \frac{\alpha}{P}$$

$$= \frac{D_\alpha \dfrac{\alpha}{Q}}{(S_P - D_P) \cdot \dfrac{P}{Q}} = \frac{e_{Q,\alpha}}{e_{S,P} - e_{Q,P}}. \qquad (10.36)$$

Because all of the elasticities in this equation may be available from empirical studies, this equation can be a convenient way to make rough estimates of the effects of various events on equilibrium prices. As an example, suppose again that α represents consumer income and that there is interest in predicting how an increase in income affects the equilibrium price of, say, automobiles. Suppose empirical data suggest that $e_{Q,I} = e_{Q,\alpha} = 3.0$, $e_{Q,P} = -1.2$ (these figures are from Table 10.3) and assume that $e_{S,P} = 1.0$. Substituting these figures into Equation 10.36 yields

$$e_{P,\alpha} = \frac{e_{Q,\alpha}}{e_{S,P} - e_{Q,P}} = \frac{3.0}{1.0 - (-1.2)}$$

$$= \frac{3.0}{2.2} = 1.36. \qquad (10.37)$$

The empirical elasticity estimates therefore suggest that each 1 percent rise in consumer incomes results in a 1.36 percent rise in the equilibrium price of automobiles. Estimates of other kinds of shifts in supply or demand can be similarly modeled by manipulating Equations 10.32 and 10.33 and obtaining empirical estimates of the necessary parameters.

 EXAMPLE 10.4

Equilibria with Constant Elasticity Functions

An even more complete analysis of supply-demand equilibrium can be provided if we use specific functional forms. Constant elasticity functions are especially useful for this purpose. Suppose the demand for automobiles is given by

$$Q_D(P, I) = 0.1\, P^{-1.2}\, I^3, \qquad (10.38)$$

where price (P) is measured in dollars as is real family income (I). The supply function for automobiles is

$$Q_S(P, w) = 6{,}400\, Pw^{-.5}, \qquad (10.39)$$

where w is the hourly wage of automobile workers. Notice that the elasticities assumed here are those used previously in the text ($e_{Q,P} = -1.2$, $e_{Q,I} = 3.0$, and $e_{S,P} = 1$). If the values for the "exogenous" variables I and w are \$20,000 and \$25, respectively, demand-supply equilibrium requires

$$Q_D = .1\, P^{-1.2}\, I^3 = 8 \times 10^{11}\, P^{-1.2}$$
$$= Q_S = 6{,}400\, Pw^{-.5} = 1{,}280\, P \qquad (10.40)$$

or

$$P^{2.2} = 8 \times 10^{11}/1{,}280 = 6.25 \times 10^8$$

or

$$P^* = 9,957$$
$$Q^* = 1,280 \cdot P^* = 12,745,000. \qquad (10.41)$$

Hence, the initial equilibrium in the automobile market has a price of nearly $10,000 with about 13 million cars being sold.

A shift in demand. A 10 percent increase in real family income, all other factors remaining constant, would shift the demand function to

$$Q_D = 1.06 \times 10^{12} \, P^{-1.2} \qquad (10.42)$$

and, proceeding as before,

$$P^{2.2} = 1.06 \times 10^{12}/1,280 = 8.32 \times 10^8 \qquad (10.43)$$

or

$$P^* = 11,339$$
$$Q^* = 14,514,000. \qquad (10.44)$$

As we predicted earlier, the 10 percent rise in real income raised car prices by nearly 14 percent. In the process, quantity sold increased by about 1.77 million automobiles.

A shift in supply. An exogenous shift in automobile supply as a result, say, of changing auto workers' wages would also affect market equilibrium. If wages were to rise to $30 per hour, the supply function would shift to

$$Q_s \, (P, w) = 6,400 \, P(30)^{-.5} = 1,168 \, P \qquad (10.45)$$

and returning to our original demand function (with $I = \$20,000$) would yield

$$P^{2.2} = 8 \times 10^{11}/1,168 = 6.85 \times 10^8 \qquad (10.46)$$

or

$$P^* = 10,381$$
$$Q^* = 12,125,000. \qquad (10.47)$$

The 20 percent rise in wages, therefore, led to a 4.3 percent rise in auto prices and a decline in sales of more than 600,000 units. Changing equilibria in many types of markets can be approximated by using this general approach together with empirical estimates of the relevant elasticities.

Query: Do the results of changing auto workers' wages agree with what might have been predicted using an equation similar to Equation 10.36?

Long-run analysis

We saw in Chapter 8 that, in the long run, a firm may adapt all of its inputs to fit market conditions. For long-run analysis, therefore, we should use the firm's long-run cost curves. A profit-maximizing firm that is a price taker will produce the output level for which price is equal to long-run marginal cost (*MC*). However, we must consider a second and ultimately more important influence on price in the long run: the entry of entirely new firms into the industry or the exit of existing firms from the industry. In mathematical terms, we must allow the number of firms, *n*, to vary in response to economic incentives. The perfectly competitive model assumes that there are no special costs of entering or exiting from an industry. Consequently, new firms will be lured into any market in which (economic) profits are positive. Similarly, firms will leave any industry in which profits are negative. The entry of new firms will cause the short-run industry supply curve to shift outward, because there are now more firms producing than there were previously. Such a shift will cause market price (and industry profits) to fall. The process will continue until no firm contemplating entering the industry is able to earn a profit.[7] At that point, entry will cease and an equilibrium number of firms will be in the industry. A similar argument can be made for the case in which some of the firms in an industry are suffering short-run losses. Some firms will choose to leave the industry, and this will cause the supply curve to shift to the left. Market price will rise, thus restoring profitability to those firms remaining in the industry.

Equilibrium conditions

For the purpose of this chapter, we shall assume that all the firms in an industry have identical cost curves; that is, no firm controls any special resources or technologies.[8] Because all firms are identical, the equilibrium long-run position requires that each firm earn exactly zero economic profits. In graphic terms, the long-run equilibrium price must settle at the low point of each firms' long-run average total cost curve. Only at this point do the two equilibrium conditions $P = MC$ (which is required for profit maximization) and $P = AC$ (which is required for zero profit) hold. It is important to emphasize, however, that these two equilibrium conditions have rather different origins. Profit maximization is a goal of firms. The $P = MC$ rule therefore derives from the behavioral assumptions we have made about firms and is similar to the output decision rule used in the short run. The zero-profit condition is not a goal for firms. Firms obviously would prefer to have large, positive profits. The long-run operation of the market, however, forces all firms to accept a level of zero economic profits ($P = AC$) because of the willingness of firms to enter and to leave an industry in response to the possibility of making supranormal returns. Although the firms in a perfectly competitive industry may earn either positive or negative profits in the short run, in the long run only a level of zero profits will prevail. Hence, we can summarize this analysis by the following definition:

DEFINITION

Long-run competitive equilibrium. A *perfectly competitive industry* is in *long-run equilibrium* if there are no incentives for profit-maximizing firms to enter or to leave the industry. This will occur when the number of firms is such that $P = MC = AC$ and each firm operates at the low point of its long-run average cost curve.

Long-run equilibrium: constant-cost case

To discuss long-run pricing in detail, we must make an assumption about how the entry of new firms into an industry affects the prices of firms' inputs. The simplest assumption we might make is that entry has no effect on the prices of those inputs—perhaps because the industry is a relatively small hirer in its various input markets. Under this assumption, no matter how many firms enter (or leave) an industry, each firm will retain the same set of

---

[7]Remember that we are using the economists' definition of profits here. These profits represent a return to the owner of a business in excess of that which is strictly necessary to keep him or her in the business. Hence, when we talk about a firm earning "zero" profits, we mean that no entrepreneurial income is being earned in excess of that which could be earned from alternative investments.

[8]If firms have different costs, very low-cost firms can earn positive long-run profits, and such extra profits will be reflected in the price of the resource that accounts for the firm's low costs. In this sense the assumption of identical costs is not very restrictive, because an active market for the firm's inputs will ensure that average costs (which include opportunity costs) are the same for all firms. See also the discussion of Ricardian rent later in this chapter.

cost curves with which it started. This assumption of constant input prices may not be tenable in many important cases, which we will look at in the next section. For the moment, however, we wish to examine the equilibrium conditions for a *constant-cost industry*.

Initial equilibrium

Figure 10.7 demonstrates long-run equilibrium for an industry. For the market as a whole (Figure 10.7b), the demand curve is given by D and the short-run supply curve by SS. The short-run equilibrium price is therefore P_1. The typical firm (Figure 10.7a) will produce output level q_1, because at this level of output, price is equal to short-run marginal cost (SMC). In addition, with a market price of P_1, output level q_1 is also a long-run equilibrium position for the firm. The firm is maximizing profits, because price is equal to long-run marginal costs (MC). Figure 10.7a also implies our second long-run equilibrium property: Price is equal to long-run average costs (AC). Consequently, economic profits are zero, and there is no incentive for firms either to enter or to leave the industry. The market depicted in Figure 10.7 is therefore in both short-run and long-run equilibrium. Firms are in equilibrium because they are maximizing profits, and the number of firms is stable because economic profits are zero. This equilibrium will tend to persist until either supply or demand conditions change.

Responses to an increase in demand

Suppose now that the market demand curve in Figure 10.7b shifts outward to D'. If SS is the relevant short-run supply curve for the industry, then in the short run, price will rise to P_2. The typical firm, in the short run, will choose to produce q_2 and will earn profits on this level of output. In the long run, these profits will attract new firms into the market. Because of the constant-cost assumption, this entry of new firms will have no effect on

---

FIGURE 10.7   **Long-Run Equilibrium for a Perfectly Competitive Industry: Constant-Cost Case**

An increase in demand from D to D' will cause price to rise from P_1 to P_2 in the short run. This higher price will create profits in the industry, and new firms will be drawn into the market. If it is assumed that the entry of these new firms has no effect on the cost curves of the firms in the industry, new firms will continue to enter until price is pushed back down to P_1. At this price, economic profits are zero. The long-run supply curve (LS) will therefore be a horizontal line at P_1. Along LS, output is increased by increasing the number of firms, each producing q_1.

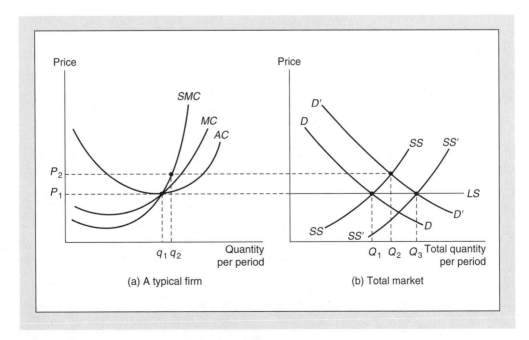

(a) A typical firm   (b) Total market

input prices. New firms will continue to enter the market until price is forced down to the level at which there are again no pure economic profits. The entry of new firms will therefore shift the short-run supply curve to SS', where the equilibrium price (P_1) is reestablished. At this new long-run equilibrium, the price-quantity combination P_1, Q_3 will prevail in the market. The typical firm will again produce at output level q_1, although now there will be more firms than in the initial situation.

Infinitely elastic supply

We have shown that the *long-run supply curve* for the constant-cost industry will be a horizontal straight line at price P_1. This curve is labeled LS in Figure 10.7b. No matter what happens to demand, the twin equilibrium conditions of zero long-run profits (because free entry is assumed) and profit maximization will ensure that no price other than P_1 can prevail in the long run.[9] For this reason, P_1 might be regarded as the "normal" price for this commodity. If the constant-cost assumption is abandoned, however, the long-run supply curve need not have this infinitely elastic shape, as we show in the next section.

 EXAMPLE 10.5

Infinitely Elastic Long-Run Supply

Handmade bicycle frames are produced by a number of identically sized firms. Total (long-run) monthly costs for a typical firm are given by

$$C(q) = q^3 - 20q^2 + 100q + 8,000, \qquad (10.48)$$

where q is the number of frames produced per month. Demand for handmade bicycle frames is given by

$$Q_D = 2,500 - 3P, \qquad (10.49)$$

where Q_D is the quantity demanded per month and P is the price per frame. To determine the long-run equilibrium in this market, we must find the low point of the typical firm's average cost curve. Because

$$AC = \frac{C(q)}{q} = q^2 - 20q + 100 + \frac{8,000}{q} \qquad (10.50)$$

and

$$MC = \frac{\partial C(q)}{\partial q} = 3q^2 - 40q + 100, \qquad (10.51)$$

and we know this minimum occurs where $AC = MC$, we can solve for this output level:

$$q^2 - 20q + 100 + \frac{8,000}{q} = 3q^2 - 40q + 100$$

or

$$2q^2 - 20q = \frac{8,000}{q}, \qquad (10.52)$$

which has a convenient solution of $q = 20$. With a monthly output of 20 frames, each producer has a long-run average and marginal cost of $500. This, then, is the long-run equilibrium price of bicycle frames (handmade frames cost a bundle, as any cyclist can attest).

With $P = \$500$, Equation 10.49 shows $Q_D = 1,000$. The equilibrium number of firms is therefore 50. When each of these 50 firms produces 20 frames per month, supply will precisely balance what is demanded at a price of $500.

If demand in this problem were to increase to

$$Q_D = 3,000 - 3P, \qquad (10.53)$$

we would expect long-run output and the number of frames to increase. Assuming that entry into the frame market is free and that such entry does not alter costs for the typical bicycle maker, the long-run equilibrium price will remain at $500 and a total of 1,500 frames per month will be demanded. That will require 75 frame makers, so 25 new firms will enter the market in response to the increase in demand.

Query: Presumably, the entry of frame makers in the long run is motivated by the short-run profitability of the industry in response to the increase in demand. Suppose each firm's short-run costs were given by $SC = 50q^2 - 1,500q + 20,000$. Show that short-run profits are zero when the industry is in long-term equilibrium. What are the industry's short-run profits as a result of the increase in demand?

Shape of the long-run supply curve

Contrary to the short-run situation, long-run analysis has very little to do with the shape of the (long-run) marginal cost curve. Rather, the zero-profit condition centers attention on the low point of the long-run average cost curve as the factor most relevant to long-run price determination. In the constant-cost case, the position of this low point does not change as new firms enter the industry. Consequently, if input prices do not change only one price can prevail in the long run regardless of how demand shifts—the long-run supply curve is horizontal at this price. Once the constant-cost assumption is abandoned, this need not be the case. If the entry of new firms causes average costs to rise, the long-run supply curve will have an upward slope. On the other hand, if entry causes average costs to decline, it is even possible for the long-run supply curve to be negatively sloped. We shall now discuss these possibilities.

Increasing cost industry

The entry of new firms into an industry may cause the average costs of all firms to rise for several reasons. New and existing firms may compete for scarce inputs, thus driving up their prices. New firms may impose "external costs" on existing firms (and on themselves) in the form of air or water pollution, and new firms may increase the demand for tax-financed services (police forces, sewage treatment plants, and so forth), and the required taxes may show up as increased costs for all firms. Figure 10.8 demonstrates two market equilibria in such an *increasing cost industry*. The initial equilibrium price is P_1. At this price the typical firm produces q_1, and total industry output is Q_1. Suppose now that the demand curve for the industry shifts outward to D'. In the short run, price will rise to P_2, since this is where D' and the industry's short-run supply curve (SS) intersect. At this price the typical firm will produce q_2 and will earn a substantial profit. This profit then attracts new entrants into the market and shifts the short-run supply curve outward.

Suppose that this entry of new firms causes the cost curves of all firms to rise. The new firms may compete for scarce inputs, thereby driving up the prices of these inputs. A typical firm's new (higher) set of cost curves is shown in Figure 10.8b. The new long-run equilibrium price for the industry is P_3 (here $P_3 = MC = AC$), and at this price Q_3 is

FIGURE 10.8   **An Increasing Cost Industry Has a Positively Sloped Long-Run Supply Curve**

Initially, the market is in equilibrium at P_1, Q_1. An increase in demand (to D') causes price to rise to P_2 in the short run, and the typical firm produces q_2 at a profit. This profit attracts new firms into the industry. The entry of these new firms causes costs for a typical firm to rise to the levels shown in (b). With this new set of curves, equilibrium is reestablished in the market at P_3, Q_3. By considering many possible demand shifts and connecting all the resulting equilibrium points, the long-run supply curve (LS) is traced out.

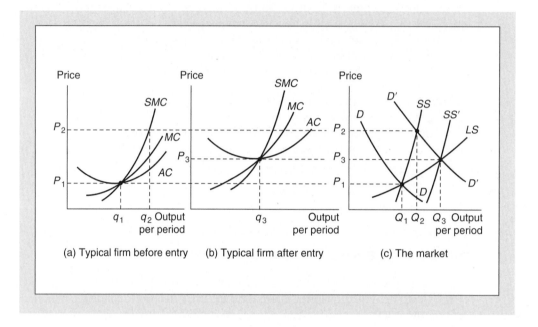

(a) Typical firm before entry   (b) Typical firm after entry   (c) The market

demanded. We now have two points (P_1, Q_1 and P_3, Q_3) on the long-run supply curve. All other points on the curve can be found in an analogous way by considering all possible shifts in the demand curve. These shifts will trace out the long-run supply curve LS. Here LS has a positive slope because of the increasing cost nature of the industry. Notice that the LS curve is flatter (more elastic) than the short-run supply curves. This indicates the greater flexibility in supply response that is possible in the long run. Still, the curve is upward sloping, so price rises with increasing demand. This situation is probably quite common; we will have more to say about it in later sections.

Decreasing cost industry

Not all industries exhibit constant or increasing costs. In some cases, the entry of new firms may reduce the costs of firms in an industry. For example, the entry of new firms may provide a larger pool of trained labor from which to draw than was previously available, thus reducing the costs associated with the hiring of new workers. Similarly, the entry of new firms may provide a "critical mass" of industrialization, which permits the development of more efficient transportation and communications networks. Whatever the exact reason for the cost reductions, the final result is illustrated in the three panels of Figure 10.9. The initial market equilibrium is shown by the price-quantity combination P_1, Q_1 in Figure 10.9c. At this price the typical firm produces q_1 and earns exactly zero in economic profits. Now suppose that market demand shifts outward to D'. In the short run, price will increase to P_2 and the typical firm will produce q_2. At this price level, positive profits are being earned. These profits cause new entrants to come into the market. If this entry causes costs to decline, a new set of cost curves for the typical firm might resemble those shown in Figure 10.9b. Now the new equilibrium price is P_3; at this price, Q_3 is demanded. By considering all possible shifts in demand, the long-run supply curve, LS,

FIGURE 10.9   **A Decreasing Cost Industry Has a Negatively Sloped Long-Run Supply Curve**

Initially, the market is in equilibrium at P_1, Q_1. An increase in demand to D' causes price to rise to P_2 in the short run, and the typical firm produces q_2 at a profit. This profit attracts new firms to the industry. If the entry of these new firms causes costs for the typical firm to fall, a set of new cost curves might look like those in (b). With this new set of curves, market equilibrium is reestablished at P_3, Q_3. By connecting such points of equilibrium, a negatively sloped long-run supply curve (LS) is traced out.

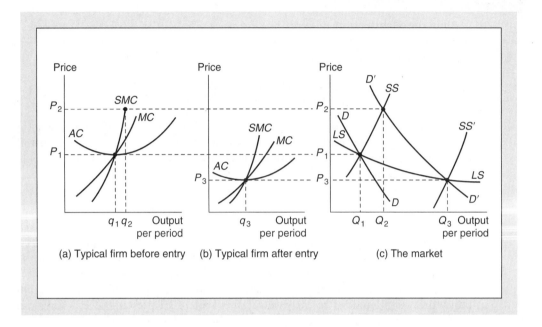

(a) Typical firm before entry   (b) Typical firm after entry   (c) The market

can be traced out. This curve has a negative slope because of the decreasing cost nature of the industry. Therefore, as output expands, price falls. This possibility has been used as the justification for protective tariffs to shield new industries from foreign competition. It is assumed (only occasionally correctly) that the protection of the "infant industry" will permit it to grow and ultimately to compete at lower world prices.

Classification of long-run supply curves

Thus we have shown that the long-run supply curve for a perfectly competitive industry may assume a variety of shapes. The principal determinant of the shape is the way in which the entry of firms into the industry affects all firms' costs. The following definitions cover the various possibilities:

DEFINITION

Constant, increasing, and decreasing cost industries. An industry supply curve exhibits one of three shapes:

Constant cost: Entry does not affect input costs; the long-run supply curve is horizontal at the long-run equilibrium price.

Increasing cost: Entry increases input costs; the long-run supply curve is positively sloped.

Decreasing cost: Entry reduces input costs; the long-run supply curve is negatively sloped.

Now we show how the shape of the long-run supply curve can be further quantified.

Long-run elasticity of supply

The long-run supply curve for an industry incorporates information on internal firm adjustments to changing prices and changes in the number of firms and input costs in response to profit opportunities. All of these supply responses are summarized in the following elasticity concept:

DEFINITION

Long-run elasticity of supply. The *long-run elasticity of supply* ($e_{LS,P}$) records the proportionate change in long-run industry output in response to a proportionate change in product price. Mathematically,

$$e_{LS,P} = \frac{\text{percentage change in } Q}{\text{percentage change in } P} = \frac{\partial Q_{LS}}{\partial P} \cdot \frac{P}{Q_{LS}}. \qquad (10.54)$$

The value of this elasticity may be positive or negative, depending on whether the industry exhibits increasing or decreasing costs. As we have seen, in the constant-cost case, $e_{LS,P}$ is infinite, because industry expansions or contractions can occur without having any effect on product prices.

Empirical estimates

It is obviously important to have good empirical estimates of long-run supply elasticities. These indicate whether production can be expanded with only a slight increase in relative price (that is, supply is price elastic) or whether expansions in output can occur only if relative prices rise sharply (that is, supply is price inelastic). Such information can be used to assess the likely effect of shifts in demand on long-run prices and to evaluate alternative policy proposals intended to increase supply. Table 10.2 presents several long-run supply elasticity estimates. These relate primarily (though not exclusively) to natural resources

TABLE 10.2	Selected Estimates of Long-Run Supply Elasticities
Agricultural acreage	
Corn	0.18
Cotton	0.67
Wheat	0.93
Aluminum	Nearly infinite
Chromium	0–3.0
Coal (eastern reserves)	15.0–30.0
Natural gas (U.S. reserves)	0.20
Oil (U.S. reserves)	0.76
Urban housing	
Density	5.3
Quality	3.8

SOURCES: Agricultural acreage—M. Nerlove, "Estimates of the Elasticities of Supply of Selected Agricultural Commodities," *Journal of Farm Economics* 38 (May 1956): 496–509. Aluminum and chromium—estimated from U.S. Department of Interior, *Critical Materials Commodity Action Analysis* (Washington, DC: U.S. Government Printing Office, 1975). Coal—estimated from M. B. Zimmerman, "The Supply of Coal in the Long Run: The Case of Eastern Deep Coal," MIT Energy Laboratory Report No. MITEL 75–021 (September 1975). Natural gas—based on estimate for oil (see text) and J. D. Khazzoom, "The FPC Staff's Econometric Model of Natural Gas Supply in the United States," *The Bell Journal of Economics and Management Science* (Spring 1971): 103–17. Oil—E. W. Erickson, S. W. Millsaps, and R. M. Spann, "Oil Supply and Tax Incentives," *Brookings Papers on Economic Activity* 2 (1974): 449–78. Urban housing—B. A. Smith, "The Supply of Urban Housing," *Journal of Political Economy* 40 (August 1976): 389–405.

because economists have devoted considerable attention to the implications of increasing demand for the prices of such resources. As the table makes clear, these estimates vary widely depending on the spatial and geological properties of the particular resources involved. All of the estimates, however, suggest that supply does respond positively to price.

Comparative statics analysis of long-run equilibrium

Earlier in this chapter we showed how to develop a simple comparative statics analysis of changing short-run equilibria in competitive markets. By using estimates of the long-run elasticities of demand and supply, exactly the same sort of analysis can be conducted for the long run as well.

For example, the hypothetical auto market model in Example 10.4 might serve equally well for long-run analysis, though some differences in interpretation might be required. Indeed, in applied models of supply and demand it is often not clear whether the author intends his or her results to reflect the short run or the long run, and some care must be taken to understand how the issue of entry is being handled.

Industry structure

One aspect of the changing long-run equilibria in a perfectly competitive market that is obscured by using a simple supply-demand analysis is how the number of firms varies as market equilibria change. Because, as we will see in Part 5, the functioning of markets may in some cases be affected by the number of firms, and because there may be direct public policy interest in entry and exit from an industry, some additional analysis is required. In this section we will examine in detail determinants of the number of firms in the constant-cost case. Brief reference will also be made to the increasing-cost case, and some of the problems for this chapter examine that case in more detail.

Shifts in demand

Because the long-run supply curve for a constant-cost industry is infinitely elastic, analyzing shifts in market demand is particularly easy. If the initial equilibrium industry, output is Q_0 and q^* represents the output level for which the typical firm's long-run average cost is minimized, the initial equilibrium number of firms (n_0) is given by

$$n_0 = \frac{Q_0}{q^*}. \tag{10.55}$$

A shift in demand that changes equilibrium output to Q_1 will, in the long run, change the equilibrium number of firms to

$$n_1 = \frac{Q_1}{q^*}, \tag{10.56}$$

and the change in the number of firms is given by

$$n_1 - n_0 = \frac{Q_1 - Q_0}{q^*}. \tag{10.57}$$

That is, the change in the equilibrium number of firms is completely determined by the extent of the demand shift and by the optimal output level for the typical firm.

Changes in input costs

Even in the simple constant-cost industry case, analyzing the effect of an increase in an input price (and hence an upward shift in the infinitely elastic long-run supply curve) is relatively complicated. First, in order to calculate the decline in industry output, it is necessary to know both the extent to which minimum average cost is increased by the input price rise and how such an increase in the long-run equilibrium price affects total quantity

An Increase in an Input Price May Change Long-Run Equilibrium Output for the Typical Firm

An increase in the price of an input will shift average and marginal cost curves upward. The precise effect of these shifts on the typical firm's optimal output level (q^*) will depend on the relative magnitudes of the shifts.

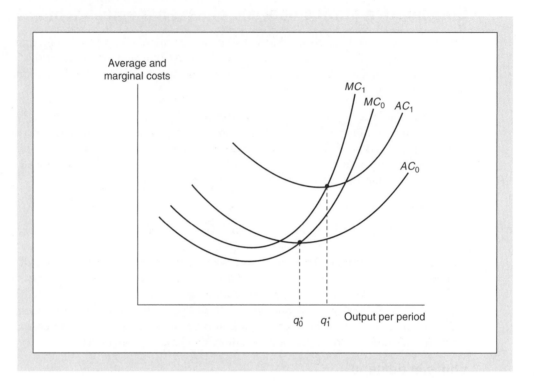

demanded. Knowledge of the typical firm's average cost function and of the price elasticity of demand permits such a calculation to be made in a straightforward way. But an increase in an input price may also change the minimum average cost output level for the typical firm. Such a possibility is illustrated in Figure 10.10. Both the average and marginal costs have been shifted upward by the input price increase, but because average cost has shifted up by a relatively greater extent than the marginal cost, the typical firm's optimal output level has increased from q_0^* to q_1^*. If the relative sizes of the shifts in cost curves were reversed, however, the typical firm's optimal output level would have fallen.[10] Taking account of this change in optimal scale, Equation 10.57 becomes

$$n_1 - n_0 = \frac{Q_1}{q_1^*} - \frac{Q_0}{q_0^*},\qquad (10.58)$$

and a number of possibilities arise.

---

[10]A mathematical proof proceeds as follows. Optimal output, q^*, is defined such that

$$AC(v, w, q^*) = MC(v, w, q^*).$$

Differentiating both sides of this expression, by, say, v, yields

$$\frac{\partial AC}{\partial v} + \frac{\partial AC}{\partial q^*} \cdot \frac{\partial q^*}{\partial v} = \frac{\partial MC}{\partial v} + \frac{\partial MC}{\partial q^*} \cdot \frac{\partial q^*}{\partial v};$$

but $\partial AC/\partial q^* = 0$, because average costs are minimized. By manipulating terms, we have

$$\frac{\partial q^*}{\partial v} = \left\{\frac{\partial MC}{\partial q^*}\right\}^{-1} \cdot \left[\frac{\partial AC}{\partial v} - \frac{\partial MC}{\partial v}\right].$$

Since $\partial MC/\partial q > 0$ at the minimum AC, $\partial q^*/\partial v$ will be positive or negative, depending on the sizes of the relative shifts in the AC and MC curves.

If $q_1^* \geq q_0^*$, the decline in quantity brought about by the rise in market price will definitely cause the number of firms to fall. However, if $q_1^* < q_0^*$, the result will be indeterminate. Industry output will fall, but optimal firm size also will fall, so the ultimate effect on the number of firms depends on the relative magnitude of these changes. A decline in the number of firms still seems the most likely outcome when an input price increase causes industry output to fall, but an increase in n is at least a theoretical possibility.

EXAMPLE 10.6

Rising Input Costs and Industry Structure

A rise in costs for bicycle frame makers will alter the equilibrium described in Example 10.5, but the precise effect on market structure will depend on how costs increase. The effects of an increase in fixed costs are fairly clear—the long-run equilibrium price will rise and the size of the typical firm will also increase. This latter effect occurs because a rise in fixed costs raises AC but not MC. To ensure that the equilibrium condition for $AC = MC$ holds, output (and MC) must also rise. For example, if a rise in shop rents causes the typical frame maker's costs to increase to

$$C(q) = q^3 - 20q^2 + 100q + 11,616, \qquad (10.59)$$

it is an easy matter to show that $MC = AC$ when $q = 22$. The rise in rent has therefore increased the efficient scale of bicycle frame operations by 2 bicycle frames per month. At $q = 22$, long-run average and marginal cost is 672, and that will be the long-run equilibrium price for frames. At this price

$$Q_D = 2,500 - 3P = 484, \qquad (10.60)$$

so there will be room in the market now for only 22 (= 484 ÷ 22) firms. The rise in fixed costs resulted not only in an increase in price but also in a significant reduction in the number of frame makers (from 50 to 22).

Increases in other types of input costs may, however, have more complex effects. Although a complete analysis would require an examination of frame makers' production functions and their related input choices, we can provide a simple illustration by assuming that a rise in some variable input prices causes the typical firm's total cost function to become

$$C(q) = q^3 - 8q^2 + 100q + 4,950. \qquad (10.61)$$

Now

$$MC = 3q^2 - 16q + 100$$

and

$$AC = q^2 - 8q + 100 + \frac{4,950}{q}. \qquad (10.62)$$

Setting $MC = AC$ yields

$$2q^2 - 8q = \frac{4,950}{q}, \qquad (10.63)$$

(continued)

EXAMPLE 10.6 CONTINUED

which has a solution of $q = 15$. This particular change in the total cost function has therefore significantly reduced the optimal size for frame shops. With $q = 15$, Equations 10.62 show $AC = MC = 535$, and with this new long-run equilibrium price,

$$Q_D = 2,500 - 3P = 895. \qquad (10.64)$$

These 895 frames will, in equilibrium, be produced by about 60 firms ($895 \div 15 = 59.67$—problems don't always work out evenly!). Even though the increase in costs results in a higher price, the equilibrium number of frame makers expands from 50 to 60 because the optimal size of each shop is now smaller.

Query: How do the total, marginal, and average functions derived from Equation 10.61 differ from those in Example 10.5? Are costs always greater (for all levels of q) for the former cost curve? Why is long-run equilibrium price higher with the former curves? (See footnote 10 for a formal discussion.)

Producer surplus in the long run

In Chapter 9 we described the concept of short-run producer surplus, which represents the return to a firm's owners in excess of what would be earned if output were zero. We showed that this consisted of the sum of short-run profits plus short-run fixed costs. Because in long-run equilibrium profits are zero and there are no fixed costs, all such short-run surplus is eliminated. Owners of firms are indifferent about whether they are in a particular market, because they could earn identical returns on their investments elsewhere. Suppliers of firms' inputs may not be indifferent about the level of production in a particular industry, however. In the constant-cost case, of course, input prices are assumed to be independent of the level of production on the presumption that inputs can earn the same amount in alternative occupations. But in the increasing-cost case, entry will bid up some input prices and suppliers of these inputs will be made better off. Consideration of these price effects leads again to the notion of producer surplus:

DEFINITION

> **Producer surplus.** Producer surplus is the extra return that producers make by making transactions at the market price over and above what they would earn if nothing were produced. It is illustrated by the size of the area below the market price and above the supply curve.

Although this is the same definition we introduced in Chapter 9, the context is now somewhat different. Now the "extra returns that producers make" should be interpreted as meaning "the higher prices that productive inputs receive." For short-run producer surplus, the gainers from market transactions are firms who are able to cover fixed costs and may earn profits over their variable costs. For long-run producer surplus we must penetrate back into the chain of production in order to identify who the ultimate gainers from market transactions are.

It is perhaps surprising that long-run producer surplus can be shown graphically in much the same way as short-run producer surplus. It is given by the area above the *long-run* supply curve and below equilibrium market price. In the constant-cost case, long-run supply is infinitely elastic and this area will equal zero, showing that returns to inputs are independent of the level of production. With increasing costs, however, long-run supply will be positively sloped and input prices will be bid up as industry output expands. Because this notion of long-run producer surplus is widely used in applied analysis (see Chapter 11), we will provide a formal development.

Ricardian rent

Long-run producer surplus can be most easily illustrated with a situation first described by David Ricardo in the early part of the nineteenth century.[11] Assume there are many parcels of land on which a particular crop might be grown. These range from very fertile land (low costs of production) to very poor, dry land (high costs). The long-run supply curve for the crop is constructed as follows. At low prices only the best land is used. As output increases, higher-cost plots of land are brought into production because higher prices make it profitable to use this land. The long-run supply curve is positively sloped because of the increasing costs associated with using less fertile land.

Market equilibrium in this situation is illustrated in Figure 10.11. At an equilibrium price of P^*, owners of both the low-cost and the medium-cost firms earn (long-run) profits. The "marginal firm" earns exactly zero economic profits. Firms with even higher costs stay out of the market because they would incur losses at a price of P^*. Profits earned by the intramarginal firms can persist in the long run, however, because they reflect a return to a unique resource—low-cost land. Free entry cannot erode these profits even over the long term. The sum of these long-run profits constitutes long-run producer surplus as given by area P^*EB in panel (d) of Figure 10.11. Equivalence of these areas can be shown by recognizing that each point in the supply curve in panel (d) represents minimum average cost for some firm. For each such firm, $P - AC$ represents profits per unit of output. Total long-run profits can then be computed by summing over all units of output.[12]

Capitalization of rents

The long-run profits for the low-cost firms in Figure 10.11 will often be reflected in prices for the unique resources owned by those firms. In Ricardo's initial analysis, for example, one might expect fertile land to sell for more than an untillable rock pile. Because such prices will reflect the present value of all future profits, these profits are said to be "capitalized" inputs' prices. Examples of capitalization include such disparate phenomena as the higher prices of nice houses with convenient access for commuters, the high value of rock and sport stars' contracts, and the lower value of land near toxic waste sites. Notice that in all of these cases it is market demand that determines rents—these rents are not traditional input costs that indicate foregone opportunities.

---

[11]See David Ricardo, *The Principles of Political Economy and Taxation* (1817; reprinted London: J. M. Dent and Son, 1965), Chapters 2 and 32.

[12]More formally, suppose that firms are indexed by i ($i = 1, \ldots n$) from lowest to highest cost and that each firm produces q^*. In the long-run equilibrium, $Q^* = n^* q^*$ (where n^* is the equilibrium number of firms and Q^* is total industry output). Suppose also the inverse of the supply function (competitive price as a function of quantity supplied) is given by $P = P(Q)$. Because of the indexing of firms, price is determined by the highest cost firm in the market, $P = P(iq^*) = AC_i$ and $P^* = P(Q^*) = P(n^*q^*)$. Now, in long-run equilibrium, profits for firm i are given by

$$\pi_i = (P^* - AC_i)q^*,$$

and total profits are given by

$$\pi = \int_0^{n^*} \pi_i di = \int_0^{n^*} (P^* - AC_i)q^* \, di$$

$$= \int_0^{n^*} P^* \, q^* \, di - \int_0^{n^*} AC_i q^* \, di$$

$$= P^* n^* \, q^* - \int_0^{n^*} P(iq^*) q^* \, di$$

$$= P^* \, Q^* - \int_0^{Q^*} P(Q) dQ,$$

which is the shaded area in panel (d) of Figure 10.11.

| FIGURE 10.11 | **Ricardian Rent** |

Owners of low-cost and medium-cost land can earn long-run profits. Long-run producers' surplus represents the sum of all these rents—area *P*EB* in panel (d). Usually Ricardian rents will be capitalized into input prices.

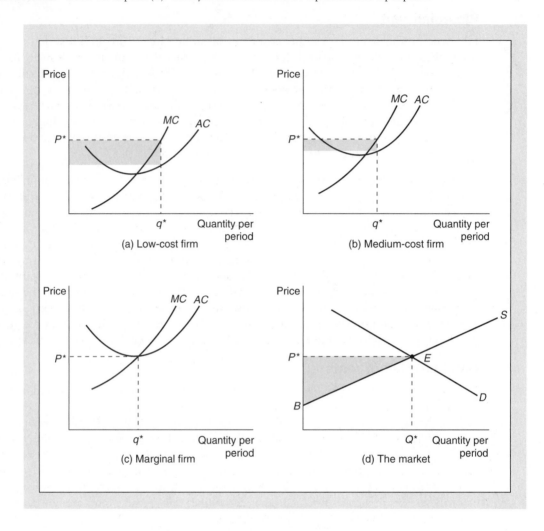

(a) Low-cost firm

(b) Medium-cost firm

(c) Marginal firm

(d) The market

Input supply and long-run producer surplus

It is the scarcity of low-cost inputs that creates the possibility of Ricardian rent. If low-cost farmland were available at infinitely elastic supply, there would be no such rent. More generally, any input that is "scarce" (in the sense that it has a positively sloped supply curve to a particular industry) will obtain rents in the form of earning a higher return than would be obtained if industry output were zero. In such cases, increases in output not only raise firms' costs (and thereby the price for which the output will sell), but also generate factor rents for inputs. The sum of all such rents is again measured by the area above the long-run supply curve and below equilibrium price. Changes in the size of this area of long-run producer surplus indicate changing rents earned by inputs to the industry. Notice that although long-run producer surplus is measured using the market supply curve, it is inputs to the industry that actually receive this surplus. Empirical measurements of changes in long-run producer surplus are widely used in applied welfare analysis to indicate how suppliers of various inputs fare as conditions change. Problem 10.7 and several of the problems in Chapter 11 provide some numerical illustrations of the connection between input rents and long-run producer surplus.

SUMMARY

In this chapter we have developed a detailed model of competitive price determination in a single market. This model of supply and demand, which was first articulated by Alfred Marshall in the latter part of the nineteenth century, is at the heart of much of microeconomic analysis. Its principal properties include the following:

- In the short run, equilibrium prices are established by the interaction of what demanders are willing to pay (as reflected by the market demand curve) and what firms are willing to produce (as reflected by the short-run market supply curve). These prices are treated as fixed in both demanders' and suppliers' decision-making processes.

- A shift in either demand or supply will cause the equilibrium price to change. The extent of such a change will depend on the slopes of the various curves and can be modeled using fairly simple comparative statics techniques.

- Firms may earn positive profits in the short run. Because fixed costs must always be paid, firms will choose a positive output providing revenues exceed variable costs.

- In the long run the number of firms is variable in response to profit opportunities. The assumption of free entry and exit implies that the firms in a competitive industry will earn zero economic profits in the long run ($P = AC$). Because firms also seek maximum profits, the equality $P = MC = AC$ implies that firms will operate at the low points of their long-run average cost curves.

- The shape of the long-run supply curve depends on how entry and exit affect firms' input costs. In the constant-cost case, input prices do not change and the long-run supply curve is horizontal. If entry raises input costs, the long-run supply curve will have a positive slope.

- Changes in long-run market equilibrium will also change the number of firms. Precise predictions about the extent of these changes is made difficult by the possibility that the minimum average cost level of output may be affected by changes in input costs or by technical progress.

- If changes in the long-run equilibrium in a market change the prices of inputs to that market, this will affect the welfare of suppliers of those inputs. Such changes can be measured by changes in the value of long-run producer surplus.

PROBLEMS

10.1

Suppose there are 100 identical firms in a perfectly competitive industry. Each firm has a short-run total cost function of the form

$$C(q) = \frac{1}{300} q^3 + 0.2q^2 + 4q + 10.$$

a. Calculate the firm's short-run supply curve with q as a function of market price (P).

b. On the assumption that there are no interaction effects among costs of the firms in the industry, calculate the short-run industry supply curve.

c. Suppose market demand is given by $Q = -200P + 8,000$. What will be the short-run equilibrium price-quantity combination?

10.2

Suppose there are 1,000 identical firms producing diamonds and the total-cost function for each firm is given by

$$C(q) = q^2 + wq,$$

where q is the firm's output level and w is the wage rate of diamond cutters.

a. If $w = 10$, what will be the firm's (short-run) supply curve? What is the industry's supply curve? How many diamonds will be produced at a price of 20 each? How many more diamonds would be produced at a price of 21?

b. Suppose the wages of diamond cutters depend on the total quantity of diamonds produced and the form of this relationship is given by

$$w = 0.002Q,$$

where Q represents total industry output, which is 1,000 times the output of the typical firm.

   In this situation, show that the firm's marginal cost (and short-run supply) curve depends on Q. What is the industry supply curve? How much will be produced at a price of 20? How much more will be produced at a price of 21? What do you conclude about the shape of the short-run supply curve?

10.3

A perfectly competitive market has 1,000 firms. In the very short run, each of the firms has a fixed supply of 100 units. The market demand is given by

$$Q = 160,000 - 10,000P.$$

a. Calculate the equilibrium price in the very short run.

b. Calculate the demand schedule facing any one firm in this industry.

c. Calculate what the equilibrium price would be if one of the sellers decided to sell nothing or if one seller decided to sell 200 units.

d. At the original equilibrium point, calculate the elasticity of the industry demand curve and the elasticity of the demand curve facing any one seller.

Suppose now that in the short run, each firm has a supply curve that shows the quantity the firm will supply (q_i) as a function of market price. The specific form of this supply curve is given by

$$q_i = -200 + 50P.$$

Using this short-run supply response, answer questions (a) through (d) above.

10.4

Suppose the demand for frisbees is given by

$$Q = 100 - 2P$$

and the supply by

$$Q = 20 + 6P.$$

a. What will be the equilibrium price and quantities for Frisbees?

b. Suppose the government levies a tax of $4 per Frisbee. Now what will be the equilibrium quantity, the price consumers will pay, and the price firms will receive? How is the burden of the tax shared by buyers and sellers?

c. How would your answers to parts (a) and (b) change if the supply curve were instead

$$Q = 70 + P?$$

What do you conclude by comparing these two cases? (See Chapter 11 for a further discussion of tax incidence theory.)

10.5

Wheat is produced under perfectly competitive conditions. Individual wheat farmers have U-shaped, long-run average cost curves that reach a minimum average cost of $3 per bushel when 1,000 bushels are produced.

a. If the market demand curve for wheat is given by

$$Q_D = 2,600,000 - 200,000P,$$

where Q_D is the number of bushels demanded per year and P is the price per bushel, in long-run equilibrium what will be the price of wheat, how much total wheat will be demanded, and how many wheat farms will there be?

b. Suppose demand shifts outward to

$$Q_D = 3,200,000 - 200,000P.$$

If farmers cannot adjust their output in the short run, what will market price be with this new demand curve? What will the profits of the typical farm be?

c. Given the new demand curve described in part (b), what will be the new long-run equilibrium? (That is, calculate market price, quantity of wheat produced, and the new equilibrium number of farms in this new situation.)

d. Graph your results.

10.6

A perfectly competitive industry has a large number of potential entrants. Each firm has an identical cost structure such that long-run average cost is minimized at an output of 20 units ($q_i = 20$). The minimum average cost is $10 per unit. Total market demand is given by

$$Q = 1,500 - 50P.$$

a. What is the industry's long-run supply schedule?

b. What is the long-run equilibrium price (P^*)? The total industry output (Q^*)? The output of each firm (q^*)? The number of firms? And the profits of each firm?

c. The short-run total-cost function associated with each firm's long-run equilibrium output is given by

$$C(q) = 0.5q^2 - 10q + 200.$$

Calculate the short-run average and marginal cost function. At what output level does short-run average cost reach a minimum?

d. Calculate the short-run supply function for each firm and the industry short-run supply function.

e. Suppose now that the market demand function shifts upward to $Q = 2,000 - 50P$. Using this new demand curve, answer part (b) for the very short run when firms cannot change their outputs.

f. In the short run, use the industry short-run supply function to recalculate the answers to (b).

g. What is the new long-run equilibrium for the industry?

10.7

Suppose that the demand for stilts is given by

$$Q = 1,500 - 50P$$

and that the long-run total operating costs of each stilt-making firm in a competitive industry are given by

$$C(q) = 0.5q^2 - 10q.$$

Entrepreneurial talent for stilt making is scarce. The supply curve for entrepreneurs is given by

$$Q_S = 0.25w,$$

where w is the annual wage paid.

Suppose also that each stilt-making firm requires one (and only one) entrepreneur (hence, the quantity of entrepreneurs hired is equal to the number of firms). Long-run total costs for each firm are hence given by

$$C(q,w) = 0.5q^2 - 10q + w.$$

a. What is the long-run equilibrium quantity of stilts produced? How many stilts are produced by each firm? What is the long-run equilibrium price of stilts? How many firms will there be? How many entrepreneurs will be hired, and what is their wage?

b. Suppose that the demand for stilts shifts outward to

$$Q = 2,428 - 50P.$$

Answer the questions posed in part (a).

c. Because stilt-making entrepreneurs are the cause of the upward sloping long-run supply curve in this problem, they will receive all rents generated as industry output expands. Calculate the increase in rents between parts (a) and (b). Show that this value is identical to the change in long-run producer surplus as measured along the stilt supply curve.

10.8

Suppose that the long-run total cost function for the typical mushroom producer is given by

$$C(q,w) = wq^2 - 10q + 100,$$

where q is the output of the typical firm and w represents the hourly wage rate of mushroom pickers. Suppose also that the demand for mushrooms is given by

$$Q = -1,000P + 40,000,$$

where Q is total quantity demanded and P is the market price of mushrooms.

a. If the wage rate for mushroom pickers is $1, what will be the long-run equilibrium output for the typical mushroom picker?

b. Assuming that the mushroom industry exhibits constant costs and that all firms are identical, what will be the long-run equilibrium price of mushrooms, and how many mushroom firms will there be?

c. Suppose the government imposed a tax of $3 for each mushroom picker hired (raising total wage costs, w, to $4). Assuming that the typical firm continues to have costs given by

$$C(q,w) = wq^2 - 10q + 100,$$

how will your answers to parts (a) and (b) change with this new, higher wage rate?

d. How would your answers to (a), (b), and (c) change if market demand were instead given by

$$Q = -1,000P + 60,000?$$

SUGGESTIONS FOR FURTHER READING

Knight, F. H. *Risk, Uncertainty and Profit,* Chaps. 5 and 6. Boston: Houghton Mifflin, 1921.
Classic treatment of the role of economic events in motivating industry behavior in the long run.

Marshall, A. *Principles of Economics.* 8th ed., Book 5, Chaps. 1, 2, and 3. New York: Crowell-Collier and Macmillan, 1920.
Classic development of the supply-demand mechanism.

Mas-Colell, A., M. D. Whinston, and J. R. Green. *Microeconomic Theory,* Chap. 10. New York. Oxford University Press, 1995.
Provides a compact analysis at a high level of theoretical precision. There is a good discussion of situations where competitive markets may not reach an equilibrium

Reynolds, L. G. "Cut-Throat Competition." *American Economic Review 30* (December 1940): 736–47.
Critique of the notion that there can be "too much" competition in an industry.

Robinson, J. "What Is Perfect Competition?" *Quarterly Journal of Economics 49* (1934): 104–20.
Critical discussion of the perfectly competitive assumptions.

Stigler, G. J. "Perfect Competition, Historically Contemplated." *Journal of Political Economy 65* (1957): 1–17.
Fascinating discussion of the historical development of the competitive model.

Varian, H. R. *Microeconomic Analysis,* 3rd ed., Chap. 13. New York: W. W. Norton, 1995.
A terse, but instructive coverage of many of the topics in this chapter. The importance of entry is stressed, though the precise nature of the long-run supply curve is a bit obscure.

EXTENSIONS

Demand Aggregation and Estimation

In Chapters 4 through 6 we showed that the assumption of utility maximization implies several properties for individual demand functions:

- The functions are continuous;
- The functions are homogeneous of degree zero in all prices and income;
- Income-compensated substitution effects are negative, and
- Cross-price substitution effects are symmetric.

In this extension we will examine the extent to which these properties would be expected to hold for aggregated market demand functions and what, if any, restrictions should be placed on such functions. In addition, we illustrate some other issues that arise in estimating these aggregate functions and some results from such estimates.

E10.1 Continuity

The continuity of individual demand functions clearly implies the continuity of market demand functions. But there are situations in which market demand functions may be continuous whereas individual functions are not. Consider the case where goods—such as an automobile—must be bought in large, discrete units. Here individual demand may be discontinuous, but the aggregated demands of many people may be (nearly) continuous.

E10.2 Homogeneity and income aggregation

Because each individual's demand function is homogeneous of degree zero in all prices and income, market demand functions are also homogeneous of degree zero in all prices and *individual* incomes. However, market demand functions are not necessarily homogeneous of degree zero in all prices and *total* income.

To see when demand might depend just on total income, suppose individual i's demand for X is given by

$$x_i = a_i(P) + b(P)y_i \qquad i = 1, n, \qquad \text{(i)}$$

where P is the vector of all market prices, $a_i(P)$ is a set of individual-specific price effects, and $b(P)$ is a marginal propensity-to-spend function that is the same across all individuals (although the value of this parameter may depend on market prices). In this case the market demand functions will depend on P and on total income.

$$\Upsilon = \sum_{i=1}^{n} y_i. \qquad \text{(ii)}$$

This shows that market demand reflects the behavior of a single "typical" consumer. Gorman (1959) shows that this is the most general form of demand function that can represent such a typical consumer.

E10.3 Cross-equation constraints

Suppose a typical individual buys k items and that expenditures on each are given by

$$p_j x_j = \sum_{i=1}^{k} a_{ij} p_i + b_j y \qquad j = 1, k. \qquad \text{(iii)}$$

If expenditures on these k items exhaust total income, that is,

$$\sum_{j=1}^{k} p_j x_j = y, \qquad \text{(iv)}$$

summing over all goods shows that

$$\sum_{j=1}^{k} a_{ij} = 0 \ (\textit{for all } i) \qquad \text{(v)}$$

and that

$$\sum_{j=1}^{k} b_j = 1 \qquad \text{(vi)}$$

for each person. This implies that researchers are generally not able to estimate expenditure functions for k goods independently. Rather, some account must be taken of relationships between the expenditure functions for different goods.

E10.4 Econometric practice

The degree to which these theoretical concerns are reflected in the actual practices of econometricians varies widely. At the least sophisticated level, an equation similar to (iii) might be estimated directly using ordinary least squares (OLS), with little attention to the ways in which the assumptions might be violated. Various elasticities could be calculated directly from this equation, although because of the linear form used these would not be constant for changes in p_i or y. A constant elasticity formulation of Equation iii would be

$$\ln(p_j x_j) = \sum_{i=1}^{k} a_{ij} \ln(p_i) + b_j \ln y \quad j = 1, k, \text{ (vii)}$$

and here price and income elasticities would be given directly by

$$
\begin{aligned}
e_{x_j, p_j} &= 1 + a_{ij} \\
e_{x_j, p_i} &= a_{ij} \qquad (i \neq j) \qquad \text{(viii)} \\
e_{y_j, y} &= b_j,
\end{aligned}
$$

respectively. Notice here, however, that no specific attention is paid to biases introduced by use of aggregate income or by the disregard of possible cross-equation restrictions such as those in Equations v and vi. Further restrictions are also implied by the homogeneity of each of the demand functions ($\sum_{i=1}^{k} a_{ij} + b_j = -1$), although this restriction too is often disregarded in the development of simple econometric estimates.

More sophisticated studies of aggregated demand equations seek to remedy these problems by explicit consideration of potential income distribution effects and by the estimation of entire systems of demand equation. Theil (1971, 1975)

provides a good introduction to some of the procedures used.

Econometric results

Table 10.3 reports a number of economic estimates of representative price and income elasticities drawn from a variety of sources. The original sources for these estimate should be consulted to determine the extent to which the authors have been attentive to the theoretical restrictions outlined previously. Overall, these estimates accord fairly well with intuition—the demand for transatlantic air travel is more price classic than is the demand for medical care, for example. Perhaps somewhat surprising are the high price and income elasticities for owner-occupied housing, because "shelter" is often regarded in everyday discussion as a necessity. The very high estimated income elasticity of demand for automobiles probably conflates the measurement of both quantity and quality demanded. But it does suggest why the automobile industry is so sensitive to the business cycle.

References

Gorman, W. M. "Separable Utility and Aggregation." *Econometrica* (November 1959): 469–81.

Shafer, W., and H. Sonnenschein. "Market Demand and Excess Demand Functions." In K. J. Arrow and M. D. Intriligator, eds., *Handbook of Mathematical Economics,* vol. II. Amsterdam: North-Holland, 1982, pp. 671–93.

Stoker, T. M. "Empirical Approaches to the Problem of Aggregation over Individuals." *Journal of Economic Literature* (December 1993): 1827–74.

Theil, H. *Principles of Econometrics.* New York: John Wiley & Sons, 1971, pp. 326–46.

———. *Theory and Measurement of Consumer Demand,* vol. 1. Amsterdam: North-Holland, 1975, chaps. 5 and 6.

| TABLE 10.3 | Representative Price and Income Elasticities of Demand |

	Price Elasticity	Income Elasticity
Food	−0.21	+0.28
Medical services	−0.18	+0.22
Housing		
Rental	−0.18	+1.00
Owner occupied	−1.20	+1.20
Electricity	−1.14	+0.61
Automobiles	−1.20	+3.00
Gasoline	−0.55	+1.60
Beer	−0.26	+0.38
Wine	−0.88	+0.97
Marijuana	−1.50	0.00
Cigarettes	−0.35	+0.50
Abortions	−0.81	+0.79
Transatlantic air travel	−1.30	+1.40
Imports	−0.58	+2.73
Money	−0.40	+1.00

SOURCES: Food: H. Wold and L. Jureen, *Demand Analysis* (New York: John Wiley & Sons, 1953): 203. Medical services: income elasticity from R. Andersen and L. Benham, "Factors Affecting the Relationship Between Family Income and Medical Care Consumption." in Herbert Klarman, ed. *Empirical Studies in Health Economics* (Baltimore: Johns Hopkins Press, 1970). Price elasticity from W. C. Manning et al., "Health Insurance and the Demand for Medical Care: Evidence from a Randomized Experiment," *American Economic Review* (June 1987): 251–77. Housing: income elasticities from F. de Leeuw, "The Demand for Housing," *Review for Economics and Statistics* (February 1971); price elasticities from H. S. Houthakker and L. D. Taylor, *Consumer Demand in the United States* (Cambridge, MA: Harvard University Press, 1970): 166–67. Electricity, R. F. Halvorsen, "Residential Demand for Electricity," unpublished Ph.D. dissertation, Harvard University, December 1972. Automobiles: Gregory C. Chow, *Demand for Automobiles in the United States* (Amsterdam: North Holland, 1957). Gasoline: C. Dahl "Gasoline Demand Survey," *Energy Journal* 7 (1986): 67–82. Beer and wine: J. A. Johnson, E. H. Oksanen, M. R. Veall, D. Fritz, "Short-Run and Long-Run Elasticities for Candian Consumption of Alcoholic Beverages," *Review of Economics and Statistics* (February 1992): 64–74. Marijuana: T. C. Misket and F. Vakil, "Some Estimate of Price and Expenditure Elasticities Among UCLA Students," *Review of Economics and Statistics* (November 1972): 474–75. Cigarettes: F. Chalemaker, "Rational Addictive Behavior and Cigarette Smoking," *Journal of Political Economy* (August 1991): 722–42. Abortions: M. H. Medoff, "An Economic Analysis of the Demand for Abortions," *Economic Inquiry* (April 1988): 253–59. Transatlantic air travel: J. M. Cigliano, "Price and Income Elasticities for Airline Travel," *Business Economics* (September 1980): 17–21. Imports: M. D. Chinn, "Beware of Econometricians Bearing Estimates," *Journal of Policy Analysis and Management* (Fall 1991): 546–67. Money: "Long-Run Income and Interest Elasticities of Money Demand in the United States," *Review of Economics and Statistics* (November 1991): 665–74. Price elasticity refers to interest rate elasticity.

Chapter 11

APPLIED COMPETITIVE ANALYSIS

The model of a perfectly competitive market we developed in the previous chapter provides the basis for much applied microeconomic analysis. Using these principles of supply and demand has proven to be a good way to get started in an investigation of many real-world markets. In this chapter we provide a brief description of some of these uses. Before beginning, two warnings may be appropriate. First, our analysis here will look only at a single market; that is, we will employ a partial equilibrium approach. In Chapter 12 we explore a series of general equilibrium models that permit an investigation of repercussions in many markets simultaneously. In such models some of the simple results of supply and demand analysis may not hold. Similarly, a warning about the strict assumptions that underlie the competitive model should also be kept in mind. The most important such assumption is that of price-taking behavior on the part of both suppliers and demanders. When economic actors have some influence on market price, alternative models are required. Several such models are examined in Part 5 of this book.

Economic efficiency and welfare analysis

Long-run competitive equilibria may have the desirable property of allocating resources "efficiently." Although we will have far more to say about this concept in a general equilibrium context in Chapter 12, here we can offer a partial equilibrium description of why the result might hold. Remember from Chapter 5 that the area below a demand curve and above market price represents consumer surplus—the extra utility consumers receive from choosing to purchase a good voluntarily rather than being forced to do without it. Similarly, as we saw in Chapter 10, producer surplus is measured as the area below market price and above the long-run supply curve, which represents the extra return that productive inputs receive rather than having no transactions in the good. Overall then, the area between the demand curve and the supply curve represents the sum of consumer and producer surplus. It measures the total additional value obtained by market participants by being able to make market transactions in this good. It seems clear that this total area is maximized at the competitive market equilibrium.

A graphic proof

Figure 11.1 shows a simplified proof. Given the demand curve (D) and the long-run supply curve (S), the sum of consumer and producer surplus is given by distance AB for the first unit produced. Total surplus continues to increase as additional output is produced up

FIGURE 11.1   **Competitive Equilibrium and Consumer/Producer Surplus**

At the competitive equilibrium (Q^*) the sum of consumer surplus (shaded lighter gray) and producer surplus (shaded darker) is maximized. For an output level less than Q^*, say, Q_1, there is a deadweight loss of consumer and producer surplus given by area *FEG*.

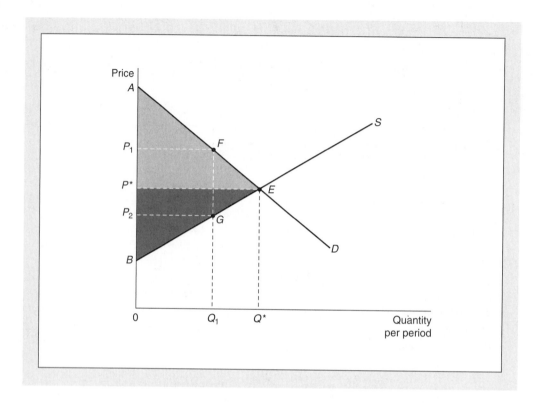

to the competitive equilibrium level, Q^*. This level of production will be achieved when price is at the competitive level, P^*. Total consumer surplus is represented by the light shaded area in the figure, total producer surplus by the darker shaded area. Clearly, for output levels less than Q^*, (say, Q_1), total surplus would be reduced. One sign of this misallocation is that at Q_1, demanders would value an additional unit of output at P_1, whereas marginal costs would be given by P_2. Because $P_1 > P_2$, total welfare would clearly increase by producing one more unit of output. A transaction that involved trading this extra unit at any price between P_1 and P_2 would be mutually beneficial—both parties would gain.

The total welfare loss that occurs at output level Q_1 is given by area *FEG*. The distribution of surplus at output level Q_1 will depend on the precise (nonequilibrium) price that prevails in the market. At a price of P_1 consumer surplus would be reduced substantially to area AFP_1, whereas producers might actually gain because producer surplus is now P_1FGB. At a low price such as P_2 the situation would be reversed, with producers being much worse off than they were initially. Hence the distribution of the welfare losses from producing less than Q^* will depend on the price at which transactions are conducted. The size of the total loss, however, is given by *FEG*, regardless of the price settled upon.[1]

---

[1]Increases in output beyond Q^* also clearly reduce welfare. See Problem 11.1.

A mathematical proof

Mathematically, we wish to maximize

consumer surplus + producer surplus   **(11.1)**

$$= [U(Q) - PQ] + [PQ - \int_0^Q P(Q)\ dQ] = U(Q) - \int_0^Q P(Q)\ dQ,$$

where $U(Q)$ is the utility function of the representative consumer and $P(Q)$ is the long-run supply relation. In long-run equilibria along the long-run supply curve, $P(Q) = AC = MC$. Maximization of Equation 11.1 with respect to Q yields

$$U'(Q) = P(Q) = AC = MC,$$ **(11.2)**

so maximization occurs where the marginal value of Q to the representative consumer is equal to market price. But this is precisely the competitive supply-demand equilibrium, because the demand curve represents consumers' marginal valuations, whereas the supply curve reflects marginal (and, in long-term equilibrium, average) cost.

Applied welfare analysis

The conclusion that the competitive equilibrium maximizes the sum of consumer and producer surplus mirrors a series of more general economic efficiency "theorems" we will examine in Chapter 12. Describing the major caveats that attach to these theorems is best delayed until that more extended discussion. Here we are more interested in showing how the competitive model is used to examine the consequences of changing economic conditions on the welfare of market participants. Usually such welfare changes are measured by looking at changes in consumer and producer surplus.

 EXAMPLE 11.1

Welfare Loss Computations

Use of consumer and producer surplus notions makes possible the explicit calculation of welfare losses from restrictions on voluntary transactions. In the case of linear demand and supply curves, this computation is especially simple because the areas of loss are frequently triangular. For example, if demand is given by

$$Q_D = 10 - P$$ **(11.3)**

and supply by

$$Q_S = P - 2,$$ **(11.4)**

market equilibrium occurs at the point $P^* = 6$, $Q^* = 4$. Restriction of output to $\bar{Q} = 3$ would create a gap between what demanders are willing to pay ($P_D = 10 - Q = 7$) and what suppliers require ($P_S = 2 + \bar{Q} = 5$). The welfare loss from restricting transactions is given by a triangle with a base of 2 (= $P_D - P_S = 7 - 5$) and a height of 1 (the difference between Q^* and $\bar{Q}$). Hence the welfare loss is one dollar if P is measured in dollars per unit and Q is measured in units. More generally, the loss will be measured in the units in which $P \cdot Q$ is measured.

Computations with constant elasticity curves. More realistic results can usually be obtained by using constant elasticity demand and supply curves based on econometric studies. In Example 10.4, we examined such a model of the U.S. automobile market. We can

(continued)

EXAMPLE 11.1 CONTINUED

simplify that example a bit by assuming P is measured in thousands of dollars, Q in millions of automobiles, and that demand is given by

$$Q_D = 200 \ P^{-1.2} \qquad (11.5)$$

and supply by

$$Q_S = 1.3 \ P. \qquad (11.6)$$

Equilibrium in the market is given by $P^* = 9.87$, $Q^* = 12.8$. Suppose now that government policy restricts automobile sales to 11 (million) to control emissions of pollutants. An approximation to the direct welfare loss from such a policy can be found by the triangular method used earlier.

With $\bar{Q} = 11$, $P_D = (11/200)^{-.83} = 11.1$, $P_S = 11/1.3 = 8.46$. Hence, the welfare loss "triangle" is given by $.5(P_D - P_S)(Q^* - \bar{Q}) = .5(11.1 - 8.46)(12.8 - 11) = 2.38$. Here the units are those of P times Q: billions of dollars. The approximate[2] value of the welfare loss is therefore $2.4 billion, which might be weighed against the expected gain from emissions control.

Distribution of loss. In the automobile case, the welfare loss is shared about equally by consumers and producers. An approximation for consumers' losses is given by $.5(P_D - P^*)(Q^* - \bar{Q}) = .5(11.1 - 9.87)(12.8 - 11) = 1.11$, and for producers by $.5(9.87 - 8.46)(12.8 - 11) = 1.27$. Because the price elasticity of demand is somewhat greater (in absolute value) than the price elasticity of supply, consumers incur less than half the loss and producers somewhat more than half. With a more price elastic demand curve, consumers would incur a smaller share of the loss.

Query: How does the size of the total welfare loss from a quantity restriction depend on the elasticities of supply and demand? What determines how the loss will be shared?

Price controls and shortages

Sometimes governments may seek to control prices at below equilibrium levels. Although adoption of such policies may be based on noble motives, the controls deter long-run supply responses and create welfare losses for both consumers and producers. A simple analysis of this possibility is provided by Figure 11.2. Initially the market is in long-run equilibrium at P_1, Q_1 (point E). An increase in demand from D to D' would cause the price to rise to P_2 in the short run and encourage entry by new firms. Assuming this market is characterized by increasing costs (as reflected by the positively sloped, long-run supply curve, LS), price would fall somewhat as a result of this entry, ultimately settling at P_3. If these price changes were regarded as undesirable, the government could, in principle, prevent them by imposing a legally enforceable ceiling price of P_1. This would cause firms to continue to supply their previous output (Q_1) and, because at P_1 demanders now want to purchase Q_4, there will be a shortage, given by $Q_4 - Q_1$.

---

[2] A more precise estimate of the loss can be obtained by integrating $P_D - P_S$ over the range $Q = 11$ to $Q = 12.8$. With exponential demand and supply curves, this integration is often easy. In the present case, the technique yields an estimated welfare loss of 2.28, thereby showing that the triangular approximation is not too bad, even for relatively large price changes. In later analysis, therefore, we will primary use such approximations.

FIGURE 11.2   Price Controls and Shortages

A shift in demand from D to D' would raise price to P_2 in the short run. Entry over the long run would yield a final equilibrium of P_3, Q_3. Controlling the price at P_1 would prevent these actions and yield a shortage of $Q_4 - Q_1$. Relative to the uncontrolled situation, the price control yields a transfer from producers to consumers (area P_3CEP_1) and a deadweight loss of forgone transactions given by the two areas $AE'C$ and $CE'E$.

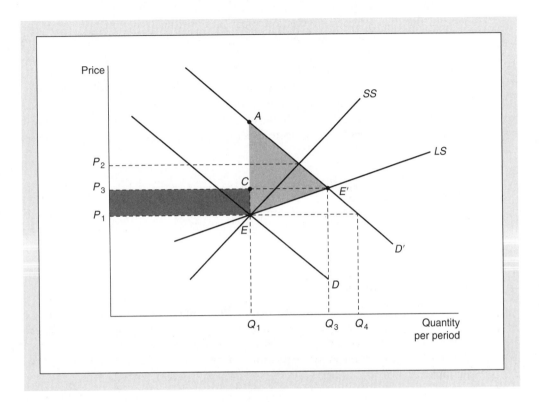

Welfare evaluation

The welfare consequences of this price-control policy can be evaluated by comparing consumer and producer surplus measures prevailing under this policy to those that would have prevailed in the absence of controls. First, the buyers of Q_1 gain consumer surplus given by area P_3CEP_1 because they can buy this good at a lower price than would exist in an uncontrolled market. This gain reflects a pure transfer from producers out of the amount of producer surplus that would exist without controls. What current consumers have gained from the lower price, producers have lost. Although this transfer does not represent a loss of overall welfare, it does clearly affect the relative well-being of the market participants.

Second, the area $AE'C$ represents the value of additional consumer surplus that would have been attained without controls. Similarly, the area $CE'E$ reflects additional producer surplus available in the uncontrolled situation. Together, these two areas (that is, area $AE'E$) represent the total value of mutually beneficial transactions that are prevented by the government policy of controlling price. This is, therefore, a measure of the pure welfare costs of that policy.

Disequilibrium behavior

The welfare analysis depicted in Figure 11.2 also suggests some of the types of behavior that might be expected as a result of the price-control policy. Assuming that observed market outcomes are generated by

$$Q(P_1) = \min\ [Q_D(P_1),\ Q_S(P_1)], \tag{11.7}$$

suppliers will be content with this outcome, but demanders will not because they will be forced to accept a situation of excess demand. They have an incentive to signal their dissatisfaction to suppliers through increasing price offers. Such offers may not only tempt existing suppliers to make illegal transactions at higher than allowed prices, but may encourage new entrants to make such transactions. It is this kind of activity that leads to the prevalence of black markets in most instances of price control. Modeling the resulting transactions is difficult for two reasons. First, these may involve non–price taking behavior because the price of each transaction must be individually negotiated rather than set by "the market." Second, nonequilibrium transactions will often involve imperfect information. Any pair of market participants will usually not know what other transactors are doing, although such actions may affect their welfare by changing the options available. Some progress has been made modeling such disequilibrium behavior using game theory techniques (see Chapter 15). However, other than the obvious prediction that transactions will occur at prices above the price ceiling, no very generally results have been obtained.[3] The types of black market transactions undertaken will depend on the specific institutional details of the situation.

Tax incidence analysis

The partial equilibrium model of competitive markets has also been widely used to study the impact of taxes. Although, as we will point out, these applications are necessarily limited by their inability to analyze tax effects that spread through many markets, they do provide important insights on a number of issues.

A mathematical model

The effect of a per unit tax can be most easily studied using the mathematical model of supply and demand that was introduced in Chapter 10. Now, however, we need to make a distinction between the price paid by demanders (P_D) and the price received by suppliers (P_S), because a per-unit tax (t) introduces a "wedge" between these two magnitudes of the form:

$$P_D - P_S = t \qquad (11.8)$$

or, in terms of the small price changes we wish to examine,

$$dP_D - dP_S = dt. \qquad (11.9)$$

Maintenance of equilibrium in the market requires

$$dQ_D = dQ_S,$$

or

$$D_P dP_D = S_P dP_S, \qquad (11.10)$$

where D_P, S_P are the price derivatives of the demand and supply functions, respectively. We can use Equations 11.9 and 11.10 to solve for the effect of the tax on P_D:

$$D_P dP_D = S_P dP_S = S_P(dP_D - dt). \qquad (11.11)$$

Hence

$$\frac{dP_D}{dt} = \frac{S_P}{S_P - D_P} = \frac{e_S}{e_S - e_D}, \qquad (11.12)$$

---

[3]See J. Bénassy, "Nonclearing Markets: Microeconomic Concepts and Macroeconomic Applications," *Journal of Economic Literature* (June 1993): 732–61.

where e_S and e_D represent the price elasticities of supply and demand, respectively, and the final equation is derived by multiplying numerator and denominator by P/Q. A similar set of manipulations for the change in supply price gives

$$\frac{dP_S}{dt} = \frac{e_D}{e_S - e_D}.$$ (11.13)

Because $e_D \le 0$, $e_S \ge 0$, these calculations provide the obvious results

$$\frac{dP_D}{dt} \ge 0$$
$$\frac{dP_S}{dt} \le 0.$$ (11.14)

If $e_D = 0$ (demand is perfectly inelastic), $dP_D/dt = 1$ and the per-unit tax is completely paid by demanders. Alternatively, if $e_D = -\infty$, $dP_S/dt = -1$ and the tax is wholly paid by producers. More generally, dividing Equation 11.13 by Equation 11.12 yields

$$-\frac{dP_S/dt}{dP_D/dt} = -\frac{e_D}{e_S},$$ (11.15)

which shows that the actor with the less elastic responses (in absolute value) will experience most of the price change occasioned by the tax.

A welfare analysis

Figure 11.3 permits a simplified welfare analysis of the tax incidence issue. Imposition of the unit tax, t, creates a vertical wedge between the supply and demand curves, and quantity traded declines to Q^{**}. Demanders incur a loss of consumer surplus given by area $P_D FEP^*$, of which $P_D FHP^*$ is transferred to the government as a portion of total tax revenues. The balance of total tax revenues ($P^* HGP_S$) is paid by producers, who incur a total loss of producer surplus given by area $P^* EGP_S$. Notice that the reduction in combined consumer and producer surplus exceeds total tax revenues collected by area FEG. This area represents a "deadweight" loss that arises because some mutually beneficial transactions are discouraged by the tax. In general, the sizes of all of the various areas illustrated in Figure 11.3 will be affected by the price elasticities involved. To determine the final incidence of the producers' share of the tax would require an explicit analysis of input markets—the burden of the tax would be reflected in reduced rents for those inputs characterized by relatively inelastic supply. More generally, a complete analysis of the incidence question requires a general equilibrium model that can treat many markets simultaneously. We discuss such models in the next chapter.

Deadweight loss and elasticity

All non-lump-sum taxes involve deadweight losses because they alter the behavior of economic actors. The size of such losses will depend in a rather complex way on the elasticities of demand and supply in the market. A linear approximation to the deadweight loss accompanying a small tax, dt, is given by

$$DW = -.5(dt)(dQ).$$ (11.16)

But from the definition of elasticity, we know

$$dQ = e_D dP_D \cdot Q_0/P_0,$$ (11.17)

where Q_0 and P_0 are the pretax values for quantity and price, respectively. Combining Equations 11.17 and 11.12 yields

$$dQ = e_D[e_S/(e_S - e_D)]\, dt\, Q_0/P_0,$$ (11.18)

FIGURE 11.3   **Tax Incidence Analysis**

Imposition of a specific tax of amount *t* per unit creates a "wedge" between the price consumers pay (P_D) and what suppliers receive (P_S). The extent to which consumers or producers pay the tax depends on the price elasticities of demand and supply.

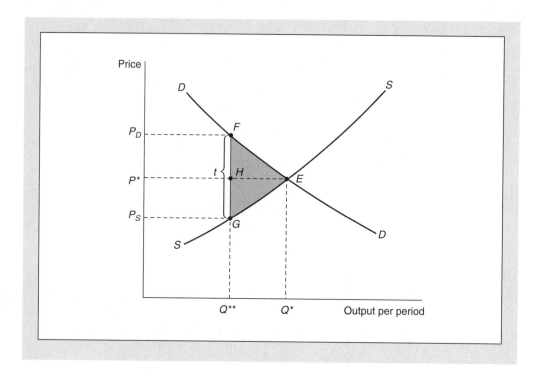

and substitution into Equation 15.16 provides a final expression for the loss:

$$DW = -.5\left(\frac{dt}{P_0}\right)^2 [e_D e_S/(e_S - e_D)]P_0 Q_0. \qquad (11.19)$$

Clearly, deadweight losses are zero in cases in which either e_D or e_S is zero because then the tax does not alter the quantity of the good traded. More generally, deadweight losses are smaller in situations where e_D or e_S is small. In principle, Equation 11.19 can be used to evaluate the deadweight losses accompanying any complex tax system. This information might provide some insights on how a tax system could be designed to minimize the overall "excess burden" involved in collecting a needed amount of tax revenues. Notice also that DW is proportional to the square of the tax rate—marginal excess burden increases with the tax rate.

Transaction costs

Although we have developed this discussion in terms of tax incidence theory, models incorporating a wedge between buyers' and sellers' prices have a number of other applications in economics. Perhaps the most important of these concern costs associated with making market transactions. In some cases these costs may be explicit. Most real estate transactions, for example, take place through a third-party broker, who charges a fee for the service of bringing buyer and seller together. Similar explicit transaction fees occur in the trading of stocks and bonds, boats and airplanes, and practically everything that is solid at auction. In all of these instances, buyers and sellers are willing to pay an explicit fee to an agent or broker who facilitates the transaction. In other cases transaction costs

EXAMPLE 11.2

The Deadweight Loss from Taxes

In Example 11.1 we examined the loss of consumer and producer surplus that would occur if automobile sales were cut from their equilibrium level of 12.8 (million) to 11 (million). An auto tax of $2,640 (i.e., 2.64 thousand dollars) would accomplish this reduction because it would introduce exactly the wedge between demand and supply price that was calculated previously. Because we have assumed $e_D = -1.2$ and $e_S = 1.0$ in Example 11.1, and initial spending on automobiles is approximately $126 (billion), Equation 11.19 predicts that the deadweight loss from the auto tax would be

$$DW = .5\left(\frac{2.64}{9.87}\right)^2 (1.2/2.2)(126) = 2.46. \qquad (11.20)$$

This loss of 2.46 billion dollars is approximately the same as the loss from emissions control calculated in Example 11.1. It might be contrasted to total tax collections, which in this case amount to $29 billion ($2,640 per automobile times 11 million automobiles in the post-tax equilibrium). Here, the deadweight loss equals approximately 8 percent of total tax revenues collected.

Marginal burden. An incremental increase in the auto tax would be relatively more costly in terms of deadweight losses. Suppose the government decided to round the auto tax upward to a flat $3,000 per car. In this case, car sales would drop to approximately 10.7 (million). Tax collections would amount to $32.1 billion, an increase of $3.1 billion over what was computed previously. Equation 11.20 can be used to show that deadweight losses now amount to $3.17 billion—an increase of $0.71 billion above the losses experienced with the lower tax. At the margin then, additional deadweight losses amount to about 23 percent (0.72/3.1) of additional revenues collected. Hence marginal and average excess burden computations may differ significantly.

Query: Can you explain intuitively why the marginal burden of a tax exceeds its average burden? Under what conditions would the marginal excess burden of a tax exceed additional tax revenues collected?

may be largely implicit. Individuals trying to purchase a used car, for example, will spend considerable time and effort reading classified advertisements and examining vehicles, and these activities amount to an implicit cost of making the transaction.

To the extent that transaction costs are on a per-unit basis (as they are in the real estate, securities, and auction examples), our previous taxation example applies exactly. From the point of view of the buyers and sellers, it makes little difference whether t represents a per-unit tax or a per-unit transaction fee, because the analysis of the fee's effect on the market will be the same. That is, the fee will be shared between buyers and sellers, depending on the specific elasticities involved. Trading volume will be lower than in the absence of such fees.[4] A somewhat different analysis would hold, however, if transaction

---

[4]This analysis does not consider possible benefits obtained from brokers. To the extent that these services are valuable to the parties in the transaction, demand and supply curves will shift outward to reflect this value. Hence trading volume may actually expand with the availability of services that facilitate transactions, although the costs of such services will continue to create a wedge between sellers' and buyers' prices.

costs were a lump-sum amount per transaction. In that case individuals would seek to reduce the number of transactions made, but the existence of the charge would not affect the supply-demand equilibrium itself. For example, the cost of driving to the supermarket is mainly a lump-sum transaction cost on shopping for groceries. The existence of such a charge may not significantly affect the price of food items or the amount of food consumed (unless it tempts people to grow their own), but the charge will cause individuals to shop less frequently, to buy larger quantities on each trip, and to hold larger inventories of food in their homes than would be the case in the absence of such a cost.

Effects on the attributes of transactions

More generally, taxes or transaction costs may affect some attributes of transactions more than others. In our formal model, we assumed that such costs were based only on the physical quantity of goods sold. The desire of suppliers and demanders to minimize costs therefore led them to reduce quantity traded. When transactions involve several dimensions (such as quality, risk, or timing), taxes or transaction costs may affect some or all of these dimensions, depending on the precise basis on which the costs are assessed. For example, a tax on quantity may cause firms to upgrade product quality, or information-based transaction costs may encourage firms to produce less risky, standardized commodities. Similarly, a per-transaction cost (travel costs of getting to the store) may cause individuals to make fewer but larger transactions (and hold larger inventories). The possibilities for these various substitutions will obviously depend on the particular circumstances of the transaction. We will examine several examples of cost-induced changes in attributes of transactions in later chapters.[5]

Trade restrictions

Restrictions on the flow of goods in international commerce have effects similar to those we just examined for taxes. Impediments to free trade may reduce mutually beneficial transactions and cause a variety of transfers among the various parties involved. Once again the competitive model of supply and demand is frequently used to study these effects.

Gains from international trade

Figure 11.4 illustrates the domestic demand and supply curves for a particular good, say, shoes. In the absence of international trade, the domestic equilibrium price of shoes would be P^* and quantity would be Q^*. Although this equilibrium would exhaust all mutually beneficial transactions between domestic shoe producers and domestic demanders, opening of international trade presents a number of additional options. If world shoe prices, P_W, are less than the prevailing domestic price P^*, the opening of trade will cause prices to fall to this world level.[6] This drop in price will cause quantity demanded to increase to Q_1, whereas quantity supplied by domestic producers will fall to Q_2. Imported shoes will amount to $Q_1 - Q_2$. In short, what shoes domestic producers do not supply at the world price are instead provided by foreign sources.

The shift in the market equilibrium from E_0 to E_1 causes a large increase in consumer surplus given by area $P^*E_0E_1P_W$. Part of this gain reflects a transfer from domestic shoe producers (area $P^*E_0A\ P_W$), and part represents an unambiguous welfare gain (area E_0E_1A). The source of consumer gains here is obvious—buyers get shoes at a lower price than was previously available in the domestic market. As in our analysis of taxation, losses of producer surplus are experienced by those inputs that give the long-run supply curve its upward slope. If, for example, the domestic shoe industry experiences increasing costs

[5]For the classic treatment of this topic, see Y. Barzel, An "Alternative Approach to the Analysis of Taxation," *Journal of Political Economy* (December 1976): 1177–97.

[6]Throughout our analysis we will assume this country is a price taker in the world market and can purchase all of the imports it wishes without affecting the price, P_W. For an analysis of an upward sloping supply curve for imports, see Problem 11.10.

| FIGURE 11.4 | **Opening of International Trade Increases Total Welfare** |

Opening of international trade lowers price from P^* to P_W. At P_W domestic producers supply Q_2 and demanders buy Q_1. Imports amount to $Q_1 - Q_2$. The lower price results in a transfer from domestic producers to consumers (shaded lighter gray) and a net gain of consumer surplus (shaded darker gray).

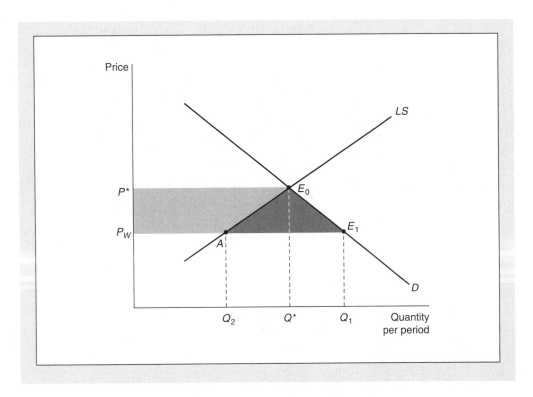

because shoemaker wages are driven up as industry output expands, the decline in output from Q^* to Q_2 as a result of trade will reverse this process, causing shoemaker wages to fall.

Tariff protection and the politics of trade

Shoemakers are unlikely to take wage losses arising from shoe imports lying down. Instead, they will press the government for protection from the flood of imported footwear. Because the loss of producer surplus is experienced by relatively few individuals, whereas consumer gains from trade are spread across many shoe buyers, shoemakers may have considerably greater incentives to organize opposition to imports than consumers would have to organize to keep trade open. The result may be the adoption of protectionist measures.

Historically, the most important type of protection employed has been a tariff: a tax on the imported good. The effects of such a tax are shown in Figure 11.5. Now comparisons begin from the free-trade equilibrium, E_1. Imposition of a per-unit tariff on shoes for domestic buyers of amount t raises the effective price to $P_W + t = P_R$. This price rise causes quantity demanded to fall from Q_1 to Q_3, whereas domestic production expands from Q_2 to Q_4. The total quantity of shoe imports falls from $Q_1 - Q_2$ to $Q_3 - Q_4$. Because each imported pair of shoes is now subject to a tariff, total tariff revenues are given by the area BE_2DC, measured by $t(Q_3 - Q_4)$.

Imposition of the tariff on imported shoes creates a variety of welfare effects. Total consumer surplus is reduced by area $P_RE_2E_1P_W$. Part of this, as we have seen, is transferred into tariff revenues and part is transferred into increased domestic producers' surplus (area P_RBAP_W). The two triangles, BCA and E_2E_1D, represent losses of consumer surplus that are not transferred to

FIGURE 11.5   **Effects of a Tariff**

Imposition of a tariff of amount t raises price to $P_R = P_W + t$. This results in collection of tariff revenue (area BE_2DC), a transfer from consumers to producers (area P_RBAP_W), and two triangles measuring deadweight loss (shaded). A quota has similar effects, though in this case no revenues are collected.

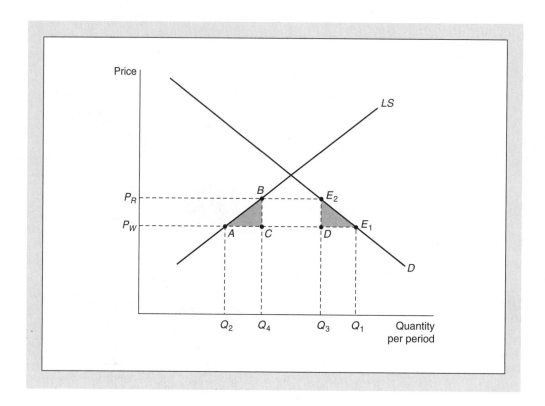

anyone; these are a deadweight loss from the tariff and are similar to the excess burden imposed by any tax. All of these areas can be measured if good empirical estimates of the domestic supply and demand elasticities for imported goods are available, as we now show.

Quantitative estimates of deadweight losses

Estimates of the sizes of the welfare loss triangle in Figure 11.5 can be readily calculated. Because $P_R = (1 + t)P_W$, the proportional change in quantity demanded brought about by this price rise is given by

$$\frac{Q_3 - Q_1}{Q_1} = \frac{P_R - P_W}{P_W} \cdot e_D = te_D \tag{11.21}$$

and the area of triangle E_2E_1D is given by

$$DW_1 = .5(P_R - P_W)(Q_1 - Q_3) = -.5t^2e_DP_WQ_1. \tag{11.22}$$

Similarly, the loss in consumer surplus represented by area BCA is given by

$$DW_2 = .5(P_R - P_W)(Q_4 - Q_2) = .5t^2e_SP_WQ_2. \tag{11.23}$$

Notice that the values of both DW_1 and DW_2 are convex functions of the tariff rate (t) and each depends on the initial value of total revenues. When imports initially represent a large share of the domestic market and e_D and e_S are of similar sizes (in absolute value), this suggests that DW_1 will generally be the larger of the two deadweight losses. These losses may sometimes be large relative to total transfers to producers (area P_RBAP_W), thereby leading to rather large estimates for the "costs" of some tariffs relative to the value of production benefits generated.

Other types of trade protection

Many other types of trade restrictions can be illustrated by adapting the tariff model we have already developed in Figure 11.5. A quota that limits imports to $Q_3 - Q_4$ would have effects that are very similar to those shown in the figure: market price would rise to P_R; a substantial transfer from consumers to domestic producers would occur (area $P_R BAP_W$); and there would be deadweight losses represented by the triangles BCA and $E_2 E_1 D$. With a quota, however, no revenues are collected by the government, so the loss of consumer surplus represented by area $BE_2 DC$ must go elsewhere. It might be captured by owners of import licenses or by foreign producers, depending on how quota rights are assigned. Nonquantitative restrictions such as inspection or testing requirements also impose cost and time delays that can be treated as an "implicit" tariff on imports. Figure 11.5 can easily be adapted to illustrate the effects of these impediments to trade.

 EXAMPLE 11.3

Trade and Tariffs

These various aspects of trade policy can be illustrated with our simplified model of the automobile market. As we have shown previously, with a demand function given by

$$Q_D = 200P^{-1.2} \tag{11.24}$$

and supply by

$$Q_S = 1.3P, \tag{11.25}$$

the domestic market has a long-run equilibrium of

$$P^* = 9.87 \tag{11.26}$$
$$Q^* = 12.8.$$

If automobiles were available at a world price of 9 (thousand dollars), demand would expand to $Q_D = 14.3$, whereas domestic supply would shrink to $Q_S = 11.7$. Imports would amount to 2.6 (million) cars. As shown in Figure 11.4, consumers would gain significantly by the availability of imports (consumer surplus would expand by approximately 11.8 billion dollars), although a significant portion of this gain (10.7 billion) would represent a transfer from domestic producers to consumers.

Effects of a tariff. If pressure from domestic producers leads the government to adopt, say, a $500 tariff, the world price of cars will rise to 9.5 (thousand dollars), quantity demanded will contract (to 13.4), and domestic supply will expand (to 12.4). Imports would contract to 1.0 (million) cars. The welfare effects of these changes can be calculated directly, or can be approximated by the expressions in Equations 11.22 and 11.23. A direct calculation of DW_1 yields[7]

$$DW_1 = .5\,(.5)\,(14.3 - 13.4) = 0.225, \tag{11.27}$$

and for DW_2, we have

$$DW_2 = .5\,(.5)\,(12.4 - 11.7) = 0.175. \tag{11.28}$$

Hence the total deadweight loss from the tariff (0.4 billion) is approximately equal to total tariff revenue (0.5 billion).

(continued)

---

[7]Because the tariff here is approximately $t = .055$, Equation 11.22 yields an approximate value of DW_1 of 0.234, whereas Equation 11.23 shows $DW_2 = 0.159$. The estimated total deadweight loss is approximately 0.4 billion.

EXAMPLE 11.3 CONTINUED

Effects of a quota. An automobile import quota of 1 million cars would have identical effects to that of a $500 tariff. Equilibrium price would rise by $500, and there would be a large transfer from domestic consumers to domestic producers. Deadweight losses of $0.4 billion would also be the same as before. Now, however, there would be no tariff revenues. The $0.5 billion loss in consumer surplus will instead be transferred to whomever can appropriate the rights to import cars. Because the right to import a car is worth $500, it seems likely there will be active interest in acquiring such rights.

Query: What is the total transfer from consumers to producers as a result of the auto tariff or quota in this problem? Who would ultimately receive this transfer?

SUMMARY

In this chapter we have shown how the competitive model can be used to investigate a wide range of economic activities and policies. Some of the general lessons from these applications include:

- The concepts of consumer and producer surplus provide useful ways of analyzing the effects of economic changes on the welfare of market participants. Changes in consumer surplus represent changes in the overall utility consumers receive from consuming a particular good. Changes in long-run producer surplus represent changes in the returns product inputs receive.

- Price controls involve both transfers between producers and consumers and losses of transactions that could benefit both consumers and producers.

- Tax incidence analysis concerns the determination of which economic actor ultimately bears the burden of a tax. In general, this incidence will fall mainly on the actors who exhibit inelastic responses to price changes. Taxes also involve deadweight losses that constitute an "excess" burden in addition to the burden imposed by the actual tax revenues collected.

- Transaction costs can sometimes be modeled as taxes. Both taxes and transaction costs may affect the attributes of transactions depending on the basis on which the costs are incurred.

- Trade restrictions such as tariffs or quotas create transfers between consumers and producers and deadweight losses of economic welfare. The effects of many types of trade restrictions can be modeled as being equivalent to a per-unit tariff.

PROBLEMS

11.1

Suppose that the demand for broccoli is given by

$$Q = 1,000 - 5P,$$

where Q is quantity per year measured in hundreds of bushels and P is price in dollars per hundred bushels. The long-run supply curve for broccoli is given by

$$Q = 4P - 80.$$

a. Show that the equilibrium quantity here is $Q = 400$. At this output, what is the equilibrium price? How much in total is spent on broccoli? What is consumer surplus at this equilibrium? What is producer surplus at this equilibrium?

b. How much in total consumer and producer surplus would be lost if $Q = 300$ instead of $Q = 400$?

c. Show how the allocation between suppliers and demanders of the loss of total consumer and producer surplus described in part (b) depends on the price at which broccoli is sold. How would the loss be shared if $P = 140$? How about if $P = 95$?

d. What would be the total loss of consumer and producer surplus if $Q = 450$ rather than $Q = 400$? Show that the size of this total loss also is independent of the price at which the broccoli is sold.

11.2

The handmade snuffbox industry is composed of 100 identical firms, each having short-run total costs given by

$$STC = 0.5q^2 + 10q + 5$$

and short-run marginal costs by

$$SMC = q + 10,$$

where q is the output of snuffboxes per day.

a. What is the short-run supply curve for each snuffbox maker? What is the short-run supply curve for the market as a whole?

b. Suppose the demand for total snuffbox production is given by

$$Q = 1,100 - 50P.$$

What will be the equilibrium in this marketplace? What will each firm's total short-run profits be?

c. Graph the market equilibrium and compute total short-run producer surplus in this case.

d. Show that the total producer surplus you calculated in part (c) is equal to total industry profits plus industry short-run fixed costs.

11.3

The perfectly competitive videotape copying industry is composed of many firms that can copy five tapes per day at an average cost of $10 per tape. Each firm must also pay a royalty to film studios, and the per-film royalty rate (r) is an increasing function of total industry output (Q) given by

$$r = .002Q.$$

Demand is given by

$$Q = 1,050 - 50P.$$

a. Assuming the industry is in long-run equilibrium, what will be the equilibrium price and quantity of copied tapes? How many tape firms will there be? What will the per-film royalty rate be?

b. Suppose demand for copied tapes increases to

$$Q = 1,600 - 50P.$$

Now, what is the long-run equilibrium price and quantity for copied tapes? How many tape firms are there? What is the per-film royalty rate?

c. Graph these long-run equilibria in the tape market and calculate the increase in producer surplus between the situations described in parts (a) and (b).

d. Show that the increase in producer surplus is precisely equal to the increase in royalties paid as Q expands incrementally from its level in part (b) to its level in part (c).

11.4

Consider again the market for broccoli described in Problem 11.1.

a. Suppose demand for broccoli shifted outward to

$$Q = 1{,}270 - 5P.$$

What would be the new equilibrium price and quantity in this market?

b. What would be the new levels of consumer and producer surplus in this market?

c. Suppose the government had prevented the price of broccoli from rising from its equilibrium level of Problem 11.1. Describe how the consumer and producer surplus measures described in part (b) would be reallocated or lost entirely.

11.5

Returning once more to the broccoli market described in Problem 11.1, suppose the government instituted a $45 per-hundred-bushel tax on broccoli.

a. How would this tax affect equilibrium in the broccoli market?

b. How would this tax burden be shared between buyers and sellers of broccoli?

c. What is the excess burden of this tax?

d. Suppose now the demand for broccoli shifted to

$$Q = 2{,}200 - 15P.$$

Answer parts (a) and (b) for this alternative demand curve.

e. Suppose now that the broccoli market is characterized by the original demand curve described in Problem 11.1, but the supply curve is

$$Q = 10P - 800.$$

Answer parts (a) and (b) for this case.

f. What do you conclude by comparing these three cases of tax incidence we have examined for the broccoli market?

11.6

Suppose the government imposed a $3 tax on snuffboxes in the industry described in Problem 11.2.

a. How would this tax change the market equilibrium?

b. How would the burden of this tax be shared between snuffbox buyers and sellers?

c. Calculate the total loss of producer surplus as a result of the taxation of snuffboxes. Show that this loss equals the change in total short-run profits in the snuffbox industry. Why don't fixed costs enter into this computation of the change in short-run producer surplus?

11.7

Suppose that the government institutes a $5.50 per-film tax on the film copying industry described in Problem 11.3.

a. Assuming that the demand for copied films is that given in part (a) of Problem 11.3, how will this tax affect the market equilibrium?

b. How will the burden of this tax be allocated between consumers and producers? What will be the loss of consumer and producer surplus?

c. Show that the loss of producer surplus as a result of this tax is borne completely by the film studios. Explain your result intuitively.

11.8

The domestic demand for portable radios is given by

$$Q = 5,000 - 100P,$$

where price (P) is measured in dollars and quantity (Q) is measured in thousands of radios per year. The domestic supply curve for radios is given by

$$Q = 150P.$$

a. What is the domestic equilibrium in the portable radio market?

b. Suppose portable radios can be imported at a world price of $10 per radio. If trade were unencumbered, what would the new market equilibrium be? How many portable radios would be imported?

c. If domestic portable radio producers succeeded in getting a $5 tariff implemented, how would this change the market equilibrium? How much would be collected in tariff revenues? How much consumer surplus would be transferred to domestic producers? What would the deadweight loss from the tariff be?

d. How would your results from part (c) be changed if the government reached an agreement with foreign suppliers to "voluntarily" limit the portable radios they export to 1,250,000 per year? Explain how this differs from the case of a tariff.

11.9

In Example 11.3 we showed that the deadweight loss from a tariff of $500 on imported autos was approximately equal to the amount of tariff revenues collected. How would the marginal excess burden from increasing the tariff to $600 compare with the marginal tariff revenues collected? Explain your result intuitively.

11.10

In our analysis of tariffs we assumed that the country in question faced a perfectly elastic supply curve for imports. Now assume this country faces a positively sloped supply curve for imported goods.

a. Show graphically how the level of imports will be determined.

b. Use your graph from part (a) to demonstrate the effects of a tariff in this market.

c. Carefully identify the sources of the various changes in consumer and producer surplus that are brought about by the tariff in part (b).

d. Show how the deadweight losses brought about by the tariff in this case will depend on the elasticity of demand and the elasticities of supply of domestic and imported goods.

SUGGESTIONS FOR FURTHER READING

Arnott, R. "Time for Revision on Rent Control?" *Journal of Economic Perspectives* (Winter 1995): 99–120.
Provides an assessment of actual "soft" rent-control policies and provides a rationale for them.

Bosworth, B., and G. Burtless. "Effective Tax Reform in Labor Supply, Investments, and Saving." *Journal of Economic Perspectives* (Winter 1992): 3–75.
Illustrates how the impact of taxes can be modeled in a variety of markets.

deMelo, J., and D. G. Tarr. "The Welfare Costs of U.S. Quotas in Textiles, Steel, and Autos." *Review of Economics and Statistics* (August 1990): 489–97.
A nice study of the quota question in a general equilibrium context. Finds that the quotas studied have the same quantitative effects as a tariff rate of about 20 percent.

Salanie, B. *The Economics of Taxation.* Cambridge, MA: MIT Press, 2003.
This provides a compact study of many issues in taxation. Describes a few simple models of incidence and develops some general equilibrium models of taxation.

Chapter 12

GENERAL EQUILIBRIUM AND WELFARE

The partial equilibrium models of perfect competition that were introduced in Chapters 10 and 11 are clearly inadequate for describing all of the effects that occur when changes in one market have repercussions in other markets. They are therefore also inadequate for making very general welfare statements about how well market economies perform. Instead, what is needed is an economic model that permits us to view many markets simultaneously. In this chapter we will develop a very simple version of such a model and use it to explore a variety of welfare questions. Although our use of this model does permit some progress to be made, it should be stated at the outset that general equilibrium analysis is one of the most complex topics in microeconomics, and we will only scratch its surface. The references to this chapter suggest some ways in which the theory might be pursued further and the Extensions to the chapter show how general equilibrium models can be applied to the real world.

Perfectly competitive price system

The model we will develop in this chapter is primarily an elaboration of the supply-demand mechanism we presented in Chapter 10. Here we will assume that all markets are of the type described in that chapter and refer to such a set of markets as a *perfectly competitive price system.* The assumption is that there is some large number of homogeneous goods in this simple economy. Included in this list of goods are not only consumption items but also factors of production. Each of these goods has an *equilibrium price,* established by the action of supply and demand.[1] At this set of prices, every market is cleared in the sense that suppliers are willing to supply that quantity which is demanded and consumers will demand that quantity which is supplied. We also assume that there are no transaction or transportation charges and that both individuals and firms have perfect knowledge of prevailing market prices.

The law of one price

Because of the zero transactions cost and perfect information assumptions, each good obeys the law of one price: A homogeneous good trades at the same price no matter who buys it or

---

[1]One aspect of this market interaction should be made clear from the outset. The perfectly competitive market determines only relative (not absolute) prices. In this chapter, we speak primarily of relative prices. It makes no difference whether the prices of apples and oranges are $.10 and $.20, respectively, or $10 and $20. The important point in either case is that two apples can be exchanged for one orange in the market.

which firm sells it. If one good traded at two different prices, demanders would rush to buy the good where it was cheaper, and firms would try to sell all their output where the good was more expensive. These actions in themselves would tend to equalize the price of the good. In the perfectly competitive market, then, each good must have only one price. This is why we may speak unambiguously of *the* price of a good.

Assumptions about perfect competition

The perfectly competitive model assumes that people and firms react to prices in specific ways:

1. There are assumed to be a large number of people buying any one good. Each person takes all prices as given and adjusts his or her behavior to *maximize utility,* given the prices and his or her budget constraint. People may also be suppliers of productive services (for example, labor), and in such decisions they also regard prices as given.[2]

2. There are assumed to be large number of firms producing each good, and each firm produces only a small share of the output of any one good. In making input and output choices, firms are assumed to operate to *maximize profits.* The firms treat all prices as given when making these profit-maximizing decisions.

These various assumptions should be familiar because we have been making them throughout this book. Our purpose here is to show how an entire economic system operates when all markets work in this way.

A simple graphical model of general equilibrium

We begin our analysis with a very simple graphical model of general equilibrium involving only two goods, which we will call *x* and *y*. This model will prove very useful because it incorporates many of the features of far more complex general equilibrium representations of the economy. We will make extensive use of the model any time a multimarket analysis is needed.

General equilibrium demand

Ultimately, demand patterns in an economy are determined by individuals' preferences. For our simple model we will assume that all individuals have identical preferences, which can be represented by an indifference curve map[3] defined over quantities of the two goods, *x* and *y*. The benefit of this approach for our purposes is that this indifference curve map (which is identical to the ones used in Chapters 3–6) shows how individuals rank consumption bundles containing both goods. These rankings are precisely what we meant by "demand" in a general equilibrium context. Of course, we cannot actually illustrate which bundles of commodities will be chosen until we know the budget constraints that demanders face. Because incomes are generated as individuals supply labor, capital, and other resources to the production process, we must delay this illustration until we have examined the forces of production and supply in our model.

General equilibrium supply

Developing a notion of general equilibrium supply in this two-good model is a somewhat more complex process than describing the demand side of the market because we have not thus far illustrated production and supply of two goods simultaneously. Our approach is to use the familiar production possibility curve (see Chapter 1) for this purpose. By de-

---

[2]Because one price represents the wage rate, the relevant budget constraint is in reality a time constraint. For a discussion, see Chapter 16.

[3]There are some technical problems in using a single indifference curve map to represent the preferences of an entire community of individuals. In this case the marginal rate of substitution (that is, the slope of the community indifference curve) will depend on how the available goods are distributed among individuals: The increase in total *y* required to compensate for a one-unit reduction in *x* will depend on which specific individual(s) the *x* is taken from. Although we will not discuss this issue in detail here, it has been widely examined in the international trade literature.

tailing the way in which this curve is constructed, we can also use this construction to examine the ways in which markets for outputs and inputs are related.

Edgeworth box diagram

Construction of the production possibility curve for two outputs (x and y) begins with the assumption that there are fixed amounts of capital and labor inputs that must be allocated to the production of the two goods. The possible allocations of these inputs can be illustrated with an Edgeworth box diagram with dimensions given by the total amounts of capital and labor available.

In Figure 12.1 the length of the box represents total labor-hours and the height of the box represents total capital-hours. The lower left-hand corner of the box represents the "origin" for measuring capital and labor devoted to production of good x. The upper right-hand corner of the box represents the origin for resources devoted to y. Using these conventions, any point in the box can be regarded as a fully employed allocation of the available resources between goods x and y. Point A, for example, represents an allocation in which the indicated number of labor-hours are devoted to x production together with a specified number of hours of capital. Production of good y uses whatever labor and capital are "left over." Point A in Figure 12.1, for example, also shows the exact amount of labor and capital used in the production of good y. Any other point in the box has a similar interpretation. Thus, the Edgeworth box shows every possible way the existing capital and labor might be used to produce x and y.

FIGURE 12.1   **Construction of an Edgeworth Box Diagram for Production**

The dimensions of this diagram are given by the total quantities of labor and capital available. Quantities of these resources devoted to x production are measured from origin O_x; quantities devoted to y are measured from O_y. Any point in the box represents a fully employed allocation of the available resources to the two goods.

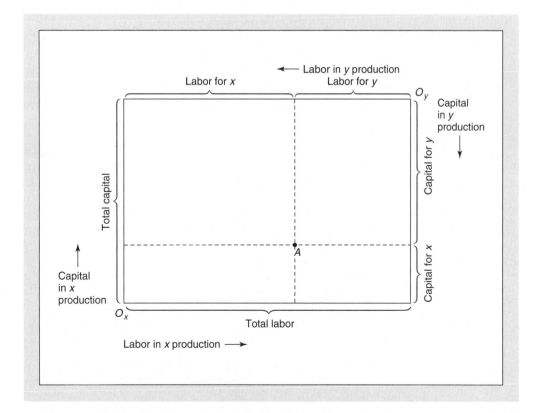

FIGURE 12.2   Edgeworth Box Diagram of Efficiency in Production

This diagram adds production isoquants for *x* and *y* to Figure 12.1. It then shows technically efficient ways to allocate the fixed amounts of *k* and *l* between the production of the two outputs. The line joining O_x and O_y is the locus of these efficient points. Along this line the *RTS* (of *l* for *k*) in the production of good *x* is equal to the *RTS* in the production of *y*.

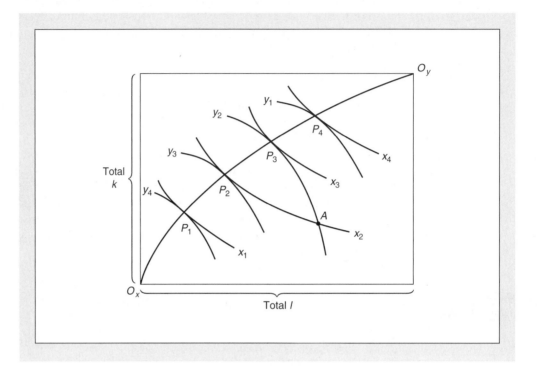

Efficient allocations

Many of the allocations shown in Figure 12.1 are technically inefficient in that it is possible to produce both more *x* and more *y* by shifting capital and labor around a bit. In our model we assume that competitive markets will not exhibit such inefficient input choices (for reasons we will explore in more detail later in the chapter). Hence we wish to discover the efficient allocations in Figure 12.1, because these illustrate the actual production outcomes in this model. To do so, we introduce isoquant maps for good *x* (using O_x as the origin) and good *y* (using O_y as the origin), as shown in Figure 12.2. In this figure it is clear that the arbitrarily chosen allocation *A* is inefficient. By reallocating capital and labor one can produce both more *x* than x_2 and more *y* than y_2.

The efficient allocations in Figure 12.2 are those such as P_1, P_2, P_3, and P_4, where the isoquants are tangent to one another. At any other points in the box diagram, the two goods' isoquants will intersect, and we can show inefficiency as we did for point *A*. At the points of tangency, however, this kind of unambiguous improvement cannot be made. In going from P_2 to P_3, for example, more *x* is being produced, but at the cost of less *y* being produced, so P_3 is not "more efficient" than P_2—both of the points are efficient. Tangency of the isoquants for good *x* and good *y* implies that their slopes are equal. That is, the *RTS* of capital for labor is equal in *x* and *y* production. Later we will show how competitive input markets will lead firms to make such efficient input choices.

The curve joining O_x and O_y that includes all of these points of tangency therefore shows all of the efficient allocations of capital and labor. Points off this curve are inefficient in that unambiguous increases in output can be obtained by reshuffling inputs be-

FIGURE 12.3   **Production Possibility Frontier**

The production possibility frontier shows the alternative combinations of *x* and *y* that can be efficiently produced by a firm with fixed resources. The curve can be derived from Figure 12.2 by varying inputs between the production of *x* and *y* while maintaining the conditions for efficiency. The negative of the slope of the production possibility curve is called the rate of product transformation (*RPT*).

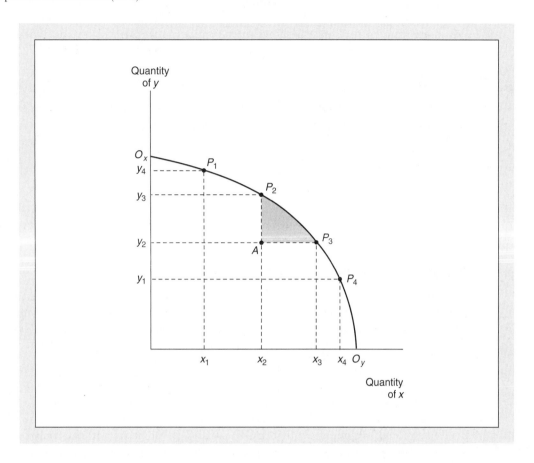

tween the two goods. Points in $O_x O_y$ are all efficient allocations, however, because more *x* can be produced only by cutting back on *y* production and vice versa.

Production possibility frontier

The efficiency locus in Figure 12.2 shows the maximum output of *y* that can be produced for any preassigned output of *x*. We can use this information to construct a *production possibility frontier*, which shows the alternative outputs of *x* and *y* that can be produced with the fixed capital and labor inputs. In Figure 12.3 the $O_x O_y$ locus has been taken from Figure 12.2 and transferred onto a graph with *x* and *y* outputs on the axes. At O_x, for example, no resources are devoted to *x* production; consequently, *y* output is as large as is possible with the existing resources. Similarly, at O_y, the output of *x* is as large as possible. The other points on the production possibility frontier (say, P_1, P_2, P_3, and P_4) are derived from the efficiency locus in an identical way. Hence we have derived the following definition:

DEFINITION

Production possibility frontier. The *production possibility frontier* shows those alternative combinations of two outputs that can be produced with fixed quantities of inputs if those inputs are employed efficiently.

Rate of product transformation

The slope of the production possibility frontier shows how x output can be substituted for y output when total resources are held constant. For example, for points near O_x on the production possibility frontier, the slope is a small negative number, say, $-\frac{1}{4}$, implying that by reducing y output by 1 unit, x output could be increased by 4. Near O_y, on the other hand, the slope is a large negative number, say, -5, implying that y output must be reduced by 5 units to permit the production of one more x. The slope of the production possibility frontier, then, clearly shows the possibilities that exist for trading y for x in production. The negative of this slope is called the *rate of product transformation* (RPT):

Rate of product transformation. The *rate of product transformation (RPT)* between two outputs is the negative of the slope of the production possibility frontier for those outputs. Mathematically,

$$RPT \text{ (of } x \text{ for } y) = -\text{slope of production possibility frontier}$$

$$= -\frac{dy}{dx} \text{ (along } O_xO_y\text{).} \tag{12.1}$$

The RPT records how x can be technically traded for y while continuing to keep the available productive inputs efficiently employed.

Shape of the production possibility frontier

The production possibility frontier illustrated in Figure 12.3 exhibits an increasing RPT. For output levels near O_x, relatively little y must be sacrificed to obtain one more x ($-dy/dx$ is small). Near O_y, on the other hand, additional x may be obtained only by substantial reductions in y output ($-dy/dx$ is large). In this section we will show why this concave shape might be expected to characterize most production situations.

A first step in that analysis is to recognize that RPT is equal to the ratio of the marginal cost of x (MC_x) to the marginal cost of y (MC_y). Intuitively, this result is obvious. Suppose, for example, that x and y are produced only with labor. If it takes two labor-hours to produce one more x, we might say that MC_x is equal to 2. Similarly, if it takes only one labor-hour to produce an extra y, MC_y is equal to 1. But in this situation it is clear that the RPT is 2: Two y must be forgone to provide enough labor so that x may be increased by 1 unit. Hence, the RPT is indeed equal to the ratio of the marginal costs of the two goods.

More formally, suppose that the costs (say, in terms of the "disutility" experienced by factor suppliers) of any output combination are denoted by $C(x, y)$. Along the production possibility frontier, $C(x, y)$ will be constant because the inputs are in fixed supply. Hence we can write the total differential of the cost function as

$$dC = \frac{\partial C}{\partial x} \cdot dx + \frac{\partial C}{\partial y} \cdot dy = 0 \tag{12.2}$$

for changes in x and y along the production possibility frontier. Manipulating Equation 12.2 yields

$$RPT = -\frac{dy}{dx} \text{ (along } O_xO_y\text{)} = \frac{\partial C/\partial x}{\partial C/\partial y} = \frac{MC_x}{MC_y}, \tag{12.3}$$

which was precisely what we wished to show: The RPT is a measure of the relative marginal costs of the two goods.

To demonstrate reasons why the RPT might be expected to rise for clockwise movements along the production possibility frontier, we can proceed by showing why the ratio of MC_x to MC_y should rise as x output expands and y output contracts. We first present two relatively simple arguments that apply only to special cases; then we turn to a more sophisticated general argument.

Diminishing returns

The most common rationale offered for the concave shape of the production possibility frontier is the assumption that both goods are produced under conditions of diminishing returns. Hence increasing the output of good x will raise its marginal cost, whereas decreasing the output of y will reduce its marginal cost. Equation 12.3 then shows that the *RPT* will increase for movements along the production possibility frontier from O_x to O_y. A problem with this explanation, of course, is that it applies only to cases in which both goods exhibit diminishing returns to scale, and that assumption is at variance with the theoretical reasons for preferring the assumption of constant or even increasing returns to scale we have mentioned elsewhere in this book.

Specialized inputs

If some inputs were "more suited" for x production than for y production (and vice versa), the concave shape of the production frontier also could be explained. In that case, increases in x output would require drawing progressively less suitable inputs into the production of that good. Marginal costs of x therefore would rise. Marginal costs for y, on the other hand, would fall, as smaller output levels for y would permit the use of only those inputs most suited for y production. Such an argument might apply, for example, to a farmer with a variety of types of land under cultivation in different crops. In trying to increase the production of any one crop, the farmer would be forced to grow it on increasingly unsuitable parcels of land. Although this type of specialized input assumption has considerable importance in explaining a variety of real-world phenomena, it is nonetheless at variance with our general assumption of homogeneous factors of production. It cannot serve as a fundamental explanation for concavity.

Differing factor intensities

Even if inputs are homogeneous and production functions exhibit constant returns to scale, the production possibility frontier will be concave if goods x and y use inputs in different proportions.[4] In the production box diagram of Figure 12.2, for example, good x is *capital intensive* relative to good y. That is, at every point along the O_xO_y contract curve, the ratio of k to l in x production exceeds the ratio of k to l in y production: The bowed curve O_xO_y is always above the main diagonal of the Edgeworth box. If, on the other hand, good y had been relatively capital intensive, the O_xO_y contract curve would have been bowed downward below the diagonal. Although a formal proof that unequal factor intensities result in a concave production possibility frontier will not be presented here, it is possible to suggest intuitively why that occurs. Consider any two points on the frontier O_xO_y in Figure 12.3—say, P_1 (with coordinates x_1, y_4) and P_3 (with coordinates x_3, y_2). One way of producing an output combination "between" P_1 and P_3 would be to produce the combination

$$\frac{x_1 + x_3}{2}, \quad \frac{y_4 + y_2}{2}.$$

Because of the constant returns-to-scale assumption, that combination would be feasible and would fully utilize both factors of production. The combination would lie at the midpoint of a straight-line chord joining points P_1 and P_3. Although such a point is feasible, it is not efficient, as can be seen by examining points P_1 and P_3 in the box diagram of Figure 12.2. Because of the bowed nature of the contract curve, production at a point midway between P_1 and P_3 would be off the contract curve: Producing at a point such as P_2 would provide more of both goods. The production possibility frontier in Figure 12.3

[4]If, in addition to homogeneous factors and constant returns to scale, each good also used k and l in the same proportions under optimal allocations, the production possibility frontier would be a straight line.

must therefore "bulge out" beyond the straight line P_1P_3. Because such a proof could be constructed for any two points on O_xO_y, we have shown that the frontier is concave; that is, the *RPT* increases as the output of good X increases. When production is reallocated in a northeast direction along the O_xO_y contract curve (in Figure 12.3), the capital-labor ratio decreases in the production of *both* x and y. Because good x is capital intensive, this change raises MC_x. On the other hand, because good y is labor intensive, MC_y falls. Hence the relative marginal cost of x (as represented by the *RPT*) rises.

Opportunity cost and supply

The production possibility curve therefore demonstrates that there are many possible efficient combinations of the two goods and that producing more of one good necessitates cutting back on the production of some other good. This is precisely what economists mean by the term *opportunity cost*. The cost of producing more x can be most readily measured by the reduction in y output that this entails. The cost of one more unit of x is therefore best measured as the *RPT* (of x for y) at the prevailing point on the production possibility frontier. The fact that this cost increases as more x is produced represents the formulation of supply in a general equilibrium context.

 EXAMPLE 12.1

Concavity of the Production Possibility Frontier

In this example we look at two characteristics of production functions that may cause the production possibility frontier to be concave.

Diminishing returns. Suppose that the production of both x and y depends only on labor input and that the production functions for each of these goods are

$$x = f(l_x) = l_x^{0.5}$$
$$y = f(l_y) = l_y^{0.5}. \qquad (12.4)$$

Hence, production of each of these goods exhibits diminishing returns to scale. If total labor supply is limited by

$$l_x + l_y = 100, \qquad (12.5)$$

then simple substitution shows that the production possibility frontier is given by

$$x^2 + y^2 = 100 \text{ for } x, y \geq 0. \qquad (12.6)$$

In this case then, the frontier is a quarter-circle and is concave. The *RPT* can be calculated by taking the total differential of the production possibility frontier:

$$2xdx + 2ydy = 0 \text{ or } RPT = \frac{-dy}{dx} = \frac{-(-2x)}{2y} = \frac{x}{y}, \qquad (12.7)$$

and this slope increases as x output increases. A numerical illustration of concavity starts by noting that the points $(10, 0)$ and $(0, 10)$ both lie on the frontier. A straight line joining these two points would also include the point $(5, 5)$, but that point lies below the frontier. If equal amounts of labor are devoted to both goods, production is $x = y = \sqrt{50}$, which yields more of both goods than the midpoint.

Factor intensity. To show how differing factor intensities yields a concave production possibility frontier, suppose that the two goods are produced under constant returns to scale, but with different Cobb-Douglas production functions:

$$x = f(k, l) = k_x^{0.5}l_x^{0.5}$$
$$y = g(k, l) = k_y^{0.25}l_y^{0.75}. \qquad (12.8)$$

Suppose also that total capital and labor are constrained by

$$k_x + k_y = 100 \qquad l_x + l_y = 100. \qquad (12.9)$$

It is easy to show that

$$RTS_x = \frac{k_x}{l_x} = \kappa_x \qquad RTS_y = \frac{3k_y}{l_y} = 3\kappa_y, \qquad (12.10)$$

where $\kappa_i = k_i/l_i$. Being located on the production possibility frontier requires $RTS_x = RTS_y$ or $\kappa_x = 3\kappa_y$. That is, no matter how total resources are allocated to production, being on the production possibility frontier requires that x be the capital-intensive good (because, in some sense, capital is more productive in x production than in y production). The capital-labor ratios in the production of the two goods are also constrained by the available resources:

$$\frac{k_x + k_y}{l_x + l_y} = \frac{k_x}{l_x + l_y} + \frac{k_y}{l_x + l_y} = \alpha\kappa_x + (1-\alpha)\kappa_y = \frac{100}{100} = 1, \quad (12.11)$$

where $\alpha = l_x/(l_x + l_y)$—that is, α is the share of total labor devoted to x production. Using the condition that $\kappa_x = 3\kappa_y$ we can find the input ratios of the two goods in terms of the overall allocation of labor:

$$\kappa_y = \frac{1}{1 + 2\alpha} \qquad \kappa_x = \frac{3}{1 + 2\alpha}, \qquad (12.12)$$

and now we are in a position to phrase the production possibility frontier in terms of the share of labor devoted to x production:

$$x = \kappa_x^{0.5}l_x = \kappa_x^{0.5}\alpha(100) = 100\alpha\left(\frac{3}{1 + 2\alpha}\right)^{0.5}$$

$$y = \kappa_y^{0.25}l_y = \kappa_y^{0.25}(1-\alpha)(100) = 100(1-\alpha)\left(\frac{1}{1 + 2\alpha}\right)^{0.25}. \qquad (12.13)$$

We could push this algebra even further to eliminate α from these two equations to get an explicit functional form for the production possibility frontier that involves only x and y, but we can show concavity with what we already have. First, notice that if $\alpha = 0$ (x production gets no labor or capital inputs), then we have $x = 0$, $y = 100$. With $\alpha = 1$, we get $x = 100$, $y = 0$. Hence, a linear production possibility frontier would include the point (50, 50). But if $\alpha = 0.39$, say,

$$x = 100\alpha\left(\frac{3}{1 + 2\alpha}\right)^{0.5} = 39\left(\frac{3}{1.78}\right)^{0.5} = 50.6$$

$$y = 100(1-\alpha)\left(\frac{1}{1 + 2\alpha}\right)^{0.25} = 61\left(\frac{1}{1.78}\right)^{0.25} = 52.8, \qquad (12.14)$$

which shows that the actual frontier is bowed outward beyond a linear frontier. It is worth repeating that both of the goods in this example are produced under constant returns to scale and the two inputs are fully homogeneous. It is only the differing input intensities involved in the production of the two goods that yields the concave production possibility frontier.

Query: How would an increase in the total amount of labor available shift the production possibility frontiers in these examples?

Determination of equilibrium prices

Given these notions of demand and supply in our simple two-good economy, we can now illustrate how equilibrium prices are determined. Figure 12.4 shows the production possibility frontier for the economy (*PP*), and the set of indifference curves represents individuals' preferences for these goods. First, consider the price ratio p_x/p_y. At this price ratio, firms will choose to produce the output combination x_1, y_1. Profit-maximizing firms will choose the more profitable point on *PP*. At x_1, y_1 the ratio of the two goods' prices (p_x/p_y) is equal to the ratio of the goods' marginal costs (the *RPT*), so profits are maximized there. On the other hand, given this budget constraint (line *C*)[5] individuals will demand x_1', y_1'. Consequently, with these prices, there is an excess demand for good x (individuals demand more than is being produced), whereas there is an excess supply of good y. The workings of the marketplace will cause p_x to rise and p_y to fall. The price ratio p_x/p_y will rise; the price line will take on a steeper slope. Firms will respond to these price changes by moving clockwise along the production possibility frontier; that is, they will increase their production of good x and decrease their production of good y. Similarly,

---

FIGURE 12.4   **Determination of Equilibrium Prices**

With a price ratio given by p_x/p_y, firms will produce x_1, y_1; society's budget constraint will be given by line *C*. With this budget constraint, individuals demand x_1' and y_1'; that is, there is an excess demand for good x, and an excess supply of good y. The workings of the market will move these prices toward their equilibrium levels p_x^*, p_y^*. At those prices, society's budget constraint will be given by line C^*, and supply and demand will be in equilibrium. The combination x^*, y^* of goods will be chosen.

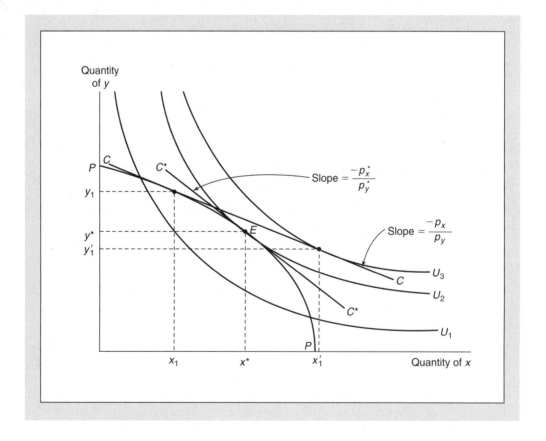

---

[5]It is important to recognize why the budget constraint has this location. Because p_x and p_y are given, the value of total production is $p_x \cdot x_1 + p_y \cdot y_1$. This is the value of "GDP" in the simple economy pictured in Figure 12.4. It is also, therefore, the total income accruing to people in society. Society's budget constraint therefore passes through x_1, y_1 and has a slope of $-p_x/p_y$. This is precisely the budget constraint labeled *C* in the figure.

individuals will respond to the changing prices by substituting y for x in their consumption choices. These actions of both firms and individuals, then, serve to eliminate the excess demand for x and the excess supply of y as market prices change.

Equilibrium is reached at x^*, y^* with a price ratio of p_x^*/p_y^*. With this price ratio,[6] supply and demand are equilibrated for both good x and good y. Given p_x and p_y, firms will produce x^* and y^* in maximizing their profits. Similarly, with a budget constraint given by C^*, individuals will demand x^* and y^*. The operation of the price system has cleared the markets for both x and y simultaneously. This figure therefore provides a "general equilibrium" view of the supply-demand process for two markets working together. For this reason we will make considerable use of this figure in our subsequent analysis.

Comparative statics analysis

As in our partial equilibrium analysis, the equilibrium price ratio p_x^*/p_y^* illustrated in Figure 12.4 will tend to persist until either preferences or production technologies change. This competitively determined price ratio reflects these two basic economic forces. If preferences were to shift, say, toward good x, p_x/p_y would rise, and a new equilibrium would be established by a clockwise move along the production possibility curve. More x and less y would be produced to meet these changed preferences. Similarly, technical progress in

---

FIGURE 12.5   **Effects of Technical Progress in *X* Production**

Technical advances that lower marginal costs of x production will shift the production possibility frontier. This will generally create income and substitution effects that cause the quantity of x produced to increase (assuming x is a normal good). Effects on the production of y are ambiguous because income and substitution effects work in opposite directions.

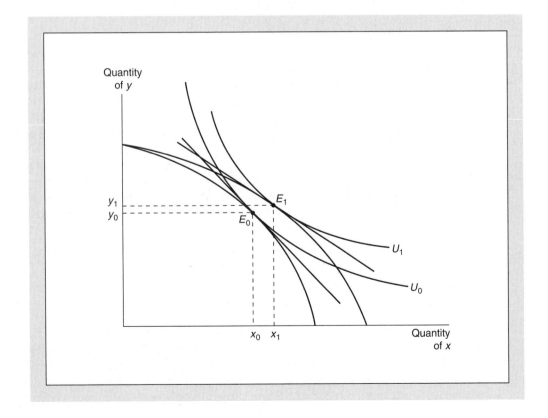

---

[6]Notice again that competitive markets determine only equilibrium relative prices. Determination of the absolute price level requires the introduction of money into this barter model.

the production of good x would shift the production possibility curve outward, as illustrated in Figure 12.5. This would tend to lower the relative price of x and increase the quantity of x consumed (assuming x is a normal good). In the figure the quantity of y consumed also increases as a result of the income effect arising from the technical advance; but a slightly different drawing of the figure could have reversed that result if the substitution effect had been dominant. Example 12.2 looks at a few such effects.

 EXAMPLE 12.2

Comparative Statics in a General Equilibrium Model

To explore how general equilibrium models work, let's start with a simple example based on the production possibility frontier in Example 12.1. In that example we assumed that production of both goods was characterized by decreasing returns $x = l_x^{0.5}$ $y = l_y^{0.5}$ and that total labor available was given by $l_x + l_y = 100$. The resulting production possibility frontier was given by $x^2 + y^2 = 100$ and $RPT = x/y$. To complete this model we assume that the typical individual's utility function is given by $U(x, y) = x^{0.5} y^{0.5}$, so the demand functions for the two goods are

$$x = x(p_x, p_y, I) = 0.5I/p_x$$
$$y = y(p_x, p_y, I) = 0.5I/p_y. \qquad (12.15)$$

Base case equilibrium. Profit maximization by firms requires that $p_x/p_y = MC_x/MC_y = RPT = x/y$, and utility-maximizing demand requires that $p_x/p_y = y/x$. So equilibrium requires that $x/y = y/x$, or $x = y$. Inserting this result into the equation for the production possibility frontier shows that

$$x^* = y^* = \sqrt{50} = 7.07 \text{ and } p_x/p_y = 1. \qquad (12.16)$$

This is the equilibrium for our base case with this model.

The budget constraint. The budget constraint that faces individuals is not especially transparent in this illustration, so it may be useful to discuss it explicitly. In order to bring some degree of absolute pricing into the model, let's consider all prices in terms of the wage rate, w. Because total labor supply is 100, total labor income is $100w$. But, because of the diminishing returns assumed for production, each firm also earns profits. For firm x, say, the total-cost function is $C(w, x) = wl_x = wx^2$, so $p_x = MC_x = 2wx = 2w\sqrt{50}$. The profits for firm x are therefore $\pi_x = (p_x - AC_x)x = (p_x - wx)x = wx^2 = 50w$. A similar computation shows that profits for firm y are also given by $50w$. Because general equilibrium models must obey the national income identity, we assume that consumers are also shareholders in the two firms and treat these profits also as part of their spendable incomes. Hence, total consumer income is

$$\text{Total Income} = \text{Labor Income} + \text{Profits}$$
$$= 100w + 2(50w) = 200w. \qquad (12.17)$$

This income will just permit consumers to spend $100w$ on each good by buying $\sqrt{50}$ units at a price of $2w\sqrt{50}$. So, the model is internally consistent.

A shift in supply. There are only two ways in which this base case equilibrium can be disturbed: (1) By changes in "supply"—that is, by changes in the underlying technology of this economy; or (2) by changes in "demand"—that is, by changes in preferences. Let's first consider changes in technology. Suppose that there is technical improvement in x production so that the production function is $x = 2l_x^{0.5}$. Now the production possibility frontier is given by

$$\frac{x^2}{4} + y^2 = 100 \text{ and } RPT = x/4y. \text{ Proceeding as before to find the equilibrium in this model:}$$

$$(\text{supply}) \ p_x/p_y = x/4y \text{ and } (\text{demand}) \ p_x/p_y = y/x, \quad (12.18)$$

so $x^2 = 4y^2$ and the equilibrium is

$$x^* = 2\sqrt{50}\, y^* = \sqrt{50}, \; p_x/p_y = 1/2. \qquad (12.19)$$

Technical improvements in x production have caused its relative price to fall and consumption of this good to rise. As in many examples with Cobb-Douglas utility, the income and substitution effects of this price decline on y demand are precisely offsetting. Technical improvements clearly make consumers better off, however. Whereas previously utility was given by $U(x, y) = x^{0.5}\, y^{0.5} = \sqrt{50} = 7.07$, now it has increased to $U(x, y) = x^{0.5}\, y^{0.5} = (2\sqrt{50})^{0.5}\,(\sqrt{50})^{0.5} = \sqrt{2} \cdot \sqrt{50} = 10$. Technical change has increased consumer welfare substantially.

A shift in demand. If consumer preferences were to switch to favor good y as $U(x, y) = x^{0.1}\, y^{0.9}$, demand functions would be given by $x = 0.1I/p_x$ and $y = 0.9I/p_y$, and demand equilibrium would require $p_x/p_y = y/9x$. Returning to the original production possibility frontier to arrive at an overall equilibrium, we have

$$\text{(supply) } p_x/p_y = x/y \text{ and (demand) } p_x/p_y = y/9x, \quad (12.20)$$

so $9x^2 = y^2$ and the equilibrium is given by

$$x^* = \sqrt{10}\; y^* = 3\sqrt{10} \text{ and } p_x/p_y = 1/3. \qquad (12.21)$$

Hence, the decline in demand for x has significantly reduced its relative price. Notice that in this case, however, we cannot make a welfare comparison to the previous cases because the utility function has changed.

Query: What are the budget constraints in these two alternative scenarios? How is income distributed between wages and profits in each case? Explain the differences intuitively.

General equilibrium modeling and factor prices

This very simple general equilibrium model therefore reinforces Marshall's observations about the importance of both supply and demand forces in the price determination process. By providing an explicit connection between the markets for all goods, the general equilibrium model makes it possible to examine more complex questions about market relationships than is possible by looking at only one market at a time. General equilibrium modeling also permits an examination of the connections between goods and factor markets; we can illustrate that with an important historical case.

The corn laws debate

High tariffs on grain imports were imposed by the British government following the Napoleonic wars. Debate over the effects of these "corn laws" dominated the analytical efforts of economists between the years 1829 and 1845. A principal focus of the debate concerned the effect that elimination of the tariffs would have on factor prices, a question that continues to have relevance today, as we will see.

The production possibility frontier in Figure 12.6 shows those combinations of grain (x) and manufactured goods (y) that could be produced by British factors of production. Assuming (somewhat contrary to actuality) that the corn laws completely prevented trade, market equilibrium would be at E with the domestic price ratio given by p_x^*/p_y^*. Removal of the tariffs would reduce this price ratio to p_x'/p_y'. Given that new ratio, Britain would produce combination A and consume combination B. Grain imports would amount to

FIGURE 12.6   **Analysis of the Corn Laws Debate**

Reduction of tariff barriers on grain would cause production to be reallocated from point E to point A. Consumption would be reallocated from E to B. If grain production is relatively capital intensive, the relative price of capital would fall as a result of these reallocations.

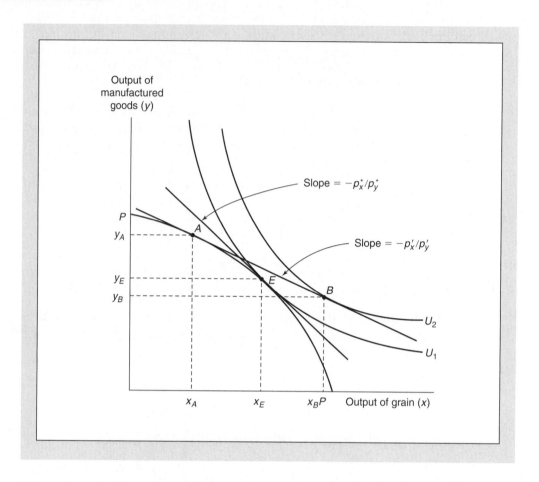

$x_B - x_A$, and these would be financed by export of manufactured goods equal to $y_A - y_B$. Overall utility for the typical British consumer would be increased by the opening of trade. Use of the production possibility diagram therefore demonstrates the implications that relaxing the tariffs would have for the production of both goods.

Trade and factor prices

By referring back to the Edgeworth production box diagram that lies behind the production possibility frontier (Figure 12.2), it is also possible to analyze the effect of tariff reductions on factor prices. The movement from point E to point A in Figure 12.6 is similar to a movement from P_3 to P_1 in Figure 12.2, where production of x is decreased and production of y is increased.

This figure also records the reallocation of capital and labor made necessary by such a move. If we assume that grain production is relatively capital intensive, the movement from P_3 to P_1 causes the ratio of k to l to rise in both industries.[7] This in turn will cause the relative price of capital to fall (and the relative price of labor to rise). Hence

---

[7]In the corn laws debate, attention actually centered on the factors, land and labor.

we conclude that repeal of the corn laws would be harmful to capital owners (that is, landlords) and helpful to laborers. It is not surprising that landed interests fought repeal of the laws.

Political support for trade policies

The possibility that trade policies may affect the relative incomes of various factors of production continues to exert a major influence on political debates about such policies. In the United States, for example, exports tend to be intensive in their use of skilled labor, whereas imports tend to be intensive in unskilled labor input. By analogy to our discussion of the corn laws, therefore, it might be expected that further movements toward free trade policies would result in rising relative wages for skilled workers and in falling relative wages for unskilled workers. It is not surprising therefore that unions representing skilled workers (the machinists or aircraft workers) tend to favor free trade, whereas unions of unskilled workers (those in textiles, shoes, and related businesses) tend to oppose it.[8]

Existence of general equilibrium prices

So far we have more or less assumed that competitive markets can reach an equilibrium in which the forces of supply and demand are balanced in all markets simultaneously. But, given the assumptions we have made, such a simultaneous solution is by no means ensured. Beginning with the nineteenth-century investigations by Leon Walras, economists have used increasingly sophisticated tools to examine whether a set of prices that equilibrates all markets exists and, if so, how this set of prices can be found. In this section we will explore some aspects of this question.

A simple mathematical model

The essential aspects of the modern solution to the Walrasian problem can be demonstrated for the case where no production takes place. Suppose there are n goods, in absolutely fixed supply, in this economy and that they are distributed in some way among the individuals in society. Let S_i $(i = 1, \ldots, n)$ be the total supply of good i available, and let the price of good i be represented by p_i $(i = 1, \ldots, n)$. The total demand for good i depends on all the prices, and this function represents the sum of the individuals' demand functions for good i. This total demand function is denoted by

$$D_i(p_1, \ldots, p_n)$$

for $i = 1, \ldots, n$.

Because we are interested in the whole set of prices $p_1, \ldots, p_n$, it will be convenient to denote this whole set by P. Hence the demand functions can be written as

$$D_i(P).$$

Walras' problem then can be stated formally as: Does there exist an *equilibrium set of prices* (P^*) such that

$$D_i(P^*) = S_i \tag{12.22}$$

for all values of i? The question posed by Walras is whether a set of prices exists for which supply is equal to demand *in all markets simultaneously*.

---

[8]The finding that the opening of trade will raise the relative price of the abundant factor is called the Stolper-Samuelson theorem after the economists who rigorously proved it in the 1950s.

Excess demand functions

In what follows it will be more convenient to work with excess demand functions for good i at any set of prices (P), which are defined to be[9]

$$ED_i(P) = D_i(P) - S_i. \quad i = 1, n \tag{12.23}$$

Using this notation, the equilibrium conditions can be rewritten as

$$ED_i(P^*) = D_i(P^*) - S_i = 0. \ i = 1, n \tag{12.24}$$

This condition states that at the equilibrium prices, excess demand is to be equal to zero in all markets.[10]

Walras himself noted several interesting features about the system of Equation 12.24. First, as we have already shown, the demand functions (and hence the excess demand functions) are *homogeneous of degree zero*. If all prices were to double (including the wages of labor), the quantity demanded of every good would remain unchanged. Hence we can only hope to establish equilibrium relative prices in a Walrasian-type model. A second assumption made by Walras was that the demand functions (and therefore the excess demand functions) are *continuous*; if prices were to change by only a small amount, quantities demanded would change by only a small amount. The assumptions of homogeneity and continuity are direct results of the theory of consumer behavior that we studied in Part 2.

Walras' law

A final observation that Walras made is that the n excess demand functions are not independent of one another. The equations are related by the formula

$$\sum_{i=1}^{n} p_i \cdot ED_i(P) = 0. \tag{12.25}$$

Equation 12.25 is usually called *Walras' law*. The equation states that the "total value" of excess demand is zero at *any* set of prices. There can be neither excess demand for all goods together nor excess supply. Proving Walras' law is a simple matter, although it is necessary to introduce some cumbersome notation. The proof rests on the fact that each individual in the economy is bound by a budget constraint. A simple example of the proof is given in the footnote;[11] the generalization of this proof is left to the reader.

Walras' law, it should be stressed, holds for any set of prices, not just for equilibrium prices. The law can be seen to apply trivially to an equilibrium set of prices, because each of the excess demand functions will be equal to zero at this set of prices. Walras' law

---

[9]Although we will not do so, supply behavior can be introduced here by making S_i depend on P also.

[10]This equilibrium condition will be slightly amended later to allow for goods whose equilibrium price is zero.

[11]Suppose that there are two goods (A and B) and two individuals (Smith and Jones) in society. Let D_A^S, D_B^S, S_A, S_B^S be Smith's demands and supplies of A and B and use a similar notation for Jones' demands and supplies. Smith's budget constraint may be written as

$$p_A D_A^S + p_B D_B^S = p_A S_A^S + p_B S_B^S$$

or

$$p_A(D_A^S - S_A^S) + p_B(D_B^S - S_B^S) = 0$$

or

$$p_A ED_A^S + p_B ED_B^S = 0,$$

where ED_A^S and ED_B^S represent the excess demand of Smith for A and B, respectively.

A similar budget constraint holds for Jones:

$$p_A ED_A^J + p_B ED_B^J = 0,$$

and therefore, letting ED_A and ED_B represent total excess demands for A and B, it must be the case that

$$p_A \cdot (ED_A^S + ED_A^J) + p_B \cdot (ED_B^S + ED_B^J) = p_A \cdot ED_A + p_B \cdot ED_B = 0.$$

This is Walras' law exactly as it appears in Equation 12.25.

shows that the equilibrium conditions in n markets are not independent. We do not have n independent equations in n unknowns (the n prices). Rather, Equation 12.24 represents only $(n-1)$ independent equations, and hence we can hope to determine only $(n-1)$ of the prices. But this is what would have been expected in view of the homogeneity property of the demand functions. We can hope to determine only equilibrium *relative prices;* nothing in this model permits the derivation of absolute prices.

Walras' proof of the existence of equilibrium prices

Having recognized these technical features of the system of excess demand equations, Walras turned to the question of the existence of a set of equilibrium (relative) prices. He tried to establish that the n equilibrium conditions of Equation 12.24 were sufficient, in this situation, to ensure that such a set of prices would in fact exist, and therefore that the exchange model had a consistent theoretical framework. A first indication that this existence of equilibrium prices might be ensured is provided by a simple counting of equations and unknowns. The market equilibrium conditions provide $(n-1)$ *independent* equations in $(n-1)$ unknown relative prices. Hence the elementary algebra of solving simultaneous linear equations suggests that an equilibrium solution might exist.

Unfortunately, as Walras recognized, the act of solving for equilibrium prices is not nearly as simple a matter as counting equations and unknowns. First, the equations are not necessarily linear. Hence the standard conditions for the existence of solutions to simultaneous linear equations do not necessarily apply in this case. Second, from consideration of the economics of the problem, it is clear that all the equilibrium prices must be nonnegative. A negative price has no meaning in the context of this problem. To attack these two difficulties, Walras developed a very tedious proof, which involved solving for equilibrium prices in a series of successive approximations. Without presenting Walras' proof in detail, it is instructive to see how he approached the problem.

Start with some initial, arbitrary set of prices. Holding the other $(n-1)$ prices constant, find the equilibrium price in the market for good 1. Call this "provisional" equilibrium price p_1'. Now, holding p_1' and the other $(n-2)$ prices constant, solve for the equilibrium price in the market for good 2. Call this price p_2'. Notice that in changing p_2 from its initial position to p_2', the price initially calculated for market 1 need no longer be an equilibrium price, because good 1 may be a substitute or a complement to good 2. This is a reflection of the fact that the system of equations is indeed simultaneous. Using the provisional prices p_1' and p_2', solve for a provisional p_3'. The proof proceeds in this way until a complete set of provisional relative prices has been calculated.

In the second iteration of Walras' proof, $p_2', \ldots, p_n'$ are held constant while a new equilibrium price is calculated for the first good. Call this new provisional price p_1''. Proceeding as outlined above, an entire new set of provisional relative prices $(p_1'', \ldots, p_n'')$ can be calculated. The proof continues to iterate in this way until a reasonable approximation to a set of equilibrium prices is achieved.

The importance of Walras' proof is its ability to demonstrate the simultaneous nature of the problem of finding equilibrium prices. It is, however, a cumbersome proof and is generally not used today. More recent work has used some relatively simple tools of advanced mathematics to demonstrate the existence of equilibrium prices in a formal and elegant way. To demonstrate such a proof, one advanced mathematical theorem must be described.

Brouwer's fixed-point theorem

Because this section is purely mathematical, it is perhaps best to plunge right in by stating Brouwer's theorem:

Any continuous mapping $[F(X)]$ of a closed, bounded, convex set into itself has at least one fixed point (X^*) such that $F(X^*) = X^*$.

FIGURE 12.7   A Graphical Illustration of Brouwer's Fixed-Point Theorem

Because any continuous function must cross the 45° line somewhere in the unit square, this function must have a point for which $f(x^*) = x^*$. This point is called a "fixed point."

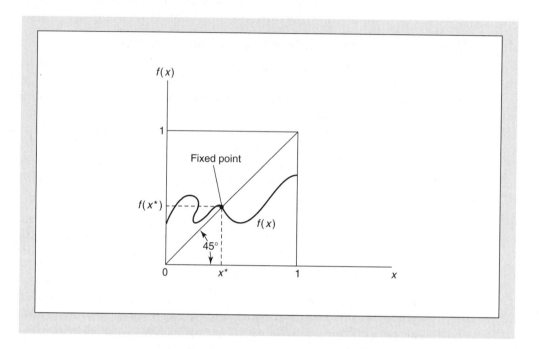

Before analyzing this theorem on a word-by-word basis, perhaps an example will aid in understanding the terminology. Suppose that $f(x)$ is a continuous function defined on the interval $[0, 1]$ and that $f(x)$ takes on values also on the interval $[0, 1]$. This function then obeys the conditions of Brouwer's theorem; it must be the case that there exists some x^* such that $f(x^*) = x^*$. This fact is demonstrated in Figure 12.7. It is clear from this figure that any function, as long as it is continuous (as long as it has no "gaps"), must cross the 45° line somewhere. This point of crossing is a *fixed point*, because f maps this point (x^*) into itself.

To study the more general meaning of the theorem, it is first necessary to define the terms *mapping, closed, bounded,* and *convex*. Definitions of these concepts will be presented in an extremely intuitive, nonrigorous way, because the costs of mathematical rigor greatly outweigh its possible benefits for the purposes of this book.

A *mapping* is a rule that associates the points in one set with points in another (or possibly the same) set. The most commonly encountered mappings are those that associate one point in n-dimensional space with some other point in n-dimensional space. Suppose that F is the mapping we wish to study. Then let X be a point for which the mapping is defined; the mapping associates X with some other point $Y = F(X)$. If a mapping is defined over a subset of an n-dimensional space (S), and if every point in S is associated (by the rule F) with some other point in S, the mapping is said to map S *into* itself. In Figure 12.7 the function f maps the unit interval into itself. A mapping is *continuous* if points that are "close" to each other are mapped into other points that are "close" to each other.

The *Brouwer fixed-point theorem* considers mappings defined on certain kinds of sets. These sets are required to be closed, bounded, and convex. Perhaps the simplest way to describe such sets is to say that they look like (n-dimensional analogies of) soap bubbles. They are *closed* in the sense that they contain their boundaries; the sets are *bounded* because none of their dimensions is infinitely large; and they are *convex* because they have no indentations in them. A technical description of the properties of such sets can be found in any elementary topology book.[12] For our purposes, however, it is only necessary to recognize that Brouwer's theorem is intended to apply to certain types of conveniently shaped sets. In order to use the theorem to prove the existence of equilibrium prices, therefore, we must first describe the set of points that has these desirable properties.

Proof of the existence of equilibrium prices

The key to applying Brouwer's theorem to the exchange model just developed is to choose a suitable way for "normalizing" prices. Because only relative prices matter in the exchange model, it is convenient to assume that prices have been defined so that the sum of all prices is 1. Mathematically, for any arbitrary set of prices $(p_1, \ldots, p_n)$, we can instead deal with *normalized* prices of the form[13]

$$p_i' = \frac{p_i}{\sum\limits_{i=1}^{n} p_i}. \tag{12.26}$$

These new prices will retain their original relative values $(p_i'/p_j' = p_i/p_j)$ and will sum to 1:

$$\sum_{i=1}^{n} p_i' = 1. \tag{12.27}$$

Because of the homogeneity of degree zero of all the excess demand functions, this kind of normalization can always be made. Hence, for the remainder of this proof, it will be assumed that the feasible set of prices (call this set S) is composed of all possible combinations of n nonnegative numbers that sum to 1. To avoid complex notation, we shall drop the special symbols we have been using for such prices.

This set, S, is the one to which we can apply Brouwer's theorem. The set S is closed, bounded, and convex.[14] To apply Brouwer's theorem, it is necessary to define a continuous mapping of S into itself. By a judicious choice of this mapping, it is possible to show that the fixed point dictated by the theorem is in fact a set of equilibrium relative prices.

Free goods

Before demonstrating the details of the proof, we must redefine what is meant by an "equilibrium set of prices." We do not really require that excess demand be exactly equal to zero in every market for an equilibrium. Rather, goods may exist for which the markets are in equilibrium but for which the available supply exceeds demand; there is negative excess demand. For this to be the case, however, it is necessary that the price of this particular good be zero. Hence, the equilibrium conditions of Equation 12.24 may be rewritten to take account of such *free goods:*

$$\begin{aligned} ED_i(P^*) &= 0 \quad \text{for } p_i^* > 0 \\ ED_i(P^*) &\leq 0 \quad \text{for } p_i^* = 0. \end{aligned} \tag{12.28}$$

Notice that such a set of equilibrium prices continues to obey Walras' law.

---

[12]For a development of the mathematics used in general equilibrium theory, see the references at the end of this chapter.

[13]One additional assumption must be made here; that is, at least one of the prices is nonzero. In economic terms this means that at least one good is scarce. Without this assumption a normalization of prices would not be possible—but, then again, studying economics in such a case would be unnecessary, because there would be no economic problem of scarcity.

[14]In two dimensions the set simply would be a straight line joining the coordinates $(0, 1)$ and $(1, 0)$. In three dimensions the set would be a triangular-shaped plane with vertices at $(0, 0, 1)$, $(0, 1, 0)$, and $(1, 0, 0)$. It is easy to see that each of these sets is closed, bounded, and convex.

Mapping the set of prices into itself

Using this definition of equilibrium and remembering that prices have been normalized to sum to 1, it is now possible to construct a continuous function that transforms one set of prices into another. The function to be defined builds on the Walrasian idea that in order to achieve equilibrium, prices of goods in excess demand should be raised, whereas those in excess supply should have their prices lowered. Hence, we define the mapping $F(P)$ for any (normalized) set of prices, P, such that the ith component of $F(P)$, denoted by $F^i(P)$, is given by

$$F^i(P) = p_i + ED_i(P) \tag{12.29}$$

for all i. The mapping then performs the necessary task of appropriately raising and lowering prices. If, at p_i, good i is in excess demand [$ED_i(P) > 0$], the price p_i is raised, whereas if excess demand is negative, p_i is reduced. Because the excess demand functions are assumed to be continuous, this mapping will also be continuous. Two problems with the mapping of Equation 12.29 remain. First, nothing ensures that the new prices will be nonnegative. Hence, the mapping must be redefined to be

$$F^i(P) = \text{Max } [p_i + ED_i(P), 0] \tag{12.30}$$

for all i. The term *Max* here simply means that the new prices defined by the mapping F must be either positive or zero; prices are not allowed to go negative. The mapping of Equation 12.30 is also continuous.

A second problem with the mapping of Equation 12.30 is that the recalculated prices are not necessarily normalized; they will not sum to 1. It would be a simple matter, however, to normalize these new prices so they do sum to 1.[15] To avoid introducing additional notation, assume that this normalization has been done and therefore

$$\sum_{i=1}^{n} F^i(P) = 1. \tag{12.31}$$

Application of Brouwer's theorem

With this normalization, then, F satisfies the conditions of the Brouwer fixed-point theorem. It is a continuous mapping of the set S into itself. Hence there exists a point (P^*) that is mapped into itself. For this point,

$$p_i^* = \text{Max } [p_i^* + ED_i(P^*), 0] \tag{12.32}$$

for all i.

---

[15]To accomplish this normalization, it is first necessary to show that not all of the transformed prices will be zero; it is necessary to show that $p_i + ED_i(P) > 0$ for some i. This can be proved by contradiction. Assume that $p_i + ED_i(P) \leq 0$ for all i. Multiply this expression by p_i and sum over all values of i, giving

$$\sum_{i=1}^{n} p_i^2 + \sum_{i=1}^{n} p_i ED_i(P) \leq 0.$$

But

$$\sum_{i=1}^{n} p_i ED_i = 0$$

by Walras' law. Hence

$$\sum_{i=1}^{n} p_i^2 \leq 0,$$

and this implies that $p_i = 0$ for all i. However, we have already ruled out this situation (see footnote 13), and have therefore poved that at least one of the transformed prices must be positive.

But this says that P^* is an equilibrium set of prices: for $p_i^* > 0$,

$$p_i^* = p_i^* + ED_i(P^*)$$

or

$$ED_i(P^*) = 0; \tag{12.33}$$

and for $p_i^* = 0$,

$$p_i^* + ED_i(P^*) \le 0$$

or

$$ED_i(P^*) \le 0. \tag{12.34}$$

We have therefore shown that the set of excess demand functions does in fact possess an equilibrium solution consisting of nonnegative prices. The simple exchange model developed here is consistent in that the market supply and demand functions necessarily have a solution. The homogeneity and continuity properties of the demand functions and the ability of Walras' law to tie together supply and demand are jointly responsible for this result.

Generalizations

Although this proof is a relatively old one in the field of general equilibrium theory, it does exhibit features of much of the more recent literature in this field. In particular, practically all modern proofs use Walras' law and rely on some type of fixed-point theorem. More recent work has tended to focus on ways in which the proof of the existence of general equilibrium prices can be generalized to situations involving more complex supply assumptions and on how equilibrium prices can actually be computed. In later chapters of this book, we will examine some of these alternative supply assumptions, such as cases of imperfect competition and problems caused by "public goods" (which we define later in this chapter). The Extensions to this chapter show some of the ways in which general equilibrium models have been applied using computers.

 EXAMPLE 12.3

A General Equilibrium with Three Goods

The economy of Oz is composed only of three precious metals: (1) silver, (2) gold, and (3) platinum. There are 10 (thousand) ounces of each metal available. The demand for gold is given by

$$D_2 = -2\frac{p_2}{p_1} + \frac{p_3}{p_1} + 11$$

and for platinum by $\qquad\qquad\qquad\qquad\qquad$ (12.35)

$$D_3 = -\frac{p_2}{p_1} - 2\frac{p_3}{p_1} + 18.$$

Notice that the demands for gold and platinum depend on the relative prices of the two goods and that these demand functions are homogeneous of degree zero in all three prices. Notice also that we have not written out the demand function for silver but, as we will show, it can be derived from Walras' law.

(continued)

EXAMPLE 12.3 CONTINUED

Equilibrium in the gold and platinum markets requires that demand equal supply in both markets simultaneously:

$$-2\frac{p_2}{p_1} + \frac{p_3}{p_1} + 11 = 10$$

$$-\frac{p_2}{p_1} - 2\frac{p_3}{p_1} + 18 = 10. \tag{12.36}$$

This system of simultaneous equations can be solved rather easily as

$$\frac{p_2}{p_1} = 2 \qquad \frac{p_3}{p_1} = 3. \tag{12.37}$$

In equilibrium, therefore, gold will have a price twice that of silver, and platinum a price three times that of silver. The price of platinum will be 1.5 times that of gold.

Walras' law and the demand for silver. Because Walras' law must hold in this economy, we know

$$p_1 ED_1 = -p_2 ED_2 - p_3 ED_3. \tag{12.38}$$

Solving Equations 12.36 for the excess demands (by moving the fixed supplies to the left-hand side) and substituting into Walras' law yields

$$p_1 ED_1 = 2\frac{p_2^2}{p_1} - \frac{p_2 p_3}{p_1} - p_2 + \frac{p_2 p_3}{p_1} + 2\frac{p_3^2}{p_1} - 8p_3 \tag{12.39}$$

or

$$ED_1 = 2\frac{p_2^2}{p_1^2} + 2\frac{p_3^2}{p_1^2} - \frac{p_2}{p_1} - 8\frac{p_3}{p_1}. \tag{12.40}$$

As expected, this function is homogeneous of degree zero in the relative prices, and the market for silver is also in equilibrium ($ED_1 = 0$) at the relative prices computed previously. (Check this yourself!)

A change in supply. If gold supply decreases to 7 and platinum supply increases to 11, we would expect relative prices to change. It seems likely that the relative price of gold will rise. Similarly, because the rise in gold price will reduce the demand for platinum and platinum supply has increased, the relative price of platinum should fall. But that will reduce the demand for gold, so the end result is ambiguous—clearly, a simultaneous solution is called for. In fact, the solution to

$$-2\frac{p_2}{p_1} + \frac{p_3}{p_1} + 11 = 7 \tag{12.41}$$

and

$$-\frac{p_2}{p_1} - 2\frac{p_3}{p_1} + 18 = 11 \tag{}$$

is

$$\frac{p_2}{p_1} = 3 \qquad \frac{p_3}{p_1} = 2. \tag{12.42}$$

So the price of gold rises relative to both silver and platinum. The price of platinum falls relative to that of silver. All of these effects can be captured only in a simultaneous model.

Query: Is the silver market still in equilibrium given the new supplies of gold and platinum?

The efficiency of perfect competition

Although most people recognize the equilibrium properties of the competitive price system (after all, prices usually do not fluctuate widely from day to day), they see little overall pattern to the resulting allocation of resources. The relationships described by the competitive model are so complex it is hard to believe that any desirable outcome will emerge from the chaos. This view provides an open-ended rationale to tinker with the system—because the results of market forces are chaotic, surely human societies can do better through careful planning.

Smith's invisible hand hypothesis

It took the genius of Adam Smith to challenge this view, which was probably the prevalent one in the eighteenth century. To Smith, the competitive market system represented the polar opposite from chaos. Rather, it provided a powerful "invisible hand" that ensured resources would find their way to where they were most valued, thereby enhancing the "wealth" of the nation. In Smith's view, reliance on the economic self-interest of individuals and firms would result in a (perhaps surprisingly) desirable social outcome.

Smith's initial insights gave rise to modern welfare economics. Specifically, his widely quoted "invisible hand" image provided the impetus for what is now called the "First Theorem of Welfare Economics"—that there is an exact correspondence between the efficient allocation of resources and the competitive pricing of these resources. Here we will investigate this correspondence in some detail. We begin by defining economic efficiency in a variety of contexts. These definitions, all of which draw on the work of the nineteenth-century economist Vilfred Pareto, have already been described briefly in earlier chapters; our goal here is to draw these discussions together and illustrate their underlying relationship to the competitive allocation of resources.

Pareto efficiency

We begin with Pareto's definition of economic efficiency.

DEFINITION

Pareto efficient allocation. An allocation of resources is *Pareto efficient* if it is not possible (through further reallocations) to make one person better off without making someone else worse off.

The Pareto definition then identifies particular allocations as being "inefficient" if unambiguous improvements are possible. Notice that the definition does not require interperson comparisons of utility. "Improvements" are defined by individuals themselves.

Efficiency in production

An economy is efficient in production if it is on its production possibility frontier. Formally, we can use Pareto's terminology to define productive efficiency as follows:

> **Productive efficiency.** An allocation of resources is *efficient in production* (or "technically efficient") if no further reallocation would permit more of one good to be produced without necessarily reducing the output of some other good.

As for Pareto efficiency itself, it is perhaps easiest to grasp this definition by studying its converse—an allocation would be inefficient if it were possible to move existing resources around a bit and get additional amounts of one good and no less of anything else. With technically efficient allocations, no such unambiguous improvements are possible. The trade-offs among outputs necessitated by movements along the production possibility frontier reflect the technically efficient nature of all of the allocations on the frontier.

Technical efficiency is an obvious precondition for overall Pareto efficiency. Suppose resources were allocated so that production was inefficient; that is, production was occurring at a point inside the production possibility frontier. It would then be possible to produce more of at least one good and no less of anything else. This increased output could be given to some lucky person making him or her better off (and no one else worse off). Hence, inefficiency in production is also Pareto inefficiency. As we shall see in the next section, however, technical efficiency does not guarantee Pareto efficiency. An economy can be efficient at producing the wrong goods—devoting all available resources to producing left shoes would be a technically efficient use of those resources, but surely some Pareto improvement could be found in which everyone would be better off.

A discussion of efficiency in production and its relationship to the production possibility frontier is somewhat more complex than our simple presentation earlier in this chapter might imply. Because production is divided among many firms, we must be concerned not only with the ways in which a single firm uses its resources (as we essentially were earlier), but also with how resources are allocated among firms. To facilitate this examination, we will break the question down into three separate issues: (1) resource allocation within a single firm; (2) allocation of productive resources among firms; and (3) coordination of firms' output choices. All of these allocational problems must be solved if production is to take place on the production possibility frontier.

Efficient choice of inputs for a single firm

In Figure 12.2 we examined the situation of a firm having fixed inputs of capital and labor. There we showed that the firm will have allocated these inputs efficiently if they are fully employed and if the rate of technical substitution (RTS) between capital and labor is the same for every output the firm produces. Previously, we developed a detailed graphical proof of this assertion; here we will use a mathematical approach. Assume the firm produces two goods, x and y, and that the total available inputs of capital and labor are given by k and l. The production function for good x is given by

$$x = f(k_x, l_x), \tag{12.43}$$

where k_x and l_x are capital and labor devoted to x production. If we assume full employment, $k_y = \bar{k} - k_x$, $l_y = \bar{l} - l_x$, and the production function for good y is

$$y = g(k_y, l_y) = g(\bar{k} - k_x, \bar{l} - l_x). \tag{12.44}$$

Technical efficiency requires that x output be as large as possible for any predetermined value of y output (say, $\bar{y}$). Setting up the Lagrangian expression for this constrained maximum problem yields

$$\mathscr{L} = f(k_x, l_x) + \lambda[\bar{y} - g(\bar{k} - k_x, \bar{l} - l_x)]. \qquad (12.45)$$

Differentiation with respect to k_x, l_x, and λ gives the following first-order conditions for a constrained maximum:

$$\frac{\partial \mathscr{L}}{\partial k_x} = f_k + \lambda g_k = 0$$

$$\frac{\partial \mathscr{L}}{\partial l_x} = f_l + \lambda g_l = 0 \qquad (12.46)$$

$$\frac{\partial \mathscr{L}}{\partial \lambda} = \bar{y} - g(\bar{k} - k_x, \bar{l} - l_x) = 0.$$

Moving the terms in λ to the right-hand side of the first two of these equations, we have

$$\frac{f_k}{f_l} = \frac{g_k}{g_l}, \qquad (12.47)$$

and, using the result (from Chapter 7) that the RTS is the ratio of the inputs' marginal productivities, that implies[16]

$$RTS_x (k \text{ for } l) = RTS_y (k \text{ for } l). \qquad (12.48)$$

This is precisely the result we showed graphically in Figure 12.2.

Efficient allocation of resources among firms

Resources must also be allocated in some efficient way among firms to ensure overall productive efficiency. Intuitively, resources should be allocated to those firms where they can be most efficiently used. More precisely, the condition for efficient allocation is that the marginal physical product of any resource in the production of a particular good is the same no matter which firm produces that good.

A mathematical proof of this rule is straightforward. Suppose there are two firms producing the same good (x) and their production functions are given by $f_1(k_1, l_1)$ and $f_2(k_2, l_2)$. Assume also that total supplies of capital and labor are given by $\bar{k}$ and $\bar{l}$. The allocational problem is then to maximize

$$x = f_1(k_1, l_1) + f_2(k_2, l_2), \qquad (12.49)$$

subject to the constraints

$$k_1 + k_2 = \bar{k}$$

$$l_1 + l_2 = \bar{l}. \qquad (12.50)$$

Upon substituting the constraints into Equation (12.49), the maximization problem becomes

$$x = f_1(k_1, l_1) + f_2(\bar{k} - k_1, \bar{l} - l_1). \qquad (12.51)$$

---

[16]These results hold only for an interior maximum in which both inputs are actually used to produce both goods. If that were not the case, these first-order conditions would have to be amended.

First-order conditions for a maximum are

$$\frac{\partial x}{\partial k_1} = \frac{\partial f_1}{\partial k_1} + \frac{\partial f_2}{\partial k_1} = \frac{\partial f_1}{\partial k_1} - \frac{\partial f_2}{\partial k_2} = 0$$

$$\frac{\partial x}{\partial l_1} = \frac{\partial f_1}{\partial l_1} + \frac{\partial f_2}{\partial l_1} = \frac{\partial f_1}{\partial l_1} - \frac{\partial f_2}{\partial l_2} = 0$$

(12.52)

or

$$\frac{\partial f_1}{\partial k_1} = \frac{\partial f_2}{\partial k_2}$$

and

$$\frac{\partial f_1}{\partial l_1} = \frac{\partial f_2}{\partial l_2},$$

(12.53)

as was to be shown.

 EXAMPLE 12.4

Gains from Efficiently Allocating Labor

To examine the quantitative gains in output from allocating resources efficiently, suppose two rice farms have production functions of the simple form

$$q = k^{1/4} \, l^{3/4},$$

(12.54)

but one rice farm is more mechanized than the other. If capital for the first farm is given by $k_1 = 16$ and for the second farm by $k_2 = 625$, we have

$$q_1 = 2l_1^{3/4}$$
$$q_2 = 5l_2^{3/4}.$$

(12.55)

If the total labor supply is 100, an equal allocation of labor to these two farms will provide total rice output of

$$Q = q_1 + q_2 = 2(50)^{3/4} + 5(50)^{3/4} = 131.6.$$

(12.56)

The efficient allocation is found by setting the marginal productivities equal:

$$\frac{\partial q_1}{\partial l_1} = \left(\frac{3}{2}\right) l_1^{-1/4} = \frac{\partial q_2}{\partial l_2} = \frac{15}{4} l_2^{-1/4}.$$

(12.57)

Hence, for efficiency labor should be allocated so that

$$l_1 = \left(\frac{5}{2}\right)^{-4} l_2 = .0256 l_2.$$

(12.58)

Given the greater capitalization of farm 2, practically all of the available labor should be devoted to it. With 100 units of labor, 97.4 units should be allocated to farm 2 with only 2.6 units to farm 1. In this case total output will be

$$Q = q_1 + q_2 = 2(2.6)^{3/4} + 5(97.4)^{3/4} = 159.1.$$

(12.59)

This represents a gain of more than 20 percent over the rice output obtained under the equal allocation.

Query: Suppose capital were not fixed in this problem. How should capital *and* labor be allocated between the two farms?

FIGURE 12.8   **Graphical Demonstration of Efficient Output Choice**

If two firms' rates of product transformation differ, total output can be increased by moving these firms toward equalization of those rates. In the figure, firm A is relatively efficient at producing cars, and firm B is relatively efficient at producing trucks. If each firm were to specialize in its efficient product, total output could be increased.

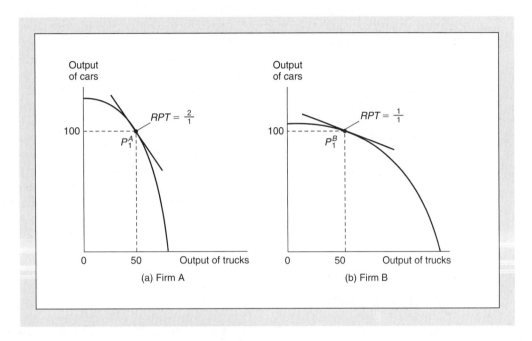

(a) Firm A

(b) Firm B

Efficient choice of output by firms

Although resources may be efficiently allocated within a firm and among all firms, there is still one other condition of efficient production that must be obeyed: Firms must produce efficient combinations of outputs. Roughly speaking, firms that are good at producing hamburgers should produce hamburgers and those good at producing cars should produce cars.

A mathematical derivation of the condition required for this result is straightforward. Suppose there are two outputs (x and y) each produced by two firms, and the production possibility frontiers for these firms are given in explicit form by

$$y_i = f_i(x_i) \qquad \text{for } i = 1,2. \tag{12.60}$$

The overall optimization problem, then, is to produce the maximum amount of x for any given value of y (say, y^*). Setting up the Lagrangian for this problem as

$$\mathcal{L} = x_1 + x_2 + \lambda[y^* - f_1(x_1) - f_2(x_2)] \tag{12.61}$$

yields the simple first-order condition:

$$\partial f_1/\partial x_1 = \partial f_2/\partial x_2. \tag{12.62}$$

In words, the rate of product transformation should be the same for all firms producing these two goods.

This result is shown graphically in Figure 12.8. There two firms have opted for output combinations on their respective production possibility curves with unequal *RPT*s. Because firm A's *RPT* is 2, it could increase car production by 2 (to 102) by reducing truck output by 1 (to 99). Firm B could expand truck output to 51 by reducing car output to 99. Hence total output of cars has increased from 200 to 201 whereas truck output has remained at 100. Such gains in production are always possible when *RPT*s differ.

Theory of comparative advantage

One of the most important applications of this conclusion is in the study of international trade, where it is used as the basis for the *theory of comparative advantage*. This theory was first proposed by Ricardo, who argued that countries should specialize in producing those goods of which they are relatively more efficient producers.[17] The countries should then trade with the rest of the world to obtain needed commodities. If countries do specialize in this way, total world production will be greater than if each country tried to produce a balanced bundle of goods. To demonstrate this fact, let us look again at Figure 12.8. Now we can take the two production possibility curves to represent those of two different countries with fixed resources. Points P_1^A and P_1^B may represent the countries' pretrade production choices. Because the *RPT* differs between the two countries, world output could be increased by having country A produce more cars and country B produce more trucks. The countries should proceed to specialize in this way until their *RPT*s are equilibrated. With country A specializing in car production, it can trade with country B to get the trucks it needs; similarly, B can trade with A for cars. Because total world output has been increased as a result of specialization, both countries may now be better off. This is the logic that provides intellectual support for the belief that "free trade is the best policy." It is important to note that the analysis uses only information about the product transformation rates between the two goods in each country, not about marginal productivity differences between countries. It is possible that a country could have an "absolute" advantage in the production of every good (in the sense that its marginal productivity of labor in the production of *every* good exceeded that of its trading partner), but such a country would still benefit from specialization and trade.

Efficiency in product mix

Technical efficiency is not a sufficient condition for Pareto efficiency. Demand must also be brought into the story. It does little good for an economy to be an efficient producer of yo-yos and xylophones if no one wants these goods. In order to ensure Pareto efficiency, we need some way to tie individuals' preferences and production possibilities together. The condition necessary to ensure that the right goods are produced is that the *marginal rate of substitution* for any two goods must be *equal* to the *rate of product transformation* of the two goods. Simply phrased, the psychological rate of trade-off between the two goods in people's preferences must be equal to the rate at which they can be traded off in production.

A graphical proof

Figure 12.9 illustrates the requirement for efficiency in product mix for a very simple case, a single person economy. It assumes that the one person in this economy (Robinson Crusoe?) produces only two goods (x and y). (This analysis could also apply to an economy of many individuals with identical preferences.) Those combinations of x and y that can be produced are given by the production possibility frontier *PP*. Any point on *PP* represents a point of technical efficiency. By superimposing the individual's indifference map on Figure 12.9, however, we see that only one point on *PP* provides maximum utility. This point of maximum utility is at *E*, where the curve *PP* is tangent to the individual's highest indifference curve, U_2. At this point of tangency, the individual's *MRS* (of x for y) is equal to the technical *RPT* (of x for y); hence, this is the required condition for overall efficiency. Notice that point *E* is preferred to every other point that is efficient in a productive sense. In fact, for any point (other than point *E*), such as *F*, on the curve *PP*, there exist points that are inefficient but are preferred to *F*. In Figure 12.9, the "inefficient" point *G* is preferred to the "efficient" point *F*. It would be preferable from the individual's point of view to produce inefficiently rather than be forced to produce the "wrong" combination of goods in an efficient way. Point *E* (which is efficiently produced) is superior to any such "second-best" solutions.

---

[17]See D. Ricardo, *The Principles of Political Economy and Taxation* (1817; reprint ed., London: J. M. Dent and Son, 1965), pp. 81–93.

FIGURE 12.9   **Efficiency in Product Mix in a Robinson Crusoe Economy**

In a single-person economy, the curve *PP* represents those combinations of *x* and *y* that can be produced. Every point on *PP* is efficient in a production sense. However, only the output combination at point *E* is a true utility maximum for the individual. At *E* the individual's *MRS* is equal to the rate at which *x* can technically be traded for *y* (*RPT*).

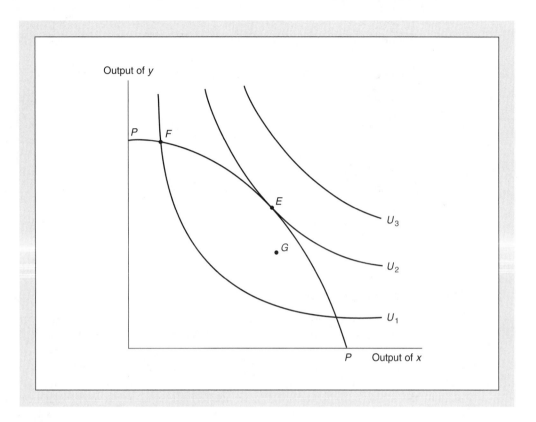

A mathematical proof

To demonstrate this result mathematically, assume again there are only two goods (*x* and *y*) and one individual in society (again Robinson Crusoe) whose utility function is given by $U(x, y)$. Assume also that this society's production possibility frontier can be written in implicit form as $T(x, y) = 0$. Robinson's problem is to maximize utility subject to this production constraint. Setting up the Lagrangian expression for this problem yields

$$\mathscr{L} = U(x, y) + \lambda[T(x, y)], \qquad (12.63)$$

and the first-order conditions for an interior maximum are

$$\frac{\partial \mathscr{L}}{\partial x} = \frac{\partial U}{\partial x} + \lambda \frac{\partial T}{\partial x} = 0$$

$$\frac{\partial \mathscr{L}}{\partial y} = \frac{\partial U}{\partial y} + \lambda \frac{\partial T}{\partial y} = 0 \qquad (12.64)$$

$$\frac{\partial \mathscr{L}}{\partial \lambda} = T(x, y) = 0.$$

Combining the first two of these equations yields

$$\frac{\partial U/\partial x}{\partial U/\partial y} = \frac{\partial T/\partial x}{\partial T/\partial y} \qquad (12.65)$$

or

$$MRS \ (x \ \text{for} \ y) = -\frac{dy}{dx} \ (\text{along} \ T) = RPT \ (x \ \text{for} \ y), \qquad (12.66)$$

as Figure 12.9 illustrated. We have shown that only if individuals' preferences are taken into account will resources be allocated in a Pareto efficient way. Without such an explicit reference to preferences, it would be possible, by reallocating production, to raise at least one person's utility without reducing anyone else's.

Competitive prices and efficiency—the First Theorem of Welfare Economics

The essence of the relationship between perfect competition and the efficient allocation of resources can easily be summarized. Attaining a Pareto efficient allocation of resources requires that (except when corner solutions occur) the rate of trade-off between any two goods, say, x and y, should be the same for all economic agents. In a perfectly competitive economy, the ratio of the price of x to the price of y provides this common rate of trade-off to which all agents will adjust. Because prices are treated as fixed parameters in both individuals' utility-maximizing decisions and firms' profit-maximizing decisions, all trade-off rates between x and y will be equalized to the rate at which x and y can be traded in the market (P_x/P_y). Because all agents face the same prices, all trade-off rates will be equalized and an efficient allocation will be achieved. This is the "First Theorem of Welfare Economics."

Efficiency in production

To show that competitive pricing can lead to efficiency in production, consider first the requirement that a firm have identical rates at which it can trade one input for another (the rate of technical substitution, RTS) in all those outputs it produces. This is ensured by the existence of perfectly competitive markets for inputs. In minimizing costs the firm will equate the RTS between any two inputs, say, labor and capital, to the ratio of their competitive rental prices (w/v). This will be true for any output the firm happens to produce; hence the firm will be equating all its RTSs to the common price ratio w/v. In this way, without any external direction, the firm will be led to adopt efficient input proportions in a decentralized way.

Efficiency in production also requires that every firm that produces a particular good, say, x, has identical marginal productivities of labor in the production of x. In Chapter 9 we showed that a profit-maximizing firm will hire additional units of any input (say, labor) up to the point at which its marginal contribution to revenues is equal to the marginal cost of hiring the input. If we let p_x represent the price of the good being sold and f^1 and f^2 represent the production functions for two firms that produce x, profit maximization requires that

$$p_x f_l^1 = w$$

and

$$p_x f_l^2 = w. \qquad (12.67)$$

Because both firms face both the same price for x and the same competitive wage rate, these equations imply

$$f_l^1 = f_l^2. \qquad (12.68)$$

Consequently, every firm will have the same marginal productivity of labor in the production of x. The market has succeeded in bringing about an efficient allocation of each input among firms.

Finally, the requirement is that the rate of product transformation (RPT—this is the rate at which one output can be traded for another in production) between any two goods be the same for all firms. That a perfectly competitive price system will ensure this can be most easily shown by recalling that the RPT (of x for y) is equal to the ratio of the marginal cost of x (MC_x) to that of y (MC_y). But each profit-maximizing firm will produce that output level for which marginal cost is equal to the market price. Therefore $p_x = MC_x$ and $p_y = MC_y$ for every firm, and hence $MC_x/MC_y = p_x/p_y$ for all firms.

This discussion demonstrates that the profit-maximizing, decentralized decisions of many firms can achieve technical efficiency in production without any central direction. Competitive market prices act as signals to unify the multitude of decisions firms make into one coherent, efficient pattern. Relying on the self-interest of profit-maximizing entrepreneurs is a theoretically plausible way of prompting the production sector to act efficiently.

Efficiency in product mix

Proving that perfectly competitive markets lead to efficiency in the relationship between production and preferences is also straightforward. Because the price ratios quoted to consumers are the same ratios the market presents to firms, the MRS shared by all individuals will be identical to the RPT shared by all firms. This will be true for any pair of goods. Consequently, an efficient mix of goods will be produced. Again, notice the two important functions that market prices perform. First, they ensure supply and demand will be equalized for all goods. If a good were produced in too great amounts, a market reaction would set in (its price would fall) that would cut back on production of the good and shift resources into other employment. The equilibrating of supply and demand in the market therefore ensures there will be neither excess demand nor excess supply. Second, equilibrium prices provide market trade-off rates for both firms and individuals to use as parameters in their decisions. Because these trade-off rates are identical for firms and individuals, efficiency is ensured.

A graphical proof

Our discussion of general equilibrium modeling earlier in this chapter provides precisely the tools required to show this result graphically. Figure 12.10 repeats Figure 12.4, but now we are more interested in the efficiency properties of the general equilibrium solution illustrated. Given the production possibility frontier PP and preferences represented by the indifference curves, it is clear that x^*, y^* represents the efficient output mix (compare this figure to Figure 12.9). Possibly x^*, y^* could be decided upon in a centrally planned economy if the planning board had adequate information about production possibilities and individuals' preferences. Alternatively, reliance on competitive markets and the self-interest of firms and individuals will also lead to this allocation. Only with a price ratio of p_x^*/p_y^* will supply and demand be in equilibrium in this model, and that equilibrium will occur at the efficient product mix, E. Smith's invisible hand ensures not only that production is technically efficient (that output combinations lie on the production possibility frontier), but also that the forces of supply and demand lead to the Pareto efficient output combination. More-complex models of competitive equilibrium price determination reach essentially the same conclusion.[18]

Laissez-faire policies

In its most dogmatic expression, the correspondence between competitive equilibrium and Pareto efficiency provides "scientific" support for the laissez-faire position taken by many economists. For example, Smith's assertion that

> the natural effort of every individual to better his own condition, when suffered to exert itself with freedom and security, is so powerful a principle that it is alone, and without any assistance, not only capable of carrying on the society to wealth and prosperity, but of surmounting a hundred impertinent obstructions with which the folly of human laws too often encumbers its operations.[19]

---

[18]See, for example, K. J. Arrow and F. H. Hahn, *General Competitive Analysis* (San Francisco: Holden-Day, 1971), chaps. 4 and 5.
[19]A. Smith, *The Wealth of Nations* (New York: Random House, Modern Library Edition, 1937), p. 508.

EXAMPLE 12.5

Efficiency and Inefficiency

The efficiency of competitive pricing can be shown with the simple general equilibrium models examined in Example 12.2. Each of the allocations found in that example are efficient given the preferences and productive technology that underlies them. That is, in each case utility is as large as possible given the production possibility frontier.

The base case allocation ($x^* = y^* = \sqrt{50}$) is technically feasible in both of the other cases illustrated in Example 12.2, but it is not the best use of resources. For the situation where there is technical progress in the production of good x, the base case allocation now lies inside the production possibility frontier. The allocation ($x^* = y^* = 10$) clearly is Pareto-superior to the base case. Another way to see this is, if we hold y^* constant at $\sqrt{50}$, it is possible to produce $x^* = 2\sqrt{50}$ once the technical progress in good x is taken into account. Opting for the base case allocation would forgo a substantial amount of x production (of course, only $x^* = y^* = 10$ is truly efficient given the new technology).

The base case allocation would also be inefficient when preferences shift toward good y. With the new utility function, the base case would yield

$$U(x, y) = x^{0.1}y^{0.9} = (50)^{0.05}(50)^{0.45} = (50)^{0.5} = 7.07. \quad (12.69)$$

Alternatively, the optimal allocation [$x^* = (10)^{0.5}$, $y^* = 3(10)^{0.5}$] yields utility of

$$U(x, y) = x^{0.1}y^{0.9} = (10)^{0.05}(3)^{0.9}(10)^{0.45} = (3)^{0.9}(10)^{0.5} = 8.50. \quad (12.70)$$

Clearly, efficiency requires that preferences and technology be tied together properly.

The excess burden of a tax, again. As an illustration of how general equilibrium analysis can be used to show the same kinds of welfare effects we illustrated in Chapter 11, consider again the modeling of taxation. Suppose that the government is unhappy with our base case scenario because it believes people should not consume so much of good x. To address this concern, the government places a 200 percent tax on good x, but maintains purchasing power by rebating the tax proceeds to consumers in a lump sum. To model this tax, we let p_x/p_y be the price ratio without the tax—this is the ratio firms see. Consumers, on the other hand, see a price ratio of $3p_x/p_y$—that is, they must pay the firm p_x and the government $2p_x$ whenever they buy a unit of good x. Now equilibrium is described by

$$\text{(supply)} \ p_x/p_y = x/y \text{ and (demand)} \ 3p_x/p_y = y/x. \quad (12.71)$$

Hence, $x/y = y/3x$ or $y^2 = 3x^2$. Substituting this into the production possibility frontier yields the following after-tax equilibrium:

$$x^* = 5, \ y^* = 5\sqrt{3}, \ p_x/p_y = 1/\sqrt{3} = 0.58. \quad (12.72)$$

Post-tax utility in this situation is

$$U(x, y) = x^{0.5} \ y^{0.5} = 5(3)^{0.25} = 6.58. \quad (12.73)$$

The reduction in utility from 7.07 to 6.58 is a measure of the excess burden of this tax. Here, because tax proceeds are rebated to consumers, there is no other burden of this tax. The welfare loss arises solely because the tax discourages x consumption by creating a wedge between what consumers pay for the good and what producers receive for it.

Query: Explain the various components of the consumer's budget constraint in the tax example studied here.

FIGURE 12.10   **Competitive Equilibrium and Efficiency in Output Mix**

Although all of the output combinations on PP are technically efficient, only combination x^*, y^* is Pareto optimal. A competitive equilibrium price ratio of p_x^*/p_y^* will lead this economy to this Pareto efficient solution.

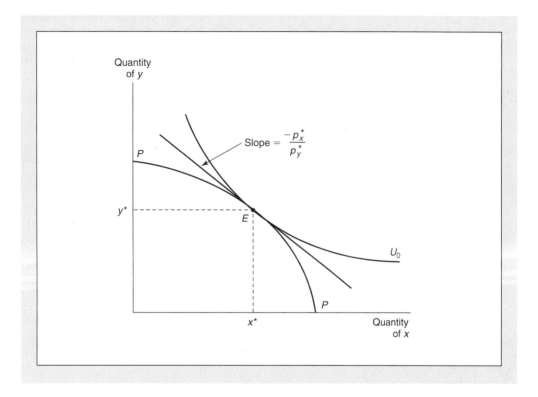

has much theoretical validity. Again, as Smith noted, it is not the "public spirit" of the baker that provides bread for individuals' consumption. Rather, bakers (and other producers) operate in their own self-interest in responding to market signals. Individuals also respond to these signals in deciding how to allocate their incomes. Government intervention in this smoothly functioning process may only result in a loss of Pareto efficiency.

Such a sweeping conclusion, of course, vastly overstates the general applicability of the simple model we have been using. No one should attempt to draw policy recommendations from a theoretical structure that pays so little attention to the institutional details of the real world. Still, the efficiency properties of the competitive system do provide a benchmark, a place to start to examine reasons why competitive markets may fail.

Departing from the competitive assumptions

Factors that may distort the ability of competitive markets to achieve efficiency can be classed into four general groupings that include most of the interesting cases: (1) imperfect competition, (2) externalities, (3) public goods, (4) imperfect information. Here we provide a brief summary of these groupings; we will return to them in later chapters.

Imperfect competition

"Imperfect competition" includes all those situations in which economic agents exert some market power in determining price. In this case, as we will see in Part 5, these agents will take such effects into account in their decisions. A firm that faces a downward-sloping demand curve for its product, for example, will recognize that the marginal revenue from selling one more unit is less than the market price of that unit. Because it is the marginal return to its decisions that motivates the profit-maximizing firm, marginal revenue rather than market price becomes the important magnitude. Market prices no longer carry the informational content required to achieve Pareto efficiency. Other cases of market power result in similar informational shortcomings.

Externalities

The competitive price system can also fail to allocate resources efficiently when there are interactions among firms and individuals that are not adequately reflected in market prices. Perhaps the prototype example is the case of a firm that pollutes the air with industrial smoke and other debris. Such a situation is termed an *externality:* It is an interaction between the firm's level of production and individuals' well-being that is not accounted for by the price system. A more complete discussion of the nature of externalities will be presented in Chapter 20, but here we can describe why the presence of such nonmarket interactions interferes with the ability of the price system to allocate resources efficiently. With externalities, market prices no longer reflect all of a good's costs of production. There is a divergence between *private* and *social* marginal cost, and these extra social costs (or possibly benefits) will not be reflected in market prices. Hence market prices will not carry the information about true costs that is necessary to establish an efficient allocation of resources. As we will show in Chapter 20, most of the study of environmental economics is concerned with potential ways to ameliorate the effects of such discrepancies.

Public goods

A similar problem in pricing occurs in the case of "public" goods. These are goods, such as national defense, which (usually) have two properties that make them unsuitable for production in markets. First, the goods are *nonrival,* in that additional people can consume the benefits of them at zero cost. This property suggests that the "correct" price for such goods is zero—obviously a problem if they are going to be produced profitably. A second feature of many public goods is *nonexclusion*—extra individuals cannot be precluded from consuming the good. Hence, in a market context, most consumers will adopt a "free rider" stance—waiting for some "other guy" to pay. Both of these technical features of public goods pose substantial problems for market economies. These problems are also examined in Chapter 20.

Imperfect information

Our discussion of the efficiency of perfectly competitive pricing has implicitly assumed that both suppliers and demanders know the equilibrium prices at which transactions occur. If economic actors are uncertain about prices or if markets cannot reach equilibrium, there is no reason to expect that the efficiency property of competitive pricing will be retained. There are, of course, many ways in which imperfect information may affect market outcomes. And, once it is admitted that information may be imperfect, it is important to construct models of how information is obtained and used by suppliers and demanders. To examine all of these issues here would take us too far away from our primary goals. In Chapter 19, however, we return to the topic of imperfect information by looking in detail at this rapidly expanding area of economic research.

These four impediments to efficiency suggest that one should be very careful in applying the First Theorem of Welfare Economics to actual policy choices. As we will discuss in later chapters, there may be good reason to interfere with market outcomes on efficiency grounds. There are also, of course, many bad reasons to interfere with markets—there are undoubtedly situations where the lessons of the First Theorem should be followed. The role of microeconomic analysis is to provide a systematic way of sorting through these cases.

Distribution

Although the First Theorem of Welfare Economics ensures that (under certain conditions) competitive markets will achieve allocations, there is no guarantee that these allocations will achieve any sort of fair distribution of welfare among individuals. As A. K. Sen has pointed out, an allocation of resources may be Pareto efficient "even when some people are rolling in luxury and others are near starvation, as long as the starvers cannot be made better off without cutting into the pleasures of the rich. . . . In short, a society can be Pareto optimal and still be perfectly disgusting."[20] Although a formal treatment of social welfare economics is beyond the scope of this book, here we will look briefly at the nature of the distributional issue.

An exchange economy

To study distribution in its simplest setting, assume there are only two people in society, Smith and Jones. Assume also that the total quantities of two goods (x and y) to be distributed among these people are in fixed supply. Now we can use the Edgeworth box diagram introduced earlier in this chapter to illustrate all possible allocations of these goods between Smith and Jones. In Figure 12.11 the dimensions of the Edgeworth box are given by the total quantities of the goods available. Smith's indifference curves are drawn with origin O_S, and Jones's indifference curves are drawn with origin O_J. Any point within the box represents a possible allocation of the goods to these two people, and we can use the indifference curves to evaluate the utility derived by each person from such allocations.

Mutually beneficial transactions

Any point within the Edgeworth box at which the *MRS* for Smith is unequal to that for Jones offers an opportunity for Pareto improvements. Consider the potential allocation A in Figure 12.11. This point lies on the point of intersection of Smith's indifference curve U_S^1 and

---

FIGURE 12.11   **Edgeworth Box Diagram of Pareto Efficiency in Exchange**

The points on the curve O_S, O_J are efficient in the sense that at these allocations Smith cannot be made better off without making Jones worse off, and vice versa. An allocation such as A, on the other hand, is inefficient because both Smith and Jones can be made better off by choosing to move into the shaded area. Notice that along O_S, O_J the *MRS* for Smith is equal to that for Jones. The line O_S, O_J is called the *contract curve*.

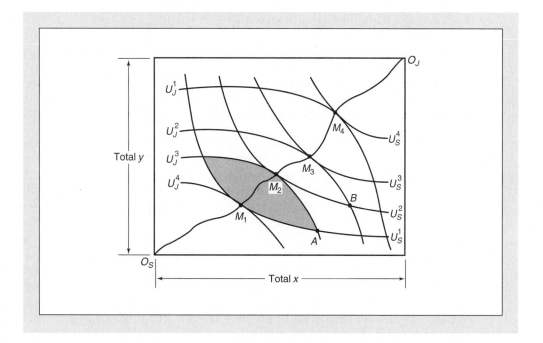

---

[20]A. K. Sen, *Collective Choice and Social Welfare* (San Francisco: Holden-Day, 1970), p. 22.

Jones's indifference curve U_J^3. Obviously, the marginal rates of substitution (the slopes of the indifference curves) are not equal at A. Any allocation in the oval-shape shaded area represents a mutually beneficial trade for these two people—they can both move to a higher level of utility by adopting a trade that moves them into this area. When the marginal rates of substitution of Smith and Jones are equal, however, such mutually beneficial trades are not available. The points M_1, M_2, M_3, and M_4 in Figure 12.11 indicate tangencies of these individuals' indifference curves, and movement away from such points must make at least one of the people worse off. A move from M_2 to A, for example, reduces Smith's utility from U_S^2 to U_S^1 even though Jones is made no worse off by the move. Alternatively, a move from M_2 to B makes Jones worse off, but keeps the utility level of Smith constant. In general, then, these points of tangency do not offer the promise of additional mutually beneficial trading and are therefore Pareto efficient.

Contract curve

The set of all the Pareto efficient allocations in an Edgeworth box diagram is called the *contract curve*. In Figure 12.11 this set of points is represented by the line running from O_S to O_J and includes the tangencies M_1, M_2, M_3, and M_4 (and many other such tangencies). Points off the contract curve (such as A or B) are inefficient, and mutually beneficial trades are possible. But, as its name implies, the contract curve represents the exhaustion of all such trading opportunities. Even a move along the contract curve (say, from M_1 to M_2) cannot represent a mutually beneficial trade because there will always be a winner (Smith) and a loser (Jones). These observations may be summarized as follows:

> **Contract curve.** In an exchange economy, all efficient allocations of existing goods lie along a (multidimensional) *contract curve*. Points off that curve are necessarily inefficient, because individuals can be made unambiguously better off by moving to the curve. Along the contract curve, however, individuals' preferences are rivals in the sense that one individual's situation may be improved only if someone else is made worse off.

Exchange with initial endowments

In our previous discussion we assumed that fixed quantities of the two goods could be allocated in any way conceivable. A somewhat different analysis would hold if the individuals participating in the exchange possessed specific quantities of the goods at the start. There would still be the definite possibility that each person could benefit from voluntary trade, because it is unlikely the initial allocations would be efficient ones. On the other hand, neither person would engage in a trade that would leave him or her worse off than would be the case without trading. Hence only a portion of the contract curve can be regarded as allocations that might result from voluntary exchange.

These ideas are illustrated in Figure 12.12. The initial endowments of Smith and Jones are represented by point A in the Edgeworth box. As before, the dimensions of the box are taken to the total quantities of the two goods available. The contract curve of efficient allocations is represented by the line O_S, O_J. Let the indifference curve of Smith, which passes through point A, be called U_S^A and, similarly, let Jones's indifference curve through A be denoted by U_J^A. Notice that at point A, the individuals' indifference curves are not tangent, and therefore the initial endowments are not efficient. Neither Smith nor Jones will accept trading outcomes that give a utility level of less than U_S^A or U_J^A, respectively. It would be preferable for an individual to refrain from trading rather than accept such an inferior outcome. Thus, if we focus only on efficient allocations, only those between M_1 and M_2 on the contract curve can occur as a result of free exchange. The range of efficient outcomes from voluntary exchange has been narrowed by considering the initial endowments with which the individuals enter into trading. If the initial distribution of goods favors Jones, any final allocation will also favor Jones, because it is in Jones's interest to refuse to accept bargains that provide less utility.

FIGURE 12.12   **Exchange with Initial Endowments**

If individuals start with initial endowments (such as those represented by point A), neither would be willing to accept an allocation that promised a lower level of utility than point A does. Smith would not accept any allocation below U_S, and Jones would not accept any allocation below U_J^A. Therefore, not every point on the contract curve can result from free exchange. Only the efficient allocations between M_1 and M_2 are eligible if each individual is free to refrain from trading and we require that the final allocation be efficient.

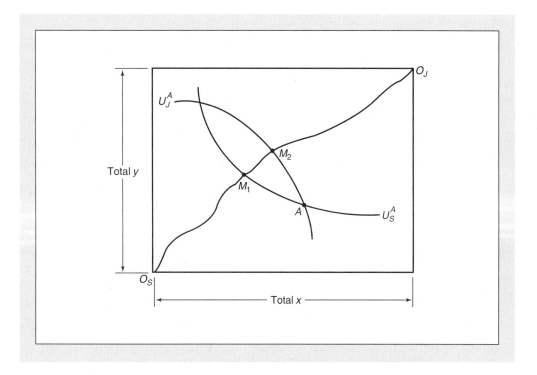

The distributional dilemma and the Second Theorem of Welfare Economics

This, then, is the distributional dilemma in its most abstract setting. If initial endowments are skewed in favor of some economic actors, the Pareto efficient allocations promised by the competitive price system will also tend to favor those actors. Voluntary transactions cannot overcome large differences in initial endowments, and some sort of transfers (possibly lump sum) will be needed to attain more equal results.

These thoughts lead to what is sometimes called the "Second Theorem of Welfare Economics." In general terms, the theorem states that any desired distribution of welfare among the individuals in an economy can be achieved in an efficient manner through competitive pricing if initial endowments are adjusted appropriately. It is this theorem that allows economists to make a sharp distinction between the efficiency issues that arise in a particular economic problem and the equity issues that arise in that problem. Put simply, economists frequently argue for using the efficiency properties of competitive prices to "make the pie as big as possible" and then to adjust the resulting distribution to be "fair" through the use of lump-sum transfers. Unfortunately, implementing the required lump-sum transfers may often be easier said than done—virtually all tax/transfer systems have real efficiency costs. Hence, the First and Second Theorems of Welfare Economics are not a cure-all for every economic policy question. Still, there are many cases where both efficiency and equity concerns suggest reliance on competitive pricing, so interference in market transactions to achieve distributional goals is not always a forgone conclusion. Rather, the correct application of applied welfare economics to any issue requires an independent assessment of both allocational and distributional issues.

EXAMPLE 12.6

A Two-Person Exchange Economy

To fix these ideas, consider an exchange economy in which there are exactly 1,000 soft drinks (x) and 1,000 hamburgers (y). If we let Smith's utility be represented by

$$U_S(x_S, y_S) = x_S^{2/3}\, y_S^{1/3} \tag{12.74}$$

and Jones's utility by

$$U_J(x_J, y_J) = x_J^{1/3}\, y_J^{2/3}, \tag{12.75}$$

we can compute the efficient ways of allocating soft drinks and hamburgers. Notice at the start that Smith has a relative preference for soft drinks, whereas Jones tends to prefer hamburgers, as reflected by the differing exponents in the utility functions of the two individuals. We might therefore expect that efficient allocations would give relatively more soft drinks to Smith and relatively more hamburgers to Jones.

To find the efficient points in this situation, suppose we let Smith start at any preassigned utility level, U_S. Our problem now is to choose x_S, y_S, x_J, and y_J to make Jones's utility as large as possible given Smith's utility constraint. Setting up the Lagrangian for this problem yields

$$\begin{aligned}\mathscr{L} &= U_J(x_J, y_J) + \lambda\,[\,U_S(x_S, y_S) - \overline{U}_S\,] \\ &= x_J^{1/3}\, y_J^{2/3} + \lambda\,(x_S^{2/3}\, y_S^{1/3} - \overline{U}_S).\end{aligned} \tag{12.76}$$

Remember that Jones simply gets what Smith doesn't, and vice versa. Hence

$$x_J = 1000 - x_S$$

and

$$y_J = 1000 - y_S. \tag{12.77}$$

Our Lagrangian is therefore a function of only the two variables x_S and y_S:

$$\mathscr{L} = (1000 - x_S)^{1/3}\,(1000 - y_S)^{2/3} + \lambda\,(x_S^{2/3} y_S^{1/3} - \overline{U}_S). \tag{12.78}$$

The first-order conditions for a maximum are

$$\begin{aligned}\frac{\partial \mathscr{L}}{\partial x_S} &= -\frac{1}{3}\left(\frac{1000 - y_S}{1000 - x_S}\right)^{2/3} + \frac{2\lambda}{3}\left(\frac{y_S}{x_S}\right)^{1/3} = 0 \\ \frac{\partial \mathscr{L}}{\partial y_S} &= -\frac{2}{3}\left(\frac{1000 - x_S}{1000 - y_S}\right)^{1/3} + \frac{\lambda}{3}\left(\frac{x_S}{y_S}\right)^{2/3} = 0.\end{aligned} \tag{12.79}$$

Moving the terms in λ to the right side of these equations and dividing the top equation by the bottom gives[21]

$$\frac{1}{2}\left(\frac{1000 - y_S}{1000 - x_S}\right) = 2\left(\frac{y_S}{x_S}\right) \tag{12.80}$$

or

$$\frac{x_S}{(1000 - x_S)} = \left(\frac{4 y_S}{1000 - y_S}\right), \tag{12.81}$$

---

[21]Notice that Equation 12.80 is a restatement of the condition that the individuals' marginal rates of substitution must be equal for an efficient allocation. That is, *MRS* (for Smith) $= (\partial U_S/\partial x)/(\partial U_S/\partial y) = 2(y/x)$ and *MRS* (for Jones) $= (\partial U_J/\partial x)/(\partial U_J/\partial y) = 1/2\,(y/x)$.

which is our required condition for efficiency. We can now use Equation 12.81 to calculate any number of Pareto efficient allocations. In Table 12.1 we have done so for a few values of x_S ranging from 0 to 1,000 (that is, for situations in which Smith gets nothing to situations where he or she gets everything).

Pareto efficiency. To illustrate why points off this contract curve are inefficient, consider an initial allocation in which Smith and Jones share x and y equally. With 500 units of each item, both Smith and Jones receive a utility of 500 (assuming that such utility measurement is meaningful). But, by using your basic scientific calculator, it is a relatively simple matter to show that there are many allocations on the contract curve that offer more utility to both people. Table 12.1 shows that this is nearly true for the allocations where Smith gets 600 or 700 soft drinks, and the precise boundaries of such mutually beneficial trades can be easily calculated. For example, consider $x_S = 660$, $y_S = 327$, $x_J = 340$, and $y_J = 673$. For this allocation Smith's utility is 522 and Jones's is 536. Both are clearly better off than at the initial allocation, and one might expect some sort of trading to take place that moves them toward the contract curve.

Effects of initial endowments. To see how initial endowments may restrict the range of Pareto efficient solutions in this economy, suppose Smith starts in a very favorable position with $x_S = 800$, $y_S = 800$. Then Jones gets $x_J = 200$, $y_J = 200$, and the initial utility levels are $U_S = 800$, $U_J = 200$. There are Pareto improvements that might be made from these initial endowments, but none of them will improve Jones's situation very much. For example, if we hold Smith's utility at 800, the efficient allocation $x_S = 884$, $y_S = 657$, $x_J = 116$, $y_J = 343$ will increase Jones's utility from 200 to 239. But that is the best that Jones can do given the constraint that Smith cannot be made worse off. The efficiency gains to Jones, while significant, do very little to move the overall allocation toward more equal outcomes.

Query: Would different preferences for the two people in this example offer greater scope for equalizing outcomes from voluntary transactions? Are there any preferences for Smith and Jones for which voluntary transactions would lead to equality even from very unequal initial allocations?

TABLE 12.1   **Pareto Efficient Allocations of 1,000 Soft Drinks and 1,000 Hamburgers to Smith and Jones**

x_S	y_S	$U_S = x_S^{2/3} y_S^{1/3}$	$x_J = 1000 - x_S$	$y_J = 1000 - y_S$	$U_J = x_J^{1/3} y_J^{2/3}$
0	0	0	1000	1000	1000
100	27	65	900	973	948
200	59	133	800	941	891
300	97	206	700	903	830
400	143	284	600	857	761
500	200	368	500	800	684
600	273	461	400	727	596
700	368	565	300	632	493
800	500	684	200	500	368
900	692	825	100	308	212
1000	1000	1000	0	0	0

SUMMARY

This chapter has provided a general exploration of Adam Smith's conjectures about the efficiency properties of competitive markets. We began with a description of how to model many competitive markets simultaneously and then used that model to make a few statements about welfare. Some of the highlights of this rather long chapter were:

- Preferences and production technologies provide the building blocks upon which all general equilibrium models are based. One particularly simple version of such a model uses individual preferences for two goods together with a concave production possibility frontier for those two goods.

- Competitive markets can establish equilibrium prices by making marginal adjustments in prices in response to information about the demand and supply for individual goods. Walras' Law ties markets together so that such a solution is assured (in most cases).

- Competitive prices will result in a Pareto-efficient allocation of resources. This is the First Theorem of Welfare Economics.

- Factors that will interfere with competitive markets' abilities to achieve efficiency include: (1) market power; (2) externalities; (3) existence of public goods; and (4) imperfect information.

- Competitive markets need not yield equitable distributions of resources, especially when initial endowments are very skewed. In theory any desired distribution can be attained through competitive markets accompanied by lump-sum transfers. But there are many practical problems in implementing such transfers.

PROBLEMS

12.1

Suppose the production possibility frontier for guns (x) and butter (y) is given by

$$x^2 + 2y^2 = 900.$$

a. Graph this frontier

b. If individuals always prefer consumption bundles in which $y = 2x$, how much x and y will be produced?

c. At the point described in part (b), what will be the *RPT* and hence what price ratio will cause production to take place at that point? (This slope should be approximated by considering small changes in x and y around the optimal point.)

d. Show your solution on the figure front part (a).

12.2

The purpose of this problem is to examine the relationship among returns to scale, factor intensity, and the shape of the production possibility frontier.

Suppose there are fixed supplies of capital and labor to be allocated between the production of good x and good y. The production function for x is given by

$$x = k^\alpha l^\beta$$

and for y by
$$y = k^\gamma l^\delta,$$

where the parameters α, β, γ, δ will take on different values throughout this problem.

Using either intuition, a computer, or a formal mathematical approach, derive the production possibility frontier for x and y in the following cases:

    a. $\alpha = \beta = \gamma = \delta = \frac{1}{2}$.

    b. $\alpha = \beta = \frac{1}{2}, \gamma = \frac{1}{3}, \delta = \frac{2}{3}$.

    c. $\alpha = \beta = \frac{1}{2}, \gamma = \delta = \frac{2}{3}$.

    d. $\alpha = \beta = \gamma = \delta = \frac{2}{3}$.

    e. $\alpha = \beta = .6, \gamma = .2, \delta = 1.0$.

    f. $\alpha = \beta = .7, \gamma = .6, \delta = .8$.

Do increasing returns to scale always lead to a convex production possibility frontier? Explain.

12.3

The country of Podunk produces only wheat and cloth, using as inputs land and labor. Both are produced by constant returns-to-scale production functions. Wheat is the relatively land-intensive commodity.

    a. Explain, in words or with diagrams, how the price of wheat relative to cloth *(p)* determines the land-labor ratio in each of the two industries.

    b. Suppose that p is given by external forces (this would be the case if Podunk were a "small" country trading freely with a "large" world). Show, using the Edgeworth box, that if the supply of labor increases in Podunk, the output of cloth will rise and the output of wheat will fall.

12.4

Suppose two individuals (Smith and Jones) each have 10 hours of labor to devote to producing either ice cream (x) or chicken soup (y). Smith's utility function is given by

$$U_S = x^{.3}y^{.7},$$

whereas Jones' is given by

$$U_J = x^{.5}y^{.5}.$$

The individuals do not care whether they produce x or y, and the production function for each good is given by

$$x = 2l$$

$$y = 3l,$$

where l is the total labor devoted to production of each good. Using this information,

    a. What must the price ratio, p_x/p_y, be?

    b. Given this price ratio, how much x and y will Smith and Jones demand? (*Hint:* Set the wage equal to 1 here.)

    c. How should labor be allocated between x and y to satisfy the demand calculated in part (b)?

12.5

Suppose there are only three goods (x_1, x_2, and x_3) in an economy and that the excess demand functions for x_2 and x_3 are given by

$$ED_2 = -3p_2/p_1 + 2p_3/p_1 - 1$$
$$ED_3 = 4p_2/p_1 - 2p_3/p_1 - 2.$$

a. Show that these functions are homogeneous of degree zero in p_1, p_2, and p_3.

b. Use Walras' law to show that if $ED_2 = ED_3 = 0$, ED_1 also must be 0. Can you also use Walras' law to calculate ED_1?

c. Solve this system of equations for the equilibrium relative prices p_2/p_1 and p_3/p_1. What is the equilibrium value for p_3/p_2?

12.6

Suppose that Robinson Crusoe produces and consumes fish *(F)* and coconuts *(C)*. Assume that during a certain period he has decided to work 200 hours and is indifferent as to whether he spends this time fishing or gathering coconuts. Robinson's production for fish is given by

$$F = \sqrt{l_F}$$

and for coconuts by

$$C = \sqrt{l_C},$$

where l_F and l_C are the number of hours spent fishing or gathering coconuts. Consequently,

$$l_C + l_F = 200.$$

Robinson Crusoe's utility for fish and coconuts is given by

$$\text{utility} = \sqrt{F \cdot C}.$$

a. If Robinson cannot trade with the rest of the world, how will he choose to allocate his labor? What will the optimal levels of *F* and *C* be? What will his utility be? What will be the *RPT* (of fish for coconuts)?

b. Suppose now that trade is opened and Robinson can trade fish and coconuts at a price ratio of $p_F/p_C = 2/1$. If Robinson continues to produce the quantities of *F* and *C* in part (a), what will he choose to consume, given the opportunity to trade? What will his new level of utility be?

c. How would your answer to part (b) change if Robinson adjusts his production to take advantage of the world prices?

d. Graph your results for parts (a), (b), and (c).

12.7

Consider an economy with just one technique available for the production of each good:

Good	Food	Cloth
Labor per unit output	1	1
Land per unit output	2	1

a. Suppose land is unlimited, but labor equals 100. Write and sketch the production possibility frontier.

b. Suppose labor is unlimited, but land equals 150. Write and sketch the production possibility frontier.

c. Suppose labor equals 100 and land equals 150. Write and sketch the production possibility frontier. (*Suggestion:* What are the intercepts of the production possibility frontier? When is land fully employed? Labor? Both?)

d. Explain why the production possibility frontier of part (c) is concave.

e. Sketch the relative price of food as a function of its output in case (c).

f. If consumers insist on trading 4 units of food for 5 units of cloth, what is the relative price of food? Why?

g. Explain why production is exactly the same at a price ratio of $p_F/p_C = 1.1$ as at $p_F/p_C = 1.9$.

h. Suppose capital is also required for producing food and clothing and that capital requirements per unit of food and per unit of clothing are 0.8 and 0.9, respectively. There are 100 units of capital available. What is the production possibility curve in this case? Answer part (e) for this case.

12.8

In the country of Ruritania there are two regions, A and B. Two goods (x and y) are produced in both regions. Production functions for region A are given by

$$x_A = \sqrt{l_x}$$
$$y_A = \sqrt{l_y}.$$

l_x and l_y are the quantity of labor devoted to x and y production, respectively. Total labor available in region A is 100 units. That is,

$$l_x + l_y = 100.$$

Using a similar notation for region B, production functions are given by

$$x_B = \frac{1}{2}\sqrt{l_x}$$

$$y_B = \frac{1}{2}\sqrt{l_y}.$$

There are also 100 units of labor available in region B:

$$l_x + l_y = 100.$$

a. Calculate the production possibility curves for regions A and B.

b. What condition must hold if production in Ruritania is to be allocated efficiently between regions A and B (assuming labor cannot move from one region to the other)?

c. Calculate the production possibility curve for Ruritania (again assuming labor is immobile between regions). How much total y can Ruritania produce if total x output is 12? *Hint:* A graphical analysis may be of some help here.

12.9

Smith and Jones are stranded on a desert island. Each has in his possession some slices of ham (H) and cheese (C). Smith is a very choosy eater and will eat ham and cheese only in the fixed proportions of 2 slices of cheese to 1 slice of ham. His utility function is given by $U_S = \min(H, C/2)$.

Jones is more flexible in his dietary tastes and has a utility function given by $U_J = 4H + 3C$. Total endowments are 100 slices of ham and 200 slices of cheese.

a. Draw the Edgeworth box diagram that represents the possibilities for exchange in this situation. What is the only exchange ratio that can prevail in any equilibrium?

b. Suppose Smith initially had $40H$ and $80C$. What would the equilibrium position be?

c. Suppose Smith initially had $60H$ and $80C$. What would the equilibrium position be?

d. Suppose Smith (much the stronger of the two) decides not to play by the rules of the game. Then what could the final equilibrium position be?

12.10

In Example 12.6 each individual has an initial endowment of 500 units of each good.

a. Express the demand for Smith and Jones for goods x and y as functions of p_x and p_y and their initial endowments.

b. Use the demand functions from part (a) together with the observation that total demand for each good must be 1,000 to calculate the equilibrium price ratio, p_x/p_y, in this situation. What are the equilibrium consumption levels of each good by each person?

c. How would the answers to this problem change for the following initial endowments?

	Smith's Endowment		Jones's Endowment	
	x	y	x	y
i.	0	1000	1000	0
ii.	600	600	400	400
iii.	400	400	600	600
iv.	1000	1000	0	0

Explain the reason for these varying results.

SUGGESTIONS FOR FURTHER READING

Arrow, K. J., and F. H. Hahn. *General Competitive Analysis,* Chaps. 1, 2, and 4. Amsterdam: North-Holland, 1978.
Sophisticated mathematical treatment of general equilibrium analysis. Each chapter has a good literary introduction.

Debreu, G. "Existence of Competitive Equilibrium." In K. J. Arrow and M. D. Intriligator, eds., *Handbook of Mathematical Economics,* vol. 2. Amsterdam: North-Holland, 1982, pp. 697–743.
Fairly difficult survey of existence proofs based on fixed-point theorems. Contains a comprehensive set of references.

Debreu, G. *Theory of Value.* New York: John Wiley & Sons, 1959.
Basic reference, difficult mathematics. Does have a good introductory chapter on the mathematical tools used.

Ginsburgh, V., and M. Keyzer. *The Structure of Applied General Equilibrium Models.* Cambridge, MA: MIT Press, 1997.

Detailed discussions of the problems in implementing CGE models. Some useful references to the empirical literature.

Harberger, A. "The Incidence of the Corporate Income Tax." *Journal of Political Economy* (January/February 1962): 215–40.

Nice use of a two-sector general equilibrium model to examine the final burden of a tax on capital.

Mas-Colell, A., M. D. Whinston, and J. R. Green. *Microeconomic Theory.* Oxford: Oxford University Press, 1995.

Part Four is devoted to general equilibrium analysis. Chapters 17 (existence) and 18 (connections to game theory) are especially useful. Chapters 19 and 20 pursue several of the topics in the Extensions to this chapter.

Salanie, B. *Microeconomic Models of Market Failure.* Cambridge, MA: MIT Press, 2000.

Nice summary of the theorems of welfare economics along with detailed analyses of externalities, public goods, and imperfect competition.

Sen, A. K. *Collective Choice and Social Welfare,* Chaps. 1 and 2. San Francisco: Holden-Day, 1970.

Basic reference on social choice theory. Early chapters have a good discussion of the meaning and limitations of the Pareto efficiency concept.

EXTENSIONS

Computable General Equilibrium Models

Recent improvements in computer technology have made it feasible to develop computable general equilibrium (CGE) models of considerable detail. These may involve literally hundreds of industries and individuals, each with somewhat different technologies or preferences. The general methodology employed with these models is to assume various forms for production and utility functions, then choose particular parameters of those functions based on empirical evidence. Numerical general equilibrium solutions are then generated by the models and compared to real-world data. After "calibrating" the models to reflect reality, various policy elements in the models are varied as a way of providing general equilibrium estimates of the overall impact of those policy changes. In this extension we briefly review a few of these types of applications.

E12.1 Trade models

One of the first uses for applied general equilibrium models was to the study of the impact of trade barriers. Because much of the debate over the effects of such barriers (or of their reduction) focuses on impacts on real wages, such general equilibrium models are especially appropriate for the task.

Two unusual features tend to characterize such models. First, because the models often have an explicit focus on domestic versus foreign production of specific goods, it is necessary to introduce a large degree of product differentiation into individuals' utility functions. That is, "U.S. textiles" are treated as being different from "Mexican textiles" even though, in most trade theories, textiles might be treated as homogeneous goods. Modelers have found they must allow for only limited substitutability among such goods if their models are to replicate actual trade patterns.

A second feature of CGE models of trade is the interest in incorporating increasing returns-to-scale technologies into their production sectors. This permits the models to capture one of the primary advantages of trade for smaller economies. Unfortunately, introduction of the increasing returns-to-scale assumption also requires that the models depart from perfectly competitive, price-taking assumptions. Often some type of markup pricing, together with Cournot-type imperfect competition (see Chapter 14), is used for this purpose.

North American Free Trade

Some of the most extensive CGE modeling efforts have been devoted to analyzing the impact of the North American Free Trade Agreement (NAFTA). Virtually all of these models find that the agreement offered welfare gains to all of the countries involved. Gains for Mexico accrued primarily because of reduced U.S. trade barriers on Mexican textiles and steel. Gains to Canada came primarily from an increased ability to benefit from economies of scale in certain key industries. Brown (1992) surveys a number of CGE models of North American free trade and concludes that gains on the order of 2–3 percent of GDP might be experienced by both of these countries. For the United States, gains from NAFTA might be considerably smaller, but even in this case, significant welfare gains were found to be associated with the increased competitiveness of domestic markets.

E12.2 Tax and transfer models

A second major use of CGE models is to evaluate potential changes in a nation's tax and transfer policies. For these applications, considerable care must be taken in modeling the factor supply side of the models. For example, at the margin, the effects of rates of income taxation (either positive or negative) can have important labor supply effects that only a general equilibrium approach can model properly. Similarly, tax/transfer policy can also affect savings and investment decisions, and for these too it may be necessary to adopt more detailed modeling procedures (for example, differentiating individuals by age so as to examine effects of retirement programs).

The Dutch MIMIC model

Probably the most elaborate tax/transfer CGE model is that developed by the Dutch Central

Planning Bureau—the Micro Macro Model to Analyze the Institutional Context (MIMIC). This model puts emphasis on social welfare programs and on some of the problems they seek to ameliorate (most notably unemployment, which is missing from many other CGE models). Gelauff and Graaflund (1994) summarize the main features of the MIMIC model. They also use it to analyze such policy proposals as the 1990s tax reform in the Netherlands and potential changes to the generous unemployment and disability benefits in that country.

E12.3 Environmental models

CGE models are also appropriate for understanding the ways in which environmental policies may affect the economy. In such applications the production of pollutants is considered as a major side effect of the other economic activities in the model. By specifying environmental goals in terms of a given reduction in these pollutants, it is possible to use these models to study the economic costs of various strategies for achieving these goals. One advantage of the CGE approach is to provide some evidence on the impact of environmental policies on income distribution— a topic largely omitted from more narrow, industry-based modeling efforts.

Assessing CO_2 reduction strategies

Concern over the possibility that CO_2 emissions in various energy-using activities may be contributing to global warming has led to a number of plans for reducing these emissions. Because the repercussions of such reductions may be widespread and varied, CGE modeling is one of the preferred assessment methods. Perhaps the most elaborate such model is that developed by the OECD—the General Equilibrium Environmental Model (GREEN) model. The basic structure of this model is described by Burniaux, Nicoletti, and Oliviera-Martins (1992). The model has been used to simulate various policy options that might be adopted by European nations to reduce CO_2 emissions, such as institution of a carbon tax or increasingly stringent emissions regulations for automobiles and power plants. In general, these simulations suggest that economic costs of these policies would be relatively modest given the level of restrictions currently anticipated. But most of the policies would have adverse distributional effects that may require further attention through government transfer policy.

E12.4 Regional and urban models

A final way in which CGE models can be used is to examine economic issues that have important spatial dimensions. Construction of such models requires careful attention to issues of transportation costs for goods and moving costs associated with labor mobility, because particular interest is focused on where transactions occur. Incorporation of these costs into CGE models is in many ways equivalent to adding extra levels of product differentiation, because these affect the relative prices of otherwise homogeneous goods. Calculation of equilibria in regional markets can be especially sensitive to how transport costs are specified.

Changing government procurement

CGE regional models have been widely used to examine the local impact of major changes in government spending policies. For example, Holtman, Robinson, and Subramanian (1996) use a CGE model to evaluate the regional impact of reduced defense expenditures on the California economy. They find that the size of the effects depends importantly on the assumed costs of migration for skilled workers. A similar finding is reported by Bernat and Hanson (1995), who examine possible reductions in U.S. price-support payments to farms. Although such reductions would offer overall efficiency gains to the economy, they could have significant negative impacts on rural areas.

References

Bernat, G. A., and K. Hanson. "Regional Impacts of Farm Programs: A Top-Down CGE Analysis." *Review of Regional Studies* (Winter 1995): 331–50.

Brown, D. K. "The Impact of North American Free Trade Area: Applied General Equilibrium Models." In N. Lustig, B. P. Bosworth, and R. Z. Lawrence, eds., *North American Free Trade: Assessing the Impact*. Washington, DC: The Brookings Institution, 1992, pp. 26–68.

Burniaux, J. M., G. Nicoletti, and J. Oliviera-Martins. "Green: A Global Model for Quantifying the Costs of Policies to Curb CO_2 Emissions." *OECD Economic Studies* (Winter 1992): 49–92.

Gelauff, G. M. M., and J. J. Graaflund. *Modeling Welfare State Reform*. Amsterdam: North Holland, 1994.

Hoffman, S., S. Robinson, and S. Subramanian. "The Role of Defense Cuts in the California Recession: Computable General Equilibrium Models and Interstate Fair Mobility." *Journal of Regional Science* (November 1996): 571–95.

Part 5

MODELS OF IMPERFECT COMPETITION

CHAPTER 13   MODELS OF MONOPOLY

CHAPTER 14   TRADITIONAL MODELS OF IMPERFECT COMPETITION

CHAPTER 15   GAME THEORY MODELS OF PRICING

One of the most important assumptions made throughout Part 4 was that both suppliers and demanders were price takers. All economic actors were assumed to exert no influence on prices, and therefore prices were treated as fixed parameters in their decisions. This behavioral assumption was crucial to most of our analysis, especially that related to the efficiency properties of the competitive price system. In this part, we will explore the consequences of dropping the price-taking assumption for suppliers of goods.

We begin our examination of imperfect competition in Chapter 13 with the case of a single supplier of a good. Such a supplier is called a monopoly. *This supplier faces the entire market demand curve for its product and can choose to operate at any point on that demand curve. That is, the monopoly supplier can choose whatever price-quantity combination on the demand curve it finds most profitable. Its activities are constrained only by the nature of the demand curve for its product, not by the behavior of rival producers. This then is the polar opposite case from perfect competition, in which the existence of many suppliers enforces price-taking behavior on any one firm.*

In Chapter 14 we move from the relatively simple case of monopoly to market structures involving a "few" firms. As we shall see, adding additional suppliers (even if we restrict ourselves to two-firm models of duopoly) makes matters much more complicated. In such cases any one firm does not face the total market demand curve, but, rather, faces a demand curve for its own output that will have properties determined in part by its rivals' behavior—the demand curve for GM cars depends in part on what Ford and Toyota do. To develop a realistic model, therefore, requires that some assumption be made about how one firm believes its rivals behave.

The issues of intrafirm rivalry and product differentiation introduced in Chapter 14 can also be approached formally as applications of the theory of games. In Chapter 15 we provide a general introduction to this topic. We show how many strategic situations can be interpreted in game-theoretic terms and illustrate how the notion of market equilibrium has important analogies in these models.

Chapter 13

MODELS OF MONOPOLY

A monopoly *is a single firm that serves an entire market. This single firm faces the market demand curve for its output. Using its knowledge of this demand curve, the monopoly makes a decision on how much to produce. Unlike the perfectly competitive firm's output decision (which has no effect on market price), the monopoly's output decision will, in fact, determine the good's price. In this sense monopoly markets and markets characterized by perfect competition are polar opposite cases.*

At times it is more convenient to treat monopolies as having the power to set prices. Technically, a monopoly can choose that point on the market demand curve at which it prefers to operate. It may choose either market price or quantity, but not both. In this chapter we will usually assume that monopolies choose the quantity of output that maximizes profits and then settle for the market price that the chosen output level yields. It would be a simple matter to rephrase the discussion in terms of price setting, and in some places we shall do so.

Barriers to entry

Given these conventions we have the following:

DEFINITION

Monopoly. A *monopoly* is a single supplier to a market. This firm may choose to produce at any point on the market demand curve.

The reason a monopoly exists is that other firms find it unprofitable or impossible to enter the market. *Barriers to entry* are therefore the source of all monopoly power. If other firms could enter a market, the firm would, by definition, no longer be a monopoly. There are two general types of barriers to entry: technical barriers and legal barriers.

Technical barriers to entry

A primary technical barrier is that the production of the good in question may exhibit decreasing marginal (and average) costs over a wide range of output levels. The technology of production is such that relatively large-scale firms are low-cost producers. In this situation (which is sometimes referred to as *natural monopoly*) one firm may find it profitable to drive others out of the industry by cutting prices. Similarly, once a monopoly has been established, entry will be difficult because any new firm must produce at relatively low levels of output and therefore at relatively high average costs. It is important to stress that the range of declining costs need only be "large" relative to the market in question. Declining costs on some absolute scale are not necessary. For example, the production and delivery of concrete does not exhibit declining marginal costs over a broad range of output when compared to the total U.S. market. However, in any particular small town, declining marginal costs may permit a monopoly to be established. The high costs of transportation in this industry tend to isolate one market from another.

Another technical basis of monopoly is special knowledge of a low-cost productive technique. But the problem for the monopoly that fears entry is keeping this technique uniquely to itself. When matters of technology are involved, this may be extremely difficult, unless the technology can be protected by a patent (see below). Ownership of unique resources, such as mineral deposits or land locations, or the possession of unique managerial talents may also be a lasting basis for maintaining a monopoly.

Legal barriers to entry

Many pure monopolies are created as a matter of law rather than as a matter of economic conditions. One important example of a government-granted monopoly position is in the legal protection of a product by a patent or copyright. Prescription drugs, computer chips, and Disney animated movies are examples of profitable products that are shielded (for a time) from direct competition by potential imitators. Because the basic technology for these products is uniquely assigned to one firm, a monopoly position is established. The defense made of such a governmentally granted monopoly is that the patent and copyright system makes innovation more profitable and therefore acts as an incentive. Whether the benefits of such innovative behavior exceed the costs of having monopolies is an open question that has been much debated by economists.

A second example of a legally created monopoly is the awarding of an exclusive franchise to serve a market. These franchises are awarded in cases of public utility (gas and electric) service, communications services, the post office, some television and radio station markets, and a variety of other situations. The argument usually put forward in favor of creating these franchised monopolies is that the industry in question is a natural monopoly: Average cost is diminishing over a broad range of output levels, and minimum average cost can be achieved only by organizing the industry as a monopoly. The public utility and communications industries are often considered good examples. Certainly, that does appear to be the case for local electricity and telephone service where a given network probably exhibits declining average cost up to the point of universal coverage. But recent deregulation in telephone services and electricity generation show that, even for these industries, the natural monopoly rationale may not be all-inclusive. In other cases, franchises may be based largely on political rationales. This seems to be true for the postal service in the United States and for a number of nationalized industries (airlines, radio and television, banking) in other countries.

Creation of barriers to entry

Although some barriers to entry may be independent of the monopolist's own activities, other barriers may result directly from those activities. For example, firms may develop unique products or technologies and take extraordinary steps to keep these from being copied by competitors. Or firms may buy up unique resources to prevent potential entry. The De Beers cartel, for example, controls a high fraction of the world's diamond mines. Finally, a would-be monopolist may enlist government aid in devising barriers to entry. It may lobby for legislation that restricts new entrants so as to "maintain an orderly market," or for health and safety regulations that raise potential entrants' costs. Because the monopolist has both special knowledge of its business and significant incentives to pursue these goals, it may have considerable success in creating such barriers to entry.

The attempt by a monopolist to erect barriers to entry may involve real resource costs. Maintaining secrecy, buying unique resources, and engaging in political lobbying are all costly activities. A full analysis of monopoly should involve not only questions of cost minimization and output choice (as under perfect competition), but also an analysis of profit-maximizing entry barrier creation. However, we will not provide a detailed investigation of such questions here.[1] Instead, we will generally assume that the monopolist can do nothing to affect barriers to entry and that the firm's costs are therefore similar to what a competitive firm's costs would be. At times, however, we will mention some of the complications raised by the possibility of expenditures incurred to protect a monopolist's market. A more complete discussion of these "rent-seeking" expenditures is presented in Chapter 21.

Profit maximization and output choice

To maximize profits, a monopoly will choose to produce that output level for which marginal revenue is equal to marginal cost. Because the monopoly, in contrast to a perfectly competitive firm, faces a negatively sloped market demand curve, marginal revenue will be less than the market price. To sell an additional unit, the monopoly must lower its price on all units to be sold if it is to generate the extra demand necessary to absorb this marginal unit. The profit-maximizing output level for a firm is then the level Q^* in Figure 13.1. At that level marginal revenue is equal to marginal costs, and profits are maximized.

FIGURE 13.1   **Profit Maximization and Price Determination for a Monopoly**

A profit-maximizing monopolist produces that quantity for which marginal revenue is equal to marginal cost. In the diagram this quantity is given by Q^*, which will yield a price of P^* in the market. Monopoly profits can be read as the rectangle of P^*EAC.

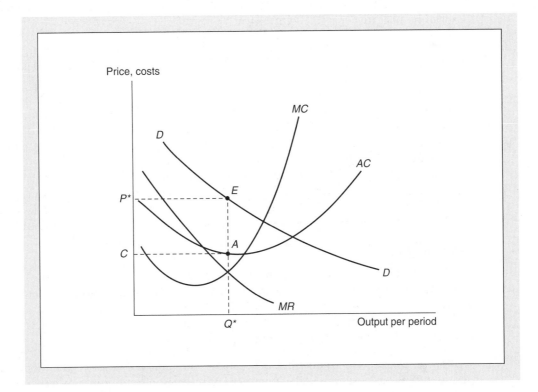

---

[1]For a simple treatment, see R. A. Posner, "The Social Costs of Monopoly and Regulation," *Journal of Political Economy 83* (August 1975): 807–27.

Given the monopoly's decision to produce Q^*, the demand curve D indicates that a market price of P^* will prevail. This is the price that demanders as a group are willing to pay for the output of the monopoly. In the market, an equilibrium price-quantity combination of P^*, Q^* will be observed. Assuming $P^* > AC$, this output level will be profitable, and the monopolist will have no incentive to alter output levels unless demand or cost conditions change. Hence we have the following principle:

OPTIMIZATION PRINCIPLE

Monopolist's output. A monopolist will choose to produce that output for which marginal revenue equals marginal cost. Because the monopolist faces a downward-sloping demand curve, market price will exceed marginal revenue and the firm's marginal cost at this output level.

The inverse elasticity rule, again

In Chapter 9 we showed that the assumption of profit maximization implies that the gap between a price of a firm's output and its marginal cost is inversely related to the price elasticity of the demand curve facing the firm. Applying Equation 9.13 to the case of monopoly yields

$$\frac{P - MC}{P} = -\frac{1}{e_{Q,P}},\tag{13.1}$$

where now we use the elasticity of demand for the entire market ($e_{Q,P}$) because the monopoly is the sole supplier of the good in question. This observation leads to two general conclusions about monopoly pricing. First, a monopoly will choose to operate only in regions in which the *market* demand curve is elastic ($e_{Q,P} < -1$). If demand were inelastic, marginal revenue would be negative and could not therefore be equated to marginal cost (which presumably is always positive). Equation 13.1 also shows that $e_{Q,P} > -1$ implies an (implausible) negative marginal cost.

A second implication of Equation 13.1 is that the firm's "markup" over marginal cost (measured as a fraction of price) depends inversely on the elasticity of market demand. If, for example, $e_{Q,P} = -2$, Equation 13.1 shows that $P = 2MC$, whereas if $e_{Q,P} = -10$, $P = 1.11MC$. Notice also that if the elasticity of demand were constant along the entire demand curve, the proportional markup over marginal cost would remain unchanged in response to changes in input costs. Market price, therefore, moves proportionally to marginal cost—increases in marginal cost will prompt the monopoly to increase its price proportionally, and decreases in marginal cost will cause the monopoly to reduce its price proportionally. Even if elasticity is not constant along the demand curve, it seems clear from Figure 13.1 that increases in marginal cost will increase price (though not necessarily in the same proportion). So long as the demand curve facing the monopoly is downward sloping, upward shifts in MC will prompt the monopoly to reduce output and thereby obtain a higher price.[2]

Monopoly profits

Total profits earned by the monopolist can be read directly from Figure 13.1. These are shown by the rectangle P^*EAC and again represent the profit per unit (price minus average cost) times the number of units sold. These profits will be positive if market price exceeds average total cost. If $P^* < AC$, however, the monopolist can only operate at a long-term loss and will decline to serve the market.

Because, by assumption, no entry is possible into a monopoly market, the monopolist's positive profits can exist even in the long run. For this reason some authors refer to the prof-

---

[2]The comparative statics of a shift in the demand curve facing the monopolist are not so clear, however, and no unequivocal prediction about price can be made. For an analysis of this issue, see the discussion that follows and Problem 13.4.

its that a monopoly earns in the long run as *monopoly rents*. These profits can be regarded as a return to that factor that forms the basis of the monopoly (a patent, a favorable location, or a dynamic entrepreneur, for example); hence another possible owner might be willing to pay that amount in rent for the right to the monopoly. The potential for profits is the reason why some firms pay other firms for the right to use a patent and why concessioners at sporting events (and on some highways) are willing to pay for the right to the concession. To the extent monopoly rights are given away at below their true market value (as in radio and television licensing), the wealth of the recipients of those rights is increased.

Although a monopoly may earn positive profits in the long run,[3] the size of such profits will depend on the relationship between the monopolist's average costs and the demand for its product. Figure 13.2 illustrates two situations in which the demand, marginal revenue, and marginal cost curves are rather similar. As Equation 13.1 suggests, the price–marginal cost markup is about the same in these two cases. But average costs in Figure 13.2a are considerably lower than in Figure 13.2b. Although the profit-maximizing decisions are similar in the two cases, the level of profits ends up being quite different. In Figure 13.2a the monopolist's price (P^*) exceeds the average cost of producing Q^* (labeled AC^*) by a large extent, and significant profits are obtained. In Figure 13.2b, however, $P^* = AC^*$ and the monopoly earns zero economic profits, the largest amount possible in this case. Hence, large profits from a monopoly are not inevitable, and the actual extent of economic profits may not always be a good guide to the significance of monopolistic influences in a market.

| FIGURE 13.2 | **Monopoly Profits Depend on the Relationship Between the Demand and Average Cost Curves** |

Both of the monopolies in this figure are equally "strong," if by this we mean they produce similar divergences between market price and marginal cost. However, because of the location of the demand and average cost curves, it turns out that the monopoly in (a) earns high profits whereas that in (b) earns no profits. Consequently, the size of profits is not a measure of the strength of a monopoly.

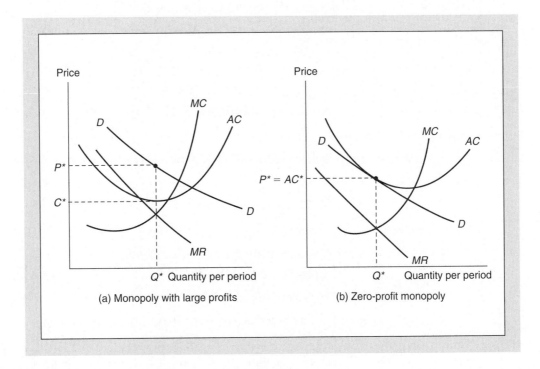

(a) Monopoly with large profits   (b) Zero-profit monopoly

---

[3]As in the competitive case, the profit-maximizing monopolist would be willing to produce at a loss in the short run as long as market price exceeds average variable cost.

There is no monopoly supply curve

In the theory of perfectly competitive markets we presented in Part 4, it was possible to speak of an industry supply curve. We constructed the long-run supply curve by allowing the market demand curve to shift and observing the supply curve that was traced out by the series of equilibrium price-quantity combinations. This type of construction is not possible for monopolistic markets. With a fixed market demand curve, the supply "curve" for a monopoly will be only one point, namely, that price-quantity combination for which $MR = MC$. If the demand curve should shift, the marginal revenue curve would also shift, and a new profit-maximizing output would be chosen. However, connecting the resulting series of equilibrium points on the market demand curves would have little meaning. This locus might have a very strange shape, depending on how the market demand curve's elasticity (and its associated MR curve) changes as the curve is shifted. In this sense the monopoly firm has no well-defined "supply curve." Each demand curve is a unique profit-maximizing opportunity for a monopolist.

 EXAMPLE 13.1

Monopoly with Linear Demand

Suppose the market for Olympic-quality Frisbees (Q, measured in Frisbees bought per year) has a linear demand curve of the form

$$Q = 2,000 - 20P \qquad (13.2)$$

or

$$P = 100 - Q/20, \qquad (13.3)$$

and that the costs of a monopoly Frisbee producer are given by

$$C(Q) = .05Q^2 + 10,000. \qquad (13.4)$$

To maximize profits, this producer chooses that output level for which $MR = MC$. To solve this problem we must phrase both MR and MC as functions of Q alone. To do so, write total revenue as

$$P \cdot Q = 100Q - Q^2/20. \qquad (13.5)$$

Consequently

$$MR = 100 - Q/10 = MC = .1Q \qquad (13.6)$$

and

$$Q^* = 500 \qquad P^* = 75. \qquad (13.7)$$

At the monopoly's preferred output level,

$$C(Q) = .05(500)^2 + 10,000 = 22,500$$
$$AC = 22,500/500 = 45. \qquad (13.8)$$

Using this information we can calculate profits by

$$\pi = (P^* - AC) \cdot Q^* = (75 - 45) \cdot 500 = 15,000. \qquad (13.9)$$

Notice that at this equilibrium there is a large markup between price (75) and marginal cost ($MC = .1Q = 50$). As long as entry barriers prevent a new firm from producing Olympic-quality Frisbees, however, this gap and positive economic profits can persist indefinitely.

An illustration of the inverse elasticity rule. To see that the inverse elasticity rule holds, we need to compute the elasticity of demand at the monopoly's equilibrium point:

$$e_{Q,P} = \frac{\partial Q}{\partial P} \cdot \frac{P}{Q} = -20\left(\frac{75}{500}\right) = -3. \qquad (13.10)$$

So, by Equation 13.1

$$\frac{P - MC}{P} = \frac{1}{3}$$

or

$$P = \frac{3}{2} MC, \qquad (13.11)$$

which is indeed the relationship between the equilibrium price (75) and the monopoly's marginal cost (50).

Query: How would an increase in fixed costs from 10,000 to 12,500 affect the monopoly's output plans? How would profits be affected? Suppose total costs were to shift to $C(Q) = .075\, Q^2 + 10,000$. How would the equilibrium change?

Monopoly and resource allocation

In Chapter 12 we briefly mentioned why the presence of monopoly distorts the allocation of resources. Because the monopoly produces a level of output for which $MC = MR < P$, the market price of its good no longer conveys accurate information about production costs. Hence, consumers' decisions will no longer reflect true opportunity costs of production, and resources will be misallocated. In this section we explore this misallocation in some detail in a partial equilibrium context.

Basis of comparison

To evaluate the allocational effect of a monopoly, we need a precisely defined basis of comparison. A particularly useful comparison is provided by the perfectly competitive, constant-cost industry. In this case, as we showed in Chapter 10, the industry's long-run supply curve will be infinitely elastic with price equal to both marginal and average cost. It is convenient to think of a monopoly as arising from the "capture" of such a competitive industry and to treat the individual firms that constituted the competitive industry as now being single plants in the monopolist's empire. A prototype case would be John D. Rockefeller's purchase of most of the U.S. petroleum refineries in the late nineteenth century and his decision to operate them as part of the Standard Oil trust. We can then compare the performance of this monopoly to the performance of the previously competitive industry to arrive at a statement about the welfare consequences of monopoly.

A graphical analysis

Figure 13.3 shows a simple linear demand curve for a product produced by a constant-cost industry. If this market were competitive, output would be Q^*—that is, production would occur where price is equal to long-run average and marginal cost. Under a simple single-price monopoly, output would be Q^{**}, because this is the level of production for which marginal revenue is equal to marginal cost. The restriction in output

FIGURE 13.3   Allocational and Distributional Effects of Monopoly

Monopolization of this previously competitive market would cause output to be reduced from Q^* to Q^{**}. Consumer expenditures and productive inputs worth AEQ^*Q^{**} are reallocated to the production of other goods. Consumer surplus equal to $P^{**}BAP^*$ is transferred into monopoly profits. There is a deadweight loss given by BEA.

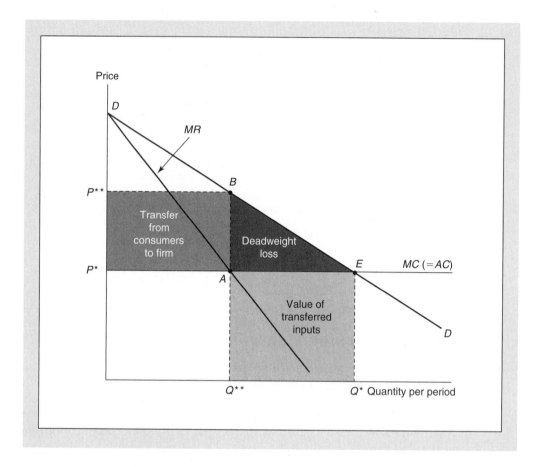

from Q^* to Q^{**} represents the misallocation brought about through monopolization. The total value of resources released by this output restriction is shown in Figure 13.3 as area AEQ^*Q^{**}. Essentially, the monopoly closes down some of the plants that were operating in the competitive case. These transferred inputs can be productively employed elsewhere, so area AEQ^*Q^{**} is not a social loss.

The restriction in output from Q^* to Q^{**} involves a total loss in consumer surplus of $P^{**}BEP^*$. Part of this loss is captured by the monopoly as profits. These profits are measured by $P^{**}BAP^*$, and they reflect a transfer of income from consumers to the firm. As for any transfer, difficult issues of equity arise in attempting to assess whether or not such a transfer is "equitable." There is no ambiguity about the loss in consumers' surplus given by area BEA, however, because this loss is not transferred to anyone. It is a pure "deadweight" loss and represents the principal measure of the allocational harm of the monopoly.[4]

To illustrate the nature of this deadweight loss, consider Example 13.1, in which we calculated an equilibrium price of $75 and a marginal cost of $50. This gap between price and marginal cost is an indication of the efficiency-improving trades that are forgone through

---

[4]If the monopolized industry has a positively sloped long-run supply curve, some of the deadweight losses will also be reflected in reduced rents for inputs arising from the monopolist's restriction in output.

monopolization. Undoubtedly, there is a would-be buyer who is willing to pay, say, $60 for an Olympic Frisbee, but not $75. A price of $60 would more than cover all of the resource costs involved in Frisbee production, but the presence of the monopoly prevents such a mutually beneficial transaction between Frisbee users and the providers of Frisbee-making resources. For this reason, the monopoly equilibrium is not Pareto optimal—an alternative allocation of resources would make all parties better off. Economists have made many attempts to estimate the overall cost of these deadweight losses in actual monopoly situations. Most of these estimates are rather small when viewed in the context of the whole economy.[5] Allocational losses are larger, however, for some narrowly defined industries.

 EXAMPLE 13.2

Welfare Losses and Elasticity

The allocational effects of monopoly can be characterized fairly completely in the case of constant marginal costs and a constant price elasticity demand curve. To do so, assume that constant marginal (and average) costs for a monopolist are given by c and that the demand curve has a constant elasticity form of

$$Q = P^e, \tag{13.12}$$

where e is the price elasticity of demand ($e < -1$). We know the competitive price in this market will be

$$P_c = c \tag{13.13}$$

and the monopoly price is given by

$$P_m = \frac{c}{1 + \dfrac{1}{e}}. \tag{13.14}$$

The consumer surplus associated with any price (P_0) can be computed as

$$
\begin{aligned}
CS &= \int_{P_0}^{\infty} Q(P)\,dP \\
&= \int_{P_0}^{\infty} P^e\,dP \\
&= \left. \frac{P^{e+1}}{e+1} \right|_{P_0}^{\infty} \\
&= -\frac{P_0^{e+1}}{e+1}.
\end{aligned}
\tag{13.15}
$$

Hence, under perfect competition,

$$CS_c = -\frac{c^{e+1}}{e+1}, \tag{13.16}$$

and, under monopoly,

$$CS_m = -\frac{\left(\dfrac{c}{1 + \dfrac{1}{e}}\right)^{e+1}}{e+1}. \tag{13.17}$$

---

[5]The classic study is A. Harberger, "Monopoly and Resource Allocation," *American Economic Review* (May 1954): 77–87. Harberger estimates that such losses constitute about 0.1 percent of gross national product.

EXAMPLE 13.2 CONTINUED

Taking the ratio of these two surplus measures yields

$$\frac{CS_m}{CS_c} = \left(\frac{1}{1 + \frac{1}{e}}\right)^{e+1}.$$

(13.18)

If $e = -2$, for example, this ratio is $\frac{1}{2}$—consumer surplus under monopoly is half what it is under perfect competition. For more-elastic cases this figure falls a bit (because output restrictions under monopoly are more significant). For elasticities closer to -1, the ratio increases.

Profits. The transfer from consumer surplus into monopoly profits can also be computed fairly easily in this case. Monopoly profits are given by

$$\pi_m = P_m Q_m - c Q_m = \left(\frac{c}{1 + \frac{1}{e}} - c\right) Q_m$$

$$= \left(\frac{-\frac{c}{e}}{1 + \frac{1}{e}}\right) \cdot \left(\frac{c}{1 + \frac{1}{e}}\right)^e = -\left(\frac{c}{1 + \frac{1}{e}}\right)^{e+1} \cdot \frac{1}{e}.$$

(13.19)

Dividing this expression by Equation 13.16 yields

$$\frac{\pi_m}{CS_c} = \left(\frac{e+1}{e}\right)\left(\frac{1}{1 + \frac{1}{e}}\right)^{e+1} = \left(\frac{e}{1+e}\right)^e.$$

(13.20)

For $e = -2$, this ratio is $\frac{1}{4}$. Hence one-fourth of the consumer surplus enjoyed under perfect competition is transferred into monopoly profits. The deadweight loss from monopoly in this case is therefore also $\frac{1}{4}$ of the level of consumer surplus under perfect competition.

Query: Suppose $e = -1.5$. What fraction of consumer surplus is lost through monopolization? How much is transferred into monopoly profits? Why do these results differ from the case $e = -2$?

Monopoly, product quality, and durability

The market power enjoyed by a monopoly may be exercised along dimensions other than the market price of its product. If the monopoly has some leeway in the type, quality, or diversity of the goods it produces, it would not be surprising if the firm's decisions were to differ from those that might prevail under a competitive organization of the market. Whether a monopoly will produce higher-quality or lower-quality goods than would be produced under competition is unclear, however. It all depends on the nature of consumer demand and the firm's costs.

A formal treatment of quality

Suppose consumers' willingness to pay for quality (X) is given by the inverse demand function $P(Q, X)$, where

$$\partial P/\partial Q < 0, \ \partial P/\partial X > 0.$$

If the costs of producing Q and X are given by $C(Q, X)$, the monopoly will choose Q and X to maximize

$$\pi = P(Q, X)Q - C(Q, X). \tag{13.21}$$

The first-order conditions for a maximum are

$$\frac{\partial \pi}{\partial Q} = P(Q, X) + Q \frac{\partial P}{\partial Q} - C_Q = 0 \tag{13.22}$$

$$\frac{\partial \pi}{\partial X} = Q \frac{\partial P}{\partial X} - C_X = 0. \tag{13.23}$$

The first of these equations repeats the usual rule that marginal revenue equals marginal cost for output decisions. The second equation states that when Q is appropriately set, the monopoly should choose that level of quality for which the marginal revenue attainable from increasing the quality of its output by one unit is equal to the marginal cost of making such an increase. As might have been expected, the assumption of profit maximization requires the monopolist to proceed to the margin of profitability along all of the dimensions it can. Notice, in particular, that the marginal demander's valuation of quality per unit is multiplied by the monopolist's output level.

The level of product quality that will be opted for under competitive conditions will also be the one that maximizes net social welfare:

$$SW = \int_0^{Q^*} P(Q, X)dQ - C(Q, X), \tag{13.24}$$

where Q^* is the output level determined through the competitive process of marginal cost pricing given X. Differentiation of Equation 13.24 with respect to X yields the first-order condition for a maximum:

$$\frac{\partial SW}{\partial X} = \int_0^{Q^*} P_X(Q, X)dQ - C_X = 0. \tag{13.25}$$

The difference between the quality choice specified in Equation 13.23 and Equation 13.25 is that the former looks at the marginal valuation of one more unit of quality assuming Q is at its profit-maximizing level, whereas the latter looks at the marginal value of quality averaged across all output levels.[6] Therefore even if a monopoly and a perfectly competitive industry chose the same output level, they might opt for differing quality levels because each is concerned with a different margin in its decision making. Only by knowing the specifics of the problem, however, is it possible to predict the direction of these differences. For an example, see Problem 13.10.

---

[6]The average marginal valuation (AV) of product quality is given by

$$AV = \int_0^{Q^*} P_X(Q, X)dQ/Q.$$

Hence $Q \cdot AV = C_X$ is the quality rule adopted to maximize net welfare under perfect competition. Compare this to Equation 13.23.

The durability of durable goods

Much of the research on the effect that monopolization has on quality has focused on durable goods. These are goods such as automobiles, houses, or refrigerators that provide services to their owners over several periods rather than being completely consumed soon after they are bought. The element of time that enters into the theory of durable goods leads to many interesting problems and paradoxes. Initial interest in the topic started with the question of whether monopolies would produce goods that lasted as long as would similar goods produced under perfect competition. The intuitive notion that monopolies would "underproduce" durability (just as they choose an output below the competitive level) was soon shown to be incorrect by the Australian economist Peter Swan[7] in the early 1970s.

Swan's insight was to view durable goods demand as being the demand for a flow of services (i.e., automobile transportation) over several periods. He argued that both a monopoly and a competitive market would seek to minimize the cost of providing this flow to consumers. The monopoly would, of course, choose an output level that restricted the flow of services so as to maximize profits, but, assuming constant returns to scale in production, there is no reason that durability per se would be affected by market structure. This result is sometimes referred to as "Swan's independence assumption." Output decisions can be treated independently from decisions about product durability.

Subsequent research on the Swan result has focused on showing how it can be undermined by different assumptions about the nature of a particular durable good or by relaxing the implicit assumption that all demanders are the same. For example, the result depends importantly on how durable goods deteriorate. The simplest type of deterioration is illustrated by a durable good such as a light bulb that provides a constant stream of services until it becomes worthless. With this type of good, Equations 13.23 and 13.25 are identical, so Swan's independence result holds. Even when goods deteriorate smoothly, the independence result continues to hold if a constant flow of services can be maintained by simply replacing what has been used—this requires that new goods and old goods be perfect substitutes and infinitely divisible. Outdoor house paint may, more or less, meet this requirement. On the other hand, most goods clearly do not. It is just not possible to replace a run-down refrigerator with, say, half of a new one. Once such more complex forms of deterioration are considered, Swan's result may not hold because we can no longer fall back upon the notion of providing a given flow of services at minimal cost over time. In these more complex cases, however, it is not always the case that a monopoly will produce less durability than will a competitive market—it all depends on the nature of the demand for durability.

Time inconsistency and heterogeneous demand

Focusing on the service flow from durable goods provides important insights on durability, but it does leave an important question unanswered—when should the monopoly produce the actual durable goods needed to provide the desired service flow? Suppose, for example, that a light bulb monopoly decides that its profit-maximizing output decision is to supply the services provided by 1 million 60-watt bulbs. If the firm decides to produce 1 million bulbs in the first period, what is it to do in the second period (say, before any of the original bulbs burn out)? Because the monopoly chooses a point on the service demand curve where $P > MC$, it has a clear incentive to produce more bulbs in the second period by cutting price a bit. But consumers can anticipate this, so they may reduce their first period demand, waiting for a bargain. Hence, the monopoly's profit-maximizing plan will unravel. Ronald Coase was the first economist to note this "time inconsistency" that arises when a monopoly produces a durable good.[8] Coase argued that its presence would

[7]P. L. Swan, "Durability of Consumption Goods," *American Economic Review* (December 1970): 884–94.

[8]R. Coase, "Durability and Monopoly," *Journal of Law and Economics* (April 1972): 143–49.

severely undercut potential monopoly power—in the limit, competitive pricing is the only outcome that can prevail in the durable goods case. Only if the monopoly can succeed in making a credible commitment not to produce more in the second period can it succeed in its plan to achieve monopoly profits on the service flow from durable goods.

Recent modeling of the durable goods question has examined how a monopolist's choices are affected in situations where there are different types of demanders.[9] In such cases, questions about the optimal choice of durability and about credible commitments become even more complicated. Not only must the monopolist settle on an optimal scheme for each category of buyers, but it must also ensure that the scheme intended for, say, type 1 demanders is not also attractive to type 2 demanders. Studying these sorts of models would take us too far afield, but some illustrations of how such "incentive compatible constraints" work are provided in the Extensions to this chapter. Clearly further work is needed if we are to understand fully the complex pricing schemes adopted by multiproduct durable goods producers such as Microsoft or Panasonic.

Price discrimination

In some circumstances a monopoly may be able to increase profits by departing from a single-price policy for its output. The possibility of selling identical goods at different prices is called price discrimination.[10]

DEFINITION

Price discrimination. A monopoly engages in *price discrimination* if it is able to sell otherwise identical units of output at different prices.

Whether a price discrimination strategy is feasible depends crucially on the inability of buyers of the good to practice arbitrage. In the absence of transactions or information costs, the "law of one price" implies that a homogeneous good must sell everywhere for the same price. Consequently, price discrimination schemes are doomed to failure because demanders who can buy from the monopoly at lower prices will be more attractive sources of the good for those who must pay high prices than is the monopoly itself. Profit-seeking middlemen would destroy any discriminatory pricing scheme. When resale is costly (or can be prevented entirely), however, price discrimination becomes possible.

First-degree or perfect price discrimination

If each buyer can be separately identified by a monopolist, it may be possible to charge each the maximum price he or she would willingly pay for the good. This strategy of *perfect* (or *first-degree*) price discrimination would then extract all available consumer surplus, leaving demanders as a group indifferent between buying the monopolist's good or doing without it. The strategy is illustrated in Figure 13.4. The figure assumes that buyers are arranged in descending order of willingness to pay. The first buyer is willing to pay up to P_1 for Q_1 units of output, so the monopolist charges P_1 and obtains total revenues of $P_1 Q_1$, as indicated by the lightly shaded rectangle. A second buyer is willing to pay up to P_2 for $Q_2 - Q_1$ units of output, so the monopolist obtains total revenue of $P_2(Q_2 - Q_1)$ from this buyer. Notice that for this strategy to succeed, the second buyer must be unable to resell the output he or she buys at P_2 to the first buyer (who pays $P_1 > P_2$).

The monopolist will proceed in this way up to the point at which the marginal buyer is no longer willing to pay the good's marginal cost (labeled *MC* in Figure 13.3). Hence

---

[9]For a summary, see M. Waldman, "Durable Goods Theory for Real World Markets," *Journal of Economic Perspectives* (Winter 2003): 131–54.

[10]A monopoly may also be able to sell differentiated products at differential price-cost margins. Here, however, we treat price discrimination only for a monopoly that produces a single, homogeneous product.

FIGURE 13.4   Perfect Price Discrimination

Under perfect price discrimination, the monopoly charges a different price to each buyer. It sells Q_1 units at P_1, $Q_2 - Q_1$ units at P_2, and so forth. In this case the firm will produce Q^*, and total revenues will be DEQ^*0.

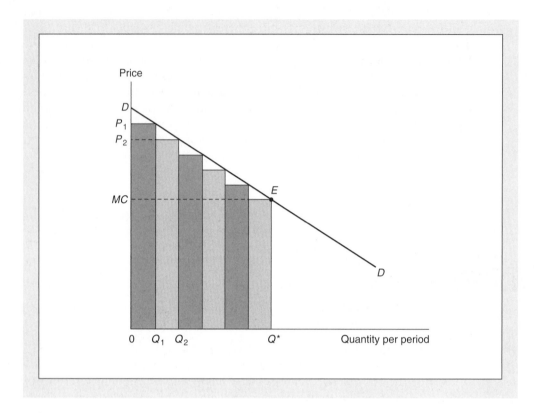

total quantity produced will be Q^*. Total revenues collected will be given by the area DEQ^*0. All consumer surplus has been extracted by the monopolist and there is no deadweight loss in this situation. (Compare Figures 13.3 and 13.4.) The allocation of resources under perfect price discrimination is therefore efficient, though it does entail a large transfer from consumer surplus into monopoly profits.

 EXAMPLE 13.3

First-Degree Price Discrimination

Consider again the Frisbee monopolist in Example 13.1. Because there are relatively few high-quality Frisbees sold, the monopolist may find it possible to discriminate perfectly among a few world-class flippers. In this case it will choose to produce that quantity for which the marginal buyer pays exactly the marginal cost of a Frisbee:

$$P = 100 - Q/20 = MC = .1Q. \tag{13.26}$$

Hence

$$Q^* = 666$$

and, at the margin, price and marginal cost are given by

$$P = MC = 66.6. \tag{13.27}$$

Now we can compute total revenues by integration:

$$R = \int_0^{Q^*} P(Q)\,dQ = 100Q - \frac{Q^2}{40}\bigg|_0^{666} \tag{13.28}$$

$$= 55{,}511$$

and total costs as

$$C(Q) = .05Q^2 + 10{,}000 = 32{,}178. \tag{13.29}$$

Total profits are given by

$$\pi = R - C = 23{,}333, \tag{13.30}$$

which represents a substantial increase over the single-price policy examined in Example 13.1 (which yielded 15,000).

Query: What is the maximum price any Frisbee buyer pays in this case? Use this to obtain a geometric definition of profits.

Third-degree price discrimination through market separation

First-degree price discrimination poses a considerable information burden for the monopoly—it must know the demand function for each potential buyer. A less stringent requirement would be to assume the monopoly can separate its buyers into relatively few identifiable markets (such as "rural-urban," "domestic-foreign," or "prime-time–off-prime") and pursue a separate monopoly pricing policy in each market.[11] Knowledge of the price elasticities of demand in these markets is sufficient to pursue such a policy. The monopoly then sets price in each market according to the inverse elasticity rule. Assuming that marginal cost is the same in all markets, this results in a pricing policy in which

$$P_i\left(1 + \frac{1}{e_i}\right) = P_j\left(1 + \frac{1}{e_j}\right) \tag{13.31}$$

or

$$\frac{P_i}{P_j} = \frac{\left(1 + \dfrac{1}{e_j}\right)}{\left(1 + \dfrac{1}{e_i}\right)}, \tag{13.32}$$

where P_i and P_j are the prices charged in markets i and j, which have price elasticities of demand given by e_i and e_j. An immediate consequence of this pricing policy is that the profit-maximization price will be higher in markets in which demand is less elastic. If, for example, $e_i = -2$ and $e_j = -3$, Equation 13.32 shows that $P_i/P_j = 4/3$—prices will be one-third higher in the less elastic market.

Figure 13.5 illustrates this result for two markets that the monopoly can serve at constant marginal cost (MC). Demand is less elastic in market 1 than in market 2, hence the

---

[11]Market-separating price discrimination is also referred to as *third-degree* price discrimination. We will take up *second-degree* price discrimination in the next section.

FIGURE 13.5   **Separated Markets Raise the Possibility of Third-Degree Price Discrimination**

If two markets are separate, a monopolist can maximize profits by selling his or her product at different prices in the two markets. This would entail choosing that output for which $MC = MR$ in each of the markets. The diagram shows that the market that has a less elastic demand curve will be charged the higher price by the price discriminator.

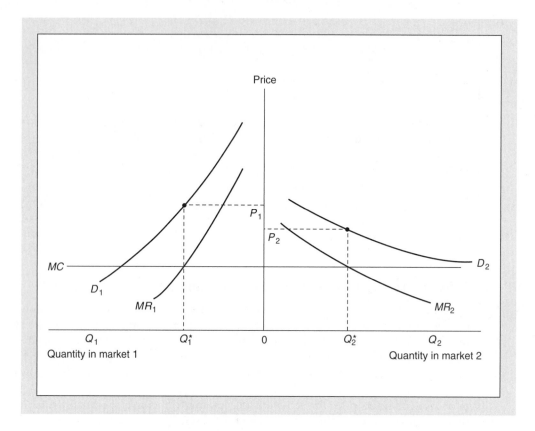

gap between price and marginal revenue is larger in the former market. Profit maximization requires that the firm produce Q_1^* in market 1 and Q_2^* in market 2, resulting in a higher price in the less elastic market. So long as arbitrage between the two markets can be prevented, this price difference can persist. The two-price discriminatory policy is clearly more profitable for the monopoly than would be a single-price policy, because the firm could always opt for such a policy should market conditions warrant a single price.

The welfare consequences of third-degree price discrimination is, in principle, ambiguous. Relative to a single-price policy, the discriminating policy requires raising price in the less elastic market and reducing it in the more elastic one. Hence, the changes have an off-setting effect on total allocational losses. A more complete analysis suggests the intuitively plausible conclusion that the multiple-price policy will be allocationally superior to a single-price policy only in situations in which total output is increased through discrimination. Example 13.4 illustrates the simple case of linear demand curves for which the multiple-price policy always results in greater allocational losses.[12]

---

[12]For a detailed discussion, see R. Schmalensee, "Output and Welfare Implications of Monopolistic Third-Degree Price Discrimination," *American Economic Review* (March 1981): 242–47.

EXAMPLE 13.4

Third-Degree Price Discrimination

Suppose the demand curves in two separated markets are given by

$$Q_1 = 24 - P_1$$

and

$$Q_2 = 24 - 2P_2, \qquad (13.33)$$

and that a monopoly can serve both of these markets at a constant marginal cost of 6. Profit maximization in the two markets requires

$$MR_1 = 24 - 2Q_1 = 6 = MR_2 = 12 - Q_2, \qquad (13.34)$$

so the optimal choices are

$$Q_1 = 9$$
$$Q_2 = 6. \qquad (13.35)$$

Prices that prevail in the two markets are then[13]

$$P_1 = 15$$
$$P_2 = 9. \qquad (13.36)$$

Profits for the monopoly following a two-price policy are

$$\pi = (P_1 - 6)Q_1 + (P_2 - 6)Q_2 = 81 + 18 = 99. \qquad (13.37)$$

The allocational impact of this policy can be evaluated by calculating the deadweight losses in the two markets. Because demand in market 1 at $P = MC = 6$ is 18 and competitive output would be 12 in market 2, such losses are given by

$$DW_1 = .5(P_1 - MC)(18 - Q_1) = .5(15 - 6)(18 - 9) = 40.5 \qquad (13.38)$$

and

$$DW_2 = .5(P_2 - MC)(12 - Q_2) = .5(9 - 6)(12 - 6) = 9. \qquad (13.39)$$

Single price policies. This third-degree price discrimination solution is sustainable so long as market separation can be maintained. But demanders in market 1 will look enviously at the lower prices being paid in market 2 and may seek some sort of redress. One possibility would be to press government regulators to require that all goods be sold at a single price. In this case the monopolist's optimal choice is to continue its pricing policy in market 1 ($P_1 = 15$, $Q_1 = 9$). This decision would preclude any sales in market 2 because the maximum that a market 2 demander is willing to pay is $P_2 = 12$. This solution would clearly be nonoptimal, however—it would increase the loss in consumer surplus in market 2 with no gain to participants in market 1.

An alternative approach would be to eliminate whatever barrier separates these two markets so that the monopolist would have to treat all demanders identically. In this case, market demand would become

$$Q = Q_1 + Q_2 = 48 - 3P. \qquad (13.40)$$

(continued)

---

[13]At these prices, $e_1 = -15/9$, $e_2 = -2(9/6) = -3$. Hence these choices obey Equation 13.32, because $P_1/P_2 = 5/3$.

EXAMPLE 13.4 CONTINUED

Now the marginal revenue function facing the firm is

$$MR = 16 - 2\,Q/3. \tag{13.41}$$

Hence, profit maximization requires $Q = 15$, $P = 11$. Because merging these markets has made demand more sensitive to price, the monopolist opts for a lower price than under the single-price regulatory scheme. Notice also that profits ($\pi = (P - 6) \cdot Q = 75$) are lower in this case than in either of the prior two cases. Total deadweight losses are also smaller in this case:

$$DW = 0.5 \cdot (P - 6) \cdot (30 - Q) = 0.5 \cdot (5) \cdot (15) = 37.5. \tag{13.42}$$

Query: Notice that the merged-market equilibrium quantity is the same as in the market-separation equilibrium ($Q = 15$). Is this always true with linear demand curves? What does this imply about the efficiency of third-degree price discrimination with such demand?

Second-degree price discrimination through price schedules

The examples of price discrimination examined in the previous section require the monopoly to separate demanders into a number of categories and choose a profit-maximizing price for each such category. An alternative approach would be for the monopoly to choose a (possibly rather complex) price schedule that provides incentives for demanders to separate themselves depending on how much they wish to buy. Such schemes include quantity discounts, minimum purchase requirements or "cover" charges, and tie-in sales. These plans would be adopted by a monopoly if they yielded greater profits than would a single-price policy, after accounting for any possible costs of implementing the price schedule. Because the schedules will result in demanders paying different prices for identical goods, this form of (second degree) price discrimination is feasible only when there are no arbitrage possibilities.

Two-part tariffs

One form of pricing schedule that has been extensively studied is a linear two-part tariff, under which demanders must pay a fixed fee for the right to consume a good and a uniform price for each unit consumed. The prototype case, first studied by Walter Oi, is an amusement park (perhaps Disneyland) that sets a basic entry fee coupled with a stated marginal price for each amusement used.[14] Mathematically, this scheme can be represented by the tariff any demander must pay to purchase q units of a good:

$$T(q) = a + pq, \tag{13.43}$$

where a is the fixed fee and p is the marginal price to be paid. The monopolist's goal then is to choose a and p to maximize profits, given the demand for this product. Because the average price paid by any demander is given by

$$\bar{p} = \frac{T}{q} = \frac{a}{q} + p, \tag{13.44}$$

---

[14] W. Y. Oi, "A Disneyland Dilemma: Two-Part Tariffs for a Mickey Mouse Monopoly," *Quarterly Journal of Economics* (February 1971): 77–90. Interestingly, the Disney empire once used a two-part tariff but abandoned it because the costs of administering the payment schemes for individual rides became too high. Like other amusement parks, Disney moved to a single-admissions-price policy (which still provided them with ample opportunities for price discrimination, especially with the multiple parks at Disney World).

this tariff is feasible only when those who pay low average prices (those for whom q is large) cannot resell the good and those who must pay high average prices (those for whom q is small).

One feasible approach described by Oi for establishing the parameters of this linear tariff would be for the firm to set the marginal price, p, equal to MC and then set a so as to extract the maximum consumer surplus from a given set of buyers. One might imagine buyers being arrayed according to willingness to pay. The choice of $p = MC$ would then maximize consumer surplus for this group, and a could be set equal to the surplus enjoyed by the least eager buyer. He or she would then be indifferent about buying the good, but all other buyers would experience net gains from the purchase.

This feasible tariff might not be the most profitable, however. Consider the effects on profits of a small increase in p above MC. This would result in no net change in the profits earned from the least willing buyer. Quantity demanded would drop slightly at the margin where $p = MC$, and some of what had previously been consumer surplus (and therefore part of the fixed fee, a) would be converted into variable profits since now $p > MC$. For all other demanders, profits would be increased by the price rise. Although each will pay a bit less in fixed charges, profits per unit bought will rise to a greater extent.[15] In some cases it is possible to make an explicit calculation of the optimal two-part tariff. Example 13.5 provides an illustration. More generally, however, optimal schedules will depend on a variety of contingencies. Some of the possibilities are examined in the Extensions to this chapter.

 EXAMPLE 13.5

Two-Part Tariffs

In order to illustrate the mathematics of two-part tariffs, let's return to the demand equations introduced in Example 13.4, but now assume that they apply to two specific demanders:

$$q_1 = 24 - p_1$$
$$q_2 = 24 - 2p_2, \qquad (13.45)$$

where now the p's refer to the marginal prices faced by these two buyers.[16]

An Oi tariff. Implementing the two-part tariff suggested by Oi would require the monopolist to set $p_1 = p_2 = MC = 6$. Hence, in this case, $q_1 = 18$, $q_2 = 12$. With this marginal price, demander 2 (the least eager of the two) obtains consumer surplus of 36 [$= 0.5 \cdot (12 - 6) \cdot 12$]. That is the maximal entry fee that might be charged without causing this person to leave the market. Consequently, the two-part tariff in this case would be $T(q) = 36 + 6q$. If the monopolist opted for this pricing scheme, its profits would be

$$\pi = R - C = T(q_1) + T(q_2) - AC(q_1 + q_2) \qquad (13.46)$$
$$= 72 + 6 \cdot 30 - 6 \cdot 30 = 72.$$

These fall short of those obtainable with all of the pricing schemes discussed in Example 13.4.

The optimal tariff. The optimal two-part tariff in this situation can be computed by noting that total profits with such a tariff are $\pi = 2a + (p - MC)(q_1 + q_2)$. Here the entry fee,

(*continued*)

---

[15]This follows because $q_i(mc) > q_1(mc)$, where $q_i(mc)$ is the quantity demanded when $p = MC$ for all except the least willing buyer (person 1). Hence the gain in profits from an increase in price above MC $\Delta p q_i(mc)$, exceeds the loss in profits from a smaller fixed fee, $\Delta p q_1(mc)$.

[16]The theory of utility maximization that underlies these demand curves is that the quantity demanded is determined by the marginal price paid, whereas the entry fee, a, determines whether $q = 0$ might be optimal instead.

EXAMPLE 13.5 CONTINUED

a, must equal the consumer surplus obtained by person 2. Inserting the specific parameters of this problem yields

$$\pi = 0.5 \cdot 2q_2(12 - p) + (p - 6)(q_1 + q_2)$$
$$= (24 - 2p)(12 - p) + (p - 6)(48 - 3p) \qquad (13.47)$$
$$= 18p - p^2.$$

Hence, maximum profits are obtained when $p = 9$ and $a = 0.5(24 - 2p)(12 - p) = 9$. Therefore the optimal tariff is $T(q) = 9 + 9q$. With this tariff, $q_1 = 15$, $q_2 = 6$, and the monopolist's profits are 81 $[= 2(9) + (9 - 6) \cdot (15 + 6)]$. The monopolist might opt for this pricing scheme if it were under political pressure to have a uniform pricing policy and to agree not to price demander 2 "out of the market." The two-part tariff permits a degree of differential pricing ($\bar{p}_1 = 9.60$, $\bar{p}_2 = 9.75$) but appears "fair" since all buyers face the same schedule.

Query: Suppose a monopolist could choose a different entry fee for each demander. What pricing policy would be followed?

Regulation of monopoly

The regulation of natural monopolies is an important subject in applied economic analysis. The utility, communications, and transportation industries are highly regulated in most countries, and devising regulatory procedures that cause these industries to operate in a desirable way is an important practical problem. Here we will examine a few aspects of the regulation of monopolies that relate to pricing policies.

Marginal cost pricing and the natural monopoly dilemma

Many economists believe it is important for the prices charged by regulated monopolies to reflect marginal costs of production accurately. In this way the deadweight loss may be minimized. The principal problem raised by an enforced policy of marginal cost pricing is that it will require natural monopolies to operate at a loss. Natural monopolies, by definition, exhibit decreasing average costs over a broad range of output levels. The cost curves for such a firm might look like those shown in Figure 13.6. In the absence of regulation the monopoly would produce output level Q_A and receive a price of P_A for its product. Profits in this situation are given by the rectangle $P_A ABC$. A regulatory agency might instead set a price of P_R for the monopoly. At this price, Q_R is demanded, and the marginal cost of producing this output level is also P_R. Consequently, marginal cost pricing has been achieved. Unfortunately, because of the negative slope of the firm's average cost curve, the price P_R (= marginal cost) falls below average costs. With this regulated price, the monopoly must operate at a loss of $GFEP_R$. Because no firm can operate indefinitely at a loss, this poses a dilemma for the regulatory agency: Either it must abandon its goal of marginal cost pricing, or the government must subsidize the monopoly forever.

Two-tier pricing systems

One way out of the marginal cost pricing dilemma is the implementation of a multi-price system. Under such a system the monopoly is permitted to charge some users a high price while maintaining a low price for marginal users. In this way the demanders paying the high price in effect subsidize the losses of the low-price customers. Such a pricing scheme

FIGURE 13.6   **Price Regulation for a Decreasing Cost Monopoly**

Because natural monopolies exhibit decreasing average costs, marginal costs fall below average costs. Consequently, enforcing a policy of marginal cost pricing will entail operating at a loss. A price of P_R, for example, will achieve the goal of marginal cost pricing but will necessitate an operating loss of $GFEP_R$.

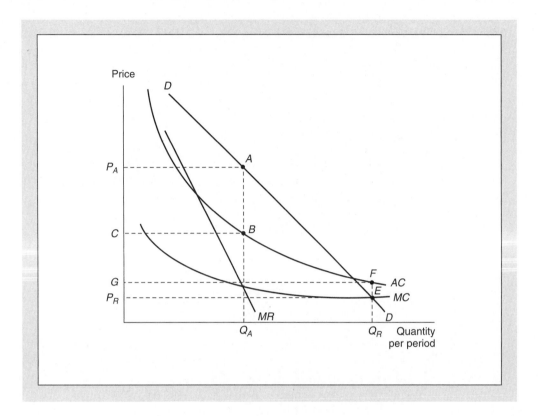

is shown in Figure 13.7. Here the regulatory commission has decided that some users will pay a relatively high price, P_1. At this price, Q_1 is demanded. Other users (presumably those who would not buy the good at the P_1 price) are offered a lower price, P_2. This lower price generates additional demand of $Q_2 - Q_1$. Consequently, a total output of Q_2 is produced at an average cost of A. With this pricing system, the profits on the sales to high-price demanders (given by the rectangle P_1DBA) balance the losses incurred on the low-priced sales ($BFEC$). Furthermore, for the "marginal user," the marginal cost pricing rule is being followed: It is the "intramarginal" user who subsidizes the firm so it does not operate at a loss. Although in practice it may not be so simple to establish pricing schemes that maintain marginal cost pricing and cover operating costs, many regulatory commissions do use price schedules that intentionally discriminate against some users (for example, businesses) to the advantage of others (consumers).

Rate of return regulation

Another approach followed in many regulatory situations is to permit the monopoly to charge a price above marginal cost that is sufficient to earn a "fair" rate of return on investment. Much analytical effort is then devoted to defining the "fair" rate concept and to developing ways in which it might be measured. From an economic point of view, some of the most interesting questions about this procedure concern how the regulatory activity affects the firm's input choices. If, for example, the rate of return allowed to firms exceeds what owners might obtain on investment under competitive circumstances, there will be an incentive to use relatively more capital input than would truly minimize costs. Or if

FIGURE 13.7   **Two-Tier Pricing Schedule**

By charging a high price (P_1) to some users and a low price (P_2) to others, it may be possible for a regulatory commission to (1) enforce marginal cost pricing and (2) create a situation where the profits from one class of user (P_1DBA) subsidize the losses of the other class (*BFEC*).

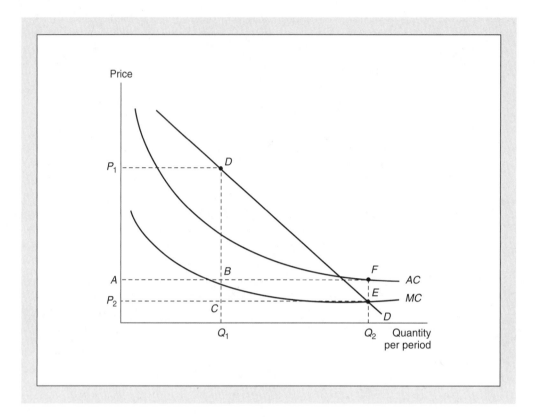

regulators typically delay in making rate decisions, firms may be given incentives to minimize costs that would not otherwise exist. We will now briefly examine a formal model of such possibilities.[17]

A formal model

Suppose a regulated utility has a production function of the form

$$q = f(k, l). \tag{13.48}$$

This firm's actual rate of return on capital is then defined as

$$s = \frac{pf(k, l) - wl}{k}, \tag{13.49}$$

where p is the price of the firm's output (which depends on q) and w is the wage rate for labor input. If s is constrained by regulation to be equal to, say, $\bar{s}$, then the firm's problem is to maximize profits

$$\pi = pf(k, l) - wl - vk \tag{13.50}$$

---

[17]This model is based on H. Averch and L. L. Johnson, "Behavior of the Firm Under Regulatory Constraint," *American Economic Review* (December 1962): 1052–69.

subject to this regulatory constraint. Setting up the Lagrangian expression for this problem yields

$$\mathscr{L} = pf(k, l) - wl - vk + \lambda[wl + \bar{s}k - pf(k, l)].\qquad(13.51)$$

Notice that if $\lambda = 0$, regulation is ineffective and the monopoly behaves like any profit-maximizing firm. If $\lambda = 1$, Equation 13.51 reduces to

$$\mathscr{L} = (\bar{s} - v)k,\qquad(13.52)$$

which, assuming $\bar{s} > v$ (which it must be if the firm is not to earn less than the prevailing rate of return on capital elsewhere), means this monopoly will hire infinite amounts of capital—an implausible result. Hence, $0 < \lambda < 1$. The first-order conditions for a maximum are

$$\frac{\partial \mathscr{L}}{\partial l} = pf_l - w + \lambda(w - pf_l) = 0$$

$$\frac{\partial \mathscr{L}}{\partial k} = pf_k - v + \lambda(\bar{s} - pf_k) = 0\qquad(13.53)$$

$$\frac{\partial \mathscr{L}}{\partial \lambda} = wl + \bar{s}k - pf(k, l) = 0.$$

The first of these conditions implies that the regulated monopoly will hire additional labor input up to the point at which $pf_l = w$—a result that holds for any profit-maximizing firm. For capital input, however, the second condition implies

$$(1 - \lambda)pf_k = v - \lambda\bar{s}\qquad(13.54)$$

or

$$pf_k = \frac{v - \lambda\bar{s}}{1 - \lambda} = v - \frac{\lambda(\bar{s} - v)}{1 - \lambda}.\qquad(13.55)$$

Because $\bar{s} > v$ and $\lambda < 1$, Equation 13.55 implies

$$pf_k < v.\qquad(13.56)$$

The firm will hire more capital (and achieve a lower marginal productivity of capital) than it would under unregulated conditions. "Overcapitalization" may therefore be a regulatory-induced misallocation of resources for some utilities. Although we shall not do so here, it is possible to examine other regulatory questions using this general analytical framework.

Dynamic views of monopoly

The static view that monopolistic practices distort the allocation of resources provides the principal economic rationale for favoring antimonopoly policies. Not all economists believe that the static analysis should be determinant, however. Some authors, most notably J. A. Schumpeter, have stressed the beneficial role that monopoly profits can play in the process of economic development.[18] These authors place considerable emphasis on innovation and the ability of particular types of firms to achieve technical advances. In this context the profits that monopolistic firms earn provide funds that can be invested in research and development. Whereas perfectly competitive firms must be content with a normal return on invested capital, monopolies have "surplus" funds with which to undertake the risky process of research. More important, perhaps, the possibility of attaining a monopolistic position, or the desire to maintain such a position, provides an important incentive to keep one step ahead of potential competitors. Innovations in new products and

---

[18]See, for example, J. A. Schumpeter, *Capitalism, Socialism and Democracy,* 3rd ed. (New York: Harper & Row, 1950), especially Chapter 8.

cost-saving production techniques may be integrally related to the possibility of monopolization. Without such a monopolistic position, the full benefits of innovation could not be obtained by the innovating firm.

Schumpeter stresses the point that the monopolization of a market may make it less costly for a firm to plan its activities. Being the only source of supply for a product eliminates many of the contingencies that a firm in a competitive market must face. For example, a monopoly may not have to spend as much on selling expenses (advertising, brand identification, and visiting retailers, for example) as would be the case in a more competitive industry. Similarly, a monopoly may know more about the specific demand curve for its product and may more readily adapt to changing demand conditions. Of course, whether any of these purported benefits of monopolies outweigh their allocational and distributional disadvantages is an empirical question. Issues of innovation and cost savings cannot be answered by recourse to a priori arguments. Detailed investigation of real-world markets is a necessity.

SUMMARY

In this chapter we have examined models of markets in which there is only a single monopoly supplier. Unlike the competitive case we investigated in Part 4, monopoly firms do not exhibit price-taking behavior. Instead, the monopolist can choose the price-quantity combination on the market demand curve that is most profitable. A number of consequences then follow from this market power:

- The most profitable level of output for the monopolist is the one for which marginal revenue is equal to marginal cost. At this output level, price will exceed marginal cost. The profitability of the monopolist will depend on the relationship between price and average cost.

- Relative to perfect competition, monopoly involves a loss of consumer surplus for demanders. Some of this is transferred into monopoly profits, whereas some of the loss in consumer supply represents a deadweight loss of overall economic welfare. It is a sign of Pareto inefficiency.

- Monopolists may opt for different levels of quality than would perfectly competitive firms. Durable goods monopolists may be constrained by markets for used goods.

- A monopoly may be able to increase its profits further through price discrimination—that is, charging different prices to different categories of buyers. The ability of the monopoly to practice price discrimination depends on its ability to prevent arbitrage among buyers.

- Governments often choose to regulate natural monopolies (firms with diminishing average costs over a broad range of output levels). The type of regulatory mechanisms adopted can affect the behavior of the regulated firm.

PROBLEMS

13.1

A monopolist can produce at constant average and marginal costs of $AC = MC = 5$. The firm faces a market demand curve given by $Q = 53 - P$.

a. Calculate the profit-maximizing price-quantity combination for the monopolist. Also calculate the monopolist's profits.

b. What output level would be produced by this industry under perfect competition (where price = marginal cost)?

c. Calculate the consumer surplus obtained by consumers in case (b). Show that this exceeds the sum of the monopolist's profits and the consumer surplus received in case (a). What is the value of the "deadweight loss" from monopolization?

13.2

A monopolist faces a market demand curve given by

$$Q = 70 - P.$$

a. If the monopolist can produce at constant average and marginal costs of $AC = MC = 6$, what output level will the monopolist choose in order to maximize profits? What is the price at this output level? What are the monopolist's profits?

b. Assume instead that the monopolist has a cost structure where total costs are described by

$$C(Q) = .25Q^2 - 5Q + 300.$$

With the monopolist facing the same market demand and marginal revenue, what price-quantity combination will be chosen now to maximize profits? What will profits be?

c. Assume now that a third cost structure explains the monopolist's position, with total costs given by

$$C(Q) = .0133Q^3 - 5Q + 250.$$

Again, calculate the monopolist's price-quantity combination that maximizes profits. What will profit be? (*Hint:* Set $MC = MR$ as usual and use the quadratic formula to solve the second-order equation for Q.)

d. Graph the market demand curve, the MR curve, and the three marginal cost curves from parts (a), (b), and (c). Notice that the monopolist's profit-making ability is constrained by (1) the market demand curve (along with its associated MR curve) and (2) the cost structure underlying production.

13.3

A single firm monopolizes the entire market for widgets and can produce at constant average and marginal costs of

$$AC = MC = 10.$$

Originally, the firm faces a market demand curve given by

$$Q = 60 - P.$$

a. Calculate the profit-maximizing price-quantity combination for the firm. What are the firm's profits?

b. Now assume that the market demand curve shifts outward (becoming steeper) and is given by

$$Q = 45 - .5P.$$

What is the firm's profit-maximizing price-quantity combination now? What are the firm's profits?

c. Instead of the assumptions of part (b), assume that the market demand curve shifts outward (becoming flatter) and is given by

$$Q = 100 - 2P.$$

What is the firm's profit-maximizing price-quantity combination now? What are the firm's profits?

d. Graph the three different situations of parts (a), (b), and (c). Using your results, explain why there is no real supply curve for a monopoly.

13.4

Suppose the market for Hula Hoops is monopolized by a single firm.

a. Draw the initial equilibrium for such a market.

b. Now suppose the demand for Hula Hoops shifts outward slightly. Show that, in general (contrary to the competitive case), it will not be possible to predict the effect of this shift in demand on the market price of Hula Hoops.

c. Consider three possible ways in which the price elasticity of demand might change as the demand curve shifts—it might increase, it might decrease, or it might stay the same. Consider also that marginal costs for the monopolist might be rising, falling, or constant in the range where $MR = MC$. Consequently, there are nine different combinations of types of demand shifts and marginal cost slope configurations. Analyze each of these to determine for which it is possible to make a definite prediction about the effect of the shift in demand on the price of Hula Hoops.

13.5

Suppose a monopoly market has a demand function in which quantity demanded depends not only on market price (P) but also on the amount of advertising the firm does (A, measured in dollars). The specific form of this function is

$$Q = (20 - P)(1 + 0.1A - 0.01A^2).$$

The monopolistic firm's cost function is given by

$$C = 10Q + 15 + A.$$

a. Suppose there is no advertising ($A = 0$). What output will the profit-maximizing firm choose? What market price will this yield? What will be the monopoly's profits?

b. Now let the firm also choose its optimal level of advertising expenditure. In this situation, what output level will be chosen? What price will this yield? What will the level of advertising be? What are the firm's profits in this case?

Hint: Part (b) can be worked out most easily by assuming the monopoly chooses the profit-maximizing price rather than quantity.

13.6

The taxation of monopoly can sometimes produce results different from those that arise in the competitive case. This problem looks at some of those cases. Most of these can be analyzed by using the inverse elasticity rule (Equation 9.13 or 13.1).

a. Consider first an ad valorem tax on the price of a monopoly's good. This tax reduces the net price received by the monopoly from P to $P(1 - t)$—where t is the proportional tax rate. Show that with a linear demand curve and constant marginal cost the imposition of such a tax causes price to rise by less than the full extent of the tax.

b. Suppose that the demand curve in part (a) were a constant elasticity curve. Show that the price would now increase by precisely the full extent of the tax. Explain the difference between these two cases.

c. Describe a case where the imposition of an ad valorem tax on a monopoly would cause the price to rise by more than the tax.

d. A specific tax is a fixed amount per unit of output. If the tax rate is τ per unit, total tax collections are τQ. Show that the imposition of a specific tax on a monopoly will reduce output more (and increase price more) than will the imposition of an ad valorem tax that collects the same tax revenue.

13.7

Suppose a monopoly can produce any level of output it wishes at a constant marginal (and average) cost of $5 per unit. Assume the monopoly sells its goods in two different markets separated by some distance. The demand curve in the first market is given by

$$Q_1 = 55 - P_1,$$

and the demand curve in the second market is given by

$$Q_2 = 70 - 2P_2.$$

a. If the monopolist can maintain the separation between the two markets, what level of output should be produced in each market, and what price will prevail in each market? What are total profits in this situation?

b. How would your answer change if it only cost demanders $5 to transport goods between the two markets? What would be the monopolist's new profit level in this situation?

c. How would your answer change if transportation costs were zero and the firm was forced to follow a single-price policy?

d. Suppose the firm could adopt a linear two-part tariff under which marginal prices must be equal in the two markets but lump-sum entry fees might vary. What pricing policy should the firm follow?

13.8

Suppose a perfectly competitive industry can produce widgets at a constant marginal cost of $10 per unit. Monopolized marginal costs rise to $12 per unit because $2 per unit must be paid to lobbyists to retain the widget producers' favored position. Suppose the market demand for widgets is given by

$$Q_D = 1,000 - 50P.$$

a. Calculate the perfectly competitive and monopoly outputs and prices.

b. Calculate the total loss of consumer surplus from monopolization of widget production.

c. Graph your results and explain how they differ from the usual analysis.

13.9

Suppose the government wished to combat the undesirable allocational effects of a monopoly through the use of a subsidy.

a. Why would a lump-sum subsidy not achieve the government's goal?

b. Use a graphical proof to show how a per-unit-of-output subsidy might achieve the government's goal.

c. Suppose the government wishes its subsidy to maximize the difference between the total value of the good to consumers and the good's total cost. Show that to achieve this goal it should set

$$\frac{t}{P} = -\frac{1}{e_{Q,P}},$$

where t is the per-unit subsidy and P is the competitive price. Explain your result intuitively.

13.10

Suppose a monopolist produces alkaline batteries that may have various useful lifetimes (X). Suppose also that consumers' (inverse) demand depends on batteries' lifetimes and quantity (Q) purchased according to the function

$$P(Q, X) = g(X \cdot Q),$$

where $g' < 0$. That is, consumers care only about the product of quantity times lifetime. They are willing to pay equally for many short-lived batteries or few long-lived ones. Assume also that battery costs are given by

$$C(Q, X) = C(X)Q,$$

where $C'(X) > 0$. Show that in this case the monopoly will opt for the same level of X as does a competitive industry even though levels of output and prices may differ. Explain your result.

(*Hint:* Treat XQ as a composite commodity.)

SUGGESTIONS FOR FURTHER READING

Posner, R. A. "The Social Costs of Monopoly and Regulation." *Journal of Political Economy 83* (1975): 807–27.
> *An analysis of the probability that monopolies may spend resources on the creation of barriers to entry and therefore may have higher costs than perfectly competitive firms.*

Schumpeter, J. A. *Capitalism, Socialism and Democracy,* 3rd ed. New York: Harper & Row, 1950.
> *Classic defense of the role of the entrepreneur and economic profits in the economic growth process.*

Spence, M. "Monopoly, Quality, and Regulation." *Bell Journal of Economics* (April 1975): 417–29.
> *Develops the approach to product quality used in this text and provides a detailed analysis of the effects of monopoly.*

Stigler, G. J. "The Theory of Economic Regulation." *Bell Journal of Economics and Management Science 2* (Spring 1971): 3.
> *Early development of the "capture" hypothesis of regulatory behavior—that the industry captures the agency supposed to regulate it and uses that agency to enforce entry barriers and further enhance profits.*

Tirole, J. *The Theory of Industrial Organization,* Chaps. 1–3. Cambridge, MA: MIT Press, 1989.
> *A complete analysis of the theory of monopoly pricing and product choice.*

Varian, H. R. *Microeconomic Analysis,* 3rd ed., chap. 14. New York: W. W. Norton, 1992.
> *Provides a succinct analysis of the role of incentive compatibility constraints in second-degree price discrimination.*

EXTENSIONS

Optimal Tariff Schedules

In Chapter 13 we examined a few simple illustrations of ways in which a monopoly may increase profits by practicing second-degree price discrimination—that is, by establishing price (or "outlay") schedules that prompt buyers to separate themselves into distinct market segments. Here we will pursue this topic a bit further, because the study of optimal tariff schedules has a wide variety of applications to many areas of microeconomic theory.

Structure of the problem

To examine issues related to price schedules in a simple context for each demander, we define the "valuation function" as

$$V_i(q) = P_i(q) \cdot q + S_i, \qquad \text{(i)}$$

where $P_i(q)$ is the inverse demand function for individual i and S_i is consumer surplus. Hence V_i represents the total value to individual i of undertaking transactions of amount q, which includes total spending on the good plus the value of consumer surplus obtained. Here we will assume that there are only two demanders[1] or homogeneous groups of demanders and that person 1 has stronger preferences for this good than person 2, in the sense that

$$V_1(q) > V_2(q) \qquad \text{(ii)}$$

for all values of q. The monopolist is assumed to have constant marginal costs (denoted by c) and chooses a tariff (revenue) schedule, $T(q)$, that maximizes profits given by

$$\pi = T(q_1) + T(q_2) - c(q_1 + q_2), \qquad \text{(iii)}$$

where q_i represents the quantity chosen by person i. In selecting a price schedule that successfully differentiates among consumers, the monopolist faces two "incentive compatibility" constraints. To ensure that the low-demand person (2) is actually served, it is necessary that

$$V_2(q_2) - T(q_2) \geq 0. \qquad \text{(iv)}$$

That is, person 2 must derive a net benefit from his or her optimal choice, q_2. Person 1, the high-

demand individual, must also obtain a net gain from his or her chosen consumption level (q_1) and must prefer this choice to the output choice made by person 2:

$$V_1(q_1) - T(q_1) \geq V_1(q_2) - T(q_2). \qquad \text{(v)}$$

If the monopolist does not recognize this constraint, it may find that person 1 opts for the portion of the price schedule intended for person 2, thereby destroying the goal of obtaining self-selected market separation. Given this general structure, we can proceed to illustrate a number of interesting features of the monopolist's problem.

E13.1 Pareto superiority

Permitting the monopolist to depart from a simple, single-price scheme offers the possibility of adopting "Pareto superior" tariff schedules under which all parties to the transaction are made better off. For example, suppose the monopolist's profit-maximizing price is P_M. At this price, person 2 consumes q_2^M and receives a net value from this consumption of

$$V_2(q_2^M) - P_M q_2^M. \qquad \text{(vi)}$$

A tariff schedule for which

$$T(q) = P_M q \text{ for } q \leq q_2^M$$

and

$$T(q) = A + \bar{P}q \text{ for } q > q_2^M, \qquad \text{(vii)}$$

where $A > 0$ and $c < \bar{P} < P_M$, may yield both increased profits for the monopolist and increased welfare for person 1. Specifically, consider values of A and $\bar{P}$ such that

$$A + \bar{P}q_1^M = P_M q_1^M$$

or

$$A = (P_M - \bar{P})q_1^M, \qquad \text{(viii)}$$

where q_1^M represents consumption of person 1 under a single-price policy. In this case then, A and $\bar{P}$ are set so that person 1 can still afford to buy q_1^M under this new price schedule. Because $\bar{P} < P_M$, however, he or she will opt for $q_1^* > q_1^M$. Because person 1 could have bought q_1^M but chose q_1^* instead, he or she must be better off

---

[1]Generalizations to many demanders are nontrivial. For a discussion, see Wilson (1993), Chapters 2–5.

under the new schedule. The monopoly's profits are now given by

$$\pi = A + \bar{P}q_1 + P_M q_2^M - c(q_1 + q_2^M) \quad \text{(ix)}$$

and

$$\pi - \pi_M = A + \bar{P}q_1 - P_M q_1^M - c(q_1 - q_1^M), \quad \text{(x)}$$

where π_M is the monopoly's single-price profits $[= (P_M - c)(q_1^M + q_2^M)]$. Substitution for A from Equation viii shows

$$\pi - \pi_M = (\bar{P} - c)(q_1 - q_1^M) > 0. \quad \text{(xi)}$$

Hence, this new price schedule also provides more profits to the monopoly, some of which might be shared with person 2. The price schedule is Pareto superior to a single monopoly price. The notion that multipart schedules may be Pareto superior has been used not only in the study of price discrimination, but also in the design of optimal tax schemes and auction mechanisms (see Willig, 1978).

Pricing a farmland reserve

The potential Pareto superiority of complex tariff schedules was used by R. B. W. Smith (1995) to estimate a least cost method for the U.S. government to finance a Conservation Reserve Program for farmland. The specific plan the author studies would maintain a 34-million-acre reserve out of production in any given year. He calculates that use of carefully constructed (nonlinear) tariff schedules for such a program might cost only $1 billion annually.

E13.2 Tied sales

Sometimes a monopoly will market two goods together. This situation poses a number of possibilities for discriminatory pricing schemes. Consider, for example, laser printers that are sold with toner cartridges or electronic game players sold with patented additional games. Here the pricing situation is similar to that examined in Chapter 13—usually consumers buy only one unit of the basic product (the printer or camera) and thereby pay the "entry" fee. Then they consume a variable number of tied products (toner and film). Because our analysis in Chapter 13 suggests that the monopoly will choose a price for its tied product that exceeds marginal cost, there will be a welfare loss relative to a situation in which the tied good is produced competitively. Perhaps for this reason, tied sales are prohibited by law in some cases. Prohibition may not necessarily increase welfare, however, if the monopoly declines to serve low-demand consumers in the absence of such a practice (Oi, 1971).

Automobiles and wine

One way in which tied sales can be accomplished is through creation of a multiplicity of quality variants that appeal to different classes of buyers. Automobile companies have been especially ingenious at devising quality variants of their basic models (for example, the Honda Accord comes in DX, LX, EX, and SX configurations) that act as tied goods in separating buyers into various market niches. A 1992 study by J. E. Kwoka examines one specific U.S. manufacturer (Chrysler) and shows how market segmentation is achieved through quality variation. The author calculates that significant transfer from consumer surplus to firms occurs as a result of such segmentation.

Generally, this sort of price discrimination in a tied good will be infeasible if that good is also produced under competitive conditions. In such a case the tied good will sell for marginal cost, and the only possibility for discriminatory behavior open to the monopolist is in the pricing of its basic-good (that is, by varying "entry fees" among demanders). In some special cases, however, choosing to pay the entry fee will confer monopoly power in the tied good on the monopolist even though it is otherwise reduced under competitive conditions. For example, Locay and Rodriguez (1992) examine the case of restaurants' pricing of wine. Here group decisions to patronize a particular restaurant may confer monopoly power to the restaurant owner in the ability to practice wine price discrimination among buyers with strong grape preferences. The owner is constrained by the need to attract groups of customers to the restaurant, however, so the power to price discriminate is less than under the pure monopoly scenario.

References

Kwoka, J. E. "Market Segmentation by Price-Quality Schedules: Some Evidence from Automobiles." *Journal of Business* (October 1992): 615–28.

Locay, L., and A. Rodriguez. "Price Discrimination in Competitive Markets." *Journal of Political Economy* (October 1992): 954–68.

Oi, W. Y. "A Disneyland Dilemma: Two-Part Tariffs on a Mickey Mouse Monopoly." *Quarterly Journal of Economics* (February 1971): 77–90.

Smith, R. B. W. "The Conservation Reserve Program as a Least Cost Land Retirement Mechanism." *American Journal of Agricultural Economics* (February 1995): 93–105.

Willig, R. "Pareto Superior Non-Linear Outlay Schedules." *Bell Journal of Economics* (January 1978): 56–69.

Wilson, W. *Nonlinear Pricing*. Oxford: Oxford University Press, 1993.

Chapter 14

TRADITIONAL MODELS OF IMPERFECT COMPETITION

In this chapter we examine models of price determination in markets that fall between the polar extremes of perfect competition and monopoly. Although no single model can be used to explain all possible forms of such imperfect competition, we will examine a few of the basic elements common to many of the models in current use. To that end we will focus on three specific topics: (1) pricing of homogeneous goods in markets in which there are relatively few firms; (2) product differentiation and advertising in such markets; and (3) the effect that entry and exit possibilities have on long-run outcomes in imperfectly competitive markets. In a sense, then, this chapter concerns how the assumptions of the perfectly competitive model can be relaxed and what the results of changing those assumptions are. In this analysis, conclusions from the perfectly competitive model provide a useful benchmark because departures from the competitive norm may involve efficiency losses. Two specific criteria we will use in this comparison are (1) whether prices under imperfect competition equal marginal costs, and (2) whether, in the long run, production occurs at minimum average cost. We will see that imperfectly competitive markets often lack one or both of these desirable features of perfect competition. Many of these same topics are reexamined from the perspective of game theory in Chapter 15.

Pricing under homogeneous oligopoly

In this section we will examine the general theory of price determination in markets in which relatively few firms produce a single homogeneous product. As before, we will assume that the market is perfectly competitive on the demand side; that is, there are assumed to be many demanders, each of whom is a price taker. We will also assume that there are no transaction or information costs, so the good in question obeys the law of one price and we may speak unambiguously of *the* good's price. Later in this chapter we will relax this assumption when we consider product differentiation. In this section we will also assume that there are a fixed number of n identical firms (where n is taken to be a relatively small number). Later, we will consider a numerical example of duopoly (in which $n = 2$), but for the moment there is no reason to restrict our analysis to any specific number. Throughout this section we will assume that n is fixed, but later in the chapter we will allow n to vary through entry and exit in response to firms' profitability.

Basic structure of the model

The output of each firm in our model will be denoted by $q_i (i = 1 \ldots n)$. Because firms are assumed to be identical, symmetry in costs will usually require that these outputs are equal, although it would be a simple matter to allow for some differences among firms. The inverse demand function for the good being examined will be denoted by $f(Q)$, and this shows the price, P, that demanders as a group are willing to pay for any particular level of industry output. That is,

$$P = f(Q) = f(q_1 + q_2 + \cdots + q_n). \tag{14.1}$$

Each firm's decision problem is to maximize its own profits (π_i), given the market price of the good and the firm's total costs, which are denoted by $C_i(q_i)$. Hence, the firm's goal is to maximize

$$
\begin{aligned}
\pi_i &= Pq_i - C_i(q_i) \\
&= f(Q)q_i - C_i(q_i) \\
&= f(q_1 + q_2 + \cdots + q_n)q_i - C_i(q_i).
\end{aligned} \tag{14.2}
$$

Most of the issues discussed in this section ultimately center around how firms make this profit-maximizing output choice. In perhaps overly simple mathematical terms, the results will depend on precisely what is assumed about how Equation 14.2 should be differentiated to solve for a profit maximum. In economic terms, the central question concerns how one firm assumes other firms react to its decisions.

Four possible models will be examined here. These are summarized in the following definitions. We will see that these different models yield rather different results and that equilibria arising from the conjectural variations model are generally indeterminate except in a few special cases.

DEFINITION

Oligopoly pricing models. *Quasi-competitive model:* Assumes price-taking behavior by all firms (P is treated as fixed).

Cartel model: Assumes firms can collude perfectly in choosing industry output (and, therefore P).

Cournot model: Assumes that firm i treats firm j's output as fixed in its decisions ($\partial q_j / \partial q_i = 0$).

Conjectural variations model: Firm i assumes that firm j's output will respond to variations in its output ($\partial q_j / \partial q_i \neq 0$).

Quasi-competitive model

As was the case under perfect competition, each firm in the quasi-competitive model is a price taker. That is, each firm assumes (possibly incorrectly) that its decisions will not affect market price. In this case the first-order condition for profit maximization is that

$$\frac{\partial \pi_i}{\partial q_i} = P - \frac{\partial C_i(q_i)}{\partial q_i} = 0 \tag{14.3}$$

or

$$P = MC_i(q_i) \qquad (i = 1, n). \tag{14.4}$$

These n supply equations, together with the market-clearing demand equation,

$$P = f(Q) = f(q_1 + q_2 + \cdots + q_n), \tag{14.5}$$

will ensure that this market arrives at the short-run competitive solution. That solution is illustrated for the case of constant marginal costs as point C in Figure 14.1. Although n

| **FIGURE 14.1** | **Alternative Solutions to the Oligopolistic Pricing Problem** |

Market equilibrium under an oligopoly can occur at many points on the demand curve. In this figure (which assumes that marginal costs are constant over all output ranges), the quasi-competitive equilibrium occurs at point C, the cartel equilibrium at point M, and the Cournot solution at point A. Many other solutions may occur between points M and C, depending on the specific assumption made about firms' strategic interrelationships

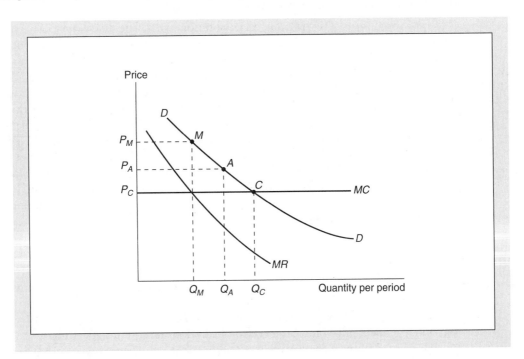

may be a small number, the assumption of price-taking behavior in this case results in a competitive outcome.

Cartel model

Of course, the assumption of price-taking behavior may be particularly inappropriate in industries with few firms in which each firm recognizes that its decisions have an obvious effect on price. An alternative assumption would be that firms as a group recognize they can affect price and manage to coordinate their decisions so as to achieve monopoly profits. In this case the cartel acts as a multiplant monopoly and chooses $q_1, q_2, \ldots, q_n$ so as to maximize total industry profits.

$$\pi = PQ - [C_1(q_1) + C_2(q_2) + \cdots + C_n(q_n)] \tag{14.6}$$

$$= f(q_1 + q_2 + \cdots + q_n)[q_1 + q_2 + \cdots + q_n] - \sum_{i=1}^{n} C_i(q_i). \tag{14.7}$$

The first-order conditions for a maximum are that

$$\frac{\partial \pi}{\partial q_i} = P + (q_1 + q_2 + \cdots + q_n)\frac{\partial P}{\partial q_i} - MC_i(q_i) = 0 \tag{14.8}$$

$$= MR(Q) - MC_i(q_i) = 0 \tag{14.9}$$

Notice that MR can be written as a function of the combined output of all firms because its value is the same no matter which firm's output level is changed. At the profit-maximizing point this common marginal revenue will be equated to each firm's marginal production cost. Assuming these marginal costs are equal and constant for all firms, the output choice is indicated by point M in Figure 14.1. Because this coordinated plan requires a specific output level for each firm, the plan will also dictate how monopoly profits earned by the cartel are to be shared. In the aggregate these profits will be as large as possible, given the market demand curve and the industry's cost structure.

Viability of the cartel solution

There are three problems with this cartel solution. First, and most obviously, such monopolistic decisions may be illegal. In the United States, for example, Section I of the Sherman Act (1890) outlaws "conspiracies in restraint of trade," so would-be cartel members may expect a visit from the FBI. Similar laws exist in many other countries. A second problem with the cartel solution is that it requires that a considerable amount of information be available to the directors of the cartel—specifically, they must know the market demand function and each individual firm's marginal cost function. This information may be costly to obtain, and some cartel members may be reluctant to provide it. Finally, and most important, the cartel solution is fundamentally unstable. Because each cartel member will produce an output level for which $P > MC_i$, each will have an incentive to expand output. If the directors of the oligopoly are not able to police such "chiseling," the monopolistic solution may collapse. The difficulties of the OPEC cartel in dictating precise target output levels to its members attest to these problems. In the next chapter we will examine the stability of cartel pricing strategies in more detail.

Cournot solution

One of the first researchers to develop a model of markets containing few firms was the French economist Augustin Cournot, who presented a formal analysis of duopoly behavior in 1838.[1] In our notation Cournot assumed that each firm recognizes that its own decisions about q_i affect price but that its own output decisions do not affect those of any other firm. That is, each firm recognizes that $\partial P / \partial q_i \neq 0$ but assumes that $\partial q_j / \partial q_i = 0$ for all $j \neq i$. Using these assumptions, the first-order conditions for a profit maximum in our model are

$$\frac{\partial \pi_i}{\partial q_i} = P + q_i \frac{\partial P}{\partial q_i} - MC_i(q_i) = 0 \qquad (14.10)$$

(for all $i = 1, n$). Notice from this equation that the firm assumes that changes in q_i affect its total revenue only through the direct effect on the market price of its own sales. Hence the equation differs both from the cartel solution (where the effect of a change in price on total industry revenues is taken into account—see Equation 14.8) and from the conjectural variations case, discussed next, in which indirect effects of firm i's output on firm j's output are taken into account. In general, the n equations in 14.10, together with the market-clearing demand Equation 14.5, will permit an equilibrium solution for the variables q_1, $q_2, \ldots, q_n$ and P. An examination of the profit-maximizing Equation 14.10 shows that as long as marginal costs are increasing (as they generally must be for a true profit maximum), each firm's output in the Cournot solution will exceed the cartel output because the "firm-specific" marginal revenue in that equation is larger than the market-marginal revenue notion in Equation 14.8. On the other hand, the firm's output will fall short of the competitive output because the term $q_i \cdot \partial P / \partial q_i$ in Equation 14.10 is negative. Market equilibrium will therefore occur at a point such as A in Figure 14.1. At this point price exceeds marginal cost, but output is higher and industry profits lower than in the monopoly case.

In general, it might also be supposed that the greater the number of firms in the industry, the closer the equilibrium point will be to the competitive point C. With a larger number of firms the term $q_i \cdot \partial P / \partial q_i$ in Equation 14.10 approaches zero, and the equa-

[1]A. Cournot, *Researches into the Mathematical Principles of the Theory of Wealth*, trans. N. T. Bacon (New York: Macmillan, 1897).

tion therefore comes to resemble the quasi-competitive solution. For an illustration[2] of this limit property of the Cournot model, see Example 14.1 later in the chapter. It should be noted that the Cournot equilibrium described here is also a Nash equilibrium in output strategies. For more on game-theoretic formulations of the pricing problem, see Chapter 15.

Conjectural variations model

So far our models of oligopolistic price determination have not allowed for strategic interactions among firms. In markets with few firms, that is a particularly untenable assumption. Ford must obviously take some account of how Toyota will respond to its pricing and output decisions; all other software companies must worry about what Microsoft will do; and members of the OPEC cartel must be concerned with new oil exploration throughout the world. The problem faced by economic theorists is how to capture these strategic considerations in some sort of tractable analytical model. One approach relies on game theory to examine strategic choices in a simplified setting. In the next chapter we will illustrate how such tools can be applied to the analysis of duopolistic markets. Here we explore some of the ways in which strategic concerns can be integrated into the models we have already developed.

The primary way of building strategic concerns into our model is by considering the assumptions that might be made by one firm about other firms' behavior. In mathematical terms, we wish to examine the possible assumptions that firm i might make about how its decisions might affect those of firm j. Specifically, for each firm i we are concerned with the assumed value of the derivative $\partial q_j / \partial q_i$ for all firms j other than firm i itself. Because the value of this derivative will be speculative, models based on various assumptions about its value are termed *conjectural variations* models; that is, they are concerned with firm i's "conjectures" about firm j's output variations.

Thus far in our models we have assumed that $\partial q_j / \partial q_i = 0$ for all $j \neq i$. We therefore have assumed no strategic interaction among firms. Once this assumption is relaxed, each firm's profit-maximizing decision becomes more complex. Now the first-order condition for maximizing Equation 14.2 becomes

$$\frac{\partial \pi_i}{\partial q_i} = P + q_i \left[\frac{\partial P}{\partial q_i} + \sum_{j \neq i} \frac{\partial P}{\partial q_j} \cdot \frac{\partial q_j}{\partial q_i} \right] - MC_i(q_i) = 0. \qquad (14.11)$$

That is, the firm must now not only be concerned with how its own output affects market price directly, but also must consider how variations in its own output will affect market price through effects on other firms' output decisions. Because any number of plausible assumptions might be made about such responses, there is no generally accepted theory of the type of equilibrium likely to emerge from the responses given by Equation 14.11. A few interesting models have been developed for the duopoly case, and we will demonstrate a simple numerical example of these later

Price leadership model

One tractable form of the conjectural variations model is based on the assumption that the market in question is composed of a single price leader and a fringe of quasi-competitive competitors. Assuming the leader is firm 1, a mathematical representation of this market would include a price-taking reaction such as that given by Equation 14.4 for firms 2 . . . *n,* with only firm 1 requiring a complex reaction function of the type given by Equation 14.11. A graphical analysis of such a market is provided by

[2]For a formal discussion of these issues, see J. Friedman, "Oligopoly Theory," in K. J. Arrow and M. D. Intriligator, eds., *Handbook of Mathematical Economics,* vol. 2 (Amsterdam: North-Holland, 1982).

| **FIGURE 14.2** | **Formal Model of Price Leadership Behavior** |

The curve $D'D'$ shows the demand curve facing the price leader; it is derived by subtracting what is produced by the competitive fringe of firms (SC) from market demand (DD). Given $D'D'$, the firm's profit-maximizing output level is Q_L, and a price of P_L will prevail in the market.

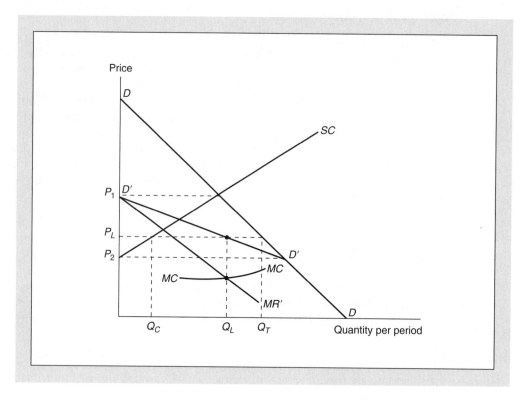

Figure 14.2. The demand curve in the figure represents the total demand curve for the industry's product, and the supply curve SC represents the supply decisions of all the $n - 1$ firms in the competitive fringe. It is simply the horizontal sum of their short-run marginal cost curves. Using these two curves, the demand curve ($D'D'$) facing the industry leader is derived as follows. For a price of P_1 or above, the leader will sell nothing, because the competitive fringe would be willing to supply all that is demanded. For prices below P_2 the leader has the market to itself, because the fringe is not willing to supply anything. Between P_2 and P_1 the curve $D'D'$ is constructed by subtracting what the fringe will supply from total market demand; that is, the leader gets that portion of demand not taken by the fringe firms.

Given the residual demand curve $D'D'$, the leader can construct its marginal revenue curve (MR') and then refer to its own marginal cost curve (MC) to determine the profit-maximizing output level, Q_L. Market price then will be P_L. Given that price, the competitive fringe will produce Q_C, and total industry output will be $Q_T (= Q_C + Q_L)$.

Of course, this model does not answer such important questions as how the price leader in an industry is chosen or what happens when a member of the fringe decides to challenge the leader for its position and profits. But the model does illustrate one tractable case of the conjectural variations model that may explain pricing behavior in some instances. For example, it has been argued that the model may at times have offered an appropriate explanation for pricing in markets such as those for prime commercial loans (here the major money center banks are the "leaders"), standardized steel products in the 1950s and 1960s (U.S. Steel was the leader), and, perhaps, the OPEC cartel (where Saudi

Arabia, by virtue of politics and geology, can play the role of leader). Of course, all such purported examples require substantial empirical investigation to determine the validity and scope of the price leadership model.

EXAMPLE 14.1

Cournot's Natural Spring Duopoly

As a numerical example of some of these ideas, we will consider a very simple case in which there are no production costs and only two firms. Following Cournot's nineteenth-century example of two natural springs, we assume each spring owner has a large supply of (possibly healthful) water and faces the problem of how much to provide to the market. The demand for spring water is given by the linear demand curve

$$Q = q_1 + q_2 = 120 - P \qquad (14.12)$$

and is illustrated in Figure 14.3. We will now examine various market equilibria along this demand curve.

Quasi-competitive solution. Because each firm has zero marginal costs, the quasi-competitive solution will result in a market price of zero. Total demand will be 120. In this particular example the division of output between the two springs is indeterminate because each has zero marginal cost over all output ranges. The quasi-competitive output level is indicated by point C in Figure 14.3.

Cartel solution. The cartel solution to this example can be found by maximizing total industry revenue (and profits):

$$\pi = PQ = 120Q - Q^2. \qquad (14.13)$$

The first-order condition for a maximum is

$$\frac{\partial \pi}{\partial Q} = 120 - 2Q = 0$$

or

$$Q = 60$$
$$P = 60$$
$$\pi = 3,600. \qquad (14.14)$$

Again, the precise division of these output levels and profits between the two springs is indeterminate. The cartel solution is indicated by point M in Figure 14.3.

Cournot solution. From Equation 14.12 it is easy to see that the two firms' revenues (and profits) are given by

$$\pi_1 = Pq_1 = (120 - q_1 - q_2)q_1 = 120q_1 - q_1^2 - q_1q_2$$
$$\pi_2 = Pq_2 = (120 - q_1 - q_2)q_2 = 120q_2 - q_2^2 - q_1q_2. \qquad (14.15)$$

If each spring owner assumes the other will not react to his or her own output decisions, $\partial q_1/\partial q_2 = \partial q_2/\partial q_1 = 0$, and the first-order conditions for a maximum are

$$\frac{\partial \pi_i}{\partial q_1} = 120 - 2q_1 - q_2 = 0$$

$$\frac{\partial \pi_2}{\partial q_2} = 120 - 2q_2 - q_1 = 0. \qquad (14.16)$$

(continued)

EXAMPLE 14.1 CONTINUED

Equations 14.16 are called *reaction functions* because they show how each firm reacts to the other's output level. In equilibrium these equations must be mutually consistent—that is, each firm must produce what the other thinks it will. Given this assumption, Equations 14.16 can be solved simultaneously for the equilibrium values of q_1 and q_2 to yield

$$q_1 = q_2 = 40$$
$$P = 120 - (q_1 + q_2) = 40$$
$$\pi_1 = \pi_2 = Pq_1 = Pq_2 = 1,600. \qquad (14.17)$$

More will be supplied under the Cournot assumptions than under the cartel case, and industry profits (3,200) will be somewhat lower than when output decisions are fully coordinated. This Cournot solution is denoted by point A in Figure 14.3. In this particular case it is easy to show that as more firms are introduced into the analysis, the equilibrium

FIGURE 14.3   **Solutions to the Duopoly Problem**

Given the demand curve $Q = 120 - P$, the points M, A, S, and C represent, respectively, the cartel, Cournot, Stackelberg, and quasi-competitive solutions to the duopoly problem.

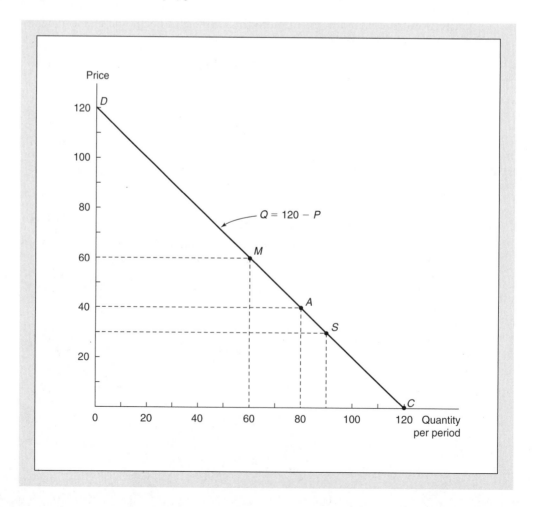

moves toward the competitive point.[3] For a somewhat more realistic case that also yields this solution, see Problem 14.2.

Query: Given that one spring owner's output is 40 in the Cournot model, why can't the other owner gain by producing more than 40 units of output? Does this conclusion conflict with our discussion of cartels where we expected chiseling whenever $P > MC$? (See Chapter 15 for a further discussion of this point.)

 EXAMPLE 14.2

Stackelberg Leadership Model

The assumption of a constant marginal cost makes the price leadership model inappropriate for Cournot's spring problem. In this case the "competitive fringe" would simply take the entire market by pricing at marginal cost (here zero), with no room left in the market for the price leader. There is, however, the possibility for a different type of strategic leadership, a possibility first recognized by the German economist Heinrich von Stackelberg.[4] Von Stackelberg examined the consequences of assuming that one firm (say, firm 1) recognized the process by which the other firm makes its output decisions. That is, he assumed that firm 1 knows (from Equation 14.16) that firm 2 chooses q_2 so that

$$q_2 = \frac{120 - q_1}{2}. \tag{14.18}$$

Firm 1 can now calculate the conjectural variation,

$$\frac{\partial q_2}{\partial q_1} = -\frac{1}{2}. \tag{14.19}$$

In words, firm 2 reduces its output by ½ unit for each unit increase in q_1. Firm 1's profit-maximization problem can now be reconsidered to take account of this reaction:

$$\pi_1 = Pq_1 = 120q_1 - q_1^2 - q_1 q_2 \tag{14.20}$$

and the first-order condition for a maximum is

$$\frac{\partial \pi_1}{\partial q_1} = 120 - 2q_1 - q_1 \frac{\partial q_2}{\partial q_1} - q_2 = 0$$

$$= 120 - \frac{3}{2} q_1 - q_2 = 0. \tag{14.21}$$

(continued)

---

[3]With n firms Equation 14.16 becomes

$$\frac{\partial \pi_i}{\partial q_i} = 120 - 2q_i - \sum_{j \neq i} q_j = 0 \qquad (i = 1, n).$$

Assuming, by symmetry, that all the q's are equal to $\bar{q}$, we have

$$\frac{\partial \pi_i}{\partial q_i} = 120 - (n + 1)\bar{q} = 0.$$

Hence, $\bar{q} = 120/(n + 1)$ and total output $= n\bar{q} = [n/(n + 1)](120)$, which approaches 120 (the competitive output) for large values of n.

[4]H. von Stackelberg, *The Theory of the Market Economy,* trans. A. T. Peacock (New York: Oxford University Press, 1952).

EXAMPLE 14.2 CONTINUED

Solving this equation simultaneously with firm 2's reaction function (Equation 14.18) yields equilibrium values different from those in the Cournot model:

$$q_1 = 60$$
$$q_2 = 30$$
$$P = 120 - (q_1 + q_2) = 30 \qquad (14.22)$$
$$\pi_1 = Pq_1 = 1,800$$
$$\pi_2 = Pq_2 = 900.$$

Firm 1 has been able to increase its profits by using its knowledge of firm 2's reactions. Firm 2's profits have been seriously eroded in this process. This solution is shown as point *S* on the demand curve presented in Figure 14.3.

Choice of the leader and ruinous competition. One ambiguous feature of the Stackelberg model is the absence of any theory of how the leader is chosen. If each firm assumes that the other is a follower, each will produce 60 and will be disappointed at the final outcome (with total output of 120, market price, in the present example, will fall to zero). On the other hand, if each acts as a follower, the situation reverts to the Cournot equilibrium. From the Stackelberg perspective, however, the Cournot equilibrium is unstable: Each firm can perceive the benefits of being a leader and may try to choose its output accordingly. As we will see in Chapter 15, we need to explore the game theoretic aspects of this problem further if we are to evaluate all of the possibilities that may arise.

Query: Why does the first spring owner's decision to increase output raise profits here whereas it did not in the case proposed in the query to Example 14.1?

Product differentiation

Up to this point we have been assuming that the oligopolistic firms being examined produce a homogeneous output. Demanders were therefore assumed to be indifferent about which firm's output they bought, and the law of one price was assumed to hold in the market. Such an assumption is widely at variance with many real-world markets. Firms often devote considerable resources to differentiating their products from those of their competitors through such devices as quality and style variations, warranties and guarantees, special service features, and product advertising. All of these activities require firms to employ additional resources, and firms will choose to do so if profits are thereby increased. Such attempts at product variation also will result in a relaxation of the law of one price, because now the market will consist of goods that vary from firm to firm and demanders may have preferences about which supplier to patronize. That possibility introduces a certain fuzziness into what we mean by the "market for a good." Now there are many closely related, but not identical, products being produced. For example, once it is recognized that toothpaste brands vary somewhat from supplier to supplier, should we consider all these products to be in the same market? Or should we differentiate, say, among fluoridated products, gels, striped toothpaste, smokers' toothpaste, and so forth? Or, consider the problem of spatial differentiation. Because demanders will be closer to some sellers than to others, they may view nearby sellers more favorably because buying from them involves lower transportation charges. Here we will assume the market is composed of *n* firms, each producing a slightly different product, but that these products can usefully be considered a single-product group. This notion can be made more precise as follows:

Product group. The outputs of a set of firms constitute a *product group* if the substitutability in demand among the products (as measured by the cross-price elasticity) is very high relative to the substitutability between those firms' outputs and other goods generally.

Although this definition has its own ambiguities (arguments about the definition of a product group often dominate antitrust proceedings, for example), it should suffice for our purposes.[5] Now we will proceed to offer a formal but simplified analysis of pricing within the market for such a product group.

Firms' choices

Again we will assume that there are n firms competing in a particular product group. Now, however, each firm can choose the amount it spends on attempting to differentiate its product from those of its competitors. We will denote the resources used by the ith firm for this purpose by z_i, which might include spending on special options, quality, brand advertising, or moving to a favorable location. The firm's costs now are given by

$$\text{total costs} = C_i(q_i, z_i). \tag{14.23}$$

Because there are n slightly different goods in the product group, we must allow for the possibility of different market prices for each of these goods. Such prices will be denoted by $p_1, \ldots, p_n$ (although some of these may be equal). The demand facing the ith firm shows how price received depends on quantity produced by that firm (q_i), on prices being charged by all other firms (p_j for $j \neq i$), and on the ith firm's and all other firms' attempts to differentiate their products ($z_j, j = 1, n$). In its most general form then,

$$p_i = g(q_i, p_j, z_i, z_j), \tag{14.24}$$

where the terms p_j and z_j are intended to include all other prices and differentiation activities, respectively. Presumably, $\partial p_i / \partial q_i \leq 0$, $\partial p_i / \partial p_j \geq 0$, $\partial p_i / \partial z_i \geq 0$, and $\partial p_i / \partial z_j \leq 0$. That is, the demand curve facing the individual firm is downward sloping and is shifted outward by price increases by its competitors. Product differentiation activities by the ith firm may also shift demand outward, whereas such activities by competitors will shift demand inward.

The ith firm's profits are given by

$$\pi_i = p_i q_i - C_i(q_i, z_i), \tag{14.25}$$

and in the simple case where $\partial z_j / \partial q_i$, $\partial z_j / \partial z_i$, $\partial p_j / \partial q_i$, and $\partial p_j / \partial z_i$ are all zero, the first-order conditions for a maximum are

$$\frac{\partial \pi_i}{\partial q_i} = p_i + q_i \frac{\partial p_i}{\partial q_i} - \frac{\partial C_i}{\partial q_i} = 0 \tag{14.26}$$

$$\frac{\partial \pi_i}{\partial z_i} = q_i \frac{\partial p_i}{\partial z_i} - \frac{\partial C_i}{\partial z_i} = 0. \tag{14.27}$$

Equation 14.26 is a restatement of the marginal revenue equals marginal cost condition for a profit maximum. Equation 14.27 shows that, as for any input, additional differentiation activities should be pursued up to the point at which the additional revenues they generate are equal to their marginal costs.[6]

---

[5]A more precise definition might be built around the "attribute" concept introduced in Chapter 6. Under this approach, goods that share a common set of attributes would constitute a product group.

[6]For an alternative statement, see Problem 14.4.

Market equilibrium

Although this description of firms' choices seems straightforward, these choices are actually quite complex. Because the demand curve facing any one firm depends on the prices and product differentiation activities of its competitors, that demand curve may shift often, and its position at any particular time may be only partly understood. As in the Cournot model, the firm must make some assumptions in order to make decisions. And, as in the conjectural variations model, whatever one firm decides to do may affect its competitors' actions. Hence, the differentiated oligopoly model poses even more complex strategic issues than did the models we examined for the homogeneous good case. Not surprisingly, few definitive conclusions can be reached about the nature of the market equilibria that result from such a situation. We illustrate one type of equilibrium in spatially differentiated markets in Example 14.3, and take up Chamberlin's model of monopolistic competition later in this chapter. Problem 14.6 and several of the game theory models described in Chapter 15 also offer insights about product differentiation.

 EXAMPLE 14.3

Spatial Differentiation

To develop a simple model of product differentiation, consider the case of ice cream stands located on a beach—a problem first studied by H. Hotelling in the 1920s.[7] Figure 14.4 shows this (linear) beach with two ice cream stands located at points A and B. Assume demanders are located uniformly along the beach, one at each unit of length, and that each buys exactly one ice cream cone per period. Ice cream cones are assumed to be costless to produce, but carrying them back to one's beach umbrella results in a cost c per unit of distance traveled (because the ice cream melts). If we let p_A be stand A's price and p_B be stand B's price, a person located at point E will be indifferent between stands A and B if

$$p_A + cx = p_B + cy. \qquad (14.28)$$

As Figure 14.4 shows,

$$a + x + y + b = L, \qquad (14.29)$$

where L is the length of the beach. The coordinate of point E is therefore

$$x = \frac{p_B - p_A + cy}{c} \qquad (14.30)$$

$$= \frac{p_B - p_A}{c} + L - a - b - x \qquad (14.31)$$

or

$$x = \frac{1}{2}\left(L - a - b + \frac{p_B - p_A}{c}\right) \qquad (14.32)$$

and

$$y = \frac{1}{2}\left(L - a - b + \frac{p_A - p_B}{c}\right). \qquad (14.33)$$

Profits for the two firms are

$$\pi_A = p_A(a + x) = \frac{1}{2}(L + a - b)p_A + \frac{p_A p_B - p_A^2}{2c} \qquad (14.34)$$

---

[7]H. Hotelling, "Stability in Competition," *Economic Journal* (January 1929): 41–57.

FIGURE 14.4   **Spatial Differentiation and Pricing**

Ice cream stands are located at points A and B along a linear beach of length L. In equilibrium, consumers to the left of E will patronize stand A; those to the right will patronize stand B. Different prices will prevail at the two stands. If the stands can relocate, they may move to the center of the beach or to the ends depending on the strategic assumptions made.

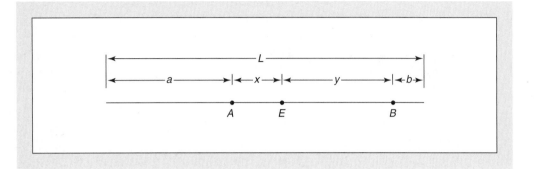

and

$$\pi_B = p_B(b + y) = \frac{1}{2}(L - a + b)p_B + \frac{p_A p_B - p_B^2}{2c}. \quad (14.35)$$

Each firm will choose its own price so as to maximize profits:

$$\frac{\partial \pi_A}{\partial p_A} = \frac{1}{2}(L + a - b) + \frac{p_B}{2c} - \frac{p_A}{c} = 0$$

$$\frac{\partial \pi_B}{\partial p_B} = \frac{1}{2}(L - a + b) + \frac{p_A}{2c} - \frac{p_B}{c} = 0. \quad (14.36)$$

These can readily be solved for

$$p_A = c\left(L + \frac{a - b}{3}\right)$$

$$p_B = c\left(L - \frac{a - b}{3}\right). \quad (14.37)$$

In general, these prices will depend on the precise location of the two stands and will differ from each other. For example, if we assume that the beach is 100 yards long, $a = 40$ yards, $b = 10$ yards, and $c = \$.01$ per yard, then

$$p_A = .01\left(100 + \frac{30}{3}\right)$$

$$= \$1.10$$

$$p_B = .01\left(100 - \frac{30}{3}\right) \quad (14.38)$$

$$= \$.90$$

These price differences arise only from the locational aspects of this problem—cones themselves are identical and costless. Because A is somewhat more favorably located

(*continued*)

EXAMPLE 14.3 CONTINUED

than *B*, it can charge a higher price for its cones without losing too much business to *B*. Using Equation 14.32 shows

$$x = \frac{1}{2}(100 - 40 - 10 - 20) = 15, \qquad (14.39)$$

so stand *A* sells 55 cones (despite its higher price) whereas *B* sells only 45. At point *E* a consumer is indifferent between walking 15 yards to *A* and paying $1.10 or walking 35 yards to *B* and paying $.90. The solution is inefficient in that a consumer slightly to the right of *E* would incur a shorter walk by patronizing *A*, but chooses *B* because of *A*'s power to set higher prices.

Locational choices. Perhaps the most important insights to be gained from this example arise if we allow the ice cream stands to change their locations at zero cost. That is, we allow the firms to change the nature of the product they are offering (theoretically, location plays the role of z_i in Equation 14.27). Analysis of this possibility formally raises a number of complexities, so an intuitive discussion may suffice. If we focus only on the number of ice cream cones sold, it seems clear that each stand has an incentive to move to the center of the beach. Any stand that opts for an off-center position is subject to its rival moving between it and the center and taking a large share of the market. This effect resembles the tendency of political candidates to move toward the center on controversial issues—opting for an off-center position makes a candidate vulnerable to moves that allow his or her rival to take a majority of the vote. In the case of product differentiation, such motives tend to encourage a similarity of products.

But the ice cream cone firms here care more about profits than market share. Moving closer to one's rival causes a decline in consumers' willingness to pay for locational advantages; hence, profits will fall from such a move. Ultimately, therefore, the firms' optimal locational decisions will depend on the specifics of consumers' demands for spatially differentiated products, and, in some cases, maximal differentiation (location at the ends of the beach) may be the result.[8] Whatever the locational choices that result in a sustainable equilibrium, it seems unlikely the firms would opt for the socially optimal locations that minimize total travel cost.[9]

Query: In this problem would it matter if ice cream cones could be produced at constant marginal cost? Suppose cone production were subject to increasing marginal cost?

---

[8]See C. d'Aspremont, J. Gabszewicz, and J. Thisse, "On Hotelling's Stability in Competition," *Econometrica* (September 1979): 1145–51.

[9]Total walking costs to *A* are

$$\int_0^a z\,dz + \int_0^x z\,dz = (a^2 + x^2)/2.$$

Similarly, costs of walking to *B* are $(b^2 + y^2)/2$. The sum of these is minimized when

$$a = x = b = y = L/4.$$

Entry

The possibility of new firms entering an industry plays an important role in the development of the theory of perfectly competitive price determination. It ensures that any long-run profits will be eliminated by new entrants and that firms will produce at the low points of their long-run average cost curves. Under conditions of oligopoly, the first of these forces continues to operate. To the extent that entry is possible, long-run profits are constrained. If entry is completely costless, long-run economic profits will be zero (as in the competitive case).

Zero-profit equilibrium

Whether firms in an oligopolistic industry with free entry will be directed to the low point of their average cost curves depends on the nature of the demand curve facing them. If firms are price takers, the analysis given for the competitive case carries over directly: Because $P = MR = MC$ for profit maximization with price taking, and because $P = AC$ if entry is to result in zero profits, production will take place where $MC = AC$ (that is, at minimum average cost).

If oligopolistic firms have some control over the price they receive (perhaps because each produces a slightly differentiated product), each firm will face a downward-sloping demand curve and the competitive analysis may not hold. Entry may still reduce profits to zero, but now production at minimum average cost is not ensured. This situation is illustrated in Figure 14.5. Initially, the demand curve facing the firm is given by *dd*, and economic profits are being earned. New firms will be attracted by these profits, and their entry will shift *dd* inward (because there are now a larger number of firms to contend with a given market demand curve). Indeed, entry can reduce profits to zero by shifting the demand curve to *d'd'*. The level of output that maximizes profits with this demand curve

---

FIGURE 14.5   **Entry Reduces Profitability in an Oligopoly**

Initially, the demand curve facing the firm is *dd*. Marginal revenue is given by *mr*, and q^* is the profit-maximizing output level. If entry is costless, new firms attracted by the possibility for profits may shift the firm's demand curve inward to *d'd'*, where profits are zero. At output level q', average costs are not a minimum, and the firm exhibits excess capacity given by $q_m - q'$.

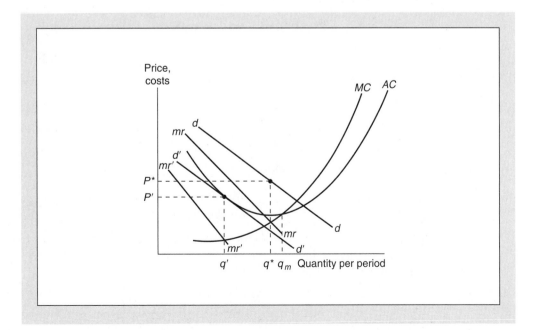

(q') is not, however, the same as that level at which average costs are minimized (q_m). Rather, the firm will produce less than that "efficient" output level and will exhibit "excess capacity," given by $q_m - q'$. Some economists have hypothesized that this outcome characterizes industries such as service stations, convenience stores, and fast-food franchisers, where product differentiation is prevalent but entry is relatively costless.

EXAMPLE 14.4

Monopolistic Competition

The zero-profit equilibrium illustrated in Figure 14.5 was first described by Edward Chamberlin, who termed his model *monopolistic competition*.[10] In this model, each firm produces a slightly differentiated product and entry is costless. As a numerical example, suppose there are n firms in a market and that each firm has the same total cost schedule of the form:

$$c_i = 9 + 4q_i. \tag{14.40}$$

Each firm also faces a demand curve for its product of the form

$$q_i = -.0.01(n-1)p_i + 0.01\sum_{j \neq i} p_j + \frac{303}{n}, \tag{14.41}$$

where p_j is the prices charged by other firms and n is the number of firms in the industry. Notice that the demand curve for each firm is a downward-sloping function of its own price and depends positively on the prices charged by its competitors. Here we will define an equilibrium for this industry to be a situation in which prices must be equal ($p_i = p_j$ for all i and j). Other models allow some price dispersion to exist even in equilibrium, perhaps because of spatial or other types of differentiation. Because in our equilibrium $p_i = p_j$, it is clear that $q_i = 303/n$ and $Q = nq_i = 303$. This solution holds for any n.

Equilibrium market structure. To find equilibrium n, we first examine each firm's profit-maximizing choice of p_i. Because

$$\pi_i = p_i q_i - c_i, \tag{14.42}$$

the first-order condition for a maximum is

$$\frac{\partial \pi_i}{\partial p_i} = -.02(n-1)p_i + .01\sum_{j \neq i} p_j + \frac{303}{n} \tag{14.43}$$
$$+ .04(n-1) = 0,$$

so

$$p_i = \frac{.5 \sum_{j \neq i} p_j}{n-1} + \frac{303}{.02(n-1)n} + 2. \tag{14.44}$$

Applying the equilibrium condition $p_j = p_i$ yields

$$p_i = \frac{30,300}{(n-1)(n)} + 4. \tag{14.45}$$

Notice that price approaches marginal cost (4) as n gets large here. Hence, this model has a competitive solution as a limiting case. Equilibrium n is determined by the zero-profit condition (because entry is unconstrained)

$$p_i q_i - c_i = 0. \tag{14.46}$$

---

[10]See E. Chamberlin, *The Theory of Monopolistic Competition* (Cambridge, MA: Harvard University Press, 1933).

Substituting into this expression the value for p_i found in Equation 14.44 and the value for q calculated in Equation 14.41 gives

$$\frac{30,300 \cdot 303}{n^2(n-1)} + \frac{4(303)}{n} = 9 + \frac{4(303)}{n}, \qquad (14.47)$$

or $n = 101$. The final equilibrium is therefore

$$\begin{aligned} p_i &= p_j = 7 \\ q_i &= 3 \qquad\qquad (14.48) \\ \pi_i &= 0. \end{aligned}$$

Nature of the equilibrium. In the equilibrium calculated in Equation 14.48, each firm has $p_i = AC_i$ but $p_i > MC_i = 4$. In addition, because

$$AC_i = 4 + \frac{9}{q_i}, \qquad (14.49)$$

each firm has diminishing average costs throughout all output ranges, so production does not occur at minimum average cost. Each firm's zero-profit equilibrium would therefore resemble Figure 14.5. The features of this equilibrium prompted Chamberlin's hypothesis that monopolistic competition is Pareto inefficient.

If each potential entrant faces a demand function similar to that in Equation 14.41, the equilibrium described in Equation 14.48 is sustainable. No new firm would find it profitable to enter this industry. This view of sustainability may be too narrow, however. By adopting a fairly large-scale production plan, a potential entrant could achieve relatively low average costs in this model (with $q = 9$, $AC = 5$, for example). This low average cost gives the potential entrant considerable leeway in pricing its product so as to tempt customers of existing firms to switch allegiances.[11]

Query: What is the Pareto-efficient solution for this market? How might the efficient solution depend on the nature of demanders' utility?

Contestable markets and industry structure

The conclusion that the Chamberlin zero-profit equilibrium pictured in Figure 14.5 is sustainable in the long run has been challenged by several economists.[12] They argue that the model neglects the effects of *potential entry* on market equilibrium by focusing only on the behavior of actual entrants. They therefore reintroduce to economics the distinction, first made by H. Demsetz, between competition *in* the market and competition *for* the market by showing that the latter concept provides a more appropriate perspective for analyzing the free entry assumption.[13] Within this broader perspective the "invisible hand" of competition becomes even more constraining on firms' behavior, and perfectly competitive equilibria are more likely to emerge.

[11]More generally, Chamberlin's model of monopolistic competition can be viewed as seriously incomplete because it does not specify the precise reasons why the demand curve facing each firm is downward sloping. Assuming that the slope arises from some sort of brand name, reputational, or locational differences among goods, a more complete model should address firms' choices among such strategies. For one example of such analysis, see Problem 14.6.

[12]See W. J. Baumol, "Contestable Markets: An Uprising in the Theory of Industry Structure," *American Economic Review* (March 1982): 1–19, and W. J. Baumol, J. C. Panzar, and R. D. Willig, *Contestable Markets and the Theory of Industry Structure* (San Diego, CA: Harcourt Brace Jovanovich, 1982).

[13]H. Demsetz, "Why Regulate Utilities?" *Journal of Law and Economics* (April 1968): 55–65.

The expanded examination of entry begins by defining a "perfectly contestable market":

Perfectly contestable market. A market is *perfectly contestable* if entry and exit are absolutely free. Equivalently, a perfectly contestable market is one in which no outside potential competitor can enter by cutting price and still make profits (because if such profit opportunities existed, potential entrants would take advantage of them).

A perfectly contestable market then drops the perfectly competitive assumption of price-taking behavior but expands a bit upon the concept of free entry by permitting potential entrants to operate in a hit-and-run manner, snatching up whatever profit opportunities are available. Such an assumption, as we will point out below, is not necessarily accurate in many market situations, but it does provide a different starting place for a simplified theory of pricing.

The equilibrium illustrated in Figure 14.5 is unsustainable in a perfectly contestable market, provided two or more firms are already in the market. In such a case a potential hit-and-run entrant could turn a quick profit by taking all the first firm's sales by selling q' at a price slightly below P' and making up for the loss this would entail by selling further marginal increment in output to the other firm(s)' customers at a price in excess of marginal cost. That is, because the equilibrium in Figure 14.5 has $P > MC$, it permits a would-be entrant to take away one zero-profit firm's market and encroach a bit on other firms' markets where, at the margin, profits are attainable. The only type of market equilibrium that would be impervious to such hit-and-run tactics would be one in which firms earn zero profits and price at marginal costs. As we saw in Chapter 10, this requires that firms produce at the low points of their long-run average cost curves where $P = MC = AC$. Even in the absence of price-taking behavior in markets with relatively few firms, perfect contestability provides an "invisible hand" that guides market equilibrium to a competitive-type result.

Market structure

This perfectly contestable analysis can be taken one step further by showing how industry structure is determined. If, as in Chapter 10, we let q^* represent that output level for which average costs are minimized and Q^* represent the total market demand for the commodity when price equals minimal average cost, then the equilibrium number of firms in the industry is given by

$$n = \frac{Q^*}{q^*},\qquad\qquad (14.50)$$

and, contrary to the perfectly competitive case, this number may be relatively small. In Figure 14.6, for example, exactly four firms fulfill the market demand for Q^*, and the perfectly contestable assumption will ensure competitive behavior, even though these firms may recognize strategic relationships among themselves. The ability of potential entrants to seize any possible opportunities for profit sharply constrains the types of behavior that are possible and thereby provides a determinate equilibrium market structure.

Barriers to entry

All of the analysis presented so far in this section has been predicated on the assumptions of free entry and exit. When various barriers prevent such flexibility, these results must be modified. Possible barriers to entry in the oligopoly case include many of those already discussed in connection with monopoly in the previous chapter. They

FIGURE 14.6   **Perfect Contestability and Industry Structure**

In a perfectly contestable market, equilibrium requires that $P = MC = AC$. The number of firms is completely determined by market demand (Q^*) and by the output level that minimizes average cost (q^*).

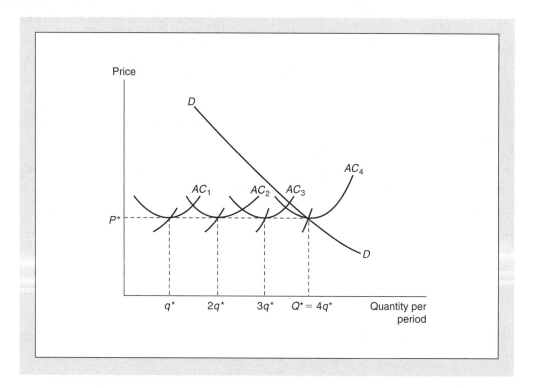

also include those arising specifically out of some features of oligopolistic markets. Product differentiation, for example, may raise entry barriers by promoting strong brand loyalty. Or producers may so proliferate their brands that no room remains for would-be entrants to do anything different (this has been alleged to be true in the ready-to-eat breakfast cereal industry). The possibility of strategic pricing decisions may also deter entry if existing firms can convince firms wishing to enter that it would be unprofitable to do so. Firms may, for a time, adopt lower, entry-deterring prices in order to accomplish this goal, with the intent of raising prices once potential entrants disappear (assuming they do).

Finally, the completely flexible type of hit-and-run behavior assumed in the contestable markets theory may be subject to two other types of barriers in the real world. First, some types of capital investments made by firms may not be reversible. A firm cannot build an automobile assembly plant for a week's use and then dismantle it at no loss. In this case there are exit costs that will make recurrent raids on the industry unprofitable. Of course, in other cases, such as the trucking industry, capital may be easily rented for short periods and exit will then pose few costs. Second, the contestable markets model requires that quantity demanded respond instantly to price differentials. If, instead, demanders switch slowly to a new product, potential entrants cannot attain market penetration quickly, and their ability to discipline firms in the market will be constrained. The importance of all such restrictions for market behavior is ultimately an empirical question.

EXAMPLE 14.5

A Contestable Natural Monopoly

Suppose the total cost of producing electric power (Q, measured in thousands of kilowatt hours) is given by

$$C(Q) = 100Q + 8,000. \tag{14.51}$$

Obviously, this function exhibits declining average cost over all output ranges, so electricity production is a natural monopoly. The demand for electricity depends on its price (in dollars per thousand kilowatt hours) according to

$$Q_D = 1,000 - 5P. \tag{14.52}$$

If a single electricity producer behaves as a monopolist, it will choose a profit-maximizing quantity by

$$MR = 200 - \frac{2Q}{5} = MC = 100 \tag{14.53}$$

or

$$Q_m = 250$$
$$P_m = 150. \tag{14.54}$$

At this monopoly choice, profits will be 4,500 (= $R - C$ = 37,500 − 33,000). These profits provide a tempting target for would-be entrants into the electric industry. If there are no entry barriers (the existing company does not have an exclusive franchise, for example), such an entrant can offer electricity customers a lower price and still cover costs. The monopoly solution in Equations 14.54 may not therefore represent a viable equilibrium.

A contestable solution. If electricity production is fully contestable, the only price viable under the threat of potential entry is average cost. Only with average cost pricing will potential entrants have no incentive to threaten the monopolist's position. We can find this equilibrium by

$$Q = 1,000 - 5P = 1,000 - 5(AC)$$
$$= 1,000 - 5\left(100 + \frac{8,000}{Q}\right), \tag{14.55}$$

which results in the quadratic expression

$$Q^2 - 500Q + 40,000 = 0. \tag{14.56}$$

Factoring gives

$$(Q - 400)(Q - 100) = 0, \tag{14.57}$$

but only the $Q = 400$ solution is a sustainable entry deterrent. Under contestability, therefore, the market equilibrium is

$$Q_c = 400$$
$$P_c = 120. \tag{14.58}$$

Contestability has increased consumer welfare considerably from what it was under the monopoly solution. Indeed, the contestable solution is precisely what might have been chosen by a regulatory commission interested in average cost pricing.

Query: Is consumer surplus as large as possible in this case given the constraint that no subsidies are being provided to electric power producers? How might consumer surplus be increased further through an appropriate subsidy?

SUMMARY

Many markets fall between the polar extremes of perfect competition and monopoly. In this chapter we began our examination of such markets by introducing some of the most widely used models. We have seen that in such imperfectly competitive markets, each firm must take its rivals' actions into account in making decisions, and this adds a considerable conjectural element to the analysis. In Chapter 15 we will continue to explore these interrelations through the use of game theory models. Here we reached for general conclusions about modeling markets with relatively few firms:

- Markets with few firms offer potential profits through the formation of a monopoly cartel. Such cartels may, however, be unstable and costly to maintain because each member has an incentive to chisel on price.

- In markets with few firms, output and price decisions are interdependent. Each firm must consider its rivals' decisions. Modeling such interdependence is difficult because of the need to consider conjectural variations.

- The Cournot model provides a tractable approach to oligopoly markets, but neglects important strategic issues.

- Product differentiation can be analyzed in a standard profit-maximization framework. With differentiated products, the law of one price no longer holds, and firms may have somewhat more leeway in their pricing decisions.

- Entry conditions are important determinants of the long-run sustainability of various market equilibria. With perfect contestability, equilibria may resemble perfectly competitive ones even though there are relatively few firms in the market.

PROBLEMS

14.1

Assume for simplicity that a monopolist has no costs of production and faces a demand curve given by

$$Q = 150 - P.$$

a. Calculate the profit-maximizing price-quantity combination for this monopolist. Also calculate the monopolist's profits.

b. Suppose a second firm enters the market. Let q_1 be the output of the first firm and q_2 the output of the second. Market demand is now given by

$$q_1 + q_2 = 150 - P.$$

Assuming this second firm also has no costs of production, use the Cournot model of duopoly to determine the profit-maximizing level of production for each firm as well as the market price. Also calculate each firm's profits.

c. How do the results from parts (a) and (b) compare to the price and quantity that would prevail in a perfectly competitive market? Graph the demand and marginal revenue curves and indicate the three different price-quantity combinations on the demand curve.

14.2

A monopolist can produce at constant average (and marginal) costs of $AC = MC = 5$. The firm faces a market demand curve given by

$$Q = 53 - P.$$

a. Calculate the profit-maximizing price-quantity combination for this monopolist. Also calculate the monopolist's profits.

b. Suppose a second firm enters the market. Let q_1 be the output of firm 1 and q_2 the output of firm 2. Market demand now is given by

$$q_1 + q_2 = 53 - P.$$

Assuming firm 2 has the same costs as firm 1, calculate the profits of firms 1 and 2 as functions of q_1 and q_2.

c. Suppose (after Cournot) each of these two firms chooses its level of output so as to maximize profits on the assumption that the other's output is fixed. Calculate each firm's "reaction function," which expresses desired output of one firm as a function of the other's output.

d. On the assumption in part (c), what is the only level for q_1 and q_2 with which both firms will be satisfied (what q_1, q_2 combination satisfies both reaction curves)?

e. With q_1 and q_2 at the equilibrium level specified in part (d), what will be the market price, the profits for each firm, and the total profits earned?

f. Suppose now there are n identical firms in the industry. If each firm adopts the Cournot strategy toward all its rivals, what will be the profit-maximizing output level for each firm? What will be the market price? What will be the total profits earned in the industry? (All these will depend on n.)

g. Show that when n approaches infinity, the output levels, market price, and profits approach those that would "prevail" in perfect competition.

14.3

Use the analysis developed in this chapter to explain the following industrial behavior:

a. Banks announce a widely publicized prime rate and change it only occasionally.

b. Apple and IBM computers are not compatible.

c. Insurance companies continue to solicit automobile insurance business in spite of their plea that "we lose money on every policy we write."

d. U.S. automobiles were of very low quality in the 1960s and 1970s, but quality improved in the late 1980s.

14.4

Suppose a firm's costs for dollars spent on product differentiation (or advertising) activities (z) and quantity (q) can be written as

$$C = g(q) + z \qquad g'(q) > 0,$$

and that its demand function can be written as

$$q = q(p, z).$$

Show that the firm's profit-maximizing choices for p and z will result in spending a share of total revenues on z given by

$$\frac{z}{pq} = -\frac{e_{q,z}}{e_{q,p}}.$$

(This condition was derived by R. Dorfman and P. Steiner in "Optimal Advertising and Optimal Quality," *American Economic Review* [December 1954]: 826–36.)

14.5

One way of measuring the size distribution of firms is through the use of the Herfindahl Index, which is defined as

$$H = \sum \alpha_i^2,$$

where α_i is the share of firm i in total industry revenues. Show that if all firms in the industry have constant returns-to-scale production functions and follow Cournot output decisions (Equation 14.10), the ratio of total industry profits to total revenue will equal the Herfindahl Index divided by the price elasticity of demand. What does this result imply about the relationship between industry concentration and industry profitability?

14.6

S. Salop provides an instructive model of product differentiation. He asks us to conceptualize the demand for a product group as varying along a circular spectrum of characteristics (the model can also be thought of as a spatial model with consumers located around a circle). Demanders are located at each point on this circle and each demands one unit of the good. Demanders incur costs if they must consume a product that does not precisely meet the characteristics they prefer. As in the Hotelling model, these costs are given by tx (where x is the "distance" of the consumer's preferred characteristic from the characteristics being offered by the nearest supplier and t is the cost incurred per unit distance). Initially there are n firms each with identical cost functions given by $C_i = f + cq_i$. For simplicity we assume also that the circle of characteristics has a circumference of precisely 1 and that the n firms are located evenly around the circle at intervals of $1/n$.

a. Each firm is free to choose its own price (p), but is constrained by the price charged by its nearest neighbor (p^*). Explain why the extent of any one firm's market (x) is given by the equation

$$p + tx = p^* + t[(1/n) - x].$$

b. Given the pricing decision illustrated in part (a), this firm sells $q_i = 2x$ because it has a market on "both sides." Calculate the profit-maximizing price for this firm as a function of p^*, c, and t.

c. Assuming symmetry among all firms will require that all prices are equal, show that this results in an equilibrium in which $p = p^* = c + t/n$. Explain this result intuitively.

d. Show that in equilibrium the profits of the typical firm in this situation are $\pi_i = t/n^2 - f$.

e. Assuming free entry, what will be the equilibrium level of n in this model?

f. Calculate the optimal level of differentiation in this model—defined as that number of firms (and products) that minimizes the sum of production costs plus demander distance costs. Show that this number is precisely half the number calculated in part (e). Hence, this model suffers from "over-differentiation." (For a further exploration of this model, see S. Salop "Monopolistic Competition with Outside Goods," *Bell Journal of Economics,* Spring 1979, pp. 141–56.)

14.7

Suppose demand for crude oil is given by

$$Q = -2,000P + 70,000,$$

where Q is the quantity of oil in thousands of barrels per year and P is the dollar price per barrel. Suppose also that there are 1,000 identical small producers of crude oil, each with marginal costs given by

$$MC = q + 5,$$

where q is the output of the typical firm.

a. Assuming each small oil producer acts as a price taker, calculate the market supply curve and the market equilibrium price and quantity.

b. Suppose a practically infinite supply of crude oil is discovered in New Jersey by a would-be price leader and can be produced at a constant average and marginal cost of $15 per barrel. Assuming the supply behavior of the competitive fringe described in part (a) is not changed by this discovery, how much should the price leader produce in order to maximize profits? What price and quantity will now prevail in the market?

c. Graph your results. Does consumer surplus increase as a result of the New Jersey oil discovery? How does consumer surplus after the discovery compare to what would exist if the New Jersey oil were supplied competitively?

14.8

Suppose a firm is considering investing in research that would lead to a cost-saving innovation. Assuming the firm can retain this innovation solely for its own use, will the additional profits from the lower (marginal) costs be greater if the firm is a competitive price taker or if the firm is a monopolist? Develop a careful graphical argument. More generally, develop a verbal analysis to suggest whether competitive or monopoly firms are more likely to adopt cost-saving innovations. (For an early analysis of this issue, see W. Fellner, "The Influence of Market Structure on Technological Progress," *Quarterly Journal of Economics* [November 1951]: 560–67.)

14.9

The demand for telephones in a midsize city is given by

$$Q = 1,000 - 50P,$$

where Q is the number of homes buying service (in thousands) and P is the monthly connect charge (in dollars). Phone system costs are given by

$$C = 550 \ln (.1Q - 20) \text{ for } Q > 200.$$

a. Is telephone production a natural monopoly in this city?

b. What output level will an unregulated monopoly produce in this situation? What price will be charged? What will monopoly profits be?

c. If there is active (contestable) competition for the city franchise, what price will prevail?

SUGGESTIONS FOR FURTHER READING

Bain, J. S. *Barriers to New Competition*. Cambridge, MA: Harvard University Press, 1956.
Classic treatment of the theory of entry barriers together with some empirical detail.

Baumol, W. J., J. C. Panzar, and R. D. Willig. *Contestable Markets and the Theory of Industry Structure*. San Diego, CA: Harcourt Brace Jovanovich, 1982.
Detailed theoretical treatment of recent theories of contestable markets.

Mas-Collel, A., M. D. Whinston, and J. R. Green. *Microeconomic Theory*. New York. Oxford University Press. 1995.
Chapter 12 has nice summaries of several models of spatial differentiation.

Scherer, F. M. *Industrial Market Structure and Economic Performance,* 2nd ed. Chicago: Rand McNally, 1980.
Major industrial organization text. Encyclopedic coverage. Not as analytical as the more recent Tirole text.

Schmalensee, R. *The Economics of Advertising,* Chap. 1. Amsterdam: North-Holland, 1972.
Good summary of theories of advertising together with some empirical investigations (especially of cigarette advertising).

Shy, Oz. *Industrial Organization: Theory and Applications*. Cambridge, MA: MIT Press, 1995.
Chapter 7 offers extended treatments of models of differentiated products, including detailed treatment of several location models.

Stiglitz, J., and G. F. Mathewson, eds. *New Developments in the Analysis of Market Structure*. Cambridge, MA: MIT Press, 1986.
Contains a number of useful review articles and discussions. Especially recommended are those by Baumol et al. (Contestability), Schmalensee (Advertising), and Stiglitz (Competition and Research and Development Incentives).

Tirole, J. *The Theory of Industrial Organization*. Cambridge, MA: MIT Press, 1988.
Complete treatment of a variety of models of imperfect competition. Particularly useful sections on product differentiation and nonprice competition.

Chapter 15

GAME THEORY MODELS OF PRICING

Many of the strategic issues that arise in modeling markets with only a few sellers can be studied using the tools of game theory. In this chapter we will look at some of these applications. First, however, we must introduce some of the basic concepts of game theory and show how equilibrium is defined in a game theory model.

Basic concepts

Game theory models seek to portray complex strategic situations in a highly simplified and stylized setting. Much like the other models in this book, game theory models abstract from most of the personal and institutional details of a problem in order to arrive at a representation of the situation that is mathematically tractable. This ability to get to the "heart" of the problem is the greatest strength of this type of modeling.

Any situation in which individuals or firms must make strategic choices and in which the final outcome will depend on what each actor chooses to do can be viewed as a *game*. All games have three basic elements: (1) players; (2) strategies; and (3) payoffs. Games may be *cooperative*, in which players can make binding agreements, or *noncooperative*, where such agreements are not possible. Here we will be concerned primarily with noncooperative games. The basic elements listed below are included in such games.

Players

Each decision maker in a game is called a *player*. These players may be individuals (as in poker games), firms (as in markets with few firms), or entire nations (as in military conflicts). All players are characterized as having the ability to choose from among a set of possible actions they might take.[1] Usually, the number of players is fixed throughout the "play" of a game, and games are often characterized by the number of players (that is, two-player, three-player, or *n*-player games). In this chapter we will primarily study two-player games and will denote these

---

[1] Sometimes one of the players in a game is taken to be "nature." For this player, actions are not "chosen" but rather occur with certain probabilities. For example, the weather may affect the outcomes of a game, but it is not "chosen" by nature. Rather, particular weather outcomes are assumed to occur with various probabilities. Games against nature can be analyzed using the methods developed in Chapters 18 and 19.

players by *A* or *B*. One of the important assumptions usually made in game theory (as in most of economics) is that the specific identity of the players is irrelevant. There are no "good guys" or "bad guys" in a game, and players are not assumed to have any special abilities or shortcomings. Each player is simply assumed to choose the course of action that yields the most favorable outcome, after taking the actions of his or her opponent into account.

Strategies

Each course of action open to a player during a game is called a *strategy*. Depending on the game being examined, a strategy may be a very simple action (take another card in blackjack) or a very complex one (build a laser-based antimissile defense), but each strategy is assumed to be a well-defined, specific course of action.[2] Usually, the number of strategies available to each player will be small; many aspects of game theory can be illustrated for situations in which each player has only two strategies available. In noncooperative games, players cannot reach binding agreements with each other about what strategies they will play—each player is uncertain about what the other will do.

Payoffs

The final returns to the players of a game at its conclusion are called "payoffs." Payoffs are usually measured in levels of utility obtained by the players, although monetary payoffs (say, profits for firms) are often used instead. In general, it is assumed that players can rank the payoffs of a game ordinally from most preferred to least preferred and will seek the highest ranked payoff attainable. Payoffs incorporate all aspects associated with outcomes of a game; these include explicit monetary payoffs and implicit feelings by the players about the outcomes, such as whether they are embarrassed or gain self-esteem. Players prefer payoffs that offer more utility to those that offer less.

Notation

Usually it is not necessary to write down a game in formal notation—a literary description of the situation will do. But, for stating results in a compact way, some notation can help clarify matters. Following standard custom, we will denote a particular game *G* between two players (*A* and *B*) by

$$G[S_A, S_B, U_A(a,b), U_B(a,b)], \qquad (15.1)$$

where S_A and S_B represent the set of strategies available for players *A* and *B*, respectively, and U_A and U_B represent the utility obtained by the players when *A* and *B* choose particular strategies ($a \subset S_A$, $b \subset S_B$).

Nash equilibrium in games

In the economic theory of markets, the concept of *equilibrium* is developed to indicate a situation in which both suppliers and demanders are content with the market outcome. Given the equilibrium price and quantity, no market participant has an incentive to change his or her behavior. The question therefore arises whether there are similar equilibrium concepts in game theory models. Are there strategic choices that, once made, provide no incentives for the players to alter their behavior further? Do these equilibria then offer believable explanations of the outcome of games?

Although there are several ways to formalize equilibrium concepts in game theory, the most commonly used approach was originally proposed by Cournot (see Chapter 14) in

---

[2]In games involving a sequence of actions (for example, most board games, such as chess), a specification of strategies may involve several decision points (each move in chess). Assuming perfect knowledge of how the game is played, such complex patterns can often be expressed by choices among a large but finite set of pure strategies, each of which specifies a complete course of action until the game is completed. See our discussion of "extensive" and "normal" forms and D. M. Kreps, *Game Theory and Economic Modeling*, Chap. 3, (Oxford University Press, 1990).

the nineteenth century and generalized in the early 1950s by J. Nash.[3] Under Nash's procedure, a pair of strategies, say, (a^*, b^*), is defined to be an equilibrium if a^* represents player A's best strategy when B plays b^*, and b^* represents B's best strategy when A plays a^*. Formally, a pair of strategies is a Nash equilibrium if

$$U_A(a^*, b^*) \geq U_A(a', b^*) \text{ for all } a' \subset S_A \qquad (15.2)$$

and

$$U_B(a^*, b^*) \geq U_B(a^*, b') \text{ for all } b' \subset S_B.$$

Even if one of the players reveals the (equilibrium) strategy he or she will use, the other player cannot benefit from knowing this. For nonequilibrium strategies, this is not the case. As we shall see, if one player knows what the other's strategy will be, he or she can often benefit from that knowledge and choose another strategy. This may, in turn, reduce the payoff received by the player who has revealed his or her strategy, providing an incentive to do something else.

Not every game has a Nash equilibrium pair of strategies. And, in some cases, a game may have multiple equilibria, some of which are more plausible than others. Some Nash equilibria may not be especially desirable for the players in a game. And, in some cases, other equilibrium concepts may be more reasonable than those proposed by Nash. Still, we now have an initial working definition of equilibrium with which to start our study of game theory:

DEFINITION

Nash equilibrium strategies. A pair of strategies (a^*, b^*) represents an equilibrium solution to a two-player game if a^* is an optimal strategy for A against b^*, and b^* is an optimal strategy for B against a^*.[4]

An illustrative game

As a way of illustrating the game-theoretic approach to strategic modeling, let's examine a simple example in which two students (A and B) must decide how loudly to play their stereos in a dorm. Each person may choose to play his or her equipment either loudly (L) or softly (S). We wish to examine possible equilibrium choices in this situation. It should be stressed at the outset that this game is not especially realistic—it is intended for pedagogic purposes only.

The game in extensive form

Figure 15.1 illustrates the specific details of the dorm game. In this game "tree," the action proceeds from left to right, and each "node" represents a decision point for the person indicated there. The first move in this game belongs to A: he or she must choose a decibel level, L or S. Because B's decisions occur to the right of A's, the tree indicates that B makes the decision after A. At this stage, two versions of the game are possible depending on whether B knows what choice A made. First we will look at the case where B does not have this information. The larger oval surrounding B's two decision nodes indicates that both nodes share the same (lack of) information. B must choose L or S without knowing what A has done. Later we will examine the case where B does have this information.

The numbers at the end of each tree branch indicate payoffs, here measured in utility to these two dorm mates. Each pair of payoffs lists A's utility first. For example, the payoffs in Figure 15.1 show that if A chooses S and B chooses L, utility will be 6 for A and 4 for B. Other payoffs are interpreted similarly.

---

[3]John Nash, "Equilibrium Points in n-Person Games," *Proceedings of the National Academy of Sciences* 36 (1950): 48–49. Nash is the principal figure in the 2001 film *A Beautiful Mind*. See Problem 15.5 for a game theory example from the film.

[4]Although this definition is stated only for two-player games, the generalization to n-persons is straightforward but notationally cumbersome.

FIGURE 15.1   **The Dormitory Game in Extensive Form**

In this game, *A* chooses a loud (*L*) or a soft (*S*) stereo volume, then *B* makes a similar choice. The oval surrounding *B*'s nodes indicates that they share the same (lack of) information—*B* does not know what strategy *A* has chosen. Payoffs (with *A*'s first) are listed at the right.

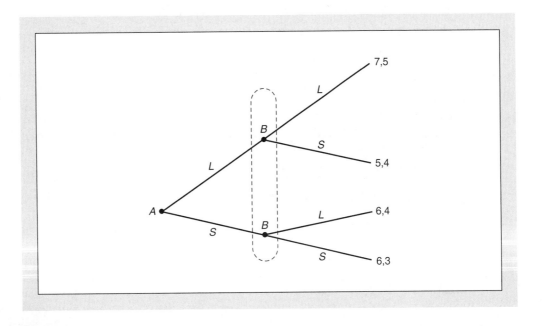

TABLE 15.1   **The Dormitory Game in Normal Form**

		B's Strategies	
		L	S
A's Strategies	L	7, 5	5, 4
	S	6, 4	6, 3

The game in normal form

Although the game tree in Figure 15.1 offers a useful visual presentation of the complete structure of a game, sometimes it is more convenient to describe games in tabular (sometimes called *normal* or *strategic*) form. Table 15.1 provides such a presentation for the dormitory game. In the table, *A*'s strategies (*S* or *L*) are shown at the left, and *B*'s strategies are shown across the top. Payoffs (again with *A*'s coming first) corresponding to the various strategic choices are shown in the body of the table. Figure 15.1 and Table 15.1 convey exactly the same information about this game, though usually it is more convenient to work with the normal form.

Dominant strategies and Nash equilibria

Table 15.1 makes clear that a loud-play strategy is a dominant strategy for person *B*. No matter what strategy *A* chooses, the *L* strategy provides greater utility to *B* than does the *S* strategy. Of course, because the structure of the game is known to both players, *A* will recognize that *B* has such a dominant strategy. Hence, *A* will opt for the strategy that does the best against *B*'s choice of *L*. As can be seen from Table 15.1, *A* will consequently also choose to play his or her music loudly (*L*). Considerations of strategy dominance, therefore, suggest that the *A:L, B:L* strategy choice will be made and that the resulting utility payoffs will be 7 (to *A*) and 5 (to *B*).

The *A:L, B:L* strategy choice also obeys the Nash criterion for equilibrium. If *A* knows that *B* will play *L*, his or her best choice is *L*. Similarly, if *B* knows *A* will play *L* his or her best choice is also *L* (indeed, because *L* is a dominant strategy for *B*, this is the best choice no matter what *A* does). The *A:L, B:L* choice, therefore, meets the symmetry required by the Nash criterion.

To see why the other strategy pairs in Table 15.1 do not meet the Nash criterion, let us consider them one at a time. If the players announce *A:S, B:L*, this provides *A* with a chance to better his or her position—if *A* knows *B* will opt for *L*, he or she can obtain greater utility by choosing *L*. The choice *A:S, B:L* is therefore not a Nash equilibrium. Neither of the two outcomes in which *B* chooses *S* meets the Nash criterion either. As we have already pointed out, no matter what *A* does, *B* can improve its utility by choosing *L* instead. Because *L* strictly dominates *S* or *B*, no outcome in which *B* plays *S* can be a Nash equilibrium.

Existence of Nash equilibria

Although the dorm game illustrated in Figure 15.1 contains a unique Nash equilibrium, that is not a general property of all two-person games. Example 15.1 illustrates a simple game (Rock, Scissors, Paper) in which no Nash equilibrium exists, and another game (Battle of the Sexes) that contains two Nash equilibria. These examples make clear, therefore, that the Nash approach may not always identify a unique equilibrium solution to a two-player game. Rather, one must explore the details of each game situation to determine whether there exist believable Nash equilibria.

 EXAMPLE 15.1

Sample Nash Equilibria

Table 15.2 illustrates two familiar games that reflect differing possibilities for Nash equilibria. Part (a) of the table depicts the children's finger game Rock, Scissors, Paper. The zero payoffs along the diagonal show that if players adopt the same strategy, no payments are made. In other cases the payoffs indicate a $1 payment from loser to winner under the usual hierarchy (Rock breaks Scissors, Scissors cut Paper, Paper covers Rock). As anyone who has played this game knows, there is no equilibrium. Any strategy pair is unstable because it offers at least one of the players an incentive to adopt another strategy. For example, (*A:* Scissors, *B:* Scissors) provides an incentive for either *A* or *B* to choose Rock. Similarly (*A:* Paper, *B:* Rock) obviously encourages *B* to choose Scissors. The irregular cycling behavior exhibited in the play of this game clearly indicates the absence of a Nash equilibrium.

Battle of the sexes. In the Battle of the Sexes game, a husband (*A*) and wife (*B*) are planning a vacation. *A* prefers mountain locations; *B* prefers the seaside. Both players prefer a vacation spent together to one spent apart. The payoffs in part (b) of Table 15.2 reflect these preferences. Here both of the joint vacations represent Nash equilibria. With (*A:* Mountain, *B:* Mountain) neither player can gain by taking advantage of knowing the other's strategy. Similar comments apply to (*A:* Seaside, *B:* Seaside). Hence this is a game with two Nash equilibria.

Query: Are any of the strategies in either of these games dominant? Why aren't separate vacations Nash equilibria in the Battle of the Sexes?

TABLE 15.2	**Two Simple Games**

(a) Rock, Scissors, Paper—No Nash Equilibria

		B's Strategies		
		Rock	Scissors	Paper
A's Strategies	Rock	0, 0	1, –1	–1, 1
	Scissors	–1, 1	0, 0	1, –1
	Paper	1, –1	–1, 1	0, 0

(b) Battle of the Sexes—Two Nash Equilibria

		B's Strategies	
		Mountain	Seaside
A's Strategies	Mountain	2, 1	0, 0
	Seaside	0, 0	1, 2

There are, however, certain types of two-player games in which a Nash equilibrium must exist. Intuitively, games in which the participants have a large number of strategies will often offer sufficient flexibility to ensure that at least one Nash equilibrium must exist. Such games arise in two contexts. First, games in which the strategies chosen by *A* and *B* are alternative levels of a single continuous variable include an "infinite" number of potential strategies; such games are guaranteed to have a Nash equilibrium. The most important class of such games involves games where the players are two firms that must choose the price they will charge for a single product. Some games of this type, together with illustrations of the types of Nash equilibria they exhibit, are discussed later in this chapter.

Another way in which games may contain a sufficiently "large" number of strategies is to permit players to use "mixed" strategies. In such games, there may be relatively few "pure" strategies like the ones we have been examining—perhaps only two. But each player is permitted to play these pure strategies with pre-selected probabilities. In the dorm game, for example, *A* might flip a coin to determine whether to play music loudly or softly—that is, he or she would play each strategy with probability ½. If each player can choose to play the available pure strategies with any probabilities he or she might choose, the game will be converted into one with an infinite number of (mixed) strategies and, again, the existence of a Nash equilibrium is ensured. Example 15.2 provides an illustration of how the consideration of mixed strategies can add to the Nash equilibrium outcomes in the Battle of the Sexes game we have already examined.

Unfortunately, the proof of the existence of a Nash equilibrium in two-player games with a continuum of strategies is difficult and requires a number of technical assumptions. Hence, we will not attempt to present it here. Rather, most of our analysis of two-player games will involve explicitly solving for any Nash equilibria that may exist. Interested readers may wish to explore mathematically sophisticated existence proofs on their own.[5]

---

[5]See, for example, D. Fudenberg and J. Tirole, *Game Theory* (Cambridge, MA: MIT Press, 1992), section 1.3. Proofs of the existence of Nash equilibria often use fixed-point theorems such as the one illustrated in Chapter 12.

EXAMPLE 15.2

Battle of the Sexes with Mixed Strategies

To show how the introduction of mixed strategies may add Nash equilibria to a given game, let's return to the Battle of the Sexes game in Example 15.1. Suppose that the spouses in the problem tire of constant bickering about vacations and decide to let "chance" decide. Specifically, suppose A decides to choose his mountain strategy with probability r and seaside with probability $1 - r$. Similarly, suppose B chooses her mountain strategy with probability s and seaside probability with $1 - s$. Given these probabilities, the outcomes of the game occur with the following probabilities: mountain-mountain, rs; mountain-seaside, $r(1 - s)$; seaside-mountain, $(1 - r)(s)$; and seaside-seaside $(1 - r)(1 - s)$. A's expected utility is then given by

$$E(U_A) = rs(2) + r(1 - s)(0) + (1 - r)(s)(0) + (1 - r)(1 - s)(1) \qquad (15.3)$$
$$= 1 - r - s + 3rs = 1 - s + r(3s - 1).$$

Obviously, A's optimal choice of r depends on B's probability, s. If $s < \frac{1}{3}$, utility is maximized by choosing $r = 0$. If $s > \frac{1}{3}$, A should opt for $r = 1$. And when $s = \frac{1}{3}$, A's expected utility is $\frac{2}{3}$ no matter what value of r is chosen. Figure 15.2 illustrates A's optimal choices of r given these various values of s.

For spouse B, expected utility is given by

$$E(U_B) = rs(1) + r(1 - s)(0) + (1 - s)(r)(0) + (1 - r)(1 - s)(2) \qquad (15.4)$$
$$= 2 - 2r - 2s + 3rs = 2 - 2r + s(3r - 2).$$

Now, when $r < \frac{2}{3}$, B's expected utility is maximized by choosing $s = 0$. When $r > \frac{2}{3}$, utility is maximized by choosing $s = 1$. And when $r = \frac{2}{3}$, B's expected utility is independent of what s she chooses. These optimal choices are also shown in Figure 15.2.

Nash equilibria are shown in Figure 15.2 by the intersections of the optimal response curves for A and B. That is, the intersections obey the conditions summarized in Equations 15.2. Notice that there are three such intersections. Two of these we have seen previously: $r = 0$, $s = 0$ and $r = 1$, $s = 1$ represent the joint vacation strategies we discussed in Example 15.1. But $r = \frac{2}{3}$, $s = \frac{1}{3}$ is a new Nash equilibrium that was unavailable before the introduction of mixed strategies. More generally, Figure 15.2 provides a hint of why games with a continuum of strategies must have Nash equilibria—in general, continuous optimal response functions will intersect somewhere and those intersections will be Nash equilibria.

Query: Is the mixed-strategy equilibrium illustrated in this problem particularly desirable to the players? If the spouses could cooperate to reach a decision, would they opt for such a mixed-strategy solution?

The prisoners' dilemma

Nash equilibria arise because of the strategic uncertainties inherent in a situation. Nothing guarantees that these equilibria will be especially desirable from the players' perspectives. Probably the most famous example of a two-player game with an undesirable Nash equilibrium outcome is the Prisoners' Dilemma game, first discussed by A. W. Tucker in the 1940s. The title stems from the following game situation. Two people are arrested for a

FIGURE 15.2   **Nash Equilibria in Mixed Strategies in the Battle of the Sexes Game**

With mixed strategies, A plays "mountains" with probability r, and B plays mountains with probability s. The figure shows each player's optimal choice given the other player's choice. This game has three Nash equilibria (denoted by E): (1) $r = 0$, $s = 0$; (2) $r = 1$, $s = 1$; and (3) $r = \frac{2}{3}$, $s = \frac{1}{3}$.

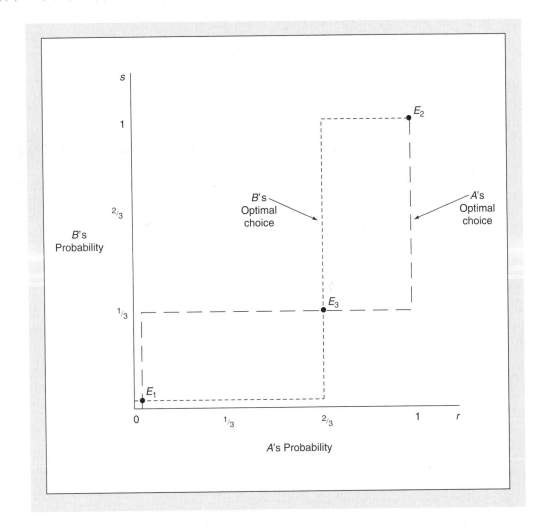

crime. The district attorney has little evidence in the case and is eager to extract a confession. She separates the suspects and tells each, "If you confess and your companion doesn't, I can promise you a reduced (six-month) sentence, whereas your companion will get 10 years. If you both confess, you will each get a three-year sentence." Each suspect also knows that if neither of them confesses, the lack of evidence will cause them to be tried for a lesser crime, for which they will receive two-year sentences. The normal-form payoff matrix for this situation is illustrated in Table 15.3. The "confess" strategy dominates for both A and B. Hence, these strategies constitute a Nash equilibrium and the district attorney's ploy looks successful. However, notice that an ironclad agreement by both prisoners not to confess would reduce their prison terms from three to two years. This "rational" solution is not stable, and each prisoner has an incentive to squeal on his or her colleague. This then is the "dilemma": Outcomes that appear to be optimal are not stable when subjected to the Nash criterion. Example 15.3 demonstrates another game, this time with an environmental twist, in which the Nash equilibrium is not especially desirable from the players' perspectives.

TABLE 15.3 **The Prisoners' Dilemma**

		B	
		Confess	Not Confess
A	Confess	A: 3 years B: 3 years	A: 6 months B: 10 years
	Not Confess	A: 10 years B: 6 months	A: 2 years B: 2 years

 EXAMPLE 15.3

The Tragedy of the Common

The term "Tragedy of the Common" has come to signify environmental problems of over-use that arise when scarce resources are treated as "common property."[6] A game-theoretic illustration of this issue can be developed by assuming that two herders (the familiar A and B) are deciding how many of the yaks in their herds to graze on the village common. The problem is that the common is quite small and can rapidly succumb to overgrazing.

In order to add some mathematical structure to this problem, let Υ_A, Υ_B represent the number of yaks that are brought to the common and suppose that the per-yak value of grazing on the common (in terms, say, of increased yak milk) is given by

$$V(\Upsilon_A, \Upsilon_B) = 200 - (\Upsilon_A + \Upsilon_B)^2. \qquad (15.5)$$

Notice that this function implies both that an extra yak reduces V ($V_i < 0$) and that this marginal effect increases with additional grazing ($V_{ii} < 0$).

To find the Nash equilibrium grazing strategies, we solve herder A's value maximization problem

$$\underset{\Upsilon_A}{\text{Max }} \Upsilon_A V = \underset{\Upsilon_A}{\text{Max }} [200\Upsilon_A - \Upsilon_A(\Upsilon_A + \Upsilon_B)^2]. \qquad (15.6)$$

The first-order condition for a maximum is

$$200 - 2\Upsilon_A^2 - 2\Upsilon_A\Upsilon_B - \Upsilon_A^2 - 2\Upsilon_A\Upsilon_B - \Upsilon_B^2 = 200 - 3\Upsilon_A^2 - 4\Upsilon_A\Upsilon_B - \Upsilon_B^2 \qquad (15.7)$$
$$= 0.$$

Similarly, for B the optimal strategy choice solves

$$200 - 3\Upsilon_B^2 - 4\Upsilon_B\Upsilon_A - \Upsilon_A^2 = 0. \qquad (15.8)$$

For a Nash equilibrium, the values for Υ_A and Υ_B must solve both Equations 15.7 and 15.8. Using the symmetry condition $\Upsilon_A = \Upsilon_B$, these can be solved as

$$200 = 8\Upsilon_A^2 = 8\Upsilon_B^2 \qquad (15.9)$$

or

$$\Upsilon_A = \Upsilon_B = 5. \qquad (15.10)$$

Hence each herder will bring 5 yaks to the common and will obtain $500[= 5 \cdot (200 - 10^2)]$ in return. Given this choice, neither herder has an incentive to change his or her behavior.

---

[6]This term was popularized by G. Hardin, "The Tragedy of the Common," *Science 162* (1968): 1243–48.

That the Nash equilibrium is not the best use of the common can be shown by noting that $\Upsilon_A = \Upsilon_B = 4$ provides greater total revenue [$544 = 4(200 - 64)$] to each herder.[7] But $\Upsilon_A = \Upsilon_B = 4$ is not a stable equilibrium. If, say, A announces $\Upsilon_A = 4$, herder B can solve Equation 15.8 as

$$3\Upsilon_B^2 + 16\Upsilon_B - 184 = 0, \tag{15.11}$$

which has a solution of 5.6 yaks. Rounding this to 6 shows that A's value would now be 400, whereas B's would be 600. As in the Prisoners' Dilemma game, $\Upsilon_A = \Upsilon_B = 4$ provides an incentive for each herder to cheat.

Query: If this game were played repetitively (say, each day), would you expect the Nash equilibrium to persist?

Cooperation and repetition

Games such as the Prisoners' Dilemma or the Tragedy of the Common suggest that cooperation among players may yield outcomes that are preferred to the Nash outcome by both players. Providing a model of cooperation in the games we have been looking at, however, is difficult, because the logic of the Nash equilibrium concept suggests that any other solution will be unstable. We could, of course, look at institutions that exist beyond a particular game (for example, the laws of contracts) to investigate how cooperative outcomes might be fostered, but that approach would divert us from the purpose of this chapter.[8] Instead, here we look at ways in which certain types of cooperative behavior might be facilitated in games that are played repeatedly. Because repetition may bring home directly to players the inefficiencies inherent in a single-period Nash equilibrium, it seems plausible that repeated play might foster cooperation. In the Prisoners' Dilemma, for example, it seems doubtful that the district attorney's ploy could succeed if used repeatedly, especially if the same suspects were always involved. Surely, even the most dim-witted criminal would eventually catch on. Similarly, it seems unlikely that the yak herders in Example 15.3 would persist in overgrazing on the common every day without eventually trying something else. To examine such possibilities, we need to develop some ways of describing games that are played over time.

A two-period game

To illustrate Nash equilibria in dynamic (multiperiod) games, we return to a reformulated version of the dormitory game presented at the beginning of this chapter. We present this new game in extensive form in order to understand its temporal aspects. Figure 15.3 repeats our prior game, but now we assume that A sets his or her decibel level first and that B can hear this before turning the stereo on. In graphical terms, the oval around B's nodes has been eliminated in Figure 15.3 to indicate this additional information. In effect, this game has now been converted into a two-period game. With this change, B's strategic choices must be phrased in a way that takes into account the information available at the start of period two. Although B will make his or her choice at the start of the game, we need to state a complete set of strategies for all the possible actions B might propose taking.

In Table 15.4 we indicate such an extended set of strategies. In all, there are four such strategies covering the possible informational contingencies. Each strategy is stated as a pair of actions indicating what B will do depending on its information. The strategy (L, L)

---

[7]Actually, the total value of the common [$\Upsilon(200 - \Upsilon^2)$] is maximized when $\Upsilon = \sqrt{66} = 8.1$, though bringing 0.1 yak to the common may require more skill than the herders have.

[8]But see the discussion of property and contracts in Chapter 20.

FIGURE 15.3	The Dormitory Game in Sequential Form

In this form of the dormitory game, *B* knows *A*'s stereo choice. Strategies for *B* must be phrased taking this information into account. (See Table 15.4.)

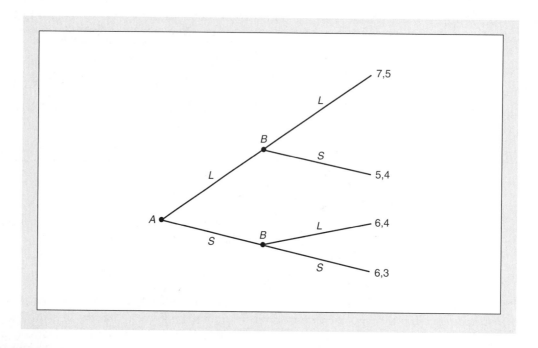

TABLE 15.4	Contingent Strategies in the Dormitory Game

		B's Strategies			
		L, L	L, S	S, L	S, S
A's Strategies	L	7, 5	7, 5	5, 4	5, 4
	S	6, 4	6, 3	6, 4	6, 3

indicates that *B* chooses *L* if *A* chooses *L* (his or her first strategy) and *L* also if *A* chooses *S* (the second strategy). Similarly (*S, L*) indicates that *B* chooses *S* if *A* chooses *L* and *B* chooses *L* if *A* chooses *S*. Although this table conveys little more than did the previous normal form for the dormitory game (Table 15.1), explicit consideration of contingent strategy choices does enable us to explore equilibrium notions for this two-period game.

Somewhat surprisingly, there are three Nash equilibria in this game: (1) *A:L, B:(L, L)*; (2) *A:L, B:(L, S)*; and (3) *A:S, B:(S, L)*. Each strategy meets the criterion of being optimal for each player given the strategy of the other. Pairs (2) and (3) are implausible, however. Each of these pairs incorporates a noncredible threat on the part of player *B*. He or she would not in fact take the specified action if in a position to do so. Consider, for example, the pair *A:L, B:(L, S)*. Under this Nash equilibrium, *B* promises to play *S* if *A* plays *S*. A glance at Figure 15.3 shows that this threat is not credible. If *B* were presented with the fact of *A* having chosen *S*, he or she will obtain utility of 3 if *S* is chosen, but 4 if *L* is chosen. The threat implicit in the (*L, S*) strategy is therefore not believable. Even though *B*'s strategy (*L, S*) is one component of a Nash equilibrium, person *A* should be able to infer the noncredibility of the threat implicit in it.

By eliminating strategies that involve noncredible threats, *A* can conclude that *B* would never play (*L, S*) or (*S, L*). Proceeding in this way, the dormitory game is reduced to the payoff matrix originally shown in Table 15.1; as we discussed, in that case *L, L* (always playing *L*) is a dominant strategy for *B*. *A* can recognize this and will opt for strategy *L*. The Nash equilibrium *A:L*, *B:(L, L)* is therefore the only one of the three in Table 15.4 that does not involve noncredible threats. Such an equilibrium is termed a *subgame perfect*, which we define more formally as follows:

DEFINITION

Subgame perfect equilibrium. A Nash equilibrium in which the strategy choices of each player do not involve noncredible threats. That is, no strategy in such an equilibrium requires a player to carry out an action that would not be in its interest at the time the choice must be made.

To understand this terminology, we note that a "subgame" is simply that portion of a larger game that begins at one decision node and includes all future actions stemming from that node. For a Nash equilibrium to qualify for subgame perfection, it must also be a Nash equilibrium in each subgame of a larger game. A Nash equilibrium that did not meet this criteria would incorporate at least one strategy that contains the threat to make a choice that the player would not actually make (according to the Nash criterion) when the game reached that point. Hence the key aspect of such subgame perfection is that this equilibrium cannot incorporate a noncredible threat.

For example, in Figure 15.3 the Nash equilibrium *A:L*, *B:(L, L)* is subgame perfect because once the game reaches either of *B*'s decision nodes, the choice *B:L* is optimal. However, the Nash equilibrium *A:L*, *B:(L, S)* is not a subgame perfect equilibrium. *B* would not actually choose *S* in the subgame stemming from his or her decision node once *A* has opted for his or her second strategy, *S*. That is, *B:S* is not a Nash equilibrium for the subgame starting at this node. Hence, what appears to be an equilibrium for this extended game by the Nash criterion does not meet the criterion for subgame perfection.

Given this refined concept of equilibrium in multiplayer games, we can now proceed to explore how cooperation might be fostered in games that are played repeatedly.

Repeated games

Many economic situations can be modeled as games that are played repeatedly. Consumers' regular purchases from a particular retailer, firms' day-to-day competition for customers, or workers' attempts to outwit their supervisors all have elements of strategic interaction that occur repetitively. In this section we study some of the formal properties of such situations.

As in the illustrative dormitory game, an important aspect of a repeated game is the expanded strategy sets that become available to the players. Not only can players select specific strategies at each stage of the game, but they also can specify strategies that indicate how outcomes from prior stages of the game will be incorporated into future play. This opens the way for the consideration of credible threats and subgame perfection.

One of the most important distinctions among repeated games is the number of repetitions incorporated in a game. In games with a fixed, finite number of repetitions, there is relatively little room for the development of innovative strategies. On the other hand, games that are to be repeated infinitely many times, or, what amounts to the same thing, repeated games in which players cannot identify a clear ending point, offer a much wider array of options.

TABLE 15.5	A Prisoners' Dilemma Game to Be Played Repeatedly

		B's Strategies	
		L	R
A's Strategies	U	1, 1	3, 0
	D	0, 3	2, 2

A prisoners' dilemma finite game illustration

Consider, for example, the game shown in Table 15.5. Here A has two strategies (U, D) as does B (L, R). Clearly, if the game is to be played only once the Nash equilibrium $A:U$, $B:L$ might be expected as an outcome. Any other strategy choice is unstable, giving at least one of the players an incentive to alter his or her behavior. Notice, however, that the payoffs under the Nash equilibrium (1, 1), are Pareto inferior to those available from the unstable strategy choice $A:D$, $B:R$, which promises payoffs (2, 2).

Suppose now that this game is to be played repeatedly for a finite number of periods, T. Any expanded strategy in which player A asserts that he or she will play D in the game's final period (say, as a result of prior plays in the game) is not credible. When period T arrives, the logic of the Nash equilibrium will assert itself and A will ultimately choose strategy U or risk seeing his or her payoff during period T become 0. Similarly, any of player B's extended set of strategies that promises to play R in the final period will contain a noncredible threat.

Hence, any subgame perfect equilibrium outcome for this game can consist only of strategies that promise to play the Nash equilibrium strategies $A:U$, $B:L$ in the final round. But the logic that applies in period T also applies in period $T-1$. Any threat by A or B to play other than their Nash equilibrium strategies in period $T-1$ is not credible. Subgame perfection requires that strategies $A:U$, $B:L$ be played in period $T-1$ as well. Continuing this proof by "backward induction" shows that the only subgame perfect equilibrium in this finite game is to require the Nash equilibrium to occur in every period. The potential gains from $A:D$, $B:R$ will remain elusive throughout the game.

A game with infinite repetitions

This logic does not work, however, if the players in this game believe it will be repeated indefinitely. In this case, each player can announce a "trigger strategy" promising to play his or her optimal cooperative strategy ($A:D$ or $B:R$) so long as the other player does. When one player deviates from this pattern, however, the game reverts to the repeating single-period Nash equilibrium.

Whether the twin trigger strategy choice represents a subgame perfect equilibrium depends on whether the threat (promise) to play cooperatively is credible. To examine the question we have to look at the subgame proceeding onward from any specific period, say K. Supposing A announces that he or she will continue to play the trigger strategy by playing cooperatively in period K, what is B's optimal response? If he or she continues to play cooperatively, payoffs of 2 can be expected to persist indefinitely. If he or she decides to "cheat" (by playing R in period K), the payoff in period K will be 3 but then fall to 1 in all future periods because cooperation has broken down and the Nash equilibrium reasserts itself. Assuming *B* discounts the future with a discount factor δ, the present value[9] of continued cooperation is

$$2 + \delta 2 + \delta^2 2 + \cdots = \frac{2}{1 - \delta}, \qquad (15.12)$$

whereas the payoff from cheating is

$$3 + \delta 1 + \delta^2 1 + \cdots = 3 + \frac{\delta}{1 - \delta}. \qquad (15.13)$$

Continued cooperation will be credible, therefore, if

$$2/(1 - \delta) > 3 + \delta/(1 - \delta), \qquad (15.14)$$

which will occur for

$$\delta > \tfrac{1}{2}. \qquad (15.15)$$

In other words, *B* will find continued cooperative play desirable providing he or she does not discount the future gains from such cooperation too highly. Example 15.4 shows that even yak herders may cooperate in some circumstances.

 EXAMPLE 15.4

The Tragedy of the Common Revisited

The overgrazing of yaks on the village common encountered in Example 15.3 may not persist in an infinitely repeated game. To simplify, assume that each herder has only two strategies available—to bring either 4 or 5 yaks to the common. Payoffs for this game can be computed from Equation 15.5 and are illustrated in Table 15.6. Here the Nash equilibrium, (*A*:5, *B*:5) is inferior to the cooperative outcome (*A*:4, *B*:4), but this latter choice is unstable when the game is played for any finite number of repetitions.

With an infinite number of repetitions, however, both players would find it attractive to adopt cooperative trigger strategies, providing

$$544/(1 - \delta) > 595 + 500/(1 - \delta), \qquad (15.16)$$

which holds for

$$\delta > 551/595 = .93. \qquad (15.17)$$

Providing the herders are reasonably farsighted (that is, have a high enough δ), cooperation is a subgame-perfect equilibrium in this infinitely repeated game.

Query: How do you interpret the discount rates (δ) required here for cooperation? Do the conditions for cooperation seem likely to be fulfilled?

---

[9]The factor δ is similar to the term $1/(1 + r)$ used in the present value formula. See Chapter 17 Appendix for details. Often, computations are easier with discount factors than with interest rates.

TABLE 15.6	Payoffs in the Repeated Yak Grazing Game

		B's Strategies	
		4	*5*
A's Strategies	4	544, 544	476, 595
	5	595, 476	500, 500

Folk theorems

These numerical illustrations suggest that cooperation may represent a subgame-perfect equilibrium in games where both players can gain unambiguously from such cooperation. That is, potential losses, such as those that occur in the Prisoners' Dilemma, may not occur if games are played repetitively. The formal statement of these general results are sometimes called *Folk Theorems* because they were widely believed by economists to be true before they were actually proven. Although there are many versions of these theorems, perhaps the most widely referenced was developed by J. Friedman in 1971.[10] He showed that any infinitely repeated game in which there exist payoffs that are preferred by both players to the payoffs attainable under a Nash equilibrium will have a subgame-perfect equilibrium that achieves these payoffs providing the players are "patient enough." Such patient players (that is, those with suitably high δs) will always find it attractive to stick to trigger strategies that promise returns long into the future. The prospect of infinite repetition succeeds in counteracting the nonoptimal outcomes guaranteed by the Nash logic in games played only a few times. Cooperative-type outcomes therefore become more believable.

Pricing in static games

We begin our analysis of pricing by looking at the simplest duopoly. Suppose there are two firms, *A* and *B*, each producing the same good at a constant marginal cost, c. The strategies for each firm consist of choosing prices, P_A and P_B, subject only to the condition that P_A and P_B must exceed c (no firm would opt to play a game that promised a certain loss). Payoffs in this game will be determined by demand conditions. Because output is homogeneous and marginal costs are constant, the firm with the lower price will gain the entire market. For simplicity we assume that if $P_A = P_B$, the firms share the market equally.

Bertrand-Nash equilibrium

In this model the only Nash equilibrium is $P_A = P_B = c$. That is, the Nash equilibrium is the competitive solution even though there are only two firms. To see why, suppose firm *A* chooses a price greater than c. The profit-maximizing response for firm *B* is to choose a price slightly less than P_A and corner the entire market. But *B*'s price, if it exceeds c, still cannot be a Nash equilibrium, because it provides *A* with further incentives for price cutting. Only by choosing $P_A = P_B = c$ will the two firms in this market have achieved a Nash equilibrium. This pricing strategy is sometimes referred to as a "Bertrand equilibrium" after the French economist who discovered it.[11]

Capacity constraints: the Cournot equilibrium

The simplicity and definiteness of the Bertrand result depend crucially on the assumptions underlying the model. If firms do not have equal costs (see Problem 15.7) or if the goods

[10]J. Friedman, "A Non-Cooperative Equilibrium for Supergames," *Review of Economic Studies* (March 1971): 1–12.

[11]J. Bertrand, "Théorie Mathematique de la Richess Sociale," *Journal de Savants* (1883): 499–508.

produced by the two firms are not perfect substitutes, the competitive result no longer holds. Other duopoly models that depart from the Bertrand result treat price competition as only the final stage of a two-stage game in which the first stage involves various types of entry or investment considerations for the firms. In Example 14.1 we examined Cournot's example of a natural spring duopoly in which each spring owner chose how much water to supply. In the present context we might assume that each firm in a duopoly must choose a certain capacity output level. Marginal costs are constant up to that level and infinite thereafter. It seems clear that a two-stage game in which firms choose capacity first (and then price) is formally identical to the Cournot analysis. The quantities chosen in the Cournot equilibrium represent a Nash equilibrium because each firm correctly perceives what the other's output will be. Once these capacity decisions are made, the only price that can prevail is that for which total quantity demanded is equal to the combined capacities of the two firms.

To see why Bertrand-type price competition will result in such a solution, suppose capacities are given by $\bar{q}_A$ and $\bar{q}_B$ and that

$$\bar{P} = D^{-1}(\bar{q}_A + \bar{q}_B), \tag{15.18}$$

where D^{-1} is the inverse demand function for the good. A situation in which

$$P_A = P_B < \bar{P} \tag{15.19}$$

is not a Nash equilibrium. With this price, total quantity demanded exceeds $\bar{q}_A + \bar{q}_B$, so any one firm could increase its profits by raising price a bit and still selling $\bar{q}_A$. Similarly,

$$P_A = P_B > \bar{P} \tag{15.20}$$

is not a Nash equilibrium. Now total sales fall short of $\bar{q}_A + \bar{q}_B$. At least one firm (say, firm A) is selling less than its capacity. By cutting price slightly, firm A can increase its profits by taking all possible sales up to $\bar{q}_A$. Of course, B will respond to a loss of sales by dropping its price a bit too. Hence, the only Nash equilibrium that can prevail is the Cournot result:[12]

$$P_A = P_B = \bar{P}. \tag{15.21}$$

In general, this price will fall short of the monopoly price but will exceed marginal cost (as was the case in Example 14.1). Results of this two-stage game are therefore indistinguishable from those arising from the Cournot model of the previous chapter.

The contrast between the Bertrand and Cournot games is striking—the former predicts competitive outcomes in a duopoly situation, whereas the latter predicts monopoly-like inefficiencies. This suggests that actual behavior in duopoly markets may exhibit a wide variety of outcomes depending on the precise way in which competition occurs. The principal lesson of the two-stage Cournot game is that, even with Bertrand price competition, decisions made prior to this final stage of a game can have an important impact on market behavior. This lesson will be reflected again in some of the game theory models of entry we describe later in this chapter.

Repeated games and tacit collusion

Earlier in this chapter we showed that players in infinitely repeated games may be able to adopt subgame-perfect Nash equilibrium strategies that yield more favorable outcomes than simply repeating a less favorable Nash equilibrium indefinitely. From the perspective of duopoly theory, the issue is whether firms must endure the Bertrand equilibrium ($P_A = P_B = c$) in each period of a repeated game or might they achieve more profitable outcomes through tacit collusion.[13]

---

[12]For completeness, it should also be noted that no situation in which $P_A \neq P_B$ can be an equilibrium. The low-price firm has an incentive to raise price and the high-price firm wishes to cut price.

[13]Explicit collusion between firms is ruled out here because we are considering only noncooperative games.

With any finite number of replications, it seems clear that the Bertrand result remains unchanged. Any strategy in which firm A, say, chooses $P_A > c$ in period T (the final period) offers B the option of choosing $P_A > P_B > c$. Hence A's threat to charge P_A in period T is noncredible. Because a similar argument applies to any period prior to T, it is clear that the only subgame-perfect equilibrium in the finitely repeated price game is the perfectly competitive one in which both firms set price equal to marginal cost in every period.

If the pricing game is to be repeated over infinitely many periods, however, twin "trigger" strategies become feasible. Under these strategies each firm, say firm A, chooses $P_A = P_M$ (where P_M is the monopoly price), providing firm B chose $P_B = P_M$ in the prior period. If B has cheated in the previous period (by setting P_B slightly below $P_A = P_M$ and obtaining all monopoly profits for itself), firm A opts for competitive pricing ($P_A = c$) in all future periods.

To determine whether these twin trigger strategies constitute a subgame-perfect equilibrium, we must ask whether they constitute a Nash equilibrium in every period (every subgame). Suppose after the pricing game has been proceeding for several periods firm B is thinking about cheating. It knows that by choosing $P_B < P_A = P_M$ it can obtain (almost all) of the single period monopoly profits, π_M, for itself. On the other hand, if B continues to collude tacitly with A, B will earn its share of the profit stream

$$(\pi_M + \delta\pi_M + \delta^2\pi_M + \cdots + \delta^n\pi_M + \cdots)/2, \qquad (15.22)$$

where δ is the discount factor applied to future profits. Because the value of this infinite stream of profits is given by $(\pi_M/2)[1/(1-\delta)]$, cheating will be unprofitable providing

$$\pi_M < (\pi_M/2)\,[1/(1-\delta)]. \qquad (15.23)$$

Some algebraic manipulation shows that this inequality holds whenever

$$\delta > \frac{1}{2}. \qquad (15.24)$$

That is, providing the firms are not too impatient in the ways in which they discount future profits, the trigger strategies represent a subgame-perfect Nash equilibrium of tacit collusion. Example 15.5 provides a numerical example.[14]

 EXAMPLE 15.5

Tacit Collusion

Suppose only two firms produce steel bars suitable for jailhouse windows. Bars are produced at a constant average and marginal cost of $10, and the demand for bars is given by

$$Q = 5,000 - 100P. \qquad (15.25)$$

Under Bertrand competition, each firm will charge a price of $10 and a total of 4,000 bars will be sold. Because the monopoly price in this market is $30, each firm has a clear incentive to consider collusive strategies. With the monopoly price, total profits each period are $40,000 (each firm's share of total profits is $20,000) so any one firm will consider a next-period price cut only if

$$\$40,000 > \$20,000\,(1/1 - \delta). \qquad (15.26)$$

If we consider the pricing period in this model to be one year and a reasonable value of δ to be 0.8,[15] the present value of each firm's future profit share is $100,000 so there is

---

[14]Many other supracompetitive price levels are sustainable under the trigger strategy for suitable values of δ.

[15]Because $\delta = (1/1 + r)$ where r is the interest rate, $\delta = .8$ implies an r of 0.25 (that is, 25 percent per year).

clearly little incentive to cheat on price. Alternatively, each firm might be willing to incur costs (say, by monitoring the other's price or by developing a "reputation" for reliability) of up to $60,000 in present value to maintain the agreement.

Tacit collusion with more firms. Viability of a trigger price strategy may depend importantly on the number of firms. With eight producers of steel bars, the gain from cheating on a collusive agreement is still $40,000 (assuming the cheater can corner the entire market). The present value of a continuing agreement is only $25,000 (= $40,000 ÷ 8 · $\frac{1}{2}$) so the trigger price strategy is not viable for any one firm. Even with three or four firms or less responsive demand conditions, the gain from cheating may exceed whatever costs may be required to make tacit collusion work. Hence, the commonsense idea that tacit collusion is easier with fewer firms is supported by this model.

Query: How does the (common) discount factor, δ, determine the maximum number of firms that can successfully collude in this problem? What is the maximum if δ = .8? How about the case when δ = .9? Explain your results intuitively.

Generalizations and limitations

The contrast between the competitive results of the Bertrand model and the monopoly results of the (infinite time period) collusive model suggests that the viability of tacit collusion in game theory models is very sensitive to the particular assumptions made. Two assumptions in our model of tacit collusion are especially important: (1) that firm *B* can easily detect whether firm *A* has cheated; and (2) that firm *B* responds to cheating by adopting a harsh response that not only punishes firm *A*, but also condemns firm *B* to zero profits forever. In more general models of tacit collusion, these assumptions can be relaxed by, for example, allowing for the possibility that it may be difficult for firm *B* to recognize cheating by *A*. Some models examine alternative types of punishment *B* might inflict on *A*—for example, *B* could cut price in some other market in which *A* also sells. Such "linked" game models have come to play an important role in the study of real world duopolies. Other categories of models explore the consequences of introducing differentiated products into models of tacit collusion or of incorporating other reasons why the demand for a firm's product may not respond instantly to price changes by its rival. As might be imagined, results of such modeling efforts are quite varied.[16] In all such models, the notions of Nash and subgame-perfect equilibria continue to play an important role in identifying whether tacit collusion can arise from strategic choices that appear viable.

Entry, exit, and strategy

The treatment of entry and exit in competitive and noncompetitive markets in previous chapters left little room for strategic considerations. A potential entrant was viewed as being concerned only with the relationship between prevailing market price and its own (average or marginal) costs. We assumed that making that comparison involved no special problems. Similarly, we assumed firms will promptly leave a market they find to be unprofitable. Upon closer inspection, however, the entry and exit issue can become considerably more complex. The fundamental problem is that a firm wishing to enter or leave a market must make some conjecture about how its action will affect market price in

---

[16]See J. Tirole, *The Theory of Industrial Organization* (Cambridge, MA: MIT Press, 1988), Chap. 6.

subsequent periods. Making such conjectures obviously requires the firm to consider what its rivals will do. What appears to be a relatively straightforward decision comparing price and cost may therefore involve a number of possible strategic ploys, especially when a firm's information about its rivals is imperfect.

Sunk costs and commitment

Many game-theoretic models of the entry process stress the importance of a firm's *commitment* to a specific market. If the nature of production requires firms to make capital investments to operate in a market and if these cannot easily be shifted to other uses, a firm that makes such an investment has committed itself to being a market participant. Expenditures on such investments are called *sunk costs,* defined more formally as follows:

DEFINITION

Sunk costs. *Sunk costs* are one-time investments that must be made to enter a market. Such investments allow the firm to produce in the market but have no residual value if the firm exits the market.

Investments in sunk costs might include expenditures such as unique types of equipment (for example, a newsprint-making machine) or job-specific training for workers (developing the skills to use the newsprint machine). Sunk costs have many characteristics similar to what we have called *fixed costs,* in that both these costs are incurred even if no output is produced. Rather than being incurred periodically, as are many fixed costs (heating the factory), sunk costs are incurred only once in connection with the entry process.[17] When the firm makes such an investment, it has committed itself to the market, and that may have important consequences for its strategic behavior.

Sunk costs, first-mover advantages, and entry deterrence

Although at first glance it might seem that incurring sunk costs by making the commitment to serve a market puts a firm at a disadvantage, in most models that is not the case. Rather, one firm can often stake out a claim to a market by making a commitment to serve it and in the process limit the kinds of actions its rivals find profitable. Many game theory models, therefore, stress the advantage of moving first, as the following example illustrates.

Other situations in which a first mover might have an advantage include investing in research and development or pursuing product differentiation strategies. In international trade theory, for example, it is sometimes claimed that protection or subsidization of a domestic industry may allow it to enter an industry first, thereby gaining strategic advantage. Similarly, pursuit of "brand proliferation" strategies by existing toothpaste or breakfast cereal companies may make it more difficult for those who come later to develop a sufficiently different product to warrant a place in the market. The success of such first-mover strategies is by no means ensured, however. Careful modeling of the strategic situation is required to identify whether moving first does offer any real advantages.

---

[17]Mathematically, the notion of sunk costs can be integrated into the per-period total-cost function as

$$C_i(q_i) = S + F_t + cq_t,$$

where S is the per-period amortization of sunk costs (for example, the interest paid for funds used to finance capital investments), F is per-period fixed costs, c is marginal cost, and q_t is per-period output. If $q_t = 0$, $C_t = S + F_t$, but if the production period is long enough, some or all of F_t may also be avoidable. No portion of S is avoidable, however.

EXAMPLE 15.6

First-Mover Advantage in Cournot's Natural Springs

Let's return again to Cournot's natural spring duopoly we studied in Examples 14.1 and 14.2. Under the Stackelberg version of this model, each firm has two possible strategies—to be a leader (produce $q_i = 60$) or a follower (produce $q_i = 30$). Payoffs under these strategies were defined in Example 14.2 and are repeated in Table 15.7.

As we noted before, here the leader-leader strategy choice for each firm proves to be disastrous. A follower-follower choice is profitable to both firms, but this choice is unstable because it gives each firm an incentive to try to be a leader. This game is not like the Prisoners' Dilemma, however, because the leader-leader option is not a Nash equilibrium—if firm A knows that B will adopt a leader strategy, its best move is to be a follower.

It is this feature of the springs duopoly game that gives rise to a first-mover advantage. With simultaneous moves, either of the two leader-follower pairs represents a Nash equilibrium. But if one firm (say B) has the opportunity to move first, it can (by choosing $q_B = 60$) dictate which of the two Nash equilibria are chosen. B's ability to choose a large plant capacity first forces A into the follower role.

Query: Suppose the springs duopoly game were repeated many times (say, by the same rivals entering many different markets), what kinds of additional outcomes might be observed?

TABLE 15.7   **Payoff Matrix for the Stackelberg Model**

		B's Strategies	
		Leader ($q_B = 60$)	Follower ($q_B = 30$)
A's Strategies	Leader ($q_A = 60$)	A: 0 B: 0	A: $1,800 B: $ 900
	Follower ($q_A = 30$)	A: $ 900 B: $1,800	A: $1,600 B: $1,600

Entry deterrence

In some cases first-mover advantages may be large enough to deter all entry by rivals. Intuitively, it seems plausible that the first mover could make the strategic choice to have a very large capacity and thereby discourage all other firms from entering the market. The economic rationality of such a decision is not clear-cut, however. In the springs duopoly model, for example, the only sure way for one spring owner to deter all entry is to satisfy the total market demand at the firm's marginal and average cost—that is, one firm would have to offer $q = 120$ at a price of zero to have a fully successful entry deterrence strategy. Obviously, such a choice results in zero profits for the incumbent firm and would not represent profit maximization. Instead, it would be better for that firm to accept some entry by following the Stackelberg leadership strategy.

With economies of scale in production, the possibility for profitable entry deterrence is increased. If the firm that is to move first can adopt a large enough scale of operation, it may be able to limit the scale of the potential entrant. The potential entrant will therefore experience such high average costs that there would be no advantage to its entering the market. Example 15.7 illustrates this possibility in the case of Cournot's natural springs. Whether this example is of general validity depends, among other factors, on whether the market is contestable. If other firms with large scales of operations elsewhere can take advantage of prices in excess of marginal cost to practice hit-and-run entry, the entry deterrence strategy will not succeed.

 EXAMPLE 15.7

Entry Deterrence in Cournot's Natural Spring

If the natural spring owners in our previous examples experience economies of scale in production, entry deterrence becomes a profitable strategy for the first firm to choose capacity. The simplest way to incorporate economies of scale into the Cournot model is to assume each spring owner must pay a fixed cost of operations. If that fixed cost is given by \$784 (a carefully chosen number!), it is clear that the Nash equilibrium leader-follower strategies remain profitable for both firms (see Table 15.7). When firm A moves first and adopts the leader's role, however, B's profits are rather small ($900 - 784 = 116$), and this suggests that firm A could push B completely out of the market simply by being a bit more aggressive.

Since B's reaction function (Equation 14.18) is unaffected by considerations of fixed costs, firm A knows that

$$q_B = \frac{120 - q_A}{2} \qquad (15.27)$$

and that market price is given by

$$P = 120 - q_A - q_B. \qquad (15.28)$$

Hence A knows that B's profits are

$$\pi_B = Pq_B - 784, \qquad (15.29)$$

which, when B is a follower (that is, when B moves second), depends only on q_A. Substituting Equation 15.27 into 15.29 yields

$$\pi_B = \left(\frac{120 - q_A}{2}\right)^2 - 784. \qquad (15.30)$$

Consequently, firm A can ensure nonpositive profits for firm B by choosing

$$q_A \geq 64. \qquad (15.31)$$

With $q_A = 64$, firm A becomes the only supplier of natural spring water. Because market price is \$56 ($= 120 - 64$) in this case, firm A's profits are

$$\pi_A = (56 \cdot 64) - 784 = 2,800, \qquad (15.32)$$

a significant improvement over the leader-follower outcome. The ability to move first coupled with the fixed costs assumed here makes entry deterrence a feasible strategy in this case.

Query: Why is the time pattern of play in this game crucial to the entry deterrence result? How does the result here contrast with our analysis of a contestable monopoly in Example 14.5?

Entry and incomplete information

So far our discussion of strategic considerations in entry decisions has focused on issues of sunk costs and output commitments. Prices were assumed to be determined through auction or Bertrand processes only after such commitments were made. A somewhat different approach to the entry deterrence question concerns the possibility of an incumbent monopoly accomplishing this goal through its pricing policy alone. That is, are there situations where a monopoly might purposely choose a low ("limit") price policy with the goal of deterring entry into its market?

In most simple cases, the limit pricing strategy does not seem to yield maximum profits nor to be sustainable over time. If an incumbent monopoly opts for a price of $P_L < P_M$ (where P_M is the profit-maximizing price), it is obviously hurting its current-period profits. But this limit price will deter entry in the future only if P_L falls below the average cost of any potential entrant. If the monopoly and its potential entrant have the same costs (and if capacity choices do not play the role they did in the previous example), the only limit price sustainable in the presence of potential entry is $P_L = AC$, adoption of which would obviously defeat the purpose of being a monopoly because profits would be zero. Hence, the basic monopoly model offers little room for entry deterrence through pricing behavior—either there are barriers to entry that allow the monopoly to sustain P_M, or there are no such barriers, in which case competitive pricing prevails.

Limit pricing and incomplete information

Believable models of limit pricing must therefore depart from traditional assumptions. The most important set of such models are those involving incomplete information. If an incumbent monopoly knows more about a particular market situation than does a potential entrant, it may be able to take advantage of its superior knowledge to deter entry. As an example, consider the game tree illustrated in Figure 15.4. Here firm A, the incumbent monopolist, may have either "high" or "low" production costs as a result of past decisions. Firm A does not actually choose its costs currently but, because these costs are not known to B, we allow for the two possibilities. Clearly, the profitability of B's entry into

---

FIGURE 15.4   **An Entry Game**

Firm A has either a "high" or a "low" cost structure that cannot be observed by B. If B assigns a subjective probability (ρ) to the possibility that A is high cost, it will enter providing $\rho > \frac{1}{4}$. Firm A may try to influence B's probability estimate.

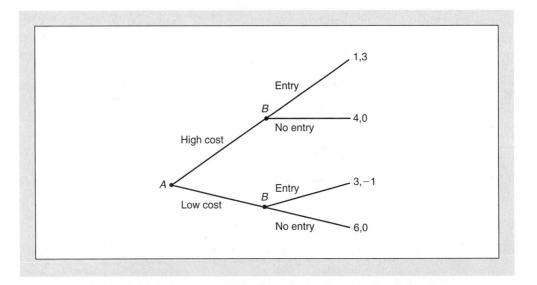

the market depends on A's costs—with high costs B's entry is profitable ($\pi_B = 3$), whereas if A has low costs, entry is unprofitable ($\pi_B = -1$). What is B to do? One possibility would be for B to use whatever information it does have to develop a subjective probability estimate of A's true cost structure. That is, B must assign probability estimates to the states of nature "low cost" and "high cost." If B assumes there is a probability ρ that A has high cost and $(1 - \rho)$ that it has low cost, entry will yield positive expected profits provided

$$E(\pi_B) = \rho(3) + (1 - \rho)(-1) > 0, \qquad (15.33)$$

which holds for

$$\rho > \frac{1}{4}. \qquad (15.34)$$

The particularly intriguing aspects of this game concern whether A can influence B's probability assessment. Clearly, regardless of its true costs, firm A is better off if B adopts the no-entry strategy, and one way to ensure that is for A to make B believe that $\rho < \frac{1}{4}$. As an extreme case, if A can convince B that it is a low-cost producer with certainty ($\rho = 0$), B will clearly be deterred from entry even if the true cost situation is otherwise. For example, if A chooses a low-price policy when it serves the market as a monopoly, this may signal to B that A's costs are low and thereby deter entry. Such strategy might be profitable for A even though it would require it to sacrifice some profits if its costs are actually high. This provides a possible rationale for low limit pricing as an entry deterrence strategy.

Unfortunately, as we will see in Chapter 19, examination of the possibilities for equilibrium signals in situations of asymmetric information raises many complexities. Because firm B knows A may create false signals, and firm A knows B will be wary of its signals, a number of solutions to this game seem possible. The viability of limit pricing as a strategy for achieving entry deterrence depends crucially on the types of informational assumptions made.[18]

Predatory pricing

Tools used to study limit pricing can also shed light on the possibility for "predatory" pricing. Ever since the formation of the Standard Oil monopoly in the late nineteenth century, part of the mythology of American business has been that John D. Rockefeller was able to drive his competitors out of business by charging ruinously low (predatory) prices. Although both the economic logic and the empirical facts behind this version of the Standard Oil story have generally been discounted[19] the possibility of encouraging exit through predation continues to provide interesting opportunities for theoretical modeling.

The structure of many models of predatory behavior is similar to that used in limit pricing models—that is, the models stress incomplete information. An incumbent firm wishes to encourage its rival to exit the market, so it takes actions intended to affect the rival's view of the future profitability of market participation. The incumbent may, for example, adopt a low-price policy in an attempt to signal to its rival that its costs are low—even if they are not. Or the incumbent may adopt extensive advertising or product differentiation activities with the intention of convincing its rival that it has economies of scale in undertaking such activities. Once the rival is convinced that the incumbent firm possesses such advantages, it may recalculate the expected profitability of its production decisions and decide to exit the market. Of course, as in the limit pricing models, such successful predatory strategies are not a forgone conclusion. Their viability depends crucially on the nature of the informational asymmetries in the market.

---

[18]For an examination of some of these issues, see P. Milgrom and J. Roberts, "Limit Pricing and Entry Under Conditions of Incomplete Information: An Equilibrium Analysis," *Econometrica* (March 1982): 443–60.

[19]J. S. McGee and others have pointed out that predatory pricing was a far less profitable strategy for Rockefeller than simply buying up his rivals at market price (which seems to have been what occurred). See J. S. McGee, "Predatory Pricing: The Standard Oil (NJ) Case," *Journal of Law and Economics* (1958): 137–69; and "Predatory Pricing Revisited," *Journal of Law and Economics* (October 1980): 289–330. Recent literature has examined whether predatory pricing can affect a rival firm's market value.

Games of incomplete information

The illustrations in the previous section suggest the desirability of extending game theory models to include cases of incomplete information. In this section we provide a brief survey of some of the ways in which this has been done.

Player types and beliefs

To generalize game theoretic ideas to reflect incomplete information, we need to introduce some new terminology. When the nature of a game's incomplete information concerns asymmetries in the information the players have about each other, this is accomplished through the introduction of player characteristics or "types."[20] Each player in a game can be one of a number of possible such types (denoted by t_A and t_B for our two players). Player types may vary along several dimensions, but for our discussion we will confine our attention to differing potential payoff (profit) functions. Usually it will be assumed each player knows his or her own payoffs, but does not know the opponent's payoffs with certainty. Hence each player must make some conjectures about what the opponent's payoffs are in order to evaluate his or her own strategic choices.

Each player's conjectures about the opponent's player types are represented by belief functions $f_A(t_B)$. These beliefs consist of player A's (say) probability estimates of the likelihood that the opponent B is of various types. As in the game tree in Figure 15.4, one player's beliefs are used to express the likelihood that the other player is on particular branches of the tree. Games of incomplete information are sometimes termed "Bayesian games" because of their use of subjective probability beliefs that were first studied by the statistician Thomas Bayes in the eighteenth century.

Given these new tools, we can generalize the notation for a game (see Equation 15.1) as

$$G[S_A, S_B, t_A, t_B, f_A, f_B, \ U_A(a, b, t_A, t_B), U_B(a, b, t_A, t_B)], \qquad (15.35)$$

where the payoffs to A and B depend not only on the strategies chosen ($a \subset S_A$, $b \subset S_B$) but also on the player types. Now we need to generalize the notion of Nash equilibrium to take this more complex game structure into account.

Bayesian-Nash equilibrium

For static (one-period) games, it is fairly simple to generalize the Nash equilibrium concept to reflect incomplete information. Because each player's payoffs depend on the (unknown) player type of the opponent, we must introduce an expected utility criteria. A strategy pair— a^*, b^*—will be a Bayesian-Nash equilibrium providing that a^* maximizes A's expected utility when B plays b^*, and vice versa. Specifically, Equations 15.2 should be modified as

$$E[U_A(a^*, b^*, t_A, t_B)] = \sum_{t_B} f_A(t_B) U(a^*, b^*, t_A, t_B)$$

$$\geq E[U_A(a', b^*, t_A, t_B)] \text{ for all } a' \subset S_A$$

and $\qquad\qquad\qquad\qquad\qquad\qquad\qquad\qquad\qquad\qquad\qquad\qquad\qquad\qquad$ (15.36)

$$E[U_B(a^*, b^*, t_A, t_B)] = \sum_{t_A} f_B(t_A) U(a^*, b^*, t_A, t_B)$$

$$\geq E[U_B(a^*, b', t_A, t_B)] \textbf{ for all } b' \subset S_B.$$

Notice here that the payoffs to each player depend on both players' types, but that A's expectations concern only his or her beliefs about B (since player A knows his or her own type). Similarly, player B knows his or her own type but must consider subjective expectations about A. Although the notation in Equation 15.36 is formidable, most applications are straightforward, involving only a few player types, as Example 15.8 illustrates.

---

[20]Information about a game may also be subject to uncertainty if a player does not know its history (that is, what moves the opponent has made in the past). Such games are termed games of "imperfect" information. Such games add new insights to many traditional game theory problems including plausible equilibrium solutions to finite, repeated prisoner dilemma games.

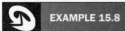
EXAMPLE 15.8

A Bayesian-Cournot Equilibrium

Suppose duopolists compete for a market in which demand is given by

$$P = 100 - q_A - q_B. \tag{15.37}$$

Suppose first that $MC_A = MC_B = 10$. Then it is a simple matter to show that the Nash (Cournot) equilibrium is $q_A = q_B = 30$ and payoffs are given by $\pi_A = \pi_B = 900$.

Imperfect information. To give this game a Bayesian flavor, assume now that $MC_A = 10$, but MC_B may be either high ($MC_B = 16$) or low ($MC_B = 4$). Suppose also that A assigns equal probabilities to these two "types" for B so that the expected marginal cost for B remains 10.

Let's start to analyze this problem by considering firm B. Because B knows there is only a single A type, it does not have to consider expectations. It chooses q_B to maximize

$$\pi_B = (P - MC_B)(q_B) = (100 - MC_B - q_A - q_B)(q_B), \tag{15.38}$$

and the first-order condition for a maximum is

$$q_B^* = (100 - MC_B - q_A)/2. \tag{15.39}$$

Notice that q_B^* depends on firm B's marginal cost, which only it knows with certainty. With high marginal costs its optimal choice is

$$q_{BH}^* = (84 - q_A)/2, \tag{15.40}$$

and with low marginal costs its optimal choice is

$$q_{BL}^* = (96 - q_A)/2. \tag{15.41}$$

Firm A must take into account that B could be either high or low cost. Its expected profits are given by

$$\pi_A = .5(100 - MC_A - q_A - q_{BH})(q_A) + .5(100 - MC_A - q_A - q_{BL})(q_A)$$
$$= (90 - q_A - .5q_{BH} - .5q_{BL})q_A. \tag{15.42}$$

The first-order condition for a profit maximum is therefore

$$q_A^* = (90 - .5q_{BH} - .5q_{BL})/2, \tag{15.43}$$

and Equations 15.40, 15.41, and 15.43 must be solved simultaneously for q_{BH}^*, q_{BL}^*, and q_A^*. A bit of algebraic manipulation yields the Bayesian-Nash equilibrium:

$$q_A^* = 30 \tag{15.44}$$
$$q_{BH}^* = 27$$
$$q_{BL}^* = 33.$$

These strategic choices constitute an *ex ante* equilibrium. After the game is played, only one market equilibrium will prevail, depending on whether firm B actually has high or low costs. But the concept of Bayesian-Nash equilibrium clarifies how the uncertainties faced by A enter into that firm's strategic choices.

Query: In this case q_A^* in the Bayesian-Nash equilibrium is the same value as in the Cournot equilibrium, with firm B's marginal cost equal to its expected value, 10. Why does this occur? Would you expect that, in general, expected values could be used in calculating Bayesian-Nash equilibria?

Existence of equilibrium

Proof of the existence of Bayesian-Nash equilibria closely parallels our earlier discussion. The previous proof is generalized by treating each player type in a static Bayesian game as a distinct player. With such an enlarged cast of players, the prior proof suggests the existence of a pure strategy Nash equilibrium in games with continuous strategies and the existence of a mixed strategy equilibrium for games where each player type has a finite set of discrete strategies. The strategy choices that comprise a Nash equilibrium in this expanded game of certainty will also constitute a Bayesian-Nash equilibrium given the beliefs of the players about the likelihood of various player types.

Mechanism design and auctions

One important way in which the concept of Bayesian-Nash equilibrium is used is in the study of the performance of various economic mechanisms; most notably, auctions. By examining equilibrium solutions under various possible auction rules, it has been possible for game theorists to devise procedures that yield desirable results in terms of obtaining high prices for goods being sold and ensuring that the goods end up in the hands of those who value them most highly. Features of auctions such as multiple bidding rounds, reservation prices, or second-price designs (where the auction winner pays the second highest bid price) can be quite complicated. Game theoretic tools help illuminate the underlying operations of such features and determine whether they encourage auction participants to reveal this true value for the good being sold. Although a thorough study of auction theory is beyond the scope of this book,[21] Example 15.9 illustrates some of the features of such models. This analysis is pursued a bit further in Problem 15.12, which looks at second-price auctions.

 EXAMPLE 15.9

An Oil Tract Auction

Suppose two firms are bidding for a tract of land that may have oil underground. Each firm has done some preliminary geological work and has decided on a potential value for the tract (V_A and V_B, respectively). The seller of the tract would obviously like to obtain the largest price possible for the land, which, in this case, would be the larger of V_A or V_B. Will a simple sealed bid auction accomplish this goal?

To develop this problem as a Bayesian game, we first need to model each firm's beliefs about the other's valuations. For simplicity, assume $0 \le V_i \le 1$ and that each firm assumes all possible values for the other firm's valuation are equally likely. In statistical terms, we assume firm A believes that V_B is uniformly distributed over the interval $[0, 1]$, and vice versa. Each firm must now decide on its bid (b_A and b_B). The gain from the auction for firm A, say, is

$$V_A - b_A \text{ if } b_A > b_B \qquad (15.45)$$

and[22]

$$0 \text{ if } b_B > b_A.$$

To derive explicit bidding strategies for each player, assume each opts to bid a fraction, $k_i\,(k_i \le 1)$ of the valuation. That is,

$$b_i = k_i V_i \qquad i = A, B. \qquad (15.46)$$

(*continued*)

---

[21]For a survey of the recent literature on auctions, see V. Krishna, *Auction Theory* (San Diego, Academic Press, 2002).
[22]To simplify the analysis we assume that the probability $b_A = b_B$ is zero.

EXAMPLE 15.9 CONTINUED

Firm *A*'s expected gain from the sale is then

$$\pi_A = (V_A - b_A) \cdot \mathbf{Prob}(b_A > b_B) \qquad (15.47)$$

and

$$\mathbf{prob}(b_A > b_B) = \mathbf{prob}(b_A > k_B V_B) = \mathbf{prob}(b_A/k_B > V_B) = b_A/k_B, \qquad (15.48)$$

where the final equality follows because of *A*'s beliefs that V_B has a uniform distribution. Hence

$$\pi_A = (V_A - b_A) \cdot b_A/k_B, \qquad (15.49)$$

which is maximized when

$$b_A = V_A/2. \qquad (15.50)$$

A similar chain of logic would conclude

$$b_B = V_B/2, \qquad (15.51)$$

so the firm with the highest valuation will win the oil tract and pay a price that is only half of that geological valuation. The auction we have described so far does not therefore result in a truthful revelation of the bidders' valuations.

Effect of additional bidders. The presence of additional bidders improves the situation, however. With $n - 1$ other bidders, firm *A*'s expected gains become

$$\pi_A = (V_A - b_A) \cdot \mathbf{Prob}(b_A > b_i, i = 1 \ldots n - 1) \qquad (15.52)$$

and (again assuming away the problem of equal bids)

$$\pi_A = 0 \text{ if } b_i > b_A \text{ for any } i \qquad (15.53)$$

If firm *A* continues to believe that each of its rival's valuations are uniformly distributed over the $[0, 1]$ interval,

$$\begin{aligned} \mathbf{Prob}(b_A > b_i, i &= 1 \ldots n) \\ &= \mathbf{Prob}(b_A > k_i V_i \qquad i = 1 \ldots n) \\ &= \prod_{i=1}^{n-1} (b_A/k_i) = b_A^{n-1}/k^{n-1}, \end{aligned} \qquad (15.54)$$

where, by symmetry, we let $k = k_i$ for all *i*. Hence

$$\pi_A = (V_A - b_A)(b_A^{n-1}/k^{n-1}), \qquad (15.55)$$

and the first-order condition for a maximum is

$$b_A = \left(\frac{n-1}{n}\right) V_A. \qquad (15.56)$$

So, as the number of bidders expands, there are increasing incentives for a truthful revelation of each firm's valuation. In the language of auction theory, sealed bid auctions are "incentive compatible," providing there are enough bidders. Notice however that this mechanism is not truth revealing because $b_A < V_A$. See Problem 15.12 and the Extensions to Chapter 21 for more on truth-revealing mechanisms.

Query: Could a seller mitigate the low valuations that arise when there are few bidders by specifying a reservation price, *r*, such that no sale is made if the maximal bid falls below *r*?

Dynamic games with incomplete information

Multiperiod and repeated games may also be characterized by incomplete information. As suggested by our informal discussion of the game depicted in Figure 15.4, the interesting additional feature of these games is that a player may be able to make inferences about the type of his or her opponent from the strategic choices the opponent makes. Hence it is necessary for players to update beliefs by incorporating the new information provided by each round of play in the game. Of course, each player is aware that his or her opponent will be doing such updating, so that too must be taken into account in deciding on a strategy. By using the method of backward induction, it is often possible to derive equilibrium strategies in such games that mirror the notion of subgame perfection we introduced in the context of repeated games with perfect information. Examination of these equilibrium concepts is an important area of current research in game theory.[23]

SUMMARY

In this chapter we have illustrated some game theory concepts and showed how they can be used to examine pricing in duopoly markets. Some of the principal results are:

- All games are characterized by a structure that involves players, strategies, and payoffs. The Nash equilibrium concept provides an intuitively attractive solution concept for many games under which each player's strategy choice is optimal given the other player's optimal choice. Not all games have unique Nash equilibria.

- Two-player noncooperative games with continuous strategy sets will usually possess one or more Nash equilibria. Games with finite strategy sets usually also have Nash equilibria in mixed strategies.

- In repeated games Nash equilibria that involve only credible threats are called *subgame-perfect equilibria*.

- Outcomes that are Pareto superior to Nash equilibria can sometimes be attainable in infinitely repeated games through the use of cooperative trigger strategies.

- In a simple single-period game, the Nash-Bertrand equilibrium implies competitive pricing with price equal to marginal cost. The Cournot equilibrium (with $p > mc$) can be interpreted as a two-stage game in which firms first select a capacity constraint.

- Tacit collusion is a possible subgame-perfect equilibrium in an infinitely repeated game. The likelihood of such equilibrium collusion diminishes with larger numbers of firms, however, because the incentive to chisel on price increases.

- Some games offer first-mover advantages. In cases involving increasing returns to scale, such advantages may result in the deterrence of all entry.

- Games of incomplete information arise when players do not know their opponents' payoff functions and must make some conjectures about them. In such Bayesian games, equilibrium concepts involve straightforward generalizations of the Nash and subgame-perfect notions encountered in games of complete information.

---

[23]For a summary, see D. Fudenberg and J. Tirole, *Game Theory* (Cambridge, MA: MIT Press, 1991), Chaps. 8–10.

PROBLEMS

15.1

Fudenberg and Tirole (1992) develop a game of stag-hunting based on an observation originally made by Rousseau. The two players in the game may either cooperate in catching a stag or each may set out on his own to catch a hare. The payoff matrix for this game is given by

		Player B	
		Stag	Hare
Player A	Stag	2, 2	0, 1
	Hare	1, 0	1, 1

a. Describe the Nash equilibria in this game.

b. Suppose B believes that A will use a mixed strategy in choosing how to hunt. How will B's optimal strategy choice depend on the probability that A will play stag?

c. Suppose this game is expanded to n players (the game Rousseau had in mind) and that all n must cooperate in order for a stag to be caught. Assuming that the payoffs for one specific player, say B, remain the same and that all the other $n - 1$ players will opt for mixed strategies, how will B's optimal strategy depend on the probabilities with which each of the other players plays stag? Explain why cooperation seems less likely in this larger game.

15.2

Players A and B have found \$100 on the sidewalk and are arguing about how it should be split. A passerby suggests the following game: "Each of you state the number of dollars that you wish (d_A, d_B). If $d_A + d_B \leq 100$ you can keep the figure you name and I'll take the remainder. If $d_A + d_B > 100$, I'll keep the \$100." Is there a unique Nash equilibrium in this game of continuous strategies?

15.3

The mixed-strategy Nash equilibrium for the Battle of the Sexes game described in Example 15.1 may depend on the numerical values of the payoffs. To generalize this solution, assume that the payoff matrix for the game is given by

		B's Strategies	
		Mountain	Seaside
A's Strategies	Mountain	$K, 1$	0, 0
	Seaside	0, 0	$1, K$

where $K \geq 1$. Show how the Nash equilibrium in mixed strategies for this game depends on the value of K.

15.4

In *A Treatise on the Family* (Cambridge: Harvard University Press, 1981), G. Becker proposes his famous Rotten Kid theorem as a game between a (potentially rotten) child, A, and his or her parent, B. A moves first and chooses an action, r, that affects his or her own income $Y_A(r)$ $(Y'_A > 0)$ and the income of the parent $Y_B(r)$ $(Y'_B < 0)$. In the second stage of the game, the parent leaves a monetary bequest of L to the child. The child cares only for his or her own utility, $U_A(Y_A + L)$, but the parent maximizes $U_B(Y_B - L) + \lambda U_A$, where $\lambda > 0$ reflects the parent's altruism toward the child. Prove that the child will opt for that value of r that maximizes $Y_A + Y_B$ even though he or she has no altruistic intentions. (*Hint:* You must first find the parent's optimal bequest, then solve for the child's optimal strategy, given this subsequent parental behavior.)

15.5

The game of "chicken" is played by two macho teens who speed toward each other on a single-lane road. The first to veer off is branded the chicken, whereas the one who doesn't turn gains peer group esteem. Of course, if neither veers, both die in the resulting crash. Payoffs to the chicken game are provided in the following table.

		B's Strategies	
		Chicken	Not Chicken
A's Strategies	Chicken	2, 2	1, 3
	Not Chicken	3, 1	0, 0

a. Does this game have a Nash equilibrium?

b. Is a threat by either not to chicken-out a credible one?

c. Would the ability of one player to firmly commit to a not-chicken strategy (by, for example, throwing away the steering wheel) be desirable for that player?

d. If you have seen the movie *A Beautiful Mind,* how might you interpret the bar scene as a game of chicken? Can you figure out what Nash's insight was?

15.6

Consider the following sealed-bid auction for a rare baseball card. Player A values the card being auctioned at $600, player B values the card at $500, and these valuations are known to each player who will submit a sealed bid for the card. Whoever bids the most will win the card. If equal bids are submitted, the auctioneer will flip a coin to decide the winner. Each player must now decide how much to bid.

a. How would you categorize the strategies in this game? Do some strategies dominate others?

b. Does this game have a Nash equilibrium? Is it unique?

c. How would this game change if each player did not know the other's valuation for the card?

15.7

Suppose firms A and B operate under conditions of constant average and marginal cost, but that $MC_A = 10$, $MC_B = 8$. The demand for the firms' output is given by

$$Q_D = 500 - 20P.$$

a. If the firms practice Bertrand competition, what will be the market price under a Nash equilibrium?

b. What will the profits be for each firm?

c. Will this equilibrium be Pareto efficient?

15.8

Two firms (*A* and *B*) are considering bringing out competing brands of a healthy cigarette. Payoffs to the companies are as shown in the table (*A*'s profits are given first):

		Firm *B*	
		Produce	Don't Produce
Firm *A*	Produce	3, 3	5, 4
	Don't Produce	4, 5	2, 2

a. Does this game have a Nash equilibrium?

b. Does this game present any first-mover advantages for either firm *A* or firm *B*?

c. Would firm *B* find it in its interest to bribe firm *A* enough to stay out of the market?

15.9

The world's entire supply of kryptonite is controlled by 20 people, with each having 10,000 grams of this potent mineral. The world demand for kryptonite is given by

$$Q = 10,000 - 1,000P,$$

where *P* is the price per gram.

a. If all owners could conspire to rig the price of kryptonite, what price would they set, and how much of their supply would they sell?

b. Why is the price computed in part (a) an unstable equilibrium?

c. Does a price for kryptonite exist that would be a stable equilibrium in the sense that no firm could gain by altering its output from that required to maintain this market price?

15.10

Suppose the demand for steel bars in Example 15.5 fluctuates with the business cycle. During expansions demand is

$$Q = 7,000 - 100P,$$

and during recessions demand is

$$Q = 3,000 - 100P.$$

Assume also that expansions and recessions are equally likely and that firms know what the economic conditions are before setting their price.

a. What is the lowest value of δ that will sustain a trigger price strategy that maintains the appropriate monopoly price during both recessions and expansions?

b. If δ falls slightly below the value calculated in part (a), how should the trigger price strategies be adjusted to retain profitable tacit collusion?

15.11

Suppose that in the Bayesian-Cournot model described in Example 15.8 the firms have identical marginal costs (10) but information about demand is asymmetric. Specifically, assume firm *A* knows the demand function (Equation 15.37) but firm *B* believes that demand may be either

$$P = 120 - q_A - q_B$$

or

$$P = 80 - q_A - q_B,$$

each with probability of 0.5. Assuming that the firms must announce their quantities simultaneously, what is the Bayesian-Nash equilibrium for this situation?

15.12

In Example 15.9 we showed that the Nash equilibrium in this first-price, sealed bid auction was for each participant to adopt a bidding strategy of $b(v) = [(n - 1)/n]v$. The total revenue a seller might expect to receive from such an auction will obviously be $[(n - 1)/n]v^*$—where v^* is the expected value of the highest valuation among the n auction participants.

a. Show that if valuations are uniformly distributed over the interval $[0, 1]$, the expected value for v^* is $n/(n + 1)$. Hence expected revenue from the auction is $(n - 1)/(n + 1)$.

   Hint: The expected value of the highest bid is given by

   $$E(v^*) = \int_0^1 vf(v)dv,$$

   where $f(v)$ is the probability density function of the probability that any particular v is the maximum among n bidders. Here $f(v) = nv^{n-1}$.

b. In a famous 1961 article ("Counterspeculation, Auctions, and Competitive Sealed Tenders," *Journal of Finance,* March 1961, pp. 8–37) William Vickrey examined second-price sealed bid auctions. In these auctions the highest bidder wins but pays the price bid by the second highest bidder. Show that the optimal bidding strategy for any participant in such an auction is to bid his or her true valuation: $b(v) = v$.

c. Show that the expected revenue provided by the second-price auction format is identical to that provided by the first-price auction studied in part (a) (this is Vickrey's "revenue equivalence theorem").

   Hint: The probability that any given valuation will be the second highest among n bidders is given by $g(v) = (n - 1)(1 - v)nv^{n-2}$. That is, the probability is given by the probability that any of $(n - 1)$ bidders will have a higher valuation $[(n - 1)(1 - v)]$ times the probability that any of n bidders will have a valuation exceeding that of $n - 2$ other bidders $[nv^{n-2}]$.

SUGGESTIONS FOR FURTHER READING

Fudenberg, D., and J. Tirole. *Game Theory.* Cambridge, MA: MIT Press, 1991.
   The later chapters provide extensive illustrations of dynamic games of imperfect information.

Gibbons, R. *Game Theory for Applied Economists.* Princeton, NJ: Princeton University Press, 1992.
   Illustrates a number of game-theoretic models relevant to topics such as bargaining, bank runs, auctions, and monetary policy. Chapter 4 on signaling equilibria is especially helpful.

Krishna, V. *Auction Theory.* San Diego: Academic Press, 2002.
   A fairly complete and up-to-date survey of the theory of auctions. Mathematics can be hard-going in spots.

Tirole, J. *The Theory of Industrial Organization.* Cambridge, MA: MIT Press, 1988.
   Game theory is used throughout Part II of this classic text. The final chapter of the book provides a convenient "user's manual" for the subject.

EXTENSIONS

Strategic Substitutes and Complements

One way to conceptualize the relationships between the choices of firms in an imperfectly competitive market is to introduce the ideas of strategic substitutes and complements. By drawing analogies to similar definitions from consumer and producer theory, game theorists define firms' activities to be *strategic substitutes* if an increase in the level of an activity (say, output, price, or spending on product differentiation) by one firm is met by a decrease in that activity by its rival. On the other hand, activities are *strategic complements* if an increase in an activity by one firm is met by an increase in that activity by its rival.

To make these ideas precise, suppose that profits for firm A (π^A) depend on the level of an activity it uses itself (S_A) and on use of a similar activity by its rival. The firm's goal, therefore, is to maximize $\pi^A(S_A, S_B)$.

E15.1 Optimality conditions and reaction functions

The first-order condition for A's choice of its own strategic activity is

$$\pi_1^A(S_A, S_B) = 0, \tag{i}$$

where the subscripts for π represent partial derivatives with respect to its various arguments. For a maximum we also require that

$$\pi_{11}^A(S_A, S_B) \leq 0. \tag{ii}$$

Obviously, the optimal choice of S_A specified by Equation i will differ for different values of S_B. We can record this relationship by A's *reaction function* (R_A)

$$S_A = R_A(S_B). \tag{iii}$$

The strategic relationship between S_A and S_B is implied by this reaction function. If $R_A' > 0$, S_A and S_B are strategic complements. If $R_A' < 0$, S_A and S_B are strategic substitutes.

E15.2 Inferences from the profit function

It is usually more convenient to use the profit function directly to examine strategic relationships. Substituting Equation iii into the first-order condition (i) gives

$$\pi_1^A = \pi_1^A [R_A(S_B), S_B] = 0. \tag{iv}$$

Partial differentiation with respect to S_B yields

$$\pi_{11}^A R_A' + \pi_{12}^A = 0. \tag{v}$$

Therefore

$$R_A' = \frac{-\pi_{12}^A}{\pi_{11}^A},$$

so, in view of the second-order condition (ii), $\pi_{12}^A > 0$ implies $R_A' > 0$ and $\pi_{12}^A < 0$ implies $R_A' < 0$. Strategic relationships can therefore be inferred directly from the derivatives of the profit function.

E15.3 The Cournot model

In the Cournot model, profits are given as a function of the two firms' quantities as

$$\begin{aligned}\pi^A &= \pi^A(q_A, q_B) \\ &= q_A P(q_A + q_B) - C(q_A).\end{aligned} \tag{vi}$$

In this case

$$\pi_1^A = q_A P' + P - C' = 0 \tag{vii}$$

and

$$\pi_{12}^A = q_A P'' + P'. \tag{viii}$$

Because $P' < 0$, the sign of π_{12}^A will depend on the concavity of the demand curve (P''). With a linear demand curve, $P'' = 0$ so π_{12}^A is clearly negative. Quantities are strategic substitutes in the Cournot model with linear demand. This will generally be true unless the demand curve is relatively convex ($P'' > 0$). For a more detailed discussion, see Bulow, Geanakoplous, and Klemperer (1985).

Voluntary export restraints

Several authors have used the strategic substitute concept in the Cournot model to examine models of trade restrictions. In these models domestic and foreign producers are treated as two "firms" vying for the domestic market. Under (Bertrand) price competition, a competitive model might be used to explain pricing in such a market, as we did in Chapter 11. But the presence of trade barriers may alter the nature of such competition. For example, a number of papers focus on the potential strategic role of "voluntary" export restraints (VERs) such as those negotiated between the United States, Hong Kong, and Taiwan over footware or between the United States and Japan over automobiles. Traditionally VERs have been viewed as virtually identical to import quotas—a restriction that would harm importing firms. But Karikari (1991) and others challenge this view by noting that the pegging of import quantities (as with VERs) may help establish a Cournot equilibrium in situations that would otherwise be unstable. Hence voluntary export restraints may indeed be "voluntary" because they yield supracompetitive profits to both parties.

E15.4 Strategic relationship between prices

If we view the duopoly problem as one of setting prices, both q_A and q_B will be functions of prices charged by the two firms:

$$q_A = D^A(P_A, P_B)$$

$$q_B = D^B(P_A, P_B). \qquad \text{(ix)}$$

Using this notation,

$$\pi^A = P_A q_A - C(q_A)$$
$$= P_A D^A(P_A, P_B) - C[D^A(P_A, P_B)]. \quad \text{(x)}$$

Hence

$$\pi_1^A = P_A D_1^A + D^A - C' D_1^A \qquad \text{(xi)}$$

and

$$\pi_{12}^A = P_A D_{12}^A + D_2^A \\ - C' D_{12}^A - C'' D_2^A D_1^A. \qquad \text{(xii)}$$

Obviously, interpreting this mass of symbols is no easy task. In the special case of constant marginal cost ($C' = 0$) and linear demand ($D_{12}^A = 0$),

the sign of π_{12}^A is given by the sign of D_2^A—that is, how increases in P_B affect q_A. In the usual case when the two goods are themselves substitutes, $D_2^A > 0$, so $\pi_{12}^A > 0$. That is, prices are strategic complements. Firms in such a duopoly would either raise or lower prices together (see Tirole, 1988).

Cartels and price wars

Use of these concepts may aid in understanding the behavior of cartels. For example, Porter (1983) develops a model of the Joint Executive Committee, a cartel of railroads that controlled eastbound grain shipments from Chicago during the 1880s. One oddity of the shipping price data is that they illustrate periodic, sharp price drops. The author rejects the notion that these were caused by slumps in demand. For example, the price declines did not appear to be associated with shipping prices on Great Lakes' steamers, a primary substitute for the railroads. Instead, the price declines appeared to be one component of the cartel's internal enforcement mechanism. Price wars were motivated by unpredictable declines in the market share of one or two market participants who used such declines as a sign of the need to reestablish market discipline. By "cheating" on their pricing, they signaled this need to other cartel participants. Hence, price wars were an important component of an overall strategy to ensure cartel stability.

References

Bulow, J., G. Geanakoplous, and P. Klemperer. "Multimarket Oligopoly: Strategic Substitutes and Complements." *Journal of Political Economy* (June 1985): 488–511.

Karikari, J. A. "On Why Voluntary Export Restraints Are Voluntary." *Canadian Journal of Economics* (February 1991): 228–33.

Porter, R. H. "A Study of Cartel Stability: The Joint Executive Committee 1880–1886." *Bell Journal of Economics* (Autumn 1983): 301–14.

Tirole, J. *The Theory of Industrial Organization.* Cambridge, MA: MIT Press, 1988, pp. 326–36.

Part 6

PRICING IN INPUT MARKETS

CHAPTER 16   LABOR MARKETS

CHAPTER 17   CAPITAL MARKETS

Our study of input demand in Chapter 9 was quite general in that it can be applied to any factor of production. In Chapters 16 and 17 we take up several issues specifically related to pricing in the labor and capital markets. Chapter 16 focuses mainly on labor supply. Most of our analysis deals with labor supply decisions of single individuals. Labor supply by unions is also considered as is the possibility that a labor market may be noncompetitive on the demand side.

In Chapter 17 the market for capital is examined. The central purpose of the chapter is to emphasize the connection between capital and the allocation of resources over time. Some care is also taken to integrate the theory of capital into the models of firms' behavior we developed in Part 3. A brief appendix to Chapter 17 presents some useful mathematical results about interest rates.

In The Principles of Political Economy and Taxation, *Ricardo wrote*

> *The produce of the earth . . . is divided among three classes of the community, namely, the proprietor of the land, the owner of the stock of capital necessary for its cultivation, and the laborers by whose industry it is cultivated. To determine the laws which regulate this distribution is the principal problem in Political Economy.**

The purpose of Part 6 is to illustrate how the study of these "laws" has advanced since Ricardo's time.

---

*D. Ricardo, *The Principles of Political Economy and Taxation* (1817; reprinted, London: J. M. Dent and Son, 1965), p. 1.

Chapter 16

LABOR MARKETS

In this chapter we examine some aspects of input pricing that are related particularly to the labor market. Because we have already discussed questions about the demand for labor (or any other input) in some detail in Chapter 9, we will be concerned primarily with analyzing the supply of labor.

Allocation of time

In Part 2 we studied the way in which an individual chooses to allocate a fixed amount of income among a variety of available goods. Individuals must make similar choices in deciding how they will spend their time. The number of hours in a day (or in a year) is absolutely fixed, and time must be used as it "passes by." Given this fixed amount of time, any individual must decide how many hours to work; how many hours to spend consuming a wide variety of goods, ranging from cars and television sets to operas; how many hours to devote to self-maintenance; and how many hours to sleep. By examining how individuals choose to divide their time among these activities, economists are able to understand the labor supply decision.

Simple two-good model

For simplicity we start by assuming there are only two uses to which an individual may devote his or her time—either engaging in market work at a real wage rate of w per hour or not working. We shall refer to nonwork time as "leisure," but this word is not meant to carry any connotation of idleness. Time not spent in market work can be devoted to work in the home, to self-improvement, or to consumption (it takes time to use a television set or a bowling ball).[1] All of those activities contribute to an individual's well-being, and time will be allocated to them in what might be assumed to be a utility-maximizing way.

More specifically, assume that an individual's utility during a typical day depends on consumption during that period (c) and on hours of leisure enjoyed (h):

$$\text{utility} = U(c, h). \tag{16.1}$$

Notice that in writing this utility function, we have used two "composite" goods, consumption and leisure. The reader should recognize that utility is in fact derived by devoting real income and time to the consumption of a wide variety of goods and services.[2] In seeking to

---

[1]Perhaps the first formal theoretical treatment of the allocation of time was given by G. S. Becker in "A Theory of the Allocation of Time," *Economic Journal 75* (September 1965): 493–517.

[2]This observation leads to the consideration of how such activities are produced in the home. For an influential survey, see R. Gronau, "Home Production: A Survey," in O. C. Ashenfelter and R. Layard, eds., *Handbook of Labor Economics* (Amsterdam: North-Holland, 1986), vol. 1, pp. 273–304.

maximize utility, the individual is bound by two constraints. The first of these concerns is available time. If we let l represent hours of work, then

$$l + h = 24. \tag{16.2}$$

That is, the day's time must be allocated either to work or to nonwork. A second constraint records the fact that the individual can purchase consumption items only by working (later in this chapter we will allow for the availability of nonlabor income). If the real hourly market wage rate the individual can earn is given by w, the income constraint is given by

$$c = wl. \tag{16.3}$$

Combining the two constraints, we have

$$c = w(24 - h) \tag{16.4}$$

or

$$c + wh = 24w. \tag{16.5}$$

This combined constraint has an important interpretation. Any person has a "full income" given by $24w$. That is, an individual who worked all the time would have this much command over real consumption goods each day. Individuals may spend their full income either by working (for real income and consumption) or by not working and thereby enjoying leisure. Equation 16.5 shows that the opportunity cost of consuming leisure is w per hour; it is equal to earnings forgone by not working.

Utility maximization

The individual's problem, then, is to maximize utility, subject to the full income constraint. Setting up the Lagrangian expression

$$\mathcal{L} = U(c, h) + \lambda(24w - c - wh), \tag{16.6}$$

the first-order conditions for a maximum are

$$\frac{\partial \mathcal{L}}{\partial c} = \frac{\partial U}{\partial c} - \lambda = 0$$
$$\frac{\partial \mathcal{L}}{\partial h} = \frac{\partial U}{\partial h} - w\lambda = 0. \tag{16.7}$$

Dividing the two lines in Equation 16.7, we get

$$\frac{\partial U / \partial h}{\partial U / \partial c} = w = MRS(h \text{ for } c). \tag{16.8}$$

Hence we have derived the following principle:

OPTIMIZATION PRINCIPLE

Utility-maximizing labor supply decision. To maximize utility, given the real wage, w, the individual should choose to work that number of hours for which the marginal rate of substitution of leisure for consumption is equal to w.

Of course, the result derived in Equation (16.8) is only a necessary condition for a maximum. As in Chapter 4, this tangency will be a true maximum provided the *MRS* of leisure for consumption is diminishing.

Income and substitution effects of a change in *w*

A change in the real wage rate (w) can be analyzed in a manner identical to that used in Chapter 5. When w rises, the "price" of leisure becomes higher—a person must give up more in lost wages for each hour of leisure consumed. The substitution effect of an increase in w on the hours of leisure therefore will be negative. As leisure becomes more expensive, there is reason to consume less of it. However, the income effect will be positive—because leisure is a normal good, the higher income resulting from a higher w will increase the demand for leisure. Thus, the income and substitution effects work in opposite directions. It is impossible to predict on a priori grounds whether an increase in w will increase or decrease the demand for leisure time. Because leisure and work are mutually exclusive ways to spend one's time, it is also impossible to predict what will happen to the number of hours worked. The substitution effect tends to increase hours worked when w increases, whereas the income effect, because it increases the demand for leisure time, tends to decrease the number of hours worked. Which of these two effects is the stronger is an important empirical question.[3]

A graphical analysis

The two possible reactions to a change in w are illustrated in Figure 16.1. In both graphs the initial wage is w_0, and the initial optimal choices of c and h are given by the point c_0, h_0. When the wage rate increases to w_1, the optimal combination moves to point c_1, h_1. This movement can be considered the result of two effects. The substitution effect is represented by the movement of the optimal point from c_0, h_0 to S and the income effect by the movement from S to c_1, h_1. In the two panels of Figure 16.1, these two effects combine to produce different results. In panel (a) the substitution effect of a change in w outweighs the income effect, and the individual demands less leisure ($h_1 < h_0$). Another way of saying this is that the individual will work longer hours when w rises.

In panel (b) of Figure 16.1 the situation is reversed. The income effect of a change in w more than offsets the substitution effect, and the demand for leisure increases ($h_1 > h_0$). The individual works shorter hours when w rises. In the cases examined in Chapter 5 this would have been considered an unusual result—when the "price" of leisure rises, the individual demands more of it. For the case of normal consumption goods, the income and substitution effects work in the same direction. Only for "inferior" goods do they differ in sign. In the case of leisure and labor, however, the income and substitution effects always work in opposite directions. An increase in w makes an individual better off because he or she is a *supplier* of labor. In the case of a consumption good, individuals are made worse off when a price rises because they are *consumers* of that good. We can summarize this analysis, as follows:

OPTIMIZATION PRINCIPLE

Income and substitution effects of a change in the real wage. When the real wage rate increases, a utility-maximizing individual may increase or decrease hours worked. The substitution effect will tend to increase hours worked as the individual substitutes earnings for leisure, which is now relatively more costly. On the other hand, the income effect will tend to reduce hours worked as the individual uses his or her increased purchasing power to buy more leisure hours.

---

[3]If the family is taken to be the relevant decision unit, even more complex questions arise about the income and substitution effects that changes in the wages of one family member, say, the husband, will have on the labor force behavior of other family members, such as the wife.

Because the individual is a supplier of labor, the income and substitution effects of an increase in the real wage rate (w) work in opposite directions in their effects on the hours of leisure demanded (or on hours of work). In (a) the substitution effect (movement to point S) outweighs the income effect, and a higher wage causes hours of leisure to decline to h_1. Hours of work therefore increase. In (b) the income effect is stronger than the substitution effect, and h increases to h_1. In this case hours of work decline.

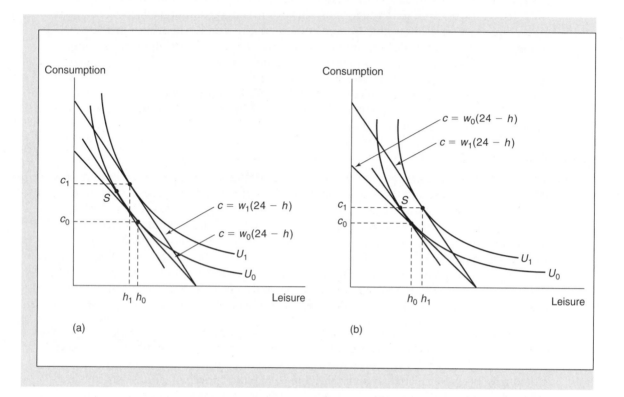

We now turn to examine a mathematical development of these responses that provides additional insights into the labor supply decision.

A mathematical analysis of labor supply

To derive a mathematical statement of labor supply decisions, it is helpful first to amend the budget constraint slightly to allow for the presence of nonlabor income. To do so, we rewrite Equation 16.3 as

$$c = wl + n, \tag{16.9}$$

where n is real nonlabor income and may include such items as dividend and interest income, receipt of government transfer benefits, or simply gifts from other persons. Indeed, n could stand for lump-sum taxes paid by this person, in which case its value would be negative.

Maximization of utility subject to this new budget constraint would yield results virtually identical to those we have already derived. That is, the necessary condition for a maximum described in Equation 16.8 would continue to hold as long as the value of n is unaffected by the labor-leisure choices being made; that is, so long as n is a "lump-sum" receipt or loss of income,[4] the only effect of introducing nonlabor income into the analysis is to shift the budget constraints in Figure 16.1 outward or inward in a parallel manner without affecting the trade-off rate between earnings and leisure.

This discussion suggests that we can write the individual's labor supply function as $l(w, n)$ to indicate that the number of hours worked will depend both on the real wage rate and on the amount of real nonlabor income received. On the assumption that leisure is a normal good, $\partial l/\partial n$ will be negative; that is, an increase in n will raise the demand for leisure and (because there are only 24 hours in the day) reduce l. To study wage effects on labor supply ($\partial l/\partial w$), we will find it helpful first to consider the dual problem to the individual's primary utility-maximization problem.

Dual statement of the problem

As we showed in Chapter 5, related to the individual's primary problem of utility maximization given a budget constraint is the dual problem of minimizing the expenditures necessary to attain a given utility level. In the present context, this problem can be phrased as choosing values for consumption (c) and leisure time ($h = 24 - l$) so that the amount of additional spending,

$$E = c - wl, \tag{16.10}$$

required to attain a given utility level [say, $U_0 = U(c, h)$] is as small as possible. As in Chapter 5, solving this minimization problem will yield exactly the same solution as solving the utility-maximization problem.

Now we can apply the envelope theorem to the minimum value for these extra expenditures calculated in the dual problem. Specifically, a small change in the real wage will change the minimum expenditures required by

$$\frac{\partial E}{\partial w} = -l. \tag{16.11}$$

Intuitively, each \$1 increase in w reduces the required value of E by \$$l$, because that is the extent to which labor earnings are increased by the wage change. This result is very similar to Shephard's lemma in the theory of production (see Chapter 9); here the result shows that a labor supply function can be calculated from the expenditure function by partial differentiation. Because utility is held constant in the dual expenditure minimization approach, this function should be interpreted as a "compensated" (constant utility) labor supply function, which we will denote by $l^c(w, U)$ to differentiate it from the uncompensated labor supply function $l(w, n)$ introduced earlier.

Slutsky equation of labor supply

Now we can use these concepts to derive a Slutsky-type equation that reflects the substitution and income effects that result from changes in the real wage. We begin by recognizing that the expenditures being minimized in the dual problem of Equation 16.11 play the role of nonlabor income in the primal utility-maximization problem. Hence, by definition, at the optimal point we have

$$l^c(w, U) = l[w, E(w, U)] = l(w, n). \tag{16.12}$$

---

[4] In many situations, however, n itself may depend on labor supply decisions. For example, the value of welfare or unemployment benefits a person can receive depends on his or her earnings, as does the amount of income taxes paid. In such cases the slope of the individual's budget constraint will no longer be reflected by the real wage but must instead reflect the *net* return to additional work after taking increased taxes and reductions in transfer payments into account. For some examples, see the Problems at the end of this chapter.

Partial differentiation of both sides of Equation 16.12 with respect to w yields

$$\frac{\partial l^c}{\partial w} = \frac{\partial l}{\partial w} + \frac{\partial l}{\partial E} \cdot \frac{\partial E}{\partial w}, \qquad (16.13)$$

and using the envelope relation from Equation 16.11 for $\partial E / \partial w$, we have

$$\frac{\partial l^c}{\partial w} = \frac{\partial l}{\partial w} - l\frac{\partial l}{\partial E} = \frac{\partial l}{\partial w} - l\frac{\partial l}{\partial n}. \qquad (16.14)$$

Introducing a slightly different notation for the compensated labor supply function,

$$\frac{\partial l^c}{\partial w} = \frac{\partial l}{\partial w}\bigg| U = U_0, \qquad (16.15)$$

and rearranging terms gives the final Slutsky equation for labor supply:

$$\frac{\partial l}{\partial w} = \frac{\partial l}{\partial w}\bigg| U = U_0 + l\frac{\partial l}{\partial n}. \qquad (16.16)$$

In words (as we have previously shown), the change in labor supplied in response to a change in the real wage can be disaggregated into the sum of a substitution effect in which utility is held constant and an income effect that is analytically equivalent to an appropriate change in nonlabor income. Because the substitution effect is positive (a higher wage increases the amount of work chosen when utility is held constant) and the term $\partial l / \partial n$ is negative, this derivation shows that the substitution and income effects work in opposite directions. The mathematical development supports the earlier conclusions from our graphical analysis and suggest at least the theoretical possibility that the labor supply curve might be "backward bending." The mathematical development also suggests that the importance of negative income effects may be greater the greater is the amount of labor itself being supplied.

 EXAMPLE 16.1

Labor Supply Functions

Individual labor supply functions can be constructed from underlying utility functions in much the same way that we constructed demand functions in Part 2. Here we will begin with a fairly extended treatment of a simple Cobb-Douglas case and then provide a shorter summary of labor supply with CES utility.

a. Cobb-Douglas utility

Suppose that an individual's utility function for consumption, c, and leisure, h, is given by

$$U(c,h) = c^\alpha h^\beta \qquad (16.17)$$

and, for simplicity, that $\alpha + \beta = 1$. This person is constrained by two equations: (1) An income constraint that shows how consumption can be financed

$$c = wl + n, \qquad (16.18)$$

where n is nonlabor income); and (2) by a total time constraint

$$l + h = 1, \qquad (16.19)$$

where we have arbitrarily set the available time to be 1. By combining the financial and time constraints into a "full income" constraint, we can arrive at the following Lagrangian expression for this utility-maximization problem:

$$\mathscr{L} = U(c, h) + \lambda(w + n - wh - c) = c^\alpha h^\beta + \lambda(w + n - wh - c). \quad (16.20)$$

First-order conditions for a maximum are

$$\frac{\partial \mathscr{L}}{\partial c} = \alpha c^{-\beta} h^\beta - \lambda = 0$$

$$\frac{\partial \mathscr{L}}{\partial h} = \beta c^\alpha h^{-\alpha} - \lambda w = 0 \quad (16.21)$$

$$\frac{\partial \mathscr{L}}{\partial \lambda} = w + n - wh - c = 0.$$

Dividing the first of these by the second yields

$$\frac{\alpha h}{\beta c} = \frac{\alpha h}{(1 - \alpha)c} = \frac{1}{w} \text{ or } wh = \frac{1-\alpha}{\alpha} \cdot c. \quad (16.22)$$

Substitution into the full income constraint then yields the familiar results

$$c = \alpha(w + n)$$
$$h = \beta(w + n)/w. \quad (16.23)$$

In words, this person spends a fixed fraction, α, of his or her full income ($w + n$) on consumption and the complementary fraction, $\beta = 1 - \alpha$, on leisure (which costs w per unit). The labor supply function for this person is then given by

$$l(w, n) = 1 - h = (1 - \beta) - \frac{\beta n}{w}. \quad (16.24)$$

b. Properties of the Cobb-Douglas labor supply function

This labor supply function shares many of the properties exhibited by consumer demand functions derived from Cobb-Douglas utility. For example, if $n = 0$, $\partial l/\partial w = 0$—this person always devotes $1 - \beta$ proportion of his or her time to working, no matter what the wage rate. Income and substitution effects of a change in w are precisely offsetting in this case, just as they are with cross-price effects in Cobb-Douglas demand functions.

On the other hand, if $n > 0$, $\partial l/\partial w > 0$. When there is positive nonlabor income, this person spends βn of it on leisure. But leisure "costs" w per hour, so an increase in the wage means that fewer hours of leisure can be bought. Hence, a rise in w increases labor supply.

Finally, notice that $\partial l/\partial n < 0$. An increase in nonlabor income allows this person to buy more leisure, so labor supply decreases. One interpretation of this result is that transfer programs (such as welfare benefits or unemployment compensation) reduce labor supply. Another interpretation is that lump-sum taxation increases labor supply. But actual tax and transfer programs are seldom lump sum—usually they affect net wage rates as well. Hence, any precise prediction requires a detailed look at how such programs affect the budget constraint.

(continued)

 **EXAMPLE 16.1 CONTINUED**

c. CES labor supply

In the Extensions to Chapter 4 we derived the general form for demand functions generated from a CES utility function. We can apply that derivation directly here to study CES labor demand. Specifically, if utility is given by

$$U(c, h) = \frac{c^\delta}{\delta} + \frac{h^\delta}{\delta}, \qquad (16.25)$$

budget share equations are given by

$$s_c = \frac{c}{w + n} = \frac{1}{(1 + w^\kappa)}$$
$$s_h = \frac{wh}{w + n} = \frac{1}{(1 + w^{-\kappa})}, \qquad (16.26)$$

where $\kappa = \delta/(\delta - 1)$. Solving explicitly for leisure gives

$$h = \frac{w + n}{w + w^{1-\kappa}} \qquad (16.27)$$

and

$$l(w, n) = 1 - h = \frac{w^{1-\kappa} - n}{w + w^{1-\kappa}}. \qquad (16.28)$$

It is perhaps easiest to explore the properties of this function by taking some examples. If $\delta = 0.5$, $\kappa = -1$ the labor supply function is

$$l(m, n) = \frac{w^2 - n}{w + w^2} = \frac{1 - n/w^2}{1 + \dfrac{1}{w}}. \qquad (16.29)$$

If $n = 0$ it is clearly the case that $\partial l/\partial w > 0$—because of the relatively high degree of substitutability between consumption and leisure in this utility function, the substitution effect of a higher wage outweighs the income effect. On the other hand, if $\delta = -1$, $\kappa = 0.5$ the labor supply function is

$$l(w, n) = \frac{w^{0.5} - n}{w + w^{0.5}} = \frac{1 - n/w^{0.5}}{1 + w^{0.5}}. \qquad (16.30)$$

Now (when $n = 0$) $\partial l/\partial w < 0$, because there is a smaller degree of substitutability in the utility function, the income effect outweighs the substitution effect in labor supply.[5]

Query: Why does the effect of nonlabor income in the CES case depend on the consumption/leisure substitutability in the utility function?

---

[5]In the Cobb-Douglas case ($\delta = 0$, $\kappa = 0$) the constant-share result (for $n = 0$) is shown by $l(w,n) = (w - n)/2w = 0.5 - n/2w$.

FIGURE 16.2 **Construction of the Market Supply Curve for Labor**

As the real wage rises, there are two reasons why the supply of labor may increase. First, higher real wages may cause each person in the market to work more hours. Second, higher wages may induce more individuals (for example, individual 2) to enter the labor market.

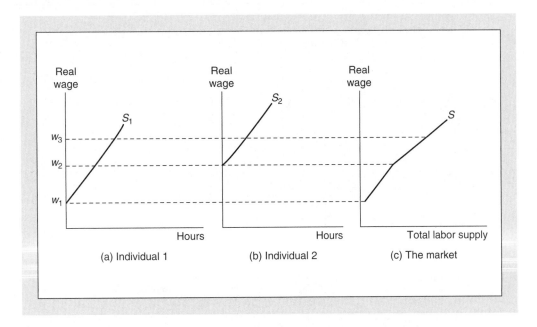

Market supply curve for labor

We can construct a market supply of labor curve from individual labor supply decisions. At each possible wage rate we add together the quantity of labor offered by each individual to arrive at a market total. One particularly interesting aspect of this procedure is that as the wage rate rises, more individuals may be induced to enter the labor force. Figure 16.2 illustrates this possibility for the simple case of two people. For a real wage below w_1 neither individual chooses to work. Consequently, the market supply curve of labor (Figure 16.2c) shows that no labor is supplied at real wages below w_1. A wage in excess of w_1 causes individual 1 to enter the labor market. However, as long as wages fall short of w_2, individual 2 will not work. Only at a wage rate above w_2 will both individuals participate in the labor market. In general, the possibility of the entry of new workers makes the market supply of labor somewhat more responsive to wage rate increases than would be the case if the number of workers was assumed to be fixed.

The most important example of higher real wage rates inducing increased labor force participation is the labor force behavior of married women in the United States in the post–World War II period. Since 1950 the percentage of working married women has increased from 32 percent to over 65 percent; economists attribute this, at least in part, to the increasing wages women are able to earn.

Labor market equilibrium

Equilibrium in the labor market is established through the interaction of individuals' labor supply decisions with firms' decisions about how much labor to hire. That process is illustrated by the familiar supply-demand diagram in Figure 16.3. At a real wage rate of w^*

FIGURE 16.3   Equilibrium in the Labor Market

A real wage of w^* creates an equilibrium in the labor market with an employment level of l^*.

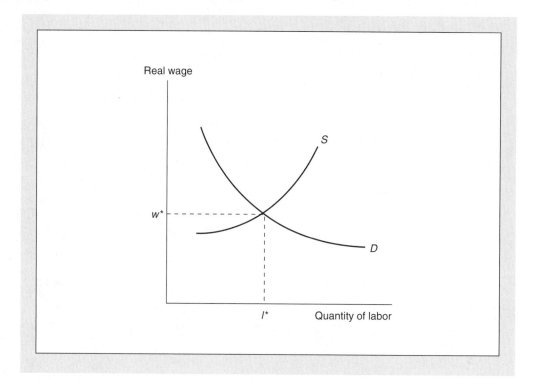

the quantity of labor demanded by firms is precisely matched by the quantity supplied by individuals. A real wage higher than w^* would create a disequilibrium in which the quantity of labor supplied is greater than the quantity demanded. There would be some involuntary unemployment at such a wage, and this may create pressure for the real wage to fall. Similarly, a real wage lower than w^* would result in disequilibrium behavior because firms would want to hire more workers than are available. In the scramble to hire workers, firms may bid up real wages to restore equilibrium.

Possible reasons for disequilibria in the labor market are a major topic in macroeconomics, especially in relationship to the business cycle. Perceived failures of the market to adjust to changing equilibria have been blamed on "sticky" real wages, inaccurate expectations by workers or firms about the price level, the impact of government unemployment insurance programs, labor market regulations and minimum wages, and intertemporal work decisions by workers. Microeconomic modeling of all of these possibilities has played a major role in recent advances in macroeconomics, though we will not pursue these topics here because that would take us away from the primary purposes of this book.

Equilibrium models of the labor market can also be used to study a number of questions about taxation and regulatory policy. For example, the tax incidence modeling illustrated in Chapter 11 can be readily adapted to the study of employment taxation. One interesting possibility that arises in the study of labor markets is that a given policy intervention may shift both demand and supply functions—a possibility we examine in Example 16.2.

EXAMPLE 16.2

Mandated Benefits

A number of recent laws have mandated that employers provide special benefits to their workers such as health insurance, paid time off, or minimum severance packages. The effect of such mandates on equilibrium in the labor market depends importantly on how the benefits are valued by workers. Suppose that prior to implementation of a mandate the supply and demand for labor are given by

$$l_S = a + bw$$
$$l_D = c - dw. \tag{16.31}$$

Setting $l_S = l_D$ yields an equilibrium wage of

$$w^* = \frac{c - a}{b + d}. \tag{16.32}$$

Now suppose that the government mandates that all firms provide a particular benefit to their workers and that this benefit costs t per unit of labor hired. Unit labor costs therefore increase to $w + t$. Suppose also that the new benefit has a monetary value to workers of k per unit of labor supplied—hence the net return from employment rises to $w + k$. Equilibrium in the labor market then requires that

$$a + b(w + k) = c - d(w + t). \tag{16.33}$$

A bit of manipulation of this expression shows that the net wage is given by

$$w^{**} = \frac{c - a}{b + d} - \frac{bk + dt}{b + d} = w^* - \frac{bk + dt}{b + d}. \tag{16.34}$$

If workers derive no value from the mandated benefit ($k = 0$), the mandate is just like a tax on employment—employees pay a share of the tax given by the ratio $d/(b + d)$ and the equilibrium quantity of labor hired falls. Qualitatively similar results will occur so long as $k < t$. On the other hand, if workers value the benefit at precisely its cost ($k = t$), the new wage falls precisely by the amount of this cost ($w^{**} = w^* - t$) and the equilibrium level of employment does not change. Finally, if workers value the benefit at more than it costs the firm to provide it ($k > t$—a situation where one might wonder why the benefit was not already provided), the equilibrium wage will fall by more than the benefit costs and equilibrium employment will increase.

Query: How would you graph this analysis? Would its conclusions depend on using linear supply and demand functions?

Wage variation

One topic that should be mentioned in connection with the supply-demand diagram in Figure 16.3 concerns how differences in workers and jobs can lead to differences in observed wages. Such wage variation has increased significantly in many economies in recent years, and examining the nature of supply and demand in the labor market can go a long way toward explaining it. Here we look briefly at two factors that are important in competitive labor markets and then we will turn to a more extended discussion of imperfect competition in the labor market.

Human capital

Because the firm's demand for labor depends on the worker's marginal productivity, differences in productivity among workers should lead to different wages. Perhaps the most important source of such productivity differences in the human capital embodied in workers. Such capital is accumulated during a worker's lifetime through formal education, other formal methods of acquiring skills (such as a job training course), on-the-job training, and general life experiences. This process has much in common with the process of investing in physical capital—a topic we take up in the next chapter. Workers invest both money and their own time in acquiring skills in the hope that those skills will pay off in the labor market. Presumably, in making decisions about undertaking these activities, workers look at the rate of return that might be expected from their investments. Only those investments in skills that promise a return higher than can be made elsewhere will be undertaken. Of course, investing in human capital is different from investing in physical capital, primarily because human capital, once acquired, cannot be divested. This makes human capital investments somewhat more risky than are more liquid investments, and consequently rates of return may be higher.[6] Because human capital human capital is both costly and raises worker productivity, it would be expected to have an unambiguously positive effect on real wages.

Compensating differentials

People obviously prefer some jobs to others. Factors such as pleasant working conditions, flexible hours, or easy commuting may make an individual willing to accept a job that pays less than others offer. This supply effect would be manifested in lower wages for such jobs. Alternatively, jobs that are unpleasant or involve significant risks will require higher wages if they are to be attractive to workers (see Problem 16.3). Such supply-induced differences in wages are termed "compensating wage differentials" because they compensate for job characteristics that workers value. The variation in such characteristics therefore explains some portion of the variation in wages.

Monopsony in the labor market

In many situations firms are not price takers for the inputs they buy. That is the supply curve for, say, labor faced by the firm is not infinitely elastic at the prevailing wage rate. It often may be necessary for the firm to offer a wage above that currently prevailing if it is to attract more employees. In order to study such situations, it is most convenient to examine the polar case of *monopsony* (a single buyer) in the labor market. If there is only one buyer in the labor market, this firm faces the entire market supply curve. To increase its hiring of labor by one more unit, it must move to a higher point on this supply curve. This will involve paying not only a higher wage to the "marginal worker," but also additional wages to those workers already employed. The marginal expense associated with hiring the extra unit of labor (ME_l) therefore exceeds its wage rate. We can show this result mathematically as follows. The total cost of labor to the firm in wl. Hence the change in those costs brought about by hiring an additional worker is

$$ME_l = \frac{\partial wl}{\partial l} = w + l\frac{\partial w}{\partial l}. \qquad (16.35)$$

---

[6]Pioneering work in the theory of human capital can be found in Gary Becker, *Human Capital: A Theoretical and Empirical Analysis with Special Reference to Education* (New York: National Bureau of Economic Research, 1964).

In the competitive case, $\partial w / \partial l = 0$ and the marginal expense of hiring one more worker is simply the market wage, w. However, if the firm faces a positively sloped labor supply curve, $\partial w / \partial l > 0$ and the marginal expense exceeds the wage. These ideas are summarized in the following definition:

DEFINITION

Marginal input expense. The *marginal expense* associated with any input (ME) is the increase in total costs of the input that results fro hiring one more unit. If the firm faces an upward-sloping supply curve for the input, the marginal expense will exceed the market price of the input.

A profit-maximizing firm will hire any input up to the point at which its marginal revenue product is just equal to its marginal expense. This result is a generalization of our previous discussion of marginalist choices to cover the case of monopsony power in the labor market. As before, any departure from such choices will result in lower profits for the firm. If, for example, $MRP_l > ME_l$, the firm should hire more workers, because such an action would increase revenues more than costs. Alternatively, if $MRP_l < ME_l$, employment should be reduced, because that would lower costs more rapidly than revenues.

Graphical analysis

The monopsonist's choice of labor input is illustrated in Figure 16.4. The firm's demand curve for labor (D) is drawn negatively sloped, as we have shown it must be.[7] Here also the ME_l curve associated with the labor supply curve (S) is constructed in much the same way that the marginal revenue curve associated with a demand curve can be constructed. Because S is positively sloped, the ME_l curve lies everywhere above S. The profit-maximizing level of labor input for the monopsonist is given by l_1, for at this level of input the profit-maximizing condition holds. At l_1 the wage rate in the market is given by w_1. Notice that the quantity of labor demanded falls short of that which would be hired in a perfectly competitive labor market (l^*). The firm has restricted input demand by virtue of its monopsonistic position in the market. The formal similarities between this analysis and that of monopoly presented in Chapter 13 should be clear. In particular, the "demand curve" for a monopsonist consists of a single point given by l_1, w_1. The monopsonist has chosen this point as the most desirable of all points on the supply curve, S. A different point will not be chosen unless some external change (such as a shift in the demand for the firm's output or a change in technology) affects labor's marginal revenue product.[8, 9]

---

[7]Figure 16.4 is intended only as a pedagogic device and cannot be rigorously defended. In particular, the curve labeled D, although it is supposed to represent the "demand" (or marginal revenue product) curve for labor, has no precise meaning for the monopsonist buyer of labor, because we cannot construct this curve by confronting the firm with a fixed wage rate. Instead, the firm views the entire supply curve, S, and used the auxiliary curve ME_l to choose the most favorable point on S. In a strict sense, there is no such thing as the monopsonist's demand curve. This is analogous to the case of a monopoly, for which we could not speak of a monopolist's "supply curve."

[8]For a detailed discussion of the comparative statics analysis of factor demand in the monopoly and monopsony cases, see W. E. Diewert, "Duality Approaches to Microeconomic Theory," in K. J. Arrow and M. D. Intriligator, eds., *Handbook of Mathematical Economics* (Amsterdam: North-Holland, 1982), vol. 2, pp. 584–590.

[9]A monopsony may also practice price discrimination in all of the ways described for a monopoly in Chapter 13.

FIGURE 16.4   Pricing in a Monopsonistic Labor Market

If a firm faces a positively sloped supply curve for labor (S), it will base its decisions on the marginal expense of additional hiring (ME_l). Because S is positively sloped, the ME_l curve lies above S. The curve S can be thought of as an "average cost of labor curve," and the ME_l curve is marginal to S. At l_1 the equilibrium condition $ME_l = MRP_l$ holds, and this quantity will be hired at a market wage rate w_1. Notice that the monopsonist buys less labor than would be bought if the labor market were perfectly competitive (l^*).

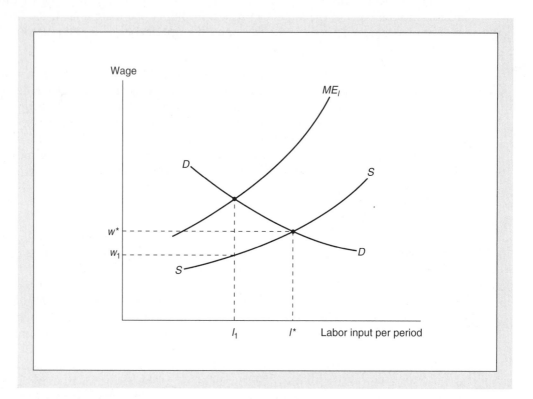

    EXAMPLE 16.3

Monopsonistic Hiring

To illustrate these concepts in a very simple context, suppose a coal mine's workers can dig two tons of coal per hour and coal sells for $10 per ton. The marginal revenue product of a coal miner is therefore $20 per hour. If the coal mine is the only hirer of miners in a local area and faces a labor supply curve of the form

$$l = 50w, \tag{16.36}$$

this firm must recognize that its hiring decisions affect wages. Expressing the total wage bill as a function of l,

$$wl = \frac{l^2}{50}, \tag{16.37}$$

permits the mine operator (perhaps only implicitly) to calculate the marginal expense associated with hiring miners:

$$ME_l = \frac{\partial wl}{\partial l} = \frac{l}{25}. \tag{16.38}$$

Equating this to miners' marginal revenue product of $20 implies that the mine operator should hire 500 workers per hour. At this level of employment the wage will be $10 per hour—only half the value of the workers' marginal revenue product. If the mine operator had been forced by market competition to pay $20 per hour, regardless of the number of miners hired, market equilibrium would have been established with $l = 1,000$ rather than the 500 hired under monopsonistic conditions.

Query: Suppose the price of coal rises to $15. How would this affect the monopsonist's hiring and the wages of coal miners? Would the miners benefit fully from the increase in their *MRP*?

Labor unions

Workers may at times find it advantageous to join together a labor union to pursue goals that can more effectively be accomplished by a group. If association with a union were wholly voluntary, we could assume that every union member derives a positive benefit from belonging. Compulsory membership (the "closed shop"), however, is often used to maintain the viability of the union organization. If all workers were left on their own to decide on membership, their rational decision might be not to join the union, and hence avoid dues and other restrictions. However, they would benefit from the higher wages and better working conditions that have been won by the union. What appears to be rational from each individual worker's point of view may prove to be irrational from a group's point of view, because the union is undermined by "free riders." Compulsory membership therefore may be a necessary means of maintaining an effective union coalition.

Unions' goals

A good starting place for our analysis of union behavior is to describe union goals. A first assumption we might make is that the goals of a union are in some sense an adequate representation of the goals of its members. This assumption avoids the problem of union leadership and disregards the personal aspirations of those leaders, which may be in conflict with rank-and-file goals. Union leaders therefore are assumed to be conduits for expressing the desires of the membership.[10] In the United States, union goals have tended to be oriented toward "bread-and-butter" issues. The programs of major unions have not emphasized the promotion of radical social change, except briefly in the early 1900s. Rather, unions have attempted to exert an effect solely in the labor market, and in this they have had some success.

In some respects, unions can be analyzed in the same way as monopoly firms. The union faces a demand curve for labor; because it is the sole source of supply, it can choose at which point on this curve it will operate. The point actually chosen by the union will obviously depend on what particular goals it has decided to pursue. Three possible choices are illustrated in Figure 16.5. For example, the union may choose to offer that quantity of labor that maximizes the total wage bill ($w \cdot l$). If this is the case, it will offer that quantity for which the "marginal revenue" from labor demand is equal to 0. This quantity is given by l_1 in Figure 16.5, and the wage rate associated with this quantity is w_1. The point E_1 is

---

[10]Much recent analysis, however, revolves around whether "potential" union members have some voice in setting union goals and how union goals may affect the desires of workers with differing amounts of seniority on the job.

FIGURE 16.5	**Three Possible Points on the Labor Demand Curve That a Monopolistic Union Might Choose**

A union has a monopoly in the supply of labor. It therefore may choose that point on the demand curve for labor that it most prefers. Three such points are shown in the figure. At point E_1 total labor payments ($w \cdot l$) are maximized; at E_2 the economic rent that workers receive is maximized; and at E_3 the total amount of labor services supplied is maximized.

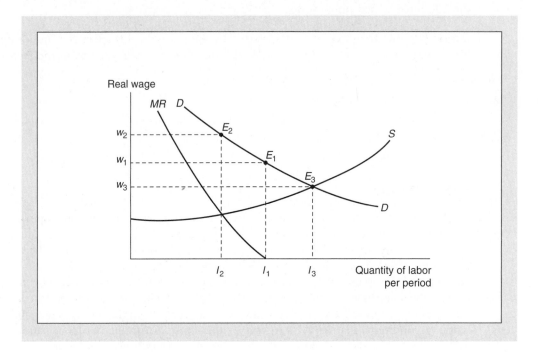

therefore the preferred wage-quantity combination. Notice that at wage rate w_1 there may be an excess supply of labor, and the union must somehow allocate available jobs to those workers who want them.

Another possible goal the union may pursue would be to choose the quantity of labor that would maximize the total economic rent (that is, wages less opportunity costs) obtained by those members who are employed. This would necessitate choosing that quantity of labor for which the additional total wages obtained by having one more employed union member (the marginal revenue) are equal to the extra cost of luring that member into the market. The union therefore should choose that quantity, l_2, at which the marginal revenue curve crosses the supply curve.[11] The wage rate associated with this quantity is w_2, and the desired wage-quantity combination is labeled E_2 in the diagram. With the wage w_2, many individuals who desire to work at the prevailing wage are left unemployed. Perhaps the union may "tax" the large economic rent earned by those who do work to transfer income to those who don't.

A third possibility would be for the union to aim for maximum employment of its members. This would involve choosing the point w_3, l_3, which is precisely the point that would result if the market were organized in a perfectly competitive way. No employment greater than l_3 could be achieved, because the quantity of labor that union members supply would be reduced for wages less than w_3.

---

[11]Mathematically, the union's goal is to choose l so as to maximize wl − (area under S), where S is the compensated supply curve for labor and reflects workers' opportunity costs in terms of forgone leisure.

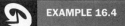 **EXAMPLE 16.4**

Modeling a Union

In Example 16.3 we examined a monopsonistic hirer of coal miners who faced a supply curve given by

$$l = 50w. \tag{16.39}$$

To study possibilities for unionization to combat this monopsonist, assume (contrary to Example 16.3) that the monopsonist has a downward-sloping marginal revenue product for labor curve of the form

$$MRP = 70 - .1l. \tag{16.40}$$

It is easy to show that without an effective union the monopsonist in this situation will choose the same wage-hiring combination it did in Example 16.3—500 workers will be hired at a wage of $10.

If the union can establish control over labor supply to the mine owner, several other options become possible. The union could press for the competitive solution, for example. A contract of $l = 583$, $w = 11.66$ would equate supply and demand. Alternatively, the union could act as a monopolist facing the demand curve given by Equation 16.40. It could calculate the marginal increment yielded by supplying additional workers as

$$\frac{d(l \cdot MRP)}{dl} = 70 - .2l. \tag{16.41}$$

The intersection between this "marginal revenue" curve and the labor supply curve (which indicates the "marginal opportunity cost" of workers' labor supply decisions) yields maximum rent to the unions' workers:

$$\frac{l}{50} = 70 - .2l \tag{16.42}$$

or

$$3{,}500 = 11l. \tag{16.43}$$

Such a calculation would therefore suggest a contract of $l = 318$ and a wage (MRP) of $38.20. The fact that both the competitive and union monopoly supply contracts differ significantly from the monopsonist's preferred contract indicates that the ultimate outcome here is likely to be determined through bilateral bargaining. Notice also that the wage differs significantly depending on which side has market power.

Query: Which, if any, of the three wage contracts described in this example might represent a Nash equilibrium.

EXAMPLE 16.5

A Union Bargaining Model

Game theory can be used to gain insights into the economics of unions. As a simple illustration, suppose a union and a firm engage in a two-stage game. In the first stage, the union sets the wage rate its workers will accept. Given this wage, the firm then chooses its employment level. This two-stage game can be solved by backward induction. Given the wage, specified by the union, w, the firm's second-stage problem is to maximize

$$\pi = R(l) - wl, \tag{16.44}$$

where R is the total revenue function of the firm expressed as a function of employment. The first-order condition for a maximum here (assuming that the wage is fixed) is the familiar

$$R'(l) = w. \tag{16.45}$$

Assuming l^* solves Equation 16.45, the union's goal is to choose w to maximize utility

$$U(w, l) = U[w, l^*(w)] \tag{16.46}$$

and the first-order condition for a maximum is

$$U_1 + U_2 l' = 0 \tag{16.47}$$

or

$$U_1/U_2 = l'. \tag{16.48}$$

In words, the union should choose w so that its *MRS* is equal to the slope of the firm's labor demand function. The w^*, l^* combination resulting from this game is clearly a Nash equilibrium.

Efficiency of the labor contract. The labor contract w^*, l^* is Pareto inefficient. To see that, notice that Equation 16.48 implies that small movements along the firm's labor demand curve (l) leave the union equally well off. But the envelope theorem implies that a decline in w must increase profits to the firm. Hence there must exist a contract, w^p, l^p (where $w^p < w^*$, $l^p > l^*$), with which both the firm and union are better off.

The inefficiency of the labor contract in this two-stage game is similar to the inefficiency of some of the repeated Nash equilibria we studied in Chapter 15. This suggests that, with repeated rounds of contract negotiations, trigger strategies might be developed that form a subgame perfect equilibrium and maintain Pareto superior outcomes. For a simple example, see Problem 16.10.

Query: Suppose the firm's total revenue function differed depending on whether the economy was in an expansion or a recession. What kinds of labor contract might be Pareto optimal?

SUMMARY

In this chapter we examined some models that focus on pricing in the labor market. Because labor demand was already treated as being derived from the profit-maximization hypothesis in Chapter 9, most of the new material here focused on labor supply. Our primary findings were:

- A utility-maximizing individual will choose to supply an amount of labor at which his or her marginal rate of substitution of leisure for consumption is equal to the real wage rate.

- An increase in the real wage creates substitution and income effects that work in opposite directions in affecting the quantity of labor supplied. This result can be summarized by a Slutsky-type equation much like the one already derived in consumer theory.

- A competitive labor market will establish an equilibrium real wage at which the quantity of labor supplied by individuals is equal to the quantity demanded by firms.

- Monopsony power by firms on the demand side of the labor market will reduce both the quantity of labor hired and the real wage. As in the monopoly case, there will also be a welfare loss.

- Labor unions can be treated analytically as monopoly suppliers of labor. The nature of labor market equilibrium in the presence of unions will depend importantly on the goals the union chooses to pursue.

PROBLEMS

16.1

Suppose there are 8,000 hours in a year (actually there are 8,760) and that an individual has a potential market wage of $5 per hour.

a. What is the individual's full income? If he or she chooses to devote 75 percent of this income to leisure, how many hours will be worked?

b. Suppose a rich uncle dies and leaves the individual an annual income of $4,000 per year. If he or she continues to devote 75 percent of full income to leisure, how many hours will be worked?

c. How would your answer to part (b) change if the market wage were $10 per hour instead of $5 per hour?

d. Graph the individual's supply of labor curve implied by parts (b) and (c).

16.2

As we saw in Chapter 16, the elements of labor supply theory can also be derived from an expenditure-minimization approach. Suppose a person's utility function for consumption and leisure takes the Cobb-Douglas form $U(c, h) = c^\alpha h^{1-\alpha}$. Then the expenditure-minimization problem is

$$\text{Minimize } c - w(24 - h) \text{ s.t. } U(c, h) = c^\alpha h^{1-\alpha} = \bar{U}.$$

a. Use this approach to derive the expenditure function for this problem.

b. Use the envelope theorem to derive the compensated demand functions for consumption and leisure.

c. Derive the compensated labor supply function. Show that $\partial l^c / \partial w > 0$.

d. Compare the compensated labor supply function from part (c) to the uncompensated labor supply function in Example 16.1 (with $n = 0$). Use the Slutsky equation to show why income and substitution effects of a change in the real wage are precisely offsetting in the uncompensated Cobb-Douglas labor supply function.

16.3

An individual receives utility from daily income (y), given by

$$U(y) = 100y - \frac{1}{2}y^2.$$

The only source of income is earnings. Hence, $y = wl$, where w is the hourly wage and l is hours worked per day. The individual knows of a job that pays \$5 per hour for a certain 8-hour day. What wage must be offered for a construction job where hours of work are random with a mean of 8 hours and a standard deviation of 6 hours to get the individual to accept this more "risky" job?

Hint: This problem makes use of the statistical identity

$$E(x^2) = \text{Var } x + E(x)^2,$$

where E means "expected value."

16.4

A family with two adult members seeks to maximize a utility function of the form

$$U(c, h_1, h_2),$$

where c is family consumption and h_1 and h_2 are hours of leisure of each family member. Choices are constrained by

$$c = w_1(24 - h_1) + w_2(24 - h_2) + n,$$

where w_1 and w_2 are the wages of each family member and n is nonlabor income.

a. Without attempting a mathematical presentation, use the notions of substitution and income effects to discuss the likely signs of the cross-substitution effects $\partial h_1 / \partial w_2$ and $\partial h_2 / \partial w_1$.

b. Suppose that one family member (say, individual 1) can work in the home, thereby converting leisure hours into consumption according to the function

$$c_1 = f(h_1),$$

where $f' > 0, f'' < 0$. How might this additional option affect the optimal division of work among family members?

16.5

A welfare program for low-income people offers a family a basic grant of \$6,000 per year. This grant is reduced by \$.75 for each \$1 of other income the family has.

a. How much in welfare benefits does the family receive if it has no other income? If the head of the family earns \$2,000 per year? How about \$4,000 per year?

b. At what level of earnings does the welfare grant become zero?

c. Assume the head of this family can earn \$4 per hour and that the family has no other income. What is the annual budget constraint for this family if it does not participate in the welfare program? That is, how are consumption (c) and hours of leisure (h) related?

d. What is the budget constraint if the family opts to participate in the welfare program? (Remember, the welfare grant can only be positive.)

e. Graph your results from parts (c) and (d).

f. Suppose the government changes the rules of the welfare program to permit families to keep 50 percent of what they earn. How would this change your answer to parts (d) and (e)?

g. Using your results from part (f), can you predict whether the head of this family will work more or less under the new rules described in part (f)?

16.6

Suppose demand for labor is given by

$$l = -50w + 450$$

and supply is given by

$$l = 100w,$$

where l represents the number of people employed and w is the real wage rate per hour.

a. What will be the equilibrium levels for w and l in this market?

b. Suppose the government wishes to raise the equilibrium wage to $4 per hour by offering a subsidy to employers for each person hired. How much will this subsidy have to be? What will the new equilibrium level of employment be? How much total subsidy will be paid?

c. Suppose instead that the government declared a minimum wage of $4 per hour. How much labor would be demanded at this price? How much unemployment would there be?

d. Graph your results.

16.7

Carl the clothier owns a large garment factory on an isolated island. Carl's factory is the only source of employment for most of the islanders, and thus Carl acts as a monopsonist. The supply curve for garment workers is given by

$$l = 80w,$$

where l is the number of workers hired and w is their hourly wage. Assume also that Carl's labor demand (marginal revenue product) curve is given by

$$l = 400 - 40MRP_l.$$

a. How many workers will Carl hire to maximize his profits, and what wage will he pay?

b. Assume now that the government implements a minimum wage law covering all garment workers. How many workers will Carl now hire, and how much unemployment will there be if the minimum wage is set at $4 per hour?

c. Graph your results.

d. How does a minimum wage imposed under monopsony differ in results as compared with a minimum wage imposed under perfect competition (assuming the minimum wage is above the market determined wage)?

16.8

The Ajax Coal Company is the only hirer of labor in its area. It can hire any number of female workers or male workers it wishes. The supply curve for women is given by

$$l_f = 100w_f$$

and for men by

$$l_m = 9w_m^2,$$

where w_f and w_m are the hourly wage rates paid to female and male workers, respectively. Assume that Ajax sells its coal in perfectly competitive market at $5 per ton and that each worker hired (both men and women) can mine 2 tons per hour. If the firm wishes to maximize profits, how many female and male workers should be hired, and what will the wage rates for these two groups be? How much will Ajax earn in profits per hour on its mine machinery? How will that result compare to one in which Ajax was constrained (say, by market forces) to pay all workers the same wage based on the value of their marginal products?

16.9

Universal Fur is located in Clyde, Baffin Island, and sells high-quality fur bow ties throughout the world at a price of $5 each. The production function for fur bow ties (q) is given by

$$q = 240x - 2x^2,$$

where x is the quantity of pelts used each week. Pelts are supplied only by Dan's Trading Post, which obtains them by hiring Eskimo trappers at a rate of $10 per day. Dan's weekly production function for pelts is given by

$$x = \sqrt{l},$$

where l represents the number of days of Eskimo time used each week.

a. For a quasi-competitive case in which both Universal Fur and Dan's Trading Post act as price takers for pelts, what will be the equilibrium price (p_x) and how many pelts will be traded?

b. Suppose Dan acts as a monopolist, while Universal Fur continues to be a price taker. What equilibrium will emerge in the pelt market?

c. Suppose Universal Fur acts as a monopsonist, but Dan acts as a price taker. What will the equilibrium be?

d. Graph your results, and discuss the type of equilibrium that is likely to emerge in the bilateral monopoly bargaining between Universal Fur and Dan.

16.10

Following in the spirit of the labor market game described in Example 16.5, suppose the firm's total revenue function is given by

$$R = 10l - l^2$$

and the union's utility is simply a function of the total wage bill

$$U(w, l) = wl.$$

a. What is the Nash equilibrium wage contract in the two-stage game described in Example 16.5?

b. Show that the alternative wage contract $w' = l' = 4$ is Pareto superior to the contract identified in part (a).

c. Under what conditions would the contract described in part (b) be sustainable as a subgame perfect equilibrium?

SUGGESTIONS FOR FURTHER READING

Ashenfelter, O. C., and D. Card. *Handbook of Labor Economics*, vol. 3. Amsterdam: North Holland, 1999.
Contains a variety of high level essays on many labor market topics. Survey articles on labor supply and demand in volumes 1 and 2 (1986) are also highly recommended.

Becker, G. "A Theory of the Allocation of Time." *Economic Journal* (September 1965): 493–517.
One of the most influential papers in microeconomics. Becker's observations on both labor supply and consumption decisions were revolutionary.

Binger, B. R., and E. Hoffman. *Microeconomics with Calculus,* 2nd ed. Reading, MA: Addison-Wesley, 1998.
Chapter 17 has a thorough discussion of the labor supply model, including some applications to household labor supply.

Hamermesh, D. S. *Labor Demand.* Princeton: Princeton University Press, 1993.
The author offers a complete coverage of both theoretical and empirical issues. The book also has nice coverage of dynamic issues in labor demand theory.

Silberberg, E., and W. Suen. *The Structure of Economics: A Mathematical Analysis,* 3rd Ed. Boston: Irwin/McGraw-Hill, 2001.
Provides a nice discussion of the dual approach to labor supply theory.

Chapter 17

CAPITAL MARKETS

In this chapter we provide an introduction to the theory of capital. In many ways that theory resembles our previous analysis of input pricing in general—the principles of profit-maximizing input choice do not change. But capital theory adds an important time dimension to economic decision making; our goal here is to explore that extra dimension. We begin with a broad characterization of the capital accumulation process and the notion of the rate of return. Then we turn to more specific models of economic behavior over time.

Capital and the rate of return

When we speak of the capital stock of an economy, we mean the sum total of machines, buildings, and other reproducible resources in existence at some point in time. These assets represent some part of an economy's past output that was not consumed, but was instead set aside to be used for production in the future. All societies, from the most primitive to the most complex, engage in capital accumulation. Hunters in a primitive society taking time off from hunting to make arrows, individuals in a modern society using part of their incomes to buy houses, or governments taxing citizens in order to purchase dams and post office buildings are all engaging in essentially the same sort of activity: some portion of current output is being set aside for use in producing output in future periods. Present "sacrifice" for future gain is the essential aspect of capital accumulation.

Rate of return

The process of capital accumulation is pictured schematically in Figure 17.1. In both panels of the figure, society is initially consuming level c_0 and has been doing so for some time. At time t_1 a decision is made to withhold some output (amount s) from current consumption for one period. Starting in period t_2 this withheld consumption is in some way put to use producing future consumption. An important concept connected with this process is the *rate of return*, which is earned on that consumption that is put aside. In panel (a), for example, all of the withheld consumption is used to produce additional output only in period t_2. Consumption is increased by amount x in period t_2 and then returns to the long-run level c_0.

FIGURE 17.1   **Two Views of Capital Accumulation**

In (a), society withdraws some current consumption *(s)* to gorge itself (with *x* extra consumption) in the next period. The one-period rate of return would be measured by $x/s - 1$. The society in (b) takes a more long-term view and uses *s* to increase its consumption perpetually by *y*. The perpetual rate of return would be given by y/s.

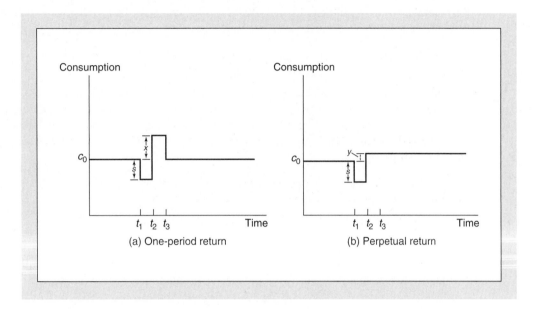

(a) One-period return   (b) Perpetual return

Society has saved in one year in order to splurge in the next year. The (one-period) rate of return from this activity would be defined as follows:

DEFINITION

Single period rate of return. The *single period rate of return* (r_1) on an investment is the extra consumption provided in period 2 as a fraction of the consumption forgone in period 1. That is,

$$r_1 = \frac{x - s}{s} = \frac{x}{s} - 1. \qquad (17.1)$$

If $x > s$ (if more consumption comes out of this process than went into it), we would say that the one-period rate of return to capital accumulation is positive. For example, if withholding 100 units from current consumption permitted society to consume an extra 110 units next year, the one-period rate of return would be

$$\frac{110}{100} - 1 = 0.10$$

or 10 percent.

In panel (b) of Figure 17.1, society takes a more long-term view in its capital accumulation. Again, an amount *s* is set aside at time t_1. Now, however, this set-aside consumption is used to raise the consumption level for all periods in the future. If the permanent level of consumption is raised to $c_0 + y$, we define the perpetual rate of return as follows:

DEFINITION

> **Perpetual rate of return.** The *perpetual rate of return* (r_∞) is the permanent increment to future consumption expressed as a fraction of the initial consumption forgone. That is,

$$r_\infty = \frac{y}{s}.$$ (17.2)

If capital accumulation succeeds in raising c_0 permanently, r_∞ will be positive. For example, suppose that society set aside 100 units of output in period t_1 to be devoted to capital accumulation. If this capital would permit output to be raised by 10 units for every period in the future (starting at time period t_2) the perpetual rate of return would be 10 percent.

When economists speak of the rate of return to capital accumulation, they have in mind something between these two extremes. Somewhat loosely we shall speak of the rate of return as being a measure of the terms at which consumption today may be turned into consumption tomorrow (this will be made more explicit soon). A natural question to ask is how the economy's rate of return is determined. Again, the equilibrium arises from the supply and demand for present and future goods. In the next section we present a simple two-period model in which this supply-demand interaction is demonstrated.

Determination of the rate of return

In this section we will describe how operation of supply and demand in the market for "future" goods establishes an equilibrium rate of return. We begin by analyzing the connection between the rate of return and the "price" of future goods. Then we show how individuals and firms are likely to react to this price. Finally, these actions are brought together (as we have done for the analysis of other markets) to demonstrate the determination of an equilibrium price of future goods and to examine some of the characteristics of that solution.

Rate of return and price of future goods

For most of our analysis in this chapter, we will assume there are only two periods to be considered—the current period (to be denoted by the subscript 0) and the next period (denoted by the subscript 1). We will use r to denote the (one-period) rate of return between these two periods. Hence, as defined in the previous section,

$$r = \frac{\Delta c_1}{\Delta c_0} - 1,$$ (17.3)

where we use the Δ notation to refer to the change in consumption in the two periods. Rewriting Equation 17.3 yields

$$\frac{\Delta c_1}{\Delta c_0} = 1 + r$$ (17.4)

or

$$\frac{\Delta c_0}{\Delta c_1} = \frac{1}{1 + r}.$$ (17.5)

The term on the left of Equation 17.5 records how much c_0 must be forgone if c_1 is to be increased by one unit; that is, the expression represents the relative "price" of one unit of c_1 in terms of c_0. So we have defined the price of future goods.[1]

DEFINITION

Price of future goods. The relative *price of future goods* (p_1) is the quantity of present goods that must be forgone to increase future consumption by one unit. That is,

$$p_1 = \frac{\Delta c_0}{\Delta c_1} = \frac{1}{1 + r}.$$

(17.6)

We now proceed to develop a demand-supply analysis of the determination of p_1. By so doing we also will have developed a theory of the determination of r, the rate of return in this simple model.

Demand for future goods

The theory of the demand for future goods is one further application of the utility-maximization model developed in Part 2 of this book. Here the individual's utility depends on present and future consumption [that is, utility = $U(c_0, c_1)$], and he or she must decide how much current wealth (W) to allocate to these two goods.[2] Wealth not spent on current consumption can be invested at the rate of return r to obtain consumption next period. As before, p_1 reflects the present cost of future consumption, and the individual's budget constraint is given by

$$W = c_0 + p_1 c_1.$$

(17.7)

This constraint is illustrated in Figure 17.2. If the individual chooses to spend all of his or her wealth on c_0, total current consumption will be W with no consumption occurring in period 2. Alternatively, if $c_0 = 0$, c_1 will be given by $W/p_1 = W(1 + r)$. That is, if all wealth is invested at the rate of return r, current wealth will grow to $W(1 + r)$ in period 2.[3]

Utility maximization

Imposition of the individual's indifference curve map for c_0 and c_1 onto the budget constraint in Figure 17.2 illustrates utility maximization. Here utility is maximized at the point c_0^*, c_1^*. The individual consumes c_0^* currently and chooses to save $W - c_0^*$ to consume next period. This future consumption can be found from the budget constraint as

$$p_1 c_1^* = W - c_0^*$$

(17.8)

or

$$c_1^* = \frac{(W - c_0^*)}{p_1}$$

(17.9)

$$= (W - c_0^*)(1 + r).$$

(17.10)

In words, wealth that is not currently consumed ($W - c_0^*$) is invested at the rate of return, r, and will grow to yield c_1^* in the next period.

---

[1]This price is identical to the discount factor introduced in connection with repeated games in Chapter 15.

[2]For an analysis of the case where the individual has income in both periods, see Problem 17.1.

[3]This observation yields an alternative interpretation of the intertemporal budget constraint, which can be written in terms of the rate of return as

$$W = c_0 + \frac{c_1}{1 + r}.$$

This illustrates the fact that it is the "present value" of c_1 that enters into the individual's current budget constraint. The concept of present value is discussed in more detail later in this chapter.

FIGURE 17.2   Individual's Intertemporal Utility Maximization

When faced with the intertemporal budget constraint $W = c_0 + p_1 c_1$, the individual will maximize utility by choosing to consume c_0^* currently and c_1^* in the next period. A fall in p_1 (an increase in the rate of return, r) will cause c_1 to rise, but the effect on c_0 is indeterminate because substitution and income effects operate in opposite directions (assuming that both c_0 and c_1 are normal goods).

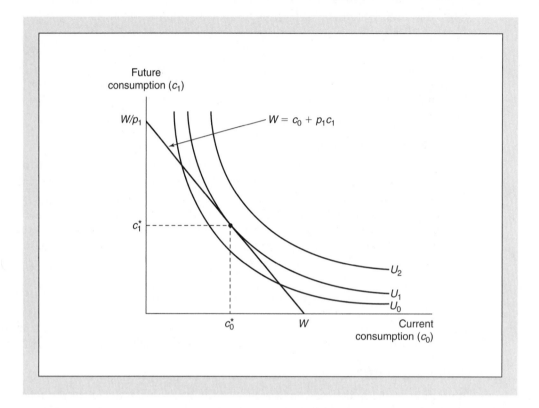

EXAMPLE 17.1

Intertemporal Impatience

Individuals' utility-maximizing choices over time will obviously depend on how they feel about the relative merits of consuming currently or waiting to consume in the future. One way of reflecting the possibility that people exhibit some impatience in their choices is to assume that the utility from future consumption is implicity discounted in the individual's mind. For example, we might assume that the utility function for consumption, $U(c)$, is the same in both periods (with $U' > 0$, $U'' < 0$), but that period 1's utility is discounted in the individual's mind by a "rate of time preference" of $1/(1 + \delta)$ (where $\delta > 0$). If the intertemporal utility function is also separable (for more discussion of this concept, see the Extensions to Chapter 6), we can write

$$U(c_0, c_1) = U(c_0) + \frac{1}{1 + \delta} U(c_1). \qquad (17.11)$$

Maximization of this function subject to the intertemporal budget constraint

$$W = c_0 + \frac{c_1}{1 + r} \qquad (17.12)$$

yields the following Lagrangian expression:

$$\mathcal{L} = U(c_0, c_1) + \lambda \left[W - c_0 - \frac{c_1}{1 + r} \right], \qquad (17.13)$$

and the first-order conditions for a maximum are

$$\frac{\partial \mathcal{L}}{\partial c_0} = U'(c_0) - \lambda = 0$$

$$\frac{\partial \mathcal{L}}{\partial c_1} = \frac{1}{1 + \delta} U'(c_1) - \frac{\lambda}{1 + r} = 0 \qquad (17.14)$$

$$\frac{\partial \mathcal{L}}{\partial \lambda} = W - c_0 - \frac{c_1}{1 + r} = 0.$$

Dividing the first and second of these and rearranging terms gives[4]

$$U'(c_0) = \frac{1 + r}{1 + \delta} U'(c_1). \qquad (17.15)$$

Because the utility function for consumption is assumed to be the same in two periods, we can conclude that $c_0 = c_1$ if $r = \delta$, that $c_0 > c_1$ if $\delta > r$ [to obtain $U'(c_0) < U'(c_1)$ requires $c_0 > c_1$], and that $c_0 < c_1$ for $r > \delta$. Whether this individual's consumption increases or decreases from period 0 to period 1 will therefore depend on exactly how impatient he or she is. Although a consumer may have a preference for present goods ($\delta > 0$), he or she may still consume more in the future than in the present if the rate of return received on savings is high enough.

Query: If two individuals are equally impatient but face different rates of return, which will exhibit the greatest increase of c_1 over c_0?

Effects of changes in *r*

A comparative statics analysis of the equilibrium illustrated in Figure 17.2 is straightforward. If p_1 falls (that is, if r rises), both income and substitution effects will cause more c_1 to be demanded, except in the unlikely event that c_1 is an inferior good. Hence, the demand curve for c_1 will be downward sloping. An increase in r effectively lowers the price of c_1, and consumption of that good thereby increases. This demand curve is labeled D in Figure 17.3.

Before leaving our discussion of individuals' intertemporal decisions, we should point out that our analysis does not permit an unambiguous statement to be made about the sign of $\partial c_0 / \partial p_1$. In Figure 17.2 substitution and income effects work in opposite directions, and no definite prediction is possible. A fall in p_1 will cause the individual to substitute c_1 for c_0 in his or her consumption plans. But the fall in p_1 raises the real value of wealth, and the income effect causes both c_0 and c_1 to increase. Phrased somewhat differently, the model illustrated in Figure 17.2 does not permit a definite prediction about how changes in the rate of return affect current-period wealth accumulation (saving). A

[4]Equation 17.15 is sometimes called the "Euler equation" for intertemporal utility maximization. Once a specific utility function is defined, the equation shows how consumption changes over time.

FIGURE 17.3   **Determination of the Equilibrium Price of Future Goods**

The point p_1^*, c_1^* represents an equilibrium in the market for future goods. The equilibrium price of future goods determines the rate of return via Equation 17.16.

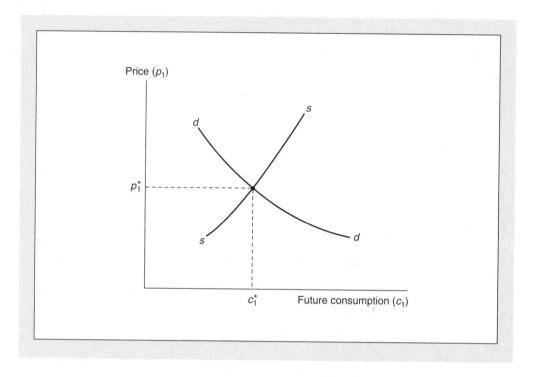

higher r produces substitution effects that favor more saving and income effects that favor less. Ultimately, therefore, the direction of the effect is an empirical question.

Supply of future goods

In one sense the analysis of the supply of future goods is quite simple. We can argue that an increase in the relative price of future goods (p_1) will induce firms to produce more of them, because the yield from doing so is now greater. This reaction is reflected in the positively sloped supply curve S in Figure 17.3. It might be expected that, as in our previous perfectly competitive analysis, this supply curve reflects the increasing marginal costs (or diminishing returns) firms experience when attempting to turn present goods into future ones through capital accumulation.

Unfortunately, delving deeper into the nature of capital accumulation runs into complications that have occupied economists for hundreds of years.[5] Basically, all of these derive from problems in developing a tractable model of the capital accumulation process. For our model of individual behavior this problem did not arise, because we could assume that the "market" quoted a rate of return to individuals so they could adapt their behavior to it. We shall also follow this route when describing firms' investment decisions later in this chapter. But to develop an adequate model of capital accumulation by firms, we must describe precisely how c_0 is "turned into" c_1, and to do so would take us too far afield into the intricacies of capital theory. Instead, we will be content to draw the supply curve in

---

[5]For a discussion of some of this debate, see M. Blaug, *Economic Theory in Retrospect*, rev. ed. (Homewood, IL: Richard D. Irwin, 1978), Chapter 12.

Figure 17.3 with a positive slope on the presumption that such a shape is intuitively reasonable. Much of the subsequent analysis in this chapter may serve to convince you that this is indeed the case.

Equilibrium price of future goods

Equilibrium in the market shown in Figure 17.3 is at p_1^*, c_1^*. At that point individuals' supply and demand for future goods are in balance, and the required amount of current goods will be put into capital accumulation to produce c_1^* in the future.[6]

There are a number of reasons to expect that p_1 will be less than 1; that is, it will cost less than the sacrifice of one current good to "buy" one good in the future. As we showed in Example 17.1, it might be argued that individuals require some reward for waiting. Everyday adages ("a bird in the hand is worth two in the bush," "live for today") and more substantial realities (the uncertainty of the future and the finiteness of life) suggest that individuals are generally impatient in their consumption decisions. Hence, capital accumulation such as that shown in Figure 17.3 will take place only if the current sacrifice is in some way worthwhile.

There are also supply reasons for believing p_1 will be less than 1. All of these involve the idea that capital accumulation is "productive": Sacrificing one good today will yield more than one good in the future. Some simple examples of the productivity of capital investment are provided by such pastoral activities as the growing of trees or the aging of wine and cheese. Tree nursery owners and vineyard and dairy operators "abstain" from selling their wares in the belief that time will make them more valuable in the future. Although it is obvious that capital accumulation in a modern industrial society is more complex than growing trees (consider building a steel mill or an electric power system), economists believe the two processes have certain similarities. In both cases investing current goods makes the production process longer and more complex and therefore improves the overall productive power of other resources used in production.

The equilibrium rate of return

We can now define the relationship of the rate of return (r) to what we have called the price of future goods by the formula

$$p_1^* = \frac{1}{1 + r}. \tag{17.16}$$

Because we believe that p_1^* will be less than 1, the rate of return (r) will be positive. For example, if $p_1^* = .9$, r will equal approximately .11, and we would say that the rate of return to capital accumulation is "11 percent." By withholding one unit of current consumption, the consumption of future goods can be increased by 1.11. The rate of return and p_1 are equivalent ways of measuring the terms on which present goods can be turned into future goods.

Rate of return, real interest rates, and nominal interest rates

The concept of the rate of return we have been analyzing so far in this chapter is sometimes used synonymously with the related concept of the "real" interest rate. In this context, both are taken to refer to the real return that is available from capital accumulation. This concept must be differentiated from the nominal interest rate actually available in

---

[6]This is a much simplified form of an analysis originally presented by I. Fisher, *The Rate of Interest* (New York: Macmillan, 1907).

financial markets. Specifically, if overall prices are expected to increase by $\dot{p}_e$ between two periods (that is, a $\dot{p}_e$ of .10 would be a 10 percent inflation rate), we would expect the nominal interest rate (R) to be given by the equation

$$1 + R = (1 + r)(1 + \dot{p}_e), \tag{17.17}$$

because a would-be lender would expect to be compensated for both the opportunity cost of not investing in real capital (r) and for the general rise in prices $(\dot{p}_e)$. Expansion of Equation 17.17 yields

$$1 + R = 1 + r + \dot{p}_e + r\dot{p}_e, \tag{17.18}$$

and assuming $r \cdot \dot{p}_e$ is small, we have the simpler approximation

$$R = r + \dot{p}_e. \tag{17.19}$$

If the real rate of return is 4 percent (.04) and the expected rate of inflation is 10 percent (.10), the nominal interest rate would be approximately 14 percent (.14). The difference, therefore, between observed nominal interest rates and real interest rates may be substantial in inflationary environments.

The firm's demand for capital

Firms rent machines in accordance with the same principles of profit maximization we derived in Chapter 9. Specifically, in a perfectly competitive market the firm will choose to hire that number of machines for which the marginal revenue product is precisely equal to their market rental rate. In this section we first investigate the determinants of this market rental rate, and we assume that all machines are rented. Later in the section, because most firms buy machines and hold them until they deteriorate rather than rent them, we shall examine the particular problems raised by such ownership.

Determinants of market rental rates

Consider a firm in the business of renting machines to other firms. Suppose the firm owns a machine (say, a car or a backhoe) that has a current market price of p. How much will the firm charge its clients for the use of the machine? The owner of the machine faces two kinds of costs: depreciation on the machine and the *opportunity cost* of having its funds tied up in a machine rather than in an investment earning the current available rate of return. If it is assumed that depreciation costs per period are a constant percentage (d) of the machine's market price and that the real interest rate is given by r, the total costs to the machine owner for one period are given by

$$pd + pr = p(r + d). \tag{17.20}$$

If we assume the machine rental market is perfectly competitive, no long-run profits can be earned by renting machines. The workings of the market will ensure that the rental rate per period for the machine (v) is exactly equal to the costs of the machine owner. Hence we have the basic result that

$$v = p(r + d). \tag{17.21}$$

The competitive rental rate is the sum of forgone interest and depreciation costs the machine's owner must pay. For example, suppose the real interest rate is 5 percent (that is, 0.05) and the physical depreciation rate is 15 percent (0.15). Suppose also that the current market price of the machine is $10,000. Then, in this simple model, the machine would have an annual rental rate of $2,000 [= $10,000 × (0.05 + 0.15)] per year; $500 of this would represent the opportunity cost of the funds invested in the machine, and the remaining $1,500 would reflect the physical costs of deterioration.

Nondepreciating machines

In the hypothetical case of a machine that does not depreciate ($d = 0$), Equation 17.21 can be written as

$$\frac{v}{P} = r. \tag{17.22}$$

In equilibrium an infinitely long-lived (nondepreciating) machine is equivalent to a perpetual bond (see the Appendix to this chapter) and hence must "yield" the market rate of return. The rental rate as a percentage of the machine's price must be equal to r. If $v/p > r$, everyone would rush out to buy machines, because renting out machines would yield more than rates of return elsewhere. Similarly, if $v/p < r$, no one would be in the business of renting out machines, because more could be made on alternative investments.

Ownership of machines

Our analysis so far has assumed that firms rent all of the machines they use. Although such rental does take place in the real world (for example, many firms are in the business of leasing airplanes, trucks, freight cars, and computers to other firms), more commonly firms own the machines they use. A firm will buy a machine and use it in combination with the labor it hires to produce output. The ownership of machines makes the analysis of the demand for capital somewhat more complex than that of the demand for labor. However, by recognizing the important distinction between a *stock* and a *flow*, we can show that these two demands are quite similar.

A firm uses *capital services* to produce output. These services are a *flow* magnitude. It is the number of machine-hours that is relevant to the productive process (just as it is labor-hours), not the number of machines per se. Often, however, the assumption is made that the flow of capital services is proportional to the *stock* of machines (100 machines, if fully employed for 1 hour, can deliver 100 machine-hours of service); therefore, these two different concepts are often used synonymously. If during a period a firm desires a certain number of machine-hours, this is usually taken to mean that the firm desires a certain number of machines. The firm's demand for capital services is also a demand for capital.[7]

A profit-maximizing firm in perfect competition will choose its level of inputs so that the marginal revenue product from an extra unit of any input is equal to its cost. This result also holds for the demand for machine-hours. The cost of capital services is given by the rental rate (v) in Equation 17.21. This cost is borne by the firm whether it rents the machine in the open market or owns the machine itself. In the former case it is an explicit cost, whereas in the latter case the firm is essentially in two businesses: (1) producing output; and (2) owning machines and renting them to itself. In this second role the firms' decisions would be the same as any other machine rental firm because it incurs the same costs. The fact of ownership, to a first approximation, is irrelevant to the determination of cost. Hence our prior analysis of capital demand applies to the owners by case as well:

OPTIMIZATION PRINCIPLE

Demand for capital. A profit-maximizing firm facing a perfectly competitive rental market for capital will hire additional capital input up to the point at which its marginal revenue product (MRP_k) is equal to the market rental rate, v. Under perfect competition

---

[7]Firms' decisions on how intensively to use a given capital stock during a period can also be analyzed, often as part of the study of business cycles.

the rental rate will reflect both depreciation costs and opportunity costs of alternative investments. Thus, we have

$$MRP_k = v = p(r + d). \qquad (17.23)$$

Theory of investment

If a firm obeys the profit-maximizing rule of Equation 17.23 and finds that it desires more capital services than can be provided by its currently existing stock of machinery, it has two choices. First, it may hire the additional machines that it needs in the rental market. This would be formally identical to its decision to hire additional labor. Second, the firm can buy new machinery to meet its needs. This second alternative is the one most often chosen; we call the purchase of new equipment by the firm *investment*.

Investment demand is an important component of "aggregate demand" in macroeconomic theory. It is often assumed this demand for plant and equipment (that is, machines) is inversely related to the real rate of interest, or what we have called the "rate of return." Using the analysis we developed in this part of the text, we can demonstrate the links in this argument. A fall in the real interest rate (r) will, ceteris paribus, decrease the rental rate on capital (Equation 17.21). Because forgone interest represents an implicit cost for the owner of a machine, a fall in r in effect reduces the price (that is, the rental rate) of capital inputs. This fall in v implies that capital has become a relatively less expensive input; this will prompt firms to increase their capital usage.

Present discounted value approach to investment decisions

When a firm buys a machine, it is in effect buying a stream of net revenues in future periods. To decide whether to purchase the machine, the firm must compute the present discounted value of this stream.[8] Only by doing so will the firm have taken adequate account of the effects of forgone interest. This provides an alternative approach to explaining the investment decision.

Consider a firm in the process of deciding whether to buy a particular machine. The machine is expected to last n years and will give its owner a stream of monetary returns (that is, marginal revenue products) in each of the n years. Let the return in year i be represented by R_i. If r is the present real interest rate, and if this rate is expected to prevail for the next n years, the present discounted value (PDV) of the net revenue flow from the machine to its owner is given by

$$PDV = \frac{R_1}{1 + r} + \frac{R_2}{(1 + r)^2} + \cdots + \frac{R_n}{(1 + r)^n}. \qquad (17.24)$$

This present discounted value represents the total value of the stream of payments provided by the machine, once adequate account is taken of the fact that these payments occur in different years. If the PDV of this stream of payments exceeds the price (p) of the machine, the firm, and other similar firms, should make the purchase. Even when the effects of the interest payments the firm could have earned on its funds had it not purchased the machine are taken into account, the machine promises to return more than its prevailing price. On the other hand, if $p > PDV$, the firm would be better off to invest its funds in some alternative that promises a rate of return of r. When account is taken of forgone interest, the machine does not pay for itself. Thus, in a competitive market the only equilibrium that can prevail is that in which the price of a machine is equal to the present discounted value of the net revenues from the machine. Only in this situation will there be

---

[8]See the Appendix to this chapter for an extended discussion of present discounted value.

neither an excess demand for machines nor an excess supply of machines. Hence, market equilibrium requires that

$$p = PDV = \frac{R_1}{1+r} + \frac{R_2}{(1+r)^2} + \cdots + \frac{R_n}{(1+r)^n}. \qquad (17.25)$$

We shall now use this condition to show two situations in which the present discounted value criterion of investment yields the same equilibrium conditions described earlier in this chapter.

Simple case

Assume first that machines are infinitely long lived and the marginal revenue product (that is, R_i) is the same in every year. This uniform return also will equal the rental rate for machines (v), because that is what another firm would pay for the machine's use during any period. With these simplifying assumptions, we may write the present discounted value from machine ownership as

$$
\begin{aligned}
PDV &= \frac{v}{(1+r)} + \frac{v}{(1+r)^2} + \cdots + \frac{v}{(1+r)^n} + \cdots \\
&= v \cdot \left(\frac{1}{(1+r)} + \frac{1}{(1+r)^2} + \cdots + \frac{1}{(1+r)^n} + \cdots \right) \\
&= v \cdot \left(\frac{1}{1 - 1/(1+r)} - 1 \right) \\
&= v \cdot \left(\frac{1+r}{r} - 1 \right) \\
&= v \cdot \frac{1}{r}.
\end{aligned}
\qquad (17.26)
$$

But in equilibrium $p = PDV$, so

$$p = v \cdot \frac{1}{r} \qquad (17.27)$$

or

$$\frac{v}{p} = r, \qquad (17.28)$$

as was already shown in Equation 17.22. For this case the present discounted value criterion gives results identical to those outlined in the previous section.

General case

Equation 17.21 can also be derived for the more general case in which the rental rate on machines is not constant over time and in which there is some depreciation. This analysis is most easily carried out by using continuous time. Suppose that the rental rate for a *new* machine at any time s is given by $v(s)$. Assume also that the machine depreciates exponentially at the rate of d.[9] The net rental rate (and the marginal revenue product) of a

---

[9]In this view of depreciation, machines are assumed to "evaporate" at a fixed rate per unit of time. This model of decay is in many ways identical to the assumptions of radioactive decay made in physics. There are other possible forms that physical depreciation might take; this is only one that is mathematically tractable.

It is important to keep the concept of physical depreciation (depreciation that affects a machine's productivity) distinct from accounting depreciation. The latter concept is important only in that the method of accounting depreciation chosen may affect the rate of taxation on the profits from a machine. From an economic point of view, however, the cost of a machine is a sunk cost: Any choice on how to "write off" this cost is to some extent arbitrary.

machine therefore declines over time as the machine gets older. In year s the net rental rate on an *old* machine bought in a previous year (t) would be

$$v(s)e^{-d(s-t)}, \tag{17.29}$$

since $s - t$ is the number of years over which the machine has been decaying. For example, suppose that a machine is bought new in 2000. Its net rental rate in 2005 then would be the rental rate earned by new machines in 2005 $[v(2005)]$ discounted by the factor e^{-5d} to account for the amount of depreciation that has taken place over the five years of the machine's life.

If the firm is considering buying the machine when it is new in year t, it should discount all of these net rental amounts back to that date. The present value of the net rental in year s discounted back to year t is therefore (if r is the interest rate)

$$e^{-r(s-t)}v(s)e^{-d(s-t)} = e^{(r+d)t}v(s)e^{-(r+d)s}, \tag{17.30}$$

because, again, $(s - t)$ years elapse from when the machine is bought until the net rental is received. The present discounted value of a machine bought in year t is therefore the sum (integral) of these present values. This sum should be taken from year t (when the machine is bought) over all years into the future:

$$PDV(t) = \int_t^\infty e^{(r+d)t}v(s)e^{-(r+d)s}ds. \tag{17.31}$$

Using the fact that in equilibrium the price of the machine at year t $[p(t)]$ will be equal to this present value, we have the following fundamental equation:

$$p(t) = \int_t^\infty e^{(r+d)t}v(s)e^{-(r+d)s}ds. \tag{17.32}$$

This rather formidable equation is simply a more complex version of Equation 17.25 and can be used to derive Equation 17.21. First rewrite the equation as

$$p(t) = e^{(r+d)t}\int_t^\infty v(s)e^{-(r+d)s}ds. \tag{17.33}$$

Now differentiate with respect to t, using the rule for taking the derivative of a product:

$$\begin{aligned}
\frac{dp(t)}{dt} &= (r + d)e^{(r+d)t}\int_t^\infty v(s)e^{-(r+d)s}ds - e^{(r+d)t}v(t)e^{-(r+d)t} \\
&= (r + d)p(t) - v(t).
\end{aligned} \tag{17.34}$$

Hence

$$v(t) = (r + d)p(t) - \frac{dp(t)}{dt}. \tag{17.35}$$

This is precisely the result shown earlier in Equation 17.21, except the term $-dp(t)/dt$ has been added. The economic explanation for the presence of this added term is that it represents the capital gains that accrue to the owner of the machine. If the machine's price can be expected to rise, for example, the owner may accept somewhat less than $(r + d)p$ for its rental.[10] On the other hand, if the price of the machine is expected to fall $[dp(t)/dt < 0]$, the owner will require more in rent than is specified in Equation 17.21. If the price of the machine is expected to remain constant over time, $dp(t)/dt = 0$ and the equations are identical. This analysis shows there is a definite relationship among the price of a machine at any time, the stream of future profits the machine promises, and the current rental rate for the machine.

---

[10]For example, rental houses in suburbs with rapidly appreciating house prices will usually rent for less than the landlord's actual costs because the landlord also gains from price appreciation.

EXAMPLE 17.2

Cutting Down a Tree

As an example of the *PDV* criterion, consider the case of a forester who must decide when to cut down a growing tree. Suppose the value of the tree at any time, t, is given by $f(t)$ (where $f'(t) > 0$, $f''(t) < 0$), and that l dollars were invested initially as payments to workers who planted the tree. Assume also that the (continuous) market interest rate is given by r. When the tree is planted, the present discounted value of the tree owner's profits is given by

$$PDV(t) = e^{-rt}f(t) - l, \qquad (17.36)$$

which is simply the difference between (the present value of) revenues and present costs. The forester's decision, then, consists of choosing the harvest date, t, to maximize this value. As always, this value may be found by differentiation:

$$\frac{dPDV(t)}{dt} = e^{-rt}f'(t) - re^{-rt}f(t) = 0, \qquad (17.37)$$

or dividing both sides by e^{-rt}:

$$f'(t) - rf(t) = 0; \qquad (17.38)$$

therefore

$$r = \frac{f'(t)}{f(t)}. \qquad (17.39)$$

Two features of this optimal condition are worth noting. First, observe that the cost of the initial labor input drops out upon differentiation. This cost is (even in a literal sense) a "sunk" cost that is irrelevant to the profit-maximizing decision. Second, Equation 17.39 can be interpreted as saying the tree should be harvested when the rate of interest is equal to the proportional rate of growth of the tree. This result makes intuitive sense. If the tree is growing more rapidly than the prevailing interest rate, its owner should leave his or her funds invested in the tree, because the tree provides the best return available. On the other hand, if the tree is growing less rapidly than the prevailing interest rate, the tree should be cut, and the funds obtained from its sale should be invested elsewhere at the rate r.

Equation 17.39 is only a necessary condition for a maximum. By differentiating Equation 17.38 again it is easy to see that it is also required that, at the chosen value of t,

$$f''(t) - rf'(t) < 0, \qquad (17.40)$$

if the first-order conditions are to represent a true maximum. Because we assumed $f'(t) > 0$ (the tree is always growing) and $f''(t) < 0$ (the growth slows over time), it is clear that this condition holds.

A numerical illustration. Suppose trees grow according to the equation

$$f(t) = e^{.4\sqrt{t}}. \qquad (17.41)$$

This equation always exhibits a positive growth rate $[f'(t) > 0]$ and, because

$$\frac{f'(t)}{f(t)} = \frac{.2}{\sqrt{t}}, \qquad (17.42)$$

(*continued*)

EXAMPLE 17.2 CONTINUED

the tree's proportional growth rate diminishes over time. If the real interest rate were, say, .04, we can solve for the optimal harvesting age as

$$r = .04 = \frac{f'(t)}{f(t)} = \frac{.2}{\sqrt{t}} \tag{17.43}$$

or

$$\sqrt{t} = \frac{.2}{.04} = 5$$

so

$$t^* = 25. \tag{17.44}$$

Up to 25 years of age, the volume of wood in the tree is increasing at a rate in excess of 4 percent per year, so the optimal decision is to permit the tree to stand. But for $t > 25$, the annual growth rate falls below 4 percent, and the forester can find better investments—perhaps planting new trees.

A change in the interest rate. If the real interest rate rises to 5 percent, Equation 17.43 would become

$$r = .05 = \frac{.2}{\sqrt{t}}, \tag{17.45}$$

and the optimal harvest age would be

$$t^* = \left(\frac{.2}{.05}\right)^2 = 16. \tag{17.46}$$

The higher real interest rate discourages investment in trees by prompting the forester to choose an earlier harvest date.[11]

Query: Suppose all prices (including those of trees) were rising at 10 percent per year. How would this change the optimal harvesting results in this problem?

Optimal resource allocation over time

The theory of capital is concerned primarily with the allocation of resources over time. Firms and individuals are led to set aside some portion of current production as capital accumulation in order to produce more in future periods. Many economic problems are of this general type; economic agents must make decisions about additions to or reductions in the level of some stock, and those decisions will affect both current and future well-being. In this section we shall examine how such decisions might be made in an optimal (that is, utility-maximizing) way.

---

[11]For further tree-related economics, see Problems 17.4 and 17.5.

The mathematical model of optimal control

Two variables are of primary interest for the problem of allocating resources over time: the stock being allocated (k) and a "control" variable (c) being used to effect increases or decreases in k. For our present discussion it is helpful to think of k as the capital stock, with c representing either the savings rate or total net investment, but many other interpretations arise in economics. Because these variables obviously will take on different values in different periods, they should be denoted as functions of time [$k(t)$ and $c(t)$]. For most of our development, however, it will be convenient not to record this functional dependence on time explicitly.

Choices of k and c will yield benefits over time to the economic agents involved. Those benefits at any point of time will be denoted by $U(k, c, t)$. The agents' goal is to maximize

$$\int_0^T U(k, c, t)dt, \tag{17.47}$$

where T denotes the time period over which decisions are to be made.

There are two types of constraints in control-theory problems. The first shows the rules by which k changes over time:

$$\frac{dk}{dt} = f(k, c, t). \tag{17.48}$$

Here the notation indicates that changes in k will depend on the level of that variable itself, on the control decisions made (c), and (possibly) on the particular point in time being observed. To avoid cumbersome notation, we adopt the convention of denoting the time derivative of any variable, x, by $\dot{x}$. Hence, the constraint given in Equation 17.48 will be written as

$$\frac{dk}{dt} = \dot{k} = f(k, c, t). \tag{17.49}$$

A second type of constraint in this maximization problem concerns initial and terminal conditions specified for the stock k. At the start of the problem, k will exist as a piece of historical data that cannot be altered, and at the conclusion of the planning period, some other type of requirement may be placed on k (for example, that k be zero). We shall write these end-point constraints as

$$k(0) = k_0$$
$$k(T) = k_T, \tag{17.50}$$

where the particular value of the constraints k_0 and k_T will depend on the nature of the problem being analyzed.

Maximum principle: an intuitive approach

The dynamic optimization problem we have described requires that we find an optimum time path for the variables k and c. That is a more difficult problem than other maximization problems discussed in this book, for which we required discovery of only a single optimal point rather than an entire time path of points. One strategy for finding a solution is to convert the dynamic problem into a "single-period" problem and then show how the solution to that simplified problem for any arbitrary point in time solves the dynamic problem as well.

To convert the dynamic problem to a single-period problem, we start by recognizing that any current decision about how the stock of k should be changed will affect both current and future well-being. An optimal choice that uses c to effect current changes in k

should balance the current costs of changing k against the future benefits of changing k and vice versa. To aid in this balancing process, we introduce a Lagrangian-type multiplier, $\lambda(t)$, which can be interpreted as the marginal change in future benefits brought about by a one-unit change in k. Therefore, $\lambda(t)$ is a measure of the (marginal) value of the stock k at the current time t. That variable (as in our other maximization problems) permits a solution that balances benefits and costs of current decisions.

Having converted the dynamic problem to a single-period one, it remains to reformulate the solution in a dynamic context. That reformulation consists of showing how $\lambda(t)$ must change over time so as to (1) keep changes in k occurring in an optimal way and (2) ensure that the end point conditions on k (Equation 17.50) are satisfied. Such a final solution will then provide a time path of values for c and k that maximizes the integral given in Equation 17.47. As an additional feature, the optimal solution will also provide a time path for the multiplier λ that will show how the marginal evaluation of k (that is, its price) changes over time.

A mathematical development

To proceed formally in the manner sketched in the previous section, we introduce the multiplier $\lambda(t)$ as a measure of the marginal value of the stock k at any instant. The total value of the stock is given by $\lambda(t)k$, and the rate of change in this value (that is, the value of gains or losses being experienced in the capital stock) is given by

$$\frac{d\lambda(t)k}{dt} = \lambda \frac{dk}{dt} + k \frac{d\lambda}{dt} = \lambda \dot{k} + k \dot{\lambda}, \qquad (17.51)$$

Hence the total net value of utility at any time (including any effect that current changes in $\dot{k}$ may have—this is what permits this single-period problem to reflect many periods) is given by

$$H = U(k, c, t) + \lambda \dot{k} + k \dot{\lambda}, \qquad (17.52)$$

where we have labeled this expression "H" to indicate its similarity to the "Hamiltonian" function encountered in formal dynamic optimization theory.[12] The function H is in some ways similar to the Lagrangian expression we have used repeatedly to solve maximization problems elsewhere in this book.

The first-order condition for choosing c to maximize H is

$$\frac{\partial H}{\partial c} = \frac{\partial U(k, c, t)}{dc} + \lambda \frac{\partial \dot{k}}{\partial c} = 0, \qquad (17.53)$$

because λ and k (as opposed to $\dot{k}$) are not dependent on the current value of c. Rewriting this first optimal condition yields

$$\frac{\partial U}{\partial c} = -\lambda \frac{\partial \dot{k}}{\partial c}. \qquad (17.54)$$

In words, for c to be optimally chosen it must be the case that the marginal increase in U from increasing c is exactly balanced by any effect such an increase has on decreasing the change in the stock of k (where such changes are evaluated at the margin by λ).

Having chosen c to maximize our augmented single-period measure of utility, we now focus on how the marginal valuation of k (that is, λ) should change over time. We can do that by asking what level of k would maximize H. Of course, in actuality k is not a choice variable at any instant—its value is determined by past history. But by "pretending" that k

---

[12] The usual Hamiltonian omits the final term in Equation 17.52. See the References at the end of this chapter.

is at its optimal value, we can infer that what the behavior of λ must be. Differentiation of H with respect to k yields

$$\frac{\partial H}{\partial k} = \frac{\partial U}{\partial k} + \lambda \frac{\partial \dot{k}}{\partial k} + \dot{\lambda} = 0 \tag{17.55}$$

as a first-order condition for a maximum. Rearranging terms gives

$$-\dot{\lambda} = \frac{\partial U}{\partial k} + \lambda \frac{\partial \dot{k}}{\partial k}. \tag{17.56}$$

This expression can be interpreted as saying that any decline in the marginal valuation of k must equal the net productivity of k in either increasing U or increasing $\dot{k}$ The value of k should be changing in a way opposite to that in which k itself impacts the sum of present and future benefits.

Bringing together the two optimal conditions, we have

$$\frac{\partial H}{\partial c} = \frac{\partial U}{\partial c} + \lambda \frac{\partial \dot{k}}{\partial c} = 0$$

$$\frac{\partial H}{\partial k} = \frac{\partial U}{\partial k} + \lambda \frac{\partial \dot{k}}{\partial k} + \dot{\lambda} = 0. \tag{17.57}$$

These show how c and λ should evolve over time so as to keep k on its optimal path.[13] Once the system of equations is started in motion, the entire time path of the relevant variables is determined. To provide a complete solution, we also need to make sure that the path of k is "feasible" in that it obeys the end-point conditions of Equation 17.50. This can usually be accomplished by adjusting the initial values for c and λ to some appropriate levels. The following example shows how this might be done.

 EXAMPLE 17.3

Exhaustible Resources

Concern with rising energy prices during the 1970s caused economists to reexamine theories of the optimal use of natural resource stocks. Because that question necessarily involves examination of the optimal time pattern for the depletion of a fixed stock of some resource (for example, oil, coal, or iron ore), it can be examined using the control theory tools we have developed.[14]

Suppose the (inverse) demand function for the resource in question is given by

$$p = p(c), \tag{17.58}$$

where p is the market price and c is the total quantity consumed during a period. For any output level c, the total utility from consumption is given by

$$U(c) = \int_0^c p(x)dx. \tag{17.59}$$

(continued)

---

[13]These are only first-order conditions for a maximum. We do not discuss second-order conditions here.
[14]The model developed here can be readily generalized to the case of renewable resources such as timber or fish.

If the rate of time preference is given by r, the optimal pattern of resource usage will be the one that maximizes

$$\int_0^T e^{-rt} U(c) dt. \tag{17.60}$$

The constraints in this problem are again of two types. First, because the stock of the resource is fixed, that stock is reduced each period by the level of consumption:

$$\dot{k} = -c. \tag{17.61}$$

In addition to this rule for changes in k, the stock of resources must also obey the endpoint constraints

$$k(0) = k_0$$

and

$$k(T) = k_T. \tag{17.62}$$

Usually, the initial stock, k_0, will represent the quantity of current "known reserves" of the resource, whereas the terminal stock, k_T, will be zero (assuming resources left in the ground have no value).

Setting up the Hamiltonian,

$$\begin{aligned} H &= e^{-rt}(U) + \lambda \dot{k} + \dot{\lambda} k \\ &= e^{-rt}(U) - \lambda c + \dot{\lambda} k, \end{aligned} \tag{17.63}$$

yields the following first-order conditions for a maximum:

$$\frac{\partial H}{\partial c} = e^{-rt} \frac{\partial U}{\partial c} - \lambda = 0 \tag{17.64}$$

$$\frac{\partial H}{\partial k} = \dot{\lambda} = 0. \tag{17.65}$$

The second equation illustrates the important result that in this problem the shadow price of the resource (λ) should stay constant over time. Because we are allocating a fixed stock, any path in which the resource had a higher shadow price in one period than in another could be improved upon (in terms of providing more utility) by reducing consumption in the period in which the shadow price is high and increasing consumption in the period in which it is low.[15]

Optimal price path. To interpret the first condition for a maximum, Equation 17.59 can be used to show that

$$\frac{\partial U}{\partial c} = p(c). \tag{17.66}$$

This condition is very similar to those from most of the utility-maximizing models in Part 2. Substituting this into Equation 17.64,

$$e^{-rt} p(c) = \lambda. \tag{17.67}$$

---

[15]One of the first authors to recognize this fundamental point was H. Hotelling, in his path-breaking article, "The Economics of Exhaustible Resources," *Journal of Political Economy 39* (April 1931): 137–75.

Because we know from our previous discussion that λ must be constant, this equation requires that the path for c be chosen so that market price rises at the rate r per period. That is precisely the sort of solution that would emerge in a competitive market. For any resource to provide an investment that is in equilibrium with other alternatives, its price must rise at the rate of interest. Any slower rate of price increase would prompt investors to put their funds into some alternative form of capital, whereas any faster rate would draw all available funds into investments in the resource. This result therefore suggests that, at least in this simple case, competitive markets will allocate natural resources efficiently over time.

A numerical illustration. End-period constraints in the natural resource case are usually handled by examining those that relate to final resource stocks. If the resource stock is to be fully depleted, it is required that the final-period price, $p(T)$, be such that demand becomes zero at that price. In most applications such a price can be found by setting it high enough so that substitutes for the resource in question totally dominate the market. For example, if it were known that solar power would totally replace petroleum energy sources in the year 2038 if oil in that year sold for more than $50 per barrel, then $50 would be the terminal price. Using that price together with Equation 17.67, the entire time path of prices can be computed [including the initial price $p(0)$]. With a real interest rate of 3 percent, equilibrium price in 2005 would be $50 \cdot e^{-.03(33)} = \$18.58$.

One final aspect of this resource-pricing problem should be noted. Throughout we have assumed that extraction costs are zero, but that should not be taken to imply that use of the resource itself is "costless." Current consumption of the resource implies lower future consumption, and this cost is no less real than actual production costs would be. Some authors refer to costs of this nature (those related to the fixed nature of the resource stock) as "user costs" or "scarcity costs." The costs are best measured by the shadow price of the resource stock, λ.

Query: Suppose extraction of oil is costly. How would this change the calculations made here?

SUMMARY

In this chapter we examined several aspects of the theory of capital, with particular emphasis on integrating that theory with the theory of the firm's demand for capital inputs. Some of the results were:

- Capital accumulation represents the sacrifice of present for future consumption. The rate of return measures the terms at which this trade can be accomplished.

- The rate of return is established through mechanisms much like those that establish any equilibrium price. The equilibrium rate of return will be positive, reflecting both individuals' relative preferences for present over future goods and the positive physical productivity of capital accumulation.

- The rate of return (or real interest rate) is an important element in the overall costs associated with capital ownership. It is an important determinant of the market rental rate on capital, v.

- Future returns on capital investments must be discounted at the prevailing real interest rate. Use of such present value notions provides an alternative way to approach studying the firm's investment decisions.

- Capital accumulation (and other dynamic problems) can be studied using the techniques of optimal control theory. Often such models will yield competitive-type results.

PROBLEMS

17.1

An individual has a fixed wealth (W) to allocate between consumption in two periods $(c_1$ and $c_2)$. The individual's utility function is given by

$$U(c_1, c_2),$$

and the budget constraint is

$$W = c_1 + \frac{c_2}{1 + r},$$

where r is the one-period interest rate.

a. Show that in order to maximize utility given this budget constraint, the individual should choose c_1 and c_2 so that the MRS (of c_1 for c_2) is equal to $1 + r$.

b. Show that $\partial c_2 / \partial r \geq 0$ but that the sign of $\partial c_1 / \partial r$ is ambiguous. If $\partial c_1 / \partial r$ is negative, what can you conclude about the price elasticity of demand for c_2?

c. How would your conclusions from part (b) be amended if the individual received income in each period $(y_1$ and $y_2)$ such that the budget constraint is given by

$$y_1 - c_1 + \frac{y_2 - c_2}{1 + r} = 0?$$

17.2

Assume an individual expects to work for 40 years and then retire with a life expectancy of an additional 20 years. Suppose also that the individual's earnings rise at a rate of 3 percent per year and that the interest rate is also 3 percent (the overall price level is constant in this problem). What (constant) fraction of income must the individual save in each working year to be able to finance a level of retirement income equal to 60 percent of earnings in the year just prior to retirement?

17.3

As scotch whiskey ages, its value increases. One dollar of scotch at year 0 is worth $V(t) = e^{2\sqrt{t} - 0.15t}$ dollars at time t. If the interest rate is 5 percent, after how many years should a person sell scotch in order to maximize the PDV of this sale?

17.4

As in Example 17.2, suppose trees are produced by applying one unit of labor at time 0. The value of the wood contained in a tree is given at any time (t) by $f(t)$. If the market wage rate is w and the real interest rate is r, what is the PDV of this production process and how should t be chosen to maximize this PDV?

a. If the optimal value of t is denoted by t^*, show that the no-pure-profit condition of perfect competition will necessitate that

$$w = e^{-rt} f(t^*).$$

Can you explain the meaning of this expression?

b. A tree sold before t^* will not be cut down immediately. Rather, it still will make sense for the new owner to let the tree continue to mature until t^*. Show that the price of a u-year-old tree will be we^{ru} and that this price will exceed the value of the wood in the tree $[f(u)]$ for every value of u except $u = t^*$ when these two values are equal.

c. Suppose a landowner has a "balanced" woodlot with one tree of "each" age from 0 to t^*. What is the value of this woodlot? (*Hint:* It is the sum of the values of all trees in the lot.)

d. If the value of the woodlot is V, show that the instantaneous interest on V (that is, $r \cdot V$) is equal to the "profits" earned at each instant by the landowner, where by profits we mean the difference between the revenue obtained from selling a fully matured tree $[f(t^*)]$ and the cost of planting a new one (w). This result shows there is no pure profit in borrowing to buy a woodlot, because one would have to pay in interest at each instant exactly what would be earned from cutting a fully matured tree.

17.5

The calculations in Problem 17.4 assume there is no difference between the decision on cutting a single tree and managing a woodlot. But managing a woodlot also involves replanting, which should be explicity modeled. To do so, assume a lot owner is considering planting a single tree at a cost w, harvesting the tree at t^*, planting another, and so forth forever. The discounted stream of profits from this activity is then

$$V = -w + e^{-rt}[f(t) - w] + e^{-r2t}[f(t) - w] \ldots$$
$$e^{-rnt}[f(t) - w] + \ldots$$

a. Show that the total value of this planned harvesting activity is given by

$$V = \frac{f(t) - w}{e^{rt} - 1} - w.$$

b. Find the value of t that maximizes V. Show that this value solves the equation

$$f'(t^*) = rf(t^*) + rV(t^*).$$

c. Interpret the results of part (b)—how do they reflect optimal usage of the "input" time? Why is the value of t^* specified in part (b) different from that in Example 17.2?

d. Suppose tree growth (measured in constant dollars) follows the logistic function

$$f(t) = 50/(1 + e^{10 - .1t}).$$

What is the maximum value of the timber available from this tree?

e. If tree growth is characterized by the equation given in part (d), what is the optimal rotation period if $r = .05$, $w = 0$? Does this period produce a "maximum sustainable" yield?

f. How would the optimal period change if r fell to .04?

(*Note:* The equation derived in part (b) is termed Faustmann's equation in forestry economics.]

17.6

This problem focuses on the interaction of the corporate profits tax with firms' investment decisions.

a. Suppose (contrary to fact) that profits were defined for tax purposes as what we have called pure economic profits. How would a tax on such profits affect investment decisions?

b. In fact, profits are defined for tax purposes as

$$\pi' = pq - wl - \textbf{depreciation,}$$

where depreciation is determined by governmental and industry guidelines that seek to allocate a machine's costs over its "useful" lifetime. If depreciation were equal to actual physical deterioration and if a firm were in long-run competitive equilibrium, how would a tax on π' affect the firm's choice of capital inputs?

c. Under the conditions of part (b), how would capital usage be affected by adoption of "accelerated depreciation" policies that specify depreciation rates in excess of physical deterioration early in a machine's life, but much lower depreciation rates as the machine ages?

d. Under the conditions of part (c), how might a decrease in the corporate profits tax affect capital usage?

17.7

A high-pressure life insurance salesman was heard to make the following argument: "At your age a \$100,000 whole life policy is a much better buy than a similar term policy. Under a whole life policy you'll have to pay \$2,000 per year for the first four years, but nothing more for the rest of your life. A term policy will cost you \$400 per year, essentially forever. If you live 35 years, you'll pay only \$8,000 for the whole life policy, but \$14,000 (= \$400 · 35) for the term policy. Surely, the whole life is a better deal."

Assuming the salesman's life expectancy assumption is correct, how would you evaluate this argument? Specifically, calculate the present discounted value of the premium costs of the two policies assuming the interest rate is 10 percent.

17.8

Suppose an individual has W dollars to allocate between consumption this period (c_0) and consumption next period (c_1) and that the interest rate is given by r.

a. Graph the individual's initial equilibrium and indicate the total value of current-period savings ($W - c_0$).

b. Suppose that after the individual makes his or her savings decision (by purchasing one-period bonds), the interest rate falls to r'. How will this alter the individual's budget constraint? Show the new utility-maximizing position. Discuss how the individual's improved position can be interpreted as resulting from a "capital gain" on his or her initial bond purchases.

c. Suppose the tax authorities wish to impose an "income" tax based on the value of capital gains. If all such gains are valued in terms of c_0 as they are "accrued," show how those gains should be measured. Call this value G_1.

d. Suppose instead that capital gains are measured as they are "realized"—that is, capital gains are defined to include only that portion of bonds that is cashed in to buy additional c_0. Show how these realized gains can be measured. Call this amount G_2.

e. Develop a measure of the true increase in utility that results from the fall in r, measured in terms of c_0. Call this "true" capital gain G_3. Show that $G_3 < G_2 < G_1$. What do you conclude about a tax policy that taxes only realized gains?

(*Note:* This problem is adapted from J. Whalley, "Capital Gains Taxation and Interest Rate Changes," *National Tax Journal* (March 1979]: 87–91.)

17.9

Example 17.3 assumed that oil was produced in a competitive market. Assuming the other conditions of the example, how would optimal resource use change if all oil were owned by a single monopoly firm?

17.10

Optimal control theory can be used to generalize the model of intertemporal consumption choice contained in Example 17.1. Consider the following simple life cycle model: An individual receives wages (w) each period and a return on his or her invested capital. Let k = capital, r = market interest rate at which the individual can borrow or lend. During each period, the individual chooses consumption (c) to maximize

$$\int_0^T U(c)e^{-pt}\,dt,$$

where ρ is the individual's rate of time preference. Given these assumptions, the intertemporal budget constraint for this problem is

$$\dot{k} = w + rk - c$$

with constraints on initial and final k of the form $k(0) = k(T) = 0$.

a. What are the necessary conditions for a maximum for this problem?

b. Under what conditions would optimal consumption rise over time? When would consumption fall over time?

c. Suppose $U(c) = \ln(c)$, what is the optimal pattern of consumption?

d. More generally, suppose

$$U(c) = \frac{c^\delta}{\delta} \quad \delta < 1.$$

What is the optimal time pattern for consumption? How does this compare to the special case in part (c)?

e. How does the optimal time pattern for consumption in this problem determine this individual's measured wealth at various points in the life cycle?

SUGGESTIONS FOR FURTHER READING

Blaug, M. *Economic Theory in Retrospect,* rev. ed., Chap. 12. Homewood, IL: Richard D. Irwin, 1978.
Good review of an Austrian capital theory and of attempts to conceptualize the capital accumulation process.

Dixit, A. K. *Optimization in Economic Theory,* 2nd ed. New York, Oxford University Press, 1990.
Extended treatment of optimal control theory in a fairly easy to follow format.

Dorfman, R. "An Economic Interpretation of Optimal Control Theory." *American Economic Review 59* (December 1969): 817–31.

Uses the approach of this chapter to examine optimal capital accumulation. Excellent intuitive introduction.

Hotelling, H. "The Economics of Exhaustible Resources." *Journal of Political Economy 39* (April 1931): 137–75.

Fundamental work on allocation of natural resources. Analyzes both competitive and monopoly cases.

Mas-Colell, A., M. D. Whinston, and J. R. Green. *Microeconomic Theory.* New York: Oxford University Press, 1995.

Chapter 20 offers extensive coverage of issues in defining equilibrium over time. The discussion of "over-lapping generations" models is especially useful.

Ramsey, F. P. "A Mathematical Theory of Saving." *Economic Journal 38* (December 1928): 542–59.

One of the first uses of the calculus of variations to solve economic problems.

Solow, R. M. *Capital Theory and the Rate of Return.* Amsterdam: North-Holland, 1964.

Lectures on the nature of capital. Very readable.

Sydsaeter, K., A. Strom, and P. Berck. *Economists' Mathematical Manual,* 3rd ed. Berlin: Springer-Verlag, 2000.

Chapter 27 provides a variety of formulas that are valuable for finance and growth theory.

Appendix to Chapter 17

THE MATHEMATICS OF COMPOUND INTEREST

The purpose of this appendix is to gather some simple results concerning the mathematics of compound interest. These results have applications in a wide variety of economic problems, ranging from macroeconomic policy to the optimal way to raise Christmas trees.

We assume there is a current prevailing market interest rate of i per period, say, one year. This interest rate is assumed to be both certain and constant over all future periods.[1] If \$1 is invested at this rate, i, and the interest is then compounded (that is, future interest is paid on post interest earned), at the end of one period \$1 will be

$$\$1 \times (1 + i),$$

at the end of two periods \$1 will be

$$\$1 \times (1 + i) \times (1 + i) = \$1 \times (1 + i)^2,$$

and at the end of n periods \$1 will be

$$\$1 \times (1 + i)^n.$$

Similarly, \$$N$ grows like

$$\$N \times (1 + i)^n$$

---

[1]The assumption of a constant i is obviously unrealistic. Because problems introduced by considering an interest rate that varies from period to period greatly complicate the notation without adding a commensurate degree of conceptual knowledge, such an analysis is not undertaken here. In many cases the generalization to a varying interest rate is merely a trivial application of the notion that any multiperiod interest rate can be regarded as resulting from compounding several single-period rates. If we let r_{ij} be the interest rate prevailing between periods i and j (where $i < j$), then,

$$1 + r_{ij} = (1 + r_{i,i+1}) + (1 + r_{i+1,i+2}) \ . \ . \ . \ (1 + r_{j-1,j}).$$

Present discounted value

The *present value* of $1 payable one period from now is

$$\frac{\$1}{(1 + i)}.$$

This is simply the amount an individual would be willing to pay now for the promise of $1 at the end of one period. Similarly, the present value of $1 payable n periods from now is

$$\frac{\$1}{(1 + i)^n},$$

and the present value of $N payable n periods from now is

$$\frac{\$N}{(1 + i)^n}.$$

The *present discounted value* of a stream of payments N_0, N_1, N_2, . . . , N_n (where the subscripts indicate the period in which the payment is to be made) is

$$PDV = N_0 + \frac{N_1}{(1 + i)} + \frac{N_2}{(1 + i)^2} + \cdots + \frac{N_n}{(1 + i)^n}. \qquad (17A.1)$$

PDV is the amount an individual would be willing to pay in return for a promise to receive the stream N_0, N_1, N_2, . . . , N_n. It represents the amount that would have to be invested now if one wished to duplicate the payment stream.

Annuities and perpetuities

An *annuity* is a promise to pay $N in each period for n periods, starting next period. The *PDV* of such a contract is

$$PDV = \frac{N}{(1 + i)} + \frac{N}{(1 + i)^2} + \cdots + \frac{N}{(1 + i)^n}. \qquad (17A.2)$$

Let $\delta = 1/(1 + i)$; then,

$$\begin{aligned} PDV &= N(\delta + \delta^2 + \cdots + \delta^n) \\ &= N\delta(1 + \delta + \delta^2 + \cdots + \delta^{n-1}) \\ &= N\delta\left(\frac{1 - \delta^n}{1 - \delta}\right). \end{aligned} \qquad (17A.3)$$

Notice that

$$\lim_{n \to \infty} \delta^n = 0.$$

Therefore, for an annuity of infinite duration,

$$PDV \text{ of infinite annuity} = \lim_{n \to \infty} PDV = N\delta\left(\frac{1}{1 - \delta}\right), \qquad (17A.4)$$

which, by the definition of δ,

$$= N\left(\frac{1}{1+i}\right)\left(\frac{1}{1-1/(1+i)}\right)$$

$$= N\left(\frac{1}{1+i}\right)\left(\frac{1+i}{i}\right) = \frac{N}{i}. \qquad (17A.5)$$

This case of an infinite-period annuity is sometimes called a *perpetuity* or a *consol*. The formula simply says that the amount that must be invested if one is to obtain $\$N$ per period forever is simply $\$N/i$, because this amount of money would earn $\$N$ in interest each period ($i \cdot \$N/i = \$N$).

The special case of a bond

An *n*-period *bond* is a promise to pay $\$N$ each period, starting next period, for *n* periods. It also promises to return the principal (face) value of the bond at the end of *n* periods. If the principal value of the bond is $\$P$ (usually $1,000 in the U.S. bond market), the present discounted value of such a promise is

$$PDV = \frac{N}{(1+i)} + \frac{N}{(1+i)^2} + \ldots + \frac{N}{(1+i)^n} + \frac{P}{(1+i)^n}. \qquad (17A.6)$$

Again, let $\delta = 1/(1+i)$; then,

$$PDV = N\delta + N\delta^2 + \cdots + (N+P)\delta^n. \qquad (17A.7)$$

Equation 17A.7 can be looked at in another way. Suppose we knew the price at which the bond is currently trading, say, B. Then we could ask what value of i gives the bond a *PDV* equal to B. To find this i we set

$$B = PDV = N\delta + N\delta^2 + \cdots + (N+P)\delta^n. \qquad (17A.8)$$

Because B, N, and P are known, we can solve this equation for δ and hence for i.[2] The i that solves the equation is called the *yield* on the bond and is the best measure of the return actually available from the bond. The yield of a bond represents the return available both from direct interest payments and from any price differential between the initial price (B) and the maturity price (P).

Notice that as i increases, *PDV* decreases. This is a precise way of formulating the well-known concept that bond prices (*PDV*'s) and interest rates (yields) are inversely correlated.

Continuous time

Thus far this approach has dealt with discrete time—the analysis has been divided into periods. Often it is more convenient to deal with continuous time. In such a case the interest on an investment is compounded "instantaneously" and growth over time is "smooth." This facilitates the analysis of maximization problems because exponential

---

[2]Because this equation is an *n*th-degree polynomial, there are in reality *n* solutions (roots). Only one of these solutions is the relevant one reported in bond tables or on calculators. The other solutions are either imaginary or unreasonable. In the present example there is only one real solution.

functions are more easily differentiated. Many financial intermediaries (for example, savings banks) have adopted (nearly) continuous interest formulas in recent years.

Suppose i is given as the (nominal) interest rate per year but half this nominal rate is compounded every six months. Then, at the end of one year, the investment of $1 would have grown to

$$\$1 \times \left(1 + \frac{i}{2}\right)^2. \tag{17A.9}$$

Notice that this is superior to investing for one year at the simple rate, i, because interest has been paid on interest; that is,

$$\left(1 + \frac{i}{2}\right)^2 > (1 + i). \tag{17A.10}$$

Consider the limit of this process—for the nominal rate of i per period, consider the amount that would be realized if i were in fact "compounded n times during the period"; let $n \rightarrow \infty$:

$$\lim_{n\to\infty}\left(1 + \frac{i}{n}\right)^n. \tag{17A.11}$$

This limit exists and is simply e^i where e is the base of natural logarithms (the value of e is approximately 2.72). It is important to note that $e^i > (1 + i)$—it is much better to have continuous compounding over the period than to have simple interest.

We can ask what continuous rate, r, yields the same amount at the end of one period as the simple rate i. We are looking for the value of r that solves the equation

$$e^r = (1 + i). \tag{17A.12}$$

Hence

$$r = \ln(1 + i). \tag{17A.13}$$

Using this formula it is a simple matter to translate from discrete interest rates into continuous ones. If i is measured as a decimal yearly rate, r is a yearly continuous rate. Table 17A.1 shows the effective annual interest rate (i) associated with selected interest rates (r) that are continuously compounded.[3] Tables similar to 17A.1 often appear in the windows of savings banks advertising the "true" yields on their accounts.

Continuous growth

One dollar invested at a continuous interest rate of r will become

$$V = \$1 \cdot e^{rT} \tag{17A.14}$$

after T years. This growth formula is a very convenient one to work with. For example, it is easy to show that the instantaneous relative rate of change in V is, as would be expected, simply given by r

$$\text{relative rate of change} = \frac{dV/dt}{V} = \frac{re^{rt}}{e^{rt}} = r. \tag{17A.15}$$

---

[3]To compute the figures in Table 17A.1 interest rates are used in decimal rather than percent form (that is, a 5 percent interest rate is recorded as 0.05 for use in Equation 17A.12).

| TABLE 17A.1 | Effective Annual Interest Rates for Selected Continuously Compounded Rates |

Continuously Compounded Rate	Effective Annual Rate
3.0%	3.05%
4.0	4.08
5.0	5.13
5.5	5.65
6.0	6.18
6.5	6.72
7.0	7.25
8.0	8.33
9.0	9.42
10.0	10.52

Continuous interest rates also are convenient for calculating present discounted values. Suppose we wished to calculate the *PDV* of $1 to be paid *T* years from now. This would be given by[4]

$$\frac{\$1}{e^{rT}} = \$1 \times e^{-rT}. \tag{17A.16}$$

The logic of this calculation is exactly the same as that used in the discrete time analysis of this appendix: future dollars are worth less than present ones.

Payment streams

One interesting application of continuous discounting occurs in calculating the *PDV* of $1 per period paid in small installments at each instant of time from today (time 0) until period *T*. Because there would be an infinite number of payments, the mathematical tool of integration must be used to compute this result:

$$PDV = \int_0^T e^{-rt} dt. \tag{17A.17}$$

What this statement says is that we are adding all the discounted dollars over the time period 0 to *T*.

The value of this definite integral is given by

$$PDV = \left. \frac{-e^{-rt}}{r} \right|_0^T$$

$$= \frac{-e^{-rT}}{r} + \frac{1}{r}. \tag{17A.18}$$

If we let *T* go to infinity, this value becomes

$$PDV = \frac{1}{r}, \tag{17A.19}$$

as was the case for the infinitely long annuity considered in the discrete case.

---

[4]In physics this formula occurs as an example of "radioactive decay." If one unit of a substance decays continuously at the rate δ, then after *T* periods, $e^{-\delta T}$ will remain. This amount never exactly reaches zero no matter how large *T* is. Depreciation can be treated the same way in capital theory.

Continuous discounting is particularly convenient for calculating the *PDV* of an arbitrary stream of payments over time. Suppose that $f(t)$ records the number of dollars to be paid during period t. Then the *PDV* of the payment at time t is

$$e^{-rt}f(t), \tag{17A.20}$$

and the *PDV* of the entire stream from the present time (year 0) until year T is given by

$$\int_0^T f(t)e^{-rt}\,dt. \tag{17A.21}$$

Often, economic agents may seek to maximize an expression such as that given in Equation 17A.21. Use of continuous time makes the analysis of such choices straightforward because standard calculus methods of maximization can be used.

Duration

The use of continuous time can also clarify a number of otherwise rather difficult financial concepts. For example, suppose we wished to know how long, on average, it takes for an individual to receive a payment from a given payment stream, $f(t)$. The present value of the stream is given by

$$V = \int_0^T f(t)e^{-rt}\,dt. \tag{17A.22}$$

Differentiation of this value by the discount factor, e^{-r} yields

$$\frac{\partial V}{\partial e^{-r}} = \int_0^T tf(t)e^{-r(t-1)}\,dt \tag{17A.23}$$

and the elasticity of this change is given by

$$e = \frac{\partial V}{\partial e^{-r}} \cdot \frac{e^{-r}}{V} = \frac{\int_0^T tf(t)e^{-rt}\,dt}{V}. \tag{17A.24}$$

Hence the elasticity of the present value of this payment stream with respect to the annual discount factor (which is similar to, say, the elasticity of bond prices with respect to changes in interest rates) is given by the ratio of the present value of a time-weighted stream of payments to an unweighted stream. Conceptually, therefore, this elasticity represents the average time an individual must wait to receive the typical payment. In the financial press this concept is termed the *duration* of the payment stream. This is an important measure of the volatility of the present value of such a stream with respect to interest rate changes.[5]

---

[5]As an example, a duration of 8 years would mean that the mean length of time that the individual must wait for the typical payment is 8 years. It also means that elasticity of the value of this stream with respect to the discount factor is 8.0. Because the elasticity of the discount factor itself with respect to the interest rate is simply $-r$, the elasticity of the value of the stream with respect to this interest rate is $-8r$. If $r = 0.05$, for example, the elasticity of the present value of the stream with respect to r is -0.40.

Part 7

UNCERTAINTY, INFORMATION, AND EXTERNALITIES

In this part we examine economic factors that may cause markets to fail to allocate resources properly. The part starts with Chapter 18 that contains a general discussion of the economic theory of behavior under uncertainty. The primary focus of the chapter is on explaining why people are usually risk averse and will therefore pay something to avoid uncertainty. In particular, they will buy insurance and, if it is fairly priced, this insurance will completely shield them against uncertainty.

Chapter 19 uses this material on behavior under uncertainty to show how imperfect information may undermine the workings of markets. Again, the focus here is mainly on insurance markets. We show how the asymmetry of information between buyers and sellers of insurance may cause problems both of moral hazard (where insured people take less than optimal precautions) and of adverse selection (where low-risk people may not be able to buy efficient amounts of insurance). The chapter also contains an analysis of the principal-agent problem in which more knowledgeable economic actors are asked to make decisions for those with less information.

Chapter 20 looks at allocational problems caused by externalities. When the actions of one person or firm affect someone else, prices do not carry adequate information to ensure efficient allocations and this chapter looks at two instances of this problem. First, it explores traditional "externalities" (such as air or water pollution). The chapter shows how such effects can be modeled and how the consequences of possible ameliorative actions can be evaluated. Chapter 20 also looks at externalities caused by "public goods"—that is, by goods that may be nonexclusive or nonrival. Again, the presentation is intended both to clarify the nature of the problems posed by such goods and to evaluate potential solutions.

Finally, Chapter 21 looks at some models of the political process. It shows that this process can in some ways be modeled in ways much like those used elsewhere in the book to model private markets. But the theory of political equilibrium is far less well developed than is the theory of market equilibrium, so the analysis here is at best suggestive.

Chapter 18

UNCERTAINTY AND RISK AVERSION

In this chapter we look at some of the basic elements that characterize individuals' motivation when making choices in uncertain situations. We show how the notion of utility can be generalized to apply to cases in which outcomes are subject to some degree of randomness. We then use this expanded concept of utility to examine the phenomenon of "risk aversion." That is, we show why individuals generally dislike uncertain situations and may be willing to pay something to reduce the uncertainty they face.

Probability and expected value

The study of individual behavior under uncertainty and the mathematical study of probability and statistics have a common historical origin in attempts to understand (and presumably to win) games of chance. The study of simple coin-flipping games, for example, has been unusually productive in mathematics and in illuminating certain characteristics of human behavior that the games exhibit. Two statistical concepts that originated in such games, and will be quite useful in the remainder of this chapter, are *probability* and *expected value*.

The *probability* of a repetitive[1] event happening is, roughly speaking, the relative frequency with which it will occur. For example, to say that the probability of obtaining a head on the flip of a fair coin is one-half means that one would expect that if a fair coin were flipped a large number of times, a head would appear in approximately one-half of the trials. Similarly, the probability of rolling a 2 on a single die is one-sixth. In approximately one out of every six rolls, a 2 will come up.

Suppose that a lottery offers n distinct prizes (some of which may be 0 or even negative), $x_1, x_2, \ldots, x_n$, and that the probabilities of winning these prizes are $\pi_1, \pi_2, \ldots, \pi_n$. If we assume that one and only one prize will be awarded to a player, it must be the case that

$$\sum_{i=1}^{n} \pi_i = 1. \tag{18.1}$$

---

[1]For repetitive events, probability is an objectively defined concept. Individuals may also attach *subjective* probabilities to nonrecurring events. For the most part, we do not distinguish between these two types of probability estimates. Additional statistical concepts are discussed in the Extensions to this chapter.

Equation (18.1) simply says that our list indicates all possible outcomes of the lottery and that one of these has to occur. To provide a measure of the average payoff in this lottery, we define expected value as follows:

Expected value. For a lottery (X) with prizes $x_1, x_2, \ldots, x_n$ and probabilities of winning $\pi_1, \pi_2, \ldots, \pi_n$, the *expected value* of the lottery is[2]

$$\text{expected value} = E(X) = \pi_1 x_1 + \pi_2 x_2 + \cdots + \pi_n x_n$$

$$= \sum_{i=1}^{n} \pi_i x_i. \tag{18.2}$$

The expected value of the lottery is a weighted sum of the prizes, where the weights are the respective probabilities. It is the size of the prize that the player will win on the average. For example, suppose that Jones and Smith agree to flip a coin once. If a head comes up, Jones will pay Smith \$1; if a tail, Smith will pay Jones \$1. From Smith's point of view, there are two prizes in this game: For a head, $x_1 = +\$1$; for a tail, $x_2 = -\$1$, where the minus sign indicates that Smith must pay. From Jones's point of view, the game is exactly the same except the signs of the outcomes are reversed. Thus, the expected value of the game is

$$\frac{1}{2} x_1 + \frac{1}{2} x_2 = \frac{1}{2}(\$1) + \frac{1}{2}(-\$1) = 0. \tag{18.3}$$

The game has an expected value of 0. If the game were to be played a large number of times, it is not likely that either player would come out very far ahead.

Now suppose that the prizes of the game were changed so that (again from Smith's point of view) $x_1 = \$10$, $x_2 = -\$1$. Smith will win \$10 if a head comes up but will lose only \$1 if a tail appears. The expected value of this game is

$$\frac{1}{2} x_1 + \frac{1}{2} x_2 = \frac{1}{2}(\$10) + \frac{1}{2}(-\$1) = \$5 - \$.50 = \$4.50. \tag{18.4}$$

If this game is played many times, Smith will certainly end up the big winner. In fact, Smith might be willing to pay Jones something for the privilege of playing the game. Games which have an expected value of 0, or those which cost their expected values (here, precisely \$4.50) for the right to play, are called (actuarially) *fair games*. A common observation is that, in many situations, people refuse to participate in actuarially fair games. This point is central to understanding developments in the theory of uncertainty and is taken up in the next section.

---

[2]If the situation being examined has continuous outcomes (for example, the change in the price of a stock measured very precisely), then we need to modify this definition a bit. If the probability that an outcome of such a random event (x) is in a small interval (dx) is given by $f(x)\, dx$, then Equation 18.1 can be modified as

$$\int_{-\infty}^{\infty} f(x)dx = 1.$$

In this case the expected value of x is given by

$$E(x) = \int_{-\infty}^{\infty} xf(x)dx.$$

In many situations (for example, when x has a normal distribution), manipulation of such expected values can be much simpler than for the discrete case. See the Extensions to this chapter for some illustrations.

Fair games and the expected utility hypothesis

People are generally unwilling to play fair games.[3] I may at times agree to flip a coin for small amounts of money, but if I were offered the chance to wager $1,000 on one coin flip, I would likely refuse. Similarly, people may sometimes pay a small amount of money to play an actuarially unfair game such as a state lottery, but they will avoid paying a great deal to play risky, but fair games.

St. Petersburg paradox

A convincing example is the "St. Petersburg paradox," which was first investigated rigorously by the mathematician Daniel Bernoulli in the eighteenth century.[4] In the St. Petersburg paradox the following game is proposed: A coin is flipped until a head appears. If a head first appears on the nth flip, the player is paid 2^n. This game has an infinite number of outcomes (a coin might be flipped from now until doomsday and never come up a head, although the likelihood of this is small), but the first few can easily be written down. If x_i represents the prize awarded when the first head appears on the ith trial, then

$$x_1 = \$2, \; x_2 = \$4, \; x_3 = \$8, \; \ldots , \; x_n = \$2^n. \tag{18.5}$$

The probability of getting a head for the first time on the ith trial is $(\frac{1}{2})^i$; it is the probability of getting $(i-1)$ tails and then a head. Hence the probabilities of the prizes given in Equation 18.5 are

$$\pi_1 = \frac{1}{2}, \pi_2 = \frac{1}{4}, \pi_3 = \frac{1}{8}, \cdots, \pi_n = \frac{1}{2^n}. \tag{18.6}$$

The expected value of the St. Petersburg paradox game is infinite:

$$\begin{aligned}
\text{expected value} &= \sum_{i=1}^{\infty} \pi_i x_i = \sum_{i=1}^{\infty} 2^i \frac{1}{2^i} \\
&= 1 + 1 + 1 + \cdots + 1 + \cdots = \infty.
\end{aligned} \tag{18.7}$$

Some introspection, however, should convince anyone that no player would pay very much (much less than infinity) to play this game. If I charged $1 billion to play the game, I would surely have no takers, despite the fact that $1 billion is still considerably less than the expected value of the game. This, then, is the paradox: Bernoulli's game is in some sense not worth its (infinite) expected dollar value.

Expected utility

Bernoulli's solution to this paradox was to argue that individuals do not care directly about the dollar prizes of a game; rather they respond to the utility these dollars provide. If we assume that the marginal utility of wealth declines as wealth increases, the St. Petersburg game may converge to a finite *expected utility* value that players would be willing to pay for the right to play. Bernoulli termed this expected utility value the *moral value* of the game because it represents how much the game is worth to the individual. Because utility may rise less rapidly than the dollar value of the prizes, it is possible that a game's moral value will fall short of its monetary expected value.

---

[3]The games discussed here are assumed to yield no utility in their play other than the prizes; hence, the observation that many individuals gamble at "unfair" odds is not necessarily a refutation of this statement. Rather, such individuals can reasonably be assumed to be deriving some utility from the circumstances associated with the play of the game. It is therefore possible to differentiate the consumption aspect of gambling from the pure risk aspect.

[4]The original Bernoulli paper has been reprinted as D. Bernoulli, "Exposition of a New Theory on the Measurement of Risk," *Econometrica 22* (January 1954): 23–36.

EXAMPLE 18.1

Bernoulli's Solution to the Paradox

Suppose, as did Bernoulli, that the utility of each prize in the St. Petersburg paradox is given by

$$U(x_i) = \ln (x_i). \qquad (18.8)$$

This natural logarithmic utility function exhibits diminishing marginal utility (that is, $U' > 0$, but $U'' < 0$), and the expected utility value of this game converges to a finite number:

$$\text{expected utility} = \sum_{i=1}^{\infty} \pi_i U(x)_i$$

$$= \sum_{i=1}^{\infty} \frac{1}{2^i} \ln(2^i). \qquad (18.9)$$

Some manipulation of this expression yields[5] the result that the expected utility value of this game is 1.39. An individual with this type of utility function might therefore be willing to invest resources that otherwise yield up to 1.39 units of utility (a certain wealth of about \$4 provides this utility) in purchasing the right to play this game. Assuming that the very large prizes promised by the St. Petersburg paradox encounter diminishing marginal utility therefore permitted Bernoulli to offer a solution to the paradox.

Query: Does Bernoulli's solution really "solve" the paradox? How would you redefine the prizes in this game so that the game would have an infinite expected utility value using the logarithmic utility function?

The von Neumann–Morgenstern theorem

In their book *The Theory of Games and Economic Behavior,* John von Neumann and Oscar Morgenstern developed mathematical models for examining the economic behavior of individuals under conditions of uncertainty.[6] To understand these interactions, it was necessary first to investigate the motives of the participants in such "games." Because the hypothesis that individuals make choices in uncertain situations based on expected utility seemed intuitively reasonable, the authors set out to show that this hypothesis could be derived from more basic axioms of "rationale" behavior. The axioms represent an attempt by the authors to generalize the foundations of the theory of individual choice to cover uncertain situations. Although most of these axioms seem eminently reasonable at first glance, many important questions about their tenability have been raised. We will not pursue these questions here, however.[7]

---

[5]Proof: Expected utility $= \displaystyle\sum_{i=1}^{\infty} \cdot 1/2^i \cdot \ln 2 = \ln 2 \sum_{i=1}^{\infty} i/2^i.$ But the value of this final infinite series can be shown to be 2.0. Hence, expected utility $= 2 \ln 2 = 1.39.$

[6]J. von Neumann and O. Morgenstern, *The Theory of Games and Economic Behavior* (Princeton, NJ: Princeton University Press, 1944). The axioms of rationality in uncertain situations are discussed in the appendix.

[7]For a discussion of some of the issues raised in the debate over the von Neumann–Morgenstern axioms, see Mark J. Machina, "Choice Under Uncertainty: Problems Solved and Unsolved," *Journal of Economic Perspectives* (Summer 1987): 121–54.

The von Neumann–Morgenstern utility index

To begin, suppose that there are n possible prizes that an individual might win by participating in a lottery. Let these prizes be denoted by $x_1, x_2, \ldots, x_n$ and assume that these have been arranged in order of ascending desirability. x_1 is therefore the least preferred prize for the individual, and x_n is the most preferred prize. Now assign arbitrary utility numbers to these two extreme prizes. For example, it is convenient to assign

$$U(x_1) = 0$$
$$U(x_n) = 1, \tag{18.10}$$

but any other pair of numbers would do equally well.[8] Using these two values of utility, the point of the von Neumann–Morgenstern theorem is to show that a reasonable way exists to assign specific utility numbers to the other prizes available. Suppose that we choose any other prize, say, x_i. Consider the following experiment. Ask the individual to state the probability, say, π_i, at which he or she would be indifferent between x_i with *certainty*, and a *gamble* offering prizes of x_n with probability π_i and x_1 with probability $(1 - \pi_i)$. It seems reasonable (although this is one of the problematic assumptions in the von Neumann–Morgenstern approach) that such a probability will exist: The individual will always be indifferent between a gamble and a sure thing, provided that a high enough probability of winning the best prize is offered. It also seems likely that π_i will be higher the more desirable x_i is; the better x_i is, the better the chance of winning x_n must be to get the individual to gamble. The probability π_i therefore represents how desirable the prize x_i is. In fact, the von Neumann–Morgenstern technique is to define the utility of x_i as the expected utility of the gamble that the individual considers equally desirable to x_i:

$$U(x_i) = \pi_i \cdot U(x_n) + (1 - \pi_i) \cdot U(x_1). \tag{18.11}$$

Because of our choice of scale in Equation 18.10 we have

$$U(x_i) = \pi_i \cdot 1 + (1 - \pi_i) \cdot 0 = \pi_i. \tag{18.12}$$

By judiciously choosing the utility numbers to be assigned to the best and worst prizes, we have been able to show that the utility number attached to any other prize is simply the probability of winning the top prizes in a gamble the individual regards as equivalent to the prize in question. This choice of utility numbers is arbitrary. Any other two numbers could have been used to construct this utility scale, but our initial choice (Equation 18.10) is a particularly convenient one.

Expected utility maximization

In line with the choice of scale and origin represented by Equation 18.10, suppose that probability π_i has been assigned to represent the utility of every prize x_i. Notice in particular that $\pi_1 = 0$, $\pi_n = 1$, and that the other utility values range between these extremes. Using these utility numbers, we can show that a "rational" individual will choose among gambles based on their expected "utilities" (that is, based on the expected value of these von Neumann–Morgenstern utility index numbers).

As an example, consider two gambles. One gamble offers x_2, with probability q, and x_3, with probability $(1 - q)$. The other offers x_5, with probability t, and x_6, with probability $(1 - t)$. We want to show that the individual will choose gamble 1 if and only if the expected utility of gamble 1 exceeds that of gamble 2. Now for the gambles:

$$\text{expected utility (1)} = q \cdot U(x_2) + (1 - q) \cdot U(x_3)$$
$$\text{expected utility (2)} = t \cdot U(x_5) + (1 - t) \cdot U(x_6). \tag{18.13}$$

---

[8]Technically, a von Neumann–Morgenstern utility index is unique only up to a choice of scale and origin—that is, only up to a "linear transformation." This requirement is more stringent than the requirement that a utility function be unique up to a monotonic transformation.

Substituting the utility index numbers (that is, π_2 is the "utility" of x_2, and so forth) gives

$$\text{expected utility (1)} = q \cdot \pi_2 + (1 - q) \cdot \pi_3$$
$$\text{expected utility (2)} = t \cdot \pi_5 + (1 - t) \cdot \pi_6. \tag{18.14}$$

We wish to show that the individual will prefer gamble 1 to gamble 2 if and only if

$$q \cdot \pi_2 + (1 - q) \cdot \pi_3 > t \cdot \pi_5 + (1 - t) \cdot \pi_6. \tag{18.15}$$

To show this, recall the definitions of the utility index. The individual is indifferent between x_2 and a gamble promising x_1 with probability $(1 - \pi_2)$ and x_n with probability π_2. We can use this fact to substitute gambles involving only x_1 and x_n for all utilities in Equation 18.14 (even though the individual is indifferent between these, the assumption that this substitution can be made is one of the most problematic of the von Neumann–Morgenstern axioms). After a bit of messy algebra, we can conclude that gamble 1 is equivalent to a gamble promising x_n with probability $q\pi_2 + (1 - q)\pi_3$, and gamble 2 is equivalent to a gamble promising x_n with probability $t\pi_5 + (1 - t)\pi_6$. The individual will presumably prefer the gamble with the higher probability of winning the best prize. Consequently, he or she will choose gamble 1 if and only if

$$q\pi_2 + (1 - q)\pi_3 > t\pi_5 + (1 - t)\pi_6. \tag{18.16}$$

But this is precisely what we wanted to show. Consequently, we have proved that an individual will choose the gamble that provides the highest level of expected (von Neumann–Morgenstern) utility. We now make considerable use of this result, which can be summarized as follows:

OPTIMIZATION PRINCIPLE

Expected utility maximization. If individuals obey the von Neumann–Morgenstern axioms of behavior in uncertain situations, they will act as if they choose the option that maximizes the expected value of their von Neumann–Morgenstern utility index.

Risk aversion

Two lotteries may have the same expected monetary value but may differ in their riskiness. For example, flipping a coin for \$1 and flipping a coin for \$1,000 are both fair games, and both have the same expected value (0). However, the latter is in some sense more "risky" than the former, and fewer people would participate in the game where the prize was winning or losing \$1,000. The purpose of this section is to discuss the meaning of the term "risky" and to explain the widespread aversion to risk.

The term *risk* refers to the variability of the outcomes of some uncertain activity.[9] If variability is low, the activity may be approximately a sure thing. With no more precise notion of variability than this, it is possible to show why individuals, when faced with a choice between two gambles with the same expected value, will usually choose the one with a smaller variability of return. Intuitively, the reason behind this is that we usually assume that the marginal utility from extra dollars of prize money (that is, wealth) declines as the prizes get larger. A flip of a coin for \$1,000 promises a relatively small gain of utility if you win but a large loss of utility if you lose. A bet of only \$1 is "inconsequential," and the gain in utility from a win approximately counterbalances the decline in utility from a loss.[10]

---

[9]Often the statistical concept of "variance" is used as a proxy for risk. See Example 18.3 and the Extensions to this chapter.

[10]An alternative, more general definition of risk aversion is that $E[U(W)] < U[E(W)]$ for any randomly distributed wealth, W. Diminishing marginal utility ensures this condition.

Risk aversion and fair bets

This argument is illustrated in Figure 18.1. Here W^* represents an individual's current wealth and $U(W)$ is a von Neumann–Morgenstern utility index that reflects how he or she feels about various levels of wealth. $U(W)$ is drawn as a concave function of W to reflect the assumption of a diminishing marginal utility. It is assumed that obtaining an extra dollar adds less to enjoyment as total wealth increases. Now suppose this person is offered two fair gambles: a 50–50 chance of winning or losing h or a 50–50 chance of winning or losing $2h$. The utility of present wealth is $U(W^*)$. The expected utility if he or she participates in gamble 1 is given by $U^h(W^*)$:

$$U^h(W^*) = \frac{1}{2}U(W^* + h) + \frac{1}{2}U(W^* - h), \qquad (18.17)$$

and the expected utility of gamble 2 is given by $U^{2h}(W^*)$:

$$U^{2h}(W^*) = \frac{1}{2}U(W^* + 2h) + \frac{1}{2}U(W^* - 2h). \qquad (18.18)$$

It is geometrically clear from the figure that[11]

$$U(W^*) > U^h(W^*) > U^{2h}(W^*). \qquad (18.19)$$

| **FIGURE 18.1** | **Utility of Wealth from Two Fair Bets of Differing Variability** |

If the utility-of-wealth function is concave (that is, exhibits a diminishing marginal utility of wealth), this person will refuse fair bets. A 50–50 bet of winning or losing h dollars, for example, yields less utility $[U^h(W^*)]$ than does refusing the bet. The reason for this is that winning h dollars means less to this individual than does losing h dollars.

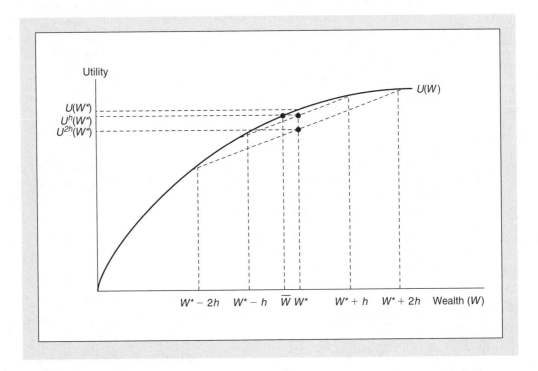

This person therefore will prefer current wealth to that wealth combined with a fair gamble and will prefer a small gamble to a large one. The reason for this is that winning a fair bet adds to enjoyment less than losing hurts. Although in this case, the prizes are equal, winning provides less extra utility than losing costs.

Risk aversion and insurance

As a matter of fact, this person might be willing to pay some amount to avoid participating in any gamble at all. Notice that a certain wealth of $\overline{W}$ provides the same utility as does participating in gamble 1. The individual will be willing to pay anything up to $W^* - \overline{W}$ to avoid participating in the gamble. This explains why people buy insurance. They are giving up a small, certain amount (the insurance premium) to avoid the risky outcome they are being insured against. The premium a person pays for automobile collision insurance, for example, provides a policy that agrees to repair his or her car should an accident occur. The widespread use of insurance would seem to imply that aversion to risk is quite prevalent. Hence, we introduce the following definition:

DEFINITION

Risk aversion. An individual who always refuses fair bets is said to be *risk averse*. If individuals exhibit a diminishing marginal utility of wealth, they will be risk averse. As a consequence, they will be willing to pay something to avoid taking fair bets.

 EXAMPLE 18.2

Willingness to Pay for Insurance

To illustrate the connection between risk aversion and insurance, consider a person with a current wealth of $100,000 who faces the prospect of a 25 percent chance of losing his or her $20,000 automobile through theft during the next year. Suppose also that this person's von Neumann–Morgenstern utility index is logarithmic—that is, $U(W) = \ln (W)$.

If this person faces next year without insurance, expected utility will be

$$\text{expected utility} = .75\, U(100{,}000) + .25\ U(80{,}000)$$
$$= .75 \ln 100{,}000 + .25 \ln 80{,}000 \quad (18.20)$$
$$= 11.45714.$$

In this situation a fair insurance premium would be $5,000 (25 percent of $20,000, assuming that the insurance company has only claim costs and that administrative costs are $0). Consequently, if this person completely insures the car, his or her wealth will be $95,000 regardless of whether the car is stolen. In this case, then,

$$\text{expected utility} = U(95{,}000)$$
$$= \ln (95{,}000) \quad (18.21)$$
$$= 11.46163.$$

This person is better off when he or she purchases fair insurance. Indeed, we can determine the maximum amount that might be paid for this insurance protection (x) by setting

$$\text{expected utility} = U(100{,}000 - x)$$
$$= \ln (100{,}000 - x) \quad (18.22)$$
$$= 11.45714.$$

Solving this equation for x yields

$$100{,}000 - x = e^{11.45714}. \quad (18.23)$$

Therefore, the maximum premium is

$$x = 5426. \tag{18.24}$$

This person would be willing to pay up to $426 in administrative costs to an insurance company (in addition to the $5,000 premium to cover the expected value of the loss). Even when these costs are paid, this person is as well off as he or she would be if forced to face the world uninsured.

Query: Suppose utility had been linear in wealth. Would this person be willing to pay anything more than the actuarially fair amount for insurance? How about the case where utility is a convex function of wealth?

Measuring risk aversion

In the study of economic choices in risky situations, it is sometimes convenient to have a quantitative measure of how averse to risk a person is. The most commonly used measure of risk aversion was initially developed by J. W. Pratt in the 1960s.[12] This risk aversion measure, $r(W)$, is defined as

$$r(W) = -\frac{U''(W)}{U'(W)}. \tag{18.25}$$

Because the distinguishing feature of risk-averse individuals is a diminishing marginal utility of wealth [$U''(W) < 0$], Pratt's measure is positive in such cases. The measure is invariant with respect to linear transformations of the utility function, and therefore not affected by which particular von Neumann–Morgenstern ordering is used.

Risk aversion and insurance premiums

Perhaps the most useful feature of the Pratt measure of risk aversion is that it is proportional to the amount an individual will pay for insurance against taking a fair bet. Suppose the winnings from such a fair bet are denoted by the random variable h (this variable may be either positive or negative). Because the bet is fair, $E(h) = 0$ (where E means "expected value"). Now let p be the size of the insurance premium that would make the individual exactly indifferent between taking the fair bet h and paying p with certainty to avoid the gamble:

$$E[U(W + h)] = U(W - p), \tag{18.26}$$

where W is the individual's current wealth. We now expand both sides of Equation 18.26 using Taylor's series.[13] Because p is a fixed amount, a linear approximation to the right-hand side of the equation will suffice:

$$U(W - p) = U(W) - pU'(W) + \text{higher order terms.} \tag{18.27}$$

---

[12]J. W. Pratt, "Risk Aversion in the Small and in the Large," *Econometrica* (January/April 1964): 122–36.

[13]Taylor's series provides a way of approximating any differentiable function around some point. If $f(x)$ has derivatives of all orders, it can be shown that

$$f(x + h) = f(x) + hf'(x) + (h^2/2)f''(x) + \text{higher order terms.}$$

The point-slope formula in algebra is a simple example of Taylor's series.

For the left-hand side, we need a quadratic approximation to allow for the variability in the gamble, h:

$$E[U(W + h)] = E[U(W) + hU'(W) + \frac{h^2}{2}U''(W)$$
(18.28)

$$+ \text{ higher order terms}]$$

$$= U(W) + E(h)U'(W) + \frac{E(h^2)}{2}U''(W)$$
(18.29)

$$+ \text{ higher order terms.}$$

Now, remembering $E(h) = 0$, dropping the higher order terms, and using the constant k to represent $E(h^2)/2$, we can equate Equations 18.27 and 18.29 as

$$U(W) - pU'(W) \cong U(W) + kU''(W)$$
(18.30)

or

$$p \cong -\frac{kU''(W)}{U'(W)} = kr(W).$$
(18.31)

That is, the amount that a risk-averse individual is willing to pay to avoid a fair bet is approximately proportional to Pratt's risk aversion measure.[14] Because insurance premiums paid are observable in the real world, these are often used to estimate individuals' risk aversion coefficients or to compare such coefficients among groups of individuals. It is therefore possible to use market information to learn quite a bit about attitudes toward risky situations.

Risk aversion and wealth

An important question is whether risk aversion increases or decreases for higher levels of wealth. Intuitively, one might think that the willingness to pay to avoid a given fair bet would decline as wealth increases, because diminishing marginal utility would make potential losses less serious for high-wealth individuals. This intuitive answer is not necessarily correct, however, because diminishing marginal utility also makes the gains from winning gambles less attractive. So the net result is indeterminate; it all depends on the precise shape of the utility function. Indeed, if utility is quadratic in wealth,

$$U(W) = a + bW + cW^2,$$
(18.32)

where $b > 0$, $c < 0$, Pratt's risk aversion measure is

$$r(W) = -\frac{U''(W)}{U'(W)} = \frac{-2c}{b + 2cW},$$
(18.33)

which, contrary to intuition, increases as wealth increases.

On the other hand, if utility is logarithmic in wealth,

$$U(W) = \ln(W) \qquad (W > 0),$$
(18.34)

we have

$$r(W) = -\frac{U''(W)}{U'(W)} = \frac{1}{W},$$
(18.35)

which does indeed decrease as wealth increases.

---

[14]In this case, the factor of proportionality is also proportional to the variance of h. For an illustration where this equation fits exactly, see Example 18.3.

The exponential utility function

$$U(W) = -e^{-AW} = -exp(-AW) \qquad (18.36)$$

(where A is a positive constant) exhibits constant absolute risk aversion over all ranges of wealth, because now

$$r(W) = -\frac{U''(W)}{U'(W)} = \frac{A^2 e^{-AW}}{Ae^{-AW}} = A. \qquad (18.37)$$

This feature of the exponential utility function can be used to provide some numerical estimates of the willingness to pay to avoid gambles, as the next example shows.

 EXAMPLE 18.3

Constant Risk Aversion

Suppose an individual whose initial wealth is W_0 and whose utility is given by the function exhibits constant absolute risk aversion is facing a 50–50 chance of winning or losing $1,000. How much ($f$) would he or she pay to avoid the risk? To find this value, we set the utility of $W_0 - f$ equal to the expected utility from the gamble:

$$-exp[-A(W_0 - f)] = -.5exp[-A(W_0 + 1,000)] \qquad (18.38)$$
$$- .5exp[-A(W_0 - 1,000)].$$

Because the factor $-exp(-AW_0)$ is contained in all of the terms in Equation 18.38, this may be divided out, thereby showing that (for the exponential utility function) the willingness to pay to avoid uncertainty is independent of initial wealth. The remaining terms

$$exp(Af) = .5exp(-1,000A) + .5exp(1,000A) \qquad (18.39)$$

can now be used to solve for f for various values of A. If $A = .0001$, $f = 49.9$—a person with this degree of risk aversion would pay about $50 to avoid a fair bet of $1,000. Alternatively, if $A = .0003$, this more risk-averse person would pay $f = 147.8$ to avoid the gamble. Because intuition suggests that these values are not unreasonable, values of the risk aversion parameter A in these ranges are sometimes used for empirical investigations.

A normally distributed risk. The constant risk aversion utility function can be combined with the assumption that a person faces a random threat to his or her wealth that follows a normal distribution (see the Extensions to this chapter for some statistical background on this concept) to arrive at a particularly simple result. Specifically, if a person's risky wealth follows a normal distribution with mean μ_W and variance σ_W^2, then the probability density function for wealth is given by $f(W) = (1/\sqrt{2\pi})e^{-z^2/2}$, where $z = [(W - \mu_W)/\sigma_W]$. If this person has a utility function for wealth given by $U(W) = -e^{-AW}$, then expected utility from his or her risky wealth is given by

$$E[U(W)] = \int_{-\infty}^{\infty} U(W)f(W)dW = \frac{1}{\sqrt{2\pi}}\int -e^{-AW}e^{-[(W-\mu_W)/\sigma]^2/2}dW. \qquad (18.40)$$

Perhaps surprisingly, this integration is not too difficult to accomplish, though it does take patience. Performing this integration and taking a variety of monotonic transformations of the resulting expression yields the final result that

$$E[U(W)] \cong \mu_W - \frac{A}{2} \cdot \sigma_W^2 \qquad (18.41)$$

(continued)

EXAMPLE 18.3 CONTINUED

Hence, expected utility is just a linear function of the two parameters of the wealth probability density function, and the individual's risk aversion parameter (A) determines the size of the negative effect of variability on expected utility. For example, suppose a person has invested his or her funds so that wealth has an expected return of \$100,000, but a standard deviation of return (σ_W) of \$10,000. With the Normal distribution, he or she might therefore expect wealth to decline below \$83,500 about 5 percent of the time and rise above \$116,500 a similar fraction of the time. With these parameters, expected utility is given by $E[U(W)] = 100,000 - \frac{A}{2}(10,000)^2$. If $A = .0001 = 10^{-4}$, expected utility is given by $100,000 - 0.5 \cdot 10^{-4} \cdot (10^4)^2 = 95,000$. Hence, this person receives the same utility from his or her risky wealth as would be obtained from a certain wealth of \$95,000. A more risk-averse person might have $A = .0003$ and in this case the "certainty equivalent" of his or her wealth would be \$85,000.

Query: Suppose this person had two ways to invest his or her wealth: Allocation 1: $\mu_W = 107,000$ $\sigma_W = 10,000$; and Allocation 2: $\mu_W = 102,000$ $\sigma_W = 2,000$. How would this person's attitude toward risk affect his or her choice between these allocations?[15]

Relative risk aversion

It seems unlikely that the willingness to pay to avoid a given gamble is independent of a person's wealth. A more appealing assumption may be that such willingness to pay is inversely proportional to wealth and that the expression

$$rr(W) = Wr(W) = -W\frac{U''(W)}{U'(W)} \tag{18.42}$$

might be approximately constant. Following the terminology proposed by J. W. Pratt,[16] the $rr(W)$ function defined in Equation 18.42 has come to be called *relative risk aversion*. The power utility function

$$U(W) = \frac{W^R}{R}\ (\text{for } R < 1, \neq 0) \tag{18.43}$$

and

$$U(W) = \ln W\ (\text{for } R = 0)$$

exhibits diminishing absolute risk aversion:

$$r(W) = -\frac{U''(W)}{U'(W)} = -\frac{(R-1)W^{R-2}}{W^{R-1}} = -\frac{(R-1)}{W} \tag{18.44}$$

but constant relative risk aversion:

$$rr(W) = Wr(W) = -(R-1) = 1 - R. \tag{18.45}$$

---

[15]This numerical example (very roughly) approximates historical data on real returns of stocks and bonds, respectively, though the calculations are illustrative only. For more details on portfolio allocation issues see the Extensions to this chapter and Problem 18.8 (together with the reference therein).
[16]Pratt, "Risk Aversion."

Empirical evidence[17] is generally consistent with values of R in the range of -3 to -1. Hence, individuals seem to be somewhat more risk averse than is implied by the logarithmic utility function, though in many applications that function provides a reasonable approximation. It is useful to note that the constant relative risk aversion utility function in Equation 18.43 has the same form as the general CES utility function we first described in Chapter 3. This provides some geometric intuition about the nature of risk aversion that we will explore later in this chapter. The function also has been used to explore the "risk premia" earned on some risky investments. We look briefly at this use in Problem 18.8.

EXAMPLE 18.4

Constant Relative Risk Aversion

An individual whose behavior is characterized by a constant relative risk aversion utility function will be concerned about proportional gains or loss of wealth. We can therefore ask what fraction of initial wealth (f) such a person would be willing to give up to avoid a fair gamble of, say, 10 percent of initial wealth. First, we assume $R = 0$ so the logarithmic utility function is appropriate. Setting the utility of this individual's certain remaining wealth equal to the expected utility of the 10 percent gamble yields

$$\ln[(1 - f)W_0] = .5 \ln(1.1 \ W_0) + .5 \ln(.9W_0). \quad (18.46)$$

Because each term contains $\ln W_0$, initial wealth can be eliminated from this expression:

$$\ln(1 - f) = .5[\ln(1.1) + \ln(.9)] = \ln(.99)^{.5}$$

so

$$(1 - f) = (.99)^{.5} = .995$$

and

$$f = .005. \quad (18.47)$$

Hence this person will sacrifice up to half of 1 percent of wealth to avoid the 10 percent gamble. A similar calculation can be used for the case $R = -2$ to yield

$$f = .015. \quad (18.48)$$

Hence this more risk-averse person would be willing to give up 1.5 percent of his or her initial wealth to avoid a 10 percent gamble.

Query: With the constant relative risk aversion function, how does this person's willingness to pay to avoid a given absolute gamble (say, of 1,000) depend on his or her initial wealth?

The state-preference approach to choice under uncertainty

Although our analysis thus far in this chapter has offered insights on a number of issues, it seems rather different from the approach we took in other chapters. The basic model of utility maximization subject to a budget constraint seems to have been lost. In order to make further progress in our examination of behavior under uncertainty, we will therefore

---

[17]Some authors write the utility function in Equation 18.43 as $U(W) = W^{1-a}/(1 - a)$ and seek to measure $a = 1 - R$, so a is positive.

develop some new techniques that will permit us to bring the discussion of such behavior back into the standard choice–theoretic framework.

States of the world and contingent commodities

We start by assuming that outcomes of any random event can be categorized into a number of *states of the world*. We cannot predict exactly what will happen, say, tomorrow, but we assume that it is possible to categorize all of the possible things that might happen into a fixed number of well-defined *states*. For example, we might make the very crude approximation of saying that the world will be in only one of two possible states tomorrow: It will be either "good times" or "bad times." One could make a much finer gradation of states of the world (involving even millions of possible states), but most of the essentials of the theory can be developed using only two states.

A conceptual idea that can be developed concurrently with the notation of states of the world is that of *contingent commodities*. These are goods delivered only if a particular state of the world occurs. "$1 in good times" is an example of a contingent commodity that promises the individual $1 in good times but nothing should tomorrow turn out to be bad times. It is even possible, by stretching one's intuitive ability somewhat, to conceive of being able to purchase this commodity—I might be able to buy from someone the promise of $1 if tomorrow turns out to be good times. Because tomorrow could be bad, this good will probably sell for less than $1. If someone were also willing to sell me the contingent commodity "$1 in bad times," then I could assure myself of having $1 tomorrow by buying the two contingent commodities "$1 in good times" and "$1 in bad times."

Utility analysis

Examining utility-maximizing choices among contingent commodities proceeds formally in much the same way we analyzed choices previously. The principal difference is that, after the fact, a person will have obtained only one contingent good (depending on whether it turns out to be good or bad times). Before the uncertainty is resolved, however, the individual has two contingent goods from which to choose and will probably buy some of each because he or she does not know which state will occur. We denote these two contingent goods by W_g (wealth in good times) and W_b (wealth in bad times). Assuming that utility is independent of which state occurs[18] and that this individual believes that good times will occur with probability π, the expected utility associated with these two contingent goods is

$$V(W_g, W_b) = \pi\, U(W_g) + (1 - \pi)\, U(W_b). \qquad (18.49)$$

This is the magnitude this individual seeks to maximize given his or her initial wealth, W.

Prices of contingent commodities

Assuming that this person can purchase a dollar of wealth in good times for p_g and a dollar of wealth in bad times for p_b, his or her budget constraint is

$$W = p_g W_g + p_b W_b. \qquad (18.50)$$

The price ratio p_g/p_b shows how this person can trade dollars of wealth in good times for dollars in bad times. If, for example, $p_g = .80$ and $p_b = .20$, the sacrifice of $1 of wealth in

---

[18]This assumption is untenable in circumstances where utility of wealth depends on the state of the world. For example, the utility provided by a given level of wealth may differ depending on whether an individual is "sick" or "healthy." We will not pursue such complications here, however. For more of our analysis, utility will be assumed to be concave in wealth: $U'(W) > 0$, $U''(W) < 0$.

good times would permit this person to buy contingent claims yielding \$4 of wealth should times turn out to be bad. Whether such a trade would improve utility will, of course, depend on the specifics of the situation. But looking at problems involving uncertainty as situations in which various contingent claims are traded is the key insight offered by the state-preference model.

Fair markets for contingent goods

If markets for contingent wealth claims are well developed and there is general agreement about the likelihood of good times (π), prices for these claims will be actuarially fair—that is, they will equal the underlying probabilities:

$$p_g = \pi$$
$$p_b = (1 - \pi), \tag{18.51}$$

Hence, the price ratio p_g/p_b will simply reflect the odds in favor of good times:

$$\frac{p_g}{p_b} = \frac{\pi}{1 - \pi}. \tag{18.52}$$

In our previous example, if $p_g = \pi = .8$ and $p_b = (1 - \pi) = .2$, then $\pi/(1 - \pi) = 4$. In this case the odds in favor of good times would be stated as "4-to-1." Fair markets for contingent claims (such as insurance markets) will also reflect these odds. An analogy is provided by the "odds" quoted in horse races. These odds are "fair" when they reflect the true probabilities that various horses will win.

Risk aversion

We are now in a position to show how risk aversion is manifested in the state-preference model. Specifically, we can show that, if contingent claims markets are fair, a utility-maximizing individual will opt for a situation in which $W_g = W_b$—that is, he or she will arrange matters so that the wealth ultimately obtained is the same no matter what state occurs.

As in previous chapters, maximization of utility subject to a budget constraint requires that this individual set the *MRS* of W_g for W_b equal to the ratio of these "goods" prices:

$$MRS = \frac{\partial V/\partial W_g}{\partial V/\partial W_b} = \frac{\pi U'(W_g)}{(1 - \pi)U'(W_b)} = \frac{p_g}{p_b}. \tag{18.53}$$

In view of the assumption that markets for contingent claims are fair (Equation 18.52), this first-order condition reduces to

$$\frac{U'(W_g)}{U'(W_b)} = 1$$

or[19]

$$W_g = W_b. \tag{18.54}$$

Hence this individual, faced with fair markets in contingent claims on wealth, will be risk averse, choosing to ensure that he or she has the same level of wealth regardless of which state occurs.

---

[19]Notice this step requires that utility be state independent and that $U'(W) > 0$.

| **FIGURE 18.2** | **Risk Aversions in the State-Preference Model** |

The line I represents the individual's budget constraint for contingent wealth claims: $W = p_g W_g + p_b W_b$. If the market for contingent claims is actuarially fair $[p_g/p_b = \pi/(1 - \pi)]$, utility maximization will occur on the certainty line where $W_g = W_b = W^*$. If prices are not actuarially fair, the budget constraint may resemble I' and utility maximization will occur at a point where $W_g > W_b$.

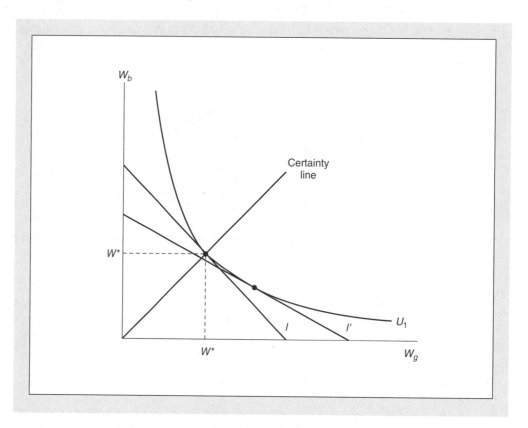

A graphic analysis

Figure 18.2 illustrates risk aversion with a graph. This individual's budget constraint (I) is shown to be tangent to the U_1 indifference curve where $W_g = W_b$—a point on the "certainty line" where wealth (W^*) is independent of which state of the world occurs. At W^* the slope of the indifference curve $[\pi/(1 - \pi)]$ is precisely equal to the price ratio p_g/p_b.

If the market for contingent wealth claims were not fair, utility maximization might not occur on the certainty line. Suppose, for example, that $\pi/(1 - \pi) = 4$ but that $p_g/p_b = 2$ because ensuring wealth in bad times proves quite costly. In this case the budget constraint would resemble line I' in Figure 18.2 and utility maximization would occur below the certainty line.[20] In this case this individual would gamble a bit by opting for $W_g > W_b$, because claims on W_b are relatively costly. Example 18.5 shows the usefulness of this approach in evaluating some of the alternatives that might be available.

[20]Because, as Equation 18.54 shows, the *MRS* on the certainty line is always $\pi/(1 - \pi)$, tangencies with a flatter slope than this must occur below the line.

EXAMPLE 18.5

Insurance in the State-Preference Model

We can illustrate the state-preference approach by recasting the auto insurance illustration from Example 18.2 as a problem involving the two contingent commodities "wealth with no theft" (W_g) and "wealth with a theft" (W_b). If, as before, we assume logarithmic utility and that the probability of a theft (that is, $1 - \pi$) is 0.25, we have

$$\text{expected utility} = .75\,U(W_g) + .25\,U(W_b) \qquad (18.55)$$
$$= .75 \ln W_g + .25 \ln W_b.$$

If the individual takes no action, utility is determined by the initial wealth endowment, $W_g^* = 100,000$, $W_b^* = 80,000$, and so,

$$\text{expected utility} = .75 \ln 100,000 + .25 \ln 80,000 \qquad (18.56)$$
$$= 11.45714.$$

To study trades away from these initial endowments, we write the budget constraint in terms of the prices of the contingent commodities, p_g and p_b:

$$p_g W_g^* + p_b W_b^* = p_g W_g + p_b W_b. \qquad (18.57)$$

Assuming these prices equal the probabilities of the two states ($p_g = .75$, $p_b = .25$) this constraint can be written

$$.75(100,000) + .25(80,000) = 95,000 = .75 W_g + .25 W_b; \qquad (18.58)$$

that is, the expected value of wealth is \$95,000, and this person can allocate this amount between W_g and W_b. Now maximization of utility with respect to this budget constraint yields $W_g = W_b = 95,000$. Consequently, the individual will move to the certainty line and receive an expected utility of

$$\text{expected utility} = \ln 95,000 = 11.46163, \qquad (18.59)$$

a clear improvement over doing nothing. To obtain this improvement, this person must be able to transfer \$5,000 of wealth in good times (no theft) into \$15,000 of extra wealth in bad times (theft). A fair insurance contract would allow this, because it would cost \$5,000 but return \$20,000 should a theft occur (but nothing should no theft occur). Notice here that the wealth changes promised by insurance— $dW_b/dW_g = 15,000/-5,000 = -3$—exactly equal the negative of the odds ratio $-\pi/(1 - \pi) = -.75/.25 = -3$.

A policy with a deductible provision. A number of other insurance contracts might be utility improving in this situation, though not all of them would lead to choices that lie on the certainty line. For example, a policy that cost \$5,200 and returned \$20,000 in case of a theft would permit this person to reach the certainty line with $W_g = W_b = 94,800$ and

$$\text{expected utility} = \ln 94,800 = 11.45953, \qquad (18.60)$$

which also exceeds the utility obtainable from the initial endowment. A policy that costs \$4,900 and requires the individual to incur the first \$1000 of a loss from theft would yield

$$W_g = 100,000 - 4,900 = 95,100 \qquad (18.61)$$
$$W_b = 80,000 - 4,900 + 19,000 = 94,100$$

(continued)

EXAMPLE 18.5 CONTINUED

and

$$\text{expected utility} = .75 \ln 95{,}100 + .25 \ln 94{,}100 \quad (18.62)$$
$$= 11.46004.$$

Although this policy does not permit this person to reach the certainty line, it is utility improving. Insurance need not be complete to offer the promise of higher utility.

Query: What is the maximum amount an individual would be willing to pay for an insurance policy under which he or she had to absorb the first $1,000 of loss?

Risk aversion and risk premiums

The state-preference model is also especially useful for analyzing the relationship between risk aversion and individuals' willingness to pay for risk. Consider two people, each of whom starts with a certain wealth, W^*. Each person seeks to maximize an expected utility function of the form

$$V(W_g, W_b) = \pi \frac{W_g^R}{R} + (1 - \pi) \frac{W_b^R}{R}. \quad (18.63)$$

Here the utility function exhibits constant relative risk aversion (see Example 18.4). Notice also that the function closely resembles the CES utility function we examined in Chapter 3 and elsewhere. The parameter R here determines both the degree of risk aversion and the degree of curvature of indifference curves implied by the function. A very risk-averse individual will have a large negative value for R and have sharply curved indifference curves, such as the curve U_1 shown in Figure 18.3. A person with more tolerance for risk will have a higher value of R and flatter indifference curves (such as U_2).[21]

Suppose now these individuals are faced with the prospect of losing h dollars of wealth in bad times. Such a risk would be acceptable to individual 2 if wealth in good times were to increase from W^* to W_2. For the very risk-averse individual 1, however, wealth would have to increase to W_1 to make the risk acceptable. The difference between W_1 and W_2 therefore indicates the effect of risk aversion on willingness to assume risk. Some of the problems in this chapter make use of this graphic device for showing the connection between preferences (as reflected by the utility function in Equation 18.63) and behavior in risky situations.

---

[21]Tangency of U_1 and U_2 at W^* is ensured, because the *MRS* along the certainty line is given by $\pi/(1 - \pi)$ regardless of the value of R.

FIGURE 18.3   **Risk Aversion and Risk Premiums**

Indifference curve U_1 represents the preferences of a very risk-averse person, whereas the person with preferences represented by U_2 is willing to assume more risk. When faced with the risk of losing h in bad times, person 2 will require compensation of $W_2 - W^*$ in good times, whereas person 1 will require a larger amount given by $W_1 - W^*$.

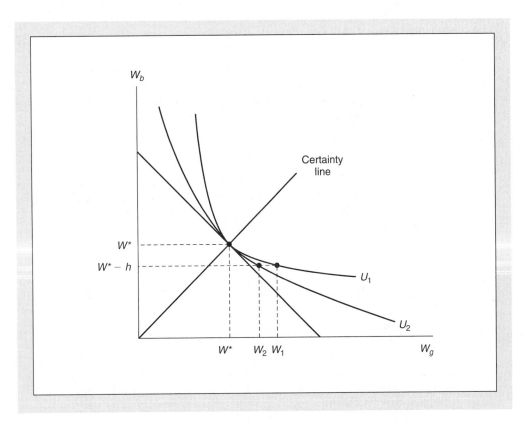

SUMMARY

In this chapter we provided some introductory material that will permit us to study individual behavior in uncertain situations. The basic results we surveyed included:

- In uncertain situations, individuals are concerned with the expected utility associated with various outcomes. If they obey the von Neumann–Morgenstern axioms, they will make choices in a way that maximizes expected utility.

- If we assume individuals exhibit a diminishing marginal utility of wealth, they will also be risk averse. That is, they will refuse to take bets that are actuarially fair.

- Risk-averse individuals will wish to insure themselves completely against uncertain events if insurance premiums are actuarially fair. They may be willing to pay actuarially unfair premiums to avoid taking risks.

- Decisions under uncertainty can be analyzed in a choice-theoretic framework by using the state-preference approach among contingent commodities. In such a model, if an individual's preferences are state independent and if prices are actuarially fair, individuals will prefer allocations along the "certainty line" that ensure the same level of wealth regardless of which state occurs.

PROBLEMS

18.1

George is seen to place an even-money $100,000 bet on the Bulls to win the NBA Championship. If George has a logarithmic utility-of-wealth function and if his current wealth is $1,000,000, what must he believe the minimum probability that the Bulls will win is?

18.2

Show that if an individual's utility-of-wealth function is convex (rather than concave, as shown in Figure 18.1), he or she will prefer fair gambles to income certainty and may even be willing to accept somewhat unfair gambles. Do you believe this sort of risk-taking behavior is common? What factors might tend to limit its occurrence?

18.3

An individual purchases a dozen eggs and must take them home. Although making trips home is costless, there is a 50 percent chance that all of the eggs carried on any one trip will be broken during the trip. The individual considers two strategies:

Strategy 1: Take all 12 eggs in one trip.

Strategy 2: Take two trips with 6 in each trip.

a. List the possible outcomes of each strategy and the probabilities of these outcomes. Show that on the average, 6 eggs will remain unbroken after the trip home under either strategy.

b. Develop a graph to show the utility obtainable under each strategy. Which strategy will be preferable?

c. Could utility be improved further by taking more than two trips? How would this possibility be affected if additional trips were costly?

18.4

Suppose there is a 50–50 chance that a risk-averse individual with a current wealth of $20,000 will contact a debilitating disease and suffer a loss of $10,000.

a. Calculate the cost of actuarially fair insurance in this situation and use a utility-of-wealth graph (such as shown in Figure 18.1) to show that the individual will prefer fair insurance against this loss to accepting the gamble uninsured.

b. Suppose two types of insurance policies were available:

(1) A fair policy covering the complete loss.

(2) A fair policy covering only half of any loss incurred.

Calculate the cost of the second type of policy and show that the individual will generally regard it as inferior to the first.

18.5

Ms. Fogg is planning an around-the-world trip on which she plans to spend $10,000. The utility from the trip is a function of how much she actually spends on it (Y), given by

$$U(Y) = \ln Y.$$

a. If there is a 25 percent probability that Ms. Fogg will lose $1,000 of her cash on the trip, what is the trip's expected utility?

b. Suppose that Ms. Fogg can buy insurance against losing the $1,000 (say, by purchasing traveler's checks) at an "actuarially fair" premium of $250. Show that her expected utility is higher if she purchases this insurance than if she faces the chance of losing the $1,000 without insurance.

c. What is the maximum amount that Ms. Fogg would be willing to pay to insure her $1,000?

18.6

In deciding to park in an illegal place, any individual knows that the probability of getting a ticket is p and that the fine for receiving the ticket is f. Suppose that all individuals are risk averse (that is, $U''(W) < 0$, where W is the individual's wealth).

Will a proportional increase in the probability of being caught or a proportional increase in the fine be a more effective deterrent to illegal parking? [*Hint:* Use the Taylor series approximation $U(W - f) = U(W) - fU'(W) + \dfrac{f^2}{2}U''(W).$]

18.7

A farmer believes there is a 50–50 chance that the next growing season will be abnormally rainy. His expected utility function has the form

$$\text{expected utility} = \frac{1}{2}\ln Y_{NR} + \frac{1}{2}\ln Y_R,$$

where Y_{NR} and Y_R represent the farmer's income in the states of "normal rain" and "rainy," respectively.

a. Suppose the farmer must choose between two crops that promise the following income prospects:

Crop	Y_{NR}	Y_R
Wheat	$28,000	$10,000
Corn	19,000	15,000

Which of the crops will he plant?

b. Suppose the farmer can plant half his field with each crop. Would he choose to do so? Explain your result.

c. What mix of wheat and corn would provide maximum expected utility to this farmer?

d. Would wheat crop insurance, available to farmers who grow only wheat, which costs $4,000 and pays off $8,000 in the event of a rainy growing season, cause this farmer to change what he plants?

18.8

For the constant relative risk aversion utility function (Equation 18.63) we showed that the degree of risk aversion is measured by $(1 - R)$. In Chapter 3 we showed that the elasticity of substitution for the same function is given by $1/(1 - R)$. Hence, the measures are reciprocals of each other. Using this result, discuss the following questions:

a. Why is risk aversion related to an individual's willingness to substitute wealth between states of the world? What phenomenon is being captured by both concepts?

b. How would you interpret the polar cases $R = 1$ and $R = -\infty$ in both the risk-aversion and substitution frameworks?

c. A rise in the price of contingent claims in "bad" times (P_b) will induce substitution and income effects into the demands for W_g and W_b. If the individual has a fixed budget to devote to these two goods, how will choices among them be affected? Why might W_g rise or fall depending on the degree of risk aversion exhibited by the individual?

d. Suppose that empirical data suggest an individual requires an average return of 0.5 percent if he or she is to be tempted to invest in an investment that has a 50–50 chance of gaining or losing 5 percent. That is, this person gets the same utility from W_0 as from an even bet on $1.055 \, W_0$ and $0.955 \, W_0$.

i. What value of R is consistent with this behavior?

ii. How much average return would this person require to accept a 50–50 chance of gaining or losing 10 percent?

Note: This part requires solving nonlinear equations, so approximate solutions will suffice. The comparison of the risk/reward trade-off illustrates what is called the "equity premium puzzle," in that risky investments seem to actually earn much more than is consistent with the degree of risk-aversion suggested by other data. See N. R. Kocherlakota, "The Equity Premium: It's Still a Puzzle" *Journal of Economic Literature* (March 1996): 42–71.

18.9

Investment in risky assets can be examined in the state-preference framework by assuming that W^* dollars invested in an asset with a certain return, r, will yield $W^*(1 + r)$ in both states of the world, whereas investment in a risky asset will yield $W^*(1 + r_g)$ in good times and $W^*(1 + r_b)$ in bad times (where $r_g > r > r_b$).

a. Graph the outcomes from the two investments.

b. Show how a "mixed portfolio" containing both risk-free and risky assets could be illustrated in your graph. How would you show the fraction of wealth invested in the risky asset?

c. Show how individuals' attitudes toward risk will determine the mix of risk-free and risky assets they will hold. In what case would a person hold no risky assets?

d. If an individual's utility takes the constant relative risk aversion form (Equation 8.62), explain why this person will not change the fraction of risky asset held as his or her wealth increases.[22]

---

[22]This problem and the next are taken from J. E. Stiglitz, "The Effects of Income, Wealth, and Capital Gains Taxation in Risk Taking," *Quarterly Journal of Economics* (May 1969), pp. 263–83.

18.10

Suppose the asset returns in Problem 18.9 are subject to taxation.

a. Show under the conditions of Problem 18.9 why a proportional tax on wealth will not affect the fraction of wealth allocated to risky assets.

b. Suppose only the returns from the safe asset were subject to a proportional income tax. How would this affect the fraction of wealth held in risky assets? Which investors would be most affected by such a tax?

c. How would your answer to part (b) change if all asset returns were subject to a proportional income tax?

(*Note:* This problem asks you to compute the *pre-tax* allocation of wealth that will result in *post-tax* utility maximization.)

SUGGESTIONS FOR FURTHER READING

Arrow, K. J. "The Role of Securities in the Optimal Allocation of Risk Bearing." *Review of Economic Studies 31* (1963): 91–96.
Introduces the state-preference concept and interprets securities as claims on contingent commodities.

———. "Uncertainty and the Welfare Economics of Medical Care." *American Economic Review 53* (1963): 941–73.
Excellent discussion of the welfare implications of insurance. Has a clear, concise, mathematical appendix. Should be read in conjunction with Pauly's article on moral hazard (see Chapter 19).

Bernoulli, D. "Exposition of a New Theory on the Measurement of Risk." *Econometrica 22* (1954): 23–36.
Reprint of the classic analysis of the St. Petersburg paradox.

Friedman, M., and L. J. Savage. "The Utility Analysis of Choice." *Journal of Political Economy 56* (1948): 279–304.
Analyzes why individuals may both gamble and buy insurance. Very readable.

Huang, Chi-fu, and R. H. Litzenberger. *Foundations for Financial Analysis.* Amsterdam: North-Holland, 1988.
Presents a good discussion of measures of "stochastic dominance" and their relationship to risk aversion.

Mas-Colell, Andreu, Michael D. Whinston, and Jerry R. Green. *Microeconomic Theory,* Chap. 6. New York: Oxford University Press, 1995.
Provides a good summary of the foundations of expected utility theory. Also examines the "state independence" assumption in detail and shows that some notions of risk aversion carry over into cases of state dependence.

Pratt, J. W. "Risk Aversion in the Small and in the Large." *Econometrica 32* (1964): 122–36.
Theoretical development of risk-aversion measures. Fairly technical treatment but readable.

Rothschild, M., and J. E. Stiglitz. "Increasing Risk: 1. A Definition." *Journal of Economic Theory 2* (1970): 225–43.
Develops an economic definition of what it means for one gamble to be "riskier" than another. A sequel article in the Journal of Economic Theory *provides economic illustrations.*

Silberberg, E. and W. Suen. *The Structure of Economics: A Mathematical Analysis,* 3rd ed. Boston. Irwin/McGraw Hill, 2001.
Chapter 13 provides a nice introduction to the relationship between statistical concepts and expected utility maximization. Also shows in detail the integration mentioned in Example 18.3.

Portfolio Theory and the Pricing of Risk

In Chapter 18 we saw that individuals will pay something to avoid uncertainty and that the extent of the sacrifice will depend on their attitudes toward risk. This suggests that the interactions of many individuals will establish a market for "risk" in which uncertainty can be reduced for a "price." The problem, then, is to devise a way of quantifying risk that is amenable to analyzing its pricing. Perhaps the most well-developed models of this process can be found in the study of capital asset pricing, where economists have extensively examined the relationship between the expected return an asset offers and the risks associated with that return. Here we will briefly summarize some basic insights from this vast topic. First, a few statistical preliminaries are required.

Statistical background

A variable x is termed a *random variable* if it takes on various values with specific probabilities. The "probability density function" for x [denoted by $f(x)$] indicates the probability that x will take on values within a narrow band, dx. Any function will serve as a probability density function, provided

$$f(x) \geq 0$$

and

$$\int_{-\infty}^{\infty} f(x)dx = 1. \tag{i}$$

Statisticians have employed a large variety of such functions to explain empirical observations. Perhaps the most useful of these is the Normal (or Gaussian) function

$$f(z) = \frac{1}{\sqrt{2\pi}} e^{-z^2/2}, \tag{ii}$$

which has the familiar bell shape, being symmetric about zero. This particular function has played a major role in the development of the theory of the pricing of risk and in many other areas of statistics.

For any random variable, x, the *mean* (or expected value) is defined as

$$\mu_x = E(x) = \int_{-\infty}^{\infty} xf(x)dx, \tag{iii}$$

and the variance of x is defined as

$$\sigma_x^2 = E[(x - \mu_x)^2] = \int_{-\infty}^{\infty} (x - \mu_x)^2 f(x)dx. \tag{iv}$$

The square root of this variance (denoted by σ_x) is termed the standard deviation of x.

For the normal distribution in Equation ii, it is a relatively simple matter to show that $\mu_z = 0$, $\sigma_z^2 = \sigma_z = 1$. This function can be generalized by noting that if

$$z = \frac{x - \mu_x}{\sigma_x} \tag{v}$$

has the distribution function in Equation ii, the variable x is said to be normally distributed with mean μ_x and standard deviation σ_x. The distribution of x is therefore completely determined by the two parameters μ_x and σ_x.

If x_i and x_j are two random variables, the *covariance* between them is defined as

$$\sigma_{ij} = E(x_i - \mu_i)(x_j - \mu_j) =$$
$$\int_{-\infty}^{\infty} \int_{-\infty}^{\infty} (x_i - \mu_x)(x_j - \mu_x)f(x_i, x_j)dx_i dx_j. \tag{vi}$$

If x_i and x_j tend to rise and fall together, σ_{ij} will be positive. If these variables tend to move in opposite directions, σ_{ij} will be negative.

If z represents a weighted average of two random variables, x_i and x_j,

$$z = \alpha x_i + (1 - \alpha)x_j \tag{vii}$$

where $0 \leq \alpha \leq 1$, then application of the various definitions shows that

$$\mu_z = \alpha\mu_i + (1 - \alpha)\mu_j \tag{viii}$$

and

$$\sigma_z^2 = \alpha^2 \sigma_i^2 + (1 - \alpha)^2\sigma_j^2 + 2\alpha (1 - \alpha)\sigma_{ij}. \tag{ix}$$

For a further development of these concepts see Freund (1992) or Hoel (1984) or any other introductory text on mathematical statistics. Here we make use of these concepts by assuming that the returns to financial assets (x_i) have a normal distribution. The mean of x_i (μ_i) indicates the expected return on asset i, whereas, as we shall see, the standard deviation of x_i (σ_i) is a starting place for discussing the risk associated with that asset. It is this variability of return that risk-averse investors seek to avoid.

E18.1 Portfolio diversification

Equation ix provides the rationale for portfolio diversification. Even if two assets have identical distributions of returns $(\mu_i = \mu_j, \sigma_i = \sigma_j)$, mixing them in a portfolio can provide a more favorable risk-reward combination. In the case where the asset returns are independent $(\sigma_{ij} = 0)$, for example, an equal weighting would yield

$$\mu_z = .5\mu_1 + .5\mu_2 = \mu_1 = \mu_2 \qquad \text{(x)}$$
$$\sigma_z^2 = .25\sigma_1^2 + .25\sigma_2^2 = .5\sigma_1^2 = .5\sigma_2^2 \qquad \text{(xi)}$$
$$\sigma_z = .707\sigma_1 = .707\sigma_2, \qquad \text{(xii)}$$

which provides the same return as holding either asset individually with reduced risk. If the assets had a negative covariance $(\sigma_{ij} < 0)$, holding both would provide even greater risk-reduction benefits.

E18.2 Efficient Portfolios

With many assets the portfolio allocation problem is to choose weights for the assets so as to minimize the standard deviation of the portfolio for each potential expected return. A solution to this optimization problem yields an efficiency frontier such as that represented by *EE* in Figure E18.1.

FIGURE E18.1   Efficient Portfolios

The frontier *EE* represents optimal mixtures of risky assets that minimize the standard deviation of the portfolio, σ, for each expected return, μ. A risk-free asset with return μ_f offers investors the opportunity to hold mixed portfolios along *PP* that mix this risk-free asset with the market portfolio, *M*.

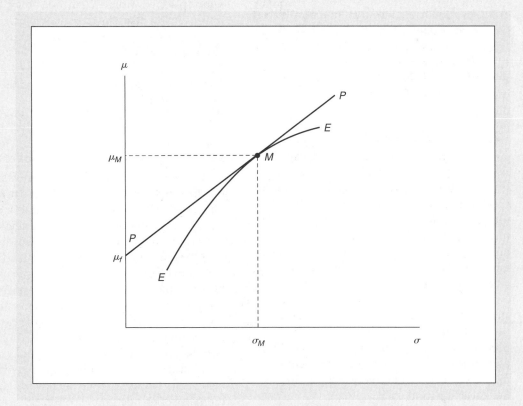

Portfolios that lie below this frontier are inferior to those on the frontier, because they offer lower expected returns for any degree of risk. Portfolio returns above the frontier are unattainable. Sharpe (1970) discusses the mathematics associated with constructing the *EE* frontier.

Mutual funds

The notion of portfolio efficiency has been widely applied to the study of mutual funds. In general, mutual funds are a good answer to small investors' diversification needs. Because such funds pool the funds of many individuals, they are able to achieve economies of scale in transactions and management costs. This permits fund owners to share in the fortunes of a much wider variety of equities than would be possible of each acted alone. But mutual fund managers have incentives of their own, so the portfolios they hold may not always be perfect representations of the risk attitudes of their clients. For example, Scharfstein and Stein (1990) develop a model that shows why mutual fund managers have incentives to "follow the herd" in their investment picks. Other studies, such as the classic investigation by Jensen (1968), find that mutual fund managers are seldom able to attain extra returns large enough to offset the expenses they charge investors. In recent years this has led many mutual fund buyers to favor "index" funds that seek simply to duplicate the market average (as represented, say, by the Standard and Poor's 500 stock index). Such funds have very low expenses and therefore permit investors to achieve diversification at minimal cost.

E18.3 Portfolio separation

If there exists a risk-free asset with expected return μ_f and $\sigma_f = 0$, optimal portfolios will consist of mixtures of this asset with risky ones. All such portfolios will lie along the line *PP* in Figure 18.1, because this shows the maximum return attainable for each value of σ for various portfolio allocations. These allocations will contain only one specific set of risky assets—the set represented by point *M*. In equilibrium this will be the "market portfolio" consisting of all capital assets held in proportion to their market valuations. This market portfolio will provide an expected return of μ_M and a standard deviation of that return of σ_M. The equation for the line *PP* that represents any mixed portfolio is given by the linear equation

$$\mu_P = \mu_f + \frac{\mu_M - \mu_f}{\sigma_M} \cdot \sigma_P. \qquad \text{(xiii)}$$

This shows that the market line *PP* permits individual investors to "purchase" returns in excess of the risk-free return ($\mu_M - \mu_f$) by taking on proportionally more risk (σ_P/σ_M). For choices on *PP* to the left of the market point, *M*, $\sigma_P/\sigma_M < 1$ and $\mu_f < \mu_P < \mu_M$. High-risk points to the right of *M*—which can be obtained by borrowing to produce a leveraged portfolio—will have $\sigma_P/\sigma_M > 1$ and will promise an expected return in excess of what is provided by the market portfolio ($\mu_P > \mu_M$). Tobin (1958) was one of the first economists to recognize the role that risk-free assets play in identifying the market portfolio and in setting the terms on which investors can obtain returns above risk-free levels.

E18.4 Individual Choices

Figure E18.2 illustrates the portfolio choices of various investors facing the options offered by the line *PP*. Individuals with low tolerance for risk (*I*) will opt for portfolios that are heavily weighted toward the risk-free asset. Investors willing to assume a modest degree of risk (*II*) will opt for portfolios close to the market portfolio. High-risk investors (*III*) may opt for leveraged portfolios. Notice that all investors face the same "price" of risk ($\mu_M - \mu_f$) with their expected returns being determined by how much relative risk (σ_P/σ_M) they are willing to incur. Notice also that the risk associated with an investor's portfolio depends only on the fraction of the portfolio invested in the market portfolio (α) since $\sigma_P^2 = \alpha^2 \sigma_M^2 + (1 - \alpha)^2 \cdot 0$. Hence, $\sigma_P/\sigma_M = \alpha$, so the investor's choice of portfolio is equivalent to his or her choice of risk.

E18.5 Capital asset pricing model

Although the analysis of E18.4 shows how a portfolio that mixes a risk-free asset with the market portfolio will be priced, it does not describe the risk-return trade-off for a single asset. Because, assuming transactions are costless, an investor can always avoid risk unrelated to the overall market by choosing to diversify with a "market portfolio," such "unsystematic" risk will not warrant any excess return. An asset will, however, earn an excess return to the extent that it contributes to overall market risk. An asset that does not yield such extra returns would not be held in the market portfolio, so it would not be held at all. This is the fundamental insight of the capital asset pricing model (CAPM).

To examine these results formally, consider a portfolio that combines a small amount (α) of an

FIGURE E18.2   Investor Behavior and Risk Aversion

Given the market options *PP*, investors can choose how much risk they wish to assume. Very risk-averse investors (U_I) will hold mainly risk-free assets, whereas risk takers (U_{III}) will opt for leveraged portfolios.

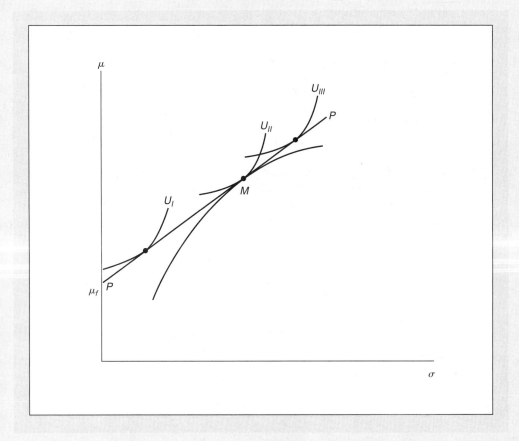

asset with a random return of *x* with the market portfolio (which has a random return of *M*). The return on this portfolio (*z*) would be given by

$$z = \alpha x + (1 - \alpha)M. \qquad \text{(xiv)}$$

The expected return is

$$\mu_z = \alpha\mu_x + (1 - \alpha)\mu_M \qquad \text{(xv)}$$

with variance

$$\sigma_z^2 = \alpha^2\sigma_x^2 + (1 - \alpha)^2\sigma_M^2 + 2\alpha(1 - \alpha)\sigma_{x,M}. \qquad \text{(xvi)}$$

But our previous analysis shows

$$\mu_z = \mu_f + (\mu_M - \mu_f) \cdot \frac{\sigma_z}{\sigma_M}. \qquad \text{(xvii)}$$

Setting Equation xv equal to xvii and differentiation with respect to α yields

$$\frac{\partial\mu_z}{\partial\alpha} = \mu_x - \mu_M = \frac{(\mu_M - \mu_F)}{\sigma_M} \frac{\partial\sigma_z}{\partial\alpha} \qquad \text{(xviii)}$$

by calculating $\dfrac{\partial\sigma_z}{\partial\alpha}$ from Equation xvi and taking the limit as α approaches zero, we get

$$\mu_x - \mu_M = \frac{(\mu_M - \mu_f)}{\sigma_M}\left(\frac{\sigma_{x,M} - \sigma_M^2}{\sigma_M}\right), \qquad \text{(xix)}$$

or, rearranging terms,

$$\mu_x = \mu_f + (\mu_M - \mu_f) \cdot \frac{\sigma_{x,M}}{\sigma_M^2}. \qquad \text{(xx)}$$

Again, risk has a reward of $\mu_M - \mu_f$, but now the quantity of risk is measured by $\sigma_{x,M}/\sigma_M^2$—this ratio of the covariance between the return *x* and the market to the variance of the market return is referred to as the *beta* coefficient for the asset. Estimated beta coefficients for financial assets are reported in many publications.

Studies of the CAPM

This version of the capital asset pricing model carries very strong implications about the determinants of any asset's expected rate of return. Because of this simplicity, the model has been subject to a large number of empirical tests. In general these find that the model's measure of systemic risk (beta) is indeed correlated with expected returns, while simpler measures of risk (for example, the standard deviation of past returns) are not. Perhaps the most influential early empirical test that reached such a conclusion was Fama and MacBeth (1973). But the CAPM itself explains only a small fraction of differences in the returns of various assets. And, contrary to the CAPM, a number of authors have found that many other economic factors significantly affect expected returns. Indeed, a prominent challenge to the CAPM comes from one of its original founders—see Fama and French (1992).

References

Fama, E. F., and K. R. French. "The Cross Section of Expected Stock Returns." *Journal of Finance* 47 (1992): 427–66.

Fama, E. F., and J. MacBeth. "Risk, Return, and Equilibrium." *Journal of Political Economy* 8 (1973): 607–36.

Freund, J. E. *Mathematical Statistics.* 5th ed. Englewood Cliffs, NJ: Prentice-Hall, 1992.

Hoel, Paul G. *Introduction to Mathematical Statistics.* 5th ed. New York: John Wiley and Sons, 1984.

Jensen, M. "The Performance of Mutual Funds in the Period 1945–1964." *Journal of Finance* (May 1968): 386–416.

Lintner, J. "The Valuation of Risk Assets and the Selection of Risky Investments in Stock Portfolios and Capital Budgets." *Review of Economics and Statistics* (February 1965): 13–37.

Scharfstein, D. S., and J. Stein. "Herd Behavior and Investment." *American Economic Review* (June 1990): 465–89.

Sharpe, W. F. *Portfolio Theory and Capital Markets.* New York: McGraw-Hill, 1970.

Tobin, J. "Liquidity Preference as Behavior Towards Risk." *Review of Economic Studies* (February 1958); 65–86.

Chapter 19

THE ECONOMICS OF INFORMATION

Information is a valuable economic resource. People who know where to buy high-quality goods cheaply can make their budgets stretch further than those who don't; farmers with access to better weather forecasting may be able to avoid costly mistakes; and government environmental regulation can be more efficient if it is based on good scientific knowledge. Although these observations about the value of information have long been recognized, formal economic modeling of information acquisition and its implications for resource allocation is fairly recent.[1] Despite its late start, the study of information economics has become one of the major areas in current research. In this chapter we briefly survey some of the principal issues raised by this research.

Properties of information

One difficulty encountered by economists who wish to study the economics of information is that "information" itself is not easy to define. Unlike the economic goods we have been studying so far, the "quantity" of information obtainable from various actions is not well defined, and what information is obtained is not homogeneous among its users. The forms of economically useful information are simply too varied to permit the kinds of price-quantity characterizations we have been using for basic consumer goods. Instead, economists who wish to study information must take some care to specify what the informational environment is in a particular decision problem (this is sometimes called the *information set*) and how that environment might be changed through individual actions. As might be expected, this approach has resulted in a vast number of models of specific situations with little overall commonality among them.

A second complication involved in the study of information concerns some technical properties of information itself. Most information is durable and retains value after it has been used. Unlike a hot dog, which is consumed only once, knowledge of a special sale can be used not only by the person who discovers it, but also by any friends with whom the information is shared. The friends then may gain from this information even though they

---

[1]The formal modeling of information is sometimes dated from the path-breaking article by G. J. Stigler, "The Economics of Information," *Journal of Political Economy* (June 1961): 213–25.

don't have to spend anything to obtain it. Indeed, in a special case of this situation, information has the characteristic of a pure *public good* (see Chapter 21). That is, the information is both *nonrival* in that others may use it at zero cost and *nonexclusive* in that no individual can prevent others from using the information. The classic example of these properties is a new scientific discovery. When some prehistoric people invented the wheel, others could use it without detracting from the value of the discovery, and everyone who saw the wheel could copy it freely.

These technical properties of information imply that market mechanisms may often operate imperfectly in allocating resources to information provision and acquisition. Standard models of supply and demand may therefore be of relatively limited use in understanding such activities. At a minimum, models have to be developed that accurately reflect the properties being assumed about the informational environment. Throughout the latter portions of this book, we will describe some of the situations in which such models are called for. Here, however, we will pay relatively little attention to supply-demand equilibria and will instead focus primarily on information issues that arise in the theory of individual choice.

The value of information

Developing models of information acquisition makes use of many of the same concepts that we introduced in connection with our study of uncertainty in the previous chapter. In many respects lack of information does represent a problem involving uncertainty for a decision maker. In the absence of perfect information, he or she may not be able to know exactly what the consequences of a particular action will be. Better information can reduce that uncertainty and therefore lead to better decisions that provide increased levels of utility.

Information and subjective possibilities

This relationship between uncertainty and information acquisition can be illustrated using the state-preference approach we introduced in the previous chapter. There we assumed that an individual forms subjective opinions about the probabilities of the two states of the world, "good times" and "bad times." In this model, information is valuable because it allows the individual to revise his or her estimates of these probabilities and to take advantage of these revisions. For example, information that foretold that tomorrow would definitely be "good times" would cause this person to revise his or her probabilities to $\pi_g = 1$, $\pi_b = 0$ and to change his or her purchases accordingly. When the information received is less definitive, the probabilities may only be changed slightly, but even small revisions may be quite valuable. If you ask some friends about their experiences with a few brands of DVD players you are thinking of buying, you may not want their opinions to dictate your choice. The prices of the players and other types of information (say, obtained from consulting *Consumer Reports*) will also affect your views. Ultimately, however, you must process all of these factors into a decision that reflects your assessment of the probabilities of various "states of the world" (in this case, the quality obtained from buying various brands).

A formal model

To illustrate how the quest for information might be integrated into a model of individual choice, suppose that information can be measured by the number of "messages" (m) "purchased." Suppose also the decision maker adjusts his or her subjective probabilities in response to these messages. Hence, π_g and π_b will be functions of m. The individual's goal now is to maximize

$$\text{expected utility} = \pi_g U(W_g) + \pi_b U(W_b) \tag{19.1}$$

subject to

$$I = p_g W_g + p_b W_b + p_m m, \tag{19.2}$$

where p_m is the per-unit cost of information messages (that is, the cost of a mechanic's time, of a phone call to gather price information, and so forth). Notice that information messages, *per se*, provide no utility in this model. Their utility only arises through their ability to change this person's decisions on how to allocate W_g and W_b. Setting up the Lagrangian for this problem,

$$\mathcal{L} = \pi_g U(W_g) + \pi_b U(W_b) + \lambda(I - p_g W_g - p_b W_b - p_m m) \qquad (19.3)$$

yields the following first-order conditions for a constrained maximum:

$$\frac{\partial \mathcal{L}}{\partial W_g} = \pi_g U'(W_g) - \lambda p_g = 0$$

$$\frac{\partial \mathcal{L}}{\partial W_b} = \pi_b U'(W_b) - \lambda p_b = 0$$

$$\frac{\partial \mathcal{L}}{\partial m} = \pi_g U'(W_g)\frac{dW_g}{dm} + \pi_b U'(W_b)\frac{dW_b}{dm} + U(W_g)\frac{d\pi_g}{dm} \qquad (19.4)$$

$$+ U(W_b)\frac{d\pi_b}{dm} - \lambda p_g \frac{dW_g}{dm} - \lambda p_b \frac{dW_b}{dm} - \lambda p_m = 0.$$

$$\frac{\partial \mathcal{L}}{\partial \lambda} = I - p_g W_g - p_b W_b - p_m m = 0.$$

The first two of these equations simply restate the optimality result derived earlier. At a maximum the (subjective) ratio of expected marginal utilities should equal the price ratio p_g / p_b. The third, complex equation represents the utility-maximizing choice for the amount of information to buy. In this model, all of the value of these messages comes from their ability to change the (subjective) probabilities of good and bad times. If the receipt of information does not change these probabilities, the two initial first-order conditions would leave the wealth allocations unchanged and the information would have no value. When new information does change probabilities, the individual must assess how much extra utility this may yield to decide how much to invest in the information itself. The trade-offs involved in this process are captured in the third equation for this maximization process. Often the principles of optimal information acquisition are more clearly illustrated with just a few discrete possibilities rather than with this sort of continuous choice model, however. A simple illustration is provided by the next example.

 EXAMPLE 19.1

The Value of Information on Prices

To illustrate how new information may affect utility maximization, let's return to one of the first models we used in Chapter 4. There we showed that if an individual consumes two goods and utility is given by $U(x, y) = x^{0.5} y^{0.5}$, the indirect utility function is

$$V(p_x, p_y, I) = \frac{I}{2 p_x^{0.5} p_y^{0.5}}. \qquad (19.5)$$

As a numerical example, we considered the case $p_x = 1$, $p_y = 4$, $I = 8$ and calculated that $V = I/2 \cdot 1 \cdot 2 = 2$. Now suppose that good y represents, say, a can of brand-name tennis balls, and this consumer knows that these can be bought at a price of either $3 or $5 from two stores he or she is considering but does not know which store charges which price. Because it is equally likely that either store has the lower price, the expected value of the

(continued)

EXAMPLE 19.1 CONTINUED

price is $4. But, because the indirect utility function is convex in price, this person receives an expected value of greater than $V = 2$ from shopping because he or she can buy more if the low-priced store is encountered. Before shopping, expected utility is

$$E[V(p_x, p_y, I)] = 0.5 \cdot V(1, 3, 8) + 0.5 \cdot V(1, 5, 8)$$
$$= 1.155 + 0.894 = 2.049. \quad (19.6)$$

If the consumer knew which store offered the lower price, utility would be even greater. If this person could buy at $p_y = 3$ with certainty, indirect utility would be $V = 2.309$ and we can use this result to calculate what the value of this information is. That is, we can ask what level of income, I^*, would yield the same utility when $p_y = 3$, as is obtained when this person must choose which store to patronize by chance. Hence we need to solve the equation

$$V(p_x, p_y, I^*) = \frac{I^*}{2 p_x^{0.5} p_y^{0.5}} = \frac{I^*}{2 \cdot 1 \cdot 3^{0.5}} = 2.049. \quad (19.7)$$

The author's calculator gives a value of $I^* = 7.098$ for this solution. Hence, this person would be willing to pay up to 0.902 (= 8 − 7.098) for the information. Notice that availability of the price information helps this person in two ways: (1) it increases the probability he or she will patronize the low-price store from 0.5 to 1.0; and (2) it permits this person to take advantage of the lower price offered by buying more.

Query: It seems odd in this problem that expected utility with price uncertainty ($V = 2.049$) is greater than utility when price takes its expected value ($V = 2$). Does this violate the assumption of risk aversion?

Asymmetry of information

One obvious implication of the study of information acquisition is that the level of information that an individual buys will depend on the per-unit price of information messages. Unlike the market price for most goods (which we usually assume to be the same for everyone), there are many reasons to believe that information costs may differ significantly among individuals. Some individuals may possess specific skills relevant to information acquisition (they may be trained mechanics, for example) whereas others may not possess such skills. Some individuals may have other types of experiences that yield valuable information, whereas others may lack that experience. For example, the seller of a product will usually know more about its limitations than will a buyer, because the seller will know precisely how the good was made and where possible problems might arise. Similarly, large-scale repeat buyers of a good may have greater access to information about it than would first-time buyers. Finally, some individuals may have invested in some types of information services (for example, by having a computer link to a brokerage firm or by subscribing to *Consumer Reports*) that make the marginal cost of obtaining additional information lower than for someone without such an investment.

All of these factors suggest that the level of information may differ among the participants in market transactions. Of course, in many instances, information costs may be low and such differences may be minor. Most people can appraise the quality of fresh vegetables fairly well just by looking at them, for example. But when information costs are high and variable across individuals, we would expect them to find it advantageous to acquire different amounts of information.

Information and insurance

The market for insurance is characterized by a number of informational asymmetries. Most of these arise from differences between buyers and sellers of insurance in their information about the uncertain event being insured against. Because buyers of insurance directly face these uncertainties, they are often in a better position to know the true likelihood of their occurrence and are frequently able to take actions that may affect that likelihood. A car owner in an urban area, for example, knows whether he or she is parking in an area where cars are likely to be stolen and could, possibly at some cost, choose to park in a safer place. Automobile insurance firms, on the other hand, find it prohibitively costly to discover how each policy holder parks and must instead base rates on an assumed average behavior. Because this type of situation is not unique to insurance markets, but characterizes a large number of transactions involving informational asymmetries, we will examine it in some detail. The concepts of "moral hazard" and "adverse selection" that we will describe are perhaps the most important discoveries of modern information theory.

Moral hazard

Individuals can take a variety of actions that influence the probability that a risky event will occur. Homeowners contemplating possible losses from fire, for example, can install sprinkler systems or keep fire extinguishers at convenient locations. Similarly, people may buy antitheft devices for cars or keep physically fit in an attempt to reduce the likelihood of illness. In these activities, utility-maximizing individuals will pursue the risk reduction up to the point at which marginal gains from additional precautions are equal to the marginal cost of these precautions.

In the presence of insurance coverage, however, this calculation may change. If a person is fully insured against losses, he or she will have a reduced incentive to undertake costly precautions and may therefore increase the likelihood of a loss occurring. In the automobile insurance case, for example, a person who has a policy that covers theft may park in less safe areas or refrain from installing antitheft devices. This behavioral response to insurance coverage is termed "moral hazard."

DEFINITION

> **Moral hazard.** The effect of insurance coverage on individuals' decisions to take actions that may change the likelihood or size of losses.

The use of the term "moral" to describe this response is perhaps unfortunate. There is nothing particularly "immoral" about the behavior being described—individuals are responding to the incentives they face. In some applications, this response might even be desirable.[2] But, because insurance providers may find it very costly to measure and evaluate such responses, moral hazard may have important implications for the allocation of resources. To examine these, we need a utility-maximizing model.

A mathematical model

Suppose a risk-averse individual faces the possibility of incurring a loss (l) that will reduce his or her initial wealth (W_0). The probability of loss is given by π, and this probability can be reduced depending on the amount (a) that an individual spends on preventative

---

[2]For example, people with medical insurance may be encouraged to seek early treatment because the insurance reduces the out-of-pocket cost of medical care.

measures. If we assume state independence, we can let $U(W)$ represent the individual's utility in both state 1 (no loss) and state 2 (loss). In the absence of insurance coverage, wealth in the two states is given by

$$
\begin{aligned}
W_1 &= W_0 - a \\
W_2 &= W_0 - a - l,
\end{aligned}
\tag{19.8}
$$

and the individual chooses a to maximize

$$
\text{expected utility} = E = (1 - \pi)U(W_1) + \pi U(W_2).
\tag{19.9}
$$

Remembering that π is a function of a, the first-order condition for a maximum is therefore

$$
\begin{aligned}
\frac{\partial E}{\partial a} &= -U(W_1)\frac{\partial \pi}{\partial a} - (1 - \pi)U'(W_1) \\
&\quad + U(W_2)\frac{\partial \pi}{\partial a} - \pi U'(W_2) = 0
\end{aligned}
\tag{19.10}
$$

or

$$
\pi U'(W_2) + (1 - \pi)U'(W_1) = [U(W_2) - U(W_1)]\frac{\partial \pi}{\partial a}.
\tag{19.11}
$$

This result has the commonsense interpretation that the individual should undertake precautionary activities up to the point at which the expected marginal utility cost (from reduced wealth) of spending one more dollar on such activities (the left side of Equation 19.11) is equal to the reduction ($\partial \pi / \partial a$ is negative) in the expected value of the utility loss that might be encountered in bad times.

Behavior with insurance and perfect monitoring

With insurance coverage the story is more complex. Now the individual may purchase insurance coverage that pays x if a loss incurs, and the premium for this coverage is given by p (which will obviously depend on x). Wealth in the two possible states is now given by

$$
\begin{aligned}
W_1 &= W_0 - a - p \\
W_2 &= W_0 - a - p - l + x,
\end{aligned}
\tag{19.12}
$$

and the individual chooses a and x to maximize expected utility. If the insurance provider could monitor precautionary activities and therefore know the probability of loss, it could charge a fair insurance premium of

$$
p = \pi x.
\tag{19.13}
$$

With such a policy

$$
\begin{aligned}
W_1 &= W_0 - a - \pi x, \\
W_2 &= W_0 - a - l + (1 - \pi)\, x.
\end{aligned}
\tag{19.14}
$$

Assuming state independence, this person can maximize expected utility by choosing x so that $W_1 = W_2$, which, as in our previous models, requires full insurance coverage (that is, $x = l$). With full coverage, the first-order condition for a utility-maximizing choice of a is

$$
\begin{aligned}
\frac{\partial E}{\partial a} &= -(1 - \pi)U'(W_1)\left(1 + l\frac{\partial \pi}{\partial a}\right) - U(W_1)\frac{\partial \pi}{\partial a} \\
&\quad - \pi U'(W_2)\left(1 + l\frac{\partial \pi}{\partial a}\right) + U(W_2)\frac{\partial \pi}{\partial a} = 0
\end{aligned}
\tag{19.15}
$$

or, using the fact that $W_1 = W_2$,

$$1 = -l\frac{\partial \pi}{\partial a}. \tag{19.16}$$

This condition is directly analogous to the one derived earlier for the uninsured case, although now, with the availability of full insurance, it can be stated more simply. At the utility-maximizing choice, the marginal cost of an extra unit of prevention (which here is just 1) should equal the marginal reduction in the expected loss provided by that extra spending. Hence, with full insurance and the actuarially fair premiums made possible by perfect monitoring, precautionary purchases are still made at the optimal levels.

The information problem and imperfect monitoring

Our analysis so far has been based on the unreasonable assumption that insurance providers know the probability that each individual will incur a loss and can therefore charge the actuarially fair premium to that person. When individuals can undertake precautionary activities, this assumption seems particularly doubtful. It would seem to require that the provider constantly monitor each person's activities to determine what his or her probability of loss is. It would require the provider to quote a different premium to each buyer to reflect his or her own precautionary activities. Obtaining such information is prohibitively costly in most circumstances, and insurers have to adopt less fully informed methods of premium setting.

In the simplest case, the insurer might set a premium based on the average probability of loss experienced by some group of people, with no variation allowed for specific individual precautionary activities.[3] With such a policy, however, each individual has an incentive to reduce his or her precautionary activities because these are costly and, in the presence of full insurance, yield no benefits in terms of utility. This result can be shown directly for the full insurance case. If $x = l$ in Equations 19.12, $W_1 = W_2$ regardless of the premium charged or the precautions undertaken. Since premiums now do not depend on a, however, it is clear that utility is maximized when $a = 0$. Even when premiums do depend partly on a, the resulting utility maximum will be characterized by too little precautionary spending and, perhaps, too much insurance. In essence then, the distorting effect of moral hazard on the allocation of resources arises from the informational asymmetry between individuals and insurance providers with respect to the ability to monitor precautions taken.[4]

  EXAMPLE 19.2

Moral Hazard and Monitoring

In several of the examples in Chapter 18, we examined an individual's decision about buying insurance against theft of a car worth $20,000. Here we look at his or her decision about whether to install an antitheft device that costs $1,950 and promises to reduce the probability of auto theft from .25 to .15. In terms of expected values, the installation clearly makes sense because the expected gain of $2,000 (.10 · 20,000) exceeds the cost of the device. Expected utility from installing the device

$$\text{expected utility} = .85 \ln (100,000 - 1,950)$$
$$+ .15 \ln (100,000 - 20,000 - 1,950) \tag{19.17}$$
$$= 11.4590$$

(*continued*)

---

[3]Another possibility is that the insurer may be able to categorize individuals into various risk categories (for example, "smokers" versus "nonsmokers," "urban" versus "rural" residents, and so forth). In the next section we examine some of the issues that arise in markets characterized by such risk clauses.

[4]If insurance providers can partly monitor precautionary spending (perhaps by observing individual insurance purchases), the analysis becomes more complex, though the possibility for inefficient resource allocation remains if this monitoring is incomplete. For a discussion, see S. Shavell, "On Moral Hazard and Insurance," *Quarterly Journal of Economics* (November 1979): 541–62.

EXAMPLE 19.2 CONTINUED

also exceeds expected utility without the device (11.4571—see Equation 18.56), so an uninsured individual will take this precaution.

Insurance and moral hazard. With insurance available, however, this may not be the case. Specifically, assume that the individual can purchase full insurance coverage for $5,200—this premium represents $5,000 for the expected loss and a $200 charge associated with administrative costs. Assume also that the insurance company makes no effort to monitor installation of antitheft devices. In this case expected utility with the insurance policy (11.4595—see Equation 18.60) exceeds expected utility with the device, so the individual will opt for buying insurance but not the device.

Monitoring of antitheft devices. If insurance providers can monitor installation of antitheft devices, the calculation will change again. Suppose it would cost $10 to determine whether an owner had installed such a device. In this case the insurance premium for a person with an antitheft device would be $3,210—$3,000 expected loss (.15 · 20,000), $200 for administrative costs, and the $10 monitoring cost. If an individual purchases such a policy (and an antitheft device), his or her wealth will be $94,840 (=100,000 – 3,210 – 1,950) with certainty because, if a theft occurs, insurance will completely cover the loss. Expected utility now is given by

$$\text{expected utility} = \ln (94{,}840) = 11.4600, \qquad (19.18)$$

which exceeds that available either from buying the antitheft device without insurance or from buying an unmonitored policy. Hence, whether the insurance availability deters all precautionary spending depends crucially on the costs of monitoring the spending.

Query: Suppose monitoring of antitheft devices costs $100 per policy and must be paid whether an individual actually installs a device. What decision would he or she make now?

Adverse selection

A second, related way in which informational asymmetries may affect market transactions arises when different individuals may have different probabilities of experiencing unfavorable outcomes. If (as in the moral hazard case) individuals know the probabilities more accurately than do insurance providers, insurance markets may not function properly because providers may not be able to set premiums based on accurate measures of expected loss. The resulting equilibria may be undesirable for many market participants.

A graphical illustration

Figure 19.1 pictures the situation of two individuals who each start with an initial wealth of W_0 and face the possibility of a loss, l. Point e represents the initial position of these individuals—they receive W_0 in state 1 (no loss) and $W_0 - l$ in state 2 (loss). Suppose that the individuals face different probabilities of loss—the high-risk individual has a probability of loss of π_H whereas the low-risk individual faces a probability of π_L (which is lower than π_H). With fair insurance and state independence (as we saw in Chapter 18), both individuals would prefer to move to the certainty line. The lines *EF* and *EG* are drawn with

FIGURE 19.1   **Equilibria with Differential Risks**

With perfect information, low-risk individuals move along the market insurance line *EF*, choosing point *F*. High-risk individuals move along *EG*, choosing point *G*. With imperfect information, both types of individuals will choose *F*, which is not viable.

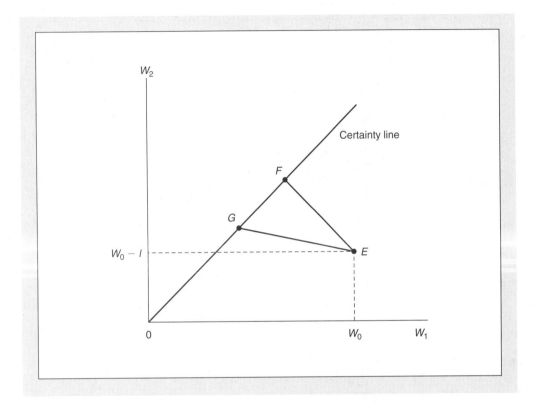

slopes $-(1 - \pi_L)/\pi_L$ and $-(1 - \pi_H)/\pi_H$, respectively, and show the market opportunities for each person to trade W_1 for W_2 by buying fair insurance.[5] The low-risk individual then maximizes utility at point *F* whereas the high-risk individual chooses point *G*.

If insurance providers have imperfect information about which individuals fall into the low- and high-risk categories, however, the solution in Figure 19.1 will be unstable. The difficulty is, of course, that point *F* provides more wealth in both states than does point *G* and will therefore be preferred by high-risk individuals. They will have an incentive to purchase insurance intended for low-risk buyers, and, in the absence of information about risk categories, the insurer will have no basis for declining to offer coverage to them. With a mixed group of clients, however, the insurer will face a higher average probability of loss than π_L and will, on average, lose money on each policy sold. Point *F* is not a viable equilibrium for a mixed client group.

Pooling

One conceivable solution would be for the insurer to offer a policy whose premium is based on the average probability of loss, $\bar{\pi} = (\pi_H + \pi_L)/2$. This pooled possibility is

---

[5]These slopes can be derived from Equation 19.14, which shows that a $1 increase in insurance (*x*) reduces W_1 by π and increases W_2 by $(1 - \pi)$. For example, if $\pi = 0.1$, $1 of insurance costs $.10 and reduces W_1 by that amount. The $1 of insurance raises W_2 by $.90 because it reimburses the $1 loss but the $.10 premium still must be paid. The slopes in Figure 19.1 are also called *odds ratios*.

FIGURE 19.2   **Impossibility of a Pooled Equilibrium**

A pooled insurance policy offers opportunities given by *EH*. A point such as *M* on this line cannot be an equilibrium, because insurance options (*N*) exist that are profitable to insurers and low-risk individuals but not to high-risk individuals.

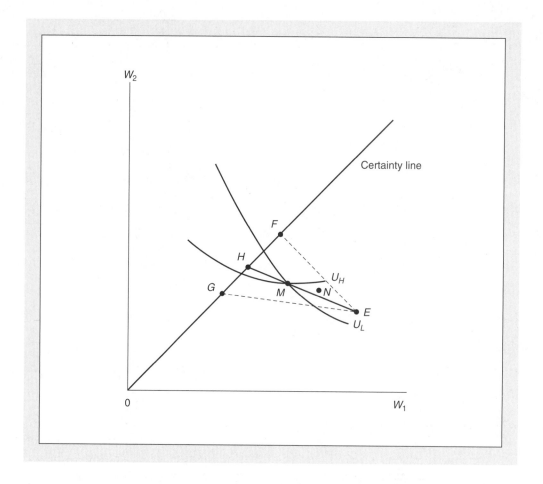

indicated by the line *EH* in Figure 19.2. Although both types of individuals will not necessarily opt for complete coverage at point *H* (since *EH* no longer accurately reflects the true probabilities each person knows he or she faces), they may settle for a policy such as *M* that provides partial coverage. But *M* cannot be a final equilibrium, because at *M* further trading opportunities exist for low-risk individuals. This can be shown as follows. At *M* the low-risk individuals' indifference curve (U_L) is steeper than the high-risk individuals' (U_H).[6] Consequently, insurance policies exist (say, *N*) that are unattractive to high-risk individuals but are attractive to low-risk individuals and profitable to insurers (because they lie below *EF*).

---

[6]Because expected utility is given by $(1 - \pi)U(W_1) + \pi U(W_2)$, the *MRS* is given by

$$\frac{-dW_2}{dW_1} = \frac{(1 - \pi)U'(W_1)}{(\pi)U(W_2)}.$$

Assuming both individuals have the same utility function and noting that each has the same wealth at *M*, the *MRS*s differ only because the underlying probabilities of loss differ. Because

$$(1 - \pi_L)/\pi_L > (1 - \pi_H)/\pi_H,$$

the low-risk individual's indifference curve will be steeper. This proof follows the analysis presented in M. Rothschild and J. Stiglitz, "Equilibrium in Competitive Insurance Markets: An Essay on the Economics of Imperfect Information," *Quarterly Journal of Economics* (November 1976): 629–50.

FIGURE 19.3   **A Separating Equilibrium**

With imperfect information, G and J represent a possible separating equilibrium. Here high-risk individuals opt for complete coverage (G), and low-risk individuals receive partial coverage (J) that is attractive to them but not to high-risk individuals.

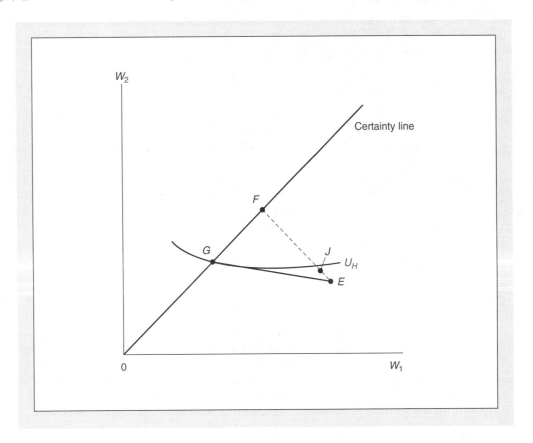

Assuming no barriers prevent the selling of fairly priced insurance, policies such as N will be offered and will attract low-risk individuals. Point M will therefore no longer be an equilibrium because the pooled probability of loss will rise above $\bar{\pi}$. In this situation, therefore, the pooled equilibrium M will not be viable.

Separating equilibria

If this market with asymmetric information is to have a viable equilibrium, it must be separated in some way—that is, high-risk individuals must have an incentive to purchase one type of insurance policy and low-risk individuals to purchase another. One such solution is illustrated in Figure 19.3. Here insurers offer policy G, and high-risk individuals respond by opting for complete insurance. If we let U_H represent the indifference curve for high-risk individuals that passes through G, any policy for low-risk persons that lies above U_H will not be viable because insurers cannot prevent those with high risks from taking advantage of it. In this situation, the best policy that low-risk individuals can obtain is one such as J. This policy lies slightly below U_H, but is economically viable (because it lies on EF) and promises more utility to low-risk individuals than does facing the world uninsured. The policies G and J, therefore, represent a separating equilibrium in this case.

This equilibrium is clearly inferior to the full information equilibrium illustrated in Figure 19.1. If insurers could determine the true risks associated with selling to specific individuals, low-risk individuals would be better off and high-risk individuals would be no worse off. Although informational asymmetries will prevent this "first best" equilibrium from being obtained, a variety of other possibilities (such as government regulations or cross-subsidization between high- and low-risk policies by insurers themselves) may yield improvements for both individuals over the equilibrium illustrated in Figure 19.3.

Market signaling

One route to such improvements involves possible attempts by low-risk individuals to inform insurers of their true status. We have seen that such individuals could clearly benefit from sharing what they know with insurers. The primary difficulty is whether the "signals" they seek to send to insurers will be believable, because high-risk individuals would also benefit if they could convince insurers that they too were low risk.

The possibility that signals may be inaccurate makes the study of the subject interesting. If insurers could simply ask each client which risk category he or she represented and get accurate replies, the informational asymmetry described in the previous section would be inconsequential. Economists have, therefore, been more interested in the possibility that insurers may be able to infer accurate probabilities by observing clients' market behavior. The proper setting may give each individual the incentive to reveal his or her true situation, and insurers may then be able to take advantage of these *market signals*. An obvious illustration is provided by the situation shown in Figure 19.3. In this equilibrium, high-risk individuals purchase type *G* policies and obtain full coverage, whereas low-risk individuals purchase type *J* policies and receive only partial coverage. The separating equilibrium, therefore, identifies an individual's risk category. Possibly, insurers could use this information to offer better policies to low-risk individuals (at least until high-risk individuals learn what is happening).

More generally, market signals may be drawn from a number of sources, provided the economic behavior being observed by insurers accurately reflects risk categories. One necessary condition for this to occur is that the costs to individuals of taking the signaling action must be related to the probability of loss. If costs were the same regardless of risk class, individuals would face similar incentives to "send" signals, and the informational value of signals would be lost. For example, it is common for insurance companies to charge higher auto insurance premiums for high-performance sports cars than for similarly priced sedans. A possible explanation is that individuals' auto purchases may indicate their driving habits—perhaps sports car owners always drive as if they were in a road race. The separating equilibrium attained from auto purchase information will be sustainable, however, only if high-risk individuals have an aversion to driving unexciting sedans. Otherwise, they may switch car purchases as a way to obtain lower cost insurance. In formal terms, auto selections are a good signal only if it is sufficiently costly (perhaps in psychological terms) for high-risk individuals to adopt the market behavior of low-risk individuals. Some of these possibilities are examined in the next example.

 EXAMPLE 19.3

Adverse Selection in Insurance

Our analysis of installation of automobile antitheft devices in Example 19.2 can also be framed as an adverse selection problem. If insurers knew which owners had installed such devices, they could price policies accordingly. Owners without the devices would face a probability of loss of 0.25 and would pay a $5,000 premium for insurance coverage (for simplicity here we assume there are no administrative costs of writing insurance). In this case the owner will fully insure and receive an expected utility of

$$\text{expected utility} = \ln (100{,}000 - 5{,}000)$$
$$= \ln (95{,}000) = 11.4616. \tag{19.19}$$

(continued)

Because we wish to focus on differing probabilities of loss and not on the cost of antitheft devices, assume that another set of owners have installed such devices at some time in the past. The cost of the device is therefore a sunk cost that will not affect the current decision. Owners with such devices have a probability of loss of 0.15 and face an actuarially fair premium of $3,000. With complete insurance, expected utility will be

$$\text{expected utility} = \ln (97,000) = 11.4825. \qquad (19.20)$$

If insurers cannot discern whether an owner has installed a device, both types of owners will purchase low-risk policies. Assuming half of all cars have the devices, the insurer will experience a 0.20 loss rate and lose an average of $1,000 per policy with a $3,000 premium. A pooled premium rate of $4,000 would clearly be attractive to high-risk owners, but low-risk owners would refuse to buy the policy because they would be better off without insurance:

$$\ln(96,000) < .85 \ln(100,000) + .15 \ln(80,000) \qquad (19.21)$$
$$11.4721 < 11.4795.$$

The pooled equilibrium is therefore not viable, because low-risk individuals would refuse to participate in it.

Separating equilibria. A situation in which high-risk individuals opt for full insurance (at a $5,000 premium) and low-risk individuals buy no insurance is a possible separating equilibrium here, but this offers opportunities for insurers to offer partial policies that would be attractive to low-risk owners. To discover the best of these, we must find a fair policy for low-risk buyers that is not attractive to high-risk buyers. Because the premium from such a policy will be $0.15x$ (where x is the amount of the loss covered), we need to solve the following inequality:

$$.75 \ln (100,000 - .15x) + .25 \ln (80,000 + .85x) < \ln(95,000), \qquad (19.22)$$

which has an approximate solution of

$$x < 3,000. \qquad (19.23)$$

Hence a low-risk policy can cover only $3,000 of a low-risk owner's loss if it is not to be too attractive to high-risk owners. The expected utility of a low-risk owner who buys such a policy (which costs $450 = .15 \cdot 3,000$) is

$$.85 \ln (99,550) + .15 \ln (82,550) = 11.4803. \qquad (19.24)$$

Although this figure exceeds the expected utility of a low-risk individual who declines to buy insurance (Equation 19.21), it falls well short of what such an individual might achieve in a full information equilibrium. Low-risk individuals might therefore invest in signaling in order to improve their situation from what it would be under this separating equilibrium. You are now asked to investigate such signaling.

Query: If only low-risk owners could buy a certificate indicating installation of an antitheft device, how much would they pay for it? How much would forged certificates have to cost to prevent high-risk owners from using them?

The principal-agent relationship

One important way in which asymmetric information may affect the allocation of resources is when one person hires another, presumably better informed, person to make decisions. Some examples of such a relationship are patients hiring physicians to decide on the proper course of medical treatments, investors hiring financial advisors to handle their money, motorists letting mechanics decide what is wrong with their cars, and stockholders hiring managers to run the companies they technically own. In all of these cases, a person with less information (the *principal*) is hiring a more informed person (the *agent*) to make decisions that will directly affect the principal's own well-being. Hence we have the following definition:

Principal-agent relationship. The hiring of one person (the agent) by another person (the principal) to make economic decisions.

It is the asymmetry of information in the principal-agent relationship that can be problematic. In this section we will explore this issue in the context of potential conflicts between owners and managers of firms in seeking maximal profits. But the relationship occurs in many other guises and there is by now a very large literature on the topic. Some basic guides to that literature are mentioned at the end of this chapter.

Conflicts in the owner-manager relationship: A graphical approach

Adam Smith understood the basic conflict between owners and managers. In *The Wealth of Nations,* he observed that "the directors of . . . companies, being the managers of other people's money than of their own, it cannot well be expected that they should watch over it with the same anxious vigilance with which [owners] watch over their own."[7] Using such famous British institutions as the Royal African Company, the Hudson's Bay Company, and the East India Company as examples, Smith went on to point out some of the consequences of management by nonowners. His observations provide an important starting point for the study of modern firms.

The main issue raised by the existence of manager-agents is illustrated in Figure 19.4, which shows the indifference curve map of a manager's preferences between the firm's profits (which are of primary interest to the owners) and various benefits (such as fancy offices or travel in the corporate jet or helicopter) that accrue mainly to the manager.[8] This indifference curve map has the same shape as those in Part 2 on the presumption that profits *and* benefits provide utility to the manager.

To construct the budget constraint the manager faces in seeking to maximize his or her utility, assume first that the manager is also the owner of this firm. If the manager chooses to have no special benefits from the job, profits will be π_{max}. Each dollar of benefits received by the manager reduces these profits by one dollar. The budget constraint will have a slope of -1, and profits will reach zero when benefits total π_{max}.

Given this budget constraint, the owner-manager maximizes utility by opting for profits of π^* and benefits of b^*. Profits of π^*, though less than π_{max}, still represent maximum profits in this situation because any other owner-manager would also wish to receive b^* in benefits. That is, b^* represents a true cost of doing business so, given these costs, the firm's manager really does maximize profits.

Agents' incentives

Now suppose that the manager is not the only owner of this firm. Instead, assume that, say, one-third of the capital of the firm is owned by the manager and the other two-thirds are owned by outside investors who play no role in operating the firm. In this case the

---

[7]Adam Smith, *The Wealth of Nations* (New York: Random House, Modern Library Edition, 1937), p. 700.

[8]Figure 19.4 is based on a figure presented in Michael C. Jensen and William H. Meckling, "Theory of the Firm: Managerial Behavior, Agency Costs and Ownership Structure," *Journal of Financial Economics* (October 1976): 305–60.

| FIGURE 19.4 | Incentives for a Manager Acting as an Agent for a Firm's Owners |

If a manager were the sole owner of a firm, π^*, b^* would be chosen because this combination of profits and benefits provides maximum utility. If the manager owns only one-third of the firm, however, the perceived budget constraint will be flatter, and b^{**}, π^{**} will be chosen.

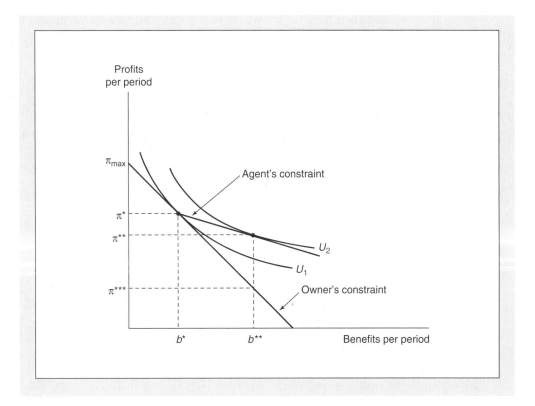

manager will act as if he or she no longer faces a budget constraint that requires that one dollar of profits be sacrificed for each dollar of benefits. Now a dollar of benefits costs the manager only \$.33 in profits, because the other \$.67 is effectively paid by the other owners in terms of reduced profits on their investment. Although the new budget constraint continues to include the point b^*, π^* (because the manager could still make the same decision a sole owner could), for benefits greater than b^* the slope of the budget constraint is only $-\frac{1}{3}$; profits from the manager's portion of the business decline by only \$.33 for each dollar in benefits received. Given this new budget constraint, the manager would choose point b^{**}, π^{**} to maximize his or her utility. Being only a partial owner of the firm causes the manager to choose a lower level of profits and a higher level of benefits than would be chosen by a sole owner.

Implications for owners

Point b^{**}, π^{**} is not attainable by this firm. Although the cost of one dollar of benefits appears to be only \$.33 in profits for the manager, in reality, of course, the benefits cost one dollar. When the manager opts for b^{**} in benefits, the loss in profits (from π^* to π^{***}) is greater for the firm as a whole than for him or her personally. The firm's owners are harmed by having to rely on an agency relationship with the firm's manager. It appears that the smaller the fraction of the firm that is owned by the manager, the greater the distortions that will be induced by this relationship. The next example illustrate this problem and describes what owners might do about it.

EXAMPLE 19.4

Using the Corporate Jet

United Biscuits, Inc., owns a fleet of corporate jets used mainly for business purposes. After firing the prior CEO for misusing the corporate fleet, the directors of UBI wish to structure a management contract that provides better incentives for cost control. All would-be applicants for the job have the same utility function for salary (s, measured in hundreds of thousands of dollars) and jet use (j, which can be only 0 or 1) of the form

$$U(s, j) = .1 \sqrt{s} + j. \tag{19.25}$$

All applicants also have job offers from other firms promising them a utility level of at most 2.0. Because excessive jet use is very costly, the directors realize that UBI profits (exclusive of the CEO's salary) will be 800 (thousand) if $j = 0$, but only 162 if $j = 1$. Hence, the directors are willing to offer the CEO up to 638 providing they can be assured he or she will not use the corporate fleet for personal use. A salary of slightly more than 400 will just be sufficient to get a potential candidate to accept a position with no jet usage ($U > 2$). That would be a more profitable contract than hiring a CEO with a required salary of 100 together with unrestricted plane use. Although this contract also offers $U > 2$, under the first contract net profits are 400 (after paying the CEO), whereas under the second they are only 62.

Contract monitoring. Unfortunately, the directors of UBI find it difficult to monitor nonbusiness jet use. If they sign a contract for 400 (and $j = 0$), the new CEO still has an incentive to use the jet, thereby raising his or her utility from 2 to 3. Such a decision would prove disastrous for the owners—with personal plane use their net profits fall to –238.

A profit-sharing contract. The owners might therefore be willing to pay something to monitor jet usage and to ensure that the terms of the high-salary contract are met. Alternatively, they could write a profit-sharing contract that might be self-enforcing. A salary promise of 50 percent of profits, for example, would be sufficient to attract a potential CEO ($U = 2.0$) provided he or she resolves not to use the jet. The candidate will realize that his or her utility will be lower with jet usage ($U = 1.9$) under such a profit-sharing contract and will presumably refrain from such behavior.

Query: How might the analysis of this contractual situation change if profits were not a "perfect signal" of jet use?

The owner-manager relationship: A mathematical analysis

We can study this example of the principal-agent relationship in a bit more detail using a mathematical approach. Suppose that the gross profits of the firm depend on some specific action (a) that a hired manager might take (that is, $\pi = \pi(a)$). The owner(s) of the firm wish to design a contract that pays the manager a salary (s) that is based on profits obtained (that is, $s = s[\pi(a)]$). For these owners, therefore, net profits are given by

$$\text{Net profits} = \pi' = \pi(a) - s[\pi(a)]. \tag{19.26}$$

Both gross and net profits are maximized when $\partial \pi / \partial a = 0$. The owners' problem then is to design a salary structure that provides an incentive for the manager to choose a value of a (say a^*) that achieves this result.

In devising a compensation plan, the owners of the firm face two issues. First, they must know the agent-manager's utility function so they can understand how he or she is affected by incentives. For example, the owners might assume that the manager's utility depends on net income, given by

$$I^M = s[(\pi(a)] - c(a) - c_0, \tag{19.27}$$

where $c(a)$ represents the costs that the manager incurs by undertaking action a ($c'(a) > 0$, $c''(a) > 0$), and c_0 represents the opportunity costs faced by the manager (such as the net benefits offered by his or her next best alternative job offer).

The second constraint faced in designing the compensation plan is that the manager must be willing to take the job. Simply put, this requires $I^M \geq 0$ because the job must provide a higher net return than does the alternative. Some authors refer to this as the "participation constraint."

The full information case

With complete information, it is relatively easy to design an optimal compensation plan. One option would be to pay no compensation unless the manager chooses a^* and to pay an amount equal to $c(a^*) + c_0$ if the optimal action is chosen. This compensation plan will just suffice to get the manager to take the job. Perhaps a more instructive alternative would be to adopt a compensation scheme under which $s(a) = \pi(a) - f$, where f is a fixed fee set to meet the participation constraint only when profits are maximized. That is, $f = \pi(a^*) - c(a^*) - c_0$. With this compensation package, the manager's income is maximized by setting $\partial s(a)/\partial a = \partial \pi/\partial a = 0$. Hence, he or she will choose $a = a^*$ and receive an income that just covers costs:

$$I^M = s(a^*) - c(a^*) - c_0 = \pi(a^*) - f - c(a^*) - c_0 = 0. \tag{19.28}$$

In the language of finance, this compensation plan makes the agent (rather than the principal) the "residual claimant" to the profits from this firm. The agent therefore maximizes profits because it is in his or her direct interest to do so.

Asymmetric information: Hidden action

These solutions for the full information case do little more than order the manager to opt for $a = a^*$. Because the relationship between managerial action and the firm's profits is fully known and because the owners know exactly what costs the manager faces, designing the compensation plan is trivial. Models of the principal-agent relationship have introduced asymmetric information into this problem in two ways. First, it is assumed that a manager's action is not directly observed and cannot be perfectly inferred from the firm's profits. Only the manager knows precisely what action he or she has chosen. This is referred to as the case of "hidden action." A second approach to modeling assumes that the agent-manager's objective function is not directly observed. This is referred to as the case of "hidden information." Here we look briefly at each of these cases.

The primary reason that the manager's action may be "hidden" is that profits depend on random factors that cannot be observed by the owner. In that case, owners will not be able to infer what action the manager has taken solely by looking at profits. One way of modeling this is to assume that there is a random element to profits so that actual profits depend on both the manager's action and on a random variable, u. That is,

$$\pi(a) = \bar{\pi}(a) + u, \tag{19.29}$$

where $\bar{\pi}$ represents the expected value of profits (which depends on the manager's actions) and u represents a normally distributed random variable with mean 0 and variance σ^2. Because owners only observe π, not $\bar{\pi}$, they can only use these actual profits in their compensation function. But this poses a problem in meeting the participation constraint.

A risk-averse manager will be concerned that actual profits may turn out badly and will decline to take the job because it provides less expected utility than does an alternative. The problem for the owner therefore is to design a compensation plan that does the best given the uncertainties involved in this problem. There are many different models of how incentive-compatible compensation plans should be designed in such circumstances. Example 19.5 looks at an especially simple case.

EXAMPLE 19.5

Incentive Plans and Risk Aversion

Suppose that the owners of the firm wish to adopt an incentive plan for risk-averse managers that involves some degree of profit sharing as a way to provide proper incentives. Such a plan might be

$$s(a) = b + d\pi(a), \tag{19.30}$$

where b and d are compensation plan parameters that are to be determined. Looking first at managerial incentives, the manager's income is now given by $I^M = s(a) - c(a) - c_0$, but this income is subject to uncertainty because of the random element associated with profits. If we assume that the manager has a constant absolute risk aversion utility function, we can use the results from Example 18.3 to derive his or her certainty equivalent income as

$$I^{CE} = b + d\bar{\pi}(a) - \frac{d^2 A\sigma^2}{2} - c(a) - c_0. \tag{19.31}$$

If the agent-manager chooses a to maximize this income, the first-order condition for a maximum is

$$\frac{\partial I^{CE}}{\partial a} = d\bar{\pi}'(a) - c'(a) = 0. \tag{19.32}$$

Hence, no matter what d the owners opt for, it will always be the case that the manager will choose his effort so that

$$d = \frac{c'(a)}{\bar{\pi}'(a)} = m(a), \tag{19.33}$$

where $m(a)$ represents the marginal cost-benefit ratio from additional effort. Because $c''(a) > 0$ and $\pi''(a) < 0$, it will be the case that $m'(a) > 0$—that is, the marginal cost-benefit ratio will increase as a increases.

To ensure that the manager will take this job, it must be the case that $I^{CE} \geq 0$. Assuming that this constraint will hold with equality, the requirement is that b be set so that

$$b = -d\bar{\pi}(a) + \frac{d^2 A\sigma^2}{2} + c(a) + c_0. \tag{19.34}$$

The principal-owners' problem now is to ensure that all of these incentives for the manager result in a profit-maximizing action being chosen. It is customary in this type of principal-agent problem to assume that the principal here is risk neutral on the assumption that owners hold fully diversified portfolios of stocks. We will adopt that practice here. In other principal-agent models, however, the assumption of risk neutrality for the principal would be inappropriate.

Using Equations 19.33 and 19.34, we can write the expected value of the owners' profits as

$$E(\pi') = (1 - d)\overline{\pi}(a) - b = \overline{\pi}(a) - \frac{m(a)^2 A\sigma^2}{2} - c(a) - c_0, \quad (19.35)$$

and the first-order condition for a maximum is

$$\frac{\partial E(\pi')}{\partial a} = \overline{\pi}'(a) - m(a)m'(a)A\sigma^2 - c'(a) = 0 \quad (19.36)$$

or

$$d = \frac{c'(a)}{\overline{\pi}'(a)} = m(a) = \frac{1}{1 + \dfrac{m'(a)A\sigma^2}{\overline{\pi}'(a)}}. \quad (19.37)$$

Three interesting conclusions can be derived from this result:

- Because of the sign conventions we have assumed, the optimal profit-sharing fraction will be between zero and one;[9]

- The optimal profit-sharing fraction is smaller the more risk averse is the agent-manager; and

- The optimal profit-sharing fraction is smaller the larger is the variance of the random element in profits.

All of these results make intuitive sense.

Query: How would you explain the presence of the term $m'(a)$ in Equation 19.37?

Hidden information

When the principal does now know the incentive structure of the agent, the kind of precise analysis in the previous example is not possible. Rather, incentive schemes must be designed on the basis of some initial assumptions about the agent's motivation, and they must be adapted as new information about those motivations is obtained. This makes it rather difficult to develop general models for this purpose. One way to approach the problem is to assume that agents are of different "types." For example, the agent types might be reflected in Example 19.5 by various values for the risk aversion parameter, A. In this case, the owner might initially set the profit-sharing fraction based on an assumed mean value for A and then observe the managers' decisions over time. The profit-sharing fraction would be adjusted as this new information became available. We will not pursue this complex topic further here, however.

---

[9]Notice that if $\sigma^2 = 0$, the optimal profit-sharing fraction is one—as we showed before, the owners should shift the residual claimant status onto the manager.

SUMMARY

In this chapter we have provided a survey of some issues that arise in modeling markets in which information is imperfect. Here these issues have been approached mainly from the point of view of an individual decision maker. Issues that arise in studying the consequences of imperfect information for the behavior of firms or for overall market performance have been mentioned only briefly. Some of our major conclusions are:

- Information is valuable because it permits individuals to increase the expected utility of their decisions. They might, therefore, be willing to pay something to acquire additional information.

- Information has a number of special properties (such as differing costs of acquisition and some aspects of a public good) that suggest that inefficiencies associated with imperfect and asymmetric information may be quite prevalent.

- The presence of asymmetric information may affect a variety of market outcomes, many of which are illustrated in the context of insurance theory. In this case, insurers may have less information about potential risks than do insurance purchasers.

- If insurers are unable to monitor the behavior of insured individuals accurately, moral hazard may arise—being insured will affect individuals' willingness to make precautionary expenditures. Such behavioral effects can arise in any contractual situation in which monitoring costs are high.

- Informational asymmetries can also lead to adverse selection in insurance markets. The resulting equilibria (if they exist) may often be inefficient in that low-risk people will be less well off than in the full information case. In some cases market signaling can reduce these inefficiencies.

- Asymmetric information may also cause some (principal) economic actors to hire others (agents) to make decisions for them. Providing the correct incentives to the agent is a difficult problem.

PROBLEMS

19.1

A farmer's tomato crop is wilting, and he must decide whether to water it. If he waters the tomatoes, or if it rains, the crop will yield $1,000 in profits; but if the tomatoes get no water, they will yield only $500. Operation of the farmer's irrigation system costs $100. The farmer seeks to maximize expected profits from tomato sales.

a. If the farmer believes there is a 50 percent chance of rain, should he water?

b. What is the maximum amount the farmer would pay to get information from an itinerant weather forecaster who can predict rain with 100 percent accuracy?

c. How would your answer to part (b) change if the forecaster were only 75 percent accurate?

19.2

In Problem 18.5, Ms. Fogg was quite willing to buy insurance against a 25 percent chance of losing $1,000 of her cash on her around-the-world trip. Suppose that people who buy such insurance tend to become more careless with their cash and that their probability of losing $1,000 rises to 30 percent. What is the actuarially fair insurance premium in this situation? Will Ms. Fogg buy insurance now? (*Note:* This problem and Problem 19.3 illustrate moral hazard.)

19.3

Problem 18.4 examined a cost-sharing health insurance policy and showed that risk-averse individuals would prefer full coverage. Suppose, however, that people who buy cost-sharing policies take better care of their own health so that the loss suffered when they are ill is reduced from $10,000 to $7,000. Now what would be the actuarially fair price of a cost-sharing policy? Is it possible that some individuals might prefer the cost-sharing policy to complete coverage? What would determine whether an individual had such preferences? (A graphical approach to this problem should suffice.)

19.4

Blue-eyed people are more likely to lose their expensive watches than are brown-eyed people. Specifically, there is an 80 percent probability that a blue-eyed individual will lose a $1,000 watch during a year, but only a 20 percent probability that a brown-eyed person will. Blue-eyed and brown-eyed people are equally represented in the population.

   a. If an insurance company assumes blue-eyed and brown-eyed people are equally likely to buy watch-loss insurance, what will the actuarially fair insurance premium be?

   b. If blue-eyed and brown-eyed people have logarithmic utility-of-wealth functions and current wealths of $10,000 each, will these individuals buy watch insurance at the premium calculated in part (a)?

   c. Given your results from part (b), will the insurance premiums be correctly computed? What should the premium be? What will the utility for each type of person be?

   d. Suppose that an insurance company charged different premiums for blue-eyed and brown-eyed people. How would these individuals' maximum utilities compare to those computed in parts (b) and (c)? (This problem is an example of adverse selection in insurance.)

19.5

Suppose there are two types of workers, high-ability workers and low-ability workers. Workers' wages are determined by their ability—high ability workers earn $50,000 per year, low-ability workers earn $30,000. Firms cannot measure workers' abilities but they can observe whether a worker has a high school diploma. Workers' utility depends on the difference between their wages and the costs they incur in obtaining a diploma.

   a. If the cost of obtaining a high school diploma is the same for high-ability and low-ability workers, can there be a separating equilibrium in this situation in which high-ability workers get high-wage jobs and low-ability workers get low wages?

   b. What is the maximum amount that a high-ability worker would pay to obtain a high school diploma? Why must a diploma cost more than this for a low-ability person if having a diploma is to permit employers to identify high-ability workers?

19.6

Suppose Molly Jock wishes to purchase a high-definition television to watch the Olympic Greco-Roman wrestling competition. Her current income is $20,000, and she knows where she can buy the television she wants for $2,000. She has heard the rumor that the same set can be bought at Crazy Eddie's (recently out of bankruptcy) for $1,700, but is unsure if the rumor is true. Suppose this individual's utility is given by

$$\text{utility} = ln(Y),$$

where Y is her income after buying the television.

   a. What is Molly's utility if she buys from the location she knows?

  b. What is Molly's utility if Crazy Eddie's really does offer the lower price?

  c. Suppose Molly believes there is a 50–50 chance that Crazy Eddie does offer the lower-priced television, but it will cost her $100 to drive to the discount store to find out for sure (the store is far away and has had its phone disconnected). Is it worth it to her to invest the money in the trip?

19.7

Suppose an individual knows that the prices of a particular color TV have a uniform distribution between $300 and $400. The individual sets out to obtain price quotes by phone.

  a. Calculate the expected minimum price paid if this individual calls n stores for price quotes.

  b. Show that the expected price paid declines with n, but at a diminishing rate.

  c. Suppose phone calls cost $2 in terms of time and effort. How many calls should this individual make in order to maximize his or her gain from search?[10]

19.8

Suppose the individual in Problem 19.7 adopts a "reservation price strategy"—that is, he or she will buy from the first retailer who meets this reservation price maximum. Under the conditions of Problem 19.7, what price should be set to maximize the gain from search?

19.9

Consider the principal-agent relationship between a patient and a physician. Suppose that the patient's utility function is given by $U^c(m, x)$, where m is medical care (whose quantity is determined by the physician) and x is other consumption goods. The patient is bound by the budget constraint $I_c = p_m m + x$, where p_m is the relative price of medical care. The physician's utility function is given by $U^d(I_d, U^p)$—that is, the physician derives utility from his or her own income and from the utility of the patient. The physician's budget constraint is $I_d = p_m m$. Show that in this situation, the physician will generally choose a level of m that is larger than a fully informed patient would choose. (*Hint:* Assume that this problem involves cardinal utility and that the physician is a "perfect altruist" in the sense that $\partial U^d / \partial U^c = 1$).

19.10

In some cases individuals may care about the date at which the uncertainty they face is resolved. Suppose, for example, that an individual knows that his or her consumption will be 10 units today (c_1) but that tomorrow's consumption (c_2) will be either 10 or 2.5, depending on whether a coin comes up heads or tails. Suppose also that the individual's utility function has the simple Cobb-Douglas form

$$U(c_1, c_2) = \sqrt{c_1 c_2}.$$

  a. If an individual cares only about the expected value of utility, will it matter whether the coin is flipped just before day 1 or just before day 2? Explain.

  b. More generally, suppose that the individual's expected utility depends on the timing of the coin flip. Specifically, assume that

$$\text{expected utility} = E_1[(E_2\{U(c_1, c_2)\})^\alpha],$$

---

[10]Problems 19.7 and 19.8 are based on material found in the Extensions to Chapter 19.

where E_1 represents expectations taken at the start of day 1, E_2 represents expectations at the start of day 2, and α represents a parameter that indicates timing preferences. Show that if $\alpha = 1$, the individual is indifferent about when the coin is flipped.

c. Show that if $\alpha = 2$, the individual will prefer early resolution of the uncertainty—that is, flipping the coin at the start of day 1.

d. Show that if $\alpha = .5$, the individual will prefer later resolution of the uncertainty (flipping at the start of day 2).

e. Explain your results intuitively and indicate their relevance for information theory. (*Note:* This problem is an illustration of "resolution seeking" and "resolution-averse" behavior. See D. M. Kreps and E. L. Porteus, "Temporal Resolution of Uncertainty and Dynamic Choice Theory," *Econometrica* [January 1978]: 185–200.)

SUGGESTIONS FOR FURTHER READING

Diamond, P., and M. Rothschild. *Uncertainty in Economics: Readings and Exercises,* revised ed. San Diego, CA: Academic Press, 1989.
    Contains reprints of many of the articles mentioned in this chapter. Also includes brief summaries of related literature and a variety of problems and exercises.

Ehrlich, I., and G. S. Becker. "Market Insurance, Self-Insurance and Self-Protection." *Journal of Political Economy* (July/August 1972): 623–58.
    Focuses on the relationship between market insurance and self-insurance (a substitute) or self-protection (a complement). Uses a state-preference approach similar to the one in Chapter 18.

Laffont, J. and D. Martimort. *The Theory of Incentives: The Principal-Agent Model.* Princeton: Princeton University Press, 2002.
    This is a complete and rather technical coverage of principal-agent models. The authors provide a nice historical introduction to the problem and also bring in issues of moral hazard and adverse selection.

Pauly, M. "The Economics of Moral Hazard: Comment." *American Economic Review* (June 1968): 531–537.
    A comment on Arrow's article on medical insurance (see Chapter 18), which uses a simple graphic argument to show how reactions to the reduced out-of-pocket costs of medical care from being insured may make complete coverage non-Pareto optimal.

Phlips, L. *The Economics of Imperfect Information.* Cambridge: Cambridge University Press, 1988.
    Covers many of the topics in this chapter. Particularly nice discussions of auctions and signaling equilibria.

Rothschild, M., and J. Stiglitz. "Equilibrium in Competitive Insurance Markets: An Essay on the Economics of Imperfect Information." *Quarterly Journal of Economics* (November 1976): 629–50.
    Presents a nice graphic treatment of the self-selection problem. Contains ingenious illustrations of various possibilities for separating equilibria.

Stigler, G. "The Economics of Information." *Journal of Political Economy* (June 1961): 213–25.
    Classic examination of the role of search in obtaining price information.

Varian, H. R. *Microeconomic Analysis,* 3rd ed. New York. W. W. Norton. 1992.
    Varian's Chapter 25 provides a fairly extensive treatment of the principal-agent model, including an illustration of how to model hidden information.

The Economics of Search

Example 19.1 illustrates how information about unknown prices is valuable to individuals. One way in which such information can be gathered is through systematic search. Calling a few discount stores when buying a big-ticket item obviously makes sense, though it seems that one could push matters too far. Checking every store in the country or adopting elaborate search schemes when purchasing toothpaste would seem nonoptimal. In this extension we look at some models of these commonsense observations.

Statistical background

As before, we need a bit of statistical background to develop a model of search behavior. If x is a random variable with a probability density function $f(x)$ (see the extensions to Chapter 18 for a discussion of random variables), then the "cumulative distribution function" $F(z)$ is defined as

$$F(z) = \int_{-\infty}^{z} f(x)dx. \qquad \text{(i)}$$

That is, $F(z)$ gives the probability that x is less than or equal to z for any given value of z. The cumulative distribution function gives an alternative way of describing the distribution of a random variable. Notice that the cumulative distribution function and the probability density function are closely related to each other since $F' = f$.

For our examination of the search issue, we assume that an individual is seeking to buy a good at the lowest possible price, but that he or she only knows the distribution of prices (p, which can only be nonnegative) being offered by various stores. That is, he or she knows $f(p)$ and $F(p)$, but not which store offers which price.

E19.1 The diminishing marginal benefit of search

Suppose this individual decides to sample (by a phone call or an actual visit) n stores, compare their prices, and buy from the cheapest one. The probability that a particular store will offer a given price (say, p_0) and that this will be lower than that offered by the $n - 1$ other stores is given by

$$[1 - F(p_0)]^{n-1} f(p_0). \qquad \text{(ii)}$$

That is, this probability is given by the probability that $p > p_0$ for $n - 1$ stores times the probability that one store offers p_0. Taking the expected value of all such prices gives the expected minimum price the searcher will pay after checking at n stores:

$$p_{\min}^{n} = \int_{0}^{\infty} [1 - F(p)]^{n-1} f(p) p \, dp. \qquad \text{(iii)}$$

Because $(1 - F)$ is less than one, this minimum price decreases as the number of stores sampled increases. It is also straightforward to show that the expected gain from adding one more store to the sample (that is, $p_{\min}^{n-1} - p_{\min}^{n}$) also diminishes as n increases.

E19.2 Costs of search

If gathering price information is costly, not all potential information will be collected. Instead, a utility-maximizing searcher will choose n so that the expected reduction in price from the nth search is exactly equal to the cost of the search, c. Because search encounters diminishing returns, increases in c will reduce the utility-maximizing value of n. Similarly, individuals who face higher search costs will pay higher expected prices. These results were first highlighted by Stigler (1960) in a famous study of used car prices.

Price dispersion

The existence of high search costs implies that markets need not necessarily obey the "law of one price." In the absence of such costs, individuals would always seek out the lowest price, ensuring that this is the only price that can prevail in equilibrium. Search costs, however, tend to separate markets, even for homogeneous goods. For example, Gaynor and Polachek (1994) find that incomplete information about physicians' prices causes patients to pay an average 30 percent more than they would with more complete price information. Additional costs from imperfect information were found to be highest for important but infrequently purchased services such as hospital follow-up visits. On the other hand, general office and pediatric visits, services that are used repeatedly, exhibited much smaller costs from imperfect price information.

There are several ways in which consumers' information costs and price dispersions can be reduced. Many states require "price posting" for products such as gasoline or prescription drugs, thereby providing a low-cost route to comparison shopping. Price advertising in the media is another low cost way to inform consumers. The U.S. Federal Trade Commission has prodded many professions, such as attorneys or real estate agents, to remove bans on price advertising. The commission argues that the primary effect of such bans on price advertising is to increase price dispersion and provide supercompetitive returns to some suppliers. Finally, consumers can reduce price dispersions themselves by purchasing price information. A number of automobile-purchase and apartment-rental services have been developed for that purpose in recent years.

E19.3 Reservation price strategy

Choosing a price search strategy on *a priori* grounds may not be optimal. If one were to encounter a surprisingly low price at, say, the fifth store sampled, it would make little sense to visit the remaining $n - 5$ ones. One sequential search strategy that is optimal in a variety of circumstances is for the individual to choose a *reservation price* (p_R) and accept the first price found that is equal to or lower than p_R. The reservation price should be chosen so that the expected gain from one more search once p_R has been achieved is equal to the cost of that search, c. That is, we wish to know the expected value of $p_R - p$ for values of $p \leq p_R$. Setting this value equal to c permits the solution of an optimal p_R.

$$c = \int_0^{p_R} (p_R - p) f(p) dp \qquad \text{(iv)}$$

Now an increase in c will cause this person to opt for a higher reservation price and he or she will visit fewer stores.[1] In this sequential strategy, just as in the fixed sample size strategy, increases in search costs reduce the amount of search individuals do.

Reservation wages

This approach to search theory has been most extensively applied to the problem of unemployed workers looking for jobs. In that application, the optimal strategy consists of choosing a minimum acceptable wage that must be met before a job is accepted. The theoretical and empirical literature on the relationship between reservation wages and job search prices is very large (see, for example, Kiefer and Neumann, 1989). Perhaps the most important finding from such studies is that reservation wages tend to decline over time as unemployment spells lengthen. There also appears to be evidence that generous unemployment benefits raise reservation wages. In most of these cases, however, reservation wages are not measured directly, but are instead inferred from the behavior of individual workers. Some economists (for example, Cox and Oaxaca, 1992) have tried to measure reservation wages (or prices) directly in controlled experiments. Although creating these experiments poses a variety of conceptual problems, evidence from them seems generally supportive of the conclusions implied by the observed search behavior of workers in the labor market.

E19.4 Distribution of prices

Optimal search strategy will also depend on the characteristics of the distribution of prices. The greater the μ_p, the greater the search intensity that will be warranted, *ceteris paribus*. Individuals will be more likely to search for expensive goods than for cheap ones. Similarly, the greater the dispersion of prices, the more search will be optimal. Obviously, if $\sigma_p = 0$ (as is implied by the "law of one price" under perfect competition), any search would be superfluous. All such results depend on an individual's knowledge of the distribution of prices before search begins, though Rothschild (1974) shows that qualitatively similar results can be derived when individuals have no *a priori* information about prices and must infer the distribution from information gathered in their search.

References

Cox, J. C., and R. L. Oaxaca. "Direct Tests of the Reservation Wage Property," *Economic Journal* (November 1992): 1423–32.

Gaynor, M., and S. W. Polachek. "Measuring Information in the Market: An Application to Physician Services." *Southern Economic Journal* (April 1994): 815–31.

Kiefer, N. M., and G. R. Neumann. *Search Models and Applied Labor Economics.* Cambridge: Cambridge University Press, 1989.

Rothschild, M. "Searching for the Lowest Price When the Distribution of Prices Is Unknown." *Journal of Political Economy* (July–August 1974): 689–711.

Stigler, G. J. "The Economics of Information." *Journal of Political Economy* (June 1961): 213–25.

---

[1] Integration by parts shows that

$$c = \int_0^{p_R} (p_R - p) f(p) dp = p_R F(p_R) - \int_0^{p_R} p f(p) dp$$
$$= \int_0^{p_R} F(p) dp,$$

which makes it clear that p_R and c are positively related.

Chapter 20

EXTERNALITIES AND PUBLIC GOODS

In Chapter 12 we looked briefly at a few problems that may interfere with the allocational efficiency of perfectly competitive markets. Here we will examine two of those problems, externalities and public goods, in more detail. This examination has two purposes. First, we wish to show clearly why the existence of externalities and public goods may distort the allocation of resources. In so doing it will be possible to illustrate some additional features of the type of information that is provided by competitive prices and some of the circumstances that may diminish the usefulness of that information. Our second reason for looking more closely at externalities and public goods is to suggest ways in which the allocational problems they pose might be mitigated. We will see that, at least in some cases, the efficiency of competitive market outcomes may be more robust than might have been anticipated.

Defining externalities

Externalities occur because economic agents have effects on third parties that are not reflected in market transactions. Chemical makers spewing toxic fumes on their neighbors, jet planes waking up people, or motorists littering the highway are, from an economic point of view, all engaging in the same sort of activity—they are having a direct effect on the well-being of others that is outside direct market channels. Such activities might be contrasted to the direct effects of markets. When I choose to purchase a loaf of bread, for example, I (perhaps imperceptibly) raise the price of bread generally, and that may affect the well-being of other bread buyers. But such effects, because they are reflected in market prices, are not true externalities and do not affect the market's ability to allocate resources efficiently.[1] Rather, the rise in the price of bread that results from my increased purchase is an accurate reflection of societal preferences, and the price rise helps ensure that the right mix of products is produced. That is not the case for toxic chemical discharges, jet noise, or litter. In these cases, market prices (of chemicals, air travel, or disposable containers) may not accurately reflect actual social costs because they may take no account of the damage being done to third parties. Information being conveyed by market prices is fundamentally inaccurate, leading to a misallocation of resources.

---

[1]Sometimes effects of one economic agent on another that take place through the market system are termed *pecuniary* externalities to differentiate such effects from the *technological* externalities we are discussing. Here the use of the term *externalities* will refer only to the latter type, because these are the only type with consequences for the efficiency of resource allocation by competitive markets.

As a summary, therefore, we have developed the following definition:

DEFINITION

Externality. An *externality* occurs whenever the activities of one economic agent affect the activities of another agent in ways that are not reflected in market transactions.

Before analyzing in detail why failing to take externalities into account can lead to a misallocation of resources, we will examine a few examples that may clarify the nature of the problem.

Interfirm externalities

To illustrate the externality issue in its simplest form, consider two firms—one producing good x and the other producing good y—where each firm uses only a single input, labor. The production of good x is said to have an external effect on the production of y if the output of y depends not only on the inputs chosen by the y-entrepreneur but also on the level at which the production of x is carried on. Notationally, the production function for good y can be written as

$$y = f(k, l; x), \tag{20.1}$$

where x appears to the right of the semicolon in the equation to show that it is an effect on production over which the y-entrepreneur has no control.[2] As an example, suppose the two firms are located on a river, with firm y being downstream from x. Suppose firm x pollutes the river in its productive process. Then the output of firm y may depend not only on the level of inputs it uses itself, but also on the amount of pollutants flowing past its factory. The level of pollutants, in turn, is determined by the output of firm x. In the production function shown by Equation 20.1, the output of firm x would have a negative marginal physical productivity $\partial y / \partial x < 0$. Increases in x output would cause less y to be produced. In the next section we return to analyze this case more fully as it is representative of most simple types of externalities.

Beneficial externalities

The relationship between two firms may be beneficial. Most examples of such positive externalities are rather bucolic in nature. Perhaps the most famous, proposed by J. Meade, involves two firms, one producing honey (raising bees) and the other producing apples.[3] Because the bees feed on apple blossoms, an increase in apple production will improve productivity in the honey industry. The beneficial effects of having well-fed bees is a positive externality to the beekeeper. In the notation of Equation 20.1, $\partial y / \partial x$ would now be positive. In the usual perfectly competitive case, the productive activities of one firm have no direct effect on those of other firms: $\partial y / \partial x = 0$.

Externalities in utility

Externalities also can occur if the activities of an economic agent directly affect an individual's utility. Most common examples of environmental externalities are of this type. From an economic perspective it makes little difference whether such effects are created by firms (in the form, say, of toxic chemicals or jet noise) or by other individuals (litter or, perhaps, the noise from a loud radio). In all such cases the amount of such activities would enter directly into the individual's utility function in much the same way as firm x's output entered into firm y's production function in Equation 20.1. As in the case of firms, such externalities may sometimes be beneficial (you may actually like the song being played on your

---

[2]We will find it necessary to redefine the assumption of "no control" considerably as the analysis of this chapter proceeds.

[3]J. Meade, "External Economies and Diseconomies in a Competitive Situation," *Economic Journal 62* (March 1952): 54–67.

neighbor's radio). So, again, a situation of no externalities can be regarded as the middle ground in which other agents' activities have no direct effect on individuals' utilities.

One special type of utility externality relevant to the analysis of social choices arises when one individual's utility depends directly on the utility of someone else. If, for example, Smith cares about Jones's welfare, we could write his or her utility function (U_S) as

$$\text{utility} = U_S(x_1, \ldots, x_n; U_J), \tag{20.2}$$

where $x_1, \ldots, x_n$ are the goods that Smith consumes and U_J is Jones's utility. If Smith is altruistic and wants Jones to be well off (as might happen if Jones were a close relative), $\partial U_S / \partial U_J$ would be positive. If, on the other hand, Smith were envious of Jones, it might be the case that $\partial U_S / \partial U_J$ would be negative; that is, improvements in Jones's utility make Smith worse off. The middle ground between altruism and envy would occur if Smith were indifferent to Jones's welfare ($\partial U_S / \partial U_J = 0$), and that is what we have usually assumed throughout this book (for a brief discussion, see the Extensions to Chapter 3).

Public goods externalities

Goods that are "public" or "collective" in nature will be the focus for our analysis in the second half of this chapter. The defining characteristic of these goods is nonexclusion; that is, once the goods are produced (either by the government or by some private entity), they provide benefits to an entire group, perhaps to everyone. It is technically impossible to restrict these benefits to the specific group of individuals who pay for them, so the benefits are available to all. As we mentioned in Chapter 12, national defense provides the traditional example. Once a defense system is established, all individuals in society are protected by it whether they wish to be or not and whether they pay for it or not. Choosing the right level of output for such a good can be a tricky process, because market signals will be inaccurate.

Externalities and allocative inefficiency

Externalities lead to inefficient allocations of resources because market prices do not accurately reflect the additional costs imposed on or benefits provided to third parties. To illustrate these inefficiencies requires a general equilibrium model because inefficient allocations in one market throw into doubt the efficiency of market-determined outcomes everywhere. Here we choose a very simple, and in some ways, rather odd general equilibrium model that allows us to make these points in a compact way. Specifically, we assume there is only one person in our simple economy and that his or her utility depends on the quantities of x and y consumed. Consumption levels of these two goods are denoted by x_c and y_c so,

$$\text{utility} = U(x_c, y_c). \tag{20.3}$$

This person has initial stocks of x and y (denoted by x^* and y^*) and can either consume these directly or use them as intermediary goods in production. To simplify matters, we assume that good x is produced using only good y, according to the production function

$$x_o = f(y_i), \tag{20.4}$$

where subscripts "o" refer to outputs and "i" refer to inputs. To illustrate externalities we assume that the output of good y depends not only on how much x is used as an input in the production process, but also on the x production level itself. Hence this would model a situation, say, where y is downriver from firm x and must cope with the pollution that production of x output creates. The production function for y is given by

$$y_o = g(x_i, x_o), \tag{20.5}$$

where $g_1 > 0$ (more x input produces more y output), but $g_2 < 0$ (additional x output reduces y output because of the externality involved).

The quantities of each good in this economy are constrained by the initial stocks available and by the additional production that takes place:

$$x_c + x_i = x_o + x^* \qquad (20.6)$$

$$y_c + y_i = y_o + y^*. \qquad (20.7)$$

Finding the efficient allocation

The economic problem for this society, then, is to maximize utility subject to the four constraints represented by Equations 20.4–20.7. To solve this problem we must introduce four Lagrangian multipliers. The Lagrangian expression for this maximization problem is

$$\mathcal{L} = U(x_c, y_c) + \lambda_1[f(y_i) - x_o] + \lambda_2[g(x_i, x_o) - y_o]$$
$$+ \lambda_3(x_c + x_i - x_o - x^*) + \lambda_4(y_c + y_i - y_o - y^*) \qquad (20.8)$$

and the six first-order conditions for a maximum are

$$\partial\mathcal{L}/\partial x_c = U_1 + \lambda_3 = 0 \qquad \text{[i]}$$
$$\partial\mathcal{L}/\partial y_c = U_2 + \lambda_4 = 0 \qquad \text{[ii]}$$
$$\partial\mathcal{L}/\partial x_i = \lambda_2 g_1 + \lambda_3 = 0 \qquad \text{[iii]}$$
$$\partial\mathcal{L}/\partial y_i = \lambda_1 f_y + \lambda_4 = 0 \qquad \text{[iv]} \qquad (20.9)$$
$$\partial\mathcal{L}/\partial x_o = -\lambda_1 + \lambda_2 g_2 - \lambda_3 = 0 \qquad \text{[v]}$$
$$\partial\mathcal{L}/\partial y_o = -\lambda_2 - \lambda_4 = 0 \qquad \text{[vi]}$$

Eliminating the λs from these equations is a straightforward process. Taking the ratio of Equations i and ii yields the familiar result.

$$MRS = U_1/U_2 = \lambda_3/\lambda_4. \qquad (20.10)$$

But Equations iii and vi also imply

$$MRS = \lambda_3/\lambda_4 = \lambda_2 g_1/\lambda_2 = g_1. \qquad (20.11)$$

Hence optimality in y production requires that the individual's MRS is consumption equal the marginal productivity of x in the production of y. This conclusion repeats the result from Chapter 12, where we showed that efficient output choice requires that dy/dx in consumption be equal to dy/dx in production.

To achieve efficiency in x production we must also consider the externality that this production poses to y. Combining Equations iv–vi gives

$$MRS = \lambda_3/\lambda_4 = (-\lambda_1 + \lambda_2 g_2)/\lambda_4 = -\lambda_1/\lambda_4 + \lambda_2 g_2/\lambda_4$$
$$= 1/f_y - g_2. \qquad (20.12)$$

Intuitively, this equation requires that the individual's MRS must also equal dy/dx obtained through x production. The first term in the expression, $1/f_y$, represents the reciprocal of the marginal productivity of y in x production—this is the first component of dy/dx as it relates to x production. The second term, g_2, represents the negative impact that added x production has on y output—this is the second component of dy/dx as it relates to x production. This final term occurs because of the need to consider the externality from x production. If g_2 were zero, Equations 20.11 and 20.12 would represent essentially the same condition for efficient production, which would apply to both x and y. With the externality, however, determining an efficient level of x production is more complex.

Inefficiency of the competitive allocation

Reliance on competitive pricing in this simple model will result in an inefficient allocation of resources. With equilibrium prices, P_x and P_y, a utility-maximizing individual would opt for

$$MRS = P_x/P_y \qquad (20.13)$$

and the profit-maximizing producer of good y would choose x input according to

$$P_x = P_y g_1. \qquad (20.14)$$

Hence efficiency condition 20.11 would be satisfied. But the producer of good x would choose y input so that

$$P_y = P_x f_y \quad \text{or} \quad P_x/P_y = 1/f_y. \qquad (20.15)$$

That is, the producer of x would disregard the externality that its production poses for y and the efficiency condition 20.12 would not be met. This failure results in an overproduction of x relative to the efficient level. This can be demonstrated by noting that the marginal product of y in producing x (f_y) is smaller under the market allocation represented by Equation 20.15 than under the optimal allocation represented by Equation 20.12. More y is used to produce x in the market allocation (and hence more x is produced) than is optimal. Example 20.1 provides a quantitative example of this nonoptimality in a partial equilibrium context.

 EXAMPLE 20.1

Production Externalities

As a partial equilibrium illustration of the losses from failure to consider production externalities, suppose two newsprint producers are located along a river. The upstream firm (x) has a production function of the form

$$x = 2,000 l_x^{1/2}, \qquad (20.16)$$

where l_x is the number of workers hired per day and x is newsprint output in feet. The downstream firm (y) has a similar production function, but its output may be affected by the chemicals firm x pours into the river:

$$\begin{aligned} y &= 2,000 l_y^{1/2}(x - x_0)^a && \text{(for } x > x_0) \\ y &= 2,000 l_y^{1/2} && \text{(for } x \le x_0), \end{aligned} \qquad (20.17)$$

where x_0 represents the river's natural capacity for pollutants. If $\alpha = 0$, x's production process has no effect on firm y, whereas if $\alpha < 0$, increase in x above x_0 cause y's output to decline.

Assuming newsprint sells for $1 per foot and workers earn $50 per day, firm x will maximize profits by setting this wage equal to labor's marginal revenue product:

$$50 = p \cdot \frac{\partial x}{\partial l_x} = 1,000 l_x^{-1/2}. \qquad (20.18)$$

The solution then is $l_x = 400$. If $\alpha = 0$ (there are no externalities), firm y will also hire 400 workers. Each firm will produce 40,000 feet of newsprint.

Effects of an externality. When firm x does have a negative externality ($\alpha < 0$), its profit-maximizing hiring decision is not affected—it will still hire $l_x = 400$ and produce

$x = 40,000$. But for firm y, labor's marginal product will be lower because of this externality. If $\alpha = -.1$ and $x_0 = 38,000$, for example, profit maximization will require

$$
\begin{aligned}
50 = p \cdot \frac{\partial y}{\partial l_y} &= 1,000 l_y^{-1/2}(x - 38,000)^{-1} \\
&= 1,000 l_y^{-1/2}(2,000)^{-1} \\
&= 468 l_y^{-1/2}.
\end{aligned}
\tag{20.19}
$$

Solving this equation for l_y shows that firm y now hires only 87 workers because of this lowered productivity. Output of firm y will now be

$$y = 2,000(87)^{1/2}(2,000)^{-1} = 8,723. \tag{20.20}$$

Because of the externality ($\alpha = .1$), newsprint output will be lower than without the externality ($\alpha = 0$).

Inefficiency. We can demonstrate that decentralized profit maximization is inefficient in this situation by imagining that firms x and y merge and the manager must decide how to allocate the combined workforce. If one worker is transferred from firm x to firm y, x output becomes

$$
\begin{aligned}
x &= 2,000(399)^{1/2} \\
&= 39,950
\end{aligned}
\tag{20.21}
$$

and for firm y

$$
\begin{aligned}
y &= 2,000(88)^{1/2}(1,950)^{-1} \\
&= 8,796.
\end{aligned}
\tag{20.22}
$$

Total output has increased by 23 feet of newsprint with no change in total labor input. The market-based allocation was inefficient because firm x did not take into account the effect of its hiring decisions on firm y.

Marginal productivity. This can be illustrated in another way by computing the true social marginal productivity of labor input to firm x. If that firm were to hire one more worker, its own output would rise to

$$x = 2,000(401)^{1/2} = 40,050. \tag{20.23}$$

As profit maximization requires, the (private) marginal value product of the 401st worker is equal to the wage. But increasing x's output now also has an effect on firm y—its output declines by about 21 units. Hence, the social marginal revenue product of labor to firm x actually amounts to only \$29 (\$50 − \$21). That is why the manager of a merged firm would find it profitable to shift some workers from firm x to y.

Query: Suppose $\alpha = +.1$. What would that imply about the relationship between the firms? How would such an externality affect the allocation of labor?

FIGURE 20.1   **Graphic Analysis of an Externality**

The demand curve for good x is given by DD. The supply curve for x represents the private marginal costs (MC) involved in x production. If x production imposes external costs on third parties, social marginal costs (MC') will exceed MC by the extent of these costs. Market equilibrium occurs at x_1 and at this output level, social marginal costs exceed what consumers pay of good x. A tax of amount t that reflects the costs of the externalities would achieve the efficient output of x—given by output level x_2.

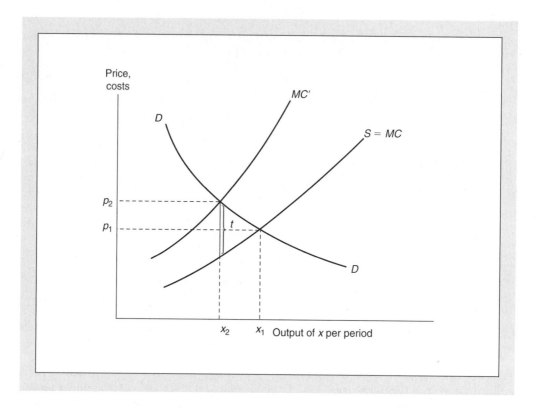

Solutions to the externality problem

Incentive-based solutions to the allocational harm of externalities start from the basic observation that output of the externality-producing activity is too high under a market-determined equilibrium. Perhaps the first economist to provide a complete analysis of this distortion was A. C. Pigou, who, in the 1920s, suggested that the most direct solution would simply be to tax the externality-creating entity.[4] All incentive-based[5] solutions to the externality problem stem from this basic insight.

A graphic analysis

Figure 20.1 provides the traditional illustration of an externality together with Pigou's taxation solution. The supply curve for good x also represents that good's private marginal costs of production (MC). When the demand for x is given by DD, the market equi-

[4]A. C. Pigou, *The Economics of Welfare* (London: MacMillan, 1920). Pigou also recognized the importance of subsidizing goods that yield positive externalities.

[5]We do not discuss purely regulatory solutions here, although the study of such solutions forms an important part of most courses in environmental economics. See W. J. Baumol and W. E. Oates, *The Theory of Environmental Policy*, 2nd ed. (Cambridge: Cambridge University Press, 1988) and the Extensions to this chapter.

librium will occur at x_1. The external costs involved in x production create a divergence between private marginal costs (MC) and overall social marginal costs (MC')—the vertical distance between the two curves represents the costs that x production poses for third parties (in our examples, only on firm y). Notice that the per-unit costs of these externalities need not be constant, independent of x-output. In the figure, for example, the size of these external costs rises as x output expands (that is, MC' and MC become further apart). At the market-determined output level, x_1, the comprehensive social marginal cost exceeds the market price, p_1, thereby indicating that the production of x has been pushed "too far." It is clear from the figure that the optimal output level is x_2 at which the market price paid for the good, p_2, now reflects all costs.

As is the case for any tax, imposition of a Pigovian tax would create a vertical wedge between the demand and supply curves for good x. In Figure 20.1 this optimal tax is shown as t. Imposition of this tax serves to reduce output to x_2, the social optimum. Tax collections equal the precise amount of external harm that x production causes. These collections might be used to compensate firm y for these costs, but that is not crucial to the analysis. Notice here that the tax must be set at the level of harm that prevails at the optimum (that is, at x_2), not at the level of harm at the original market equilibrium (x_1). That point is also made in the next example and more completely in the next section by returning to our simple general equilibrium model.

 EXAMPLE 20.2

A Pigovian Tax on Newsprint

The inefficiency in Example 20.1 arises because the upstream newsprint producer (firm x) takes no account of the effect that its production has on firm y. A suitably chosen tax on firm x can cause it to reduce its hiring to a level at which the externality vanishes. Because the river can absorb the pollutants generated with an output of $x = 38,000$, we might consider imposing a tax (t) on the firm's output that encourages it to reduce output to this level. Because output will be 38,000 if $l_x = 361$, we can calculate t from the labor demand condition:

$$(1 - t)MP_L = (1 - t)1,000(361)^{-.5} = 50 \qquad (20.24)$$

or

$$t = .05. \qquad (20.25)$$

Such a 5 percent tax would effectively reduce the price firm x receives for its newsprint to \$.95 and provide it with an incentive to reduce its hiring by 39 workers. Now, because the river can handle all of the pollutants x produces, there is no externality in the production function of firm y. It will hire 400 workers and produce 40,000 feet of newsprint per day. Notice that total newsprint output is now 78,000, a significantly higher figure than would be produced in the untaxed situation. The taxation solution provides a considerable improvement in the efficiency of resource allocation.

Query: The tax rate proposed here (0.05) seems rather small given the significant output gains obtained relative to the situation in Example 20.1. Can you explain why? Would a merged firm opt for $x = 38,000$ even without a tax?

Taxation in the general equilibrium model

The optimal Pigovian tax in our general equilibrium model is to set $t = -p_y g_2$. That is, the per-unit tax on good x should reflect the marginal harm that x does in reducing y output, valued at the market price of good y. Notice again that this tax must be based on the value of this externality at the optimal solution—because g_2 will generally be a function of the level of x output, a tax based on some other output level would be inappropriate. With the optimal tax, firm x now faces a net price for its output of $p_x - t$ and will choose y input according to

$$p_y = (p_x - t)f_y. \tag{20.26}$$

Hence the resulting allocation of resources will achieve

$$MRS = p_x/p_y = (1/f_y) + t/p_y = (1/f_y) - g_2, \tag{20.27}$$

which is precisely what is required for optimality (compare to the efficiency condition, 20.12). The Pigovian taxation solution can be generalized in a variety of ways that provide insights about the conduct of policy toward externalities. For example, in an economy with many x-producers, the tax would convey information about the marginal impact that output from any one of these would have on y output. Hence the tax scheme mitigates the need for regulatory attention to the specifics of any particular firm. It does require that regulators have enough information to set taxes appropriately—that is, they must know firm y's production function.

Pollution rights

An innovation that would mitigate the informational requirements involved with Pigovian taxation is the creation of a market for "pollution rights." Suppose, for example, that firm x must purchase from firm y rights to pollute the river they share. In this case, x's decision to purchase these rights is identical to its decision to choose its output level, because it cannot produce without them. The net revenue x receives per unit is given by $p_x - r$, where r is the payment the firm must make for each unit it produces. Firm y must decide how many rights to sell to firm x. Because it will be paid r for each right, it must "choose" x output to maximize its profits:

$$\pi_y = p_y g(x_i, x_0) + rx_0, \tag{20.28}$$

and the first-order condition for a maximum is

$$\partial\pi_y/\partial x_0 = p_y g_2 + r = 0 \quad \text{or} \quad r = -p_y g_2. \tag{20.29}$$

Equation 20.29 makes clear that the equilibrium solution to pricing in the pollution rights market will be identical to the Pigovian tax equilibrium. From the point of view of firm x it makes no difference whether a tax of amount t is paid to the government or a royalty of the same amount, r, is paid to firm y. So long as $t = r$ (a condition ensured by Equation 20.29), the same, efficient equilibrium will result.

The Coase theorem

In a famous 1960 paper, Ronald Coase showed that the key feature of the pollution rights equilibrium is that these rights be well defined and tradable with zero transaction costs.[6] The initial assignment of rights is irrelevant because subsequent trading will always yield the same, efficient equilibrium. In our example we initially assigned the rights to firm y, allowing that firm to trade them away to firm x for a per unit fee r. If the rights had been assigned to firm x instead, that firm still would have to impute some cost to using these rights themselves rather than selling them to firm y. This calculation, in combination with firm y's decision about how many such rights to buy will, again, yield an efficient result.

---

[6]R. Coase, "The Problem of Social Cost," *Journal of Law and Economics* 3 (October 1960): 1–44.

To illustrate the Coase result, assume that firm x is given x^T rights to produce (and to pollute). It can choose to use some of these to support its own production (x_0), or it may sell some to firm y (an amount given by $x^T - x_0$). Gross profits for x are given by

$$\pi_x = p_x\, x_0 + r(x^T - x_0) = (p_x - r)\, x_0 + rx^T = (p_x - r)\, f(y_i) + rx^T \quad (20.30)$$

and for y by

$$\pi y = p_y\, g(x_i,\, x_0) - r(x^T - x_0) \qquad\qquad (20.31)$$

Clearly, profit maximization in this situation will lead to precisely the same solution as in the case where firm y was assigned the rights. Because the overall total number of rights (x^T) is a constant, the first-order conditions for a maximum will be exactly the same in the two cases. This independence of initial rights assignment is usually referred to as the *Coase theorem*.

Although the results of the Coase theorem may seem counterintuitive (how can the level of pollution be independent of who initially owns the rights?), it is in reality nothing more than the assertion that, in the absence of impediments to making bargains, all mutually beneficial transactions will be completed. When transaction costs are high, or when information is asymmetric, initial rights assignments will matter, however, because the sorts of trading implied by the Coase theorem may not occur. It is therefore the limitations of the Coase theorem that provide the most interesting opportunities for further analysis. This analysis has been especially far reaching in the field of law and economics,[7] where the theorem has been applied to topics such as tort liability laws, contract law, and product safety legislation (see Problems 20.4 and 20.5).

Attributes of public goods

We now turn our attention to a related set of problems about the relationship between competitive markets and the allocation of resources—those raised by the existence of public goods. We begin by providing a precise definition of this concept and then examine why such goods pose allocational problems. We then briefly discuss potential ways in which such problems might be mitigated.

The most common definitions of public goods stress two attributes of such goods: nonexclusivity and nonrivalness. We now describe these attributes in detail.

Nonexclusivity

The first property that distinguishes public goods concerns whether individuals may be excluded from the benefits of consuming the good. For most private goods such exclusion is indeed possible: I can easily be excluded from consuming a hamburger if I don't pay for it. In some cases, however, such exclusion is either very costly or impossible. National defense is the standard example. Once a defense system is established, everyone in a country benefits from it whether they pay for it or not. Similar comments apply, on a more local level, to goods such as mosquito control or inoculation against disease programs. In these cases, once the programs are implemented, no one in the community can be excluded from those benefits whether he or she pays for them or not. Hence, we can divide goods into two categories according to the following definition:

DEFINITION

Exclusive goods. A good is *exclusive* if it is relatively easy to exclude individuals from benefiting from the good once it is produced. A good is *nonexclusive* if it is impossible, or very costly, to exclude individuals from benefiting from the good.

---

[7]The classic text is R. A. Posner, *Economic Analysis of Law*, 4th ed. (Boston: Little Brown, 1992). A more mathematical approach is T. J. Miceli, *Economics of the Law* (New York: Oxford University Press, 1997).

Nonrivalry

A second property that characterizes public goods is nonrivalry. A nonrival good is one for which additional units can be consumed at zero social marginal cost. For most goods, of course, consumption of additional amounts involves some marginal costs of production. Consumption of one more hot dog by someone, for example, requires that various resources be devoted to its production. For certain goods, however, this is not the case. Consider, for example, having one more automobile cross a highway bridge during an off-peak period. Because the bridge is already in place, having one more vehicle cross requires no additional resource use and does not reduce consumption elsewhere. Similarly, having one more viewer tune in to a television channel involves no additional cost, even though this action would result in additional consumption taking place. Therefore, we have developed the following definition:

DEFINITION

> **Nonrival goods.** A good is *nonrival* if consumption of additional units of the good involves zero social marginal costs of production.

Typology of public goods

The concepts of nonexclusion and nonrivalry are in some ways related. Many nonexclusive goods are also nonrival. National defense and mosquito control are two examples of goods for which exclusion is not possible and additional consumption takes place at zero marginal cost. Many other instances might be suggested. The concepts, however, are not identical: some goods may possess one property, but not the other. It is, for example, impossible (or at least very costly) to exclude some fishing boats from ocean fisheries, yet the arrival of another boat clearly imposes social costs in the form of a reduced catch for all concerned. Similarly, use of a bridge during off-peak hours may be nonrival, but it is possible to exclude potential users by erecting toll booths. Table 20.1 presents a cross-classification of goods by their possibilities for exclusion and their rivalry. Several examples of goods that fit into each of the categories are provided. Many of the examples, other than those in the upper left corner of table (exclusive, rival private goods), are often produced by governments. That is especially the case for nonexclusive goods because, as we shall see, it is difficult to develop ways of paying for such goods other than through compulsory taxation. Nonrival goods often are privately produced (there are, after all, private bridges, swimming pools, and highways that consumers must pay to use) as long as nonpayers can be excluded from consuming them.[8] Still, we will use a stringent definition that requires both conditions:

TABLE 20.1	**Examples Showing the Typology of Public and Private Goods**

		Exclusive	
		Yes	No
Rival	Yes	Hot dogs, automobiles, houses	Fishing grounds, public grazing land, clean air
	No	Bridges, swimming pools, satellite television transmission (scrambled)	National defense, mosquito control, justice

[8]Nonrival goods that permit imposition of an exclusion mechanism are sometimes referred to as *club goods,* because provision of such goods might be organized along the lines of private clubs. Such clubs might then charge a "membership" fee and permit unlimited use by members. The optimal size of a club is determined by the economies of scale present in the production process for the club good. For an analysis, see R. Cornes and T. Sandler, *The Theory of Externalities, Public Goods, and Club Goods* (Cambridge: Cambridge University Press, 1986).

Public good. A good is a (pure) *public good* if, once produced, no one can be excluded from benefiting from its availability and if the good is nonrival—the marginal cost of an additional consumer is zero.

Public goods and resource allocation

To illustrate the allocational problems created by public goods, we again employ a very simple general equilibrium model. In this model there are only two individuals—a single person economy would not experience problems from public goods because he or she would incorporate all of the goods' benefits into consumption decisions. We denote these two individuals by A and B. There are also only two goods in this economy. Good y is an ordinary private good, and each person begins with an allocation of this good given by y^{A*} and y^{B*}, respectively. Each person may choose to consume some of his or her y directly or to devote some portion of it to the production of a single public good, x. The amounts contributed are given by y_s^A and y_s^B, and the public good is produced according to the production function

$$x = f(y_s^A + y_s^B). \tag{20.32}$$

Resulting utilities for these two people in this society are given by

$$U^A[(x,(y^{A*} - y_s^A)], \tag{20.33}$$

and

$$U^B[(x,(y^{B*} - y_s^B)]. \tag{20.34}$$

Notice here that the level of public good production, x, enters identically into each person's utility function. This is the way in which the nonexclusivity and nonrivalry characteristics of such goods are captured mathematically. Nonexclusivity is reflected by the fact that each person's consumption of x is independent of what he or she contributes individually to its production. Nonrivalry is shown by the fact that x is the same for each person and identical to the total amount of x produced. Consumption of x benefits by A does not diminish what B can consume. These two characteristics of good x constitute the barriers to efficient production under most decentralized decision schemes, including competitive markets.

The necessary conditions for efficient resource allocation in this problem consist of choosing the levels of public goods subscriptions (y_s^A and y_s^B) that maximize, say, A's utility for any given level of B's utility. The Lagrangian expression for this problem is

$$\mathcal{L} = U^A(x, y^{A*} - y_s^A) + \lambda[U^B(x, y^{B*} - y_s^B) - K], \tag{20.35}$$

where K is a constant level of B's utility. The first-order conditions for a maximum are

$$\partial\mathcal{L}/\partial y_s^A = U_1^A f' - U_2^A + \lambda U_1^B f' = 0 \tag{20.36}$$

and

$$\partial\mathcal{L}/\partial y_s^B = U_1^A f' - \lambda U_2^B + \lambda U_1^B f' = 0. \tag{20.37}$$

A comparison of these two equations yields the immediate result that

$$\lambda U_2^B = U_2^A. \tag{20.38}$$

As might have been expected here, optimality requires that the marginal utility of y consumption for A and B be equal except for the constant of proportionality, λ. This equation may now be combined with either Equation 20.36 or 20.37 to derive the optimality condition for the production of the public good x. Using Equation 20.36, for example, gives

$$U_1^A / U_2^A + \lambda U_1^B / \lambda U_2^B = 1/f' \qquad (20.39)$$

or, more simply,

$$MRS^A + MRS^B = 1/f'. \qquad (20.40)$$

The intuition behind this condition, which was first articulated by P. A. Samuelson,[9] is that it is an adaptation of the efficiency conditions described in Chapter 12 to the case of public goods. For such goods, the MRS in consumption must reflect how much y *all* consumers would be willing to give up to get one more x, because everyone will obtain the benefits of the extra x output. Hence it is the sum of each individual's MRS that should be equated to dy/dx in production (here given by $1/f'$).

Failure of a competitive market

Production of goods x and y in competitive markets will fail to achieve this allocational goal. With perfectly competitive prices p_x and p_y, each individual will equate his or her MRS to the price ratio p_x/p_y. A producer of good x would also set $1/f'$ to be equal to p_x/p_y, as would be required for profit maximization. This behavior would not achieve the optimality condition expressed in Equation 20.40. The price ratio p_x/p_y would be "too low" in that it would provide too little incentive to produce good x. In the private market each consumer takes no account of how his or her spending on the public good benefits other consumers, so that person will devote too few resources to such production.

The allocational failure in this situation can be ascribed to the way in which private markets sum individual demands. For any given quantity the market demand curve reports the marginal valuation of a good. If one more unit were produced, it could then be consumed by someone who would value it at this market price. For public goods, the value of producing one more unit is in fact the sum of each consumer's valuation of that extra output, because all consumers will benefit from it. In this case, then, individual demand curves should be added vertically (as shown in Figure 20.2) rather then horizontally (as they are in competitive markets). The resulting price on such a public good demand curve will then reflect, for any level of output, how much an extra unit of output would be valued by all consumers. But the usual market demand curve will not properly reflect this full marginal valuation.

Inefficiency of a Nash equilibrium

An alternative approach to the production of public goods in competitive markets might rely on individuals' voluntary contributions. Unfortunately, this also will yield inefficient results. Consider the situation of person A, who is thinking about contributing s_A of his or her initial y endowment to public goods production. The utility maximization problem for A is then

$$\text{Choose } s_A \text{ to maximize } U^A[f(s_A + s_B), y^{A*} - s_A]. \qquad (20.41)$$

The first-order condition for a maximum is

$$U_1^A f' - U_2^A = 0 \text{ or } U_1^A / U_2^A = MRS^A = 1/f'. \qquad (20.42)$$

Because a similar logic will apply to person B, efficiency condition 20.40 will once more fail to be satisfied. Again the problem is that each person considers only his or her benefit from investing in the public good, taking no account of the benefits provided to

---

[9]P. A. Samuelson, "The Pure Theory of Public Expenditure." *Review of Economics and Statistics* (November 1954): 387–89.

| FIGURE 20.2 | Derivation of the Demand for a Public Good |

For a public good, the price individuals are willing to pay for one more unit (their "marginal valuations") is equal to the sum of what each individual would pay. Hence, for public goods, the demand curve must be derived by a vertical summation rather than the horizontal summation used in the case of private goods.

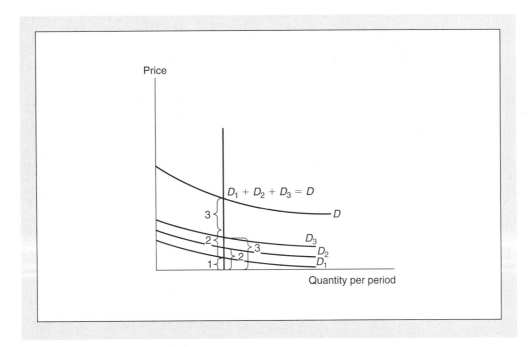

others. With many consumers, this direct benefit may be very small indeed (how much do one person's taxes contribute to national defense in the United States, for example?). In this case, any one person may opt for $s_A = 0$ and become a pure "free rider," hoping to benefit from the expenditures of others. If every person adopts this strategy, no resources will be subscribed to public goods. Example 20.3 illustrates the free-rider problem in a situation that may be all too familiar.

 EXAMPLE 20.3

Purchasing a Public Good: The Roommates' Dilemma

To illustrate the nature of the public goods problem numerically, suppose two Bohemian roommates with identical preferences derive utility from the number of paintings hung on their hovel's walls (x) and on the number of granola bars (y) they eat. The specific form of the utility function is given by

$$U_i(x, y_i) = x^{1/3}y_i^{2/3} \quad \text{(for } i = 1, 2\text{).} \qquad (20.43)$$

Notice that utility for each person depends on the total number of paintings hung and on the number of granola bars each person consumes individually. Enjoyment of paintings in this problem, therefore, constitutes a public good.

If we assume each roommate has $300 to spend and that $p_x = \$100$, $p_y = \$.20$, we can explore the consequences of various expenditure allocations. We know from previous

(continued)

EXAMPLE 20.3 CONTINUED

Cobb-Douglas examples that if each person lived alone, he or she would spend ⅓ of income on paintings ($x = 1$) and ⅔ on granola bars ($y = 1,000$).

Public goods provision and strategy. When the roommates live together, however, each must think about what the other will do. Each could, for example, assume the other will buy the paintings. In this case $x = 0$ and both people end up with a zero utility level. Alternatively, person 1 might assume that person 2 will buy no paintings. If that proves to be the case, he or she would choose to purchase one and receive a utility of

$$U_1(x, y_1) = 1^{1/3}(1,000)^{2/3} = 100, \qquad (20.44)$$

whereas person 2's utility would be

$$U_2(X, Y_2) = 1^{1/3}(1,500)^{2/3} = 131. \qquad (20.45)$$

Clearly, person 2 has gained from his or her free-rider position. Person 1's purchases provide an externality to person 2. Of course, person 2's purchases of paintings, should he or she choose to be socially conscious, would also provide an externality to person 1.

Inefficiency of allocation. That the solution obtained in Equations 20.44 and 20.45 (along with many other possibilities) is inefficient can be shown by calculating each person's marginal rate of substitution:

$$MRS_i = \frac{\partial U_i / \partial x}{\partial U_i / \partial y_i} = \frac{y_i}{2x}. \qquad (20.46)$$

Hence, at the allocations described,

$$MRS_1 = \frac{1,000}{2} = 500$$
$$MRS_2 = \frac{1,500}{2} = 750. \qquad (20.47)$$

The roommates in total would be willing to sacrifice 1,250 granola bars for one more painting—a sacrifice that would actually cost them only 500 bars combined. Relying on decentralized decision making in this case is inefficient—too few paintings are bought.

An efficient allocation. To calculate the efficient level of painting purchases, we must set the sum of each person's *MRS* equal to the goods' price ratio, because such a sum correctly reflects the trade-offs the roommates living together would make:

$$MRS_1 + MRS_2 = \frac{y_1}{2x} + \frac{y_2}{2x} = \frac{y_1 + y_2}{2x} = \frac{p_x}{p_y} = \frac{100}{.20}. \qquad (20.48)$$

Consequently,

$$y_1 + y_2 = 1,000x, \qquad (20.49)$$

which can be substituted into the combined budget constraint

$$.20(y_1 + y_2) + 100x = 600 \qquad (20.50)$$

to obtain

$$x = 2$$
$$y_1 + y_2 = 2,000. \qquad (20.51)$$

Allocating the cost of paintings. Assuming the roommates split the cost of the two paintings and use their remaining funds to buy granola bars, each will finally receive a utility of

$$U_i = 2^{1/3}1,000^{2/3} = 126. \qquad (20.52)$$

Although person 1 may not be able to coerce person 2 into such a joint sharing of cost, a 75–25 split provides a utility of

$$U_1 = 2^{1/3}750^{2/3} = 104$$
$$U_2 = 2^{1/3}1,250^{2/3} = 146, \qquad (20.53)$$

which is Pareto superior to the solution obtained when person 1 acts alone. Many other financing schemes would also yield allocations which are Pareto superior to those discussed previously. Which of these, if any, might be chosen depends on how well each roommate plays the strategic financing game.

Query: Show that in this example an efficient solution would be obtained if two people living separately decided to live together and pool their paintings. Would you expect that result to hold generally?

Lindahl pricing of public goods

An important conceptual solution to the public goods problem was first suggested by the Swedish economist E. Lindahl[10] in the 1920s. Lindahl's basic insight was that individuals might voluntarily consent to be taxed for beneficial public goods if they knew that others were also being taxed. Specifically, Lindahl assumed that each individual would be presented by the government with the proportion of a public good's cost he or she would be expected to pay and then reply (honestly) with the level of public good output he or she would prefer. In the notation of our simple general equilibrium model, individual *A*, say, would be quoted a specific percentage (α^A) and asked the level of public goods he or she would want given the knowledge that this fraction of total cost would have to be paid. To answer that question (truthfully) this person would choose that overall level of public goods output, *x*, which maximizes

$$\text{utility} = U^A[x, y^{A^*} - \alpha^A f^{-1}(x)]. \qquad (20.54)$$

The first-order condition for this utility-maximizing choice of *x* is given by

$$U_1^A - \alpha^A U_2^B(1/f') = 0 \quad \text{or} \quad MRS^A = \alpha^A/f'. \qquad (20.55)$$

Individual *B*, presented with a similar choice, would opt for a level of public goods satisfying

$$MRS^B = \alpha^B/f'. \qquad (20.56)$$

An equilibrium would then occur where $\alpha^A + \alpha^B = 1$—that is, where the level of public goods expenditure favored by the two individuals precisely generates enough in tax contributions to pay for it. Because, in that case,

$$MRS^A + MRS^B = (\alpha^A + \alpha^B)/f' = 1/f' \qquad (20.57)$$

this equilibrium would be efficient (see Equation 20.40). Hence, at least on a conceptual level, the Lindahl approach solves the public good problem. Presenting each person with the equilibrium tax share "price" will lead him or her to opt for the efficient level of public goods production.

---

[10]Excerpts from Lindahl's writings are contained in R. A. Musgrave and A. T. Peacock, eds., *Classics in the Theory of Public Finance* (London: Macmillan, 1958).

A Lindahl Solution for the Roommates

Lindahl pricing provides a conceptual solution to the roommates' problem of buying paintings in Example 20.3. If "the government" (or perhaps social convention) suggests that each roommate will pay half of painting purchases, each would face an effective price of paintings of $50. Because the utility functions for the roommates imply that $1/3$ of each person's total income of $300 will be spent on paintings, each will be willing to spend $100 on such art and will, if each is honest, report that he or she would like to have two paintings. Hence the solution will be $x = 2$, and $y_1 = y_2 = 1000$. This is indeed the efficient solution calculated in Example 20.3. The problem with this solution, of course, is that neither roommate has an incentive to truthfully report what his or her demand is for public goods given the Lindahl price. Rather, each will know that he or she would be better off by following one of the free-rider scenarios laid out in Example 20.3. As in the prisoners' dilemma studied in Chapter 15, the Lindahl solution, though Pareto optimal, is not a stable equilibrium.

Query: Although the 50–50 sharing in this example might arise from social custom, in fact the optimality of such a split is a special feature of this problem. What about this problem leads to such a Lindahl outcome? Under what conditions would Lindahl prices result in other than a 50–50 sharing?

Shortcomings of the Lindahl solution

Unfortunately, Lindahl's solution is only a conceptual one. We have already seen in our examination of the Nash equilibrium for public goods production and in our roommates' example that the incentive to be a free rider in the public goods case is very strong. This fact makes it difficult to envision how the information necessary to compute equilibrium Lindahl shares might be computed. Because individuals know their tax shares will be based on their reported demands for public goods, they have a clear incentive to understate their true preferences—in so doing they hope that the "other guy" will pay. Hence, simply asking people about their demands for public goods would not be expected to reveal their true demands. It also appears to be very difficult to design truth-revealing voting mechanisms, for reasons we will examine in the next chapter. In general, then, Lindahl's solution remains a tantalizing, but not readily achievable, target.

Local public goods

Some economists believe that demand revelation for public goods may be more tractable at the local level.[11] Because there are many communities in which individuals might reside, they can indicate their preferences for public goods (that is, for their willingness to pay Lindahl tax shares) by choosing where to live. If a particular tax burden is not utility maximizing, people can, in principle, "vote with their feet" and move to a community that does provide optimality. With perfect information, zero costs of mobility, and enough communities, therefore, the Lindahl solution may be implemented at the local level. Similar arguments apply to other types of organizations (such as private clubs) that provide

---

[11]The classic reference is C. M. Tiebout, "A Pure Theory of Local Expenditures," *Journal of Political Economy* (October 1956): 416–24.

public goods to their members—given a sufficiently wide spectrum of club offerings, an efficient equilibrium might result. Of course, the assumptions that underlie the purported efficiency of such choices by individuals are quite strict. Even minor relaxation of these assumptions may yield inefficient results because of the fragile nature of the way in which the demand for public goods is revealed.

SUMMARY

In this chapter we have examined market failures that arise from externality (or spillover) effects involved in the consumption or production of certain types of goods. In some cases it may be possible to design mechanisms to cope with these externalities in a market setting, but important limits are involved in such solutions. Some specific issues we examined were:

- Externalities may cause a misallocation of resources because of a divergence between private and social marginal cost. Traditional solutions to this divergence include mergers among the affected parties and adoption of suitable (Pigovian) taxes or subsidies.

- If transactions costs are small, private bargaining among the parties affected by an externality may bring social and private costs into line. The proof that resources will be efficiently allocated under such circumstances is sometimes called the *Coase theorem*.

- Public goods provide benefits to individuals on a nonexclusive basis—no one can be prevented from consuming such goods. Such goods are also usually nonrival in that the marginal cost of serving another user is zero.

- Private markets will tend to underallocate resources to public goods because no single buyer can appropriate all of the benefits that such goods provide.

- A Lindahl optimal tax-sharing scheme can result in an efficient allocation of resources to the production of public goods. Computation of these tax shares requires substantial information that individuals have incentives to hide, however.

PROBLEMS

20.1

A firm in a perfectly competitive industry has patented a new process for making widgets. The new process lowers the firm's average cost, meaning this firm alone (although still a price taker) can earn real economic profits in the long run.

a. If the market price is $20 per widget and the firm's marginal cost is given by $MC = .4q$, where q is the daily widget production for the firm, how many widgets will the firm produce?

b. Suppose a government study has found that the firm's new process is polluting the air and estimates the social marginal cost of widget production by this firm to be $SMC = .5q$. If the market price is still $20, what is the socially optimal level of production for the firm? What should the rate of a government-imposed excise tax be to bring about this optimal level of production?

c. Graph your results.

20.2

On the island of Pago Pago there are 2 lakes and 20 anglers. Each angler can fish on either lake and keep the average catch on his particular lake. On Lake x the total number of fish caught is given by

$$F^x = 10l_x - \frac{1}{2}l_x^2,$$

where l_x is the number of people fishing on the lake. For Lake y the relationship is

$$F^y = 5l_y.$$

a. Under this organization of society, what will be the total number of fish caught?

b. The chief of Pago Pago, having once read an economics book, believes it is possible to raise the total number of fish caught by restricting the number of people allowed to fish on Lake x. What number should be allowed to fish on Lake x to maximize the total catch of fish? What is the number of fish caught in this situation?

c. Being basically opposed to coercion, the chief decides to require a fishing license for Lake x. If the licensing procedure is to bring about the optimal allocation of labor, what should the cost of a license be (in terms of fish)?

d. Explain how this example sheds light on the connection between property rights and externalities.

20.3

Suppose the oil industry in Utopia is perfectly competitive and that all firms draw oil from a single (and practically inexhaustible) pool. Assume that each competitor believes that he or she can sell all the oil he or she can produce at a stable world price of $10 per barrel and that the cost of operating a well for one year is $1,000.

Total output per year (Q) of the oil field is a function of the number of wells (n) operating in the field. In particular,

$$Q = 500n - n^2,$$

and the amount of oil produced by each well (q) is given by

$$q = \frac{Q}{n} = 500 - n.$$

a. Describe the equilibrium output and the equilibrium number of wells in this perfectly competitive case. Is there a divergence between private and social marginal cost in the industry?

b. Suppose now that the government nationalizes the oil field. How many oil wells should it operate? What will total output be? What will the output per well be?

c. As an alternative to nationalization, the Utopian government is considering an annual license fee per well to discourage overdrilling. How large should this license fee be if it is to prompt the industry to drill the optimal number of wells?

20.4

There is considerable legal controversy about product safety. Two extreme positions might be termed *caveat emptor* (let the buyer beware) and *caveat vendor* (let the seller beware). Under the former scheme producers would have no responsibility for the safety of their products: buyers would absorb all losses. Under the latter scheme this liability assignment would be reversed: firms would be completely responsible under law for losses incurred from unsafe products. Using simple supply and demand analysis, discuss how the assignment of such liability might affect the allocation of resources. Would safer products be produced if firms were strictly liable under law? How do possible information asymmetries affect your results?

20.5

Three types of contracts are used to specify the way in which tenants on a plot of agricultural land may pay rent to the landlord. Rent may be paid (1) in money (or a fixed amount of agricultural produce), (2) as a fixed proportionate share of the crop, or (3) in "labor dues" by agreeing to work on other plots owned by the landlord. How might these alternative contract specifications affect tenants' production decisions? What sorts of transactions costs might occur in the enforcement of each type of contract? What economic factors might affect the type of contract specified in different places or during different historical periods?

20.6

Suppose a monopoly produces a harmful externality. Use the concept of consumer surplus in a partial equilibrium diagram to analyze whether an optimal tax on the polluter would necessarily be a welfare improvement.

20.7

Suppose there are only two individuals in society. The demand curve for mosquito control for person A is given by

$$q_a = 100 - p.$$

For person B the demand curve for mosquito control is given by

$$q_b = 200 - p.$$

a. Suppose mosquito control is a pure public good; that is, once it is produced, everyone benefits from it. What would be the optimal level of this activity if it could be produced at a constant marginal cost of $120 per unit?

b. If mosquito control were left to the private market, how much might be produced? Does your answer depend on what each person assumes the other will do?

c. If the government were to produce the optimal amount of mosquito control, how much will this cost? How should the tax bill for this amount be allocated between the individuals if they are to share it in proportion to benefits received from mosquito control?

20.8

Suppose there are *n* individuals in an economy with three goods. Two of the goods are pure (nonexclusive) public goods, whereas the third is an ordinary private good.

a. What conditions must hold for resources to be allocated efficiently between either of the public goods and the private good?

b. What conditions must hold for resources to be allocated efficiently between the two public goods?

20.9

Suppose the production possibility frontier for an economy that produces one public good (y) and one private good (x) is given by

$$x^2 + 100y^2 = 5{,}000.$$

This economy is populated by 100 identical individuals, each with a utility function of the form

$$\text{utility} = \sqrt{x_i y},$$

where x_i is the individual's share of private good production $(= x/100)$. Notice that the public good is nonexclusive and that everyone benefits equally from its level of production.

a. If the market for x and y were perfectly competitive, what levels of those goods would be produced? What would the typical individual's utility be in this situation?

b. What are the optimal production levels for x and y? What would the typical individual's utility level be? How should consumption of good x be taxed to achieve this result? (*Hint:* The numbers in this problem do not come out evenly, and some approximations should suffice.)

20.10

The analysis of public goods in Chapter 20 exclusively used a model with only two individuals. The results are readily generalized to n persons—a generalization pursued in this problem.

a. With n persons in an economy, what is the condition for efficient production of a public good? Explain how the characteristics of the public good are reflected in these conditions?

b. What is the Nash equilibrium in the provision of this public good to n persons? Explain why this equilibrium is inefficient. Also explain why the under-provision of this public good is more severe than in the two-person cases studied in the chapter.

c. How is the Lindahl solution generalized to n persons? Is the existence of a Lindahl equilibrium guaranteed in this more complex model?

SUGGESTIONS FOR FURTHER READING

Alchian, A., and H. Demsetz. "Production, Information Costs, and Economic Organization." *American Economic Review 62* (December 1972): 777–95.
Uses externality arguments to develop a theory of economic organizations.

Barzel, Y. *Economic Analysis of Property Rights.* Cambridge: Cambridge University Press, 1989.
Provides a graphical analysis of several economic questions that are illuminated through use of the property rights paradigm.

Cheung, S. N. S. "The Fable of the Bees: An Economic Investigation." *Journal of Law and Economics 16* (April 1973): 11–33.
Empirical study of how the famous bee–orchard owner externality is handled by private markets in the state of Washington.

Coase, R. H. "The Market for Goods and the Market for Ideas." *American Economic Review 64* (May 1974): 384–91.
Speculative article about notions of externalities and regulation in the "marketplace of ideas."

———. "The Problem of Social Cost." *Journal of Law and Economics 3* (October 1960): 1–44.
Classic article on externalities. Many fascinating historical-legal cases.

Cornes, R., and T. Sandler. *The Theory of Externalities, Public Goods, and Club Goods.* Cambridge: Cambridge University Press, 1986.
Good theoretical analysis of many of the issues raised in this chapter. Good discussions of the connections between returns to scale, excludability, and club goods.

Cropper, M. L., and W. E. Oates. "Environmental Economics: A Survey." *Journal of Economic Literature* (June 1992): 675–740.

Complete survey article with particularly useful sections on applications of hedonic price theory.

Demsetz, H. "Toward a Theory of Property Rights." *American Economic Review, Papers and Proceedings 57* (May 1967): 347–59.

Brief development of a plausible theory of how societies come to define property rights.

Mas-Colell, A., M. D. Whinston, and J. R. Green. *Microeconomic Theory.* New York: Oxford University Press, 1995.

Chapter 11 covers much of the same ground as this chapter does, though at a somewhat more abstract level.

Posner, R. A. *Economic Analysis of Law,* 5th ed. Boston: Little Brown, 1998.

In many respects the "bible" of the law and economics movement. Posner's arguments are not always economically correct, but unfailingly interesting and provocative.

Samuelson, P. A. "The Pure Theory of Public Expenditures." *Review of Economics and Statistics 36* (November 1954): 387–89.

Classic statement of the efficiency conditions for public goods production.

Pollution Abatement

Although our discussion of externalities focused on how Pigovian taxes can make goods' markets operate more efficiently, similar results also apply to the study of the technology of pollution abatement. In these Extensions we briefly review this alternative approach. We assume there are only two firms, A and B, and that their output levels (q_A and q_B respectively) are fixed throughout our discussion. It is an inescapable scientific principle that production of physical goods (as opposed to services) must obey the conservation of matter. Hence production of q_A and q_B is certain to involve some emission by-products, e_A and e_B. The physical amounts of these emissions (or, at least their harmful components) can be abated using inputs z_A and z_B (which cost p per unit). The resulting levels of emissions are given by

$$f^A(q_A, z_A) = e_A \quad \text{and} \quad f^B(q_A, z_B) = e_B, \quad \text{(i)}$$

where, for each firm's abatement function, $f_1 > 0$ and $f_2 < 0$.

E20.1 Optimal abatement

If a regulatory agency has decided that e^* represents the maximum allowable level of emissions from these firms, this level would be achieved at minimal cost by solving the Lagrangian expression

$$\mathscr{L} = pz_A + pz_B + \lambda(f^A + f^B - e^*). \quad \text{(ii)}$$

First-order conditions for a minimum are

$$p + \lambda f_2^A = 0 \quad \text{and} \quad p + \lambda f_2^B = 0. \quad \text{(iii)}$$

Hence we have

$$\lambda = -p/f_2^A = -p/f_2^B. \quad \text{(iv)}$$

This equation makes the rather obvious point that cost-minimizing abatement is achieved when the marginal cost of abatement (universally referred to as MAC in the environmental literature) is the same for each firm. A uniform standard that required equal emissions from each firm would not be likely to achieve that efficient result—considerable cost-savings might be attainable under equalization of marginal abatement costs relative to such uniform regulation.

E20.2 Emission taxes

The optimal solution described in Equation iv can be achieved by imposing an emission tax (t) equal to λ on each firm (presumably this tax would be set at a level that reflects the marginal harm that a unit of emissions causes). With this tax, each firm seeks to minimize $pz_i + tf^i(q_i, z_i)$, which does indeed yield the efficient solution

$$t = -p/f_2^A = -p/f_2^B. \quad \text{(v)}$$

Notice that, as in the analysis of Chapter 20, one benefit of the taxation solution is that the regulatory authority need not know the details of the firms' abatement functions. Rather, the firms themselves make use of their own private information in determining abatement strategies. If these functions differ significantly among firms it would be expected that emissions reductions would also differ.

Emission taxes in the United Kingdom

Hanley, Shogren, and White (1997) review a variety of emission taxation schemes that have been implemented in the United Kingdom. They show that marginal costs of pollution abatement vary significantly (perhaps as much as thirtyfold) among firms. Hence, relative to uniform regulation, the cost-savings from taxation schemes can be quite large. For example, the author's review a series of studies of the Tees estuary that report annual cost-savings in the range of £10 million (in 1976 dollars). The authors also discuss some of the complications that arise in setting efficient effluent taxes when emission streams do not have a uniform mix of pollutants or when pollutants may accumulate to dangerous levels over time.

E20.3 Tradable permits

As we illustrated in Chapter 20, many of the results achievable through Pigovian taxation can also be achieved through a tradable permit system. In this case, the regulatory agency would set the number of permits (s^*) equal to e^* and allocate these permits in some way among firms ($s_A + s_B = s^*$). Each firm then may buy or sell any number of permits desired, but must ensure that its emissions are equal to the number of permits it holds. If the market price of permits is given by p_s, each firm's problem is again to minimize

$$pz_i + p_s(e_i - s_i), \qquad \text{(vi)}$$

which yields an identical solution to that derived in Equations iv and v with $p_s = t = \lambda$. Hence the tradable permit solution would be expected to yield the same sort of cost-savings as do taxation schemes.

SO_2 trading

The U.S. Clean Air Act of 1990 established the first large-scale program of tradable emission permits. These focused on sulfur dioxide emissions with the goal of reducing acid rain arising from power plant burning of coal. Schmalensee et al. (1998) review early experiences under this program. They conclude it is indeed possible to establish large and well-functioning markets in emission permits. More than five million (one-ton) emission permits changed hands in the most recent year examined, at prices that averaged about $150 per permit. The authors also show that firms using the permit system employed a wide variety of compliance strategies. This suggests the flexibility inherent in the permit system led to considerable cost savings. One interesting aspect of this review of SO_2 permit trading is the authors' speculations about why the permit prices were only about half what had been expected. They attribute a large part of the explanation to an initial "over-investment" in emission cleaning technology by power companies in the mistaken belief that permit prices, once the system was implemented, would be in the $300–400 range. With such large fixed-cost investments, the marginal cost of removing a ton of SO_2 may have been as low as $65/ton, thereby exerting a significant downward force on permit prices.

E20.4 Innovation

Although taxes and tradable permits appear to be mathematically equivalent in the models we have been describing, this equivalence may vanish once the dynamics of innovation in pollution abatement technology is considered. Of course, both procedures offer incentives to adopt new technologies—if a new process can achieve a given emission reduction at a lower MAC, it will be adopted under either scheme. In a detailed analysis of dynamics under the two approaches, however, Milliman and Prince (1989) argue that taxation is better. Their reasoning is that the taxation approach encourages a more rapid diffusion of new abatement technology because incremental profits attainable from adoption are greater than with permits. Such rapid diffusion may also encourage environmental agencies to adopt more stringent emission targets because these targets will now more readily meet cost-benefit tests.

References

Hanley, N., J. F. Shogren, and B. White, *Environmental Economics in Theory and Practice* (New York, Oxford University Press, 1997).

Millman, S. R., and R. Prince, "Firm Incentive to Promote Technological Change in Pollution Control," *Journal of Environmental Economics and Management* (November 1989): 247–65.

Schmalensee, R., P. L. Joskow, A. D. Ellerman, J. P. Montero, and E. M. Bailey, "An Interim Evaluation of the Sulfur Dioxide Trading Program," *The Journal of Economic Perspectives* (Summer 1998): 53–68.

Chapter 21

POLITICAL ECONOMICS

Many decisions about resource allocation are made through the political process: voters may cast bal-lots on funding for local schools; elected representatives vote on budgets for public goods (such as defense) and for public transfers (welfare or unemployment compensation); and government regulatory agencies set standards for a broad range of goods, such as stock market transactions or allowable levels of air pol-lution. Traditionally economists avoided any specific analysis of such processes, arguing that they were outside the confines of standard economic analysis. In recent years, however, that view has been increas-ingly challenged as economists have sought to employ the same kinds of model building that are used to study markets to, instead, examine political decisions. In this chapter we take a brief look at this rapidly growing area of research. To set the stage for this material, we first provide a brief review of "standard" welfare economics, ending with Arrow's famous negative conclusion about the hope of finding acceptable general social welfare functions. The chapter then takes a decidedly more positivist tone by illustrating a variety of models of how the political process actually works.

Social welfare criteria

We will begin our study of the political process by examining some of the problems associated with devising welfare criteria for choosing among feasible allocations of resources. This sub-ject is the most normative branch of microeconomics, because it necessarily involves making hard choices about the utility levels of different individuals. In choosing between two alloca-tions, A and B, the problem arises that some individuals prefer A whereas others prefer B. Comparisons among people must be made in order to judge which allocation is preferable. As might be expected, there is no universally accepted criterion for making such choices.

Social welfare criteria in an exchange model

The model of efficiency in exchange developed in Chapter 12 is useful for demonstrating the problems involved in establishing social welfare criteria. Consider the Edgeworth box dia-gram in Figure 21.1. Only points on the contract curve are considered as possible candidates for a social optimum. Points off the contract curve are Pareto inefficient because both indi-viduals can be made better off. In so doing (presumably), social welfare could be improved. Along the contract curve the utilities of the two individuals (Smith and Jones) vary, and these utilities are directly competitive. Smith's utility can be increased only by decreasing

FIGURE 21.1   Edgeworth Box Diagram of Exchange

The curve O_S, O_J is the locus of efficient allocations of x and y between Smith and Jones. Allocations of this locus are dominated by those on it in that both individuals can be made better off by moving to the contract curve.

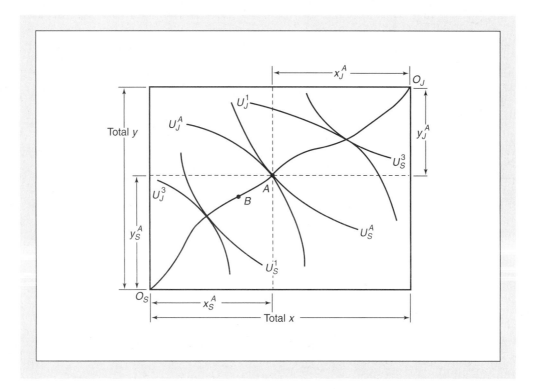

Jones's. Given this set of efficient allocations, we now wish to discuss possible criteria for choosing among them.

If we are willing to assume that utility can be compared among individuals, we can use the possible utility combinations along the contract curve in Figure 21.1 to construct[1] the utility possibility frontier shown in Figure 21.2. The curve O_S, O_J records those utility levels for Smith and Jones that are obtainable from the fixed quantities of available goods. Any utility combination (such as point C) that lies inside the curve O_S, O_J is Pareto inefficient. Using the utility possibility frontier, we can now rephrase the "problem" of welfare economics as being the development of criteria for selecting a point on this frontier.

Equality criterion

A few simple criteria for choosing a point on O_S, O_J are easily shown. One possible principle would require complete equality: Smith and Jones should enjoy the same level of welfare. This social welfare criterion would necessitate choosing point A on the utility possibility frontier. Because point A corresponds to a unique point on the contract curve, the socially optimal allocation of goods has been determined by this choice. In Figure 21.1 this allocation is seen to require that Smith gets x_S^A and y_S^A, whereas Jones gets x_J^A and y_J^A. Notice that the goods x and y are not necessarily distributed equally. It is equality of utilities that is required by the criterion, not equality of goods.

---

[1]This construction is identical to that we used in Chapter 12 to derive the production possibility frontier.

FIGURE 21.2	Utility Possibility Frontier

Assuming measurability of utility, the utility possibility frontier can be derived from Figure 21.1. This curve (O_S, O_J) shows those combinations of utility that society can achieve. Two criteria for choosing among points on O_S, O_J might be: Choose "equal" utilities for Smith and Jones (point A); or choose the utilities so that their sum is the greatest (point B). Under the Rawls criterion, the efficient allocation B would be regarded as inferior to equal allocations between D and A.

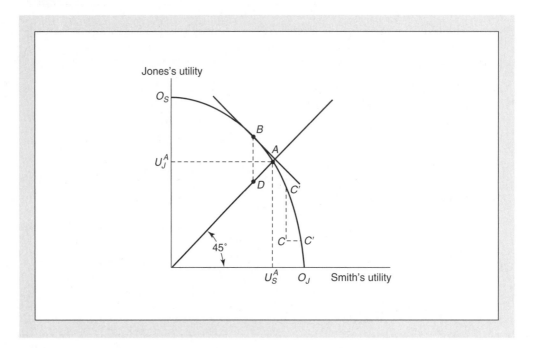

Utilitarian criterion

A similar (though not necessarily identical) criterion would be to choose that point on the utility possibility frontier for which the sum of Smith's and Jones's utilities is the greatest. This would require that the optimal point (B) be chosen to maximize ($U_J + U_S$) subject to the constraint implied by the utility possibility frontier. As before, point B would imply a certain allocation of x and y between Smith and Jones, and this allocation could be derived from Figure 21.1. Later in this chapter we will make some use of this criterion because it is commonly encountered in political analysis.

The Rawls criterion

A final criterion we can examine was first posed by the philosopher John Rawls.[2] Rawls begins by envisioning society as being in an "initial position" in which no one knows what his or her final position (and ultimate utility) will be. He then asks what kind of welfare criterion would be adopted by people who find themselves in such a position. Posed in this way, selection of a welfare criterion is a problem in behavior under uncertainty, because no one knows exactly how the criterion chosen will affect his or her personal well-being. From his initial premise Rawls concludes that individuals would be very risk averse in their selection of a criterion. Specifically, he asserts that members of society would choose to depart from perfect equality only on the condition that the worst-off person under an unequal distribution of utilities would actually be better off than under equality. In terms of Figure 21.2 unequal distributions such as B would be permitted only when the attainable equal distributions (which lie along the 45° line) were below point D.

---

[2]Rawls, *A Theory of Justice* (Cambridge, MA: Harvard University Press, 1971).

FIGURE 21.3   **Using a Social Welfare Function to Find the Social Optimum**

If we can postulate the existence of a social welfare function having the indifference curves w_1, w_2, and w_3, it is possible to conceptualize the problem of social choice. It is clear that efficiency (being an O_S, O_J) is necessary for a welfare optimum, but this is not sufficient, as may be seen by comparing points D and F.

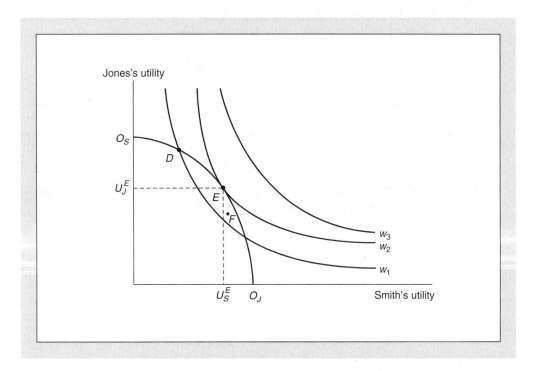

Equal distributions that lie between D and A are, according to Rawls, superior to B because the worst-off individual (Smith) is better off there than under allocation B. The Rawls criterion therefore suggests that many efficient allocations may not be socially desirable and that societies may choose equality even at considerable efficiency costs. Such a conclusion is not universally shared by economists, many of whom argue that the criteria proposed are unnecessarily risk averse. Individuals in the initial position may instead prefer to gamble that they will be the winners under an unequal final distribution, and such motives may dominate if the likelihood of being the worst-off individual is small. Still, Rawls's conception of using the "initial position" methodology to conceptualize how individuals might make social decisions is an intriguing one that has been widely used in other investigations.

Social welfare functions

A more general approach to social welfare (which as special cases includes the three criteria we discussed above) can be obtained by examining the concept of a social welfare function:[3] This function might depend only on Smith's and Jones's utility levels:

$$\text{social welfare} = W(U_S, U_J). \tag{21.1}$$

The social choice problem, then, is to allocate x and y between Smith and Jones so as to maximize W. This procedure is pictured in Figure 21.3. The curves labeled w_1, w_2, and w_3

[3]This concept was first developed by A. Bergson in "A Reformulation of Certain Aspects of Welfare Economics," *Quarterly Journal of Economics 52* (February 1938): 310–34.

represent social indifference curves, in that society is indifferent about which utility combination on a particular curve is chosen.[4] Point E is the optimal point of social welfare under the Bergson criterion. This is the highest level of w achievable with the given utility possibility frontier. As before, it is necessary to go from point E to the Edgeworth box diagram to determine the socially optimal allocation of goods.

Conflicts between efficiency and equity

Figure 21.3 demonstrates a conceptual way of choosing a distribution of utilities that maximizes social welfare. The figure again illustrates the important distinction to be made between the goals of equity and efficiency. All of the points on O_S, O_J are efficient by the Pareto criterion. However, some of the efficient points represent far more socially desirable distributions than do others. As with the Rawls criterion, there are in fact many inefficient points (such as F) that are socially preferred to efficient points (such as D). It sometimes may be in society's interest to choose seemingly inefficient allocations of resources if the truly optimal allocation (point E) is unattainable.

 EXAMPLE 21.1

Equitable Sharing

A father arrives home carrying an eight-piece pizza. How should he share it between his two ravenous teenagers? Suppose teen 1 has a utility of pizza function of the form

$$U_1 = 2\sqrt{x_1}, \tag{21.2}$$

and teen 2 (the larger of the two) has a utility function of the form

$$U_2 = \sqrt{x_2}. \tag{21.3}$$

The least-resistance option would be to share the pizza equally—four slices each. In this case $U_1 = 4$, $U_2 = 2$. Alternatively, a benevolent father recognizes teen 2's greater needs and opts for an allocation that provides equal utility. In this case $x_1 = 1.6$, $x_2 = 6.4$, $U_1 = U_2 = 2.53$. As a third simple alternative, a utilitarian father might seek to maximize the sum of his teens' utility by choosing $x_1 = 6.4$, $x_2 = 1.6$, $U_1 = 5.06$, $U_2 = 1.26$, and $U_1 + U_2 = 6.32$.

A probabilistic father. A father familiar with probability theory might turn this whole problem over to the teens to decide. But because the teens' desires are directly competitive, it is unlikely they will arrive at a unanimous decision with full information. If, however, the father offers the three possible allocations listed above and says he will flip a coin to determine who gets which portion under each, expected utility maximization would yield unanimity. Expected utilities from a coin flip that yields teen 1 either 1.6 or 6.4 pieces is

$$E(U_1) = .5(2.53) + .5(5.06) = 3.80. \tag{21.4}$$

Similarly, for teen 2,

$$E(U_2) = .5(2.53) + .5(1.26) = 1.90.$$

Hence, in this case, each teen would opt for the first, equal allocation, because each gets higher expected utility from it than from the flip.

---

[4]Under the "equality" criterion the social welfare function would have L-shaped indifference curves, whereas a utilitarian social welfare function that sought to maximize the sum of utilities would have indifference curves that are parallel straight lines with a slope of –1.

A Rawlsian father. If the father could subject each of his teens to a "veil of ignorance" so neither would know his or her identity until the pizza is served, the voting might be still different. If each teen focuses on a worst-case scenario, each would opt for the equal utility allocation because it ensures that utility will not fall below 2.53. But that may assume too much risk aversion. If each teen believes he or she has a 50–50 chance of being labeled "1" or "2," expected utilities are

$$\text{(i) } x_1 = x_2 = 4 \qquad E(U) = .5(4) + .5(2) = 3$$
$$\text{(ii) } x_1 = 1.6, \, x_2 = 6.4 \quad E(U) = .5(2.53) + .5(2.53) = 2.53 \qquad (21.5)$$
$$\text{(iii) } x_1 = 6.4, \, x_2 = 1.6 \quad E(U) = .5(5.06) + .5(1.26) = 3.16.$$

If the teens vote only on the basis of expected utility, each might now opt for the utilitarian solution (that is, iii).

Query: Might the degree of risk aversion exhibited by the teens change their voting in the Rawlsian situation, or has it already been accounted for in the calculation?

The Arrow impossibility theorem

The Bergson social welfare function, then, provides a useful tool for demonstrating particular aspects of the problem of social choice. We must recognize, however, that this tool is only a conceptual one offering little guidance for the development of practical government policy. We have so far begged the question of how such a function is established or what the properties of the function are likely to be. Here we will examine the approach to such questions taken by K. J. Arrow and others.[5]

The basic problem

Arrow views the general social welfare problem as one of choosing among several feasible "social states." It is assumed that each individual in society can rank these states according to their desirability. The question Arrow raises is, Does there exist a ranking of these states on a societywide scale that fairly records these individual preferences? Symbolically, assume there are three social states (A, B, and C) and two individuals in society (Smith and Jones). Suppose that Smith prefers A to B (we will denote this by $A \, P_S \, B$, where P_S represents the words "is preferred by Smith to") and B to C. These preferences can be written as $A \, P_S \, B$ and $B \, P_S \, C$. If Smith is to be "rational," it should then be the case that $A \, P_S \, C$: Preferences should be transitive. Suppose also that among the three states, Jones has preferences $C \, P_J \, A$, $A \, P_J \, B$, and $C \, P_J \, B$. Arrow's impossibility theorem consists of showing that a reasonable social ranking of these three states (call this ranking P) cannot exist.

The Arrow axioms

The crux of this theorem is to define what is meant by a "reasonable social ranking." Arrow assumes that any social ranking (P) should obey the following six seemingly unobjectionable axioms (here P is to be read "is socially preferred to"):

1. It must rank all social states: Either $A \, P \, B$, $B \, P \, A$, or A and B are equally desirable ($A \, I \, B$) for any two states A and B.

2. The ranking must be transitive: If $A \, P \, B$ and $B \, P \, C$ (or $B \, I \, C$), then $A \, P \, C$.

[5] See K. J. Arrow, *Social Choice and Individual Values*, 2nd ed. (New Haven, CT: Yale University Press, 1963).

3. The ranking must be positively related to individual preferences: If A is unanimously preferred to B by Smith and Jones, then A P B.

4. If new social states become feasible, this fact should not affect the social ranking of the original states. If, between A and B, A P B, then this will remain true if some new state (D) becomes feasible.[6]

5. The social preference relation should not be imposed, say, by custom. It should not be the case that A P B regardless of the tastes of individuals in society.

6. The relationship should be nondictatorial. One person's preferences should not determine society's preferences.

Arrow's proof

Arrow was able to show that these six conditions (all of which seem ethically reasonable on the surface) are not compatible with one another: no general social relationship obeying Conditions 1 to 6 exists. Using the preferences of Smith and Jones among A, B, and C, it is possible to see the kind of inconsistencies that can arise in social choice. Because B P_s C and C P_J B, it must be the case that society is indifferent between B and C (B I C). Otherwise, society's preferences would be in accord with only one individual (and against the other), and this would violate Axiom 6 requiring nondictatorship.

Because both Smith and Jones prefer A to B, Conditions 3 and 5 require that A P B. Hence, by transitivity Axiom 2, A P C. But, again, this is a violation of the nondictatorship assumption, because A P_s C but C P_J A. Thus, in this simple case, an inconsistency arises in the attempt to construct a social preference relationship. Admittedly, this example is a bit contrived, but it does illustrate clearly the problems of trying to aggregate divergent patterns of individual preferences into some reasonable social pattern. The importance of Arrow's work is to show that any social decision rule chosen must violate at least one of the postulates embodied in Axioms 1 through 6.

Significance of the Arrow theorem

Much research in social choice theory has been focused on Arrow's fundamental result and on whether it continues to hold under potential revisions in the set of basic postulates. In general, the impossibility result appears to be rather robust to modest changes in these postulates. Systems with fewer basic axioms and systems under which some of Arrow's axioms are relaxed continue to demonstrate a variety of inconsistencies. It appears that to expect methods of social choice to be at the same time rational, definitive, and egalitarian may be to expect too much. Instead, compromises are inevitable. Of course, where to make such compromises is a very difficult normative question.

Despite the negative nature of Arrow's conclusion, it should be remembered that all societies do in fact make social choices. The U.S. Congress manages to pass a budget (often at the last minute); college faculties establish curricula; and Alaskan Eskimos decide how to improve upon their communal fishing methods for the next year. Rather than examining the normative question of how such choices might be made in a socially optimal

---

[6]Condition 4 is sometimes called the axiom of the *independence of irrelevant alternatives.* More controversy has arisen over this axiom (and similar ones in the von Neumann–Morgenstern list) than any other. To see the sort of functions that are ruled out by the axiom, consider individuals voting for candidates in an election. Suppose each individual can rank these candidates in order of their desirability. An election somehow combines these individual lists into a societywide list. According to Axiom 4, the social list must have the property that if candidate X is preferred to candidate Y, this should remain true even if other candidates enter or leave the race. The most common election procedure in which each person votes only for his or her most preferred candidate may not obey the axiom because of the presence of "spoilers" in the race. For example, it is conceivable that the presence of Ralph Nader in the 2000 presidential election caused Al Gore to lose. With the "irrelevant alternative" Nader out of the race, Gore might have won. The presidential election system therefore would not obey Arrow's Axiom 4. Many authors have examined the consequences of relaxing the axiom.

way, therefore, economists have increasingly taken a positive approach, asking how decisions are actually made. That is the approach we will take now.

Direct voting and resource allocation

Voting is used as a social decision process in many institutions. In some instances individuals vote directly on policy questions. That is the case in some New England town meetings, many statewide referenda (for example, California's Proposition 13 in 1977), and for many of the national policies adopted in Switzerland. Direct voting also characterizes the social decision procedure used for many smaller groups and clubs such as farmers' cooperatives, university faculties, or the local Rotary Club. In other cases, however, societies have found it more convenient to use a representative form of government in which individuals vote directly only for political representatives, who are then charged with making decisions on policy questions. For our study of public choice theory, we will begin with an analysis of direct voting. This is an important subject not only because such a procedure applies to many cases, but also because elected representatives often engage in direct voting (in Congress, for example), and the theory we will illustrate applies to those instances as well. Later in the chapter we will take up special problems raised in studying representative government.

Majority rule

Because so many elections are conducted on a majority rule basis, we often tend to regard that procedure as a natural and, perhaps, optimal one for making social choices. But only a cursory examination should suggest that there is nothing particularly sacred about a rule requiring that a policy obtain 50 percent of the vote to be adopted. In the U.S. Constitution, for example, two-thirds of the states must adopt an amendment before it becomes law. And 60 percent of the U.S. Senate must vote to limit debate on controversial issues. Indeed, in some institutions (Quaker meetings, for example), unanimity may be required for social decisions. Our discussion of the Lindahl equilibrium concept in the previous chapter suggests there may exist a distribution of tax shares that would obtain unanimous support in voting for public goods. But arriving at such unanimous agreements is usually thwarted by emergence of the free-rider problem. Examining in detail the forces that lead societies to move away from unanimity and to choose some other determining fraction would take us too far afield here. We instead will assume throughout our discussion of voting that decisions will be made by majority rule. Readers may wish to ponder for themselves what kinds of situations might call for a decisive proportion of other than 50 percent.

The paradox of voting

In the 1780s the French social theorist M. de Condorcet observed an important peculiarity of majority rule voting systems—they may not arrive at an equilibrium but instead may cycle among alternative options. Condorcet's paradox is illustrated for a simple case in Table 21.1. Suppose there are three voters (Smith, Jones, and Fudd) choosing among three policy options. For our subsequent analysis we will assume the policy options represent three levels of spending on a particular public good [(A) low, (B) medium, or (C) high], but Condorcet's paradox would arise even if the options being considered do not have this type of ordering associated with them. Preferences of Smith, Jones, and Fudd among the three policy options are indicated in Table 21.1. These preferences give rise to Condorcet's paradox.

Consider a vote between options A and B. Here option A would win, because it is favored by Smith and Fudd and opposed only by Jones. In a vote between options A and C, option C would win, again by 2 votes to 1. But in a vote of C versus B, B would win and we would be back where we started. Social choices would endlessly cycle among the three alternatives. In subsequent votes, any choice initially decided upon could be defeated by

TABLE 21.1	Preferences That Produce the Paradox of Voting

	Choices: A—Low Spending B—Medium Spending C—High Spending		
Preferences	Smith	Jones	Fudd
	A	B	C
	B	C	A
	C	A	B

an alternative, and no equilibrium would ever be reached. In this situation the option finally chosen will depend on such seemingly nongermane issues as when the balloting stops or how items are ordered on an agenda rather than being derived in some rational way from the preferences of voters.

Single-peaked preferences and the median voter theorem

Condorcet's voting paradox arises because of the presence of a degree of irreconcilability in the preferences of voters. One therefore might ask whether restrictions on the types of preferences allowed might yield situations where equilibrium voting outcomes are more likely. A fundamental result about this probability was discovered by D. Black in 1948.[7] Black showed that equilibrium voting outcomes always occur in cases where the issue being voted upon is one-dimensional (such as how much to spend on a public good) and where voters' preferences are "single peaked." To understand what the notion of single peaked means, consider again Condorcet's paradox. In Figure 21.4 we illustrate the preferences that gave rise to the paradox by assigning hypothetical utility levels to options A, B, and C consistent with the preferences recorded in Table 21.1. For Smith and Jones, preferences are single peaked—as levels of public goods' expenditures rise, there is only one local utility-maximizing choice (A for Smith, B for Jones). Fudd's preferences, on the other hand, have two local maxima (A and C). It is these preferences that produced the cyclical voting pattern. If instead Fudd had the preferences represented by the dashed line in Figure 21.4 (where now C is the only local utility maximum), there would be no paradox. In that case, option B would be chosen because that option would defeat both A and C by votes of 2 to 1. Here B is the preferred choice of the "median" voter (Jones) whose preferences are "between" the preferences of Smith and the revised preferences of Fudd.

Black's result is quite general and applies to any number of voters. If choices are unidimensional[8] and preferences are single peaked, majority rule will result in the selection of the project that is most favored by the median voter. Therefore, that voter's preferences will determine what public choices are made. This result is a key starting point for many models of the political process. In such models the median voter's preferences dictate policy choices—either because that voter determines which policy gets a majority of votes in a direct election or the median voter will dictate choices in competitive elections in which candidates must adopt policies that appeal to this voter.

---

[7]D. Black, "On the Rationale of Group Decision Making," *Journal of Political Economy* (February 1948): 23–34.

[8]The result can be generalized a bit to deal with multidimensional policies if individuals can be characterized in their support for such policies along a single dimension.

FIGURE 21.4   **Single-Peaked Preferences and the Median Voter Theorem**

This figure illustrates the preferences in Table 21.1. Smith's and Jones's preferences are single peaked, but Fudd's have two local peaks, and these yield the voting paradox. If Fudd's instead had been single peaked (the dashed line), option B would be chosen as the preferred choice of the median voter (Jones).

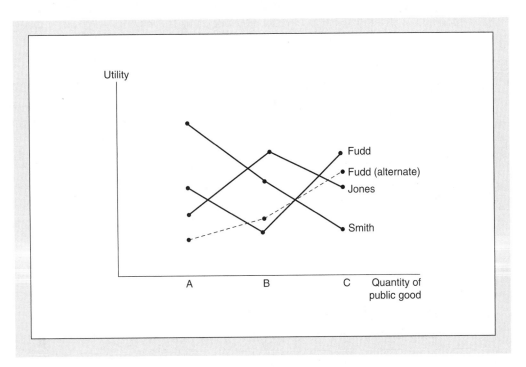

A simple political model

To illustrate how the median voter theorem is applied in political models, suppose a community is characterized by a large number (n) of voters each with an income given by y_i. The utility of each voter depends on his or her consumption of a private good (c_i) and of a public good (g) according to the additive function

$$\text{utility of person } i = U_i = c_i + f(g), \tag{21.6}$$

where $f_g > 0, f_{gc} < 0$.

Each voter must pay income taxes to finance g. Taxes are proportional to income and are imposed at a rate t. Hence each person's budget constraint is given by

$$c_i = (1 - t)\, y_i. \tag{21.7}$$

The government is also bound by a budget constraint

$$g = \sum_1^n ty_i = tny^A, \tag{21.8}$$

where y^A is average income for all voters.

Given these constraints, the utility of person i can be written as a function of his or her choice of g only:

$$U_i(g) = (y^A - g/n)\, y_i/y^A + f(g). \tag{21.9}$$

Utility maximization for person i shows that his preferred level of expenditures on the public good satisfies

$$dU_i/dg = -y_i/ny^A + f_g(g) = 0 \quad \text{or} \quad g = f_g^{-1}(y_i/ny^A). \qquad (21.10)$$

This shows that desired spending on g is inversely related to income. Because (in this model) the benefits of g are independent of income, but taxes increase with income, high-income voters can expect to have smaller net gains (or even losses) from public spending than can low-income voters.

The median voter equilibrium

If g is determined here through majority rule, its level will be chosen to be that level favored by the "mean voter." In this case voters' preferences align exactly with incomes, so g will be set at that level preferred by the voter with median income (y^m). Any other level for g would not get 50 percent of the vote. Hence, equilibrium g is given by

$$g^* = f_g^{-1}(y^m/ny^A) = f_g^{-1}[(1/n)(y^m/y^A)]. \qquad (21.11)$$

In general, the distribution of income is skewed to the right in practically every political jurisdiction in the world. With such an income distribution $y^m < y^A$, with the difference between the two measures becoming larger the more skewed is the income distribution. Hence Equation 21.11 suggests that, ceteris paribus, the more unequal is the income distribution in a direct[9] democracy, the higher will be tax rates and the greater will be spending on public goods. Similarly, laws that extend the vote to increasingly poor segments of the population would also be expected to increase such spending.

Optimality of the median voter result

Although the median voter theorem permits a number of interesting positive predictions about the outcome of voting, the normative significance of these results is more difficult to pinpoint. In this example, it is clear the result does not replicate the Lindahl voluntary equilibrium described in Chapter 20—high-income voters would not voluntarily agree to the taxes imposed.[10] The result also does not necessarily correspond to any of the welfare criteria laid out at the start of this chapter. For example, under a utilitarian social welfare criterion, g would be chosen so as to maximize the sum of utilities:

$$SW = \sum_1^n U_i = \sum \left[(y^A - g/n)y_i/y^A + f(g)\right] = ny^A - g + nf(g). \qquad (21.12)$$

The optimal choice for g is then found by differentiation:

$$dSW/dg = -1 + nf_g = 0$$

or

$$g^* = f_g^{-1}(1/n) = f_g^{-1}[(1/n)(y^A/y^A)], \qquad (21.13)$$

which shows that a utilitarian choice would opt for the level of g favored by the voter with *average* income. That output of g would be smaller than that favored by the median voter because $y^m < y^A$. In Example 21.2 we take this analysis a bit further by showing how it might apply to governmental transfer policy.

---

[9]Under representative democracy, as we shall see, we must also question whether representatives follow the will of the median voter.

[10]Although they might if the benefits of g were also proportional to income.

EXAMPLE 21.2

Voting for Redistributive Taxation

Suppose voters were considering adoption of a lump-sum transfer to be paid to every person and financed through proportional taxation. If we denote the per-person transfer by b, each individual's utility is now given by

$$U_i = c_i + b \qquad\qquad (21.14)$$

and the government budget constraint is

$$nb = tny^A \quad \text{or} \quad b = ty^A. \qquad\qquad (21.15)$$

For a voter whose income is greater than average, utility would be maximized by choosing $b = 0$, because such a voter would pay more in taxes than he or she would receive from the transfer. Any voter with less than average income will gain from the transfer no matter what the tax rate is. Hence such voters (including the decisive median voter) will opt for $t = 1$ and $b = y^A$. That is, they would vote to fully equalize incomes through the tax system. Of course, such a tax scheme is unrealistic—primarily because a 100 percent tax rate would undoubtedly create negative work incentives that reduce average income.

To capture such incentive effects, assume[11] each person's income has two components, one responsive to tax rates $[y_i(t)]$ and one not responsive (n_i). Assume also that the average value of n_i is 0, but that its distribution is skewed to the right so that $n_m < 0$. Now utility is given by

$$U_i = (1 - t) [y_i(t) + n_i] + b. \qquad\qquad (21.16)$$

Assuming that each person first optimizes over those variables (such as labor supply) that affect $y_i(t)$, the first-order condition[12] for a maximum in his or her political decisions about t and b then become (using the government budget constraint in Equation 21.15)

$$dU_i / dt = -n_i + t \, dy^A / dt = 0. \qquad\qquad (21.17)$$

Hence for voter i the optimal redistributive tax rate is given by

$$t_i = n_i / dy^A / dt. \qquad\qquad (21.18)$$

Assuming political competition under majority-rule voting will opt for that policy favored by the median voter, the equilibrium rate of taxation will be

$$t^* = n_m / dy^A / dt. \qquad\qquad (21.19)$$

Because both n_m and dy^A / dt are negative, this rate of taxation will be positive. The optimal tax will be greater the farther n_m is from its average value (that is, the more unequal income is distributed). Similarly, the larger are distortionary effects from the tax, the smaller the optimal tax. This model then poses some rather strong testable hypotheses about redistribution in the real world.

Query: Would progressive taxation be more likely to raise or lower t^* in this model?

---

[11]What follows represents a much simplified version of a model first developed by T. Romer in "Individual Welfare, Majority Voting, and the Properties of a Linear Income Tax," *Journal of Public Economics* (December 1978): 163–68.

[12]Equation 21.17 can be derived from 21.16 through differentiation and by recognizing that $dy_i / dt = 0$ because of the assumption of individual optimization.

Representative government

In representative governments, people vote for candidates, not policies. Successful candidates then vote directly in legislative bodies for the policies they prefer. Politicians' policy preferences are molded by a variety of influences, including their perceptions of what their constituents want, their view of the "public good," the forcefulness of "special interest" groups, and, ultimately, the desire to ensure their own reelection. In this section we briefly explore how policies are chosen and how such choices affect the allocation of resources.

Probabilistic voting

To study representative government, we will assume there are only two candidates for a political office. Prior to the election each candidate announces his or her "platform"—a complete listing of the policies to be followed, if elected. The candidates' platforms will be denoted by θ_1 and θ_2. To simplify things further, we will assume that candidates, once elected, actually seek to implement the platform they have stated. Of course, in reality, candidates often go back on election promises, but to study the issue of credibility would take us too far afield.

Each of the n voters in society observes the candidates' platforms and decides how to vote. If π_i represents the probability that voter i will vote for candidate 1, we will assume that

$$\pi_i = f_i[\, U_i(\theta_1) - U_i(\theta_2)],\qquad (21.20)$$

where $f' > 0$ and $U_i(\theta_j)$ represents the utility that the voter expects to obtain from the platform announced by candidate j. Because there are only two candidates[13] in the election, the probability that voter i will vote for candidate 2 is given by $1 - \pi_i$.

Nash Equilibrium in the candidate game

Candidate 1 chooses θ_1 so as to maximize the probability of his or her election:

$$\textbf{expected vote} = EV_1 = \sum_{i=1}^{n} \pi_i = \sum_{i=1}^{n} f_i[U_i(\theta_1) - U_i(\theta_2)]. \qquad (21.21)$$

Similarly, candidate 2 chooses θ_2 to maximize his or her expected votes:

$$\textbf{expected vote} = EV_2 = \sum_{i=1}^{n} (1 - \pi_i) = n - EV_1. \qquad (21.22)$$

From the perspective of game theory our voting model is therefore a *zero-sum game* with continuous strategies (the platforms, θ_1 and θ_2). The fundamental theorem of such games ensures that this game will have a Nash equilibrium set of strategies for which

$$EV_1(\theta_1, \theta_2^*) \le EV_1(\theta_1^*, \theta_2^*) \le EV_1(\theta_1^*, \theta_2). \qquad (21.23)$$

That is, candidate 1 does best against θ_2^* by choosing θ_1^*, and candidate 2 does best against θ_1^* by choosing θ_2^*. Considerations of the strategic aspects of elections, therefore, suggest that candidates will be led to equilibrium platforms and that the properties of elections can be studied by examining how these platforms are affected by changing situations.

---

[13]Here we also assume that all voters do, in fact, vote. The study of voter "turnout" is obviously quite important in the study of actual elections.

EXAMPLE 21.3

Net Value Platforms

Although it is generally difficult to quantify the various dimensions of candidates' platforms, one simple illustration is provided by "net value" platforms under which each candidate promises a unique dollar benefit (that is, value of government services less taxes paid) to each voter. For example, candidate 1 promises a net dollar benefit of θ_{1i} to each voter. The candidate is bound by a government budget constraint:

$$\sum_{i=1}^{n} \theta_{1i} = 0. \tag{21.24}$$

The candidates' goal is to choose that set of θ_{1i} that maximizes EV_1 against θ_2^*. Setting up the Lagrangian for this problem yields

$$\mathcal{L} = EV_1 + \lambda \left(\sum_{i=1}^{n} \theta_{1i} \right) \tag{21.25}$$

$$= \sum_{i=1}^{n} f_i [U(\theta_{1i}) - U(\theta_2^*)] + \lambda \left(\sum_{i=1}^{n} \theta_{1i} \right).$$

The first-order condition for the net benefits promised to voter i is given by

$$\frac{\partial \mathcal{L}}{\partial \theta_{1i}} = f_i' U_i' + \lambda = 0. \tag{21.26}$$

If the function f_i is the same for all voters, Equation 21.26 implies that candidate 1 should choose θ_{1i} so that U_i' is the same for all voters. Interestingly, this is the same policy that would be adopted by an omniscient philosopher king who sought to maximize the "utilitarian" social welfare function:

$$SW = \sum_{i=1}^{n} U_i(\theta_{1i}). \tag{21.27}$$

In this simple model, then, there is a connection between the strategic outcomes from voting for representatives and optimal resource allocations that might be suggested by specific social welfare functions. Competition among candidates in the public arena may to some extent complement Smith's invisible hand in private markets.[14]

Query: Does candidate 2 also select a utilitarian optimal platform? How would this result change if f_i differed among voters?

Money and politics

Because money has come to play an increasingly important role in elections, economists have sought to generalize the previous model to take account of campaign contributions and other types of political payoffs. There are two routes by which such payments can affect the allocation of resources through political channels. First, money spent on media advertising or on get-out-the-vote efforts may affect voters' decisions (that is, such spending

[14]Other normative properties of probabilistic voting models are discussed in P. Coughlan and S. Nitzan, "Electoral Outcomes with Probabilistic Voting and Nash Social Welfare Maxima," *Journal of Public Economics* (February 1981): 113–21.

may affect the function f_i introduced in the previous section). Second, the promise of campaign contributions may cause candidates to alter their platforms so as to appeal to special interest group contributors. Ultimately, then, the platforms chosen by candidates may not represent the pure Nash equilibrium choices implied earlier. Instead, actual platforms may represent complex trade-offs between candidates' needs to obtain campaign funding and their needs to appeal to a majority of voters. Modeling these trade-offs and inferring how various "reform" proposals might affect observed outcomes is a difficult problem in general equilibrium analysis.

Rent-seeking behavior

Elected politicians perform the role of agents in choosing policies favored by the principals in society—the voters. In this context, a perfect agent would opt for those policies that the fully informed median voter would choose were they in a position to do so. One might ask, however, if such a behavioral assumption asks too much of politicians. There seems to be no compelling reason why politicians should become selfless agents upon being elected to office. An alternative assumption is that politicians might engage in *rent-seeking activities* that seek to enhance their own welfare. Such activities could range from the banal (stealing some tax revenues) to the ingenious (disguising political rents as seemingly necessary costs of legislative activity). In terms of the political model we developed earlier in this chapter, the possibility for such "corrupt" activities would create an implicit tax wedge between the value of public goods received by voters and taxes paid. That is, extraction of a political rent r would require that the government budget constraint (Equation 21.8) be rewritten as

$$g = tny^A - r. \tag{21.28}$$

Voters would presumably take such rent-seeking activities into account in deciding on public policies, and this would likely reduce optimal values for g and t accordingly.

Political rents and electoral competition

Whether political rents can persist in an environment of open electoral competition is open to question. If candidate A announces policy $(g, t)^A$ that obeys the budget constraint in Equation 21.28, candidate B can always choose a policy $(g, t)^B$ that is more attractive to the median voter by accepting a smaller rent. Much as Bertrand price competition in our game theory models in Chapter 15 constrained competitors to marginal cost pricing, active competition among political candidates can drive political rents to zero. Only with barriers to entry (incumbent campaigning advantages, for example) or with imperfect information about politicians' activities can positive rents persist. Viewed in this way, election reform and antitrust policy have much in common.

Sources of political rents

Success in generating political rents need not arise only from within the government sector of the economy. Private citizens may seek rents for themselves by seeking help from politicians who are in the position to grant them favors. For example, suppose a firm in an otherwise competitive industry can encourage (through some sort of monetary payments) politicians to grant an exclusive franchise. The result would be a monopolization of the industry together with some of what would have been monopoly profits being transferred to the politician. The political payoff itself would not be a welfare cost to society—this would just further transfer what the monopoly had already transferred from consumers. But the deadweight loss from the creation of the monopoly (relative to the competitive situation that would have prevailed in the absence of political favoritism), together with whatever real resources went into securing the franchise, would constitute the true welfare cost of rent seeking.

Hence we have developed a general definition:

DEFINITION

Rent-seeking activities. Economic agents engage in rent-seeking activities when they use the political process to generate economic rents that would not ordinarily occur in market transactions. Such rents will be shared by politicians and private agents. The welfare costs of these activities consist of the utility losses to individuals who must accept second-best outcomes, not from size of the rents themselves or from the way in which the rents are shared.

The definition suggests that rent-seeking may be quite common and that the costs associated with such activities may be high. Example 21.4 illustrates that it is possible to use standard economic concepts to analyze such activities.

EXAMPLE 21.4

Rent Dissipation

If a number of actors compete in the same rent-seeking activity, it is possible that all available rent will be dissipated into rent seekers' costs. Suppose, for example, a monopoly might earn profits of π_m per period and a franchise for the monopoly can be obtained from a pliant government official for a bribe of B per period ($B < \pi_m$). Risk-neutral entrepreneurs will offer bribes so long as the expected gain exceeds the costs of the bribe. If each rent seeker has the same chance of winning the franchise, the number of bribers (n) will expand to the point at which

$$B = \pi_m / n. \tag{21.29}$$

Hence the total rent available will be dissipated through the bribes paid by all contestants for the franchise. If rent seekers were risk averse, or if government officials stop short of receiving the maximum bribes possible, some rent may remain for the franchise winner, however.

Query: Would rent be completely dissipated in this example if n were capped at lower than the number needed to satisfy Equation 21.29?

SUMMARY

In this chapter we surveyed some of the concepts from the economic theory of public choice. We showed that public choice mechanisms are intrinsically more difficult to evaluate than market mechanisms. Even in relatively simple situations, Pareto-inferior results may occur. For complex situations (such as voting in Congress), developing explicit models of behavior may be very difficult and evaluation must be by less formal means. In examining these issues we showed that:

- Choosing equitable allocations of resources is an ambiguous process because many potential welfare criteria might be used. In some cases achieving equity (appropriately defined) may require some efficiency sacrifices.

- Arrow's impossibility theorem shows that, given fairly general assumptions, there is no completely satisfactory social choice mechanism. The problem of social choice theory is therefore to assess the performance of relatively imperfect mechanisms.

- Direct voting and majority rule may not always yield an equilibrium. If preferences are single-peaked, however, majority rule voting on one-dimensional public questions will result in choosing policies most favored by the median voter. Such policies are not necessarily efficient, however.

- Voting in representative governments may be analyzed using the tools of game theory. In some cases candidates choices of strategies will yield Nash equilibria that have desirable normative consequences.

- Politicians may engage in opportunistic rent seeking, but this will be constrained by electoral competition.

PROBLEMS

21.1

There are 200 pounds of food that must be allocated between two sailors marooned on an island. The utility function of the first sailor is given by

$$\text{utility} = \sqrt{f_1},$$

where f_1 is the quantity of food consumed by the first sailor. For the second sailor, utility (as a function of his food consumption) is given by

$$\text{utility} = \tfrac{1}{2}\sqrt{f_2}.$$

a. If the food is allocated equally between the sailors, how much utility will each receive?

b. How should food be allocated between the sailors to ensure equality of utility?

c. How should food be allocated so as to maximize the sum of the sailors' utilities?

d. Suppose sailor 2 requires a utility level of at least 5 to remain alive. How should food be allocated so as to maximize the sum of utilities subject to the constraint that sailor 2 receive that minimum level of utility?

e. Suppose both sailors agree on a social welfare function of the form

$$W = U_1^{1/2} U_2^{1/2}.$$

How should food be allocated between the sailors so as to maximize social welfare?

21.2

In the 1930s several authors suggested a "bribe criterion" for judging the desirability of social situations. This welfare criterion states that a movement from social state A to state B is an improvement in social welfare if those who gain by this move are able to compensate those who lose sufficiently so that they will accept the change. Compensation does not actually have to be made; it is only necessary that it could be paid. If the compensation is actually made, this criterion reduces to the Pareto definition (some individuals are made better off without making anyone worse off). Hence, the criterion is novel only in that compensation is not paid by the gainers to the losers. In such a situation, does the bribe criterion seem to be "value-free," or does the criterion seem somehow to favor those who are initially rich? Can you give some simple examples?

21.3

Suppose an economy is characterized by a linear production possibility function for its two goods (x and y) of the form

$$x + 2y = 180.$$

There are two individuals in this economy, each with an identical utility function for x and y of the form

$$U(x, y) = \sqrt{xy}.$$

a. Suppose y production is set at 10. What would the utility possibility frontier for this economy be?

b. Suppose y production is set at 30. What would the utility possibility frontier be?

c. How should y production be chosen so as to ensure the "best" utility possibility frontier?

d. Under what conditions (contrary to those of this problem) might your answer to part (c) depend on the point on the utility possibility frontier being considered?

21.4

Suppose seven individuals constitute a society in which individuals cast votes for their most preferred social arrangement and that the arrangement with the greatest number of votes is always chosen. Devise an example of individual rankings of the three states A, B, and C such that state A is chosen when all three states are available but that state B is chosen if the "irrelevant" alternative C is not available. (This amounts to showing that the constitution of this society does not obey Axiom 4 in Arrow's list.) How reasonable is your example? What does it indicate about the nature of Arrow's axiom?

21.5

Suppose there are two individuals in an economy. Utilities of those individuals under five possible social states are shown in the following table:

State	Utility 1	Utility 2
A	50	50
B	70	40
C	45	54
D	53	50.5
E	30	84

Individuals do not know which number (1 or 2) they will be assigned when the economy begins operating, hence they are uncertain about the actual utility they will receive under the alternative social states. Which social state will be preferred if an individual adopts the following strategies in his or her voting behavior to deal with this uncertainty?

a. Choose that state which ensures the highest utility to the least well-off person.

b. Assume there is a 50–50 chance of being either individual and choose that state with the highest expected utility.

c. Assume that no matter what, the odds are always unfavorable such that there is a 60 percent chance of having the lower utility and a 40 percent chance of higher utility in any social state. Choose the state with the highest expected utility given these probabilities.

d. Assume there is a 50–50 chance of being assigned either number and that each individual dislikes inequality. Each will choose that state for which

$$\text{expected utility} - |U_1 - U_2|$$

is as large as possible (where the $| \ldots |$ notation denotes absolute value).

e. What do you conclude from this problem about social choices under a "veil of ignorance" as to an individual's specific identity in society?

21.6

Suppose there are three individuals in society trying to rank three social states (*A*, *B*, and *C*). For each of the methods of social choice indicated, develop an example to show how (at least) one of the Arrow axioms will be violated.

a. Majority rule without vote trading.

b. Majority rule with vote trading.

c. Point voting where each voter can give 1, 2, or 3 points to each alternative and the alternative with the highest point total is selected.

21.7

Suppose individuals face a probability of *u* that they will be unemployed next year. If they are unemployed they will receive unemployment benefits of *b*, whereas if they are employed they receive $w(1 - t)$, where *t* is the tax used to finance unemployment benefits. Unemployment benefits are constrained by the government budget constraint $ub = tw(1 - u)$.

a. Suppose the individual's utility function is given by

$$U = (y_i)^\delta / \delta,$$

where $1 - \delta$ is the degree of constant relative risk aversion. What would be the utility-maximizing choices for *b* and *t*?

b. How would the utility maximizing choices for *b* and *t* respond to changes in the probability of unemployment, *u*?

c. How would *b* and *t* change in response to changes in the risk aversion parameter δ?

21.8

The demand for gummy bears is given by

$$Q = 200 - 100p,$$

and these confections can be produced at a constant marginal cost of $.50.

a. How much will Sweettooth, Inc., be willing to pay in bribes to obtain a monopoly concession from the government for gummy bear production?

b. Do the bribes represent a welfare cost from rent seeking?

c. What is the welfare cost of this rent-seeking activity?

21.9

How does the free rider problem arise in the decision of eligible voters to vote? How might voter participation decisions affect median voter results? How might it affect probabilistic voting models?

21.10

Suppose voters based their decisions on the ratio of utilities received from two candidates—that is, Equation 21.6 would be

$$\pi_i = f_i[(U_i(\theta_1)/U_i(\theta_2))].$$

Show that the results from a game involving net value platforms would in this case maximize the Nash social welfare function

$$SW = \prod_{i=1}^{n} U_i.$$

SUGGESTIONS FOR FURTHER READING

Arrow, K. J. *Social Choice and Individual Values,* 2nd ed. New Haven, CT: Yale University Press, 1963.
Classic statement of the impossibility theorem. Extensive discussion of its general meaning.

Black, D. "On the Rationale of Group Decision Making." *Journal of Political Economy* (February 1948): 23–34. Reprinted in K. J. Arrow and T. Scitovsky, eds., *Readings in Welfare Economics.* Homewood, IL: Richard D. Irwin, 1969.
Early development of the "median voter" theorem.

Buchanan, J. M., and G. Tullock. *The Calculus of Consent.* Ann Arbor: University of Michigan Press, 1962.
Classic analysis of the properties of various voting schemes.

Drazen, A. *Political Economy in Macroeconomics.* Princeton, NJ: Princeton University Press, 2000.
Consideration of a variety of models of macroeconomic policy decision making.

Inman, R. P. "Markets, Governments and the 'New' Political Economy." In A. J. Auerbach and M. Feldstein, eds., *Handbook of Public Economics,* vol. 2. Amsterdam: North-Holland, 1987, pp. 647–777.
Extensive review of the topics covered in this chapter. Interesting use of game theory to illustrate some concepts. Good discussion of theoretical role for tax limitation provisions.

Mueller, D. *Public Choice II.* Cambridge: Cambridge University Press, 1989.
Extends the analysis of probabilistic voting in this chapter to explicitly consider political contributions and a number of other issues.

Olson, M. *The Logic of Collective Action.* Cambridge, MA: Harvard University Press, 1965.
Analyzes the effects of individual incentives on the willingness to undertake collective action. Many fascinating examples.

Persson, T., and G. Tabellini. *Political Economics: Explaining Economic Policy.* Cambridge, MA: MIT Press, 2000.
A complete summary of recent models of political choices. Covers voting models and issues of institutional frameworks.

Rawls, J. *A Theory of Justice.* Cambridge, MA: Harvard University Press, 1971.
Basic philosophical text. Makes wide use of economic concepts, especially Pareto efficiency notions and the contract curve.

Sen, A. K. *Collective Choice and Social Welfare.* San Francisco: Holden-Day, 1970.
Complete, formal analysis of collective choice issues. Has many literary sections among the more mathematical analyses.

EXTENSIONS

Voting Schemes

We saw in Chapter 21 that there is very little relationship between the results of majority rule voting for public goods and solving the demand revelation problem posed in Chapter 20. Most common voting schemes do not convey enough information about voters' preferences to permit the implementation of an efficient outcome such as that envisioned in the Lindahl equilibrium. In these Extensions we look at more complex schemes for voting that come closer to the Lindahl ideal. These are primarily of theoretical interest, however. Practical implementation could be quite resource-intensive.

E21.1 Vickrey auctions

Many voting schemes draw on the initial insights of W. Vickrey from his famous paper on second-price, sealed bid auctions[1] (1961). Vickrey's major insight was that sealed-bid auctions in which the highest bidder wins, but pays the amount bid by the next highest bidder, provided incentives to bidders to reveal their true value for the item being sold. Consider bidder i, who will receive utility u_i from a good. Under the usual first-price sealed-bid auction, this person may bid $b_i < u_i$ in the hope this will win the auction and provide a surplus of $u_i - b_i$. Hence person i has an incentive not to reveal his or her true valuation. Under a second-price sealed-bid auction, however, the highest bid from other bidders,[2] $b_{(-i)}$, is exogenous to person i. If $u_i < b_{(-i)}$, person i can bid $b_i = u_i$ and will lose the auction (which is utility-maximizing in that case). If $u_i > b_{(-i)}$ this person can still bid $b_i = u_i$ and win the auction, receiving a net gain of $u_i - b_{(-i)}$. In either case, person i's incentive is to bid truthfully—the Vickrey second-price sealed-bid auction is "truth revealing."

E21.2 The Groves mechanism

In an important 1973 paper, T. Groves proposed a way to adapt the Vickrey insight to the problem of discovering the demand for a public good. Under the Groves scheme, each voter would be asked to reveal his or her net valuation (benefits minus taxes—so net valuations could be negative) for a public good/financing plan combination. But each voter would also be offered a simultaneous transfer payment carefully chosen to ensure that he or she had an incentive to announce truthful net values. To illustrate this payment, assume there is only one public good being voted on and that the net value reported for this good by voter i is given by v_i. Each voter is promised a direct transfer of amount $t_i = \sum_{-i} v_i$ (which might itself be negative) if the project is undertaken and 0 otherwise. That is, each voter is offered a transfer that will equal the sum of all other voters' announced valuations, but the transfer will be paid only if the project is undertaken.

The problem for voter i is to choose his or her announced net valuation in such a way that the project will be undertaken if and only if $u_i + \sum_{-i} v_i > 0$. But each voter also knows that the government will in fact undertake the project if and only if $\sum_i v_i > 0$. Hence choosing $v_i = u_i$ is at least one option for stating a valuation that proves to be utility-maximizing. Because this strategy is a dominant one for each voter, the Groves mechanism will be truth revealing for all voters.

E21.3 The Clarke mechanism

The Groves procedure provides the basis for many additional voting schemes. One way in which the procedure can be generalized is to add to the original Groves transfer some other additional tax or transfer that is independent of voter i's valuation revealing process. A scheme that was proposed earlier by E. Clarke (1971) can be looked at in this way. Under this scheme, the Groves transfer is accompanied by a tax based also on other voter's evaluations. This tax

---

[1]For further details on the mathematics of such auctions, see Problem 15.10

[2]The notation $(-i)$ means all members of a group other than member i.

is set equal to $Max(\sum_{-i} v_i, 0)$. That is, the tax is equal to the sum of other voters' valuations if that sum is positive and 0 otherwise. This combined two-part transfer/tax scheme has some rather interesting properties. First, this process will also be truth-revealing—the addition of the tax does not change the truth-revealing character of the Groves transfer. Second, the Clarke scheme assigns an interesting role to "pivotal" voters. A pivotal voter is one whose reported valuation actually changes the decision for a project. For nonpivotal voters, the combined transfer/tax under the Clarke scheme is zero. Suppose, for example, that combined valuations for group $(-i)$ are highly positive so that the project will be undertaken whatever voter i reports (though, remember, this report will be truthful because of the Groves transfer). In this case, the Groves transfer and the Clarke-inspired tax would cancel, giving a net transfer/tax of zero. If the combined valuation of group $(-i)$ is so negative that it cannot be turned around by voter i, the project will not be undertaken, and both the Groves transfer and the Clarke tax will be zero. When voter i is pivotal, he or she always pays a tax, and this tax looks much like a Pigovian tax in that it compensates for the externality that voter i causes to group $(-i)$ by reversing their collective valuation. For example, suppose $\sum_{-i} v_i$ is negative but that $\sum_i v_i$ is positive. Then the project will be built, and voter i will receive a negative Groves transfer of $\sum_{-i} v_i$ and a Clarke tax of zero. That is, in this case the voter pays a tax equal to the combined negative valuations that voters in group $(-i)$ experience as a result of actually undertaking the project. Voter i's payment compensates for the negative externality that his or her pivotal vote causes. A similar tax is paid when voter i's negative valuation for a project causes it not to be built even though the project is, on net, favored by group $(-i)$. Hence the Clarke mechanism reflects much the same insights as do Pigovian taxes.

E21.4 Generalizations

The voting schemes we have been describing (which are sometimes termed *VCG mechanisms* after their three principal discoverers) can be generalized in a number of directions. For example, Mas-Colell, Whinston, and Green (1995) summarize ways in which the VCG approach can be adapted to evaluate many potential governmental projects or how different notions of equilibrium can be used to get more robust results. Other authors have investigated asymptotic properties of VCG mechanisms and conclude that the prevalence of pivotal voters approaches zero as the overall number of voters expands. One implicit assumption we have used throughout these extensions does not seem to be generalizable, however. This is the notion that the various transfers and taxes envisioned in the VCG approach can simply be added to the voter's (indirect) utility from a project without affecting allocations elsewhere in the budget.[3] Whether such assumptions about preferences provide a fairly good approximation for modeling actual political decisions is an open question.

References

Clarke, E., "Multipart Pricing of Public Goods," *Public Choice* (Fall 1971):19–33.

Groves, T., "Incentives in Teams," *Econometrica* (July 1973):617–31.

Mas-Collell, A., M. D. Whinston, and J. R. Green, *Microeconomic Theory* (New York, Oxford University Press, 1995).

Vickrey, W., "Counterspeculation, Auctions, and Competitive Sealed Tenders," *Journal of Finance* (January 1961):1–17.

---

[3]Technically, utility is assumed to be "quasi-linear" in that $u_i = U_i(c) + g_i + t_i$ where c is consumption, g_i represents the benefits of the project, and t_i represents taxes paid or transfers received.

Brief Answers to Queries

The following brief answers to the queries that accompany each example in the text may help students test their understanding of the concepts being presented.

CHAPTER 1

1.1

If price depends on quantity, differentiation of $p(q) \cdot q$ would be more complicated. This would lead to the concept of marginal revenue—a topic we encounter in many places in this book.

1.2

The reduced form in Equation 1.16 shows that $\partial p^*/\partial a = 1/225$. So, if a increases by 450, p^* should increase by 2—which is what a direct solution shows.

1.3

If $x = 9.99$, $y = 5.040$; if $x = 10.01$, $y = 4.959$.

$$\frac{\Delta y}{\Delta x} = \frac{-.081}{.02},$$

which is close to -4. Calculus results can only be approximated by discrete changes.

CHAPTER 2

2.1

The first-order condition for a maximum is $\partial \pi/\partial l = 50/\sqrt{l} - 10 = 0$, $l^* = 25$, $\pi^* = 250$.

2.2

No, only the exponential function (or a function that approximates it over a range) has constant elasticity.

2.3

These would be concentric circles centered at $x_1 = 1$, $x_2 = 2$. For $y = 10$, the "circle" is a single point.

2.4

For different constants, each production possibility frontier is a successively larger quarter ellipse centered at the origin.

2.5

$\partial y^*/\partial b = 0$ because x_1 would always be set at b for optimality, and the term $(x_1 - b)$ would vanish.

2.6

With $x_1 + x_2 = 2$, $x_1 = 0.5$, $x_2 = 1.5$. Now $y^* = 9.5$. For $x_1 + x_2 \geq 3$, the unconstrained optimum is attainable.

2.7

A circular field encloses maximal area for minimum perimeter. Proof requires a limit argument.

2.8

The local maximum is also a global maximum here. The constancy of the second derivative implies the slope of the function decreases at a constant rate.

2.9

This function resembles an inverted cone that has only one highest point.

2.10

A linear constraint would be represented by a plane in these three-dimensional figures. Such a plane would have a unique tangency to the surfaces in both Figure 2.4(a) and 2.4(c). For an unconstrained maximum, however, the plane would be horizontal, so only Figure 2.4(a) would have a maximum.

2.11

Such a transformation would not preserve homogeneity. However it would not affect the trade-off between the x's: for any constant, $k, -f_1/f_2 = x_2/x_1$.

CHAPTER 3

3.1

The derivation here holds utility constant to create an implicit relationship between y and x. Changes in x also implicitly change y because of this relationship (Equation 3.11).

3.2

The *MRS* is not changed by such a doubling in Examples 1 and 3. In Example 2 the *MRS* would be changed because $(1 + x)/(1 + y) \neq (1 + 2x)/(1 + 2y)$.

3.3

For homothetic functions, the *MRS* is the same for every point along a positively sloped ray through the origin.

3.4

The indifference curves here are "horizontally parallel." That is, for any given level of y, the *MRS* is the same no matter what the value of x is. One implication of this (as we shall see in Chapter 4) is that the effect of additional income on purchases of good y is zero—all extra income is channeled into the good with constant marginal utility (good x).

CHAPTER 4

4.1

Constant shares imply $\partial x/\partial p_y = 0$ and $\partial y/\partial p_x = 0$. Notice p_y does not enter Equation 4.23; p_x does not enter 4.24.

4.2

Budget shares are not affected by income, but they are affected by changes in relative prices. This is the case for all homothetic functions.

4.3

Since a doubling of all prices and nominal income does not change the budget constraint, it will not change utility. Indirect utility is homogeneous of degree zero in all prices and nominal income.

4.4

In the Cobb-Douglas case, with $p_y = 3$, $E(1,3,2) = 2 \cdot 1 \cdot 3^{0.5} \cdot 2 = 6.93$, so this person should have his or her income reduced by a lump-sum 1.07 to compensate for the fall in prices. In the fixed proportions case, the original consumption bundle now costs 7, so the compensation is −1.0. Notice that with fixed proportions the consumption bundle does not change, but with the Cobb-Douglas, the new choice is $x = 3.46$, $y = 1.15$ because this person takes advantage of the reduction in the price of y.

CHAPTER 5

5.1

The shares equations computed from Equations 5.5 or 5.7 show that this individual always spends all of his or her income regardless of p_x, p_y, and I. That is, the shares sum to one.

5.2

If $x = .5 \ I/p_x$, $I = 100$, $p_x = 1$ implies $x = 50$. In Equation 5.11 $x = .5(100/1) = 50$ also. If p_x rises to 2.0, the Cobb-Douglas predicts $x = 25$. The CES implies $x = 100/6 = 16.67$. The CES is more responsive to price.

5.3

Since proportional changes in p_x and p_y do not induce substitution effects, holding V constant implies that x and y will not change. That should be true for all compensated demand functions.

5.4

A larger exponent for, say, x in the Cobb-Douglas function will increase the share of income devoted to that good and increase the relative importance of the income effect in the Slutsky decomposition.

5.5

This is easiest to see in the Cobb-Douglas case for which $e_{x,p_x} = -1$ regardless of budget shares. The Slutsky equation in elasticity terms shows that, because the income effect here is $-s_x e_{x,I} = -s_x(1) = -s_x$, the compensated price elasticity is $e^c_{x,p_x} = e_{x,p_x} + s_x = -(1 - s_x)$. This occurs because proportional changes in x demand will be larger when the share devoted to that good is smaller because they are starting from a smaller base.

5.6

Typically it is assumed that demand goes to zero at some finite price when calculating total consumer surplus. The specific assumption made does not affect calculations of changes in consumer surplus.

CHAPTER 6

6.1

Since $\partial x / \partial p_y$ includes both income and substitution effects, this derivative could be 0 if the effects offset each other. The conclusion that $\partial x / \partial p_y = 0$ implies the goods must be used in fixed proportions would hold only if the income effect of this price change were 0.

6.2

Asymmetry can occur with homothetic preferences since, although substitution effects are symmetric, income effects may differ in size.

6.3

Since the relationships between p_y, p_z, and p_h never change, the maximization problem will always be solved the same way.

CHAPTER 7

7.1

Now with $k = 11$

$$q = 72,600l^2 - 1,331l^3$$
$$MP_l = 145,200l - 3,993l^2$$
$$AP_l = 72,600l - 1,331l^2.$$

In this case, AP_l now reaches its maximal value at $l = 27.3$ rather than at $l = 30$.

7.2

If $k = l$, since k and l enter f symmetrically, $f_k = f_l, f_{kk} = f_{ll}$. Hence, the numerator of Equation 7.21 will be negative if $f_{kl} > f_{ll}$. Combining Equations 7.24 and 7.25 (and remembering $k = l$) shows this holds for $k = l < 20$.

7.3

The $q = 4$ isoquant contains the points $k = 4$, $l = 0$; $k = 1$, $l = 1$; and $k = 0$, $l = 4$. It is therefore fairly sharply convex. It seems possible that a L-shaped isoquant might be reached for particular coefficients of the linear and radical terms.

7.4

Because the composite technical change factor is $\theta = \alpha\phi + (1 - \alpha)\varepsilon$, a value of $\alpha = 0.3$ implies that technical improvements in labor will be weighted more highly in determining the overall result.

CHAPTER 8

8.1

If $\sigma = 2$, $\rho = 0.5$, $k/l = 16$, $l = 8/5$, $k = 128/5$, $C = 96$.

If $\sigma = 0.5$, $\rho = -1$, $k/l = 2$, $l = 60$, $k = 120$, $C = 1080$.

Notice that changes in σ also change the scale of the production function, so the total-cost figures cannot be compared directly.

8.2

The expression for unit costs is $(v^{1-\sigma} + w^{1-\sigma})^{1/1-\sigma}$. If $w + v$ is a constant and $\sigma = 0$, the relative costs on the inputs make no difference to unit cost. For higher values of σ, greater disparities in input costs lead to cost savings because of the possibilities for input substitution.

8.3

The elasticities are given by the exponents in the cost functions and are unaffected by technical change as modeled here.

8.4

In this case σ = ∞. With $w = 4v$, cost minimization could use the inputs in any combination (for q constant) without changing costs. A rise in w would cause the firm to switch to using only capital and would not affect total costs. This shows that the impact on costs of an increase in the price of a single input depends importantly on the degree of substitution.

8.5

Because capital costs are fixed in the short run, they do not affect short-run marginal costs (in mathematical terms, the derivative of a constant is zero). Capital costs do, however, affect short-run average costs. In Figure 8.9 an increase in v would shift MC, AC, and all of the SATC curves upward, but would leave the SMC curves unaffected.

CHAPTER 9

9.1

If $MC = 5$, profit maximization requires $q = 25$. Now $P = 7.50$, $R = 187.50$, $C = 125$, and $\pi = 62.50$.

9.2

Factors other than p can be incorporated into the constant term a. These would shift D and MR but would not affect the elasticity calculations.

9.3

When w rises to 15, supply shifts inward to $q = 8P/5$. When k increases to 100, supply shifts outward to $q = 25P/6$. A change in v would not affect short-run marginal cost or the shutdown decision.

9.4

A change in v has no effect on SMC but it does affect fixed costs. A change in w would affect SMC and short-run supply.

9.5

A rise in wages for all firms would shift the market supply curve inward, raising the product price. This would cause each firm to produce more than would be the case with a constant price. The output effect in the demand for labor would therefore be somewhat smaller than the output effect discussed in the example. Still, both substitution and output effects would be negative.

CHAPTER 10

10.1

The ability to sum incomes in this linear case would require that each person have the same coefficient for income. Because each person faces the same price, aggregation requires only adding of price coefficients.

10.2

A value for β other than 0.5 would mean that the exponent of price would not be 1.0. The higher is β the more price elastic is short-run supply.

10.3

This would require making the demand curve flatter. For example, the demand curve $Q = 16,000 - 1,000P$ has the same initial equilibrium values ($P^* = 12$, $Q^* = 4,000$) as in the original problem. But with reduced supply the equilibrium is now $P^* = 12.63$, $Q^* = 3,368$.

10.4

Following steps similar to those used to derive Equation 10.36 yields

$$e_{P,\beta} = \frac{-e_{Q,\beta}}{e_{S,P} - e_{Q,P}}$$

Here $e_{Q,\beta} = e_{Q,w} = -.5$ so $e_{P,\beta} = \dfrac{-(-.5)}{2.2} = .227$.

Multiplication by .20 (since wages rose 20 percent) predicts a price rise of 4.5 percent, very close to the number in the example.

10.5

The short-run supply curve is given by $Q_S = .5P + 750$, and the short-term equilibrium price is $643. Each firm earns approximately $2,960 in profits in the short run.

10.6

Total and average costs for Equation 10.59 exceed those for Equation 10.46 for $q > 15.9$. Marginal costs for Equation 10.59 always exceed those for Equation 10.46. Optimal output is lower with Equation 10.59 than with Equation 10.46 because marginal costs increase more than average costs.

CHAPTER 11

11.1

Losses from a given restriction in quantity will be greater when supply and/or demand is less elastic. The actor with the least elastic response will bear the greater share of the loss.

11.2

An increase in t unambiguously increases dead-weight loss. Because increases in t reduce quantity, however, total tax revenues are subject to countervailing effects. Indeed, if $t/(P + t) \geq -1/e_{Q,P}$ then $dtQ/dt < 0$.

11.3

Total transfer to domestic producers is (in billions) $.5 \cdot (11.7) + .5(.5)(0.7) = 6.03$. This would be gained as rents to those inputs that give the auto supply curve its positive slope. With a quota, domestic producers may also be able to gain some portion of what would have been tariff revenue.

CHAPTER 12

12.1

An increase in labor input will shift the first frontier out uniformly. In the second case, such an increase will shift the y-intercept out farther than the x-intercept because good y uses labor intensively.

12.2

In all three scenarios the total value of output is $200w$, composed half of wages and half of profits. With the shift in supply, consumers still devote $100w$ to each good. Purchases of x are twice those of y because y costs twice as much. With the shift on demand, the consumer spends $20w$ on good x and $180w$ on good y. But good y now costs three times what x costs, so consumers buy only three times as much y as they do x.

12.3

Walras's law ensures that the silver market is in equilibrium. Recalculating Equation 16.40 gives

$$ED_1 = 2(p_2/p_1)^2 + 2(p_3/p_1)^2 - 4p_2/p_1 - 7p_3/p_1$$

or, at the new relative prices,

$$= 2(3)^2 + 2(2)^2 - 4(3) - 7(2) = 0.$$

12.4

Because each production function exhibits constant returns to scale, any allocation of capital will be efficient if labor is allocated appropriately.

12.5

Total consumer income is $300w$ which is allocated equally to each good. Firms producing good y get this as total revenue ($150w$). Firms producing good x receive only $50w$ in revenues because $100w$ goes to the government in taxes. For these firms, total (after-tax) revenue is $p_x \cdot x = 50w$. Consumer spending on good x, however, is $3p_x \cdot x = 150w$. In this case, GDP is still $200w - 50w$ in x production, $150w$ in y production. There is $100w$ in taxes and transfers, but this figure is not part of GDP.

12.6

The indifference curves are relatively flat here, implying that these individuals are quite willing to substitute one good for another. This flexibility implies a relatively narrow range of mutually beneficial trading opportunities at point A. With less flexible preferences, the number of opportunities is increased because the individuals may start trading from widely differing marginal rates of substitution.

CHAPTER 13

13.1

The increase in fixed costs would not alter the output decisions because it would not affect marginal costs. It would, however, raise AC by 5 and reduce profits to 12,500. With the new C function, MC would rise to $.15Q$. In this case, $Q^* = 400$, $P^* = 80$, $C = 22,000$, and $\pi = 10,000$.

13.2

With $e = -1.5$, the ratio of monopoly to competitive consumer surplus is 0.58 (Equation 13.18). Profits represent 19 percent of competitive consumer surplus (Equation 13.20).

13.3

If $Q = 0$, $P = 100$. Total profits are given by the triangular area between the demand curve and the MC curve, less fixed costs. This area is $.5(100)(666) = 33,333$. So $\pi = 33,333 - 10,000 = 23,333$.

13.4

Yes, output is the same because marginal revenue curves are linear too. Because output does not expand under the two-price policy, welfare cannot be increased by such a policy.

13.5

Profits would be maximized by setting marginal price equal to MC in each market and charging an entry fee of 36 in market 2 and 162 in market 1.

CHAPTER 14

14.1

With $q_2 = 40$, the residual demand facing firm 1 is $q_1 = 80 - P$. Hence, $MR = 80 - 2q_1$ so for $q_1 > 40$, $MR < 0$. Clearly, it is marginal revenue, not price, that matters for the chiseling decision.

14.2

In Example 14.1, q_2 was assumed to be constant. Now firm 2 is assumed to respond to firm 1's increase in output by reducing its own output.

14.3

Constant marginal costs would not change the nature of the problem. Increasing marginal cost would drive the firms toward more equal shares of the marketplace than result from the strategic interactions in the constant-cost case.

14.4

Efficiency requires $P = MC = AC$ unless the differentiated goods exhibit little substitutability.

14.5

Consumer surplus is as large as possible given the no-subsidy constraint. Marginal cost pricing ($P = 100$) would increase consumer surplus but would require a subsidy to cover fixed costs of $8,000.

CHAPTER 15

15.1

None of the strategies is dominant. Separate vacations are not Nash equilibria because both spouses have an incentive to switch.

15.2

Expected utility is two-thirds for each player with the mixed strategies—lower than that promised by either of the other Nash equilibria. This would not be a cooperative outcome.

15.3

See Example 15.4.

15.4

$\delta > .93$ implies a one-period interest rate of less than 7 percent. With periods of days, weeks, or months this seems quite likely.

15.5

The higher is δ, the greater the present value of the future share of monopoly profits. Hence, higher discount rates favor tacit collusion. With $\delta = .8$, at most five firms will support a collusive agreement. With $r = .10$, up to 10 firms will collude tacitly.

15.6

Repeated Follower—Follower strategies might be enforced by retaliation whenever one firm chooses leader.

15.7

If A does not have the advantage of moving first, the situation of both firms is symmetrical, and the model returns to the Stackelberg case. The analysis here differs from contestability because of the sunk-cost assumption.

15.8

Linear demand and marginal costs result in q_A^* being a linear function of q_{BH}^* and q_{BL}^*, which in turn are linear functions of B's marginal cost. With nonlinear demand or, more importantly, marginal costs, q_A^* would not necessarily be based on $E(MC_B)$.

15.9

Yes, a reservation price would change bidding strategies to raise bids so long as R (reservation price) $< V_A, V_B$.

CHAPTER 16

16.1

Nonlabor income permits the individual to "buy" leisure but the amount of such purchases depends on labor-leisure substitutability.

16.2

The conclusion does not depend on linearity. So long as the demand and supply curves are conventionally shaped the curves will be shifted vertically by the parameters t and k.

16.3

Now MRP = \$30 per hour. In this case, the monopsony will hire 750 workers, and wages will be \$15 per hour. As before, the wage remains at only half the MRP.

16.4

The monopsonist wants to be on its demand for labor curve; the union (presumably) wants to be on the labor supply curve of its members. Only the supply-demand equilibrium ($l = 583$, $w = 11.67$) satisfies both these curves. Whether this is indeed a Nash equilibrium depends, among other things, on whether the union defines its payoffs as being accurately reflected by the labor supply curve.

16.5

If the firm is risk neutral, workers risk averse, optimal contracts might have lower wages in exchange for more stable income.

CHAPTER 17

17.1

If δ is the same for two individuals, but individual 1 can obtain a higher interest rate than individual 2, $U'(c_0)/U'(c_1)$ will also be greater for individual 1 than for individual 2. Hence, c_0/c_1 will be lower for individual 1 than for individual 2.

17.2

With an inflation rate of 10 percent, the nominal value of the tree would rise at an additional 10 percent per year. But such revenues would have to be discounted by an identical amount to calculate real profits so the optimal harvesting age would not change.

17.3

Would just raise the optimal price path by marginal cost of extraction.

CHAPTER 18

18.1

If $ln\ x_i = 2^i$, the paradox can be regenerated.

18.2

With linear utility, the individual would care only about expected dollar values and would be indifferent about buying actuarially fair insurance. When utility U is a convex function of wealth ($U > 0$, $U'' > 0$), the individual prefers to gamble and will buy insurance only if it costs less than is actuarially justified.

18.3

If $A = 10^{-4}$,

$$CE(\#1) = 107,000 - 0.5 \cdot 10^{-4} \cdot (10^4)^2$$
$$= 102,000$$

$$CE(\#2) = 102,000 - 0.5 \cdot 10^{-4} \cdot 4 \cdot 10^6$$
$$= 101,800.$$

So the riskier allocation is preferred. On the other hand, if $A = 3 \cdot 10^{-4}$, the less risky allocation is preferred.

18.4

Willingness to pay is a declining function of wealth (Equation 18.44). With $R = 0$ will pay 50 to avoid a 1,000 bet if $W_0 = 10,000$, but only 5 if $W_0 = 100,000$. With $R = 2$ will pay 149 to avoid a 1,000 bet if $W_0 = 10,000$, but only 15 if $W_0 = 100,000$.

18.5

The actuarially fair price for such a policy is $.25 \cdot 19,000 = 4,750$. The maximum amount the individual would pay (X) solves the equation

$$11.45714 = .75\ ln(100,000 - x)$$
$$+ .25\ ln(99,000 - x).$$

Solving this yields an approximate value of $x = \$5,120$. This person would be willing to pay up to \$370 in administrative costs for the deductible policy.

CHAPTER 19

19.1

Although price is uncertain, the model here allows the individual to buy more y when he or she encounters a low price and less when a high price is encountered. Because V is a convex function of p_y, the mean of V for two different values of p_y exceeds the value of V at the mean of p_y. This has no relationship to risk aversion, which concerns choices among options with the same expected value.

19.2

Now insurance costs \$5,300 with no device and \$3,300 with a device. Utility with insurance and no device is $ln(94,700) = 11.4589$ so the individual prefers to install the device but buy no insurance.

19.3

Assuming only full coverage policies are offered, we need to find the value of x for which $ln\ (97,000 - x) = 11.4794$ (the value of utility for low-risk individuals without insurance). Solving this equation yields $x = 297$. To find what a forged certificate must cost (y), we use

$$ln(97,000 - y) \leq 11.4616$$

(the utility from full coverage under a high-risk policy). Solving this inequality yields $y \geq 2,003$.

19.4

In this case owners would have to try to infer improper jet use from observed profits. This would require Bayesian inference and could be modeled using the "manager type" approach.

19.5

$m'(a)$ represents the marginal change in the (marginal) cost-benefit ratio for a small change in a. Because the parameter d is intended to induce greater effort, the higher is this marginal effect the smaller the optimal d is because it is inefficient to induce the manager into taking very costly actions.

CHAPTER 20

20.1

Production of x would have a beneficial impact on y so labor would be underallocated to x by competitive markets.

20.2

The tax is relatively small because of the nature of the externality that vanishes with only a relatively minor reduction in x output. A merged firm would also find $x = 38,000$ to be a profit-maximizing choice.

20.3

The roommates' separate allocations are $x = 1$, $y = 1,000$ so they would achieve the efficient allocation if they moved in together. This results from the simple additive nature of the MRSs in the Cobb-Douglas case and would not be expected to hold generally.

CHAPTER 21

21.1

Each utility function here exhibits diminishing marginal utility. Each teen is therefore risk averse. The degree of risk aversion could only be altered by changing the assumed utility functions.

21.2

Progressive taxation should raise t^* because the median voter can gain more revenue from high income tax payers without incurring high tax costs.

21.3

Candidate 2 also selects a utilitarian optimal platform. If f_i differs among voters, candidate strategies need not maximize any simple function of utilities. A Nash equilibrium still exists, however.

21.4

Some profits might remain, or perhaps officials will raise the requested bribe to $B = \pi_m / \bar{n}$.

Solutions to Odd-Numbered Problems

Only very brief solutions to most of the odd-numbered problems in the text are given here. Complete solutions to all of the problems are contained in the *Solutions Manual,* which is available to instructors upon request.

CHAPTER 2

2.1

a. $8x, 6y$
b. 8, 12
c. $8xdx + 6ydy$.
d. $dy/dx = -4x/3y$.
e. $x = 1, U = (4)(1) + (3)(4) = 16$.
f. $dy/dx = -2/3$.
g. $U = 16$ contour line is an ellipse.

2.3

Both approaches yield $x = y = 0.5$.

2.5

a. The first-order condition for a maximum is $-gt + 40 = 0$, so $t^* = 40/g$.
b. Substitution yields $f(t^*) = -0.5g(40/g)^2 + 40(40/g) = 800/g$. So $\partial f(t^*)/\partial g = -800/g^2$.
c. This follows because $\partial f/\partial g = -0.5(t^*)^2$.
d. $\partial f/\partial g = -0.5(40/g) = -0.625$, so each 0.1 increase in g reduces maximum height by 0.0625.

2.7

a. First-order conditions require $f_1 = f_2 = 1$. Hence, $x_2 = 5$. With $k = 10, x_1 = 5$.
b. With $k = 4, x_1 = -1$.
c. $x_1 = 0, x_2 = 5$.
d. With $k = 20, x_1 = 15, x_2 = 5$. Because marginal value of x_1 is constant, every addition to k beyond 10 adds only to that variable.

2.9

b. $x_1 = kx_2^{-\beta/\alpha}$
   $k = c^{1/\alpha}$

   $$\frac{dx_1}{dx_2} < 0, \frac{d^2x_1}{dx_2^2} > 0$$

c. $\alpha + \beta > 1$,
   $f_{11} = \alpha(\alpha - 1)x_1^{\alpha-2}x_2^{\beta}$
   $f_{22} = \beta(\beta - 1)x_1^{\alpha}x_2^{\beta-2}$
   $f_{12} = \alpha\beta x_1^{\alpha-1} x_2^{\beta-1}$
   $f_{11}f_{22} - f_{12}^2 = \alpha\beta (1 - \alpha - \beta) x_1^{2\alpha-2}x_2^{2\beta-2} < 0$

CHAPTER 3

3.1

a. No
b. Yes
c. Yes
d. No
e. Yes

3.3

The shape of the marginal utility function is not necessarily an indicator of convexity of indifference curves.

3.5

a. $U(h, b, m, r) = Min(h, 2b, m, 0.5r)$.
b. A fully condimented hot dog.
c. $1.60
d. $2.10—an increase of 31 percent.
e. Price would increase only to $1.725—an increase of 7.8 percent.
f. Raise prices so that a fully condimented hot dog rises in price to $2.60. This would be equivalent to a lump-sum reduction in purchasing power.

3.7

b. Budget constraint passes through $\bar{x}, \bar{y}$.

c. No trades occur until $U_0 + k$ is reached.

3.9

It follows, since $MRS = MU_x/MU_y \cdot MU_x$ doesn't depend on y or vice versa. 3.1(b) is a counter-example.

CHAPTER 4

4.1

a. $t = 5$ and $s = 2$.

b. $t = 5/2$ and $s = 4$. Costs \$2 so needs extra \$1.

4.3

a. $c = 10$, $b = 3$, and $U = 127$.

b. $c = 4$, $b = 1$, and $U = 79$.

4.5

b. $g = I/(p_g + p_v/2)$; $v = I/(2p_g + p_v)$.

c. Utility $= m = v = I/(2p_g + p_v)$.

d. $E = m(2p_g + p_v)$.

4.7

a. $V(p_x, p_y, I) = \alpha^\alpha \beta^\beta I/p_x^\alpha p_y^\beta = \kappa \, I/p_x^\alpha p_y^\beta$.

b. $E(p_x, p_y, U) = \kappa^{-1} p_x^\alpha p_y^\beta U$.

c. Clearly $\partial E/\partial p_x$ depends on α.

4.9

a. Set $MRS = p_x/p_y$.

b. Set $\delta = 0$.

c. Use $p_x x/p_y y = (p_x/p_y)^{\delta/(\delta-1)}$

CHAPTER 5

5.1

a. $U = x + \dfrac{8}{3} y$.

b. $x = I/p_x$ if $p_x \le \dfrac{8}{3} p_y$

$x = 0$ if $p_x > \dfrac{8}{3} p_y$.

d. Changes in p_y don't affect demand until they reverse the inequality.

e. Just two points (or vertical lines).

5.3

a. It is obvious since p_x/p_y doesn't change.

b. No good is inferior.

5.5

a. $x = \dfrac{I - p_x}{2p_x}$, $y = \dfrac{I + p_x}{2p_y}$.

Hence, changes in p_y do not affect x, but changes in p_x do affect y.

b. $V = \dfrac{(I + p_x)^2}{4p_x p_y}$ and so $E = \sqrt{4p_x p_y V} - p_x$.

c. The compensated demand function for x depends on p_y, whereas the uncompensated function did not.

5.7

a. Use the Slutsky equation in elasticity form. Because there are no substitution effects, $e_{h,p_h} = 0 - s_h e_{h,I} = 0 - 0.5 = -0.5$.

b. Compensated price elasticity is zero for both goods which are consumed in fixed proportions.

c. Now $s_h = 2/3$ so $e_{h,p_h} = -2/3$.

d. For a ham and cheese sandwich *(sw)*, $e_{sw,psw} = -1$, $e_{sw,p_h} = e_{sw,p_{sw}} \cdot e_{p_{sw},p_h} = (-1) \cdot 0.5 = -0.5$.

5.9

Just follow the approaches used in the two-good cases in the text (see detailed solutions).

CHAPTER 6

6.1

a. Convert this to a Cobb-Douglas with $\alpha = \beta = .5$. Result follows from prior examples.

b. Also follows from the Cobb-Douglas.

c. Set $\partial m/\partial p_s = \partial s/\partial p_m$ and cancel the symmetric substitution effects.

d. Use the Cobb-Douglas representation.

6.3

a. $p_{bt} = 2p_b + p_t$.

b. Since p_c and I are constant, $c = I/2p_c$ is also constant.

c. Yes—since changes in p_b or p_t affect only p_{bt}.

6.5

a. $p_2 x_2 + p_3 x_3 = p_3(kx_2 + x_3)$.

b. Relative price $= (p_2 + t)/(p_3 + t)$.

Approaches $p_2/p_3 < 1$ as $t \to 0$.

Approaches 1 as $t \to \infty$.

So, an increase in t raises the relative price of x_2.

c. Does not strictly apply since changes in t change relative prices.

d. May reduce spending on x_2—the effect on x_3 is uncertain.

6.7

Show $x_i \cdot \dfrac{\partial x_j}{\partial I} = x_j \cdot \dfrac{\partial x_i}{\partial I}$ and use symmetry of

net substitution effects.

6.9

a. $U_{xy} = 0$.
b. Assured by $U_i'' < 0$.
c. No conclusion possible. Depends on $p_x x$.
d. $x^\alpha y^\beta$ is not separable, $\alpha \ln x + \beta \ln y$ is.

CHAPTER 7

7.1

a. $k = 10$ and $l = 5$.
b. $k = 8$ and $l = 8$.
c. $k = 9$, $l = 6.5$, $k = 9.5$, and $l = 5.75$ (fractions of hours).
d. The isoquant is linear between solutions (a) and (b).

7.3

a. $q = 10$, $k = 100$, $l = 100$, $C = 10,000$.
b. $q = 10$, $k = 3.3$, $l = 13.2$, $C = 8,250$.
c. $q = 12.13$, $k = 4$, $l = 16$, $C = 10,000$.
d. Carla's ability to influence the decision depends on whether she can impose any costs on the bar if she is unhappy serving the additional tables. Such ability depends on whether Carla is a draw for Cheers' customers.

7.5

Let $A = 1$ for simplicity.

a.
$$f_k = \alpha k^{\alpha-1} l^\beta > 0 \quad f_l = \beta k^\alpha l^{\beta-1} > 0$$
$$f_{kk} = \alpha(\alpha - 1)k^{\alpha-2}l^\beta < 0$$
$$f_{ll} = \beta(\beta - 1)k^\alpha l^{\beta-2} < 0$$
$$f_{kl} = f_{lk} = \alpha\beta k^{\alpha-1}l^{\beta-1} > 0.$$

b. $e_{q,k} = f_k \cdot k/q = \alpha \quad e_{q,l} = f_l \cdot l/q = \beta$.
c. $f(tk, tl) = t^{\alpha+\beta} f(k,l) \dfrac{\partial f(tk,tl)}{\partial t} \cdot \dfrac{t}{f(k,l)} = (\alpha + \beta)t^{\alpha+\beta}$. At $t = 1$ this is just $\alpha + \beta$.

d., e. Apply the definitions using the derivatives from part (a).

7.7

a. $\beta_0 = 0$.
b. $MP_k = \beta_2 + \frac{1}{2}\beta_1 \sqrt{l/k}$; $MP_L = \beta_3 + \frac{1}{2}\beta_1 \sqrt{k/l}$.
c. In general, σ is not constant. If $\beta_2 = \beta_3 = 0$, $\sigma = 1$. If $\beta_1 = 0$, $\sigma = \infty$.

7.9

Apply the theorem to f_k, which is homogeneous of degree 0. With many inputs, "most" cross-partials must be positive.

CHAPTER 8

8.1

The draftsman is right because the minimum of SAC curves occurs where the slope is zero. In the constant-returns-to-scale case, both are correct.

8.3

a., b. $q = 150 \quad J = 25 \quad MC = 4$
$q = 300 \quad J = 100 \quad MC = 8$
$q = 450 \quad J = 225 \quad MC = 12$

8.5

a. $q = 2\sqrt{k \cdot l} \quad k = 100$, $q = 20\sqrt{l}$, $l = q^2/400$

$$SC = vk + wl = 100 + \frac{q^2}{100}$$
$$SAC = \frac{SC}{q} = \frac{100}{q} + \frac{q}{100}.$$

b. $SMC = \dfrac{q}{50}$. If $q = 25, SC$

q	SC	SAC	SMC
25	106.25	4,25	50
50	125	2.5	1
100	200	2	2
200	500	2.5	4

c., d. As long as the marginal cost of producing one more unit is below the average-cost curve, average costs will be falling. Similarly, if the marginal cost of producing one more unit is higher than the average cost, then average costs will be rising. Therefore, the SMC curve must intersect the SAC curve at its lowest point.
e. $C = v\bar{k} + wq^2/4\bar{k}$.
f. $\bar{k} = \dfrac{q}{2} w^{1/2} v^{1/2}$.
g. $C = qw^{1/2}v^{1/2}$.
h. Yields an envelope relationship.

8.7

a. $C = q^{1/\gamma}[(v/a)^{1-\sigma} + (w/b)^{1-\sigma}]^{1/1-\sigma}$.
b. $C = qa^{-a}b^{-b}v^a w^b$.
c. $wl/vk = b/a$.

d. $l/k = \left[\dfrac{(v/a)}{(w/b)}\right]^{\sigma}$ so $wl/vk = (v/w)^{\sigma-1}(b/a)^{\sigma}$.

Labor's relative share is an increasing function of b/a. If $\sigma > 1$, labor's share moves in the same direction as v/w. If $\sigma < 1$, labor's relative share moves in the opposite direction to v/w. This accords with intuition on how substitutability should affect shares.

8.9

a. $l = \dfrac{\partial C}{\partial w} = \dfrac{2}{3} q \left(\dfrac{v}{w}\right)^{1/3}$.

$k = \dfrac{1}{3} q \left(\dfrac{w}{v}\right)^{2/3}$.

b. $q = Bl^{2/3}k^{1/3}$ where B is a constant.

CHAPTER 9

9.1

a. $q = 50$.
b. $\pi = 200$.
c. $q = 5P - 50$.

9.3

a., b. $q = a + bP$ $P = q/b - a/b$,
$R = P_q = (q^2 - aq)/b$, $mr = 2q/b - a/b$, and the mr curve has double the slope of the demand curve, so $d - mr = -q/b$.
c. $mr = P(1 + 1/e) = P(1 + 1/b)$.
d. It follows since $e = \partial q/\partial P \cdot P/q$.

9.5

a. $C = wq^2/4$
b. $\pi(P, w) = P^2/w$
c. $q = 2P/w$
d. $l(P,w) = P^2/w^2$

9.7

a. Diminishing returns is needed to ensure that a profit-maximizing output choice exists.
b. $C(q,v,w) = (w + v)q^2/100$ $\Pi(P,v,w) = 25P^2/(w + v)$.
c. $q = \partial\Pi/\partial P = 50P/(w + v) = 20$. $\Pi = 6,000$.
d. $q = 30$, $\Pi = 13,500$.

9.9

b. Diminishing returns is needed to ensure increasing marginal cost.
c. σ determines how firms adapt to disparate input prices.
d. $q = \dfrac{\partial\Pi}{\partial P} = \dfrac{1}{1 - \gamma} KP^{\gamma/1-\gamma}(v^{1-\sigma} + w^{1-\sigma})^{\gamma/(1-\sigma)(\gamma-1)}$.
The size of σ does not affect the supply elasticity, but greater substitutability implies that increases in one input price will shift the supply curve less.
e. See detailed solutions.

CHAPTER 10

10.1

a. $q = 10\sqrt{P} - 20$.
b. $Q = 1,000\sqrt{P} - 2,000$.
c. $P = 25$; $Q = 3,000$.

10.3

a. $P = 6$.
b. $q = 60,000 - 10,000P$.
c. $P = 6.01$, $P = 5.99$.
d. $e_{Q,P} = -600$.
   a' $P = 6$.
   b' $Q = 359,800 - 59,950P$.
   c' $P = 6.002$; $P = 5.998$.
   d' $e_{Q,P} = -.6$; $e_{q,P} = -3,597$.

10.5

a. $P = 3$, $Q = 2,000,000$, and $n = 2,000$ farms.
b. $P = 6$ and $\pi = 3,000$/farm.
c. $P = 3$, $Q = 2,600,000$, and $n = 2,600$ farms.

10.7

a. $n = 50$, $Q = 1,000$, $q = 20$, $P = 10$, and $w = 200$.
b. $n = 72$, $Q = 1,728$, $q = 24$, $P = 14$, and $w = 288$.
c. The increase for the makers = $5,368. The linear approximation for the supply curve yields approximately the same result.

CHAPTER 11

11.1

a. $P = 120$, $PQ = 48,000$, $CS = 16,000$, and $PS = 20,000$.
b. Loss = 2,250.
c. $P = 140$, $CS = 9,000$, and $PS = 24,750$.
   $P = 95$, $CS = 22,500$, and $PS = 11,250$.
d. Loss = 562.50.

11.3

a. $P = 11$, $Q = 500$, and $r = 1$.
b. $P = 12$, $Q = 1,000$, and $r = 2$.
c. $\Delta PS = 750$.
d. Δ rents $= 750$.

11.5

a. $P_D = 140$, $P_S = 95$, $P_D - P_S = t = 45$; $Q = 300$.
b. Total tax $= 13,500$.
   Consumers pay 6,000; producers pay 7,500.
   Producers pay 56 percent.
c. 2,250
d. $P_D = 129.47$; $P_S = 84.47$; $Q = 258$. Total tax $= 11,610$, producers pay 79 percent.
e. $P_D = 150$; $P_S = 105$; $Q = 250$.
   Total tax $= 11,250$; consumers pay 67 percent.

11.7

a. $Q = 250$; $r = 0.5$; $P_S = 10.5$; $P_D = 16$.
b. Total tax $= 1,375$; consumer tax $= 1,250$; producer tax $= 125$; loss of $CS = 1,875$; loss of $PS = 187.5$.
c. Loss $= .5(250) + .5(.5)(250) = 187.5$. This is the total loss of PS in part (b). Occurs since only reason for upward sloping supply is upward slope of film royalties supply.

11.9

The price rises to 9.6. Total tariff revenue actually falls to .462 ($ billion). $DW_1 = .315$ and $DW_2 = .234$. Hence, DW increases by .147, a 37 percent increase from Example 16.3.

CHAPTER 12

12.1

b. If $y = 2x$, $x^2 + 2(2x)^2 = 900$; $9x^2 = 900$; $x = 10$, $y = 20$.
c. If $x = 9$ on the production possibility frontier,

$$y = \sqrt{\frac{819}{2}} = 20.24$$

If $x = 11$ on the frontier, $y = \sqrt{\frac{779}{2}} = 19.74$.

Hence, RPT is approximately $-\dfrac{\Delta y}{\Delta x} = \dfrac{-(-0.50)}{2}$
$= .25$.

12.3

a. Use the production possibility frontier, then the Edgeworth box.
b. If p doesn't change, the land-labor ratio must stay the same in each industry. This can happen only if production of the labor-intensive commodity expands.

12.5

a. Doubling prices does not change ED.
b. $p_1 ED_1 = -[-3p_2^2 + 6p_2 p_3 - 2p_3^2 - p_1 p_2 - 2p_1 p_3]/p_1$.
c. $p_2/p_1 = 3$; $p_3/p_1 = 5$; $p_3/p_2 = \dfrac{5}{3}$.

12.7

Let $F =$ Food, $C =$ Cloth.

a. Labor constraint $F + C = 100$.
b. Land constraint $2F + C = 150$.
c. Outer frontier satisfies both constraints.
d. Frontier is concave because it must satisfy both constraints. Since the $RPT = 1$ for the labor constraint and 2 for the land constraint, the production possibility frontier of part (c) exhibits an increasing RPT; hence it is concave.
e. Constraints intersect at $F = 50$, $C = 50$. For

$F < 50 \dfrac{dC}{dF} = -1$ so $\dfrac{P_F}{P_C} = 1$. For $F > 50$

$\dfrac{dC}{dF} = -2$ so $\dfrac{P_F}{P_C} = 2$.

f. If for consumers $\dfrac{dC}{dF} = -\dfrac{5}{4}$ so $\dfrac{P_F}{P_C} = \dfrac{5}{4}$.
g. If $P_F/P_C = 1.9$ or $P_F/P_C = 1.1$, will still choose $F = 50$, $C = 50$ since both price lines "tangent" to production possibility frontier at its kink.
h. $.8F + .9C = 100$. Capital constraint: $C = 0$ $F = 125$, $F = 0$ $C = 111.1$. This results in the same PPF since capital constraint is nowhere binding.

12.9

a. The contract curve is a straight line. Only equilibrium price ratio is $P_H/P_C = 4/3$.
b. Initial equilibrium on the contract curve.
c. Not on the contract curve—equilibrium is between $40H$, $80C$ and $48H$, $96C$.
d. Smith takes everything; Jones starves.

CHAPTER 13

13.1

a. $Q = 24$, $P = 29$, and $\pi = 576$.
b. $MC = P = 5$ and $Q = 48$.
c. Consumers' surplus $= 1,152$. Under monopoly, consumer surplus $= 288$, profits $= 576$, deadweight loss $= 288$.

13.3

a. $Q = 25$, $P = 35$, and $\pi = 625$.
b. $Q = 20$, $P = 50$, and $\pi = 800$.
c. $Q = 40$, $P = 30$, and $\pi \doteq 800$.

13.5

a. $P = 15$, $Q = 5$, $C = 65$, and $\pi = 10$.
b. $A = 3$, $P = 15$, $Q = 6.05$, and $\pi = 12.25$.

13.7

a. $Q_1 = 25$, $P_1 = 30$, $Q_2 = 30$, $P_2 = 20$, and $\pi = 1{,}075$.
b. $P_1 = 26.66$, $P_2 = 21.66$, and $\pi = 1{,}058.33$.
c. $P_1 = P_2 = 23.33$, $\pi = 1008.33$, $Q_1 = 31.67$ and $Q_2 = 23.33$.
d. $P_i = \alpha_i + mq_i$.
Set $m = 5$, $\alpha_1 = 1{,}250$, and $\alpha_2 = 900$.

13.9

a. The government wants output to increase toward $P = MC$, but the lump-sum subsidy doesn't affect $MR = MC$ for the monopoly firm.
b. This will shift the MC curve downward.
c. Use $MR = P(1 + 1/e)$.

CHAPTER 14

14.1

a. $Q = 75$, $P = 75$, and $\pi = 5{,}625$.
b. $q_1 + q_2 = 50$, $P = 50$, and $\pi_1 = \pi_2 = 2{,}500$.
c. Under perfect competition, $P = 0$ and $Q = 150$.

14.3

a. Price leadership.
b. Price discrimination (by sellers), though Apple's strategy appears not viable in the long run. Why?
c. Probably incorrect accounting.
d. International competition.

14.5

Multiply by q_i / PQ—this shows that under Cournot competition, more concentrated industries are more profitable.

14.7

a. $P = 25$, $Q = 20{,}000$, and total $Q_s = \sum_1^{1{,}000} q = 1{,}000P - 5{,}000$.
b. $P = 20$, $Q = 30{,}000$, and q (for leader) = 15,000.
c.

Price	Consumer Surplus
25	100,000
20	225,000
15	400,000

14.9

a. Yes, MC is declining.
b. $Q = 450$, $P = 11$, and $\pi = 3{,}341$.
c. $P = AC = 2.4$ (approximate).

CHAPTER 15

15.1

a. Stag-stag and hare-hare are both Nash equilibria.
b. If p = probability A plays stage, B will choose stag if $p > \frac{1}{2}$.
c. Require $p^{(n-1)} > \frac{1}{2}$ for cooperation.

15.3

Mixed strategy Nash equilibrium is $s = 1/(K + 1)$, $r = K/(K + 1)$.

15.5

a. There are two Nash equilibria here: A: Chicken, B: Not Chicken; and A: Not Chicken, B: Chicken.
b. The threat "Not Chicken" is not credible against a firm commitment by one's opponent to Not Chicken.
c. Such a commitment would achieve a desirable result assuming the opponent has not made such a commitment also.
d. Although the scene is subject to many interpretations (it is unclear that the movie maker had any idea what the point of the scene is), one is that approaching the most desirable woman is a game of chicken. The disastrous Nash equilibrium might be avoided by implementing some form of first-stage game.

15.7

a. $P = 10 - \epsilon$, $q_A = 0$, and $q_B = 300$.
b. $\pi_A = 0$, $\pi_B = 600$.
c. Inefficient because $P > MC_B$.

15.9

a. $P = 5$ $Q = 5{,}000$ $q = 250$.
b. If one firm sells $q = 251$, it increases its profits.
c. With 20 cartel members, only a very low price is stable ($P = .3$). With fewer members, a higher price is stable.

15.11

Follow procedure in Example 15.8. Gives $q_A^* = 30$ $q_{BH}^* = 40$ $q_{BC}^* = 20$.

CHAPTER 16

16.1

a. Full income = 40,000. l = 2,000 hours.
b. l = 1,400 hours.
c. l = 1,700 hours.
d. Supply is asymptotic to 2,000 hours as w rises.

16.3

$E[U(y_{job1})] = 100 \cdot 40 - 0.5 \cdot 1,600 = 3,200$.

$E[U(y_{job2})] = E[U(wh)] = E[100wh - 0.5(wh)^2]$
$= 800w - 0.5 \cdot [36w^2 + 64w^2] = 800w - 50w^2$.

Setting this equal to 3,200 and using quadratic formula yields $w = 8$.

16.5

a. Grant = 6,000 − .75 (I).
   If $I = 0$ Grant = 6,000.
   $I = 2,000$ Grant = 4,500.
   $I = 4,000$ Grant = 3,000.
b. Grant = 0 when 6,000 − .75I = 0, I = 6,000/.75 = 8,000.
c. Assume there are 8,000 hours in the year. Full Income = 4 × 8,000 = 32,000 = $c + 4h$.
d. Full Income
   = 32,000 + grant
   = 32,000 + 6,000 − .75 · 4(8,000 − h)
   = 38,000 − 24,000 + 3h = $c + 4h$
   or 14,000 = $c + h$ for $I < 8,000$. That is; for $h < 6,000$ hours welfare grant creates a kink in the budget constraint at 6,000 hours of leisure.

16.7

a. For $ME_l = MRP_l$, $\dfrac{l}{40} = 10 - \dfrac{l}{40}$ so $\dfrac{2l}{40} = 10$
   $l = 200$.

   Get w from supply curve: $w = \dfrac{l}{80} = \dfrac{200}{80} =$ $2.50.
b. For Carl, the marginal expense of labor now equals the minimum wage—w_m = $4.00. Setting this equal to the MRP yields l = 240.
c. Under perfect competition, a minimum wage means higher wages but fewer workers employed. Under monopsony, a minimum wage may result in higher wages *and* more workers employed.

16.9

a. Since $q = 240x - 2x^2$, total revenue is $5q = 1,200x - 10x^2$. $MRP = \dfrac{\partial TR}{\partial x} = 1,200 - 20x$.

Production of pelts $x = \sqrt{l}$. Total cost = $wl = 10x^2$. Marginal Cost = $\dfrac{\partial C}{\partial x} = 20x$. Under competition, price of pelts = $MC = 20x$, $MRP = p_x = MC = 20x$ $x = 30$, $p_x = 600$.

b. From Dan's perspective, demand for pelts = $MRP = 1,200 - 20x$, $R = p_x \cdot x = 1,200x - 20x^2$.
Marginal revenue: $\dfrac{\partial R}{\partial x} = 1,200 - 40x$ set equal to marginal cost = 20x. Yields $x = 20$, $p_x = 800$.
c. From UF's perspective, supply of pelts = $MC = 20x = p_x$, total cost = $p_x x = 20x^2$ and $ME_x = \dfrac{\partial C}{\partial x} = 40x$. So $ME_x = 40x = MRP_x = 1,200 - 20x$ with a solution of $x = 20$, $p_x = 400$.

CHAPTER 17

17.1

b. Income and substitution effects work in opposite directions. If $\partial c_1/\partial r < 0$, c_2 is price elastic.
c. Budget constraint passes through y_1, y_2, and rotates through this point as r changes. Income effect depends on whether $y_1 > c_1$ or $y_1 < c_1$ initially.

17.3

25 years.

17.5

a., b. See detailed solutions.
c. Here t^* is lower than in Example 17.2 because rotations involve additional opportunity costs.
d. $f(t)$ is asymptotic to 50 as $t \to \infty$.
e. $t^* = 100$ years. Maximum sustainable yield is not defined here since tree always grows. Notice that $f(t) = 25$ at the maximum, however, not 50.
f. $t^* = 104.1$.

17.7

PDV (whole life) = \$6,304.
PDV (term) = \$3,879.
Salesman is wrong.

17.9

Now MR should rise at the rate of interest. If demand is constant elasticity, however, $MR = kP$ so with same end price, price path will be same as in the competitive case.

CHAPTER 18

18.1

$P = .525$.

18.3

a. one trip: expected value = $.5 \cdot 0 + .5 \cdot 12 = 6$. two trip: expected value = $.25 \cdot 0 + .5 \cdot 6 + .25 \cdot 12 = 6$.
b. Two-trip strategy preferred because of smaller variance.
c. Adding trips reduces variance, but at a diminishing rate. So desirability depends on the trips' cost.

18.5

a. $E(U) = .75 \ ln(10,000) + .25 \ ln(9,000) = 9.1840$.
b. $E(U) = ln(9,750) = 9.1850$—insurance is preferable.
c. \$260

18.7

a. Plant corn.
b. Yes, a mixed crop should be chosen. Diversification increases variance, but takes advantage of wheat's high yield.
c. 44 percent wheat, 56 percent corn.
d. The farmer would only plant wheat.

18.9

a. Use Figure 18.5.
b., c. Examine the curvature of the constant RRA function.
d. It follows, because the constant RRA function is homothetic in W.

CHAPTER 19

19.1

a. Yes
b. \$50
c. 0

19.3

Cost = \$1,750.
Now expected utility = $.5 U(18,250) + .5 U(14,750)$, which may exceed $U(15,000)$.

19.5

a. No
b. \$20,000. It must cost low-ability workers more to provide no incentive to buy it, too.

19.7

a., b. $p_{min} = 300 + 100/(n + 1)$.
c. Set $-dp_{min}/dn = 2$, $n^* = 7$.

19.9

Patient utility maximization: $U_1^c / U_2^c = p_m$.

Doctor optimization: $U_1^d p_m + U_2^d [U_1^c - p_m U_2^c] = 0$. If $U_2^d = 1$, this requires $p_m = U_1^c/(U_2^c - U_1^d)$. Relative to patient maximization, this requires a smaller U_1^c. Hence, the doctor chooses more medical care than would a fully informed consumer.

CHAPTER 20

20.1

a. $P = 20$ and $q = 50$.
b. $P = 20$, $q = 40$, $MC = 16$, and tax = 4.

20.3

a. $n = 400$. The externality arises because one well's drilling affects all wells' output.
b. $n = 200$.
c. Fee = 2,000/well.

20.5

An essay question. Should consider: services are provided by parties, risks, information costs, incentives under the various contracts, and so forth.

20.7

a. Set $q_a = q_b$ and $Q = 90$.
b. Free rider problem might result in $Q = 0$.
c. Total cost = 10,800. If tax based on marginal valuation, a pays 900, b pays 9,900.

20.9

a. If each person is a free rider, utility will be 0.
b. $y = 5$, $x = 50$, $x/100 = 0.5$, and utility = $\sqrt{2.5}$.

CHAPTER 21

21.1

a. 100 each, $U_1 = 10$ and $U_2 = 5$.
b. $f_1 = 40$ and $f_2 = 160$.
c. $f_1 = 160$ and $f_2 = 40$.
d. $f_1 = f_2 = 100$.
e. $f_1 = f_2 = 100$.

21.3

a. $x = 160$; $(U_1 + U_2)^2 = 1{,}600$.
b. $(U_1 + U_2)^2 = 3{,}600$.
c. Max $2xy$ subject to $x + 2y = 180$; $x = 90$; $y = 45$; $(U_1 + U_2)^2 = 4{,}050$.
d. If utility possibility frontiers were to intersect, use the other envelope of the frontiers.

21.5

a. D
b. E
c. B
d. A
e. Choice depends on criteria used.

21.7

a. Choose b, t so that y is same in each state. Requires $t = u$.
b. b always $= (1 - t)w$, $t = u$.
c. No. Because this person is risk averse, he or she will always opt for equal income in each state.

21.9

Those with most to gain would vote. It could change Nash equilibrium strategies.

Glossary of Frequently Used Terms

Some of the terms that are used frequently in this book are defined below. The reader may wish to use the index to find those sections of the text that give more complete descriptions of these concepts.

Adverse Selection   When buyers and sellers have asymmetric information about market transactions, trades actually completed may be biased to favor the actor with better information.

Arrow Impossibility Theorem   Fundamental result of social choice theory: any social decision rule must violate at least one of the axioms of rational choice that Arrow developed.

Bertrand Equilibrium   Equilibrium in duopoly price-setting game.

Ceteris Paribus Assumption   The assumption that all other relevant factors are held constant when examining the influence of one particular variable in an economic model. Reflected in mathematical terms by the use of partial differentiation.

Coase Theorem   Result attributable to R. Coase: if bargaining costs are zero, an efficient allocation of resources can be attained in the presence of externalities through reliance on bargaining among the parties involved.

Compensated Demand Function   Function showing relationship between the price of a good and the quantity consumed while holding real income (or utility) constant. Denoted by $x^c(p_x, p_y, U)$.

Compensating Variation   The compensation required to restore a person's original utility level when prices change.

Compensating Wage Differentials   Differences in real wages that arise when the characteristics of occupations cause workers in their supply decisions to prefer one job over another.

Complements (Gross)   Two goods such that if the price of one rises, the quantity consumed of the other will fall. Goods x and y are gross complements if $\partial x / \partial p_y < 0$. See also Substitutes (Gross).

Complements (Net)   Two goods such that if the price of one rises, the quantity consumed of the other will fall, holding real income (utility) constant. Goods x and y are net complements if

$$\partial x / \partial p_y \big|_{U = \overline{U}} < 0.$$

Such compensated cross-price effects are symmetric, that is,

$$\partial x / \partial p_y \big|_{U = \overline{U}} = \partial y / \partial p_x \big|_{U = \overline{U}}.$$

See also Substitutes (Net). Also called Hicksian substitutes and complements.

Composite Commodity   A group of goods whose prices all move together—the relative prices of goods in the group do not change. Such goods can be treated as a single commodity in many applications.

Concave Function   A function that lies everywhere below its tangent plane.

Constant-Cost Industry   An industry in which expansion of output and entry by new firms has no effect on the cost curves of individual firms.

Constant Returns to Scale   See Returns to Scale.

Consumer Surplus   The area below the Marshallian demand curve and above market price. Shows what an individual would pay for the right to make voluntary transactions at this price. Changes in consumer surplus can be used to measure the welfare effects of price changes.

Contestable Market   A market in which entry and exit are absolutely free. Markets subject to such "hit-and-run" entry and exit will produce where $P = MC = AC$ even if there are not a large number of firms.

Contingent Input Demand   See Input Demand Functions.

Contour Line   The set of points along which a function has a constant value. Useful for graphing three-dimensional functions in two dimensions. Individuals' indifference curve maps and firms' production isoquant maps are examples.

Contract Curve   The set of all the efficient allocations of goods among those individuals in an exchange economy. Each of these allocations has the property that no one individual can be made better off without making someone else worse off.

Cost Function   *See* Total Cost Function.

Cournot Equilibrium   Equilibrium in duopoly quantity-setting game. A similar concept applies to an *n*-person game.

Deadweight Loss   A loss of mutually beneficial transactions. Losses in consumer and producer surplus that are not transferred to another economic agent.

Decreasing Cost Industry   An industry in which expansion of output generates cost-reducing externalities that cause the cost curves of those firms in the industry to shift downward.

Decreasing Returns to Scale   *See* Returns to Scale.

Demand Curve   A graph showing the ceteris paribus relationship between the price of a good and the quantity of that good purchased. A two-dimensional representation of the demand function $x = x(p_x, p_y, I)$. This is referred to as "Marshallian" demand to differentiate it from the compensated (Hicksian) demand concept.

Diminishing Marginal Productivity   *See* Marginal Physical Product.

Diminishing Marginal Rate of Substitution   *See* Marginal Rate of Substitution.

Discrimination, Price   Occurs whenever a buyer or seller is able to use its market power effectively to separate markets and to follow a different price policy in each market. *See also* Price Discrimination.

Duality   The relationship between any constrained maximization problem and its related "dual" constrained minimization problem.

Economic Efficiency   Exists when resources are allocated so that no activity can be increased without cutting back on some other activity. *See also* Pareto-Efficient Allocation.

Edgeworth Box Diagram   A graphic device used to demonstrate economic efficiency. Most frequently used to illustrate the contract curve in an exchange economy, but also useful in the theory of production.

Elasticity   A unit-free measure of the proportional effect of one variable on another. If $y = f(x)$, then $e_{y,x} = \partial y / \partial x \cdot x / y$.

Entry Conditions   Characteristics of an industry that determine the ease with which a new firm may begin production. Under perfect competition, entry is assumed to be costless, whereas in a monopolistic industry there are significant barriers to entry.

Envelope Theorem   A mathematical result: the change in the maximum value of a function brought about by a change in a parameter of the function can be found by partially differentiating the function with respect to the parameter (when all other variables take on their optimal values).

Equilibrium   A situation in which no actors have an incentive to change their behavior. At an equilibrium price, the quantity demanded by individuals is exactly equal to that which is supplied by all firms.

Euler's Theorem   A mathematical theorem: if $f(x_1, \ldots, x_n)$ is homogeneous of degree k, then

$$f_1 x_1 + f_2 x_2 + \ldots + f_n x_n$$
$$= k f(x_1, \ldots, x_n).$$

Exchange Economy   An economy in which the supply of goods is fixed (that is, no production takes place). The available goods, however, may be reallocated among individuals in the economy.

Expansion Path   The locus of those cost-minimizing input combinations that a firm will choose to produce various levels of output (when the prices of inputs are held constant).

Expected Utility   The average utility expected from a risky situation. If there are n outcomes, $x_1, \ldots, x_n$ with probabilities $p_1, \ldots, p_n$ ($\sum p_i = 1$), then the expected utility is given by

$$E(U) = p_1 U(x_1) + p_2 U(x_2)$$
$$+ \ldots + p_n U(x_n).$$

Expenditure Function   A function derived from the individual's dual expenditure minimization problem. Shows the minimum expenditure necessary to achieve a given utility level:

$$\text{expenditures} = E(p_x, p_y, U).$$

Externality   An effect of one economic agent on another that is not taken into account by normal market behavior.

First-Order Conditions   Mathematical conditions that must necessarily hold if a function is to take on its maximum or minimum value. Usually show that any activity should be increased to the point at which marginal benefits equal marginal costs.

Fixed Costs   Costs that do not change as the level of output changes in the short run. Fixed costs are in many respects irrelevant to the theory of short-run price determination. *See also* Variable Costs.

General Equilibrium Model   A model of an economy that portrays the operation of many markets simultaneously.

Giffen's Paradox   A situation in which the increase in a good's price leads individuals to consume more of the good. Arises because the good in question is inferior and because the income effect induced by the price change is stronger than the substitution effect.

Homogeneous Function   A function, $f(x_1, x_2, \ldots, x_n)$, is homogeneous of degree k if

$$f(m x_1, m x_2, \ldots, m x_n)$$
$$= m^k f(x_1, x_2, \ldots, x_n).$$

Homothetic Function A function that can be represented as a monotonic transformation of a homogeneous function. The slopes of the contour lines for such a function depend only on the ratios of the variables that enter the function, not on their absolute levels.

Income and Substitution Effects Two analytically different effects that come into play when an individual is faced with a changed price for some good. Income effects arise because a change in the price of a good will affect an individual's purchasing power. Even if purchasing power is held constant, however, substitution effects will cause individuals to reallocate their expectations. Substitution effects are reflected in movements along an indifference curve, whereas income effects entail a movement to a different indifference curve. *See also* Slutsky Equation.

Increasing Cost Industry An industry in which the expansion of output creates cost-increasing externalities, which cause the cost curves of those firms in the industry to shift upward.

Increasing Returns to Scale *See* Returns to Scale.

Indifference Curve Map A contour map of an individual's utility function showing those alternative bundles of goods from which the individual derives equal levels of welfare.

Indirect Utility Function A representative of utility as a function of all prices and income.

Individual Demand Curve The ceteris paribus relationship between the quantity of a good an individual chooses to consume and the good's price. A two-dimensional representation of $x = x(p_x, p_y, I)$ for one person.

Inferior Good A good that is bought in smaller quantities as an individual's income rises.

Inferior Input A factor of production that is used in smaller amounts as a firm's output expands.

Input Demand Functions These functions show how input demand for a profit-maximizing firm is based on input prices and on the demand for output. The input demand function for labor, for example, can be written as $l = l(P, v, w)$, where P is the market price of the firm's output. *Contingent* input demand functions $[l^c(v, w, q)]$ are derived from cost minimization and do not necessarily reflect profit-maximizing output choices.

Isoquant Map A contour map of the firm's production function. The contours show the alternative combinations of productive inputs that can be used to produce a given level of output.

Kuhn-Tucker Conditions First-order conditions for an optimization problem in which inequality constraints are present. These are generalizations of the first-order conditions for optimization with equality constraints.

Limit Pricing Choice of low-price strategies to deter entry.

Lindahl Equilibrium A hypothetical solution to the public goods problem: the tax share that each individual pays plays the same role as an equilibrium market price in a competitive allocation.

Long Run *See* Short Run–Long Run Distinction.

Lump-sum Principle The demonstration that general purchasing power taxes or transfers are more efficient than taxes or subsidies on individual goods.

Marginal Cost (MC) The additional cost incurred by producing one more unit of output: $MC = \partial C / \partial q$.

Marginal Physical Product (MP) The additional output that can be produced by one more unit of a particular input while holding all other inputs constant. It is usually assumed that an input's marginal productivity diminishes as additional units of the input are put into use while holding other inputs fixed. If $q = f(k, l)$, $MP_l = \partial q / \partial l$.

Marginal Rate of Substitution (MRS) The rate at which an individual is willing to trade one good for another while remaining equally well off. The MRS is the absolute value of the slope of an indifference curve. $MRS = -dy/dx \big|_{U = \bar{U}}$.

Marginal Revenue (MR) The additional revenue obtained by a firm when it is able to sell one more unit of output. $MR = \partial p \cdot q / \partial q = p(1 + 1/e_{q,p})$.

Marginal Revenue Product (MRP) The extra revenue that accrues to a firm when it sells the output that is produced by one more unit of some input. In the case of labor, for example, $MRP_l = MR \cdot MP_l$.

Marginal Utility (MU) The extra utility that an individual receives by consuming one more unit of a particular good.

Market Demand The sum of the quantities of a good demanded by all individuals in a market. Will depend on the price of the good, prices of other goods, each consumer's preferences, and on each consumer's income.

Market Period A very short period over which quantity supplied is fixed and not responsive to changes in market price.

Monopoly An industry in which there is only a single seller of the good in question.

Monopsony An industry in which there is only a single buyer of the good in question.

Moral Hazard The effect of insurance coverage on individuals' decisions to undertake activities that may change the likelihood of incurring losses.

Nash Equilibrium Strategies A set of strategies (a^*, b^*) in a two-player game such that a^* is optimal for A against b^* and b^* is optimal for B against a^*.

Normal Good   A good for which quantity demanded increases (or stays constant) as an individual's income increases.

Normative Analysis   Economic analysis that takes a position on how economic actors or markets should operate.

Oligopoly   An industry in which there are only a few sellers of the good in question.

Opportunity Cost Doctrine   The simple, though far-reaching, observation that the true cost of any action can be measured by the value of the best alternative that must be forgone when the action is taken.

Output and Substitution Effects   Come into play when a change in the price of an input that a firm uses causes the firm to change the quantities of inputs it will demand. The substitution effect would occur even if output were held constant, and it is reflected by movements along an isoquant. Output effects, on the other hand, occur when output levels change and the firm moves to a new isoquant.

Paradox of Voting   Illustrates the possibility that majority rule voting may not yield a determinate outcome but may instead cycle among alternatives.

Pareto-Efficient Allocation   An allocation of resources in which no one individual can be made better off without making someone else worse off.

Partial Equilibrium Model   A model of a single market that ignores repercussions in other markets.

Perfect Competition   The most widely used economic model: there are assumed to be a large number of buyers and sellers for any good, and each agent is a price taker. *See also* Price Taker.

Positive Analysis   Economic analysis that seeks to explain and predict actual economic events.

Present Discounted Value (*PDV*)   The current value of a sum of money that is payable sometime in the future. Takes into account the effect of interest payments.

Price Discrimination   Selling identical goods at different prices. Requires sellers to have the ability to prevent resale. There are three types: first degree—selling each unit at a different price to the individual willing to pay the most for it ("perfect price discrimination"); second degree—adopting price schedules that give buyers an incentive to separate themselves into differing price categories; third degree—charging different prices in separated markets.

Price Elasticity   Most important application of the elasticity concept, this reflects the proportional change in quantity demanded in response to a proportional change in price: If $q = f(p, \ldots)$, $e_{q,p} = \partial q / \partial p \cdot p/q$.

Price Taker   An economic agent that makes decisions on the assumption that these decisions will have no effect on prevailing market prices.

Principal-Agent Relationship   The hiring of one person (the agent) by another person (the principal) to make economic decisions.

Prisoner's Dilemma   Originally studied in the theory of games but has widespread applicability. The crux of the dilemma is that each individual, faced with the uncertainty of how others will behave, may be led to adopt a course of action that proves to be detrimental for all those individuals making the same decision. A strong coalition might have led to a solution preferred by everyone in the group.

Producer Surplus   The extra return that producers make by making transactions at the market price over and above what they would earn if nothing were produced. It is illustrated by the size of the area below the market price and above the supply curve.

Production Function   A conceptual mathematical function that records the relationship between a firm's inputs and its outputs. If output is a function of capital and labor only, this would be denoted by $q = f(k, l)$.

Production Possibility Frontier   The locus of all the alternative quantities of several outputs that can be produced with fixed amounts of productive inputs.

Profit Function   The relationship between a firm's maximum profits (Π^*) and the output and input prices it faces:

$$\Pi^* = \Pi^*(P, v, w).$$

Profits   The difference between the total revenue a firm receives and its total economic costs of production. Economic profits equal zero under perfect competition in the long run. Monopoly profits may be positive, however.

Property Rights   Legal specification of ownership and the rights of owners.

Public Good   A good that once produced is available to all on a nonexclusive basis. Many public goods are also nonrival—additional individuals may benefit from the good at zero marginal costs.

Quasi-concave Function   A function for which the set of all points for which $f(X) > k$ is convex.

Rate of Product Transformation (*RPT*)   The rate at which one output can be traded for another in the productive process while holding the total quantities of inputs constant. The *RPT* is the absolute value of the slope of the production possibility frontier.

Rate of Return   The rate at which present goods can be transformed into future goods. For example, a one-period rate of return of 10 percent implies that forgoing 1 unit of output this period will yield 1.10 units of output next period.

Rate of Technical Substitution (RTS) The rate at which one input may be traded off against another in the productive process while holding output constant. The RTS is the absolute value of the slope of an isoquant.

$$RTS = -\frac{dk}{dl}\bigg|_{q = q_0}.$$

Rent Payments to a factor of production that are in excess of that amount necessary to keep it in its current employment.

Rent-Seeking Activities Economic agents engage in rent-seeking activities when they utilize the political process to generate economic rents that would not ordinarily occur in market transactions.

Rental Rate The cost of hiring one machine for one hour. Denoted by v in the text.

Returns to Scale A way of classifying production functions that records how output responds to proportional increases in all inputs. If a proportional increase in all inputs causes output to increase by a smaller proportion, the production function is said to exhibit decreasing returns to scale. If output increases by a greater proportion than the inputs, the production function exhibits increasing returns. Constant returns to scale is the middle ground where both inputs and outputs increase by the same proportions. Mathematically, if $f(mk, ml) = m^k f(k, l)$, $k > 1$ implies increasing returns, $k = 1$ constant returns, and $k < 1$ decreasing returns.

Risk Aversion Unwillingness to accept fair bets. Arises when an individual's utility of wealth function is concave [that is, $U'(W) > 0$, $U''(W) < 0$]. Absolute risk aversion is measured by $r(W) = \dfrac{-U''(W)}{U'(W)}$. Relative risk aversion is measured by

$$rr(W) = \frac{-WU''(W)}{U'(W)}.$$

Second-Order Conditions Mathematical conditions required to ensure that points for which first-order conditions are satisfied are indeed true maximum or true minimum points. These conditions are satisfied by functions that obey certain convexity assumptions.

Shephard's Lemma Application of the envelope theorem, which shows that a consumer's compensated demand functions and a firm's (constant output) input demand functions can be derived from partial differentiation of expenditure functions or total cost functions, respectively.

Shifting of a Tax Market response to the imposition of a tax that causes the incidence of the tax to be on some economic agent other than the one who actually pays the tax.

Short Run–Long Run Distinction A conceptual distinction made in the theory of production that differentiates between a period of time over which some inputs are regarded as being fixed and a longer period in which all inputs can be varied by the producer.

Signaling Actions taken by individuals in markets characterized by adverse selection in an effort to identify their true risk categories.

Slutsky Equation A mathematical representation of the substitution and income effects of a price change on utility-maximizing choices:

$$\partial x/\partial p_x = \partial x/\partial p_x\big|_{U = \bar{U}} - x\frac{\partial x}{\partial I}.$$

Social Welfare Function A hypothetical device that records societal views about equity among individuals.

Subgame Perfect Equilibrium A Nash equilibrium in which the strategy choices of each player do not involve noncredible threats.

Substitutes (Gross) Two goods such that if the price of one increases, more of the other good will be demanded. That is x and y are gross substitutes if $\partial x/\partial p_y > 0$. *See also* Complements; Slutsky Equation.

Substitutes (Net) Two goods such that if the price of one increases, more of the other good will be demanded if utility is held constant. That is, x and y are net substitutes if

$$\partial x/\partial p_y\big|_{U = \bar{U}} > 0.$$

Net substitutability is symmetric in that

$$\partial x/\partial p_y\big|_{U = \bar{U}} = \partial y/\partial p_x\big|_{U = \bar{U}}.$$

See also Complements; Slutsky Equation.

Substitution Effects *See* Income and Substitution Effects; Output and Substitution Effects; Slutsky Equation.

Sunk Costs One-time investments that must be made in order to enter a market.

Supply Function For a profit-maximizing firm, a function that shows quantity supplied (q) as a function of output price (P) and input prices (v, w):

$$q = q(P, v, w).$$

Supply Response Increases in production prompted by changing demand conditions and market prices. Usually a distinction is made between short-run and long-run supply responses.

Tacit Collusion Choice of cooperative (monopoly) strategies without explicit collusion.

Total Cost Function The relationship between (minimized) total costs, output, and input prices

$$C = C(v, w, q).$$

Utility Function   A mathematical conceptualization of the way in which individual rank alternative bundles of commodities. If there are only two goods, x and y, utility is denoted by

$$\text{utility} = U(x, y).$$

Variable Costs   Costs that change in response to changes in the level of output being produced by a firm. This is in contrast to fixed costs, which do not change.

von Neumann–Morgenstern Utility   A ranking of outcomes in uncertain situations such that individuals choose among these outcomes on the basis of their expected utility values.

Wage   The cost of hiring one worker for one hour. Denoted by w in the text.

Walrasian Price Adjustment   The assumption that markets are cleared through price adjustments in response to excess demand or supply.

Zero-Sum Game   A game in which winnings for one player are losses for the other player.

Index

Author names are in italics. Glossary terms are bolded.